Gamification Learning Framework for Cybersecurity Education

Vasaki Ponnusamy
Higher Colleges of Technology, UAE

Noor Zaman Jhanjhi
Taylor's University, Malaysia

Kiran Adnan
Universiti Tunku Abdul Rahman, Malaysia

IGI Global
Scientific Publishing
Publishing Tomorrow's Research Today

Vice President of Editorial — Melissa Wagner
Director of Acquisitions — Mikaela Felty
Director of Book Development — Jocelynn Hessler
Production Manager — Mike Brehm
Cover Design — Jose Rosado

Published in the United States of America by
IGI Global Scientific Publishing
701 East Chocolate Avenue
Hershey, PA, 17033, USA
Tel: 717-533-8845
Fax: 717-533-7115
Website: https://www.igi-global.com E-mail: cust@igi-global.com

Library of Congress Cataloging-in-Publication Data

Names: Ponnusamy, Vasaki, 1974- editor
http://id.loc.gov/vocabulary/relators/edt
http://id.loc.gov/authorities/names/n2015067862
http://id.loc.gov/rwo/agents/n2015067862 | Zaman, Noor, 1972- editor
http://id.loc.gov/vocabulary/relators/edt
http://id.loc.gov/authorities/names/n2011087732
http://id.loc.gov/rwo/agents/n2011087732 | Adnan, Kiran, 1984- editor
http://id.loc.gov/vocabulary/relators/edt
http://id.loc.gov/authorities/names/n2025026176
http://id.loc.gov/rwo/agents/n2025026176
Title: Gamification learning framework for cybersecurity education / edited by Vasaki Ponnusamy, Noor Zaman Jhanjhi, Kiran Adnan.
Description: Hershey, PA : Information Science Reference, [2026] | Includes bibliographical references and index.
Identifiers: LCCN 2025005783 (print) | LCCN 2025005784 (ebook) | ISBN 9798337304793 ebook | ISBN 9798337304779 h/c | ISBN 9798337304786 s/c
Subjects: LCSH: Computer security--Psychological aspects
http://id.loc.gov/authorities/subjects/sh2023002816 |
Gamification--Research | Computer security--Computer-assisted instruction
Classification: LCC QA76.9.A25 (ebook) | LCC QA76.9.A25 G3575 2026 (print) |
DDC 005.8 23/eng/20250--dc25
LC record available at https://lccn.loc.gov/2025005783
British Cataloguing in Publication Data
A Cataloguing in Publication record for this book is available from the British Library.

Table of Contents

Detailed Table of Contents

convergence of gamification and cybersecurity education, emphasizing the efficacy of simulations, serious games, and competitive settings such as Capture the Flag (CTF) challenges. Emerging technologies, including artificial intelligence (AI), virtual reality (VR), and augmented reality (AR), are analyzed for their capacity to develop immersive, adaptable training environments. Ethical considerations, such as inclusivity and data protection, are also examined, highlighting the necessity for equal and effective training programs.

In the cybersecurity ecosystem, gamification has transformed the way people learn by incorporating interactive learning approaches that have improved engagement levels, dedication, and retention. Gamification approach presents promising possibilities to address challenges faced by traditional methods that are unable to cope-up with technical complexities of cybersecurity educational domain. The shifting ethics and threats in cyberspace have inevitably led to the need for experiential learning that can foster a connection among peers and encourages communication skills by infusing game components into learning. The game components such as points, levels, reward systems, competition, co-operation, and narrative to build compelling educational experiences whereby many of the skills that sustain high demand, continuously learning and problem-solving traditions get shaped and practiced.

The chapter explores the potential of gamification and behaviour design in cybersecurity training, highlighting its potential to enhance engagement and retention. It combines psychological concepts like reward systems, intrinsic motivation, and social rivalry with basic mechanics like points, badges, leaderboards, and challenges. By incorporating safe practices into routine tasks, behaviour design enhances these programs. Examples include "Capture the Flag" challenges, AI-powered customized training programs, and simulated phishing attempts. However, gamification and behaviour design have drawbacks, such as excessive dependence on external rewards, privacy issues, and reluctance to adapt. To overcome these challenges, leadership support, open policies, and a balance between internal and external motivators are essential. The chapter presents a model framework for creating gamified cybersecurity programs, emphasizing adaptive designs and ongoing improvement. Future trends like VR/AR integration and AI personalisation highlight the opportunity for further innovation.

Game-based learning platforms are reshaping how professionals prepare for cybersecurity certifications. Certifications like CISSP, CEH, and CompTIA Security+ are essential for career growth, but traditional training methods often lack engagement. Game-based learning provides an innovative alternative, incorporating interactive content, real-time feedback, and practical simulations to enhance knowledge retention and skill development. This chapter explores the foundational features of game-based platforms, including levels, leaderboards, challenges, and rewards, as well as their role in bridging theoretical knowledge with hands-on practice through virtual labs and simulations. It highlights the alignment of game activities with certification objectives, enabling learners to focus on domains such as ethical hacking and incident response. Furthermore, adaptive learning techniques ensure personalized experiences that cater to individual skill levels.

Cyber-attacks are also getting sophisticated with the passage of time and cybersecurity threats are evolving continuously. . Higher Learning Institutions should focus on creating interest towards cybersecurity education but there is still a lack of evidence showing the positive co-relation between cybersecurity education framework and interest towards the field. A games-based approach can be paradigm shift in cybersecurity education which can instill creativity and fun towards learning. The main initiative of this research is to introduce some game-based cybersecurity activities in higher learning institution and to see the positive outcome towards such approach. Several game-based activities were conducted in our higher learning institution and data were collected to study the effectiveness of the approach. The findings show positive co-relation between game-based activities and interest towards the field and future work will be based on classifying such game based activities and developing a framework as guideline for cybersecurity education in Malaysia.

The increasing complexity and volume of cyber threats have necessitated a shift in cybersecurity education towards more dynamic, practical, and personalized learning approaches. This chapter explores the intersection of Artificial Intelligence (AI) and gamification in cybersecurity education, emphasizing how AI technologies enhance traditional training environments. By enabling adaptive challenge generation, real-time feedback, personalized learning paths, and intelligent assessment, AI transforms static educational games into responsive, data-driven systems. It presents detailed case studies demonstrating how AI-infused gamified platforms are being applied across academic, corporate, and training settings. It also investigates emerging applications such as affective computing and AI-supported collaboration. Ethical challenges related the gamified learning are critically examined. The chapter offers insights into the ethical considerations necessary for designing robust and evidence-based gamified systems that can effectively prepare learners for real-world demands.

The rise in cybersecurity threats has made it crucial for Higher Education Institutions (HEIs) to strengthen their security measures. This research presents a comprehensive framework to help HEIs enhance their cybersecurity posture by addressing sector-specific challenges. The framework includes governance and leadership, risk assessment, technical controls, awareness and training, incident response, and external collaboration. By integrating these elements, HEIs can build a resilient cybersecurity strategy. This study draws on existing literature, best practices, and industry standards to offer practical guidance. The framework enables institutions to assess their current security status, identify vulnerabilities, and implement targeted improvements. By adopting this approach, HEIs can proactively mitigate risks, safeguard sensitive data, and strengthen defenses against cyber threats. It serves as a valuable resource for policymakers, administrators, and cybersecurity professionals in higher education.

Nowadays cybersecurity threats are continuously growing at a large rate. So, traditional training methods are not sufficient for the practical learning which is required for protection from the various cyber-attacks. The use of gamified learning in cybersecurity is the need of an hour. Gamified learning provides an energetic approach for the cybersecurity training by using gamification in education contents. In this chapter, the role of gamified learning platforms in cybersecurity is discussed. It focuses on various important points such as how a learner can be engaged in a better way with the help of gamification, how technical skills can be delivered better with the concept of gamified learning, how retention can be improved, and real feedbacks. It also describes various features such as tracking of performance, customized contents, opening of various learning platforms etc. In this chapter, various limitations of gamified environments are also discussed. This chapter also explores the future of cybersecurity education with gamification.

Educational games reside at the intersection of pedagogy, technology, and play. This chapter offers an in-depth exploration of educational game design, examining its theoretical underpinnings, fundamental design elements, and implementation strategies. Drawing on research from cognitive psychology, game studies, and instructional design, this chapter delineates how effective game mechanics, narrative structures, adaptive feedback systems, and user-centered interfaces can converge with robust educational content. Through case studies and contemporary examples, we present a framework for integrating curriculum objectives into engaging and interactive game experiences. The chapter concludes with a discussion of emerging technologies and future directions, providing educators and designers with guidance for creating transformative learning environments.

The chapter entitled "Measuring Success: Evaluating Learning Outcomes in Gamified Cybersecurity Training" begins the discussion with the background of cybersecurity and the problems being faced by industry due to lack of highly skilled cybersecurity professionals. This scarcity can be minimized by developing better training programs through gamified approach. It has been found that this approach is more productive compared to traditional conventional methods of teaching as cybersecurity comprises more technical content which is more abstract to conceive unless hands on practical approach is implemented hence a gamified approach which facilitates the learners with fun, more focus on learning minimizing student retention and making learning process more engaging and productive.

This research investigates the application of gamification elements with deep learning methods to improve cybersecurity training, in this case, awareness of social engineering attacks. A quasi-experimental approach was utilized, where 125 undergraduate students were assigned to game-learning and lecture-learning groups. The research utilized the Ant Colony Optimization (ACO) algorithm in feature selection, maximizing dataset quality for examination. A Bi-Stacked Gated Recurrent Unit (Bi-Stacked GRU) model was employed to individualize learning processes by monitoring interaction patterns and dynamically adapting training material. Rewards, challenges, and immediate feedback were incorporated into gamification components to infuse motivation into learners and support cybersecurity topics. Outcomes indicated that gamified, interactive learning significantly impacted comprehension and memorization of social engineering attack methods by participants against lecture-based training.

Preface

In today's hyperconnected digital landscape, cybersecurity has become a cornerstone of organizational resilience and national security. Yet, as cyber threats grow in complexity, so too does the challenge of preparing a skilled workforce capable of defending against them. Traditional cybersecurity education often struggles with engagement, retention, and practical application issues that gamification is uniquely positioned to address. *Gamification Learning Framework for Cybersecurity Education* presents a groundbreaking exploration of how game-inspired methodologies can transform cybersecurity training, making it more immersive, interactive, and effective.

This book is a collaborative effort by leading researchers, educators, and industry practitioners who share a common vision: to revolutionize cybersecurity education through gamification. By integrating game mechanics, such as competition, rewards, storytelling, and real-world simulations, into learning environments, we can foster deeper engagement, accelerate skill acquisition, and cultivate a proactive security mindset. The 17 chapters in this volume provide a comprehensive examination of gamification's role in cybersecurity, spanning theoretical foundations, practical implementations, and emerging trends powered by artificial intelligence (AI), augmented reality (AR), and adaptive learning technologies.

KEY THEMES AND CONTRIBUTIONS

The book is structured into four broad thematic sections, each addressing critical dimensions of gamified cybersecurity education:

Theoretical Foundations and Frameworks

The opening chapters establish the conceptual underpinnings of gamification in cybersecurity. *Foundations of Gamification in Cybersecurity Education* (Chapter 3) explore how game mechanics enhance cognitive retention and motivation. *A Comprehensive Framework for Strengthening Cybersecurity in Higher Education Institutions* (Chapter 8) offers a systematic approach for integrating gamification into curricula.

Innovative Technologies and Methodologies

Cutting-edge technologies are reshaping how gamification is applied in cybersecurity training. *Augmented and Virtual Reality in Gamified Cybersecurity Education* (Chapter 1) and *Artificial Intelligence-Based Gamification* (Chapter 7) demonstrate how immersive and adaptive learning environments can simulate real-world threats. *Gamification Tools for Social Engineering Attack Awareness* (Chapter 16) showcases AI-driven approaches to personalized and dynamic learning experiences.

Practical Applications and Case Studies

Several chapters focus on real-world implementations and strategies. *Game-Based Learning Platforms for Cybersecurity Certifications* (Chapter 5) and *Gamification for Continuous Security Training in DevSecOps* (Chapter 12) highlight industry applications, while *Designing Engaging Cybersecurity Challenges* (Chapter 9) provides actionable insights for educators. *Increasing the Awareness and Participation of Young Women in Cybersecurity* (Chapter 10) addresses diversity and inclusion through gamified outreach.

Assessment and Future Directions

Measuring the efficacy of gamification is crucial for continuous improvement. *Measuring Success: Evaluating Learning Outcomes* (Chapter 15) presents robust evaluation frameworks.

WHO SHOULD READ THIS BOOK?

This book is designed for a multidisciplinary audience, including:

- **Cybersecurity educators** seeking innovative teaching methodologies.

- **Instructional designers** developing gamified training modules.
- **Corporate trainers** in IT and security roles aim to enhance workforce readiness.
- **Policymakers** interested in modernizing cybersecurity education frameworks.
- **Students and professionals** looking for engaging ways to master cybersecurity concepts.

We invite you to explore these transformative approaches and join us in redefining cybersecurity education for the future.

Noor Zaman Jhanjhi,
Vasaki Ponnusamy,
Kiran Adnan

Acknowledgement

First of all, we are thankful to God for everything, and then we extend our heartfelt gratitude to all contributors, reviewers, and institutions whose support made this book possible. Special thanks to Taylor's University for fostering an environment of innovation, and to our families for their unwavering encouragement throughout this journey. This work reflects a shared vision for transformative cybersecurity education.

Chapter 1
Augmented and Virtual Reality in Gamified for Cybersecurity Education

Siva Raja Sindiramutty
https://orcid.org/0009-0006-0310-8721
Taylor's University, Malaysia

Noor Zaman Jhanjhi
https://orcid.org/0000-0001-8116-4733
Taylor's University, Malaysia

Sayan Kumar Ray
Taylors University, Malaysia

ABSTRACT

Teaching cybersecurity isn't just about handing over textbooks or running through slide decks; it's about creating an environment where skills are truly tested, refined, and mastered. Enter augmented reality (AR) and virtual reality (VR), technologies that pull learners out of theory and immerse them in scenarios where mistakes feel real, and lessons stick. This chapter explores how AR and VR elevate gamified cybersecurity education. AR overlays digital insights onto real-world environments, allowing trainees to visualise network vulnerabilities in real time. VR, on the other hand, dives deeper, throwing participants into fully simulated breaches, where they test their mettle against relentless attackers. Together, they create a learning space where mistakes are safe, but the pressure feels real. We'll walk through case studies where universities and corporations are using these tools to turn cybersecurity training into a collaborative, engaging experience.

DOI: 10.4018/979-8-3373-0477-9.ch001

INTRODUCTION

The Need for Innovative Cybersecurity Education

The Growing Demand for Skilled Cybersecurity Professionals

I once watched a friend, fresh out of university with a degree in IT, utterly freeze during his first cybersecurity assignment. He had the theory down but lacked the hands-on skills to handle the rapidly escalating threat. It's a story that's becoming far too common. As cyberattacks grow in sophistication, the need for skilled professionals capable of responding effectively has skyrocketed. Unfortunately, many traditional programs are falling short. Think about this: while tech-savvy hackers are sharpening their tools, students are often stuck dissecting outdated case studies. There's a glaring gap between what's taught and what's needed. A recent report revealed that nearly 3.5 million cybersecurity jobs remain unfilled globally (Olosunde, 2014). Meanwhile, companies are grappling with real-world consequences, from data breaches to paralyzed infrastructure (Toledano, 2024; Alex et al., 2022).

Cybersecurity education needs to shift gears. Imagine courses where students battle real-time simulations of ransomware attacks or practice patching IoT vulnerabilities under pressure. Programs could mirror gaming environments, engaging learners while building critical problem-solving skills. This isn't just about plugging skill gaps—it's about creating warriors who are prepared for battle. And here's the thing: the stakes are personal. Your bank account, health records, and even the power grid rely on these professionals. We need better education not because it's an industry buzzword, but because it's a lifeline for the digital world we depend on. Figure 1 shows challenges with the traditional teaching method.

Figure 1. Challenges with traditional teaching methods

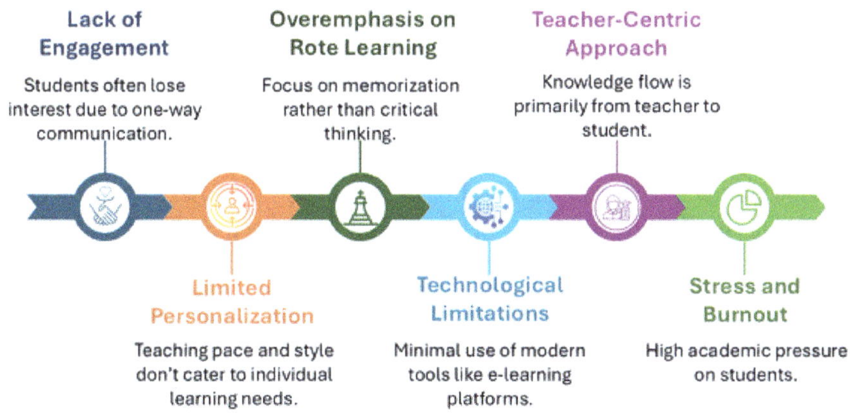

Challenges with Traditional Teaching Methods

I'll never forget sitting in a stuffy lecture hall, listening to a professor drone on about firewalls—while half the class scrolled social media. It felt like learning to swim by reading about water. Traditional teaching methods often rely on lectures, rigid syllabi, and theoretical content, leaving students unprepared for the fast-changing world of cybersecurity (LeBlanc, 2021; Alferidah & Jhanjhi, 2020). These methods fail to connect with the reality of cyberattacks, which rarely follow a script.

In many programs, there's too much focus on memorization rather than hands-on experience. While students can recite definitions of phishing, they're often stumped when asked to identify or counter an actual attack (Thompson et al., 2018; Alkinani et al., 2021). Moreover, classrooms tend to isolate subjects—network security here, and cryptography there—without emphasizing how these fields interlock during a real breach. Another issue is the lack of collaboration and critical thinking exercises. Cybersecurity isn't a solo sport; professionals often work in teams, analyzing threats and crafting layered defences together. Yet, traditional methods don't simulate that kind of dynamic. What's more, outdated curricula lag behind cybercriminals who innovate faster than academic updates can keep up. This gap means graduates enter the workforce unequipped to handle emerging threats like AI-driven malware or deepfake scams (Shwartz, 2021; Babbar et al., 2021). It's like sending a knight into battle with a dull sword—well-intentioned but doomed.

The Role of Gamification in Cybersecurity Education

Brief Overview of Gamification Concepts

Playing a cybersecurity simulation game once during a workshop, and it was way more effective than any lecture I had ever attended. The whole experience of defending a network against hackers and racing against time made the concepts stick with me. That's the magic of gamification—turning serious learning into something interactive and engaging. In cybersecurity education, it's been a game-changer (pun intended). Students, professionals, and even curious amateurs learn to recognize threats, analyze vulnerabilities, and practice defensive strategies in scenarios that feel real.

Gamification involves using game-like elements, like leaderboards, points, badges, or challenges, in non-game settings to drive motivation and retention (Kachhi, 2024; Brohi et al., 2020). Cybersecurity training platforms often include attack-and-defense setups or "capture the flag" challenges, where participants compete to solve puzzles or fix vulnerabilities (Hamza et al., 2024). These setups not only make the lessons memorable but also lower the fear of failure by creating a safe space for mistakes. Real-world simulations build confidence too—like when an intern told me they felt prepared to handle a phishing attack because they'd "practised" during one of these games. Figure 2 shows benefits of gamification

The impact extends beyond students. Organizations use gamified training to upskill their staff and reduce security risks (Buckley & Jorge, 2024; Chesti et al., 2020). The collaborative spirit and sense of accomplishment these tools foster can even make cybersecurity, which can be dry, almost…fun.

Figure 2. Benefits of gamification

Why Augmented Reality (AR) and Virtual Reality (VR)?

Advantages of Immersive Technologies in Learning Environments

Augmented Reality (AR) and Virtual Reality (VR) bring a refreshing spark to learning environments. These tools create immersive spaces where students can interact with content in a way traditional classrooms rarely allow (Serrano-Ausejo & Mårell-Olsson, 2023). I once tried a VR headset at a tech demo, and it felt like stepping into another world—it's hard to forget. Imagine students exploring ancient ruins or conducting virtual chemistry experiments without worrying about breaking a single beaker. It's not just cool—it's effective. Research shows that AR and VR boost engagement and make complex topics easier to grasp (Çeken & Taşkın, 2024; Dogra et al., 2021).

Teachers see the magic, too. These technologies allow them to break away from flat PowerPoint slides and dive into interactive 3D environments. One teacher I know uses AR to bring biology lessons to life, showing students detailed virtual organs they can explore from every angle. The results? Higher retention rates and students asking for more.

Sure, there's always a question of cost or accessibility, but studies suggest the benefits often outweigh the investment (Cevikbas et al., 2023; Fatima-Tuz-Zahra et al., 2020). And let's be real—kids already love tech. Why not meet them where they are? Whether it's learning physics through virtual roller coasters or practising public speaking in a simulated audience, AR and VR are turning classrooms into places students look forward to.

Scope of Paper

The paper focuses on advancing cybersecurity education by employing augmented and virtual reality (AR/VR) technologies. Its primary scope is higher education, targeting undergraduate and postgraduate students. This choice is deliberate, as these levels often house programs dedicated to cultivating future cybersecurity professionals. Universities have integrated AR/VR into their curricula to address the growing need for hands-on training, bridging the gap between theoretical knowledge and real-world applications. These immersive tools simulate cyberattacks, allowing learners to identify vulnerabilities and apply defence mechanisms in realistic settings.

The approach extends beyond conventional teaching methods, fostering interactive learning. For instance, AR can project simulated network threats in a classroom, while VR offers fully immersive scenarios for penetration testing or ransomware response. By utilizing these technologies, students not only learn but also practice skills in a controlled environment, gaining confidence and competence.

Although the primary focus remains on higher education, the paper also briefly explores applications in corporate training. These initiatives emphasize upskilling employees and preparing them for evolving cyber threats, highlighting the broader potential of AR/VR technologies. However, the spotlight firmly stays on university-level programs, reflecting their critical role in preparing the next wave of cybersecurity experts. This emphasis underscores the importance of integrating cutting-edge tools in academic settings to meet the industry's ever-growing demands.

Chapter Contribution

This chapter is pertinent to the area of augmented and virtual reality in gamified for cybersecurity education. First, it describes an overview of the need for innovative cybersecurity education and outlines the role of gamification in cybersecurity education with a brief overview of gamification concepts and the advantages of immersive technologies in learning environments. The chapter then investigates comparison: AR vs. VR in gamified education, key differences and complementary roles in cybersecurity education.

Furthermore, the chapter presents a immersion in realistic cybersecurity scenarios and interactive problem-solving and engagement through game mechanics. It also discusses AR for cyber threat awareness and VR for simulated attack and defense scenarios ns combining AR and VR for collaborative learning and discusses on case study on success stories of educational institutions using AR and VR in cybersecurity program. Lastly, the section provides a glimpse of challenges and limitations and ai integration, haptic feedback, and improved accessibility and collaboration with global certification bodies.

Chapter Organization

In the first section, we will cover an insight into the the need for innovative cybersecurity education and why augmented reality (AR) and virtual reality VR) needed in education. In section 2 we go understanding AR and VR in cyber security education. In section 3 we discuss common gamification elements enhanced by AR and VRfor digital curriculum and applications of AR and VR in cybersecurity training in section 4. Section 5 delves into case studies and success stories. Section 6 will explain the challenges and pitfalls in AR/VR application. In final section will discuss future trends in AR/VR for cybersecurity education

UNDERSTANDING AR AND VR IN CYBERSECURITY EDUCATION

What is AR?

Overview and Examples of AR Applications in Learning

I remember seeing my nephew explore a 3D model of the solar system through an app. He wasn't just looking; he was moving planets around and zooming in on Jupiter's storm like he was there. That's augmented reality (AR) in education—a technology blending digital visuals with the real world, making learning feel alive. It's not just about making things "cool." AR changes how students interact with content. For instance, apps like *Google Expeditions* let users tour historical landmarks virtually, while *Anatomy 4D* allows students to explore human anatomy by pointing their devices at a printed diagram (Aldeeb et al., 2024; Gopi et al., 2021).

AR also supports skill-building. Think about medical students practicing surgeries using AR-guided tools, or language learners interacting with virtual tutors who respond to their pronunciation (Xu et al., 2024). Classrooms that once relied on flat textbooks are now filled with interactive layers of information that adapt to individual learning speeds and styles (Kraglund-Gauthier, 2015).

But there's something personal here too. I've noticed how even reluctant learners become curious when AR tools are used. It's as though tech bridges the gap between dull content and real-world applications. And honestly, that excitement—seeing kids light up over a virtual frog dissection or a simulated physics experiment—reminds me why education needs to keep exploring these tools.

What is VR?

Overview and Examples of VR Applications in Learning

Virtual reality (VR) is one of those technologies that seems like science fiction until you see it in action—especially in a classroom. My nephew, a fifth grader, recently put on a VR headset to "visit" ancient Rome during a history lesson, and the excitement in his voice afterwards said it all. This is what VR does: it transforms learning into an immersive adventure. Students don't just study; they experience.

Take medical training. Aspiring surgeons can practice complicated procedures without stepping into an operating room (Charlet, 2024; Gouda et al., 2022). In biology, students can explore the human body in 3D, dissecting organs virtually—no smell, no mess (Kartal, 2008). In architecture, VR allows future designers to walk through their blueprints before a single brick is laid (Kasture, 2024; Humayun et al., 2022). Even language learners are stepping into VR simulations to practice conversations in virtual marketplaces or cafés, which is far more engaging than flipping through flashcards (Shin, 2021). But what hits home for me is the accessibility. A friend's child, who struggles with traditional teaching methods, uses VR to learn at his own pace. It's not perfect—glitches happen, and headsets can be pricey—but the potential to inspire and educate is worth the hiccups. When learning becomes a story you live, you never forget it. Figure 3 shows applications of AR and VR in cybersecurity training.

Figure 3. Applications of AR and VR in cybersecurity training

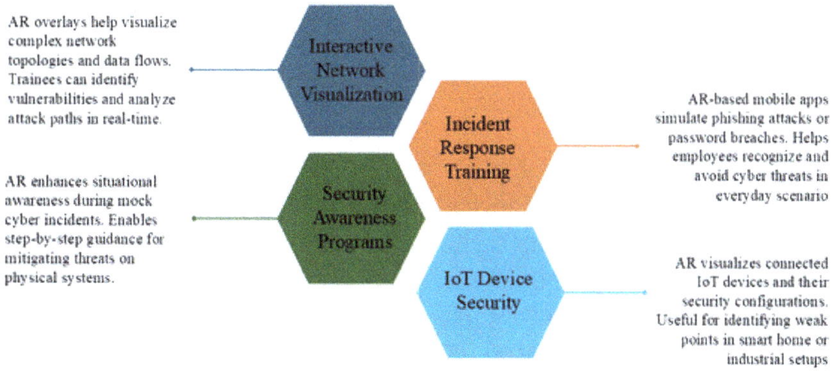

Comparison: AR vs. VR in Gamified Education

Key Differences and Complementary Roles in Cybersecurity Education

When it comes to gamified learning in cybersecurity, augmented reality (AR) and virtual reality (VR) offer their twists on engagement, yet they play off each other beautifully when combined. I once watched a group of students in a cybersecurity workshop use AR to simulate phishing attack scenarios on their phones while another team wore VR headsets to navigate a virtual corporate network riddled with vulnerabilities. It was fascinating—and chaotic. Table 1 shows AR vs VR in education application.

Table 1. AR and VR comparison

Feature	Augmented Reality (AR)	Virtual Reality (VR)
Hardware	Overlays digital content onto the real world.	Requires VR headsets and sometimes motion controllers.
Level of Immersion	Partially immersive; user remains in the real world.	Fully immersive; user is isolated from the real world.
Cost	Affordable.	Expensive

continued on following page

Table 1. Continued

Feature	Augmented Reality (AR)	Virtual Reality (VR)
Accessibility	Easier to integrate into existing devices	Limited by the need for specific VR headsets.
Interactivity	Users interact with real and digital objects.	Users interact solely with the virtual environment.
Learning Applications	Enhances real-world environments	Simulates complex scenarios

AR shines in overlaying digital elements onto the real world, which makes it great for hands-on tasks. Imagine students using AR to scan QR codes during a simulated ransomware attack or visualizing network security layers in their physical environment. It's practical and mobile, requiring just a smartphone or tablet. On the other hand, VR throws students into fully immersive environments (Maebela & Dehinbo, 2024; Jhanjhi et al., 2021). They can "sit" in a hacker's chair, break into a network, and explore the consequences of a breach—all without actual damage. It's a safe space for trial and error.

But what's exciting is how they complement each other. AR is perfect for bite-sized, real-world exercises—quick lessons in spotting phishing attempts, for example. VR, meanwhile, can simulate high-stakes scenarios like defending against botnets in a controlled, virtual setting (Khan et al., 2024; Kumar et al., 2021). Together, they create a learning experience that's both practical and deeply immersive. The result? Students who are not just tech-savvy but also battle-tested.

GAMIFICATION ELEMENTS ENHANCED BY AR AND VR IN DIGITAL CURRICULUM

Immersion in Realistic Cybersecurity Scenarios

Replicating Real-World Environments for Incident Response Training

Imagine putting on a headset and finding yourself in a bustling office under a ransomware attack. There's the CEO pacing, IT staff frantically typing, and your phone buzzing with alerts. It's stressful, chaotic—and incredibly effective. This is how gamification, blended with AR and VR, replicates high-pressure environments to train for real-world cybersecurity incidents (Rana & Chicone, 2024; Lim et al., 2019).

Gamification alone, like point systems or leaderboards, helps engagement. But mix it with AR/VR and the realism skyrockets. You're not just learning; you're living the scenario. Studies highlight how such experiences lead to better retention and decision-making during actual incidents (Yadav, 2024). And the realism isn't just visual—it's procedural. Participants must execute proper triage steps, communicate under stress, and handle cascading events, skills rarely mastered through traditional methods.

That said, I noticed during one demo that the "virtual stress" was almost too much for some attendees. A colleague confessed it felt eerily like a real breach they'd faced years ago. Still, the upside is undeniable. Research shows that immersive gamified setups increase learners' confidence and adaptability in complex situations (Aldalur, 2024; Nayyar et al., 2021). These tools aren't a novelty—they're setting new benchmarks for cybersecurity training. They prepare us not just to respond but to anticipate, adapt, and improve. If only we had these tools back during that workshop, it would've been less "PowerPoint snooze" and more "bring it on."

Interactive Problem-Solving

Gamified Challenges for Threat Identification and Mitigation

Gamification, when combined with Augmented Reality (AR) and Virtual Reality (VR), is transforming how we approach cybersecurity challenges, particularly in the realm of threat identification and mitigation. Picture this: you're in a VR world, tasked with spotting a security breach hidden in a virtual network. You have to find the flaw before it spreads, making it a high-stakes race against time. This immersive, game-like experience brings a new level of engagement to problem-solving (Khalid et al., 2024; Shah et al., 2022).

The integration of AR and VR enhances the interactive nature of these challenges. Instead of passively receiving information, users are actively involved, facing threats head-on in a simulated environment (Sharma, 2024). It's no longer just theory – it's about applying knowledge in real-time. I've seen firsthand how this hands-on approach improves understanding and retention, as players must think critically to outsmart potential attackers. It's not just fun, it's effective. VR's ability to simulate a wide range of scenarios allows users to learn by doing, which is far more impactful than reading a report on how threats unfold (Oigara, 2024; Sharma et al., 2021). Gamified challenges also offer instant feedback, showing the results of your decisions as you go. This helps identify weaknesses and refines your decision-making (Johnson et al., 2021). In the case of security, players can test their responses to various scenarios, making it a great way to practice identifying and mitigating threats without the fear of real-world consequences.

Engagement Through Game Mechanics

Achievements, Leaderboards, and Multiplayer Collaboration

The fusion of gamification mechanics like achievements, leaderboards, and multiplayer collaboration with augmented reality (AR) and virtual reality (VR) has redefined how users engage in digital environments. Achievements have always worked as motivators, but AR and VR take this a step further by immersing individuals in interactive spaces. When I tried a VR learning module that rewarded small milestones with visual fireworks, the satisfaction felt tangible—more like unlocking something in real life than just a pop-up notification on a screen. Research supports this; users feel greater accomplishment when digital rewards are tied to immersive experiences (Hammami, 2024; Singhal et al., 2020).

Leaderboards fuel competitiveness but can also foster connection (Cao & Cheng, 2024). Imagine a virtual leaderboard projected on AR glasses during a fitness game, where you see your rank compared to friends sweating beside you—there's a shared experience in both triumph and defeat. While a traditional leaderboard often feels impersonal, AR allows real-time engagement with fellow participants, making the competition livelier (Lu et al., 2021).

Multiplayer collaboration adds another layer of magic. VR platforms enable users to work together in environments that feel realistic, like solving puzzles or simulating work tasks (Yamijala et al., 2024). A group of students solving virtual escape rooms learned faster when collaboration became a game element (Park et al., 2025). It's not about isolation anymore—VR and AR strengthen teamwork by replicating the feeling of being together physically (Ramya & Ramamoorthy, 2024). These elements are more than gimmicks; they transform dull tasks into meaningful activities. AR and VR inject excitement, whether in education, training, or entertainment. When game mechanics tap into the human need for achievement and connection, engagement skyrockets.

How Gamified Aligns with Futuristic Metaverse

Gamification relies on rewards, challenges, and progression mechanics, while AR and VR add layers of immersion (Bhowmik, 2024). When combined, they align well with the Metaverse's vision—a shared, immersive digital environment. Imagine unlocking achievements in a virtual world or collaborating with classmates as avatars to solve problems. Studies have shown that such interactions encourage teamwork, creativity, and problem-solving (Damaševičius & Sidekerskienė, 2024).

Take leaderboards in VR simulations, for instance. They can push students to revisit concepts they struggled with and improve performance (Fabre et al., 2024; Hussain et al., 2024). AR overlays, like highlighting historical landmarks or molecular structures during lessons, make learning visual and engaging, connecting with students who might tune out otherwise (Shorman, 2024). Plus, the Metaverse promises a persistent digital space where learning can continue across devices and locations, blending play and education seamlessly (Jagatheesaperumal et al., 2024). Of course, this shift isn't just about kids. Teachers are learning to navigate these tools, often hilariously fumbling with headsets in training sessions. I watched one such video during a seminar, where a teacher exclaimed, "How do I get out of this virtual cave?!" It's clear we're still figuring this out, but that's part of the charm.

The possibilities are thrilling, from creating gamified lesson plans to building schools within the Metaverse. If a single AR app can excite one student, imagine what a connected, gamified Metaverse could do.

APPLICATIONS OF AR AND VR IN CYBERSECURITY TRAINING

AR for Cyber Threat Awareness

Real-Time Visualization of Network Attacks and Vulnerabilities

Virtual and Augmented Reality (VR and AR) are pushing cybersecurity training into exciting territory (Kumar et al., 2023; Sindiramutty, 2024). Imagine staring at a screen of blinking numbers and charts. That's traditional cybersecurity—dry, abstract, and uninspiring. AR changes this by giving trainees real-time, visual representations of cyber threats (Iyer et al., 2024). Think of it like wearing glasses that don't just show attacks happening but make you feel them. A simulated network attack unfolds right before your eyes: nodes light up, vulnerabilities appear as glaring holes, and invisible hacker worms through a firewall.

Real-time visualization brings clarity that spreadsheets and charts can't. In one AR training tool, vulnerabilities appear as glowing red spots in a virtual network (Irene, 2024). When an attack happens, it's no longer abstract—you watch the breach spread like fire across connected systems. This form of training helps cybersecurity teams grasp the urgency of patching weaknesses. On a broader scale, AR encourages teamwork (Vairamani, 2024; Sindiramutty et al., 2023). Picture a team huddled around a virtual map where threats unfold in real time. Everyone sees the same data, discusses the next move, and learns where to reinforce their systems.

That kind of shared awareness speeds up decision-making, especially during high-pressure scenarios.

Compared to VR's full immersion, AR stands out because it mixes virtual threats with the physical environment. Imagine walking through your actual server room, and weak points are highlighted like clues in a video game. Training becomes a hands-on experience, embedding lessons more deeply than any manual could.

VR for Simulated Attack and Defense Scenarios

Immersive Experiences Like Penetration Testing and Red Teaming

I remember hearing about a company that used virtual reality (VR) for its red teaming exercises. It wasn't your usual run-of-the-mill "sit at the desk and simulate an attack" deal. Team members would put on VR headsets and dive into a world where they could see firewalls as literal walls and malware as glowing orbs threatening to breach the system. Sounds futuristic, right? But this is where cybersecurity training is headed.

VR makes simulations feel real. Instead of relying on PowerPoint slides or basic hacking exercises, VR offers environments where security professionals can practice defending against simulated ransomware attacks or phishing schemes (Qawasmeh et al., 2024; Sindiramutty et al., 2024; Ravichandran et al., 2024). They can walk through a virtual data centre, hunt for vulnerabilities, and even simulate social engineering attacks. It's like a playground for defenders and attackers alike but with none of the real world. On the other hand, augmented reality (AR) steps in when physical spaces intersect with cyber threats (You et al., 2023; Sindiramutty, Jhanjhi, Tan, et al., 2023). Imagine standing in your office and seeing digital overlays showing potential security weaknesses, like an unlocked server room or a rogue device connected to the network. It feels like you're in a sci-fi movie, but it's surprisingly practical.

These tools don't just prepare cybersecurity teams; they immerse them. And while no one claims VR or AR can replace hands-on experience entirely, they offer something traditional training doesn't: adrenaline-pumping scenarios and the freedom to make mistakes without costly repercussions. With these technologies, cybersecurity isn't just a skill—it's an adventure.

Combining AR and VR for Collaborative Learning

Mixed-Reality Environments for Teamwork Exercises

When I first tried virtual reality, it was for gaming. But the moment I saw how immersive it was, I thought, "This could teach teamwork better than any slideshow." In cybersecurity training, AR and VR have stepped up as tools to mimic real-world scenarios (Chauhan & Sachdeva, 2024; Waheed et al., 2024). Picture a mixed-reality room where your team is trying to fend off a simulated ransomware attack. It's not just a flashy tool; it forces people to think and act like they would in a genuine crisis. These simulations provide a safe space to fail, learn, and retry without risking actual systems.

AR and VR bring collaboration to life by breaking down traditional barriers (Creed et al., 2023; Manchuri et al., 2024). One group might wear VR headsets to visualize a cyberattack unfolding, while another uses AR overlays on their devices to analyze the "infected" systems. Everyone works together, despite being miles apart. The result? A training session where you're not just learning alone but solving problems as a team. Studies show this kind of mixed-reality approach improves retention and quick decision-making.

Let's not overlook the emotional aspect. Something is humbling about "failing" a simulated attack in front of your peers. I once saw someone struggle to fix a fake breach, only to laugh nervously and admit, "Well, that's a new kind of pressure!" This kind of experience builds trust and accountability, key traits for real-world cybersecurity.

Ultimately, AR and VR don't just teach you facts; they shape how teams handle the unpredictable. And honestly, who doesn't remember lessons learned through a bit of chaos?

CASE STUDIES AND SUCCESS STORIES

Educational Institutions Using AR/VR in Educational Program

Examples of Universities and Their Gamified AR/VR Initiatives

Several universities have embraced AR/VR technology to enhance cybersecurity programs by gamifying learning experiences. It's exciting to see how these tools make complex ideas not just digestible but engaging. At Johns Hopkins University, students explore AR simulations that study body painting, allowing them to practice the Enhancement of Anatomical Education in real time (Barmaki et al., 2019;

Azam et al., 2023). It feels less like traditional learning and more like diving into a high-stakes game—only with significant real-world implications. Figure 4 shows educational institution which uses AR/VR in the education.

Figure 4. Educational institutions using AR/VR in educational programs

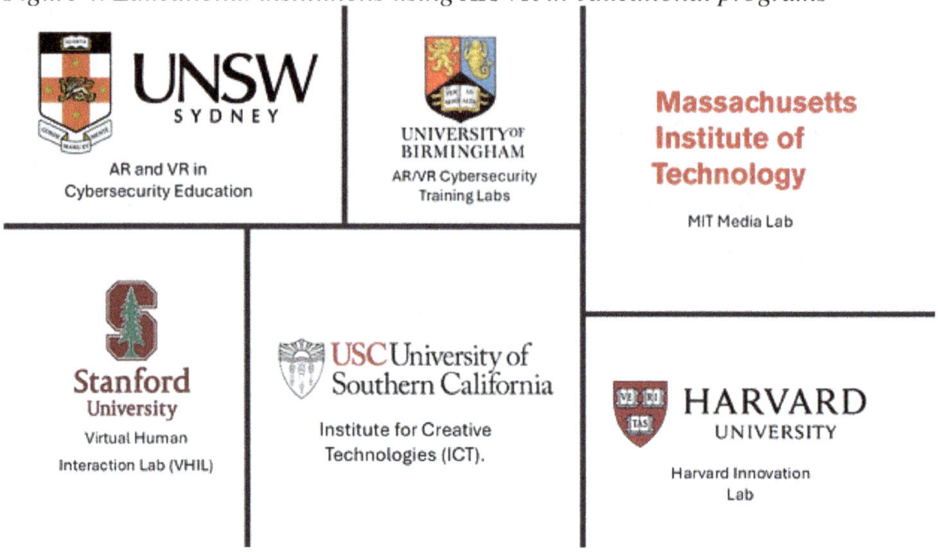

Stanford University's VR Lab has taken things up a notch. Their virtual environments replicate dental education (Mauricio et al., 2024; Sindiramutty, Tan, et al., 2024; Linqiang et al., 2024). I remember reading how one student remarked, "It felt like I was inside a company server room, trying not to panic while finding solutions" That kind of immersive pressure is invaluable because cybersecurity professionals often work under real pressure.

The University of Southern California integrates Virtual Reality Labs into ethical hacking modules. Students wear VR headsets to enhance cybersecurity skills through immersive VR simulations (Admin, 2024; Ying et al., 2024). It's the perfect marriage of the digital and physical worlds—like hacking meets augmented puzzles—and it makes learning so much less abstract.

Then there's RWTH Aachen University in Germany. The Cybernetics Lab at RWTH Aachen University in Germany offers a virtual reality-based course, "VR-2Sec: Exploring and Securing Virtual and Augmented Reality," which focuses on cybersecurity aspects related to VR and augmented reality (AR) (Sabina, n.d.). One student joked in an interview, "I'm finally applying my gaming skills to something my parents approve of!" That relatability helps break down barriers to learning.

These success stories prove that AR/VR doesn't just add flair. It builds confidence, sharpens skills, and prepares students for real cyber challenges. With more universities adopting similar programs, classrooms may soon look less like traditional lectures and more like action-packed cyber arenas.

Industry Training Programs with AR/VR Components

Corporate Use Cases and Employee Feedback

Companies are increasingly using AR/VR in their employee training programs, and the results are, quite frankly, hard to ignore. Take Walmart, for instance—they introduced VR modules to train employees for the chaos of Black Friday (Motala et al., 2024; Sheng et al., 2024). Rather than leaving workers to learn under pressure, trainees practised handling surges of customers in a virtual store. Employees reported feeling less anxious during the actual event, with many saying the immersive training boosted their confidence. That's a win by any standard.

In a similar vein, UPS drivers now train using VR to navigate risky driving scenarios (Baker & Baker, 2023; Weiqi et al., 2024). Instead of watching safety videos, drivers experience road hazards up close, making the training far more memorable. One driver shared how the virtual scenarios felt eerily real—a car cutting in suddenly or a child running into the street—but he preferred the simulated stress to real-life danger. Interestingly, the feedback wasn't about the tech itself but how the training stuck with them long after.

Even more creative, companies like Accenture are using AR to teach soft skills (Simon, 2023). Picture this: an employee negotiates with a virtual client, testing their communication style in real-time and an employee might be more willing to make mistakes with AI clients than human trainers—and that honesty led to noticeable improvements.

Of course, it's not perfect. Some employees find the headsets uncomfortable, while others complain about motion sickness (Bursztein et al., 2024; Sindiramutty, Jhanjhi, Tan, Khan, et al., 2024). But these kinks are minor compared to the bigger picture: AR/VR training sticks because people remember what they experience, not just what they're told. And that kind of learning feels like a game-changer.

Provide a Comparative Analysis of Adopting Gaming Technology and Without Gaming Technology

Incorporating gaming in education blends entertainment with learning, which tends to capture attention far more effectively than traditional methods. Games provide instant feedback, making them engaging and interactive (Besalti & Smith,

2024; Seng et al., 2024). Concepts like virtual rewards and progress tracking also motivate students, especially younger ones, to stick with challenging subjects (Gkintoni et al., 2024; Jun et al., 2024; Kiyani et al., 2024).

On the other hand, without gaming, education often leans on lectures, textbooks, and standard assignments. Sure, these methods work—they're tried and tested—but they lack the energy and excitement that games can bring. Kids today are growing up in a digital-first world; sitting through a lecture doesn't quite match the thrill of levelling up in a game. Still, the absence of gaming tools can encourage focus and discipline, which some argue is just as important as engagement.

Table 2. Comparison analysis of gaming and non-gaming technology

Aspect	With Gaming Technology	Without Gaming Technology
Engagement	Gaming makes learning interactive and fun, holding students' attention through instant feedback and rewards (Sun et al., 2023)	Traditional methods rely on lectures and textbooks, which can feel monotonous and less engaging for many students.
Motivation	Features like virtual rewards and progress tracking encourage students to tackle challenging subjects (Kurni & G, 2024)	Motivation often depends on external factors like grades and parental or teacher encouragement.
Learning Style	Interactive games cater to visual and hands-on learners, making complex concepts easier to grasp (Lee et al., 2023).	Effective for students who prefer quiet environments and structured, step-by-step approaches.
Drawbacks	Overemphasis on entertainment can distract from core learning objectives. Some students may not respond well to flashy tools.	Can feel outdated and uninspiring, especially for students accustomed to digital-first experiences
Discipline	Focused on engagement, gaming may not always teach patience or discipline effectively.	Encourages habits of focus, consistency, and discipline through less distracting methods
Real-World Relevance	Prepares students for tech-driven environments by blending learning with familiar digital interfaces.	Builds foundational skills but may struggle to connect with modern, fast-paced, tech-savvy lifestyles

Table 2 shows a comparison analysis of gaming and non-gaming approaches in education. While gaming technology transforms classrooms into interactive spaces, traditional methods bring structure and focus. Combining both approaches can offer a balanced, effective way to engage diverse learners while preparing them for future challenges.

CHALLENGES AND LIMITATIONS

High Costs of AR/VR Implementation

Devices, Software, and Development

High costs remain one of the biggest hurdles for AR/VR adoption, particularly when you consider devices, software, and development expenses (Pujiono et al., 2024). I remember hearing about a small design startup that hoped to integrate VR into their projects. They were excited about the possibilities, but the price tags quickly dampened the mood. High-end VR headsets like the Meta Quest Pro or HTC Vive can cost thousands of dollars (Burden & Savin-Baden, 2024). Add powerful computers to run the software smoothly, and the expenses grow fast. For many small businesses, that alone is a deal-breaker. Figure 5 shows challenges and limitations of using AR/VR.

Figure 5. Challenges and limitations using AR/VR

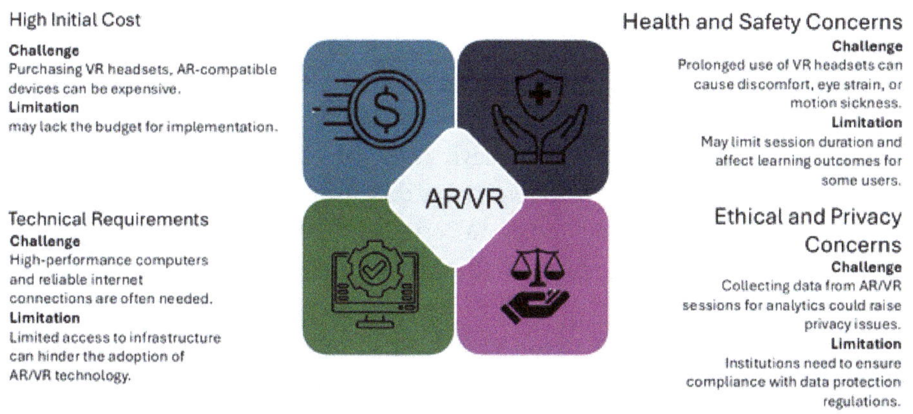

Software development doesn't make things any easier. Custom AR/VR solutions require skilled developers, which doesn't come cheap. Many firms also face subscription fees for software licenses or tools like Unity and Unreal Engine. These costs add up, creating a barrier for companies with limited budgets. And it's not just businesses feeling the pinch—schools and hospitals exploring AR/VR for education or therapy also hit funding walls.

On top of that, building content isn't as simple as snapping photos. Creating 3D environments or interactive simulations demands time, talent, and money. Small errors during development can delay projects and inflate budgets further. I once saw a VR demo glitch mid-presentation, and it was as awkward as it was expensive to fix.

Even when companies can afford the tech, there's the matter of user experience. Devices are often bulky and uncomfortable, which limits how long people can use them. For all their potential, AR/VR tools often feel unfinished, like we're beta testers paying full price. Until devices become cheaper, lighter, and more accessible, AR/VR will stay out of reach for many.

Technical Barriers

Connectivity, Compatibility, and User Accessibility Issues

The adoption of AR and VR technologies often faces serious roadblocks, particularly when it comes to connectivity, compatibility, and user accessibility. I recently tried a VR demo at an expo, and halfway through, the visuals started lagging—a problem that made the experience frustrating instead of immersive. This is not uncommon. AR/VR systems demand high-speed internet and stable connections to handle massive data transfers in real-time (Awadallah et al., 2024). Unfortunately, many regions still lack the infrastructure to provide such connectivity, creating a significant technical hurdle.

Compatibility presents another layer of trouble. AR and VR tools often require powerful, high-end devices—think state-of-the-art smartphones, headsets, or PCs. But here's the kicker: not all users have access to these devices, and hardware variations make seamless integration tricky. For instance, an AR app designed for iOS might struggle or fail altogether on certain Android devices. The technology might be there, but without universal standards, developers are left wrestling with compatibility challenges.

Then there's accessibility, which tends to be the most overlooked issue. Beyond the obvious financial barriers—VR headsets don't come cheap—the technology can exclude individuals with disabilities. Motion sickness, caused by latency or poor frame rates, remains a widespread complaint that further limits user participation (Dong et al., 2024). It's a reminder that a technology meant to feel inclusive can sometimes do the opposite.

What stood out to me at that expo wasn't just the hiccup in the VR experience but the realization that these hurdles are very real. If connectivity gaps persist, devices stay incompatible, and accessibility concerns remain ignored, AR and VR will remain niche toys rather than transformative tools.

Measuring Learning Outcomes

Difficulty in Assessing the Effectiveness of Gamified AR/VR Training

Measuring learning outcomes in gamified AR/VR training isn't as straightforward as it sounds. When I first tried a virtual training module, the experience felt immersive—almost too immersive. I was absorbed, but was I learning? That's where the problem lies. Assessing whether someone has truly grasped a skill or concept through AR/VR isn't always clear-cut (Bhatnagar & Boruah, 2024). Traditional assessments like quizzes or surveys may miss the mark because they don't capture the deeper behavioural or cognitive changes these tools aim to create.

One major challenge is how varied learners react to these experiences. Some thrive in immersive environments, while others may find them overwhelming or distracting (Cai et al., 2019). It's a bit like giving everyone the same pair of shoes and hoping they fit—what works for one doesn't always work for another. On top of that, AR/VR experiences often emphasize engagement, which can blur the line between entertainment and actual learning outcomes. Are learners engaged because the material is effective or just because the visuals are captivating? I'd argue it's often hard to tell.

Technical limitations also play a role. If the hardware lags or the VR headset doesn't sit comfortably, frustration builds, and learning takes a backseat. Plus, measuring long-term retention is tricky. A participant might ace the task in VR but forget the skill two weeks later. I remember a colleague who excelled in a virtual factory safety module but still struggled on the real floor—the transfer just wasn't there.

Ultimately, gamified AR/VR training holds promise, but assessing its true impact remains slippery. Without effective tools to measure outcomes, we're left guessing how much value these flashy, immersive tools bring.

FUTURE DIRECTIONS IN AR/VR FOR CYBERSECURITY EDUCATION

Advances in AR/VR Technologies

AI Integration, Haptic Feedback, and Improved Accessibility

Augmented Reality (AR) and Virtual Reality (VR) technologies are carving out new spaces for cybersecurity education, blending immersive experiences with innovation (Swargiary, 2024). AI integration is at the heart of these advancements, offering personalized learning environments that adapt to users' skills and needs.

The system adjusts the difficulty in real time, challenging your knowledge while keeping you engaged. This isn't a far-fetched dream; tools like these are already in development.

Haptic feedback adds another layer of realism, making AR/VR feel less like a game and more like a hands-on training ground (Babu et al., 2024). During a simulated data breach, for instance, haptic gloves could recreate the sensation of manipulating virtual tools. This physical connection creates a deeper sense of urgency and mastery. I've heard students describe their experience with such tools as "so real it was stressful," which might just be the point—stress, after all, drives critical thinking in real-world cybersecurity scenarios.

Accessibility has also seen major strides. Lightweight AR devices and mobile VR apps make immersive learning possible even for students in rural or underserved areas (K. Lee, 2012). One study found that cost-effective AR tools improved cybersecurity training for participants with limited technical backgrounds (Chandrashekar et al., 2024). This opens doors for more people to enter the cybersecurity field, which desperately needs fresh talent.

These advances matter because cybersecurity education can't stay static. Real attacks evolve, so training methods need to feel alive—and AR/VR does exactly that. It's an exciting shift that turns learning into something learners feel, not just see or hear. I mean, if training can make you sweat a little, maybe it's doing its job.

Expanding AR/VR Use in Cybersecurity Certifications

Collaboration with Global Certification Bodies

AR/VR technologies are changing how cybersecurity training happens, adding immersive, hands-on experiences. A lot of potential lies in partnering with global certification bodies. Some organizations, like $(ISC)^2$ and CompTIA, have shown interest in leveraging AR/VR to complement traditional methods (Understanding Emerging Technology - Virtual Reality/Augmented Reality | VR / AR | CompTIA, n.d.). These tools aren't just about making learning more interactive. They bridge knowledge gaps by offering real-world simulations. Studies have even found that hands-on learning via VR can improve recall rates by up to 80% compared to textbook approaches (Moro et al., 2017).

The exciting part is the possibility of global partnerships. Certification bodies working with AR/VR developers could roll out standardized modules accessible to learners worldwide. The idea is to create uniformity—no matter where someone prepares, they get the same immersive experience. Licensing, tech compatibility, and cost can get messy. Yet, these hurdles feel like speed bumps compared to the benefits. The future of AR/VR in cybersecurity certifications isn't about replacing traditional methods; it's about levelling them up.

Ethical Implications and Data Privacy in AR/VR Education

AR and VR are quickly gaining attention in cybersecurity education, but they come with challenges that demand a careful balance between innovation and responsibility. One of the fascinating aspects of these technologies is how immersive they are—like the first time I used a VR simulation to understand network attacks. It felt like stepping into another world, dodging attacks and plugging security gaps. Yet, this immersion means sensitive data is constantly being collected, from eye movements to voice recordings (Slater & Sanchez-Vives, 2016). If these tools are not designed thoughtfully, they can create more risks than benefits.

Imagine students training in AR/VR environments, unknowingly exposing personal data (Lake et al., 2024). It's not just about passwords; it could be behavioural patterns or even emotional reactions. Who controls that data? And worse, what happens if it leaks? This isn't some sci-fi nightmare; breaches in AR/VR systems have already been reported. I still remember reading about a research lab where headset data got hacked.

Ethical dilemmas also pop up when deciding how much monitoring is too much. Letting educators track students' responses might sound practical, but it also feels like crossing a line, doesn't it? I'd feel uneasy if my learning moments—mistakes, hesitations—were analyzed like stock market trends. Studies suggest designing with minimal data collection can be a starting point.

Importance of Gaming education in the era of Metaverse.

Gaming in cybersecurity education leverages immersive scenarios to make lessons stick. Imagine exploring a simulated network under attack, where every wrong move triggers a new layer of chaos. AR and VR do more than show the theory; they let learners experience what it's like to defend systems in real time. Studies have shown that interactive environments improve knowledge retention, especially for younger learners who grew up gaming (Christopoulos et al., 2024). The rise of the metaverse is another game-changer. With virtual worlds now hosting classrooms, cybersecurity students can collaborate in environments that mimic real-world conditions (Balushi et al., 2024). Gamification doesn't just teach concepts—it builds confidence. For instance, players learning encryption techniques might solve puzzles in a VR escape room. This approach has already been linked to increased problem-solving skills and engagement. Still, it's not all shiny headsets and excitement. Some sceptics argue these methods can feel more like entertainment than education. However, educators embracing AR and VR gaming are already reporting improved outcomes, particularly when these tools are blended with traditional teaching methods (Wang & Li, 2024). The challenge now is ensuring accessibility, so students everywhere—whether in a classroom or their living room—can join the game.

CONCLUSION

Summary of AR and VR's Potential to Transform Cybersecurity Education

AR and VR have immense potential to revolutionize cybersecurity education by turning passive learning into an active, immersive experience. These technologies bridge the gap between theory and practice, allowing learners to engage with realistic cyber scenarios that would be impossible to replicate in traditional classrooms. AR enhances understanding by overlaying digital information onto real-world environments, enabling students to visualize threats and vulnerabilities in real time. VR, on the other hand, offers fully immersive environments where users can simulate high-stakes scenarios like penetration testing, red teaming, or responding to ransomware attacks.

Together, AR and VR provide a hands-on approach that builds both technical skills and critical thinking under pressure. They foster collaboration through multiplayer simulations, where students or employees can tackle complex problems as a team. The gamification of learning—complete with leaderboards, challenges, and rewards—adds an element of engagement that makes even the most daunting cybersecurity concepts accessible and enjoyable.

Beyond academia, these tools are proving invaluable in corporate training programs, helping organizations prepare employees for the fast-evolving threat landscape. While challenges such as cost, accessibility, and technical barriers remain, ongoing advancements in AR/VR technology are making these tools more practical and scalable. By transforming the way cybersecurity is taught, AR and VR are equipping the next generation of professionals to better defend the digital world.

Call for Further Research and Development in this Field

The integration of AR and VR in cybersecurity education is just beginning to scratch the surface of its full potential. While these technologies have demonstrated their ability to enhance learning through immersive and interactive experiences, significant gaps remain that require further exploration. Research is needed to refine these tools, making them more accessible, cost-effective, and adaptable to diverse educational and training environments. Developing lightweight, affordable devices and ensuring compatibility across platforms will help broaden adoption.

Additionally, studies should focus on assessing the long-term impact of AR and VR on skill retention and practical application in real-world cybersecurity challenges. Improved methods for measuring learning outcomes, beyond engagement and immediate task performance, are essential to fully understand their educational value. There is also a pressing need to address ethical concerns, such as data privacy and the potential misuse of collected information during training.

Collaboration between academia, industry, and technology developers is crucial to driving innovation in this space. Partnerships can lead to the creation of standardized modules and scalable solutions that cater to both students and professionals. By investing in further research and development, we can unlock the true potential of AR and VR, transforming cybersecurity education into a dynamic and effective force for preparing individuals to navigate an increasingly complex digital landscape.

REFERENCES

Admin, I. (2024, May 22). *Mixed Reality Lab - Institute for Creative Technologies*. Institute for Creative Technologies. https://ict.usc.edu/research/labs-groups/mixed-reality-lab/

Aldalur, I. (2024). Enhancing software development education through gamification and experiential learning with genially. *Software Quality Journal*, *33*(1), 1. Advance online publication. DOI: 10.1007/s11219-024-09699-9

Aldeeb, F. H., Sallabi, O. M., Elaish, M. M., & Hwang, G. (2024). Enhancing students' learning achievements, self-efficacy, and motivation using mobile augmented reality. *Journal of Computer Assisted Learning*, *40*(4), 1823–1837. DOI: 10.1111/jcal.12989

Alex, S. A., Jhanjhi, N., Humayun, M., Ibrahim, A. O., & Abulfaraj, A. W. (2022). Deep LSTM Model for Diabetes Prediction with Class Balancing by SMOTE. *Electronics (Basel)*, *11*(17), 2737. DOI: 10.3390/electronics11172737

Alferidah, D. K., & Jhanjhi, N. (2020). Cybersecurity Impact over Bigdata and IoT Growth. *2020 International Conference on Computational Intelligence (ICCI)*. DOI: 10.1109/ICCI51257.2020.9247722

Alkinani, M. H., Almazroi, A. A., Jhanjhi, N., & Khan, N. A. (2021). 5G and IoT Based Reporting and Accident Detection (RAD) System to Deliver First Aid Box Using Unmanned Aerial Vehicle. *Sensors (Basel)*, *21*(20), 6905. DOI: 10.3390/s21206905 PMID: 34696118

Awadallah, O., Grolinger, K., & Sadhu, A. (2024). Remote collaborative framework for real-time structural condition assessment using Augmented Reality. *Advanced Engineering Informatics*, *62*, 102652. DOI: 10.1016/j.aei.2024.102652

Azam, H., Tan, M., Pin, L. T., Syahmi, M. A., Qian, A. L. W., Jingyan, H., Uddin, M. F., & Sindiramutty, S. R. (2023). Wireless Technology Security and Privacy: A Comprehensive Study. *Preprints.org*. DOI: 10.20944/preprints202311.0664.v1

Babbar, H., Rani, S., Masud, M., Verma, S., Anand, D., & Jhanjhi, N. (2021). Load balancing algorithm for migrating switches in software-defined vehicular networks. *Computers, Materials & Continua/Computers. Computers, Materials & Continua*, *67*(1), 1301–1316. DOI: 10.32604/cmc.2021.014627

Baker, E., & Baker, E. (2023, March 30). *UPS rolls out 20 more driving and delivery training simulators.* Parcel and Postal Technology International. https://www.parcelandpostaltechnologyinternational.com/news/vehicles-fleet/ups-rolls-out-20-more-driving-and-delivery-training-simulators.html

Balushi, J. S. G. A., Palarimath, S., Mohamed, C. R., Jabri, M. I. A., & Radhakrishnan, V. (2024, October 3). *Transforming Computer Practice Teaching through Virtual Reality: Trends and Future Directions.* https://ijircst.irpublications.org/index.php/ijircst/article/view/132

Barmaki, R., Yu, K., Pearlman, R., Shingles, R., Bork, F., Osgood, G. M., & Navab, N. (2019). Enhancement of Anatomical Education using Augmented Reality: An Empirical study of Body painting. *Anatomical Sciences Education*, *12*(6), 599–609. DOI: 10.1002/ase.1858 PMID: 30648818

Besalti, M., & Smith, G. G. (2024). High School Students' Motivation to Learn Climate Change Science through Educational Computer Games. *Simulation & Gaming*, *55*(3), 527–551. DOI: 10.1177/10468781241235754

Bhatnagar, D., & Boruah, A. (2024). Virtual Reality. *Wiley*, 229–247. DOI: 10.1002/9781394200498.ch14

Bhowmik, A. K. (2024). Virtual and augmented reality: Human sensory-perceptual requirements and trends for immersive spatial computing experiences. *Journal of the Society for Information Display*, *32*(8), 605–646. DOI: 10.1002/jsid.2001

Brohi, S. N., Jhanjhi, N., Brohi, N. N., & Brohi, M. N. (2020). Key Applications of State-of-the-Art Technologies to Mitigate and Eliminate COVID-19.pdf. *TECHRxiv*. DOI: 10.36227/techrxiv.12115596.v1

Buckley, C., & Jorge, M. F. C. (2024). Upskilling for the modern workplace. [iJAC]. *International Journal of Advanced Corporate Learning*, *17*(4), 94–108. DOI: 10.3991/ijac.v17i4.51277

Burden, D., & Savin-Baden, M. (2024). *The metaverse: A Critical Introduction.* CRC Press. DOI: 10.1201/9781003395461

Bursztein, E., Brown, K. J., Sanderson, L. M., & Kelley, P. G. (2024). Leveraging Virtual Reality to Enhance Diversity, Equity and Inclusion training at Google. *ACM*, 1–7. DOI: 10.1145/3613905.3637128

Cao, C., & Cheng, S. (2024). Does competition in online games foster green behaviour in life? The relationship between gamification affordances and engagement in green behaviours. *International Journal of Human-Computer Interaction*, •••, 1–18. DOI: 10.1080/10447318.2024.2338657

Çeken, B., & Taşkın, N. (2024). Examination of multimedia learning principles in augmented reality and virtual reality learning environments. *Journal of Computer Assisted Learning*, *41*(1), e13097. Advance online publication. DOI: 10.1111/jcal.13097

Cevikbas, M., Bulut, N., & Kaiser, G. (2023). Exploring the benefits and drawbacks of AR and VR technologies for learners of mathematics: Recent developments. *Systems*, *11*(5), 244. DOI: 10.3390/systems11050244

Chandrashekar, N. D., Lee, A., Azab, M., & Gracanin, D. (2024). Understanding User Behavior for Enhancing Cybersecurity Training with Immersive Gamified Platforms. *Information (Basel)*, *15*(12), 814. DOI: 10.3390/info15120814

Charlet, M. (2024). Surgery of the future: Harnessing the power of virtual reality and augmented reality. In *Elsevier eBooks* (pp. 125–145). DOI: 10.1016/B978-0-443-24049-2.00003-0

Chauhan, S., & Sachdeva, L. (2024). Immersed in reality Secured by design — A comprehensive analysis of security measures in AR/VR environments. *arXiv (Cornell University)*. https://doi.org//arxiv.2404.16839DOI: 10.48550

Chesti, I. A., Humayun, M., Sama, N. U., & Jhanjhi, N. (2020). Evolution, Mitigation, and Prevention of Ransomware. *2020 2nd International Conference on Computer and Information Sciences (ICCIS)*. DOI: 10.1109/ICCIS49240.2020.9257708

Christopoulos, A., Styliou, M., Ntalas, N., & Stylios, C. (2024). The impact of immersive virtual reality on knowledge acquisition and adolescent perceptions in cultural education. *Information (Basel)*, *15*(5), 261. DOI: 10.3390/info15050261

Creed, C., Al-Kalbani, M., Theil, A., Sarcar, S., & Williams, I. (2023). Inclusive Augmented and Virtual Reality: A research agenda. *International Journal of Human-Computer Interaction*, *40*(20), 6200–6219. DOI: 10.1080/10447318.2023.2247614

Damaševičius, R., & Sidekerskienė, T. (2024). Virtual Worlds for Learning in Metaverse: A Narrative review. *Sustainability (Basel)*, *16*(5), 2032. DOI: 10.3390/su16052032

Dogra, V., Singh, A., Verma, S., Kavita, N., Jhanjhi, N. Z., & Talib, M. N. (2021). Analyzing DistilBERT for Sentiment Classification of Banking Financial News. In *Lecture notes in networks and systems* (pp. 501–510). DOI: 10.1007/978-981-16-3153-5_53

Dong, J., Ota, K., & Dong, M. (2024). User experience of different groups in social VR applications: An empirical study based on user reviews. *IEEE Transactions on Computational Social Systems*, *11*(6), 1–13. DOI: 10.1109/TCSS.2024.3416208

Fabre, B., Bribet, J., Lescieux, L., & Caussarieu, A. (2024). Improving efficiency in optics education with immersive virtual reality. *Optical Engineering (Redondo Beach, Calif.)*, *63*(07). Advance online publication. DOI: 10.1117/1.OE.63.7.071411

Fatima-Tuz-Zahra, N., Jhanjhi, N., Brohi, S. N., Malik, N. A., & Humayun, M. (2020). Proposing a Hybrid RPL Protocol for Rank and Wormhole Attack Mitigation using Machine Learning. *2020 2nd International Conference on Computer and Information Sciences (ICCIS)*. DOI: 10.1109/ICCIS49240.2020.9257607

Gkintoni, E., Vantaraki, F., Skoulidi, C., Anastassopoulos, P., & Vantarakis, A. (2024). Promoting Physical and Mental Health among Children and Adolescents via Gamification—A Conceptual Systematic Review. *Behavioral Sciences (Basel, Switzerland)*, *14*(2), 102. DOI: 10.3390/bs14020102 PMID: 38392455

Gopi, R., Sathiyamoorthi, V., Selvakumar, S., Manikandan, R., Chatterjee, P., Jhanjhi, N. Z., & Luhach, A. K. (2021). Enhanced method of ANN based model for detection of DDoS attacks on multimedia internet of things. *Multimedia Tools and Applications*, *81*(19), 26739–26757. DOI: 10.1007/s11042-021-10640-6

Gouda, W., Almurafeh, M., Humayun, M., & Jhanjhi, N. Z. (2022). Detection of COVID-19 based on chest x-rays using deep learning. *Health Care*, *10*(2), 343. DOI: 10.3390/healthcare10020343 PMID: 35206957

Hammami, H. (2024). Exploring the mediating role of user engagement in the relationship between immersive experiences and user satisfaction in virtual reality gaming. *International Review of Management and Marketing*, *15*(1), 9–16. DOI: 10.32479/irmm.17343

Hamza, M. A., Ejaz, U., & Kim, H. (2024). Cyber5Gym: An integrated framework for 5G cybersecurity training. *Electronics (Basel)*, *13*(5), 888. DOI: 10.3390/electronics13050888

Humayun, M., Sujatha, R., Almuayqil, S. N., & Jhanjhi, N. Z. (2022). A Transfer Learning Approach with a Convolutional Neural Network for the Classification of Lung Carcinoma. *Health Care*, *10*(6), 1058. DOI: 10.3390/healthcare10061058 PMID: 35742109

Hussain, K., Rahmatyar, A. R., Riskhan, B., Sheikh, M. U., & Sindiramutty, S. R. (2024). Threats and Vulnerabilities of Wireless Networks in the Internet of Things (IoT). *IEEE 1st Karachi Section Humanitarian Technology Conference (KHI-HTC)*, *2*, 1–8. DOI: 10.1109/KHI-HTC60760.2024.10482197

Irene, M. (2024). Policing virtual reality and promising cyber peace: an impending need for integration of cybersecurity. In *Routledge eBooks* (pp. 163–181). DOI: 10.4324/9781003517290-17

Iyer, R., Maralapalle, V. C., & Mahesh, P. (2024). Virtual reality (VR) and augmented reality (AR) in vocational training. In *Advances in educational technologies and instructional design book series* (pp. 73–92). DOI: 10.4018/979-8-3693-8252-3.ch004

Jagatheesaperumal, S. K., Ahmad, K., Al-Fuqaha, A., & Qadir, J. (2024). Advancing education through extended reality and internet of everything enabled metaverses: Applications, challenges, and open issues. *IEEE Transactions on Learning Technologies, 17*, 1–20. DOI: 10.1109/TLT.2024.3358859

Jhanjhi, N., Humayun, M., & Almuayqil, S. N. (2021). Cyber security and privacy issues in industrial internet of things. *Computer Systems Science and Engineering, 37*(3), 361–380. DOI: 10.32604/csse.2021.015206

Jun, A. Y. M., Jinu, B. A., Seng, L. K., Maharaiq, M. H. F. B. Z., Khongsuwan, W., Junn, B. T. K., Hao, A. W., & Sindiramutty, S. R. (2024). Exploring the Impact of Crypto-Ransomware on Critical Industries: Case Studies and Solutions. *Preprints.org*. DOI: 10.20944/preprints202409.1325.v1

Kachhi, Z. (2024). Gamified success. In *Advances in media, entertainment and the arts (AMEA) book series* (pp. 157–176). DOI: 10.4018/979-8-3693-8322-3.ch007

Kartal, S. (2008). *Virtual dissections in the teaching of practical biology in South African high schools.* https://ujcontent.uj.ac.za/esploro/outputs/doctoral/Virtual-dissections-in-the-teaching-of/999945407691

Kasture, A. B. (2024). THE USE OF AUGMENTED REALITY (AR) INENGINEERING AND MEDICINE. *Journal of Top Trending Technology, 01*(01), 31–42. DOI: 10.71063/DJTTT.2025.1104

Khalid, I. L., Abdullah, M. N. S., & Fadzil, H. M. (2024). A Systematic Review: Digital Learning in STEM Education. *Journal of Advanced Research in Applied Sciences and Engineering Technology, 51*(1), 98–115. DOI: 10.37934/araset.51.1.98115

Khan, N., Ahmad, K., Tamimi, A. A., Alani, M. M., Bermak, A., & Khalil, I. (2024). Explainable AI-based Intrusion Detection System for Industry 5.0: An Overview of the Literature, associated Challenges, the existing Solutions, and Potential Research Directions. *arXiv (Cornell University)*. https://doi.org//arxiv.2408.03335DOI: 10.48550

Kiyani, F. F., Hamid, B., Humayun, M., Sindiramutty, S. R. L., & Chowdhury, S. (2024). Discovery of Influential Publications Using Research Article's Usage Context. *2024 International Conference on Emerging Trends in Networks and Computer Communications (ETNCC)*, 1–7. DOI: 10.1109/ETNCC63262.2024.10767576

Kraglund-Gauthier, W. (2015). Book Review- The New Digital Shoreline: How Web 2.0 and Millennials are Revolutionizing Higher Education. *Journal of Teaching and Learning With Technology*, *80–82*, 80–82. Advance online publication. DOI: 10.14434/jotlt.v4n1.13497

Kumar, M. S., Vimal, S., Jhanjhi, N., Dhanabalan, S. S., & Alhumyani, H. A. (2021). Blockchain based peer to peer communication in autonomous drone operation. *Energy Reports*, *7*, 7925–7939. DOI: 10.1016/j.egyr.2021.08.073

Kumar, R., Jain, V., Han, G. T. W., & Touzene, A. (2023). *Immersive virtual and augmented reality in healthcare: An IoT and Blockchain Perspective*. CRC Press. DOI: 10.1201/9781003340133

Kurni, M. (2024). *G, S. K.* IoT-Enabled Gamification for Education. In The Internet of Educational Things., DOI: 10.1007/978-3-031-67387-0_10

Lake, K., Kittrick, A. M., Desselle, M., Bo, A. P. L., Abayasiri, R. M., Fleming, J., Baghaei, N., & Kim, D. D. (2024). Cyber security and privacy issues in extended reality healthcare Applications: Scoping Review (Preprint). *JMIR XR and Spatial Computing.*, *1*, e59409. DOI: 10.2196/59409

LeBlanc, P. (2021). *Students first: Equity, Access, and Opportunity in Higher Education*. Harvard Education Press.

Lee, H., Wu, T., Lin, C., Wang, W., & Huang, Y. (2023). Integrating Computational Thinking into Scaffolding Learning: An innovative approach to enhance science, technology, engineering, and mathematics Hands-On learning. *Journal of Educational Computing Research*, *62*(2), 431–467. DOI: 10.1177/07356331231211916

Lee, K. (2012). Augmented reality in education and training. *TechTrends*, *56*(2), 13–21. DOI: 10.1007/s11528-012-0559-3

Lim, M., Abdullah, A., Jhanjhi, N., Khan, M. K., & Supramaniam, M. (2019). Link Prediction in Time-Evolving Criminal Network with deep Reinforcement learning technique. *IEEE Access : Practical Innovations, Open Solutions*, *7*, 184797–184807. DOI: 10.1109/ACCESS.2019.2958873

Linqiang, Y., Sindiramutty, S. R. L., Ashraf, H., Muzammal, S. M., Balakrishnan, S. P., Gupta, S., & Kavita, N. (2024). Intelligent Household Waste Classification System Based on Machine Learning. *2024 International Conference on Emerging Trends in Networks and Computer Communications (ETNCC)*, 760–768. DOI: 10.1109/ETNCC63262.2024.10767563

Lu, Z., Shen, C., Li, J., Shen, H., & Wigdor, D. (2021). More Kawaii than a Real-Person Live Streamer: Understanding How the Otaku Community Engages with and Perceives Virtual YouTubers. *Acm*, 1–14. DOI: 10.1145/3411764.3445660

Maebela, M., & Dehinbo, J. (2024, August 27). *Enhancing Sustainable Development with the Development of a Virtual Driving License Testing System in Mabopane, South Africa*. https://papers.ssrn.com/sol3/papers.cfm?abstract_id=5059064

Manchuri, A., Kakera, A., Saleh, A., & Raja, S. (2024). pplication of Supervised Machine Learning Models in Biodiesel Production Research - A Short Review. *Borneo Journal of Sciences and Technology*. DOI: 10.35370/bjost.2024.6.1-10

Mauricio, F., Alvítez-Temoche, D., Del Aguila, E., Mayta-Tovalino, F., Silva, H., & Espinoza-Carhuancho, F. (2024). Scientometric analysis of the world scientific production on augmented and virtual reality in dental education. *The Journal of Contemporary Dental Practice*, *25*(4), 358–364. DOI: 10.5005/jp-journals-10024-3675 PMID: 38956852

Moro, C., Štromberga, Z., Raikos, A., & Stirling, A. (2017). The effectiveness of virtual and augmented reality in health sciences and medical anatomy. *Anatomical Sciences Education*, *10*(6), 549–559. DOI: 10.1002/ase.1696 PMID: 28419750

Motala, A., Youngman, A., Hancox, A., & Bravo, C. (2024). *Indigenous care VR simulations*. https://openlibrary-repo.ecampusontario.ca/xmlui/handle/123456789/2154

Nayyar, A., Gadhavi, L., & Zaman, N. (2021). Machine learning in healthcare: review, opportunities and challenges. In *Elsevier eBooks* (pp. 23–45). DOI: 10.1016/B978-0-12-821229-5.00011-2

Oigara, J. N. (2024). Exploring the use of virtual reality headsets as a learning tool for classroom instruction. In *Advances in educational technologies and instructional design book series* (pp. 153–180). DOI: 10.4018/979-8-3693-6030-9.ch006

Olosunde, B. (2014). Impact of Cybersecurity Skills Gap on the U.S. Economy and National Security. *International Journal of Innovative Science, Engineering & Technology*, *11*(12), 61–76. https://www.babatopeolosunde.com/media/sm0jo4fo/impact-of-cybersecurity-skills.pdf

Park, G. L., Hegazy, S. A., Sepe, J., Swigart, J., Burnette, M., Beltran, J., & Hernandez, C. (2025). Fostering Competencies: A scoping review of escape rooms in medical education. *Medical Science Educator*, *35*(2), 1111–1121. Advance online publication. DOI: 10.1007/s40670-024-02270-y PMID: 40352986

Pujiono, I. P., Asfahani, A., & Rachman, A. (2024). Augmented reality (AR) and virtual reality (VR): recent developments and applications in various industries. *j-innovative.org*. https://doi.org/DOI: 10.31004/innovative.v4i4.12377

Qawasmeh, S. A., AlQahtani, A. S., & Khan, M. K. (2024). Navigating Cybersecurity Training: A Comprehensive review. *arXiv (Cornell University)*. https://doi.org//arxiv.2401.11326DOI: 10.48550

Ramya, R., & Ramamoorthy, S. (2024). AI in Communication Technology and Innovation of AR/VR in Communication. In *Advances in linguistics and communication studies* (pp. 1–28). DOI: 10.4018/979-8-3693-3579-6.ch001

Rana, S., & Chicone, R. (2024). Gamification and Immersive Learning with AI. In *Fortifying for Future* (pp. 51–75). DOI: 10.1007/978-3-031-81780-9_3

Ravichandran, N., Tewaraja, T., Rajasegaran, V., Kumar, S. S., Gunasekar, S. K. L., & Sindiramutty, S. R. (2024). Comprehensive Review Analysis and Countermeasures for Cybersecurity Threats: DDoS, Ransomware, and Trojan Horse Attacks. *Preprints.org*. DOI: 10.20944/preprints202409.1369.v1

Sabina. (n.d.). *Cybernetics Lab IMA & IFU | European Monitor of Industrial Ecosystems*. European Monitor of Industrial Ecosystems. https://monitor-industrial-ecosystems.ec.europa.eu/technology-centre/cybernetics-lab-ima-ifu

Seng, Y. J., Cen, T. Y., Raslan, M. H. B. M., Subramaniam, M. R., Xin, L. Y., Kin, S. J., Long, M. S., & Sindiramutty, S. R. (2024). In-Depth Analysis and Countermeasures for Ransomware Attacks: Case Studies and Recommendations. *Preprint.org*. DOI: 10.20944/preprints202408.2261.v1

Serrano-Ausejo, E., & Mårell-Olsson, E. (2023). Opportunities and challenges of using immersive technologies to support students' spatial ability and 21st-century skills in K-12 education. *Education and Information Technologies*, *29*(5), 5571–5597. DOI: 10.1007/s10639-023-11981-5

Shah, I. A., Jhanjhi, N. Z., & Laraib, A. (2022). Cybersecurity and blockchain usage in contemporary business. In *Advances in information security, privacy, and ethics book series* (pp. 49–64). DOI: 10.4018/978-1-6684-5284-4.ch003

Sharma, R., Singh, A., Kavita, N., Jhanjhi, N. Z., Masud, M., Jaha, E. S., & Verma, S. (2021). Plant disease diagnosis and image classification using deep learning. *Computers, Materials & Continua/Computers. Materials & Continua (Print)*, *71*(2), 2125–2140. DOI: 10.32604/cmc.2022.020017

Sharma, S. (2024). Revolutionizing teacher education with Cutting-Edge Digital Solutions. In *Advances in educational marketing, administration, and leadership book series* (pp. 291–310). DOI: 10.4018/979-8-3693-6880-0.ch014

Sheng, L. T., Azman, A. B., Khan, N. A., Sindiramutty, S. R., Singh, S., & Verma, S. (2024). Reinforcement learning-based traffic signal control. *2024 International Conference on Emerging Trends in Networks and Computer Communications (ET-NCC)*, 792–798. DOI: 10.1109/ETNCC63262.2024.10767501

Shorman, D. A. (2024). *Examining the role of immersive technologies in preparing preservice elementary teachers: augmented reality, integrated STEM, teaching self-efficacy, and technology self-efficacy*. DigitalCommons@University of Nebraska - Lincoln. https://digitalcommons.unl.edu/dissunl/72/

Shwartz, S. (2021). *Evil robots, killer computers, and other myths: The Truth About AI and the Future of Humanity*. Greenleaf Book Group.

Simon, P. (2023). *Here's how workers at companies like Accenture and Walmart are using virtual reality*. Fast Company. https://www.fastcompany.com/90876215/how-workers-at-accenture-and-walmart-are-using-virtual-reality

Sindiramutty, S. R. (2024). Autonomous Threat Hunting: a future paradigm for AI-Driven Threat intelligence. *arXiv (Cornell University)*. https://doi.org//arxiv.2401.00286DOI: 10.48550

Sindiramutty, S. R., Jhanjhi, N. Z., Ray, S. K., Jazri, H., Khan, N. A., Gaur, L., Gharib, A., & Manchuri, A. R. (2023). Metaverse. In *Advances in medical technologies and clinical practice book series* (pp. 24–92). DOI: 10.4018/978-1-6684-9823-1.ch002

Sindiramutty, S. R., Jhanjhi, N. Z., Tan, C. E., Khan, N. A., Gharib, A. H., & Yun, K. J. (2023). Applications of blockchain technology in supply chain management. In *Advances in logistics, operations, and management science book series* (pp. 248–304). DOI: 10.4018/978-1-6684-7625-3.ch009

Sindiramutty, S. R., Jhanjhi, N. Z., Tan, C. E., Khan, N. A., Shah, B., & Manchuri, A. R. (2024). Cybersecurity measures for logistics industry. In *Advances in information security, privacy, and ethics book series* (pp. 1–58). DOI: 10.4018/979-8-3693-3816-2.ch001

Sindiramutty, S. R., Jhanjhi, N. Z., Tan, C. E., Yun, K. J., Manchuri, A. R., Ashraf, H., Murugesan, R. K., Tee, W. J., & Hussain, M. (2024). Data security and privacy concerns in drone operations. In *Advances in information security, privacy, and ethics book series* (pp. 236–290). DOI: 10.4018/979-8-3693-0774-8.ch010

Sindiramutty, S. R., Tan, C. E., & Wei, G. W. (2024). Eyes in the sky. In *Advances in information security, privacy, and ethics book series* (pp. 405–451). DOI: 10.4018/979-8-3693-0774-8.ch017

Singhal, V., Jain, S. S., Anand, D., Singh, A., Verma, S., Kavita, N., Rodrigues, J. J. P. C., Jhanjhi, N. Z., Ghosh, U., Jo, O., & Iwendi, C. (2020). Artificial Intelligence Enabled Road Vehicle-Train Collision Risk Assessment Framework for Unmanned railway level crossings. *IEEE Access : Practical Innovations, Open Solutions, 8*, 113790–113806. DOI: 10.1109/ACCESS.2020.3002416

Slater, M., & Sanchez-Vives, M. V. (2016). Enhancing Our Lives with Immersive Virtual Reality. *Frontiers in Robotics and AI, 3*. Advance online publication. DOI: 10.3389/frobt.2016.00074

Sun, L., Kangas, M., & Ruokamo, H. (2023). Game-based features in intelligent game-based learning environments: A systematic literature review. *Interactive Learning Environments*, •••, 1–17. DOI: 10.1080/10494820.2023.2179638

Swargiary, K. (2024). *Integrating IoT in education: (Transforming Learning Through Smart Technologies)*. EdTech Research Association.

Thompson, J. D., Herman, G. L., Scheponik, T., Oliva, L., Sherman, A., Golaszewski, E., Phatak, D., & Patsourakos, K. (2018). *Student Misconceptions about Cybersecurity Concepts: Analysis of Think-Aloud Interviews*. DigitalCommons@Kennesaw State University. https://digitalcommons.kennesaw.edu/jcerp/vol2018/iss1/5/

Toledano, S. A. (2024). *Critical infrastructure security: Cybersecurity lessons learned from real-world breaches*. Packt Publishing Ltd.

Understanding emerging Technology - Virtual Reality/Augmented Reality | VR / AR | COMPTIA. (n.d.). CompTIA. https://www.comptia.org/content/research/understanding-emerging-technology-virtual-reality-augmented-reality

Vairamani, A. D. (2024). Enhancing Social Skills Development Through Augmented Reality (AR) and Virtual Reality (VR) in Special Education. *Wiley*, 65–89. DOI: 10.1002/9781394167586.ch3

Waheed, A., Seegolam, B., Jowaheer, M. F., Sze, C. L. X., Hua, E. T. F., & Sindiramutty, S. R. (2024). Zero-Day Exploits in Cybersecurity: Case Studies and Countermeasure. *Preprints.org*. DOI: 10.20944/preprints202407.2338.v1

Wang, Q., & Li, Y. (2024). How virtual reality, augmented reality and mixed reality facilitate teacher education: A systematic review. *Journal of Computer Assisted Learning, 40*(3), 1276–1294. DOI: 10.1111/jcal.12949

Weiqi, X., Hooi, S. T. C., Sindiramutty, S. R. L., Asirvatham, D. L., Kumar, D., & Verma, S. (2024). Surface Anomaly Detection Using Machine Learning Technique. *2024 International Conference on Emerging Trends in Networks and Computer Communications (ETNCC)*, 1–7. DOI: 10.1109/ETNCC63262.2024.10767562

Xu, Q., Xiong, X., & Xu, X. (2024). *Research on Building an Open Assessment and Evaluation System for Smart Classroom Teaching Based on Computer Aided Technology*. EAI., DOI: 10.4108/eai.13-10-2023.2341337

Yadav, S. (2024). Navigating the virtual classroom with virtual reality. In *Advances in educational technologies and instructional design book series* (pp. 29–54). DOI: 10.4018/979-8-3693-6030-9.ch002

Yamijala, S. M., Nimbrain, N., & Bansal, R. (2024). Enhancing remote workspaces. In *Advances in human resources management and organizational development book series* (pp. 171–190). DOI: 10.4018/979-8-3693-6839-8.ch009

Ying, X., Murugesan, R. K., Sindiramutty, S. R., Wei, G. W., Balakrishnan, S., Kumar, D., & Verma, S. (2024). Scene Text Recognition using Deep Learning Techniques. *2024 International Conference on Emerging Trends in Networks and Computer Communications (ETNCC)*, 1–9. DOI: 10.1109/ETNCC63262.2024.10767484

You, F., Fu, Q., Yang, J., Chen, H., Cui, W., & Wang, J. (2023). Team Situation Awareness-Based Augmented Reality Head-Up Display design for security requirements. *International Journal of Human-Computer Interaction, 40*(18), 5119–5138. DOI: 10.1080/10447318.2023.2231281

Chapter 2
Enhancing Cybersecurity Skills Through Gamified Learning: Practical Applications and Strategies

Andi Asrifan
https://orcid.org/0000-0002-9934-6129
Universitas Negeri Makassar, Indonesia

Raveenthiran Vivekanantharasa
The Open University of Sri Lanka, Sri Lanka

Nurul Aini
https://orcid.org/0009-0007-7929-0512
IAIN Kediri, Indonesia

ABSTRACT

The swiftly advancing digital environment demands comprehensive cybersecurity education to counteract progressively complex threats and mitigate the expanding skills deficit in the sector. Conventional training methods frequently neglect to captivate learners and impart the practical skills essential for real-world applications. Gamified learning provides a dynamic and successful approach by incorporating game design ideas into cybersecurity training programs, markedly improving motivation, skill retention, and practical experience. This research examines the convergence of gamification and cybersecurity education, emphasizing the efficacy of simulations, serious games, and competitive settings such as Capture the Flag (CTF) challenges. Emerging technologies, including artificial intelligence (AI),

DOI: 10.4018/979-8-3373-0477-9.ch002

virtual reality (VR), and augmented reality (AR), are analyzed for their capacity to develop immersive, adaptable training environments. Ethical considerations, such as inclusivity and data protection, are also examined, highlighting the necessity for equal and effective training programs.

INTRODUCTION TO CYBERSECURITY AND GAMIFICATION

Understanding Cybersecurity

Cybersecurity has become an essential domain in a progressively digital landscape focused on safeguarding systems, networks, and data from cyber threats. Cybersecurity includes several techniques, technologies, and processes to protect information and ensure data confidentiality, integrity, and availability (Kim, 2022; Taherdoost, 2022). As enterprises increasingly depend on digital infrastructure for their operations, strong cybersecurity measures are paramount. A solitary breach can result in considerable financial losses, reputational harm, and legal consequences, necessitating that firms emphasize security in their strategic strategy.

The cybersecurity landscape is ever-changing, influenced by technological breakthroughs and the increasing sophistication of cybercriminals (Nadeem et al., 2023). Current trends encompass the escalation of ransomware assaults, wherein criminal entities encrypt data and solicit money for its decryption, with the growing incidence of phishing schemes that exploit human vulnerabilities to obtain illegal access to sensitive information. The expansion of Internet of Things (IoT) devices has increased the attack surface, posing new problems for security professionals. Organizations must also contend with compliance mandates and regulatory frameworks, such as the General Data Protection Regulation (GDPR) and the Health Insurance Portability and Accountability Act (HIPAA), which further complicate cybersecurity.

As threats increase in complexity, the demand for proficient cybersecurity experts continues to rise. Nonetheless, a significant skills gap exists in the industry, as numerous organizations encounter difficulties in locating suitable people for essential positions. Conventional training techniques frequently inadequately equip individuals with the actual experience and skills needed for effectively addressing cyber dangers (Srivatanakul & Annansingh, 2022). Gamified learning introduces a unique methodology for cybersecurity education.

Gamification utilizes game design components to improve educational experiences, rendering them more captivating and interactive. Through the integration of competition, prizes, and real-world scenarios, gamified learning can enhance comprehension of cybersecurity ideas and augment skill retention (Taherdoost,

2024). This method encourages learners and enables them to hone their abilities in a secure setting, equipping them for the obstacles they will encounter in the field.

The convergence of cybersecurity and gamification offers a distinctive potential to tackle the industry's urgent demand for proficient workers. By using gamified learning methodologies, firms can develop a workforce that is more adept at managing the intricacies of the cybersecurity domain and efficiently reducing risks.

The Role of Gamification in Learning

Gamification denotes implementing game design features and ideas in non-gaming environments to improve user engagement, motivation, and educational results (Bitrián et al., 2021). It converts conventional learning settings into engaging and participatory platforms by incorporating point systems, leaderboards, challenges, and prizes into educational encounters. This method leverages learners' inherent motivations, promoting their active and sustained engagement in educational pursuits.

The fundamentals of gamification are based on comprehending how games engage players. Essential components are explicit objectives, prompt feedback, a feeling of accomplishment, and social engagement. Games frequently offer a controlled setting where players can explore, err, and acquire knowledge without encountering real-world repercussions. By integrating these ideas into education, instructors can cultivate a more engaging and effective learning experience that promotes profound understanding and skill development (Darling-Hammond et al., 2024).

In cybersecurity training, gamified learning provides many advantages that tackle the specific issues encountered by the industry (Taherdoost, 2024; Alnajim et al., 2023). Firstly, it improves engagement. Conventional training techniques, including lectures and rote memorization, may be monotonous and unmotivating (Pandey et al., 2023). Conversely, gamified learning engages learners by offering challenges that necessitate critical thinking and problem-solving abilities, rendering the educational experience pleasant and invigorating.

Secondly, gamification fosters active learning (Murillo-Zamorano et al., 2021). Rather than passively absorbing material, learners are urged to engage actively in simulations and situations that replicate authentic cybersecurity concerns. This experiential learning enables learners to implement theoretical concepts in practical contexts, enhancing comprehension and recall.

Furthermore, gamified learning promotes peer collaboration and constructive rivalry (Dindar et al., 2021). Numerous gamified platforms integrate social components, like team challenges and leaderboards, which promote collaboration, knowledge sharing, and mutual motivation among learners. This collaborative setting promotes individual learning and fosters a sense of community, vital in cybersecurity, where teamwork is frequently needed for efficient problem-solving.

Ultimately, gamification offers instantaneous feedback, enabling learners to evaluate their performance and recognize areas for enhancement in real-time (Lampropoulos et al., 2022). This feedback loop is essential for skill enhancement, as it allows individuals to modify their learning approaches and concentrate on their deficiencies.

In conclusion, gamification is essential for improving learning experiences, especially in cybersecurity. Organizations can utilize game design features to develop engaging, interactive, and successful training programs that prepare learners to navigate the intricacies of the cybersecurity landscape. This novel strategy not only mitigates the business's skills deficit but also cultivates a culture of perpetual learning and enhancement.

Intersection of Cybersecurity and Gamification

The convergence of cybersecurity and gamification offers a significant possibility to mitigate critical training deficiencies in the cybersecurity workforce (Rana & Chicone, 2025). As cyber dangers grow more sophisticated, the demand for proficient personnel with practical capabilities is essential. Conventional training approaches cannot frequently interest learners or offer the practical experience essential for equipping them for real-world issues. Gamification, emphasizing engagement, interaction, and practical application, is a viable answer to these challenges.

Gamification mostly solves deficiencies in cybersecurity instruction by augmenting student engagement. Conventional training programs frequently depend on passive learning techniques, including lectures and textbook readings, resulting in disengagement and diminished retention rates (Gerges, 2025). Conversely, gamified learning experiences engage users in dynamic scenarios that replicate authentic cybersecurity concerns. For instance, learners may be assigned the responsibility of safeguarding a virtual network from simulated assaults, necessitating the application of their expertise in a dynamic setting. This active involvement maintains learner engagement and fosters the development of critical thinking and problem-solving abilities vital for proficient cybersecurity practice.

Furthermore, gamification facilitates individualized learning experiences. Students can advance at their speed, addressing problems commensurate with their abilities while obtaining prompt feedback on their success (Strielkowski et al., 2024). This tailored method identifies knowledge deficiencies and enables learners to concentrate on areas needing enhancement, so improving their overall cybersecurity proficiency.

Numerous case studies demonstrate the effective application of gamified learning in cybersecurity training. A prominent instance is the Capture the Flag (CTF) competitions, which test players' abilities to resolve cybersecurity-related riddles and tasks

(Zhong et al., 2024). Diverse companies and educational institutions have embraced these competitions to cultivate practical skills within a competitive yet cooperative setting. Participants acquire practical experience and develop excellent teamwork skills, reflecting the collaborative essence of actual cybersecurity operations.

Another instance is the emergence of gamified training platforms like Cybrary and Immersive Laboratories, which offer interactive laboratories and situations, enabling users to hone their abilities in a secure environment (Okolie & Okoye, 2023). These platforms include gamification components such as points, badges, and leaderboards to incentivize learners and monitor their advancement, making the educational experience pleasurable and efficient.

The convergence of cybersecurity and gamification provides novel solutions to the industry's training deficiencies. By utilizing gamified learning experiences, organizations may boost engagement, offer individualized training, and cultivate a knowledgeable workforce adept at addressing the increasing problems of cybersecurity. Successful case studies illustrate that gamification enhances learning efficacy and equips professionals to navigate the complexities of real-world cyber threats.

DESIGNING GAMIFIED LEARNING EXPERIENCES

Elements of Game Design

Creating impactful gamified learning experiences necessitates a comprehensive grasp of game design principles and their application in educational settings (Adams & Du Preez, 2024). Three fundamental elements—rules, objectives, feedback, and player motivation—are central to effective game design. Each of these components is essential for developing captivating and significant educational experiences.

Rules are the fundamental principles that dictate the operation of a game. In a gamified learning environment, explicit rules delineate participant expectations, offering structure and a framework for learners to navigate (Abdul et al. 2022). These regulations must be clear and explicit, enabling learners to comprehend the expectations and the means to succeed. In a cybersecurity training simulation, regulations may govern participants' responses to cyber threats, ensuring meaningful engagement with the subject.

Objectives delineate the aims that players endeavor to accomplish within the game. In an educational context, objectives must correspond with learning outcomes, directing students toward particular skills and knowledge (Hailikari et al., 2022). Explicit, attainable goals inspire learners by providing them with a sense of purpose and direction. For example, in a gamified cybersecurity training module, objectives may encompass accurately identifying phishing attempts or safeguarding a network against simulated attacks. This congruence improves engagement and guarantees the learning experience is pertinent and applicable to real-world contexts.

Feedback is an essential element in game design. Delivering prompt and constructive feedback enables learners to comprehend their performance and recognize areas for enhancement. In gamified learning, feedback may manifest as scores, badges, or progress indicators (Puig et al., 2023). This feedback mechanism motivates learners to contemplate their actions, modify their techniques, and persist in advancing through the content. Upon finishing a cybersecurity task, participants may obtain comprehensive feedback regarding their decision-making process, emphasizing both strengths and faults.

Comprehending player motivation is crucial for creating effective gamified learning experiences. Distinct motivators, including achievement, social engagement, or innate fascination with the subject matter drive diverse learners. Game design can leverage these motivations by integrating features such as challenges, competitiveness, and teamwork (Cascella et al., 2023). Leaderboards can cultivate competitiveness among learners, but team-based tasks can promote collaboration and knowledge exchange. Educators can enhance the learning environment's engagement and efficacy by matching game mechanics with student motivations.

In summary, game design components—rules, objectives, feedback, and comprehension of player motivation—are essential for developing effective gamified learning experiences. By strategically incorporating these elements into cybersecurity training programs, educators may improve engagement, promote skill acquisition, and eventually equip learners to manage the intricacies of the cybersecurity domain.

Creating Cybersecurity Scenarios

Creating authentic cybersecurity challenges and situations is essential for building effective gamified learning experiences. These scenarios must encapsulate the intricacies and subtleties of authentic cybersecurity risks while allowing learners to use their abilities in a secure and regulated setting. Through the simulation of genuine scenarios, educators can develop engaging and significant learning experiences that equip participants for the obstacles they will encounter in their professional lives (AbuKhousa et al., 2023).

To construct successful cybersecurity scenarios, it is imperative first to ascertain the exact skills and information that learners must acquire (Chowdhury et al., 2022). This may encompass domains like threat detection, incident response, vulnerability assessment, and risk management. Upon establishing these competencies, educators can create circumstances necessitating learners to utilize these talents in authentic contexts. A scenario may entail a simulated ransomware assault in which participants must detect the breach, evaluate the damage, and execute a response plan to alleviate the organization's impact.

Integrating real-world situations into gamified exercises is an effective method for augmenting the relevance and realism of training scenarios. By examining real cybersecurity breaches and occurrences, educators can derive essential lessons and difficulties that students may face (Ulven & Wangen, 2021). An example scenario may involve a prominent data breach, such as the Equifax incident, wherein participants must address the intricacies of detecting vulnerabilities, comprehending the attack vector, and devising a response strategy. This method not only anchors the learning experience in reality but also challenges learners to evaluate the consequences of their choices critically.

Furthermore, situations must be crafted to incorporate diverse levels of complexity and difficulty to cater to learners with differing skill sets. Educators can implement tiered tasks to ensure that all participants are sufficiently challenged while facilitating skill improvement (Giannakos et al., 2024). For instance, novices may engage in fundamental situations centered on recognizing phishing emails, whereas advanced practitioners could address intricate, multi-faceted attacks necessitating strategic reasoning and teamwork.

Moreover, integrating storytelling components can augment student engagement and immersion. By situating scenarios inside a narrative framework, educators can cultivate a more engaging experience that connects with participants (Kersting et al., 2024). A hypothetical situation may depict a fictional organization confronting a cyber threat, with players assuming roles like security analysts or incident responders. This storytelling method enhances the learning experience by fostering relatability and promoting collaboration and communication among learners.

In conclusion, developing authentic cybersecurity scenarios is crucial for impactful gamified learning experiences. By creating challenges that mirror real-world scenarios and integrating genuine components, instructors may improve engagement, promote skill application, and more effectively equip learners for the intricacies of the cybersecurity domain. This method enhances the learning experience and promotes a profound comprehension of the essential abilities required for success in the profession.

Tools and Platforms for Gamified Learning

The emergence of gamification in education has resulted in the creation of numerous tools and systems to improve learning experiences through game-like components (Cal, 2024). These tools can substantially enhance cybersecurity training programs by offering dynamic, engaging, and effective learning environments.

Comprehending the numerous alternatives and choosing the appropriate instruments is essential for optimizing the effectiveness of gamified learning.

Numerous prominent gamification tools and platforms have surfaced recently, each providing distinctive features designed to address various learning requirements. Kahoot! is a prominent platform enabling instructors to design interactive quizzes and challenges for real-time participation. This technology promotes engagement via competition and prompt feedback, rendering it suitable for reinforcing cybersecurity principles in an enjoyable and accessible way (Ramaila, 2024).

Classcraft is a notable technology that converts the classroom environment into a role-playing game, allowing students to accumulate points and awards for exemplary behavior and academic accomplishments (Krishnan et al., 2021). This platform promotes cooperation and teamwork, vital components in cybersecurity training, where experts frequently collaborate to address intricate difficulties.

Platforms dedicated to cybersecurity, such as Cybrary and Immersive Labs, provide customized gamified learning experiences centered on cybersecurity competencies (Tempestini et al., 2024). These platforms offer practical laboratories, simulations, and challenges that enable learners to engage with real-world scenarios in a regulated setting.

Through interaction with these platforms, learners can cultivate essential abilities while obtaining prompt feedback on their performance (Morris et al., 2021).

When choosing appropriate technologies for cybersecurity training, various parameters must be evaluated to guarantee efficacy and alignment with educational goals:

1. Alignment with Learning Objectives: The chosen tool must closely correspond to the particular abilities and knowledge that learners must attain. Cybersecurity training may encompass tools that provide scenarios pertaining to threat detection, incident response, or risk assessment.
2. User Engagement: The instrument must facilitate active participation and involvement among learners. Elements such as competition, prizes, and interactivity can augment motivation and motivate learners to engage deeply in the training process.
3. Flexibility and Customization: An effective gamification tool must permit customization to accommodate the specific requirements of the training program. This encompasses the capacity to develop customized scenarios, challenges, and evaluations that mirror the organization's distinct cybersecurity environment.
4. Analytics and Reporting: The capacity to monitor learner advancement and performance is crucial for assessing the training program's efficacy. Analytics tools enable educators to discern knowledge deficiencies and opportunities for enhancement.

5. Usability: The platform must be accessible and intuitive for educators and students. An intuitive interface can enhance implementation efficiency and diminish obstacles to participation.

In conclusion, choosing appropriate gamification technologies and platforms is essential for improving cybersecurity training experiences. By utilizing widely accepted tools that correspond with educational goals and integrating pertinent, engaging material, companies can develop effective gamified learning environments that equip learners for the challenges of the cybersecurity domain.

PRACTICAL APPLICATIONS OF GAMIFIED LEARNING IN CYBERSECURITY

Simulation-Based Training

Simulation-based training has become an effective instrument for improving cybersecurity competencies, allowing learners to participate in realistic scenarios that replicate genuine cyber risks (Rana & Chicone, 2025). This method enables participants to hone their abilities in a secure and regulated setting, promoting enhanced learning and skill retention. Simulation-based training offers numerous advantages, especially pertinent to cybersecurity, where the risks are significant, and the environment is perpetually changing.

A primary advantage of employing simulations is providing practical experience (Doerner & Horst, 2022). In a domain where theoretical knowledge is inadequate, simulations offer learners actual applications of their skills. Participants may investigate diverse attack vectors, safeguard against threats, and react to occurrences in real-time. This experiential learning solidifies theoretical principles and empowers learners to use their knowledge in practical contexts confidently. A simulated phishing attack can assist learners in identifying the indicators of such risks, so equipping them to respond adeptly when confronted with analogous scenarios in their jobs.

A notable benefit of simulation-based training is learning from errors without incurring real-world repercussions. Cybersecurity experts frequently encounter high-pressure scenarios for rapid decision-making (Nepal et al., 2024). Simulations enable learners to explore various tactics, commit errors, and evaluate results in a risk-free setting. This iterative learning process cultivates critical thinking and problem-solving abilities, which are vital for efficient incident response.

Numerous simulation tools have been prominent in the cybersecurity training domain, each providing distinct features that enrich the educational experience (Ahmed et al., 2024). Cybeready is a prominent platform that offers realistic simulations of cyberattacks, enabling learners to hone their abilities in a dynamic setting. Participants may partake in scenarios like network breaches, malware infections, and data exfiltration, acquiring significant insights into the methodologies employed by cybercriminals.

RangeForce is an excellent solution that provides a cloud-based training platform integrating simulations with gamified components. It is a collection of interactive laboratories that test learners' abilities to counter diverse cyber threats while they accumulate points and badges for their accomplishments. This gamified method increases engagement and fosters a competitive ethos among learners, driving them to develop their skills perpetually.

Moreover, platforms such as Immersive Labs emphasize scenario-based training that adjusts to contemporary risks. These platforms guarantee that learners possess the most pertinent skills and information by consistently upgrading their content to mirror the latest cyber occurrences. This adaptability is vital in a domain where new threats arise swiftly, and remaining educated is crucial for good cybersecurity practices.

In conclusion, simulation-based training provides substantial advantages for improving cybersecurity competencies. Organizations can enhance their workforce's preparedness for the intricacies of the cybersecurity landscape by offering practical experience, facilitating safe experimentation, and employing effective simulation tools. This method promotes skill enhancement and nurtures a proactive mentality crucial for addressing the constantly changing landscape of cyber threats.

Serious Games and Cybersecurity

Serious games have evolved as an effective method for cybersecurity training, integrating fun with education to facilitate engaging learning experiences (Zhao et al., 2024). In contrast to conventional training approaches, serious games engage participants in interactive settings that allow them to hone their skills, make decisions, and learn from the outcomes of their actions. This novel method increases engagement and fosters a more profound comprehension and recall of essential cybersecurity principles.

A prominent instance of a serious game developed for cybersecurity instruction is “Escape Room: Cybersecurity Edition.” In this game, users must collaborate to resolve puzzles and tasks that simulate real-world cybersecurity situations, such as detecting weaknesses in a network or addressing a data breach. The game is designed to promote collaboration, communication, and analytical reasoning, requiring participants to exchange insights and plans to advance. The game yields learning effects such as greater problem-solving abilities, a deeper comprehension of cybersecurity principles, and improved teamwork capabilities under duress (Pirta-Dreimane et al., 2024).

A notable serious game is "Cybersecurity Lab," created by the University of Cambridge. This game enables players to assume the position of a cybersecurity expert responsible for safeguarding a network from diverse attacks. Players must assess incoming data, recognize potential threats, and execute suitable countermeasures. The game integrates authentic situations from real cyber incidents, offering participants a pragmatic comprehension of threat identification and mitigation. The "Cybersecurity Lab" learning outcomes encompass enhanced analytical abilities, proficiency in cybersecurity tools and methodologies, and an enriched understanding of the complexity associated with safeguarding digital assets (Mohamed, 2024).

"Hacknet" is a serious game that simulates the hacker experience, enabling players to investigate the realm of cybersecurity from an alternative viewpoint. In this game, participants must traverse a sequence of hacking challenges, acquiring knowledge about network security, vulnerabilities, and the ethical ramifications of hacking. Through participation in the game, players understand the mentality of cybercriminals, enhancing their ability to defend against such attacks in their professional capacities (Martineau et al., 2024). The educational benefits from "Hacknet" encompass an augmented comprehension of hacking methodologies, refined technical proficiencies, and an increased awareness of cybersecurity ethics.

The efficacy of serious games in cybersecurity training is attributed to their capacity to generate immersive, interactive experiences that encourage learners to engage thoroughly with the content (Spatafora et al., 2024). These games impart significant knowledge and skills while promoting critical thinking, teamwork, and adaptability—crucial attributes for cybersecurity workers confronting a constantly changing threat environment.

In summary, serious games serve as an effective instrument for improving cybersecurity training. By engaging learners in authentic circumstances and encouraging active involvement, these games foster essential skills and knowledge acquisition. As enterprises increasingly acknowledge the significance of gamified learning experiences, serious games will be essential in equipping the forthcoming generation of cybersecurity professionals to confront the complexities of the digital landscape.

Competitions and Challenges

Capture the Flag (CTF) competitions have emerged as a fundamental component of cybersecurity education, offering a dynamic and competitive setting for skill enhancement (Chindrus & Caruntu, 2023). These activities compel participants to address cybersecurity-related challenges, encompassing encryption, web vulnerabilities, reverse engineering, and network exploitation. The competitive aspect of

CTFs promotes participation and cultivates teamwork, critical thinking, and real-time problem-solving—vital competencies for any cybersecurity practitioner.

CTF tournaments generally feature teams or individuals vying to capture "flags," which are concealed data elements that signify the successful resolution of a task (Zafar et al., 2024). Each task is crafted to evaluate particular abilities and knowledge, enabling participants to implement theoretical principles in actual situations. This practical experience is vital, enhancing learning and allowing participants to build confidence in their skills. For example, a challenge may necessitate players to exploit a compromised online application, granting them direct experience in recognizing and addressing security vulnerabilities.

Engaging in and organizing CTF tournaments can markedly improve the educational experience for cybersecurity students and professionals (Balon & Baggili, 2023). Hosting a CTF can foster an engaging and collaborative environment for educators and training companies, promoting teamwork among participants to address challenges. Organizers can customize challenges to correspond with certain learning objectives, guaranteeing that participants acquire pertinent abilities. Furthermore, CTFs can be structured to mirror contemporary cybersecurity trends and dangers, ensuring participants remain aware and equipped for real-world situations.

Participation in CTF tournaments provides several advantages for individuals. In addition to skill enhancement, these events facilitate networking, enabling aspiring cybersecurity professionals to engage with peers, mentors, and industry experts (Venn-Wycherley et al., 2024). Numerous CTFs are sponsored by organizations seeking to find and recruit talent, rendering participation a possible avenue for job chances. Moreover, the experience acquired through CTFs can significantly enhance resumes, demonstrating practical competencies and a dedication to ongoing education.

Prominent CTF tournaments, such DEF CON CTF and the Collegiate Penetration Testing Competition (CPTC), have garnered acclaim within the cybersecurity community (Balon & Baggili, 2023). These events draw global attendees and frequently feature industry professionals' workshops and lectures, enhancing the educational experience. The challenges in these competitions differ in complexity, accommodating both novices and experienced experts, thereby promoting an inclusive atmosphere for skill enhancement.

In summary, CTF competitions are essential for improving cybersecurity abilities via gamified educational experiences. These challenges equip participants for the intricacies of the cybersecurity market by offering a competitive platform for practical application, teamwork, and networking. As enterprises and educational institutions progressively use CTFs, they will remain a crucial element of good cybersecurity training, fostering the development of the next generation of adept professionals prepared to confront rising threats.

STRATEGIES FOR IMPLEMENTING GAMIFIED LEARNING

Setting Learning Objectives

Establishing explicit and quantifiable learning objectives is a crucial step in efficiently implementing gamified learning methodologies, especially in cybersecurity training (Chowdhury et al., 2022). Clearly, articulated objectives offer a framework for instructors and learners, guaranteeing that all activities are intentional and connected with intended outcomes. In the ever-changing realm of cybersecurity, where requisite abilities are always advancing, setting explicit objectives is crucial for optimizing the efficacy of gamified experiences.

Learning objectives must be specific, measurable, achievable, relevant, and time-bound (SMART). For example, rather of a nebulous target such as "understanding cybersecurity threats," a more efficacious objective would be to "identify and classify a minimum of five distinct categories of cybersecurity threats within one hour." This explicit and quantifiable goal establishes expectations for learners and allows teachers to evaluate progress and efficacy with precision. By concentrating on particular competencies, such as threat detection, incident response, or vulnerability assessment, businesses may guarantee that their training programs meet the most urgent requirements of their staff (Kulkov et al., 2024).

It is equally crucial to align gamified activities with organizational objectives. Cybersecurity training must align with the organization's overarching goals and should not operate in isolation (Thomas & Sule, 2023; Chowdhury et al., 2022). For instance, if a business seeks to improve its security posture, the training program must prioritize skills in risk management, incident response, and adherence to regulatory compliance. By associating gamified activities with corporate objectives, educators can establish a unified training experience that enhances individual competencies while advancing the organization's performance.

Moreover, engaging stakeholders in the objective-setting process might augment the pertinence of the training program. Involving cybersecurity specialists, management, and end-users in dialogues regarding essential skills and knowledge might provide significant insights (Pollini et al., 2022). This collaborative method guarantees that the training is customized to address the unique issues encountered by the business and that participants recognize the immediate relevance of their training to their positions.

Moreover, it is imperative to include feedback mechanisms in the learning objectives. Consistent assessments and evaluations facilitate monitoring progress toward established outcomes, enabling required adjustments to be implemented (Hager et al., 2024). This iterative procedure guarantees that the training adapts to the changing requirements of both learners and the organization.

In summary, establishing explicit and quantifiable learning objectives is an essential tactic for executing gamified learning in cybersecurity training. Educators may develop targeted, pertinent, and impactful training experiences by delineating particular outcomes and linking activities with company objectives. This strategic strategy increases individual skill development and fortifies the organization's overall cybersecurity capabilities, equipping it to handle the intricacies of the digital ecosystem.

Engaging Stakeholders

Involving stakeholders is essential for effectively implementing gamified learning methodologies, especially in cybersecurity training (Taherdoost, 2024). Securing endorsement from management and participants guarantees that the training program is endorsed, pertinent, and efficacious. By cultivating a perpetual learning and enhancement culture, organizations may optimize the advantages of gamification and strengthen their overall cybersecurity stance.

To secure management's support, it is crucial to explicitly convey the benefits of gamified learning in fulfilling the organization's cybersecurity requirements. Exhibiting data and case studies that illustrate the efficacy of gamification in skill development can aid in convincing decision-makers (Guerrero & Kalmi, 2022). For instance, showcasing the achievements of other firms that have adopted gamified training might demonstrate the potential return on investment. Moreover, linking training objectives with business goals—such as minimizing security incidents or improving regulatory compliance—can further bolster the argument for gamification.

Effective management entails their participation in the planning process. Leaders are more likely to feel committed in the program by requesting their feedback on training objectives and expected outcomes (Day et al., 2021). Consistent updates on progress and results help sustain their engagement and backing during the implementation phase, cultivating a sense of ownership over the training program.

For participants, effective engagement tactics encompass articulating the advantages of gamified learning and its relevance to their responsibilities. Emphasizing gamification's engaging and pleasurable elements can mitigate opposition to innovative training approaches (Gimenez-Fernandez et al., 2021). Moreover, providing incentives—such as awards for accomplishments or acknowledgment for involvement—can encourage learners to participate actively in the training process.

Establishing a continual learning and growth culture is vital for maintaining long-term engagement (Mlambo et al., 2021). Organizations should foster an environment that empowers employees to pursue learning opportunities, disseminate knowledge, and collaborate with peers. This can be accomplished by incorporating gamified learning into standard training regimens and offering continuous access to resources, including webinars, workshops, and online courses.

Furthermore, establishing open communication channels for participants to offer feedback on the gamified learning experience is essential. Organizations can exhibit their dedication to continuous development by heeding learner input and implementing requisite modifications (McDermott et al., 2021). This improves the training experience and emphasizes that learning is the corporation's and its employees' collective obligation.

In conclusion, including stakeholders is essential for effectively implementing gamified learning in cybersecurity training. By securing support from management and participants while cultivating a culture of continuous learning and growth, organizations can establish an environment conducive to skill development and bolster overall cybersecurity preparedness. This cooperative strategy enhances the efficacy of gamified training and fosters a more robust organizational culture in response to emerging cyber threats.

Measuring Success and Outcomes

Assessing the progress and results of gamified learning projects is essential for evaluating their efficacy and facilitating ongoing enhancement (Aliu et al., 2024). In cybersecurity training, defining explicit metrics and key performance indicators (KPIs) enables enterprises to assess the effectiveness of their gamified experiences on skill enhancement and overall cybersecurity preparedness.

Organizations must establish precise measures that correspond with their educational objectives. These metrics may encompass quantitative indicators such as completion rates, assessment scores, and duration required to accomplish tasks. Monitoring the proportion of participants who successfully finish a gamified module can yield insights regarding engagement levels and content efficacy. Furthermore, assessing the mean scores on evaluations prior to and after training might facilitate the appraisal of information retention and skill acquisition.

Qualitative indicators are also vital in evaluating the efficacy of gamified learning (Poženel et al., 2022). Collecting feedback from participants via questionnaires, interviews, or focus groups can yield significant insights into their experiences and perspectives of the program. Inquiries may center on the perceived significance of the content, the degree of involvement, and the applicability of acquired skills to practical situations. This input can identify areas for enhancement and guide subsequent revisions of the gamified experience.

Key performance indicators (KPIs) must be defined to evaluate the overall impact of gamified learning on business objectives (Pappas et al., 2021). This may encompass metrics pertaining to incident response durations, the quantity of reported security issues, and overall personnel retention rates within cybersecurity positions. A decrease in successful phishing attempts within the business may serve as a direct sign of the efficacy of gamified training aimed at threat identification and awareness.

Upon establishing measurements and KPIs, companies ought to institute a systematic evaluation process to evaluate the efficacy of their gamified learning projects (Pappas et al., 2021). This iterative method facilitates continuous modifications informed by gathered data and participant input. If participants frequently indicate that specific problems are too tough or irrelevant, educators can adjust the content to address learners' requirements more effectively.

Furthermore, businesses must acknowledge achievements and disseminate results to stakeholders to emphasize the significance of gamified learning. Emphasizing advancements in skills, engagement, and overall cybersecurity posture may sustain support for continuous training projects.

In conclusion, evaluating success and outcomes is an essential technique for executing gamified learning in cybersecurity training. By defining explicit measurements and KPIs, companies may assess the efficacy of their programs and make data-informed decisions for ongoing enhancement. Collecting participant feedback and refining the gamified experience guarantees that training stays pertinent, interesting, and aligned with business objectives, thereby improving the overall cybersecurity proficiency of the workforce.

FUTURE TRENDS AND CONSIDERATIONS IN CYBERSECURITY EDUCATION

Emerging Technologies in Gamification

As cybersecurity education progresses, emerging technologies, including artificial intelligence (AI), virtual reality (VR), and augmented reality (AR), are set to substantially improve gamified learning experiences (Pirta-Dreimane et al., 2024). These technologies provide novel methods for developing immersive, interactive, and customized training environments, revolutionizing the instruction and acquisition of cybersecurity skills.

Artificial intelligence is crucial to customizing the educational experience. AI algorithms can tailor gamified content to individual needs by assessing learner behavior, performance data, and preferences (Suresh & Dhakshina, 2024). An AI-driven platform can detect learners' difficulties with cybersecurity concepts and offer customized challenges or resources to facilitate their improvement. This degree of customization increases engagement and guarantees that learners obtain the necessary support to cultivate their abilities efficiently.

Furthermore, AI can enhance the development of realistic simulations and scenarios by producing dynamic content that mirrors contemporary cybersecurity risks. Artificial Intelligence can contemporaneously revise training modules as cyber threats progress to incorporate the most recent attack routes and methodologies (Shyaa et al., 2024). This agility is essential for ensuring that cybersecurity personnel possess the most pertinent knowledge and abilities to address emerging threats.

Virtual reality (VR) provides an immersive training experience, enabling learners to participate in authentic simulations of cybersecurity situations. Virtual reality can replicate high-pressure scenarios, such as addressing a data breach or countering a cyberattack, by immersing participants in a fully interactive 3D environment (Kourtesis, 2024). This immersive experience enhances learning and retention, allowing participants to practice their abilities in a secure yet realistic environment. Furthermore, virtual reality can improve collaboration and communication abilities when participants work together in simulated situations to address intricate problems.

Augmented reality (AR) enhances virtual reality (VR) by superimposing digital information onto the physical environment (Rauschnabel, 2021). In cybersecurity training, augmented reality can deliver contextual information during practical exercises. For instance, while learners interact with physical devices, augmented reality might present pertinent information, such as possible weaknesses or optimal security procedures, directly inside their line of sight. This prompt access to information improves situational awareness and strengthens real-time learning.

The future incorporation of these technologies into gamified cybersecurity instruction is anticipated to increase substantially. Forecasts indicate that as AI, VR, and AR technologies become more available and cost-effective, enterprises will progressively integrate them to improve their training programs (Sun & Jung, 2024). This transition will probably yield more interesting and successful educational experiences, culminating in a more proficient and equipped cybersecurity workforce.

In conclusion, upcoming technologies such as artificial intelligence, virtual reality, and augmented reality are poised to transform gamified learning experiences in cybersecurity education. These technologies will augment engagement and skill acquisition by individualizing training, generating immersive simulations, and delivering contextual information. As enterprises adopt these innovations, the future of gamification in cybersecurity training is expected to be increasingly engaging, pertinent, and efficacious, enhancing individuals' preparedness to manage the intricacies of the digital environment.

Ethical Considerations in Gamified Learning

As gamified learning increasingly gains prominence in cybersecurity education, it is crucial to examine the ethical implications associated with its application (Idierukevbe & Addo, 2024). Although gamification presents various advantages regarding engagement and skill enhancement, potential ethical concerns must be meticulously addressed to guarantee that training programs are responsible, inclusive, and effective.

A significant ethical issue in gamification activities is the possibility of manipulation. Game mechanisms, like rewards and competition, can pressure learners to perform, potentially resulting in tension or anxiety (Lomos et al., 2023). Educators must create gamified experiences that encourage healthy competitiveness and intrinsic drive, avoiding an excessively competitive atmosphere that emphasizes winning over learning. Clarity on the goals of gamified activities and the significance of collaboration helps alleviate these hazards, ensuring that participants perceive support rather than coercion.

Another ethical problem is the possibility of prejudice in gamified content. Assume that the scenarios and difficulties depicted in a gamified training program exhibit skewed viewpoints or omit specific demographics. Consequently, it may reinforce prejudices and hinder the efficacy of training for various individuals. Organizations should endeavor to produce inclusive content representing diverse experiences and viewpoints within the cybersecurity domain. Involving several stakeholders in the development process helps guarantee that the training is pertinent and accessible to all learners (Chowdhury et al., 2022).

Inclusivity and accessibility are essential elements of ethical gamified education. Organizations must ensure that their training programs include persons with diverse talents and experiences. This encompasses evaluating elements such as linguistic obstacles, learning difficulties, and degrees of prior knowledge. Creating adaptable and flexible gamified experiences can address these varied requirements (Cheng & Chau, 2022). Offering many methods to interact with content—such as written instructions, video lessons, and interactive simulations—can improve accessibility for all learners.

Moreover, enterprises must consider data privacy and security issues while deploying gamified learning platforms. Collecting and analyzing learner data can yield significant insights for enhancing training programs; however, it is crucial to manage this information carefully. Organizations must guarantee adherence to data protection requirements and emphasize the confidentiality of participants' personal information.

In conclusion, addressing ethical considerations in gamified learning is essential for developing responsible and effective cybersecurity training programs. Organizations can create gamified experiences that promote a constructive learning environment by recognizing potential challenges associated with manipulation, bias, inclusion, and data privacy. Facilitating the accessibility and relevance of training programs for all participants optimizes skill development efficacy and fosters a culture of equity and respect within cybersecurity. As gamification advances, emphasizing ethical behaviors will be crucial for optimizing its advantages and mitigating pitfalls.

Lifelong Learning and Adaptation

In the swiftly advancing domain of cybersecurity, continuous skill enhancement is paramount. Cyber threats are complex, requiring experts to remain updated on the newest technology, strategies, and best practices. The evolving landscape of cybersecurity issues highlights the necessity for dedication to continuous learning, allowing individuals to adjust to emerging risks and sustain their efficacy in safeguarding digital assets (Safitra et al., 2023).

Lifelong learning in cybersecurity entails the perpetual enhancement of knowledge and abilities throughout one's professional journey. This is especially vital as fraudsters continuously innovate methods and exploit technological flaws. Professionals must comprehend fundamental concepts and interact with developing technologies like artificial intelligence, machine learning, and cloud security (Gill et al., 2022). By cultivating a culture of perpetual education, firms may guarantee that their personnel remain adaptable and proficient in addressing emerging risks.

Gamification is essential in fostering a lifelong learning mentality. Organizations can enhance learning experiences by including gamified aspects in training programs that encourage participants to seek continuous education (Jääskä & Aaltonen, 2022). Gamified learning environments frequently include challenges, incentives, and competition, which can enhance engagement and motivation for skill acquisition. Participants may accrue points or badges for completing training modules, engaging in cybersecurity challenges, or reaching specified milestones, so reinforcing the concept that learning is an ongoing endeavor.

Furthermore, gamified learning experiences can be tailored to be adaptable, enabling learners to advance at their own speed and review subjects as necessary. This adaptability is crucial for addressing cybersecurity practitioners' varied learning preferences and timetables. Organizations can enable individuals to take control of their learning paths and pursue relevant information by offering access to diverse resources, including interactive simulations, scenario-based challenges, and collaborative projects (Ahrari et al. 2021).

Fostering a culture of lifelong learning via gamification entails enhancing collaboration and knowledge exchange among peers. Collaborative challenges and competitions can enhance camaraderie and collective problem-solving, enabling participants to learn from one another and establish a robust support network (Mathunjwa et al., 2024; Dincă et al., 2023). This collaborative atmosphere develops individual skills and fortifies the organization's cybersecurity capabilities.

In conclusion, continuous skill enhancement is paramount to cybersecurity. Organizations can utilize gamification to foster a culture of lifelong learning, thereby developing interesting and adaptive training experiences that motivate professionals to enhance their knowledge and abilities perpetually. This dedication to learning and adaptation is crucial for managing the intricacies of the cybersecurity domain, ultimately resulting in a more robust and equipped workforce capable of confronting evolving threats. As the industry progresses, cultivating a culture of continuous learning will be essential for the efficacy and success of cybersecurity programs.

CONCLUSION

Incorporating gamified learning into cybersecurity education has demonstrated a transformational method for tackling the problems of a changing digital environment. Through the integration of engagement, interactivity, and practical application, gamification effectively addresses the cybersecurity skills gap. Conventional training techniques frequently inadequately equip professionals for the intricacies of actual threats. Gamified tactics, such as simulations, serious games, and contests, offer learners practical experience, enhancing critical thinking, problem-solving, and collaboration.

Gamification offers advantages surpassing skill development and augmenting motivation and retention via competition, prizes, and prompt feedback. Platforms like Cybrary and Immersive Labs illustrate how interactive situations may simulate real-world issues, enabling learners to hone and enhance their skills in a regulated setting. Furthermore, gamified learning promotes collaboration and a culture of perpetual enhancement, which is crucial for remaining ahead of advanced cyber threats.

Innovative technologies, such as artificial intelligence, virtual reality, and augmented reality, are set to enhance the efficacy of gamified training. These advances facilitate individualized, immersive, and adaptable learning experiences, ensuring professionals remain agile and well-prepared to confront new problems. Simultaneously, ethical considerations, including inclusivity, accessibility, and data privacy, must be prioritized to establish responsible and equitable training environments.

In summary, gamified learning signifies a crucial progression in cybersecurity education, providing professionals with the necessary skills and resilience for a swiftly evolving digital landscape. By promoting dedication to continuous education and adopting creative approaches, organizations may cultivate a workforce equipped to address the intricacies of cybersecurity, thereby enhancing a safer and more secure digital future.

REFERENCES

Abdul Ghani, A. S., Abdul Rahim, A. F., Yusoff, M. S. B., & Hadie, S. N. H. (2022). Developing an interactive PBL environment via persuasive gamify elements: A scoping review. [springer.com]. *Research and Practice in Technology Enhanced Learning*, *17*(1), 21. DOI: 10.1186/s41039-022-00193-z

AbuKhousa, E., El-Tahawy, M. S., & Atif, Y. (2023). Envisioning architecture of metaverse intensive learning experience (MiLEx): Career readiness in the 21st century and collective intelligence development .... Future Internet. mdpi.com

Adams, S. P. & Du Preez, R. (2024). Supporting student engagement through the gamification of learning activities: A design-based research approach. Technology. [HTML]

Ahmed, A., Watterson, C., Alhashmi, S., & Gaber, T. (2024). How universities teach cybersecurity courses online: A systematic literature review. [frontiersin.org]. *Frontiers of Computer Science*, *6*, 1499490. DOI: 10.3389/fcomp.2024.1499490

Ahrari, S., Roslan, S., Zaremohzzabieh, Z., Mohd Rasdi, R., & Abu Samah, A. (2021). Relationship between teacher empowerment and job satisfaction: A Meta-Analytic path analysis. [tandfonline.com]. *Cogent Education*, *8*(1), 1898737. DOI: 10.1080/2331186X.2021.1898737

Aliu, J., Oke, A. E., Abayomi, T., Aigbavboa, C., & Makanjuola, S. (2024). Exploring the critical success factors for adopting gamification in the Nigerian construction sector. [HTML]. *Built Environment Project and Asset Management*, *14*(2), 184–200. DOI: 10.1108/BEPAM-08-2023-0150

Alnajim, A. M., Habib, S., Islam, M., AlRawashdeh, H. S., & Wasim, M. (2023). Exploring cybersecurity education and training techniques: A comprehensive review of traditional, virtual reality, and augmented reality approaches. [mdpi.com]. *Symmetry*, *15*(12), 2175. DOI: 10.3390/sym15122175

Balon, T. & Baggili, I. (2023). Cybercompetitions: A survey of competitions, tools, and systems to support cybersecurity education. Education and Information Technologies. springer.com

Bitrián, P., Buil, I., & Catalán, S. (2021). Enhancing user engagement: The role of gamification in mobile apps. Journal of Business Research. sciencedirect.com

Cal, Y., Mayor-Peña, F., Barrera-Animas, A. Y., Escobar-Castillejos, D., Noguez, J., & Escobar-Castillejos, D. (2024, October). Designing a gamified approach for digital design education aligned with Education 4.0. [). Frontiers Media SA. frontiersin.org]. *Frontiers in Education*, *9*, 1439879. DOI: 10.3389/feduc.2024.1439879

Cascella, M., Cascella, A., Monaco, F., & Shariff, M. N. (2023). Envisioning gamification in anesthesia, pain management, and critical care: Basic principles, integration of artificial intelligence, and simulation strategies. [springer.com]. *Journal of Anesthesia, Analgesia and Critical Care*, *3*(1), 33. DOI: 10.1186/s44158-023-00118-2 PMID: 37697415

Cheng, C. & Chau, C. (2022). Gamification-based intervention for enhancing team effectiveness and coping flexibility: Randomized controlled trial. Frontiers in Psychiatry. frontiersin.org

Chindrus, C. & Caruntu, C. F. (2023). Securing the Network: A Red and Blue Cybersecurity Competition Case Study. Information. mdpi.com

Chowdhury, N., Katsikas, S., & Gkioulos, V. (2022). Modeling effective cybersecurity training frameworks: A delphi method-based study. Computers & Security. sciencedirect.com

Darling-Hammond, L., Schachner, A. C., Wojcikiewicz, S. K., & Flook, L. (2024). Educating teachers to enact the science of learning and development. [tandfonline.com]. *Applied Developmental Science*, *28*(1), 1–21. DOI: 10.1080/10888691.2022.2130506

Day, D., Bastardoz, N., Bisbey, T., Reyes, D., & Salas, E. (2021). Unlocking human potential through leadership training & development initiatives. [sagepub.com]. *Behavioral Science & Policy*, *7*(1), 41–54. DOI: 10.1177/237946152100700105

Dincă, M., Berge, T., Oni iu, A., Thomassen, M., Lu trea, A., Luche , D., & Cra ovan, M. (2023). Immersive Team-Based Learning in Transnational Virtual Classrooms. [sciendo.com]. *European Review Of Applied Sociology*, *16*(27), 51–70. DOI: 10.2478/eras-2023-0010

Dindar, M., Ren, L., & Järvenoja, H. (2021). An experimental study on the effects of gamified cooperation and competition on English vocabulary learning. [wiley.com]. *British Journal of Educational Technology*, *52*(1), 142–159. DOI: 10.1111/bjet.12977

Doerner, R. & Horst, R. (2022). Overcoming challenges when teaching hands-on courses about Virtual Reality and Augmented Reality: Methods, techniques and best practice. Graphics and Visual Computing. sciencedirect.com

Gerges, E. (2025). Beyond Lectures: The Flipped Learning Model. In Best Practices and Strategies for Online Instructors: Insights From Higher Education Online Faculty (pp. 133-166). IGI Global Scientific Publishing. [HTML]

Giannakos, M., Azevedo, R., Brusilovsky, P., Cukurova, M., Dimitriadis, Y., Hernandez-Leo, D., & Rienties, B. (2024). The promise and challenges of generative AI in education. [tandfonline.com]. *Behaviour & Information Technology*, •••, 1–27.

Gill, S. S., Xu, M., Ottaviani, C., Patros, P., Bahsoon, R., Shaghaghi, A., Golec, M., Stankovski, V., Wu, H., Abraham, A., Singh, M., Mehta, H., Ghosh, S. K., Baker, T., Parlikad, A. K., Lutfiyya, H., Kanhere, S. S., Sakellariou, R., Dustdar, S., & Uhlig, S. (2022). AI for next generation computing: Emerging trends and future directions. [PDF]. *Internet of Things : Engineering Cyber Physical Human Systems*, *19*, 100514. DOI: 10.1016/j.iot.2022.100514

Gimenez-Fernandez, E., Abril, C., Breuer, H., & Gudiksen, S. (2021). Gamification approaches for open innovation implementation: A conceptual framework. [wiley.com]. *Creativity and Innovation Management*, *30*(3), 455–474. DOI: 10.1111/caim.12452

Guerrero, E. & Kalmi, P. (2022). Gamification strategies: a characterization using formal argumentation theory. SN Computer Science. springer.com

Hager, P., Jungmann, F., Holland, R., Bhagat, K., Hubrecht, I., Knauer, M., Vielhauer, J., Makowski, M., Braren, R., Kaissis, G., & Rueckert, D. (2024). Evaluation and mitigation of the limitations of large language models in clinical decision-making. [nature.com]. *Nature Medicine*, *30*(9), 2613–2622. DOI: 10.1038/s41591-024-03097-1 PMID: 38965432

Hailikari, T., Virtanen, V., & Vesalainen..., M. (2022). Student perspectives on how different elements of constructive alignment support active learning. ... in Higher Education. sagepub.com

Idierukevbe, I. U. & Addo, A. (2024). Bridging the Cybersecurity Skills Gap: A Gamification Model. Journal of Business Studies Quarterly. [HTML]

Jääskä, E. & Aaltonen, K. (2022). Teachers' experiences of using game-based learning methods in project management higher education. Project Leadership and Society. sciencedirect.com

Kersting, M., Bondell, J., Steier, R., & Myers, M. (2024). Virtual reality in astronomy education: Reflecting on design principles through a dialogue between researchers and practitioners. International Journal of Science Education [tandfonline.com]. *Part B*, *14*(2), 157–176.

Kim, L. (2022). Cybersecurity: Ensuring confidentiality, integrity, and availability of information. In *Nursing Informatics: A Health Informatics, Interprofessional and Global Perspective* (pp. 391–410). Springer International Publishing. [HTML] DOI: 10.1007/978-3-030-91237-6_26

Kourtesis, P. (2024). A Comprehensive Review of Multimodal XR Applications, Risks, and Ethical Challenges in the Metaverse. Multimodal Technologies and Interaction. mdpi.com

Krishnan, S. D., Norman, H., & Md Yunus, M. (2021). Online gamified learning to enhance teachers' competencies using classcraft. Sustainability. mdpi.com

Kulkov, I., Kulkova, J., Rohrbeck, R., Menvielle, L., Kaartemo, V., & Makkonen, H. (2024). Artificial intelligence-driven sustainable development: Examining organizational, technical, and processing approaches to achieving global goals. [wiley.com]. *Sustainable Development (Bradford), 32*(3), 2253–2267. DOI: 10.1002/sd.2773

Lampropoulos, G., Keramopoulos, E., Diamantaras, K., & Evangelidis, G. (2022). Augmented reality and gamification in education: A systematic literature review of research, applications, and empirical studies. applied sciences, 12(13), 6809. mdpi.com

Lomos, C., Seineke, U., Kesting, F., & Luyten, J. W. (2023). The design of incentive systems in digital game-based learning: How primary school children interact with It. Education Sciences. mdpi.com

Martineau, M., Spiridon, E., & Aiken, M. (2024). Pathways to Criminal Hacking: Connecting Lived Experiences with Theoretical Explanations. Forensic Sciences. mdpi.com

Mathunjwa, M. L., Shandu, N. M., Ndwandwe, N. K., Shongwe, N., & Linda, N. (2024, December). Beyond the Classroom: The Social Benefits of Informal Sports for First-Year Students. In The Focus Conference (TFC 2024) (pp. 560-580). Atlantis Press. atlantis-press.com DOI: 10.2991/978-94-6463-630-7_31

McDermott, O., Antony, J., Sony, M., & Daly, S. (2021). Barriers and enablers for continuous improvement methodologies within the Irish pharmaceutical industry. Processes. mdpi.com

Mlambo, M., Silén, C., & McGrath, C. (2021). Lifelong learning and nurses' continuing professional development, a metasynthesis of the literature. BMC nursing. springer.com

Mohamed Saad, A. M. A. (2024). *Adapting accountants to the AI revolution: university strategies for skill enhancement, job security and competence in accounting.* Higher Education, Skills and Work-Based Learning. [HTML]

Morris, R., Perry, T., & Wardle, L. (2021). Formative assessment and feedback for learning in higher education: A systematic review. Review of Education. wiley.com

Murillo-Zamorano, L. R., López Sánchez, J. Á., Godoy-Caballero, A. L., & Bueno Muñoz, C. (2021). Gamification and active learning in higher education: Is it possible to match digital society, academia and students' interests? [springer.com]. *International Journal of Educational Technology in Higher Education*, *18*(1), 1–27. DOI: 10.1186/s41239-021-00249-y

Nadeem, M. A., Hashmi, S., & Khan, M. A. (2023). Exploring the Interplay of Cybersecurity and cybercrime in Pakistan's Digital Landscape. [cissmp.com]. *Contemporary Issues in Social Sciences and Management Practices*, *2*(4), 207–222. DOI: 10.61503/cissmp.v2i4.94

Nepal, S., Hernandez, J., Lewis, R., Chaudhry, A., Houck, B., Knudsen, E., . . . Czerwinski, M. (2024). Burnout in Cybersecurity Incident Responders: Exploring the Factors that Light the Fire. Proceedings of the ACM on Human-Computer Interaction, 8(CSCW1), 1-35. mit.edu

Okolie, J. A. & Okoye, P. U. (2023). The Infusion of Gamification in Promoting Chemical Engineering Laboratory Classes. Encyclopedia. mdpi.com

Pandey, A., Mittal, M., Ahmad, K., & Sharma, V. (2023). New Age Teaching Pedagogy: Innovative Teaching Methods and their Impact on Educational Performance of the Students. Redefining Virtual Teaching Learning Pedagogy, 59-73. [HTML]

Pappas, G., Papamichael, I., Zorpas, A., Siegel, J. E., Rutkowski, J., & Politopoulos, K. (2021). Modelling key performance indicators in a gamified waste management tool. [mdpi.com]. *Modelling*, *3*(1), 27–53. DOI: 10.3390/modelling3010003

Pirta-Dreimane, R., Brilingaitė, A., Roponena, E., Parish, K., Grabis, J., Lugo, R. G., & Bonders, M. (2024). Try to esCAPE from cybersecurity incidents! A technology-enhanced educational approach. Technology, Knowledge and Learning, 1-30. springer.com

Pollini, A., Callari, T. C., Tedeschi, A., Ruscio, D., Save, L., Chiarugi, F., & Guerri, D. (2022). Leveraging human factors in cybersecurity: An integrated methodological approach. [springer.com]. *Cognition Technology and Work*, *24*(2), 371–390. DOI: 10.1007/s10111-021-00683-y PMID: 34149309

Poženel, M., Zrnec, A., & Lavbič, D. (2022). Measuring how motivation affects information quality assessment: A gamification approach. PloS one. plos.org

Puig, A., Rodríguez, I., Rodríguez, Á, & Gallego, I. (2023). Evaluating learner engagement with gamification in online courses. Applied Sciences. mdpi.com

Ramaila, S. (2024). Harnessing Kahoot! as an educational tool to foster meaningful teaching and learning: A systematic review. African Journal of Teacher Education. uoguelph.ca

Rana, S., & Chicone, R. (2025). AI-Enhanced Virtual and Augmented Reality for Cybersecurity Training. In Fortifying the Future: Harnessing AI for Transformative Cybersecurity Training (pp. 101-131). Cham: Springer Nature Switzerland. [HTML]

Rana, S., & Chicone, R. (2025). Gamification and Immersive Learning with AI. In Fortifying the Future: Harnessing AI for Transformative Cybersecurity Training (pp. 51-75). Cham: Springer Nature Switzerland. [HTML] DOI: 10.1007/978-3-031-81780-9_3

Rauschnabel, P. A. (2021). Augmented reality is eating the real-world! The substitution of physical products by holograms. International Journal of Information Management. sciencedirect.com

Safitra, M. F., Lubis, M., & Fakhrurroja, H. (2023). Counterattacking cyber threats: A framework for the future of cybersecurity. Sustainability. mdpi.com

Shyaa, M. A., Ibrahim, N. F., Zainol, Z., Abdullah, R., Anbar, M., & Alzubaidi, L. (2024). Evolving cybersecurity frontiers: A comprehensive survey on concept drift and feature dynamics aware machine and deep learning in intrusion detection systems. [sciencedirect.com]. *Engineering Applications of Artificial Intelligence, 137*, 109143. DOI: 10.1016/j.engappai.2024.109143

Spatafora, A., Wagemann, M., Sandoval, C., Leisenberg, M., & Vaz de Carvalho, C. (2024). An Educational Escape Room Game to Develop Cybersecurity Skills. [mdpi.com]. *Computers, 13*(8), 205. DOI: 10.3390/computers13080205

Srivatanakul, T. & Annansingh, F. (2022). Incorporating active learning activities to the design and development of an undergraduate software and web security course. Journal of Computers in Education. springer.com

Strielkowski, W., Grebennikova, V., Lisovskiy, A., Rakhimova, G., & Vasileva, T. (2024). AI-driven adaptive learning for sustainable educational transformation. Sustainable Development. wiley.com

Sun, Y. & Jung, H. (2024). Machine Learning (ML) Modeling, IoT, and Optimizing Organizational Operations through Integrated Strategies: The Role of Technology and Human .... Sustainability. mdpi.com

Suresh Babu, S., & Dhakshina Moorthy, A. (2024). Application of artificial intelligence in adaptation of gamification in education: A literature review. [HTML]. *Computer Applications in Engineering Education*, *32*(1), e22683. DOI: 10.1002/cae.22683

Taherdoost, H. (2022). Understanding cybersecurity frameworks and information security standards—a review and comprehensive overview. Electronics. mdpi.com

Taherdoost, H. (2024). Towards an Innovative Model for Cybersecurity Awareness Training. Information. mdpi.com

Tempestini, G., Merà, S., Palange, M. P., Bucciarelli, A., & Di Nocera, F. (2024). Improving the Cybersecurity Awareness of Young Adults through a Game-Based Informal Learning Strategy. [mdpi.com]. *Information (Basel)*, *15*(10), 607. DOI: 10.3390/info15100607

Thomas, G., & Sule, M. J. (2023). A service lens on cybersecurity continuity and management for organizations' subsistence and growth. Organizational Cybersecurity Journal: Practice [emerald.com]. *Process and People*, *3*(1), 18–40.

Ulven, J. B. & Wangen, G. (2021). A systematic review of cybersecurity risks in higher education. Future Internet. mdpi.com

Venn-Wycherley, M., Ralph, J., & Moller, F. (2024, July). Experiences of a Pan-Wales Initiative of Cybersecurity Education in Schools. In Annual conference on Advances in Cyber Security Education (pp. 153-169). Cham: Springer Nature Switzerland. [HTML] DOI: 10.1007/978-3-031-77524-6_9

Zafar, A., Yamin, M. M., Katt, B., & Torseth, E. (2024). All flags are not created equal: A deep look into CTF Scoring Algorithms. Expert Systems with Applications. sciencedirect.com

Zhao, T., Gasiba, T., Lechner, U., & Pinto-Albuquerque, M. (2024). Thriving in the era of hybrid work: Raising cybersecurity awareness using serious games in industry trainings. [HTML]. *Journal of Systems and Software*, *210*, 111946. DOI: 10.1016/j.jss.2023.111946

Zhong, C., Liu, H., & Kam, H. J. (2024). Mining Reddit users' perspectives on cybersecurity competitions: A mixed method approach. [HTML]. *Information and Computer Security*, *32*(5), 636–655. DOI: 10.1108/ICS-02-2023-0017

Chapter 3
Foundations of Gamification in Cybersecurity Education

Abdul Azeem Khan
https://orcid.org/0000-0003-2742-8034
Universiti Islam Sultan Sharif Ali, Brunei

Abul Fadle Maidin
Universiti Islam Sultan Sharif Ali, Brunei

Sayan Kumar Ray
TUSB, Malaysia

Bashir Riskhan
Albukhari International University, Malaysia

ABSTRACT

In the cybersecurity ecosystem, gamification has transformed the way people learn by incorporating interactive learning approaches that have improved engagement levels, dedication, and retention. Gamification approach presents promising possibilities to address challenges faced by traditional methods that are unable to cope-up with technical complexities of cybersecurity educational domain. The shifting ethics and threats in cyberspace have inevitably led to the need for experiential learning that can foster a connection among peers and encourages communication skills by infusing game components into learning. The game components such as points, levels, reward systems, competition, co-operation, and narrative to build compelling educational experiences whereby many of the skills that sustain high demand, continuously learning and problem-solving traditions get shaped and practiced.

DOI: 10.4018/979-8-3373-0477-9.ch003

INTRODUCTION

Due to rising cyber threats like data breaches, ransomware, and identity theft compromising individuals, companies, and national security, cybersecurity education has also become essential. With an increasing dependence on technology, there comes an accompanying rise in the complexity of cyberattacks, creating an industry that urgently seeks professionals that can protect sensitive information from attacks and reduce potential risk(Khan, Jhanjhi, Hamid, Omar, Amsaad, & Ashraf, 2025). To address these issues organizations need to adopt Gamified approach to empower users with necessary cybersecurity skills which can't be merely taught through theoretical concepts hence it is inevitable to have a mechanisms with which the employees and all the other stakeholders who are part of this ever changing digital landscape to get hands on experience with optimum productivity which can help all stakeholders of this seamless digital ecosystem to learn the principles of cybersecurity(Khan, Jhanjhi, & Humayun, 2022) in not only in theory but also should be able to implement and practically handle it.

Figure 1. Rising market value of gamification (2019 – 2025)

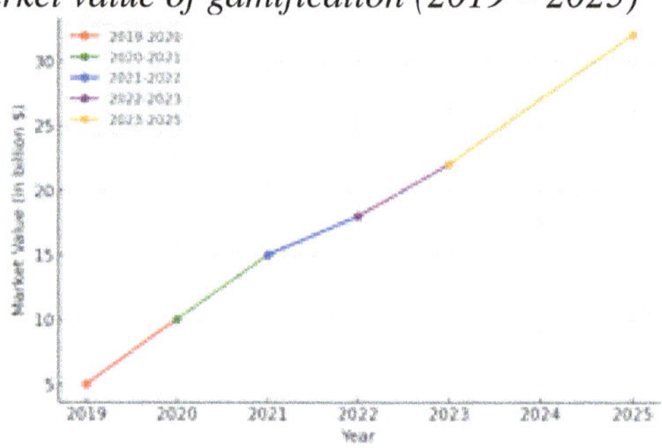

(mambo.io)

As depicted in Figure 1. there is an enormous increase in gamification tools which are in high demand and this necessity seems to be on high rise since 2019. To implement this gamification technique in cybersecurity has been a necessity as this field contains many complex concepts which seems to be abstract at a time which can't be taught just theoretically the users need to have hands on experience with optimal user engagement hence gamification has been found to be a successful approach that has yielded productive results in learning practical skills like threat analysis, security implementation, and incident response. Immersive, hands-on approaches to education that promote engagement, facilitate critical thinking, and provide real-world problem-solving abilities to combat emerging cyber threats must fill this gap(Shahid, Ashraf, Jhanjhi, & Zam, 2025).

Gamification is effective due to various psychological factors, including self-determination theory (SDT) and flow theory. Self-determination theory (SDT) suggests that experiences of autonomy, competence, and social relatedness foster greater motivation in learners which are components that are inherently foundational to gamified learning(Thompson, Melendez, Hempson-Jones, & Salvi, 2022). The theory of flow stresses balancing the challenge of a task and the level of skill required to stay engaged without experiencing frustration. Using these two theories learners can assure motivation and learning retention. Apart from it, gamification also promotes collaboration and critical thinking, which are important skills that are needed on Cybersecurity assignments and tasks. As the importance of cybersecurity education continues to grow, it is faced with critical challenges such as how to engage learners when the domain itself can be quite technical, abstract, and complicated. Conventional ways of teaching such as lectures, textbook-oriented learning, or theory-focused subjects, may not be enough to keep students engaged and motivated(Zhong, Kim, & Liu, 2024).

As comprehended a lot of cybersecurity concepts such as security frameworks, ethical-hacking, threat modeling, cryptography, network security, etc., to teach the learners there is a dire need a deep understanding of programming and mathematical logic(Santofimia et al., 2021). Technical terms in these topics could become stressful for a beginner, especially if they do not have a technical background, this can lead them to become rendered as a non-active member and at an individual level, hamper their learning. In addition to that, cybersecurity and threats are changing very rapidly and to stay abreast of the threat landscape, they need continual hands-on practice(Russo, Ribaudo, Orlich, Longo, & Armando, 2023). Traditional learning environments are often static, not allowing students to practice real world applications and reinforce their knowledge base. It restricts students from engaging with the hands-on implementation of fundamental security concepts, making it challenging for them to gain the skills required to address actual cybersecurity problems. The very first area that causes disengagement is due to there being no interactive learning models(Shukla, Singh, Sharma, Malik, & Kathuria, 2023). Rote memorization and assessments are often the focal point in traditional education methods, which may not effectively capture learners' attention or help them become critical thinkers. If learners are not engaged in their learning or given an interactive approach to explore the principles of cybersecurity, they may disengage, resulting in a lack of key concepts retention(Jin, Tu, Kim, Heffron, & White, 2018).

Figure 2. Key features of gamification

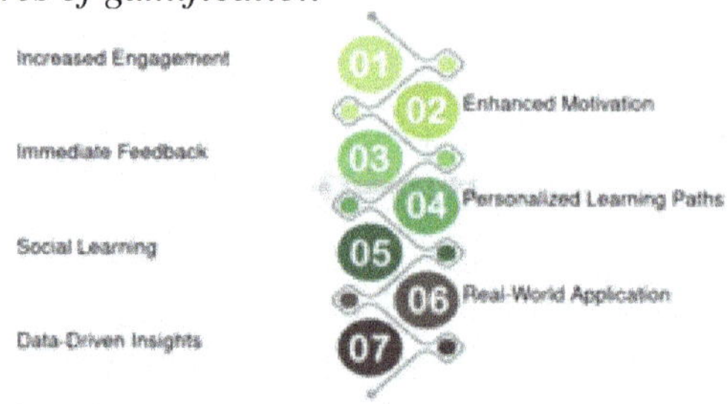

(FasterCapital, 2024)

As depicted in Figure 2 due to several benefits of gamification approach to name a few such as personalized learning paths, social learning with data driven insights through Real world applications with enhanced motivation, engagement and immediate feedback the game-based approach which is popularly known as gamification has proven to be a powerful learning mechanism to be implemented in cybersecurity education and has provided an effective solution to the problem of keeping learners engaged with complex technical topics(Karagiannis & Magkos, 2020). The use of game design elements such as contest, challenge, achievement, rewards, storytelling, etc. in an educational atmosphere to make an environment, which is exciting and interactive and improves motivation level and retention of knowledge(Kuwajima & Ishikawa, 2019). As compared to passive learning methods, gamification helps develop active participation, increases curiosity and builds analytical and problem-solving skills. Among gamification points widely used is Capture the Flag (CTF) competitions, which mimic real-world cyberattack and defense situations, enabling practical application of cybersecurity concepts(Ashraf, Jhanjhi, Brohi, & Muzafar, 2024). In a similar way cyber ranges offer virtual training environments to learners to practice on how to mitigate these threats without the risk of being attacked, thus creating adaptable professionals with practical skills(Diakoumakos, 2023).

While gamification has many benefits in cybersecurity education, it is not without challenges. Creating an experience that successfully achieves gamification should feature a game mechanic that relates directly to a specific educational goal and be scalable, accessible, and attractive making it a very challenging task. Moreover, its effect cannot be monitored although, it requires strong assessment frameworks to observe how much one implemented knowledge and absorbed skills. However, given the growing number of cybersecurity threats, incorporating gamification in education is a potent means to exceed theoretical education and being more practical in preparing future professionals for the ever-changing landscape of cybersecurity(Jelo & Helebrandt, 2022; Salama, Alturjman, Altrjman, & Al-Turjman, 2024).

WHAT IS GAMIFICATION?

Gamification is essentially incorporating game design elements and mechanics into non-game contexts to increase engagement, motivation, and learning results. Gamification is the process of incorporating game mechanics, dynamics, and aesthetics to non-game contexts, including applications in business, healthcare, education, and more, to promote participation and productivity. Gamification is based on psychological and behavioural theories about how people stay engaged and motivated with activities(Zola et al., 2025). These principles include:

1. **Intrinsic and Extrinsic Motivation:** Gamification leverages intrinsic motivation (learning for personal growth and skill acquisition) and extrinsic motivation (which brings prizes such as badges and points).
2. **Flow Theory**: Balance challenge and skill level so that the learner is engaged without being challenged too much or too little.
3. **Autonomy and Choice:** Learners are offered the freedom to make decisions.
4. **Instant Feedback & Rewards:** The learners work towards a goal and instant feedback shows them progress which improves the retention of the knowledge.
5. **Social Connection and Collaboration:** Many gamification techniques involve peer interaction, leaderboards, and competition, which promote teamwork and engagement.

Historical Context and Evolution of Gamification in Education

The gamification of education has evolved considerably from the days of red and yellow learning games and complex, AI-driven and calculating implementations. Prior to the 1980s, educators used simple Memory aids like using flashcards and quizzes, as well as role playing retention and problem-solving skills. Computer-based educational innovation in the 1980s and 1990s games became popular, with programs like Math Blaster and Oregon Trail promoting interactive digital experiences that translated concepts into tangible, actionable learning(Sharma & Sharma, 2023). From the 2000s to the 2010s, Massive Open Gamified elements (MOOCs) (Lexman & Baral, 2023) and Learning Management Systems (LMS). Addressing motivation and learning progress monitoring, gamification which comprises e.g. points, badges, leaderboards can be implemented for increased learning productivity. As Artificial Intelligence (AI), Virtual Reality (VR) and Augmented Reality (AR) are becoming more common, AR have been into place since the 2010s; gamification has also gone immersive and tailored to learners need(Vemuri, Thaneeru, & Tatikonda, 2024). Games-like immersive learning experiences have been developed to prepare hands-on and engaging education, including Capture the future cyber security professionals with battle scenarios(Aslam, 2024). Capture The Flag (CTF) competitions, and cyber ranges which further help simulate real-world cybersecurity scenarios in a virtual setting environment, while developing critical security skills without impacting any of the real-world consequences. This immediate use of any gamified process showcases a growing effort towards not just engagement, but experiential learning and mastery of a skill, effectively preparing students for whatever the more modern challenges of reality become(Zaman et al., 2022).

Table 1. Historical evolution of gamification

Time Period	Key Developments	Impact on Education
Pre-1980s	Traditional educational games (e.g., quizzes, flashcards, role-playing).	Early use of structured play to improve memorization and decision-making.
1980s-1990s	Rise of digital learning games like Math Blaster and Oregon Trail.	Introduced interactive learning and problem-solving via computer-based games.
2000s-2010s	Gamification principles (points, badges, leaderboards) integrated into MOOCs and LMS.	Increased student engagement and motivation in online learning environments.
2010s-Present	Advanced technologies like AI, VR, AR enhance gamified learning. Cybersecurity training adopts CTF competitions and cyber ranges.	Personalized learning, immersive simulations, and real-world skill application in cybersecurity and technical education.

Key Elements of Gamification: Points, Badges, Leaderboards, Challenges, and Narratives

Gamification leverages established game dynamics to produce captivating, enjoyable, and participatory learning environments. Points are a basic concept, helping learners collect points by scoring performance, giving immediate feedback, and providing an incentive to keep going. While badges serve as visual markers representing milestones, achievements, or mastery of specific skills, and motivate and recognize the learner. They are based on a competitive ranking that allows learners to see who is ahead of them, motivating social interaction and the drive to reach the highest performance. In addition to individual rewards, challenges and quests provide learners with structured tasks that require them to use problem-solving skills, develop strategies, and think critically, making the learning process more goal-oriented and immersive(Sindiramutty, Prabagaran, Jhanjhi, & Murugesan, 2024). Finally, narratives and storytelling form the building blocks for organizing and structuring educational content into engaging, relatable, and cohesive storylines, connecting engaged emotional implication meaning with educational material, promoting contextual learning, and retention. In this way, the game elements work together to establish an engaging learning environment to help simplify difficult subjects like cybersecurity, making them both meaningful and practical as learners are encouraged to not only comprehend concepts but gain direct expertise in solving real-world problems, (Luo, 2022).

Table 2. Key elements of gamification

Element	*Description*	*Educational Benefits*
Points	Numeric rewards for achievements, progress, and participation.	Provides instant feedback, encourages continued effort, and tracks progress.
Badges	Visual symbols of accomplishment for completing tasks or mastering skills.	Builds motivation and recognition, fostering a sense of achievement.
Leaderboards	Competitive ranking system displaying individual or team performance.	Encourages healthy competition and social engagement.
Challenges & Quests	Task-based activities requiring problem-solving and critical thinking.	Enhances engagement, strategy development, and practical skill application.

THE ROLE OF GAMIFICATION IN EDUCATION

Gamification has upended conventional education by morphing inactive studying into dynamic, captivating, and purposeful activities. By incorporating game elements such as scores, objectives, prizes, and narratives into instructional settings, educators can stimulate inspiration, engagement, and retention of ideas. Notably in intricate and technical areas including cybersecurity training, gamification cultivates proactive involvement and troubleshooting abilities, rendering theoretical notions more comprehensible and applicable. Complex subjects that were once dry and dull can be transformed into engaging puzzles and quests through which students must solve problems, collaborate, and apply their knowledge in a low-stakes environment. While some traditionalists remain sceptical of incorporating gameplay into learning, many students find that they are more motivated to learn and more likely to retain information in a gamified format which taps into our innate desires to set and achieve goals(Oliveira et al., 2023).

Figure 3. Human-focused approach to cybersecurity: Expanding the role of gamification

(keepnetlabs, 2025)

Psychological Theories Supporting Gamification

Gamification's effectiveness in education is deeply rooted in psychological and learning theories, particularly in theories of self-determination and flow. Self-Determination Theory suggests that people thrive when experiencing autonomy over their learning, developing competence through progress, and relating to others through shared experiences(Gil-Aciron, 2024). Gamification aligns with this by empowering students to control their journeys, earn rewards for advancing skills, and engage collaboratively. According to Flow Theory proposed by Mihaly Csikszentmihalyi, deep focus and motivation occur in a balanced state where, challenges match abilities. If tasks are too easy or hard, learners disengage through boredom or frustration. Gamification maintains this optimal engagement by dynamically tailoring difficulties to keep students immersed and inspired toward continued growth, (Xu et al., 2021).

Table 3. Key mechanisms of gamification

Mechanism	Description	Educational Benefits
Goal-Oriented Learning	Challenges, levels, and progression systems help students set and achieve incremental learning objectives, fostering a sense of accomplishment.	Provides instant feedback, encourages continued effort, and tracks progress.
Healthy Competition	Leaderboards and performance tracking motivate students to challenge themselves and their peers, increasing engagement.	Builds motivation and recognition, fostering a sense of achievement.
Personalization & Autonomy	Learners can choose their learning paths, enhancing intrinsic motivation by providing control over their educational journey.	Encourages healthy competition and social engagement.
Immediate Feedback	Timely rewards and corrective feedback reinforce learning, ensuring continuous engagement without frustration.	Enhances engagement, strategy development, and practical skill application.

Examples of Successful Gamification in Other Educational Domains

Gamification is widely applied across various fields, demonstrating its effectiveness in enhancing learning outcomes to name a few are the following discussed below:

- **Language Learning (Duolingo):** Uses points, streaks, and progress tracking to encourage consistent learning. The app's gamified format improves engagement and retention in language acquisition.
- **Medical Training (Touch Surgery):** A gamified simulation platform that allows medical students to practice surgical procedures in a risk-free environment, reinforcing theoretical knowledge through hands-on virtual training.
- **Mathematics & STEM (Khan Academy, Prodigy):** Integrates badges, challenges, and mastery levels to make problem-solving more engaging and rewarding.
- **Corporate Training & Professional Development:** Companies use game-based e-learning modules to teach cybersecurity awareness, compliance training, and leadership skills, ensuring higher retention rates than traditional methods.

In cybersecurity education, cyber ranges provide virtual environments simulating cyberattacks and defenses and they also provide learners with practical, hands-on learning in a gamified setup, which are significantly improving their readiness for real-world cybersecurity challenges(Lampropoulos & Sidiropoulos, 2024; Liu, Fathi, & Rahimi, 2024).

WHY GAMIFICATION IN CYBERSECURITY EDUCATION?

Education in cybersecurity is challenging, given the technical nature of the subject matter and the threats that are constantly evolving apart from it there is dire need for providing learners with hands-on experience. Academic subjects can often be based on theories but in cybersecurity learners must build skills such as problem-solving and critical thinking, as well as the ability to adapt to try and counter real-world threats either it can be malware attacks, phishing schemes, or data breaches(Mahmood, Akif, Ashraf, & Jhanjhi, 2024). The extremely technical nature of the field comprising encryption, network defense, and ethical hacking can be intimidating for new entrants and lead many to drop out(Jhanjhi, Khan, Ahmad, & Hussain, 2022). Moreover, the constantly changing nature of cyber threats necessitates a perpetual evolution of skills which cannot just happen through a lecture or presentation format.

Figure 4. Core principles of gamification

(Chopade, 2023)

These challenges need experiential learning; students should be working on real-life cyber cases, not passively reviewing information. Hence, this is where gamification is another big enabler turning cybersecurity awareness into game-based challenges, puzzles, and cyberattack simulations(Waseem et al.). Capture the Flag (CTF) competitions, cyber ranges, and role-based security exercises provide interactive learning. These learning mechanisms provides alternate environment that allow for real-time feedback. The gradual integration of cumulative levels of difficulty into the teaching materials, provides an opportunity to develop and fine-tune learners' cybersecurity experience. Cyber threats and ethical hacking exercises with gamification technique provides a bridge between theory and practice, consequently improving critical thinking, enhancing strategic decision making and resilience(Khan, Jhanjhi, & Sujatha, 2022; Sujatha, Prakash, & Jhanjhi, 2022).

All the aforesaid qualities are prerequisites for cybersecurity experts. Gamification prepares the future workforce with not only the essential technical skills, but also the problem-solving and adaptability abilities that will enable learners to address ever-changing cyberthreats effectively and efficiently.

CORE COMPONENTS OF A GAMIFIED CYBERSECURITY LEARNING FRAMEWORK

A gamified cybersecurity learning framework is composed of several individual elements that all contribute to improving engagement, retention of information, and working with practical skills. The first major aspect, game mechanics, includes basics such as points, levels, rewards, and progression systems that provide structured learning routes(Rege, 2015). Points can be used as instant feedback; levels can indicate when the learners have mastered a skill; rewards like badges and certificates strengthen motivation. The second element, game dynamics, defines the learning experience with new competition, collaboration, and storytelling. These platforms host healthy competition through leaderboards and CTF (Capture the Flag) competitions, as well as a focus on cooperation with cooperative challenges and cybersecurity team simulations(van Geest, Cascavilla, Hulstijn, & Zannone, 2024).

Figure 5. Gamification key design elements

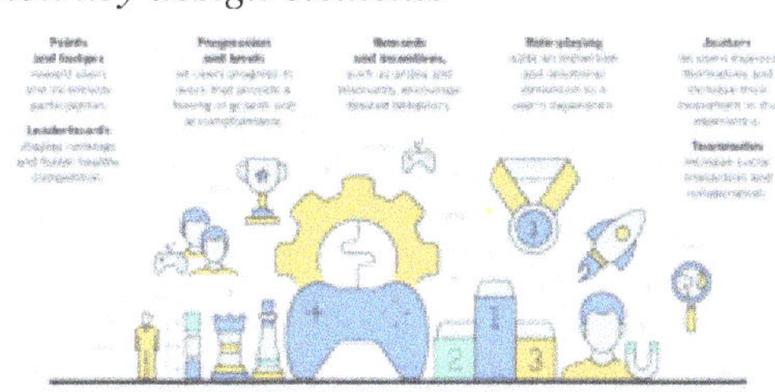

(A. S. Gillis)

Incorporating real world cyberattack scenarios, storytelling allows learners to immerse themselves in engaging, problem-solving exercises that strengthen their critical thinking skills. The third element is the varying types of players, who have different motivators in a gamified environment; achievers like to show mastery of skills and gain badges, explorers like to discover new techniques and challenges(Khan, Jhanjhi, Hamid, Omar, Amsaad, & Wassan, 2025). Personalization and inclusivity at the root of gamification pertains the fourth element, feedback mechanisms, offers immediate evaluations, progress tracking, and personalized learning trajectories. Providing immediate feedback allows learners to understand strengths and weaknesses, and adaptive learning promotes this by offering challenges relevant to the skill levels of individuals, making learning a process of balance and continuity(Kumar, Jabbar, Oudah, Khan, & Verma, 2024). Collectively, these elements constitute a responsive, engaging and high-impact learning ecosystem that closes the synergies between theory and practice, equipping individuals for the practical field in cyber engagements.

THEORETICAL FOUNDATIONS

Gamification has been well established as an effective strategy in education. These theories provide leverage in the thought process of learning and throws light on how people learn, retain and apply knowledge. Hence, incorporating these theoretical frameworks into learning and education helps educators to develop more engaging and tailored gamified educational environments that keep learners' motivation and enthusiasm balanced and prepare learners to navigate into the complexities that cybersecurity learning that the learners might face. Theoretical Foundations of Gamification in Cybersecurity Education comprise behavioral psychology, cognitive load theory and constructivist learning theory. Below is an in-depth analysis provided for these theoretical foundations, (Marougkas, Troussas, Krouska, & Sgouropoulou, 2023).

Figure 6. Theoretical foundations of learning theories

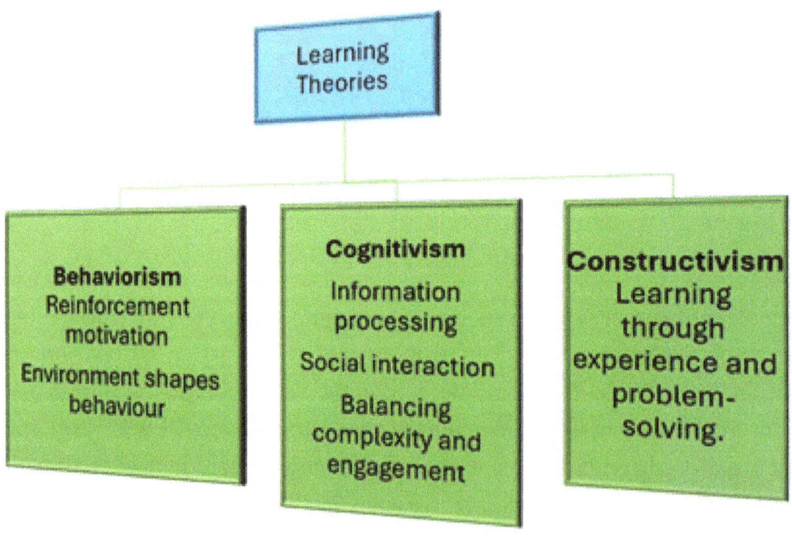

- **Behavioral Psychology**: The focus in this theoretical framework is on Reinforcement and motivation. Behavioral Psychology is among the most studied theoretical backgrounds that have been utilized for gamification. Rooted in B.F. Skinner's operant conditioning, reinforcement theory states that people tend to repeat behaviors that give them positive reinforcement in the form of rewards and avoid behaviors that prompt negative reinforcement such as punishments. Points, badges, levels, and leaderboards serve as extrinsic rewards that reinforce learning and skill adoption in gamified cybersecurity learning enabling learners for continual participation, moving through obstacles and completing activities and mastering concepts about cybersecurity in the process(Stewart, 2021).
- **Cognitive Load Theory**: Acronymized as CLT, this theory focuses on balancing complexity and engagement. It examines how our minds process information. Pioneered by John Sweller, CLT divides cognitive load into three categories: intrinsic, extraneous, and germane. Intrinsic load depends on content complexity for instance comprehending encryption algorithms. Extraneous load stems from distractions or poorly designed instruction. Germane load facilitates understanding through problem-solving. Learning cybersecurity poses challenges due to its multilayered nature. Technical specifics, analytic skills, and evolving threats strain cognitive resources. Gamification mitigates this by segmenting material into interactive, bite-sized chunks. This restart allows focused progression without overwhelm(Duran, Zavgorodniaia, & Sorva, 2022).

Figure 7. Cognitive load theory

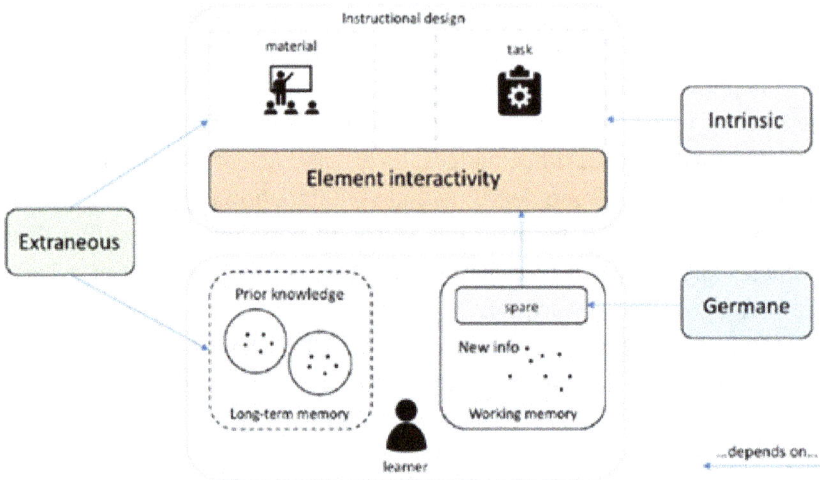

(Orru & Longo, 2019)

Customization helps too through adjustable difficulties and on-demand aids which balance intrinsic and germane loads for structured, efficient lessons. Simulated experiences like Capture the Flag enhances knowledge in practical, scenario-based exercises. These gamified exercises provide hands-on problem-solving to make abstract concepts more tangible and engaging. By incorporating CLT principles, gamification boosts retention, improves troubleshooting, and increases involvement. It helps bridge the gap between cybersecurity theory and practice(Berssanette & de Francisco, 2021).

- **Constructivist Learning Theory**: This theory focuses on Learning through experience and problem-solving. This Theory of Jean Piaget and Lev Vygotsky highlights the idea that learning is best done by engaging in exploration and problem solving, rather than through passive consumption of material. This model is also in line with experiential learning, as learners gain knowledge and understanding through exposure and interaction with actual cybersecurity issues, rather than simple memorization of the theory. For instance, cyber security gamification aligns with constructivism because learners have to secure simulated networks, act contra to malware through sandboxing, and better learn by competing against others in cybersecurity competitions. Working on the same security problems, trading ideas, and building defenses, they face problems based on reality, using teamwork and critical thought to solve problems collaboratively(Zajda & Zajda, 2021).

The task-difficulty slope established by Vygotsky within his theorized Zone of Proximity Development (ZPD) refers to tasks that can be done through guidance, but the learner can't do it independently. Here cannot be done without guidance assumes that an individual has a maximum potential for learning at a given point in time, if challenged to an appropriate degree above this threshold is capable of improving but requires the right kind of guidance outside of personal skill, a precept that underlies all gamified cybersecurity training through the scales of challenge, mentorship guidance, and in-training hints that allow an individual to amass a solid body of knowledge without overwhelming the possible learners potential(Efgivia, Rinanda, Hidayat, Maulana, & Budiarjo, 2021).

Kolb's 1969 Experiential Learning Cycle which comprises feeling, watching, thinking and doing also supports both reflection and analysis with application. Through application of this approach, assists in understanding into how learners are confronted with real-world threats that need to be analysed and conceptualized and then apply this effort to future challenges to create a self-improving cycle of learning. The combination of gamified cybersecurity and constructivism raise learners' engagement and promote problem-solving skills which in turn creates realistic understanding of cyber defence resulting in learners understanding on building systems that can work as an effective team in the implementation of technology(Wijnen-Meijer, Brandhuber, Schneider, & Berberat, 2022).

CASE STUDIES: GAMIFICATION IN CYBERSECURITY TRAINING

In fact, gamification is one of the most prominent forms of training techniques in cybersecurity, as highlighted by CTF (Capture the Flag) competitions and cyber ranges as a means to train and scale cybersecurity skills. Capture the flag (CTF) competitions simulate real-world cyberattack and defense situations that are utilized by organizations, universities, and industry events where participants solve security challenges in domains such as cryptography, network security, reverse engineering, and penetration testing(Khan, Jhanjhi, Alı, Ray, & Wassan, 2025).

Such competitions offer a great and engaging hands-on learning experience while imparting problem-solving skills, team spirit, and adaptability. Cyber ranges also provide structured, real-time training to enhance incident response, threat mitigation and digital forensics in environments that aim to simulate enterprise networks. Cyber ranges are an alternative to traditional classroom-based study, allowing learners to get hands-on experience using cybersecurity tools to explore vulnerabilities and test defense strategies that are all in a safe, completely non-production environment(Ashley et al., 2022).

Interactive, scenario-based learning modules are becoming popular among many platforms like Hack The Box, TryHackMe, NICE Cyber Ranges which are meant for beginners as well as cybersecurity professionals. These platforms leverage game mechanics such as increasing challenge, instant feedback, and competitive leader boards, to make learning both fun and focused, while gamified cybersecurity approach has proven to be effective, some obstacles and limitations remain. While CTF competition is a fantastic way to hone technical problem-solving skills, it sometimes tends to overemphasize niche challenges that don't necessarily carry over to real-world cybersecurity jobs(Marat & Marat, 2024).

Due to their nature focusing on offense such as hacking vs. defense i.e., Incident Response, risk management, compliance, many CTFs do leave some gaps in holistic cybersecurity training. Moreover, although cyber ranges are valuable for simulating real attack environments, they are also high in terms of infrastructure costs and are therefore not always available to smaller institutions. Furthermore, certain gamified platforms are devoid of personalized learning pathways, having a common one size fits all path vis-a-vis a learning compass which may leave tech novices stranded without any prior learning or a mentor(Kaplan, Zhang, & Cole, 2022).

Gamified cybersecurity training needs to achieve a fine balance between being challenging, while still being accessible and able to simulate real-world defensive scenarios and be able to deliver a training environment that is scalable and cost-effective. As such, these developments are to come they should seek to provide adaptive learning systems such as AI-driven personalization, and a more integrated approach with cybersecurity career pathways, ensuring that gamification as a method that continues to build practical, industry appealing cybersecurity capability(Chicone & Ferebee, 2020; Toccafondi, Bilancini, & Boncinelli, 2024).

CHALLENGES AND LIMITATIONS

Despite the benefits of gamification as an effective pedagogical approach to engage learners and improve cybersecurity education, it presents several challenges and limitations. A common pitfall with gamification is over-reliance on rewards, whereby learners become more interested in collecting points, badges and rankings than learning about cybersecurity. Thus, the challenge can be simply met and achieved with proper understanding and critical reflection. Furthermore, gamified learning environments can be far removed from real-world scenarios; for example, Capture the Flag (CTF) competitions primarily focus on offense that is hacking as opposed to offense, incident response, and risk management, which are essential in many professional fields of cybersecurity. Though cyber threats are evolving rapidly cybersecurity education also needs to keep pace with it but many such gamified platforms do not frequently update content which may leave learners with obsolete skills and knowledge gaps(Quayyum, 2021).

Another major challenge is addressing the needs of the full range of learners and their abilities. There are a wide range of potential learners in the cybersecurity education domain, from complete beginners to advanced professionals, necessitating different levels of difficulty and personalized paths. Nevertheless, most gamified platforms are one-size-fits-all, so they can intimidate beginners or not push advanced learners enough(Troja, DeBello, & Truong, 2023). Striking the right balance between engagement and educational rigor is also important as interactive elements help improve engagement, but too much gamification runs the risk of delivering a low-effort entertainment exercise rather than a serious learning experience on the path to mastery of cybersecurity. The game should combine structured mentorship, simulation of real-world defensive scenarios(Faith, Long, & Hamid, 2024). Apart from it, they should contain AI-driven adaptive learning which mitigates the issues of gamification in cybersecurity while motivating the learner and providing job-relevant tips and skill development as they work their way through the program. Gamification can successfully exhibit learners to real-world cybersecurity risks and career requirements provided engagement, challenge, and educational depth are balanced properly (Prümmer, van Steen, & van den Berg, 2024; van Steen & Deeleman, 2021).

FUTURE DIRECTIONS

Gamification in education needs to evolve by incorporating emerging trends and more advanced technologies to keep pace with the changing cybersecurity landscape. Among the trends are AI (Artificial Intelligence) and ML (Machine Learning) integrations that help service providers to come up with personalized gamified learning experiences. AI-powered systems can also drive the development of adaptive learning environments, analysing the performance of different learners in real time and adjusting the level of challenge, providing relevant feedback and suggesting pathways for learning according to the strengths and weaknesses of the individual. This customization gives novice learners foundational assistance while advanced users engage in challenging cybersecurity scenarios. Moreover, Virtual Reality (VR) and Augmented Reality (AR) are being used as a way to generate truly immersive cybersecurity learning experiences, mimicking authentic world cyberattack and defense conditions in a more realistic and interactive manner. These tools allow learners to play out high-pressure cybersecurity scenarios in a safe environment and help them make better decisions while applying their knowledge.

Beyond the realm of technology, a look into the future shows that gamification will be integrated with other pedagogical techniques for enhanced learning. The fact that, with the intersection of Problem Based Learning (PBL) and Experiential Learning provided with real-time scenarios can assist in training and mentorship programs. This interaction can allow the integration of hybrid models with gamification that can drive a more comprehensive learning experience more engaging and improving analytical and collaborative skills necessary for their future careers in cybersecurity. Networking with the industries can also create use cases of gamified platforms that are immersive, with engaging experience, mirroring real time cyber challenges. Compliance frameworks and ethical hacking scenario-based learning can provide learners learn exactly the job-required key skills. With ongoing innovation in cybersecurity education, the future of gamified cybersecurity training will combine AI-powered personalized learning pathways, immersive simulations, and interdisciplinary pedagogical integration, resulting in more engaging, effective, and relevant training for the next generation of cybersecurity professionals.

CONCLUSION

Gamification is considered to be a transformative approach in cybersecurity education. Cybersecurity education has evolved with the advent of gamification, where learners are now engaged in skill development through interactive methods rather than traditional learning strategies. Gamification in cybersecurity training uses the elements of game mechanics such as scorecards, leaderboards, competitions and engaging history that can make cybersecurity concepts easier to learn, motivate the learners, and build a deeper understanding which can help learners of cybersecurity domain to build cybersecurity knowledge in depth, wherein they retain it and put it into practice.

The effectiveness of gamification in learning is supported by the theoretical background of Behavioral Psychology, Cognitive Load Theory and Constructivist Learning Theory, which ensures that the learning is motivationally balanced, cognitively balanced, and driven by experience. By providing hands-on experiences in the form of Capture the Flag (CTF) competitions, cyber ranges, and other live platforms, learners not only learn and harness their skills, but also, they can have the opportunity to apply their knowledge to solve real-world problems. Thereby, enabling them to be better prepared to combat modern security threats. As gamification applies fun and exciting elements in order to engage and enhance learning through motivational rewards, lack of personalization solutions for instance like difficulty adjustment or immediate feedback and balancing fun with educational nature may limit its success.

Gamification in cybersecurity education fills the gap only to the extent that educators and organizations embrace and tailor gamified learning models to a range of skill levels and practical requirements in information security. This encompasses AI-enabled adaptive learning experiences, immersive VR/AR simulations, and structured mentorship programs to deliver personalized, industry-aligned training experiences. Furthermore, organisations should work along with cybersecurity professionals and industry leaders to ensure that gamified training environments mirror emerging cyber threats as well as effective defense mechanisms. As cybersecurity education progresses, the use of gamification will increase, demanding ongoing innovation, and research to develop this area.

Having established a comprehensive reason why gamification is key to cyber security education, the next question lies in how to design engaging and impactful cyber challenges which successfully align theory and practice. Creating gamified exercises for cybersecurity does have best practices for things like scheduled, realistic attack simulations, difficulty scaling and adaptive learning paths, which will be covered in the following chapter. It will also cover how to facilitate challenges which generate critical thinking, teamwork and strategic decision making, so that learners acquire both technical and analytical cybersecurity skills. Educators who design, craft, and administer proper gamified challenges will develop rich experiences that both teach cybersecurity principles and prepare students to face real world security challenges in a changing digital landscape.

REFERENCES

Ashley, T. D., Kwon, R., Gourisetti, S. N. G., Katsis, C., Bonebrake, C. A., & Boyd, P. A. (2022). Gamification of cybersecurity for workforce development in critical infrastructure. *IEEE Access : Practical Innovations, Open Solutions, 10*, 112487–112501. DOI: 10.1109/ACCESS.2022.3216711

Ashraf, H., Jhanjhi, N. Z., Brohi, S. N., & Muzafar, S. (2024). A Comprehensive Exploration of DDoS Attacks and Cybersecurity Imperatives in the Digital Age. In *Navigating Cyber Threats and Cybersecurity in the Logistics Industry* (pp. 236–257). IGI Global. DOI: 10.4018/979-8-3693-3816-2.ch009

Aslam, M. (2024). AI and Cybersecurity: An Ever-Evolving Landscape. *International Journal of Advanced Engineering Technologies and Innovations, 1*(1), 52–71.

Berssanette, J. H., & de Francisco, A. C. (2021). Cognitive load theory in the context of teaching and learning computer programming: A systematic literature review. *IEEE Transactions on Education, 65*(3), 440–449. DOI: 10.1109/TE.2021.3127215

Chicone, R. G., & Ferebee, S. (2020). A COMPARISON STUDY OF TWO CYBERSECURITY LEARNING SYSTEMS: FACEBOOK'S OPEN SOURCE CAPTURE THE FLAG AND CTFD. *Issues in Information Systems, 21*(1), 202–212. DOI: 10.48009/1_iis_2020_202-212

Chopade, S. (2023). How to Build a Gamification Strategy – An Expert View. Retrieved from https://www.harbingergroup.com/blogs/how-to-build-a-gamification-strategy-an-expert-view

Diakoumakos, I. (2023). *Enhancing Cyber Security Education and Training through Gamification.* Paper presented at the ACM International Conference Proceeding Series. DOI: 10.1145/3609987.3610016

Duran, R., Zavgorodniaia, A., & Sorva, J. (2022). Cognitive load theory in computing education research: A review. [TOCE]. *ACM Transactions on Computing Education, 22*(4), 1–27. DOI: 10.1145/3483843

Efgivia, M. G., Rinanda, R. A., Hidayat, A., Maulana, I., & Budiarjo, A. (2021). *Analysis of constructivism learning theory.* Paper presented at the 1st UMGESHIC International Seminar on Health, Social Science and Humanities (UMGESHIC-ISHSSH 2020). DOI: 10.2991/assehr.k.211020.032

Faith, B. F., Long, Z. A., & Hamid, S. (2024). *Promoting cybersecurity knowledge via gamification: an innovative intervention design.* Paper presented at the 2024 Third International Conference on Distributed Computing and High Performance Computing (DCHPC). DOI: 10.1109/DCHPC60845.2024.10454080

FasterCapital. (2024). Emerging Ethical Challenges in the Digital Age.

Gil-Aciron, L. A. (2024). The gamer psychology: A psychological perspective on game design and gamification. *Interactive Learning Environments*, *32*(1), 183–207. DOI: 10.1080/10494820.2022.2082489

Gillis, A. S. N. B. What is gamification? How it works and how to use it. Retrieved from https://www.techtarget.com/searchhrsoftware/definition/gamification

Jelo, M., & Helebrandt, P. (2022). *Gamification of cyber ranges in cybersecurity education.* Paper presented at the 20th Anniversary of IEEE International Conference on Emerging eLearning Technologies and Applications, ICETA 2022 - Proceedings. DOI: 10.1109/ICETA57911.2022.9974714

Jhanjhi, N., Khan, M. A., Ahmad, M., & Hussain, M. (2022). The Impact of Cyber Attacks on E-Governance During the COVID-19 Pandemic. *Cybersecurity Measures for E-Government Frameworks*, 123.

Jin, G., Tu, M., Kim, T. H., Heffron, J., & White, J. (2018). *Game based cyber-security training for High School Students.* Paper presented at the SIGCSE 2018 - Proceedings of the 49th ACM Technical Symposium on Computer Science Education. DOI: 10.1145/3159450.3159591

Kaplan, Z., Zhang, N., & Cole, S. V. (2022). *A Capture The Flag (CTF) Platform and Exercises for an Intro to Computer Security Class.* Paper presented at the Annual Conference on Innovation and Technology in Computer Science Education, ITiCSE.

Karagiannis, S., & Magkos, E. (2020). Adapting CTF challenges into virtual cybersecurity learning environments. *Information and Computer Security*, *29*(1), 105–132. DOI: 10.1108/ICS-04-2019-0050

keepnetlabs. (2025). Human-Centric Cybersecurity: Building Stronger Defenses by Focusing on People. Retrieved from https://keepnetlabs.com/blog/human-centric-cybersecurity-prioritizing-people-in-cyber-defense

Khan, A., Jhanjhi, N., Alı, G. A., Ray, S. K., & Wassan, S. (2025). Case Studies and Applications of Generative AI in Real-World Cybersecurity Scenarios.

Khan, A., Jhanjhi, N., Hamid, D. H. H., Omar, H. A. H. B. H., Amsaad, F., & Ashraf, H. (2025). Reshaping Cybersecurity for Supply Chain Sustainability in IR 4.0 and 5.0.

Khan, A., Jhanjhi, N., Hamid, D. H. H., Omar, H. A. H. B. H., Amsaad, F., & Wassan, S. (2025). Future Trends and Challenges in Cybersecurity and Generative AI. *Reshaping CyberSecurity With Generative AI Techniques*, 491-522.

Khan, A., Jhanjhi, N. Z., & Humayun, M. (2022). The Role of Cybersecurity in Smart Cities. In *Cyber Security Applications for Industry 4.0* (pp. 195–208). Chapman and Hall/CRC. DOI: 10.1201/9781003203087-9

Khan, A., Jhanjhi, N. Z., & Sujatha, R. (2022). Emerging Industry Revolution IR 4.0 Issues and Challenges. In *Cyber Security Applications for Industry 4.0* (pp. 151-169): Chapman and Hall/CRC.

Kumar, A., Jabbar, K. A., Oudah, M. Y., Khan, A. A., & Verma, R. (2024). *Applying a Machine Learning Framework to Improve the Efficacy of Network Intrusion Detection Systems.* Paper presented at the 2024 International Conference on Emerging Trends in Networks and Computer Communications (ETNCC).

Kuwajima, H., & Ishikawa, F. (2019). *Adapting square for quality assessment of artificial intelligence systems.* Paper presented at the Proceedings - 2019 IEEE 30th International Symposium on Software Reliability Engineering Workshops, ISSREW 2019. DOI: 10.1109/ISSREW.2019.00035

Lampropoulos, G., & Sidiropoulos, A. (2024). Impact of gamification on students' learning outcomes and academic performance: A longitudinal study comparing online, traditional, and gamified learning. *Education Sciences*, *14*(4), 367. DOI: 10.3390/educsci14040367

Lexman, R. R., & Baral, R. (2023). Digital twins in MOOCs: Exploring ways to enhance interactivity. *Development and Learning in Organizations.*

Liu, G. Z., Fathi, J., & Rahimi, M. (2024). Using digital gamification to improve language achievement, foreign language enjoyment, and ideal L2 self: A case of English as a foreign language learners. *Journal of Computer Assisted Learning*, *40*(4), 1347–1364. DOI: 10.1111/jcal.12954

Luo, Z. (2022). Gamification for educational purposes: What are the factors contributing to varied effectiveness? *Education and Information Technologies*, *27*(1), 891–915. DOI: 10.1007/s10639-021-10642-9

Mahmood, S., Akif, F., Ashraf, H., & Jhanjhi, N. (2024). Defense Mechanism Against Attacks Promoting Spread Of Wrong Information.

mambo.io. Gamification Statistics And Trends. Retrieved from https://mambo.io/gamification-guide/gamification-statistics-and-trends

Marat, C., & Marat, S. (2024). The role of cybersecurity education on ethical hacking.

Marougkas, A., Troussas, C., Krouska, A., & Sgouropoulou, C. (2023). Virtual reality in education: A review of learning theories, approaches and methodologies for the last decade. *Electronics (Basel), 12*(13), 2832. DOI: 10.3390/electronics12132832

Oliveira, W., Hamari, J., Shi, L., Toda, A. M., Rodrigues, L., Palomino, P. T., & Isotani, S. (2023). Tailored gamification in education: A literature review and future agenda. *Education and Information Technologies*, *28*(1), 373–406. DOI: 10.1007/s10639-022-11122-4

Orru, G., & Longo, L. (2019). *The evolution of cognitive load theory and the measurement of its intrinsic, extraneous and germane loads: a review.* Paper presented at the Human Mental Workload: Models and Applications: Second International Symposium, H-WORKLOAD 2018, Amsterdam, The Netherlands, September 20-21, 2018, Revised Selected Papers 2. DOI: 10.1007/978-3-030-14273-5_3

Prümmer, J., van Steen, T., & van den Berg, B. (2024). A systematic review of current cybersecurity training methods. *Computers & Security*, *136*, 103585. DOI: 10.1016/j.cose.2023.103585

Quayyum, F. (2021). *Cyber security education for children through gamification: Challenges and research perspectives.* Paper presented at the Methodologies and Intelligent Systems for Technology Enhanced Learning, 10th International Conference. Workshops: Volume 2. DOI: 10.1007/978-3-030-52287-2_26

Rege, A. (2015). *Multidisciplinary experiential learning for holistic cybersecurity education, research and evaluation.* Paper presented at the 2015 USENIX Summit on Gaming, Games, and Gamification in Security Education, 3GSE 2015.

Russo, E., Ribaudo, M., Orlich, A., Longo, G., & Armando, A. (2023). *Cyber Range and Cyber Defense Exercises: Gamification Meets University Students.* Paper presented at the ACM International Conference Proceeding Series. DOI: 10.1145/3617553.3617888

Salama, R., Alturjman, S., Altrjman, C., & Al-Turjman, F. (2024). *Using Gamification to Increase Healthcare Professionals' Cybersecurity Awareness.* Paper presented at the Sustainable Civil Infrastructures. DOI: 10.1007/978-3-031-78276-3_88

Santofimia, M. J., Villanueva, F. J., Litvinov, E., Viksnin, I., Fernandes, A., & Lopez, J. C. (2021). Cybersecurity in Active and Healthy Ageing Era. *Procedia Computer Science*, *192*, 2068–2076. DOI: 10.1016/j.procs.2021.08.214

Shahid, H., Ashraf, H., Jhanjhi, N., & Zam, Q.-u. A. Z. (2025). Reshaping Cybersecurity of Wireless Sensor Networks Using Energy-Optimized Approach Against Wormhole Attack. In *Reshaping CyberSecurity With Generative AI Techniques* (pp. 125-172): IGI Global.

Sharma, D., & Sharma, J. (2023). *Evolution of gamification, its implications, and its statistical impact on the society*. Paper presented at the International Conference on Emerging Trends in Design & Arts. DOI: 10.29121/shodhkosh.v4.i2SE.2023.456

Shukla, P. K., Singh, A., Sharma, A., Malik, P. K., & Kathuria, S. (2023). *Technological Powered Impersonation in MOOC Learning*. Paper presented at the Proceedings - 2023 3rd International Conference on Pervasive Computing and Social Networking, ICPCSN 2023. DOI: 10.1109/ICPCSN58827.2023.00091

Sindiramutty, S. R., Prabagaran, K. R. V., Jhanjhi, N., & Murugesan, R. K. (2024). Threat Intelligence and Information Sharing. *Utilizing Generative AI for Cyber Defense Strategies*, 191.

Stewart, M. (2021). Understanding learning: Theories and critique. In *University teaching in focus* (pp. 3–28). Routledge. DOI: 10.4324/9781003008330-2

Sujatha, R., Prakash, G., & Jhanjhi, N. Z. (2022). *Cyber Security Applications for Industry 4.0*. CRC Press. DOI: 10.1201/9781003203087

Thompson, L. A., Melendez, N., Hempson-Jones, J., & Salvi, F. (2022). *Gamification in Cybersecurity Education; the RAD-SIM Framework for Effective Learning*. Paper presented at the European Conference on Games Based Learning. DOI: 10.34190/ecgbl.16.1.504

Toccafondi, N., Bilancini, E., & Boncinelli, L. (2024). *Learning CyberSecurity with Story-Driven CTF Challenges: CyberTrials 2023*. Paper presented at the Communications in Computer and Information Science. DOI: 10.1007/978-3-031-67351-1_21

Troja, E., DeBello, J. E., & Truong, L. M. (2023). *Teaching effective and gamified cybersecurity using the metaverse: challenges and opportunities*. Paper presented at the 2023 IEEE World Engineering Education Conference (EDUNINE). DOI: 10.1109/EDUNINE57531.2023.10102900

van Geest, R. J., Cascavilla, G., Hulstijn, J., & Zannone, N. (2024). The applicability of a hybrid framework for automated phishing detection. *Computers & Security*, *139*, 103736. DOI: 10.1016/j.cose.2024.103736

van Steen, T., & Deeleman, J. R. (2021). Successful gamification of cybersecurity training. *Cyberpsychology, Behavior, and Social Networking*, *24*(9), 593–598. DOI: 10.1089/cyber.2020.0526 PMID: 34491845

Vemuri, N., Thaneeru, N., & Tatikonda, V. M. (2024). Adaptive generative AI for dynamic cybersecurity threat detection in enterprises.

Waseem, R. M., Khan, F. Z., Ahmad, M., Naseem, A., Jhanjhi, N., & Ghosh, U. Performance evaluation of aomdv on realistic and efficient vanet simulations. *Wireless Personal Communications*, 1-20.

Wijnen-Meijer, M., Brandhuber, T., Schneider, A., & Berberat, P. (2022). Implementing Kolb s experiential learning cycle by linking real experience, case-based discussion and simulation. *Journal of Medical Education and Curricular Development*, *9*, 23821205221091511. DOI: 10.1177/23821205221091511 PMID: 35592131

Xu, J., Lio, A., Dhaliwal, H., Andrei, S., Balakrishnan, S., Nagani, U., & Samadder, S. (2021). Psychological interventions of virtual gamification within academic intrinsic motivation: A systematic review. *Journal of Affective Disorders*, *293*, 444–465. DOI: 10.1016/j.jad.2021.06.070 PMID: 34252688

Zajda, J., & Zajda, J. (2021). Constructivist learning theory and creating effective learning environments. *Globalisation and education reforms: Creating effective learning environments*, 35-50.

Zaman, S. K. U., Jehangiri, A. I., Maqsood, T., Umar, A. I., Khan, M. A., Jhanjhi, N. Z., Shorfuzzaman, M., & Masud, M. (2022). COME-UP: Computation offloading in mobile edge computing with LSTM based user direction prediction. *Applied Sciences (Basel, Switzerland)*, *12*(7), 3312. DOI: 10.3390/app12073312

Zhong, C., Kim, J. B. J. B., & Liu, H. (2024). The Art of Inclusive Gamification in Cybersecurity Training. *IEEE Security and Privacy*, *22*(5), 40–51. DOI: 10.1109/MSEC.2024.3427666

Zola, F., Echeberria, X., Petisco, J., Vakakis, N., Voulgaridis, A., & Votis, K. (2025). *KINAITICS: Enhancing Cybersecurity Education Using AI-Based Tools and Gamification.* Paper presented at the Proceedings of the 2024 the 16th International Conference on Education Technology and Computers, ICETC 2024.

Chapter 4
Levelling up Security: Gamification and Behavior Design in Cybersecurity Awareness

Er. Kritika
https://orcid.org/0000-0002-1186-6032
Independent Researcher, India

ABSTRACT

The chapter explores the potential of gamification and behaviour design in cybersecurity training, highlighting its potential to enhance engagement and retention. It combines psychological concepts like reward systems, intrinsic motivation, and social rivalry with basic mechanics like points, badges, leaderboards, and challenges. By incorporating safe practices into routine tasks, behaviour design enhances these programs. Examples include "Capture the Flag" challenges, AI-powered customized training programs, and simulated phishing attempts. However, gamification and behaviour design have drawbacks, such as excessive dependence on external rewards, privacy issues, and reluctance to adapt. To overcome these challenges, leadership support, open policies, and a balance between internal and external motivators are essential. The chapter presents a model framework for creating gamified cybersecurity programs, emphasizing adaptive designs and ongoing improvement. Future trends like VR/AR integration and AI personalisation highlight the opportunity for further innovation.

DOI: 10.4018/979-8-3373-0477-9.ch004

INTRODUCTION

"Imagine an employee clicking on a phishing email, unknowingly opening the door to a major data breach—one small mistake, countless repercussions. What if, instead of fear-based lectures, we used games and behavioural insights to turn every user into a cybersecurity champion?"

The growing interconnected digital environment makes cybersecurity an essential matter which organizations with individuals need to address. Security awareness training has become essential part of modern life because technology keeps advancing while cyber threats become more sophisticated (Whitman & Mattord, 2021). This dynamic mirrors broader transformations in industry, where consumer behaviour, digital technologies, and sustainability imperatives reshape organizational operations (Rani, Guru, & Santhanam, 2024). Security systems function worst through employees and users who are therefore prioritized for threat recognition and risk mitigation education. Traditional cybersecurity training programs exist extensively yet evidence shows such methods typically do not lead users to actual behavioural change (Safa, Solms, & Futcher, 2016). This chapter demonstrates how gamification together with behaviour design tools increase user engagement while boosting memory retention and establishing safe behaviour within platforms. The implementation of behavioural principles alongside game design concepts allows security training to evolve from static information retention toward behavioural transformation of users.

Why Traditional Cybersecurity Awareness Fails?

The broad initiatives dedicated to educating users about cybersecurity show limited success since standard training programs fail to deliver expected results. Security education programs rely mostly on extensive instructional videos and sporadic workshops which yield limited user engagement results. The primary limitations of these conventional approaches include:

- Low Engagement: Security training programs are usually derided as monotonous mounted applications that produce both disinterest and disengagement among trainees (Sarkar, 2010). The structured timeslots become well-known as compulsory activities instead of offering extended learning options to staff members.
- Limited Retention: Studies demonstrate that maintained learning processes through passive methods including lectures and reader material lead to poor knowledge retention than interactive and hands-on methods (Schunk, 2012).

- Lack of Personalization: The traditional one-size-fits-all training method neglects to tailor content according to user differences and specific requirements of cybersecurity knowledge (Kirlappos, Parkin, & Sasse, 2015).
- Minimal Behaviour Change: Translating learned cybersecurity concepts into consistent user behaviour remains a fundamental challenge even with full comprehension of these principles. Training initiatives about cybersecurity at CISA (2020) have proven insufficient to stop staff from repeating password misuse or missing phishing threats.
- The current approach of security education needs radical transformation because it fails to both teach and effectively motivate users to develop secure behavioral patterns.

Gamification and Behavior Design Defined

Gamification constructs when researchers inject game-related systems like achievement points and leaderboards into habitual environments to boost user activity and determination (Deterding et al., 2011). The approach of gamification utilizes psychological principles to design cybersecurity learning programs which provide both beneficial rewards and better engagement for active student participation. Behaviour design implements organized behavioral science principles through active efforts to steer humans toward needed actions (Fogg 2009). The approach prioritizes the development of systems which support behaviour transformation through natural alignment with user motivations while streamlining processes and offering prompt action stimuli.

Both approaches share a common goal: These frameworks work simultaneously to guide and maintain user actions. Gamification concentrates on increasing user engagement and motivation yet behaviour design builds enduring behavioral patterns. These combined strategies transform passive security awareness activities into active experiences which produce meaningful results. Security systems benefit most from behaviour design alongside gamification methods because these solutions focus on the human factors that represent security's primary vulnerability points. A large number of cyber incidents stem from human errors ranging from weak passwords to malicious link clickers according to Verizon (2022). By applying gamification and behaviour design, organizations can reward users for conducting safe actions such as reporting phishing incursions and implementing multi-factor authorization features. Studies show that students learn more effectively when they receive feedback instantly in combination with rewards according to Schunk & DiBenedetto (2020).

The combination of gamification approaches with behaviour design methodology produces a robust framework for cybersecurity education programs. Through gamification users experience enticing motivational elements which aim at attracting attention combined with behaviour design principles which transform interventions into lasting behavioral modifications. Through behaviour design principles employees learn to identify phishing emails as a habit by repeating correct actions under gamified rewriting conditions. This section explores gamification fundamentals and behaviour design detection methods by analyzing their fundamental principles alongside their practical framework and corresponding cyber-awareness implementation difficulties. The following sections will:

- Describe the main elements along with psychological concepts which form gamification.
- Understand the methodology of behaviour design which builds enduring changes in human behaviour.
- Show how these approaches should integrate to create better cybersecurity training programs.
- An evaluation of possible difficulties along with ethical risks and operational hurdles needs assessment.
- A comprehensive guide must be established to design an enhanced cybersecurity awareness platform which incorporates video games and behaviour modulations.

Traditional cybersecurity awareness programs have shown increasing substantive shortcomings which led to the introduction of gamification and behaviour design as solution options. We proceed to a thorough analysis of gamification by studying its essential properties together with its psychological foundations while examining implementation examples in cybersecurity education.

UNDERSTANDING GAMIFICATION IN CYBERSECURITY AWARENESS

The fusion of game structures and aesthetic elements into non-game areas functions as an interaction strategy that activates user response (Koivisto & Hamari, 2019). Through gamification boring training content transforms into highly interactive gameplay which directs users toward enhanced learning outcomes while maintaining high engagement rates.

The success of gamification lies in its core principles, which include the use of specific game mechanics:

- Points: The system provides points that reward participants for tasks completed and specific security goals accomplished including spotting phishing messages together with reporting unsafe activities. These rewards deliver instant value by confirming positive behavior choices (Looyestyn et al., 2017).

- Leaderboards: Leaderboard interfaces present user ratings to participants by showing their performance levels which creates a competitive environment to drive users towards skill enhancement (Koivisto & Hamari, 2019).
- Badges: Achievement markers using badges enable recognition of major milestones when users finish all training content or spot a subset exercise. Billboards empower users to sense success alongside appreciation for their accomplishments.
- Challenges: The integration of challenges presents users with practical tasks which force them to utilize their acquired knowledge alongside problem-solving techniques. Identifying simulated environment vulnerabilities serves as an example challenge in this framework.
- Storytelling: Storytelling within gamification environments builds interactive scenarios which enhance participant engagement through storytelling methods. As an example security agents represent employees who safeguard vital data from cyber intruders (Hamari et al., 2016).

The training practices incorporate game elements that both enhance user participation and produce enticing outcomes that keeps participants more committed and improves their information absorption. Table 1 highlights the distinct yet complementary roles of intrinsic and extrinsic motivation in gamified cybersecurity training programs. Balancing both ensures sustained engagement and effective behavioural change.

Table 1. Comparison between intrinsic and extrinsic motivation

Aspect	Intrinsic Motivation	Extrinsic Motivation
Definition	Originates internally; driven by the inherent enjoyment or satisfaction of performing a task.	Arises from external factors such as rewards, recognition, or consequences.
Examples in Cybersecurity	Role-playing as a cybersecurity expert or solving meaningful, challenging scenarios.	Earning points, badges, or leaderboards for completing tasks like reporting phishing emails.
Engagement	Leads to deeper and sustained engagement, fostering long-term interest.	Effective for short-term engagement, especially in initial stages of training.
Retention	Encourages longer-term retention of knowledge and secure behaviour through meaningful learning.	Drives temporary participation but may not guarantee sustained interest or retention.
Focus	Encourages personal growth, creativity, and mastery of skills.	Promotes compliance and participation through tangible incentives.

continued on following page

Table 1. Continued

Aspect	Intrinsic Motivation	Extrinsic Motivation
Gamification Design	Uses elements like storytelling, autonomy, and meaningful challenges to engage users.	Incorporates points, badges, leaderboards, or other external rewards to encourage participation.
Sustainability	Offers sustainable motivation; users remain engaged even when rewards are absent.	Motivation tends to diminish when external rewards are removed.
Psychological Drivers	Driven by curiosity, autonomy, purpose, and the joy of mastery.	Driven by the desire for recognition, rewards, or competition.
Purpose	Fosters genuine behavioural change and long-term habits.	Ensures compliance and incentivizes participation in the short term.
Strengths	Encourages deep learning, creativity, and ownership of behaviours.	Effective in motivating users to engage in tasks they might not otherwise consider.
Limitations	May take time to cultivate and is less effective for uninteresting or mandatory tasks.	Less sustainable and may fail to internalize secure habits once rewards are removed.
Ideal Use	Suitable for activities requiring long-term engagement, mastery, and intrinsic satisfaction.	Best for initiating participation and driving compliance in mandatory training programs.
Balance in Gamification	Enhances the depth of engagement when paired with extrinsic motivators for initial engagement.	Provides the initial "hook" to draw users in, while intrinsic motivators sustain long-term interest.

The Psychology of Gamification: Expanding Key Principles

Gamification's success in influencing human behaviour stems from its foundation in psychology. By leveraging key principles such as reward systems, social dynamics, the need for mastery, and immediate feedback, gamification creates engaging and effective learning experiences. These principles are particularly powerful when applied to cybersecurity awareness, where behavioural change and skill-building are essential to mitigate threats.

Reward Systems and Dopamine Response

- Gamification succeeds through rewards which energize brain reward networks while stimuli reinforce targeted behaviour choices. User achievement of milestones while earning points or badges produces dopamine release which triggers rewarding brain chemicals associated with pleasure satisfaction and motivation.
- Neuroscience Perspective: Motivation together with learning depends on dopamine for normal functioning. Users who successfully accomplish their goal

followed by receiving a reward trigger their brain to form positive associations between the action and its outcome. The reinforced outcomes advance the probability that users will perform the same actions again (Zichermann & Linder, 2022).

- Gamified Cybersecurity Training Example: Staff who spot questionable emails in simulations gain points toward their team's excellence position on the standing leaderboard. The reward system offers an easy way to practice safe conduct until it becomes entrenched as habitual behaviour.
- Psychological Implications: When combined with rewards gamification creates both motivational influence and enduring commitment toward activities that users view as repetitive or troublesome. Despite being enjoyable and memorable gamification binds prize awards to safe conduct execution.

Social Competition and Collaboration

As social beings humans respond to gamification because these approaches activate friendly competition and cooperative dynamics. Leaderboards, group challenges, and team-based scenarios tap into two critical psychological needs: Offices harness human needs for recognition and the fulfilment that develops from communal goal achievement through collaboration.

- Social Competition: Leaderboards establish a competitive space which brings people together when they seek to achieve better results than their peers and teammate groups. The competitive environment builds both motivation and enhanced performance in individuals. Research data demonstrates that competitive elements boost user engagement frequency alongside task performance level enhancement (Kim et al., 2022).
- Collaboration: Users engage in collaborative problems to solve them jointly as part of collaborative challenges. Through this dynamic workplace environment teams develop stronger cohesion and build together while supporting each other's learning. CTF challenges designed as "team vs. team" matches push workers to share their cybersecurity expertise and methods while combating digital threats. Example: Teams in a gamified game defend a virtual simulated network against a cyberattack while practicing practical skills and developing collaborative abilities. Similar gamified approaches have shown success in fast fashion awareness campaigns, where social incentives and team-based sustainability missions drive user engagement (Rani et al., 2025).
- Psychological Implications: Through social competition and collaboration organizations both enhance employee engagement and develop the sense of community with shared cybersecurity responsibilities. The development of

security-conscious culture needs this approach. Employing social competition through combined collaboration in organizations enables higher engagement and establishes community bonds with unified cybersecurity responsibility. Building security-conscious culture depends heavily on this practice.

Progress and Mastery

- Through gamification the psychological need for progression and mastery comes together to deliver users meaningfully aligned achievement experiences while facilitating their constant development. Users feel motivated to enhance their skills through time when systems include reward structures along with skill trees and progressive tier frameworks.
- Sense of Progress: The system features progression mechanics which show users their advancing status through experience point achievements and level unlocks. Users stay engaged because the system shows them they are producing actual results from their input (Ryan & Deci 2020). Example: In a cybersecurity training platform users begin as "Cyber Novices" and receive upgraded status to "Cyber Experts" through successful completion of training scenarios.
- Mastery: When users gain skills through practice they develop competency which functions as an essential intrinsic motivational force. When users surmount advanced challenges their skill level increases and they feel more capable. A gain in self-confidence because of accomplishment makes individuals pursue increasingly advanced challenges. Example: A gamified simulation teaches users essential cyber defense skills by making them tackle progressively tougher digital attacks to learn identification methods alongside incident response tactics along with risk reduction strategies.
- Psychological Implications: Continuous progress together with learned capabilities form an empowerment mechanism that helps users stay precise and focused. Users experience dual benefits of instantaneous recognition for present accomplishments while developing an internal drive to keep advancing their educational pursuits because of the growth mindset environment.

Immediate Feedback

The fundamental aspect of gamification which supports learning involves immediate performance feedback. Real-time feedback loops through gamification show users exactly what happens when they take actions thus allowing them to learn from mistakes while refining their techniques.

- Role of Feedback in Learning: Security training that provides immediate feedback helps users comprehend their performance by displaying results about both successful versus unsuccessful phishing simulation outcomes. The delivery of timely feedback allows users to address mistakes quickly which prevents those mistakes from solidifying into established habits (Hamari et al., 2016). Example: A phishing simulation could trigger immediate alerts that would validate the user's correct identification of emails while providing specific explanations to support suspicious email labels.
- Error Correction and Behavioural Change: Feedback can diagnose errors and supply concrete advice which helps users excel in future activities. A gamified system would deliver encryption tactics with practical applications immediately after security test failures that support immediate acquisition of new information.
- Psychological Implications: The learning experience benefits from immediate feedback through its dynamic nature which promotes iterative learning steps. Active user participation with content boosts understanding of cybersecurity topics and speeds up the implementation of safe cybersecurity habits.

The psychological principles of reward systems, social dynamics, progression, and feedback work synergistically to create highly engaging and impactful gamified experiences. When applied to cybersecurity awareness, these principles can be integrated in the manner as highlighted in Figure 1.

Figure 1. Integrating principles for effective gamification in cybersecurity

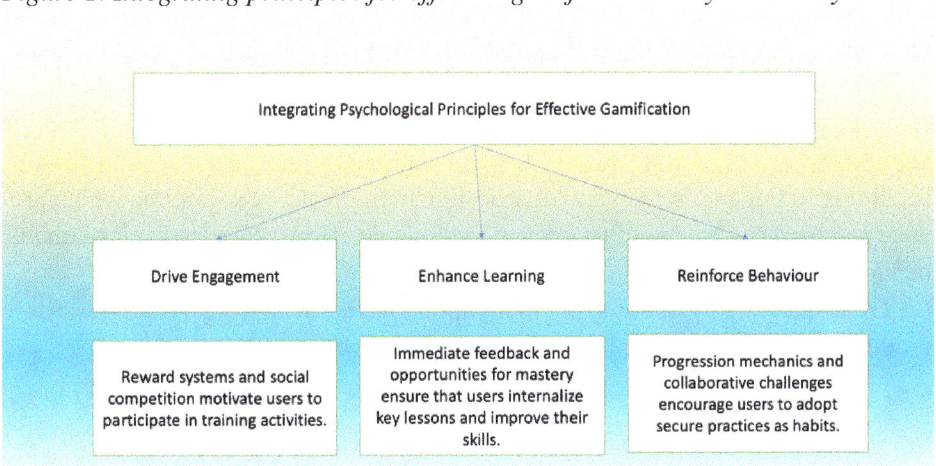

By leveraging these psychological mechanisms, gamified cybersecurity training can transform mandatory, monotonous programs into dynamic, rewarding, and memorable experiences. This approach not only improves individual performance but also fosters a security-conscious organizational culture.

INTEGRATING GAMIFICATION AND BEHAVIOR DESIGN

The combination of gamification with behaviour design models offers an efficient approach to improve cybersecurity understanding in addition to shifting safety behaviours. Through gamification people receive enjoyable rewards but behaviour design structures these rewards to shape behavioural commitments and choice patterns. These forces combine to form a unified system for producing enduring behavioural alterations among users who need to keep their activities secure and proactive.

The Synergy Between Gamification and Behavior Design

Gamification and behaviour design share overlapping goals: Interactive methods interest users while prompting them to take particular behavioural patterns. Together these approaches create better outcomes through their combined ability to use their strengths.

Gamification's Role: Through gamification people can earn points simultaneously get badges while competing on leaderboards and accepting various challenges in order to experience excitement during their learning process. Users actively connect with materials and achieve tasks because gamification simultaneously activates their natural internal drive and external incentives (Zichermann & Linder, 2022).

Behaviour Design's Role: Behaviour design analyzes psychological elements and environmental conditions which affect human conduct. Predicting user activation requires a detailed examination of triggers and behaviours together with rewards according to Fogg (2019). Behaviour design helps create interventions which produce gamified experiences that engage users while effectively creating sustainable behavioural changes.

These integrated systems bring motivation together with triggers and rewards to produce optimal behavioural results and user engagement levels.

Examples of Gamification Mechanics Aligning with Behaviour Change Principles

Mechanics That Encourage Repetition:

Gamification: Agents such as daily challenges together with streak tracking ensure sustained user participation.

Behaviour Design: According to Fogg's Behaviour Model habit formation requires constant practice. The frequency with which users experience particular interactions heightens the probability they will develop instinctive secure behaviours.

Example: Through a phishing simulation users receive rewards for identifying threats across multiple weeks thereby building their habit of scrutinizing emails.

Mechanics That Leverage Positive Reinforcement:

Gamification: Players receive badges together with points and unlock new achievements that function as immediate positive extracts for desired behaviours.

Behaviour Design: operant conditioning theory shows through Skinner's work researchers that positive reinforcement establishes desired actions through relationships with attractive effects (Skinner, 1953).

Example: The system awards employees points when they identify phishing emails which boosts their attention toward email security protection.

Mechanics That Harness Social Influence:

Gamification: Leaderboards, team-based challenges, and social recognition foster competition and collaboration.

Behaviour Design: Health behaviours get changed when influenced by the power of social norms and peer standards. Social influence makes people vigilantly protect their security because they observe others making safe behavioural choices (Kim et al., 2022).

Example: When a company implements a cybersecurity quiz leaderboard accessible to all employees it creates a dynamic competition system that drives total workforce improvement.

Mechanics That Provide Clear Feedback and Progression:

Gamification: Through quick feedback mechanisms alongside progress trackers such as rating systems or skill advancement features users maintain continuous knowledge about their application performance.

Behaviour Design: Behaviour design utilizes feedback systems to guide participants toward better responses while they study from their mistakes (Fogg, 2019).

Example: Through simulated attacks users can develop improved defensive strategies by utilizing a cybersecurity game which gives immediate feedback.

Practical Applications in Cybersecurity Training

When applying behaviur design principles to develop gamified cybersecurity training the process demands strict methodical guidelines. Here is a step-by-step process:

- Define Desired Behaviours: Design your program to teach concrete actions that users need to learn including understanding phishing attempts or creating strong passwords and directly informing security teams about incidents. Each behaviour requires breakdown with the Fogg Behaviour Model framework to identify its essential activation triggers along with user capacity elements and behavioural motivations.
- Incorporate Gamification Mechanics: Choose suitable game elements which match the target behaviour patterns. The implementation of individual achievements through points and badges exists alongside leaderboards for rival engagement and mastery objectives through challenges.
- Design Trigger Points: Embed environmental triggers which serve to initiate secure behavioural responses. Example: Online simulations should be deployed as email phishing events for staff members to receive periodic tests that improve their security awareness.
- Provide Immediate Feedback: Real-time feedback delivers performance data awarding users the ability to understand their results and study their errors. Example: Users should receive an interactive analysis which explains the warning indications along with detection methods for the phishing event after completing a simulation exercise.
- Reinforce Behaviours Through Rewards and Repetition: Initial use rewards to motivate users yet shift toward systems that trigger endogenous motivation as time passes. Example: Users receive extra points through a streak system that awards them for staying safe throughout several consecutive weeks.

- Create a Narrative for Engagement: Creating a powerful story ambassadorship delivers cybersecurity as both an individual goal and an organizational priority. Example: Your cybersecurity training program engages employees through narrative-based gameplay which simulates their work as security defenders to defend their organization against digital threats.
- Measure Outcomes and Iterate: Data analytics tools measure how users interact with your content while collecting performance metrics across different periods. Example: Assess the effectiveness of initiatives by tracking both phishing simulation success rates and training completion numbers and security incident reports. An organization should integrate secure behavioural patterns into its existing framework as a standard cultural practice.

Embedding Secure Habits into Organizational Culture

Gamified behavior design combines training activities with a cultural impact which leads to secure habit integration throughout organizations as highlighted in Figure 2.

Figure 2. Embedding secure habits

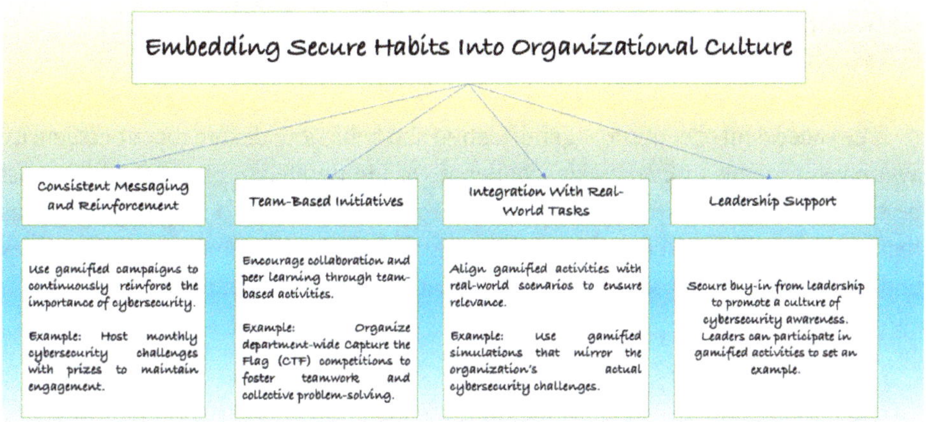

Secure habits within organizational culture harvested through gamified behaviour design helps organizations sustain proactive protection against immediate cyber threats and build resilient workforce capabilities. Organizations achieve successful cybersecurity transformation through sustained messaging and team partnership together with aligned real-world work scenarios combined with executive backing. Through these efforts organizations develop a cultural environment where safe behaviours become automatic practice enabling staff to defend against naturally developing cyber threats.

The effectiveness of integrating gamification and behaviour design can be measured through key performance indicators (KPIs):

- Improved Compliance: High completion rates of training programs along with better compliance toward established cybersecurity policies.
- Reduced Phishing Incidents: When subjects view simulated phishing links they make fewer clicks throughout the assessment.
- Enhanced Awareness: Increased recognition and reporting of potential threats.
- Engagement Metrics: Employer voices increased training completion numbers together with growing rates of gamified task completion.

Organizations reach major enhancements in cybersecurity awareness levels through their implementation of both gamification systems and behaviour design approaches that further establish a proactive security culture.

CHALLENGES AND LIMITATIONS OF GAMIFICATION AND BEHAVIOR DESIGN

The successful execution of gamification and behaviour design for cybersecurity awareness remains limited by key challenges as highlighted in Figure 3 which must be solved before ethical implementation becomes feasible. To help organizations maximize gamified system potential and navigate complex implementation challenges understanding these obstacles requires effective mitigation strategies.

Figure 3. Challenges of gamification and behaviour design

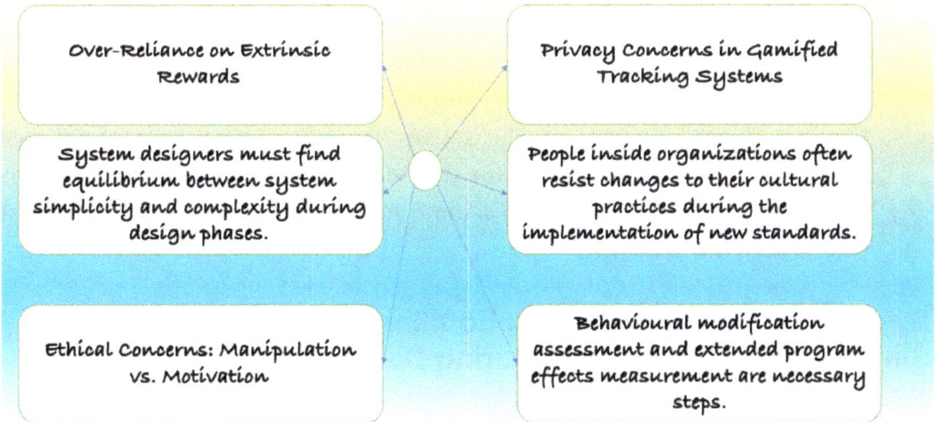

Over-Reliance on Extrinsic Rewards

The Challenge

Most gamified systems use extrinsic motivators including points alongside leaderboards and badges to keep users actively participating. The continued use of only immediate reward systems for user engagement can lead to growing disengagement because people join primarily to receive these benefits. The over-justification effect refers to a motivational post upon originally internal attention until outer incentives turning into strong distractors (Ryan & Deci, 2020).

Impact

Users typically abandon their commitment to cybersecurity training after the motivators become unavailable. The system proves ineffective in developing secure practices because external rewards do not promote enduring behavioural changes.

Mitigation Strategies

- Foster Intrinsic Motivation: Users will participate actively in gamified tasks designed with enjoyment along with meaningful content that integrates their own personal/professional goals. Simulations of real-world cybersecurity scenarios within training materials help users both gain empowerment and develop practical skills.

- Combine Rewards with Purpose: Organizations should shift their focus from awards to demonstrate the intrinsic value of safe behaviour which protect digital safety for both the organization and its users.
- Gradual Reward Reduction: The system should reduce its use of external rewards during this timeframe as users should increasingly receive rewards directly linked to their ability to achieve mastery alongside monitoring their path toward advancement.

System Designers Must Find Equilibrium Between System Simplicity and Complexity During Design Phases

The Challenge

System designers need to perform a fine line operation between constructing intuitive gamified operations that maintain user engagement. Keeping design solutions too basic leads users to lose engagement yet systems which become too intricate lose users due to complexity saturation(Hamari et al., 2016).

Impact

When designs simplify content below specific activity levels it produces insufficient engagement and restricted learning efficiencies. Users tend to avoid participating in complex systems when they become faced with confusion and frustration points.

Mitigation Strategies

- Conduct User Testing: Run trials of the gamified system using diverse employee cohorts to measure their reactions regarding system use and their engagement levels.
- Adopt a Phased Approach: Start users with simple mechanics including basic quizzes then layer complex elements as users feel more comfortable inside the system.
- Provide Clear Instructions: Each gamified game element including scoring systems and reward structures and target achievements should receive explicit explanation and simple representation.

Ethical Concerns: Manipulation vs. Motivation

The Challenge

The inherent power of gamification and behaviour design over user conduct creates problems that require ethical consideration regarding which boundaries exist between encouragement and controlling users. Relying on psychological activation techniques to a next-inducing degree for motivating participation can lead users to perceptive forced compliance or unfair treatment(Zichermann & Linder, 2022).

Impact

User experiences of manipulation alter organizational trust levels. Organizations risk deterioration of their reputation alongside lowered employee morale when ethical failures occur.

Mitigation Strategies

- Ensure Transparency: Present all purposes of gamification systems together with specific user advantages including enhanced cybersecurity understanding to users clearly.
- Promote Autonomy: Users should receive an option to engage with gamified training while multiple routes to earn success must exist to maintain learning autonomy.
- Involve Ethical Review Boards: We must work with both HR departments and ethics groups to examine gamified design elements which could generate ethical problems.

Privacy Concerns in Gamified Tracking Systems

The Challenge

The feedback along with reward delivery and progress evaluation of gamified systems depends on tracking user behaviour through their systems. Data privacy along with system security becomes a critical concern when performance or personal details are exposed to unsafe handling conditions.

Impact

When employees feel that their privacy constitutes an intrusion through gamified systems they develop decreasing levels of trust. When data management facilities are inadequate organizations become vulnerable to legal complications and face damage to their public image.

Mitigation Strategies

- Adopt Privacy-First Design: Messages should remain anonymous while preserving only those data points which support gamified functions.
- Secure Data Storage: Strong encrypted systems and owned-access protocols should both safeguard user data from unwanted breaches.
- Be Transparent About Data Usage: Show users precisely which data gets collected together with the system's current and future usage rules and information about accessibility to user details.

People Inside Organizations Often Resist Changes to their Cultural Practices During the Implementation of New Standards

The Challenge

Achieving successful gamified systems and behaviour designs need fundamental organizational cultural modifications. Operational hurdles will appear when personnel do not accept behavioural approaches as real solutions or when senior executives do not trust their worth(Hamari et al., 2016).

Impact

The refusal of employees to engage with the program weakens its ability to succeed. Leadership resistance to support gamified implementation limits both system funding and adoption potential.

Mitigation Strategies

- Engage Stakeholders Early: Restructuring the implementation process must include representative participation from employees combined with managers and senior leaders to generate acceptance and resolve concerns.
- Demonstrate Value: Demonstrative evidence from pilot projects along with positive results from various successes in gamified cybersecurity education

should be utilized to demonstrate gamification's positive effects on staff awareness about cybersecurity.
- Secure Leadership Support: Leaders should take an active part in gamified activities which serve two purposes: model commitment to the initiative while displaying their support.

Behavioral Modification Assessment and Extended Program Effects Measurement are Necessary Steps

The Challenge

Determining how gamification affects both employee behaviour and security of an organization over extended periods remains complicated despite its ability to enhance preliminary engagement(Kim et al., 2022).

Impact:

Measuring the performance outcomes of gamified systems poses complications to many organizations. Initiatives that lack measurable metrics find it difficult to prove the continued worth of gamified projects for funding.

Mitigation Strategies

- Use Multi-Metric Evaluation: Through multidimensional assessments organizations should gather numerical measurements (such as phishing incident counts and training participation rates) alongside subjective records (staff member perceptions) to benchmark program effectiveness.
- Implement Longitudinal Studies: Monitor system impact on employee behaviour through time to assess how improvements tend to persist.
- Set Clear Objectives: Establish specific measurable targets for the gamified system towards reducing phishing incidents by 50% and track continuous progress toward achievement of these goals.

Implementation of gamification combined with behaviour design for cybersecurity awareness needs thorough analysis of practical hurdles to be maximally effective. The successful implementation of engaging ethical gamified systems comes from solving problems linked to reward dependency and ethical problems and change avoidance. Organizations reach security cultural excellence when they solve these obstacles so their workforce becomes active protectors of digital domains.

DESIGNING A MODEL PROGRAM: FRAMEWORK AND IMPLEMENTATION

The Vulnerability and Cybersecurity Management Unit, in alignment with organizational objectives, facilitates a comprehensive and practical framework for developing a gamified cybersecurity awareness program within an organization through plans, tools, technologies, and strategies that enables effective measurement and evaluation of such programs.

Step Wise Procedure for Developing Gamified Cybersecurity Awareness Programs

Planning Phase

In this phase, the aim of the program is meticulously crafted, paying attention to the particular cybersecurity issues within the organization and behaviour of the end users that need to be addressed (Mitnick & Simon, 2021).

Key Steps:

- Identify Key Threats: For instance, conduct a risk assessment and identify the areas of concern, which include phishing, the presence of malware, or weak passwords which could be detrimental to the organization. If, for instance, phishing is rife, the program should be designed in a way that demonstrates mock phishing attacks so that employees can be trained on what to looks for and how to file a report on suspicious emails.
- Define Target Behaviours: Specify the secure behaviours the program wishes to achieve like reporting phishing emails, not using weak passwords, lifting locks, multi-factor authorization (MFA) and not using public Wi-Fi. Target behaviours must address other organizational security policies.
- Understand Organizational Needs: Seek opinions from relevant parties such as IT, management

Obtain input from IT teams, leadership, employees, and other stakeholders to ensure the program is responsive to their concerns and priorities. Conduct surveys or interviews to gauge current awareness levels and identify any gaps in knowledge or behaviour.

Best Practices for Planning: Apply current cybersecurity frameworks, such as NIST's CSF, to provide complete coverage (NIST, 2021). Designate risks and behaviours based on the organization's risk profile, prioritizing high-risk behaviour and threats.

Design Phase

Gamification elements and the way in which each one is designed so that it is an engaging and.

Key Elements

Game Mechanics: Use points, leaderboards & badge and challenges to motivate users. Engage in narrative storytelling to provide context and encourage engagement. To illustrate, staff members could become "cybersecurity detectives" tasked with solving data breach cases.

Behavior Design Techniques: Employ approaches to alter behaviour such as the Fogg Behaviour Model, which highlights stimuli and skills (Fogg, 2019). Apply behavioural loops (cue, routine or recompense) to reinforce secure habits. Establish a daily protocol that involves employees checking email headers, and also offer rewards for detecting phishing attempts.

Personalization and Adaptability: Customize the program according to your preferences and abilities. In addition to technical challenges, IT workers can participate in interactive phishing simulations. Maintain adaptive difficulty levels to keep users engaged without overwhelming them (Werbach & Hunter, 2021).

Accessibility and Inclusivity: Blend visual, auditory, and interactive elements to cater to different learning styles. e.g. Implement accessibility guidelines like the WCAG to ensure the platform is accessible to individuals with disabilities.

Best Practices for Design: Collect feedback from small group users to improve the program's functionality through prototype testing. Gamify and align with the organisation's brand so that it is more relatable to an.

Implementation Phase

In the implementation phase, the program is introduced, its users are engaged, and an initial evaluation is conducted.

Key Steps

Deploy the Program: Implement it in phases, starting with a group of pilots to address any bugs or user feedback prior to full implementation. Ensure that the program is effectively promoted through email, webinars, and face-to–face interactions.

Promote Engagement: Build team spirit and collaboration through leaderboards and team-based challenges. Accomplish milestones in public, such as obtaining the top score in a scam simulation, to encourage others to participate.

Monitor and Measure: Utilize dashboards to monitor performance, including participation rates, completion rates and real-time performance metrics. Acquire quantitative evaluations from users to pinpoint areas for improvement.

Best Practices for Implementation: Enable effective guidance and technical assistance for the smooth implementation. Encourage leadership participation to embody desired behaviours and demonstrate organizational dedication. Learning Tools and Technologies for Gamified Cybersecurity Training. The effectiveness of a gamified cybersecurity awareness program is determined by the selection of tools and technologies.

Tools and Technologies for Gamified Cybersecurity Training

Software Platforms and Applications

Knowledge-based Training platforms (KnowBe4 and Wombat Security) provide gamified training opportunities, including simulations, quizzes or hands-on modules (Gupta et al, 2022). Virtualizations for practice, such as IBM's Cyber Range or RangeForce, are available on Cyber Rang Platforms.

Learning Management System (LMS) Integration.

Uncomplicated integration: Add gamified programs into existing LMS platforms to pool training resources and keep track of progress. Create bespoke content using the LMS to meet the specific cybersecurity needs of an organization.

Advanced Analytics Tools

Using analytics tools, measure user engagement; identify gaps in knowledge; and track progress over time. Case studies include dashboards showing click through rates in phishing simulations, as well as statistics on suspicious activity reported by users.epi).

Metrics for Success

Quantitative and qualitative evaluations are necessary to gauge the effectiveness of a gamified awareness program focused on cybersecurity.

Key Performance Indicators (KPIs)

Estimate the percentage of workers who are exposed to simulated malware before and after their training. Phishing success rates? Rates for Incident Reporting: Track employee reports of suspicious emails or incidents. Tracking the number of employees who complete training modules.

Continuous Improvement Through Feedback Loops

Collect input from users through surveys and interviews to determine their level of interest or difficulty. By using A/B testing, you can contrast the performance of gamified elements like quizzes with scenario-based challenges. Maintain content updates to keep users informed about new threats and maintain user interest.

Long-Term Impact Metrics

Measure the longevity of secure behaviours by examining metrics such as password reset frequency or MFA adoption rates. Examine the security of an organization through external audits or penetration testing.

A gamified cybersecurity awareness program's creation and implementation necessitate careful planning, creative design (and ongoing evaluation). The use of tools, technologies, and metrics enables organizations to develop programs that not only educate employees but also incorporate secure behaviours into the organizational culture. A well-planned strategy transforms employees from inactive participants to active guardians of the organization's digital assets, ensuring long-term resilience in an ever-evolving threat environment.

FUTURE TRENDS AND OPPORTUNITIES

The future is promising for those who use gamification and behaviour design to increase awareness of cybersecurity through innovative approaches. By utilizing innovative approaches, emerging technologies are utilized by organizations to create more effective and engaging training programs. We'll go over the key trends and opportunities that will shape gamified cybersecurity training in the coming years as highlighted in figure 4.

Figure 4. Future trends an opportunities

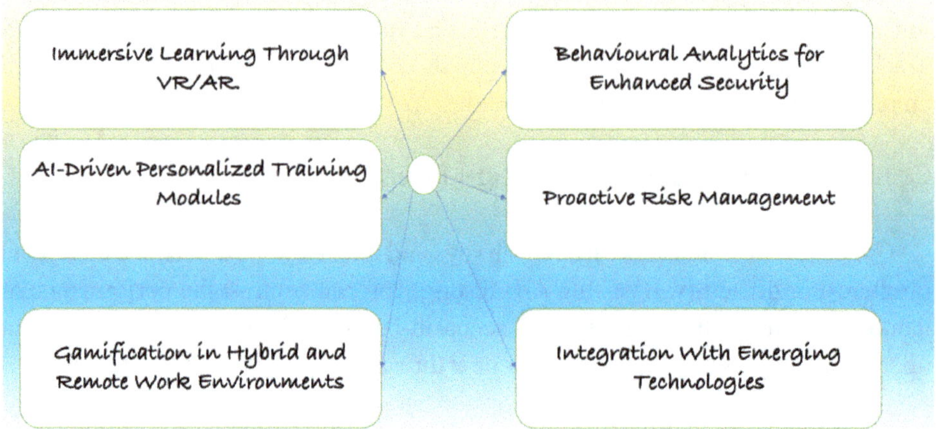

Immersive Learning Through VR/AR

Virtual reality (VR) and augmented reality have transformed learning experiences by providing immersive, interactive environments. The use of these technologies is especially advantageous in cybersecurity training, as it necessitates practical experience.

Applications of VR in Cybersecurity Training

1. Simulated Cyberattack Scenarios: VR can create realistic simulations of cyberattacks, such as ransomware incidents or phishing schemes. Users can practice responding to these threats in a controlled environment, improving their decision-making and response times. For instance, employees can experience a "live" data breach scenario, where they must identify the source of the breach and follow protocols to mitigate damage. This approach allows users to practice handling high-pressure situations, boosting their confidence and competence.
2. Training in Virtual Environments: VR-based training modules can mimic organizational networks, providing users with a sandbox to explore cybersecurity principles without risking actual systems. Example: IT teams can navigate through virtual network environments to identify vulnerabilities, test firewalls, or deploy patches.

Applications of AR in Cybersecurity Training

1. Interactive Learning: AR can overlay digital information onto physical environments, offering real-time guidance and insights. For example, employees could use AR apps to identify insecure devices in an office or review the security status of IoT devices by simply pointing their smartphones at them.
2. Hands-On Problem Solving: AR can facilitate interactive exercises, such as "spot the vulnerability" challenges. Users might scan a workstation to find potential security risks, such as weak passwords or unencrypted devices.

Benefits of VR/AR in Gamified Training

1. Increased Engagement: Immersive environments captivate learners, making training sessions more engaging and memorable (Pellas et al., 2022).
2. Real-World Application: By simulating real-world scenarios, VR/AR ensures that users can transfer their learning directly to workplace situations.
3. Enhanced Retention: Immersive experiences are proven to improve retention rates compared to traditional training methods (Clark et al., 2021).

AI-Driven Personalized Training Modules

Cybersecurity awareness programs could be revolutionized by artificial intelligence (AI) that can cater to individual needs, preferences, and performance.

Adaptive Learning Systems: Through real-time analysis of user data, AI can adjust training content and provide personalized learning opportunities. Employees who perform well in phishing simulations may be given advanced tasks, while those who do poorly may receive more basic training. The use of personalized difficulty levels ensures that users remain engaged and don't become bored (Zhou et al, 2023).

Behaviour Analytics: The ability to track user movements and identify patterns can be exploited by AI-powered systems to improve interventions. For instance, if an employee frequently engages in simulated email fraud, the system may focus on phishing awareness training. AI has the ability to identify high-risk employees by analyzing their behaviour and designing personalized training programs for them.

AI Chatbots for Real-Time Support: Virtual cybersecurity mentors can be created using AI chatbots, which offer users immediate feedback, guidance and resources. A chatbot has the potential to teach employees about safeguarding a hacked account or provide guidance on cybersecurity best practices. Additionally,

Benefits of AI Integration

1. Efficiency: AI streamlines the training process by delivering the right content to the right person at the right time.
2. Scalability: AI-powered programs can easily scale to accommodate large organizations with diverse training needs.
3. Continuous Improvement: Machine learning algorithms can analyze user feedback and program outcomes to enhance training effectiveness over time (Hamari et al., 2022).

Gamification in Hybrid and Remote Work Environments

The shift to hybrid and remote work models presents unique challenges for cybersecurity training. Gamification can address these challenges by fostering engagement and vigilance among distributed teams as listed below:

Virtual Challenges and Leaderboards: Organizations can create online platforms where employees compete in cybersecurity challenges, such as identifying phishing attempts or solving cryptographic puzzles. Leaderboards can encourage friendly competition, while team-based activities foster collaboration among remote employees.

Gamified Microlearning Modules: Gamification can be integrated into daily workflows through microlearning modules delivered via apps or collaboration tools. Example: A Slack bot could present employees with a daily "cybersecurity quiz," rewarding correct answers with virtual points or badges.

Maintaining Engagement Across Locations: Gamified systems can connect remote employees, ensuring that cybersecurity awareness remains a shared responsibility. Team competitions and global challenges encourage collaboration and create a sense of community. Virtual "cybersecurity champions" can emerge, inspiring peers to stay vigilant.

Behavioral Analytics for Enhanced Security

Behavioural analytics uses information to determine risky behaviours and to strengthen safe practices. It can be used to develop cybersecurity awareness when fused with gamification, however, when added to it, it provides incredibly useful tools. This gives organizations the opportunity to transform beyond conventional, universal training into dynamic training systems that learn about individual behaviours and learning curves, and risk profiles in real-time. Within a gamified setting, each user action (e.g. clicking on a simulated phishing message, modifying a password, turn on a multi-factor authentication) is measurable, assessable, and award-able/not-awardable. The systems of behavioural analytics use such data to identify patterns of vulnerability, discover typical response biases and identify anomalies that can indicate potential risk. The systems also detect potentially dangerous users and implement specific interventions drafted to fill the behavioural deficit.

Another vital strength is known as Behavioural Segmentation. Workers may be segmented using behavioural profiles, i.e. habitual risk takers, unconscious clickers or passive non responders and a specific cybersecurity content may be assigned to each segment. This is similar to digital marketing most commonly in segmentation tactics within consumer behaviour modelling, which is visible in areas such as experimental retail (Singh & Rani, 2024).

Performance analytics and Dashboards (Gamified) give insights and inspiration. Individual (Team) visualizations of the progress can be shared to promote competition and accountability. Safe-oriented behaviour of the teams may also be encouraged and publicly rewarded to foster a security-centered culture throughout the organization. Such systems generate a kind of cybersecurity telemetry, i.e., a constant flow of data on user behaviour that can be turned into usable intelligence by security operations centers.

Being combined with AI and Predictive Modelling makes this go a step further. Behavioural analytics platforms with AI are able to predict risky behaviour in advance by simulating the past trends. As an example, when an employee demonstrates delay in responses in simulator training and declining interest in email header information, the system could automatically book a refresher course or present real-time phishing alerts. Nevertheless, such issues as privacy and ethical considerations have to be raised openly. Monitoring and assessing the behaviour of employees including tracking them even on security grounds should not breach data protection laws or infringe the autonomy of individuals. Measure like anonymization, opt-ins, and effective communication on the use of data are necessary to retain trust.

Proactive Risk Management

The purpose of proactive risk management during cybersecurity awareness training is to locate, anticipate, and prevent dangerous events prior to its real manifestation. Gamification can provide a strong basis to implement proactive risk management by integrating risk detection in the small everyday interactions people have. Rather than utilizing periodical testing or post-compromised analyses, gamified systems also assess behavioural indicators at all times on a per-user or per-team basis and determine the level of risk by measuring factors like hesitating to complete a phishing exercise, reusing a password, or not enabled MFA, and set the risk level accordingly. These results are consumed by real-time dashboards visualising security position, and sign-posts individuals or departments at risk so that action can be brought to bear upon them.

This is even furthered in the future trends like AI-driven personalisation which learns through previous behaviours and model the possible weaknesses before they happen. An example would be the cases when the employee routinely takes a long time to report to a phishing simulation and misses optional training; the system would foresee the disengagement and trigger an adaptive nudging sequence and issue scenarios-based missions to serve as a second-chance re-engagement. These simulations may involve realistic simulations designed to meet the use case of the user or their department, position, or vulnerable areas, and presented in a form of a game where points are awarded to those who act fast and correctly.

Behaviour-triggered remediation pathways Behaviour-triggered remediation pathways is another potent instrument in forward-looking risk management. The system allows auto-enrolling the received employee who fails a phish or is highlighted by the behavioural analytics engine into a short gamified retraining scenario-based modules made up of challenges. These micro-interventions are gamified and scored so that users can basically get recognition through redeeming their risk level and earn points towards an improvement. The result of this gamified risk-loop is over time to create a growth mindset culture where failure is seen not as a punitive mark but rather as a learning point.

Effective risk management should not be just about individuals, but also organizational, where aggregated analytics of behaviour can be used to advise policy changes, hiring practices and budget, etc. To illustrate, in case analytics reveal a steady decline in the training scores of remote workers, the leadership can employ mobile-first gamified modules or introduce Android-based Slack-based micro-challenges to ensure engagement in distributed settings.

In order to have a high level of ethical integrity, systems have to be made transparent and also, privacy-conservative. Analytics on risk scores should be anonymized unless the user makes a direct choice not to have them unless an explicit agreement is made by the user not to have the analytics, and feedback mechanisms should be limited to empowerment and not tracking. The procedures of involving ethical review boards in the design of AI and gamified nudges will make the approach respectful to autonomy and willing to be trusted.

Integration With Emerging Technologies

The convergence of gamification with other technologies creates opportunities for even greater innovation:

1. Blockchain: Blockchain technology can ensure the integrity of gamified training records, providing tamper-proof evidence of compliance.
2. IoT Integration: Gamification can be extended to IoT devices, encouraging employees to secure their personal and workplace devices.
3. Gamified Incident Response Platforms: Incident response systems can incorporate gamified elements, such as tracking team performance during breach simulations.

While these trends hold immense promise, their implementation is not without challenges:

1. Cost: Emerging technologies like VR/AR can be expensive to deploy. Mitigation: Start with pilot programs to assess ROI before scaling.
2. Privacy: Behavioural analytics and AI raise concerns about employee data privacy. Mitigation: Implement transparent policies and secure data storage practices.
3. Adoption Resistance: Employees may be hesitant to adopt new technologies. Mitigation: Provide user-friendly interfaces and comprehensive training.

The future of cybersecurity training lies in harnessing the potential of gamification, behaviour design, and emerging technologies. By staying ahead of these trends, organizations can create innovative, effective, and engaging programs that empower employees to combat cyber threats. As the landscape of cybersecurity continues to evolve, embracing these opportunities is not just an option, it's a necessity for building resilient organizations. Cybersecurity ceased to be a technical issue only, it is a kind of an issue of human cognition, emotion and motivation. This chapter has shown that the old form of awareness build on passive teaching and fear based compliance can no longer keep us adequately prepared to deal with a world where there is a faster shifting of threat scenarios than of the training manuals. In order to overcome the actual vulnerability, the human factor, the organizations need to change cybersecurity learning experience into an active and stimulating one with a psychological insights.

Gamification and behavioural design is more than a new approach to learning, it is a paradigm shift. They redefine risk management, user behaviour towards threats, and how security becomes an every-day thought process rather than highlighted once a year as a tick-box activity. These strategies create secure habits that go far beyond the training room by rewarding safe behaviour, creating competition and collaboration and by inculcating learning into immersive environments. This approach can be made proactive and adaptive instead of merely reactive because of the emergence of new technologies, namely artificial intelligence, VR/AR, and behavioural analytics. They enable us to forewarn threats as they happen, make interventions more personal and, assess change in a surgical way. Since the task of spreading better awareness is achieved at ease with the combination of these instruments with gamified solutions, the additional skills acquired in the result owing to the combination of environment and tools such as resilience, confidence, and a culture of shared responsibility are not just an added value, they are an essential implementation. As organizations advance, there is no option but to turn users into the strongest defence, rather than the weakest link team. Cybersecurity is no longer an empty policy, but a practice, when employees are not only trained, but inspired, engaged and trusted. And therein is the model of secure organizations of tomorrow. Cybersecurity does not only have a technical future. It is natural. And this begins with our way of teaching, our way to motivate and our way to empower.

REFERENCES

CISA. (2020). *Cybersecurity and Infrastructure Security Agency Annual Report.* Retrieved from https://www.cisa.gov

Clark, L., Martin, K., & Nguyen, T. (2021). Gamification in hybrid work environments: Enhancing engagement and collaboration. *Journal of Workplace Learning, 33*(5), 347–361.

Deterding, S., Dixon, D., Khaled, R., & Nacke, L. (2011). From game design elements to gamefulness: defining "gamification". In *Proceedings of the 15th International Academic MindTrek Conference: Envisioning Future Media Environments* (pp. 9-15). DOI: 10.1145/2181037.2181040

Fogg, B. J. (2009). *Behaviour design: A model for creating lasting change.* Stanford University Press.

Fogg, B. J. (2019). *Tiny habits: The small changes that change everything.* Houghton Mifflin Harcourt.

Hamari, J., Koivisto, J., & Sarsa, H. (2016). Does gamification work? A literature review of empirical studies on gamification. *International Journal of Information Management, 36*(2), 162–175. DOI: 10.1016/j.ijinfomgt.2015.11.005

Hamari, J., Koivisto, J., & Sarsa, H. (2016). Does gamification work? A literature review of empirical studies on gamification. *System Sciences (HICSS), 2014 47th Hawaii International Conference on.* DOI: 10.1109/HICSS.2014.377

Hamari, J., Koivisto, J., & Sarsa, H. (2022). Does gamification work? A literature review of empirical studies on gamification. *International Journal of Human-Computer Studies, 127*, 190–204.

Kim, S., Lee, J., & Choi, Y. (2022). Gamification strategies to promote engagement in cybersecurity education. *Journal of Cybersecurity Education, 8*(1), 45–62. DOI: 10.1093/jces/xyz123

Kim, S., Song, H., & Lee, K. (2022). The role of gamification in corporate learning: Enhancing motivation and engagement. *Journal of Organizational Behavior, 43*(1), 45–59. DOI: 10.1002/job.2573

Kirlappos, I., Parkin, S., & Sasse, M. A. (2015). Learning from "Shadow Security": Why understanding non-compliance provides the basis for effective security awareness campaigns. In *Proceedings of the 2015 Workshop on Usable Security.*

Koivisto, J., & Hamari, J. (2019). The rise of motivational information systems: A review of gamification research. *Computers in Human Behavior, 99*, 98–123. DOI: 10.1016/j.chb.2019.05.033

Looyestyn, J., Kernot, J., Boshoff, K., Ryan, J., Edney, S., & Maher, C. (2017). Does gamification increase engagement with online programs? A systematic review. *PLoS One, 12*(3), e0173403. DOI: 10.1371/journal.pone.0173403 PMID: 28362821

Mitnick, K., & Simon, W. L. (2021). *The art of deception: Controlling the human element of security*. John Wiley & Sons.

Pellas, N., Fotaris, P., & Kazanidis, I. (2022). Immersive learning through VR and AR: Applications for cybersecurity training. *Computers & Education, 176*, 104363.

Rani, J., Guru, R., & Santhanam, S. (2024). *Industry evolution, current trends, and future perspectives*. In *Advances in marketing, customer relationship management, and e-services book series* (pp. 113–132). https://doi.org/DOI: 10.4018/979-8-3693-7535-8.ch006

Rani, J., Guru, R., & Santhanam, S. (2025). *AI and Environmental Stewardship*. In *Advances in computational intelligence and robotics book series* (pp. 567–582). https://doi.org/DOI: 10.4018/979-8-3693-8034-5.ch028

Ryan, R. M., & Deci, E. L. (2020). Intrinsic and extrinsic motivations: Classic definitions and new directions. *Contemporary Educational Psychology, 61*, 101860. DOI: 10.1016/j.cedpsych.2020.101860 PMID: 10620381

Ryan, R. M., & Deci, E. L. (2020). Intrinsic and extrinsic motivations: Classic definitions and new directions. *Contemporary Educational Psychology, 25*(1), 54–67. DOI: 10.1006/ceps.1999.1020 PMID: 10620381

Safa, N. S., Solms, R., & Futcher, L. (2016). Human aspects of information security in organizations. *Computers & Security, 53*, 70–80. DOI: 10.1016/j.cose.2015.10.006

Sarkar, K. R. (2010). Barriers to effective cybersecurity awareness training. *Information Management & Computer Security, 18*(1), 16–24.

Schunk, D. H. (2012). *Learning theories: An educational perspective*. Pearson Higher Ed.

Schunk, D. H., & DiBenedetto, M. K. (2020). Motivation and social-emotional learning: Theory, research, and practice. *Contemporary Educational Psychology, 60*, 101830.

Verizon. (2022). *Data Breach Investigations Report (DBIR)*. Retrieved from https://www.verizon.com

Werbach, K., & Hunter, D. (2021). *For the win: How game thinking can revolutionize your business*. Wharton Digital Press.

Whitman, M. E., & Mattord, H. J. (2021). *Principles of Information Security* (7th ed.). Cengage Learning.

Zhou, Y., Li, M., & Sun, L. (2023). AI in personalized cybersecurity training: Opportunities and challenges. *Artificial Intelligence in Education*, *34*(1), 57–73.

Zichermann, G., & Linder, J. (2022). *Gamification by Design: Implementing Game Mechanics in Web and Mobile Apps* (2nd ed.). O'Reilly Media.

Chapter 5
Game-Based Learning Platforms for Cybersecurity Certifications

Siva Raja Sindiramutty
https://orcid.org/0009-0006-0310-8721
Taylor's University, Malaysia

Noor Zaman Jhanjhi
https://orcid.org/0000-0001-8116-4733
Taylor's University, Malaysia

Mamoona Humayun
Independent Researcher, UK

ABSTRACT

Game-based learning platforms are reshaping how professionals prepare for cybersecurity certifications. Certifications like CISSP, CEH, and CompTIA Security+ are essential for career growth, but traditional training methods often lack engagement. Game-based learning provides an innovative alternative, incorporating interactive content, real-time feedback, and practical simulations to enhance knowledge retention and skill development. This chapter explores the foundational features of game-based platforms, including levels, leaderboards, challenges, and rewards, as well as their role in bridging theoretical knowledge with hands-on practice through virtual labs and simulations. It highlights the alignment of game activities with certification objectives, enabling learners to focus on domains such as ethical hacking and incident response. Furthermore, adaptive learning techniques ensure

DOI: 10.4018/979-8-3373-0477-9.ch005

personalized experiences that cater to individual skill levels.

INTRODUCTION

The Importance of Cybersecurity Certifications

Role of Certifications (e.g., CISSP, CEH, CompTIA Security+) in Career Advancement

Certifications like CISSP, CEH, and CompTIA Security+ are often described as career game-changers in cybersecurity. Certifications are like golden tickets—without them, you're not even allowed on the ride. And honestly, they weren't wrong. When recruiters see CISSP on a résumé, it's like a light bulb goes off—this person knows their stuff. Certifications signal a commitment to the profession and prove technical skills that employers value (Kamal & Ibrahim, 2025; Azam et al., 2023).

In a competitive job market, having these credentials can mean the difference between an email that starts with "We regret to inform you" and one that says, "When can you start?" They can also lead to higher salaries. A report by Glennie et al. (2024) revealed that certified professionals earn significantly more than their uncertified peers. While certifications alone don't guarantee mastery, they often open doors to specialized roles, from penetration testing to security auditing (Aslaner, 2024; Alex et al., 2022). They're not just badges; they're trust builders. One challenge, though, is the cost. I've heard peers mutter about spending thousands on exams, only to stress over recertification requirements later. But most of all it's worth it. Employers recognize the effort behind those letters and often prioritize certified candidates in hiring decisions (Penning et al., 2024; Hussain et al., 2024). Whether you're just starting or aiming to climb the corporate ladder, certifications remain a solid investment in a field that rewards expertise. Figure 1 shows the benefits of a professional certificate.

Figure 1. Benefits of professional certificate

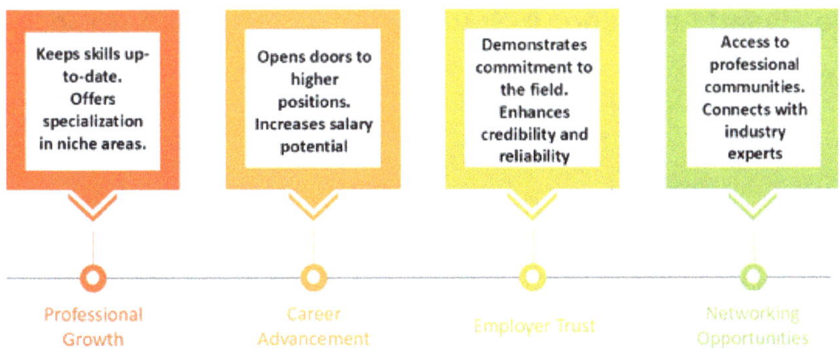

Challenges in Traditional Certification Training (e.g., Dry Content, Lack of Engagement)

When I attended my first certification course years ago, I remember being excited—until I opened the training material. It was as dry as a textbook left in the sun for a decade. The content was crammed with technical jargon, and I felt like I was reading an instruction manual for a device I'd never own. This isn't an uncommon experience. Traditional certification training often struggles with keeping learners engaged. The lack of interactivity and connection to real-world scenarios turns even the most eager participants into clock-watchers (Parks, n.d.).

Another issue is how outdated many of these courses feel. It's like watching a movie from the 90s while the world has moved on to streaming platforms. Certifications are often slow to adapt to industry changes, leaving learners stuck with the knowledge that might not be directly applicable to modern workplaces (Spiro & Bhamidi, 2024; Alferidah & Jhanjhi, 2020). Additionally, the one-size-fits-all approach doesn't work for everyone. We're all different; some thrive with hands-on activities, while others prefer discussion-based learning. Yet most certification programs ignore these differences and stick to rigid formats. What hit me hardest during these courses was isolation. Sitting in a room full of people but feeling completely disconnected—because the structure didn't encourage collaboration or sharing—was draining. Adding to the problem, there's often a pressure to memorize and regurgitate rather than truly understand the material, which diminishes long-term retention (Tripp et al., 2024; Alkinani et al., 2021). The real kicker? Despite these challenges, certifications remain a necessary evil in many industries. Imagine how much more we could learn if they felt less like chores and more like opportunities.

Game-Based Learning: A Solution to Traditional Methods

Overview of Game-based Learning (GBL) and its Benefits in Professional Education

When I first heard about game-based learning, I imagined something like video game marathons disguised as work. Turns out, it's a lot more strategic and far less about fun for fun's sake. Game-based learning (GBL) integrates game mechanics into education to make learning more engaging and interactive (Chen, 2023; Kiyani et al., 2024). Think of simulations, role-playing, or even digital games tailored to teach skills—like how pilots train in flight simulators. In professional education, GBL shifts the focus from passive consumption to active problem-solving. You're not just reading about leadership strategies; you're navigating a virtual boardroom crisis. This approach gives learners a safe space to fail, try again, and build confidence without real-world consequences (Slyman, 2024; Babbar et al., 2021). It's like practicing chess moves against an AI before facing a grandmaster.

The benefits are hard to ignore. GBL makes complex topics easier to grasp by breaking them into interactive scenarios (Springle, 2024; Brohi et al., 2020). For instance, a cybersecurity professional might learn to identify threats through a gamified simulation, gaining hands-on experience without risking actual systems (Yigit et al., 2024). It also boosts retention because people remember what they *do*, not just what they read. One of my favorite examples is how healthcare professionals use GBL to rehearse procedures. A friend of mine, a nurse, once practiced managing a patient emergency in a game environment. She said it felt like a roller coaster but admitted she learned faster than she ever did in traditional lectures. GBL also fosters collaboration. Group challenges encourage teamwork and communication, which are essential in professional environments (Medina-Merodio et al., 2024; Chesti et al., 2020). At its core, GBL isn't just about learning, it's about doing, failing, adapting, and thriving. Figure 2 shows challenges in traditional certification training.

Figure 2. Challenges in traditional certification training

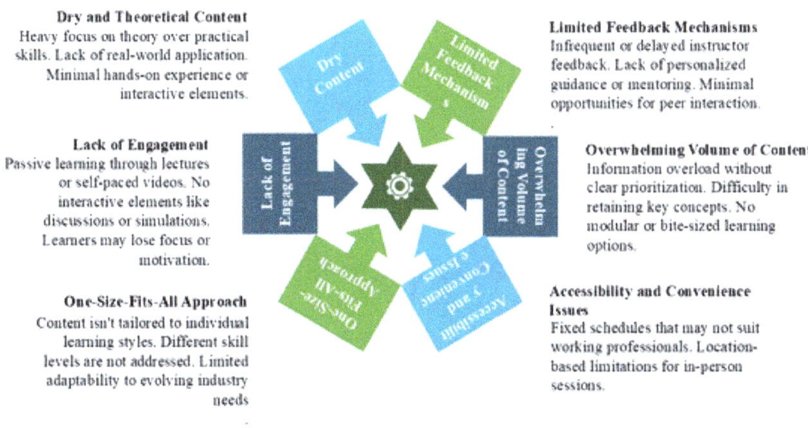

Chapter Contribution

This chapter is pertinent to the area of game-based learning platforms for cybersecurity certification. First, it describes the role of cybersecurity certification in career advancement. And outlines the challenges in traditional certification training and the overview of game-based learning and its benefits in professional education. The chapter then interactive content real-time feedback and progress tracking in game-based learning levels, leaderboards, and hands-on practicals with the simulated environment.

Furthermore, the chapter presents a mapping of game activities to certification exam domains, an Overview of a platform like TryHack me, Hack the Box, and Cyber Start, how learning increased learner retention and interest through gamified elements also discusses the cost of development and maintenance, accessibility and technical barriers. Lastly, the section presents examples of universities and the expansion of global collaboration in the GBL platform.

Chapter Organization

In the first section, we will cover an insight into the introduction to the importance of cyber security certifications. In section 2 we go down the foundation of the game-based learning platform. In section 3 we discuss designing game-based learning for certification and examples of existing platforms and tools in section 4. Section 5 delves into the benefits of game-based learning for certification preparation. Section 6 will explore to challenges in implementing a game-based learning platform. Section 7 will explain the case studies: case studies and success stories. In final section will discuss future trends in game-based cybersecurity certification training.

FOUNDATIONS OF GAME-BASED LEARNING PLATFORMS

Key Features of Game-Based Learning Platforms

Interactive Content, Real-Time Feedback, and Progress Tracking

Game-based learning platforms bring a spark of excitement to education, making learning more interactive and rewarding. At their heart, these platforms are built on three pillars: interactive content, real-time feedback, and progress tracking. Imagine being in school and struggling to stay awake in a history class. Now, picture learning the same content through an immersive game where you unlock achievements for answering questions correctly or making decisions that change the course of the story (Aly, 2024; Linqiang et al., 2024). That's the magic these platforms bring to the table.

Interactive content is a game-changer—students aren't just passive listeners anymore; they're actively engaged. Whether solving puzzles, completing quests, or collaborating with peers, they learn while immersed in the process (Song et al., 2024; Manchuri et al., 2024). Real-time feedback takes this a step further. Instant corrections and encouragement motivate learners to keep going, much like having a coach by their side. I've seen this firsthand with my nephew, who used a math app that told him immediately if he got a problem wrong and then showed him how to fix it. He loved it so much that he didn't realize he was learning.

Progress tracking is another standout feature. It's not just about grades; it's about seeing growth. When students can visualize how far they've come—whether through leaderboards, badges, or progress bars—it boosts their confidence and keeps them hooked (Alshehhi et al., 2024; Dogra et al., 2021). Teachers also benefit by identifying areas where students need extra help. These platforms don't just educate; they build resilience and curiosity. Education feels less like a chore and more like a game—one you want to win. And isn't that how learning should feel?

Core Game Mechanics Used in Cybersecurity Training

Levels, Leaderboards, Rewards, and Challenges

Cybersecurity training can be mind-numbing if it's just endless lectures and slides, but game mechanics have flipped the script. Incorporating levels, leaderboards, rewards, and challenges into the process not only makes it bearable but downright enjoyable (Philpott & Son, 2022; Mohamad & Sazali, 2018). I recently participated in a cybersecurity game, and honestly, I didn't expect to enjoy defending a virtual system against simulated attacks—but there I was, hooked.

Levels are the backbone of progression (Christopoulos & Mystakidis, 2023). They break complex topics into bite-sized chunks, letting participants build skills step by step. You don't jump into advanced threat mitigation on day one; instead, you start with basics, like recognizing phishing emails, and work your way up. Each level feels like an achievement, much like moving through the stages of a video game. Leaderboards are a game-changer for motivation (Krause et al., 2015). Seeing your name on the board—or just below a colleague's—is enough to ignite some friendly competition. But more than that, they foster collaboration. When I was stuck on a tricky challenge, my teammate offered a tip that helped me solve it, so we both moved up.

Rewards, whether they're badges, certificates, or even simple acknowledgments, keep the momentum going (Denmeade, 2015). One company I know offers gift cards to employees who complete advanced levels, and you'd be amazed at how fast they go through the training modules. And let's not forget challenges. These are where the real learning happens. Simulated attacks, time-sensitive tasks, or puzzles not only test what you've learned but also push you to think critically under pressure. They mimic real-world scenarios, making the skills stick. By weaving these mechanics into cybersecurity training, companies aren't just teaching—they're building a more alert and skilled workforce. And in today's world, isn't that the ultimate win?

The Role of Simulations in Certification Preparation

Hands-on Practice with Simulated Environments

Preparing for certifications can feel overwhelming, reading endless materials and memorizing concepts often leaves you wondering if you're truly ready. That's where simulations step in, bridging the gap between theory and practice. I remember prepping for my cybersecurity certification and feeling lost until I tackled a simulated attack scenario. It turned abstract ideas into something real, and suddenly, everything clicked.

Simulated environments provide a safe space to practice complex tasks without fear of real-world consequences (Rose et al., 2000; Girardi et al., 2024; Ravichandran et al., 2024). Whether it's setting up a firewall, detecting malware, or responding to a breach, you get hands-on experience. It's like learning to drive in a controlled setup before hitting the highway. What makes simulations so effective is their realism. These setups mimic real-world networks, complete with vulnerabilities, logs, and attack patterns. You're not just clicking through menus; you're investigating incidents and solving problems as you would on the job. This kind of active learning sticks to better than passive reading ever could. Simulations also offer immediate feedback. Make a mistake? The system shows where you went wrong and guides you on how to fix it (Girardi et al., 2024; Fatima-Tuz-Zahra et al., 2020). It's not about avoiding errors but learning from them. During my training, I botched a simulated server recovery, but seeing the consequences helped me master the steps.

Beyond technical skills, simulations build confidence. When exam questions or real-life challenges pop up, they don't feel intimidating. You've already been through the wringer in a simulated setting, so you know what to do. In certification prep, simulations aren't just tools—they're game-changers. They turn theory into action, making you not just test-ready but job-ready. Figure 3 shows the foundations of game-based learning platforms.

Figure 3. Foundations of game-based learning platforms

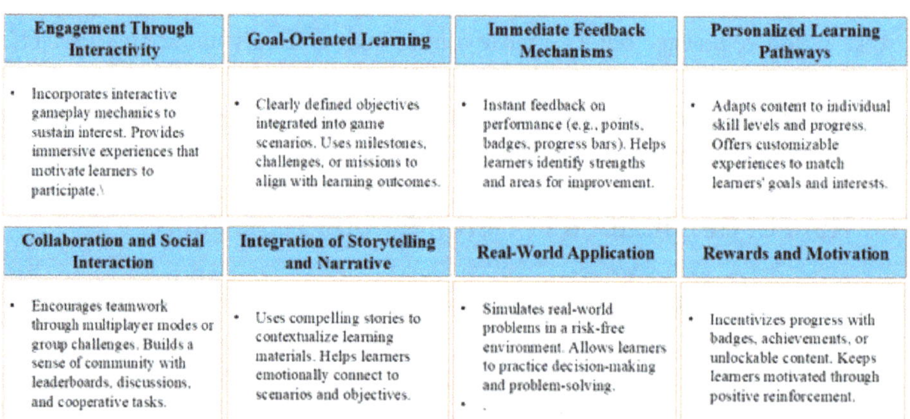

DESIGNING GAME-BASED LEARNING FOR CERTIFICATIONS

Aligning Game Content with Certification Objectives

Mapping Game Activities to Certification Exam Domains (e.g., Ethical Hacking, Incident Response)

Game-based learning has taken certification prep to another level. The trick? Aligning game content with the exam objectives so you're not just playing, you're preparing. When I was studying for my ethical hacking certification, I came across a game that simulated breaking into a system (legally, of course). Every puzzle or mission tied back to the certification domains, and it didn't feel like studying at all.

The key to effective design lies in mapping game activities directly to exam domains. Let's say the certification covers topics like network scanning, incident response, or vulnerability analysis (Edwards, 2024; Lekkala & Gurijala, 2024; Sheng et al., 2024). A well-designed game will have challenges tailored to each of these areas. For instance, you might face scenarios where you scan networks for open ports or respond to simulated breaches, sharpening skills while ticking off certification requirements. Games also provide a layered approach. Basic levels cover foundational knowledge perfect for beginners while advanced missions dive into complex scenarios, like handling ransomware or conducting penetration tests. This progression ensures learners of all levels stay engaged.

Another advantage is real-time feedback. As you tackle in-game challenges, you get immediate insights into what went right or wrong. I remember failing an incident response mission because I skipped analyzing the logs. The game flagged it, and I never made that mistake again. What makes these games so powerful is their ability to mimic exam-style thinking. Certification tests don't just ask "what" they ask "how" and "why." Games prepare you for that by embedding critical thinking into every mission. It's not just about passing the exam; it's about building confidence for the real-world tasks waiting on the other side.

Role of Adaptive Learning in Personalizing GBL Experiences

Tailoring Challenges Skill Levels and Learning Paces

Have you ever played a game that somehow seemed to know just how much to challenge you? It kept you on edge—not so hard you gave up but not so easy that you got bored. That's adaptive learning in action, and it's transforming game-based learning (GBL).

Adaptive systems adjust the difficulty, pacing, and type of challenges based on the player's skill level and progress (Sharbel & Salaimeh, 2024; Hallengren & Svensson, 2013). Imagine you're learning ethical hacking in a game. If you breeze through basic concepts like reconnaissance, the system might fast-track you to tougher tasks like privilege escalation. Struggling with incident response? The game offers simpler scenarios or hints to build your confidence. I once tried a cybersecurity training game that adjusted to my stumbling blocks—SQL injection attacks were my Achilles' heel. The game kept nudging me with targeted mini-challenges until I finally got it. By the time I moved on, I felt like a pro. This tailored approach works because it meets you where you are, respecting individual learning curves.

Feedback is another crucial piece. Adaptive GBL doesn't just serve up challenges; it tracks your actions and provides instant, meaningful feedback (Chang et al., 2024; Sindiramutty, 2024). It's like having a coach whispering, "Great job finding that vulnerability! Now, look for signs of lateral movement". This keeps learning engaging and encourages mastery. The real magic of adaptive GBL is its inclusiveness. Whether you're a beginner or an advanced learner, it ensures the experience feels relevant and rewarding (Zhou, 2024; Gopi et al., 2021). And it's not just about passing a certification, it's about creating a learning journey that's unique to you. Figure 4 shows designing game-based learning for certifications.

Figure 4. Designing game-based learning for certifications

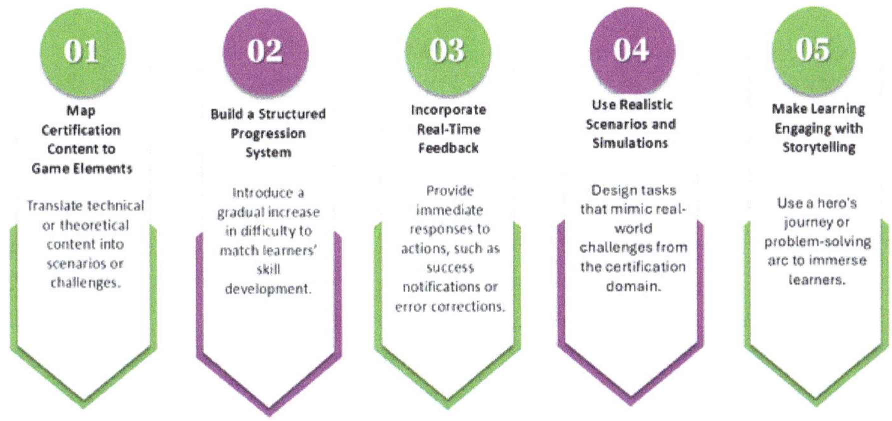

Incorporating Practical Labs into Game-Based Platforms

Using Virtual Labs to Replicate Real-World Cybersecurity Tasks

When you're learning cybersecurity, theory can only take you so far. Practical experience is where real learning happens, and virtual labs embedded in game-based platforms are a game-changer (Avci et al., 2024). These labs replicate real-world scenarios, letting you practice without the fear of breaking anything critical—or, worse, illegal. The beauty of these labs lies in their authenticity. Tasks like configuring firewalls, analyzing network traffic, or patching vulnerabilities mirror what cybersecurity professionals face daily. The added gamification elements—like time-based challenges or leaderboards—make it even more engaging (Zhao, 2024; Gouda et al., 2022). And since it's virtual, you can reset and retry, building confidence as you go. These platforms also provide guided learning paths. Struggle with penetration testing? The system might drop hints or suggest alternative strategies to help you improve without outright giving away the answer. This mix of autonomy and support keeps learners motivated while ensuring progress.

By integrating practical labs into games, learners don't just memorize concepts—they experience them (Sanzana et al., 2023; Humayun et al., 2022). And when it comes to cybersecurity, this hands-on approach bridges the gap between theoretical knowledge and the real-world challenges waiting for you in the field.

EXAMPLES OF EXISTING PLATFORMS AND TOOLS

Popular Cybersecurity Learning Games

Overview of Platforms like TryHackMe, Hack The Box, and CyberStart

Learning cybersecurity feels less like a chore when it's gamified. Platforms like **TryHackMe**, **Hack The Box**, and **CyberStart** are favorites for learners of all levels. They make even the most intimidating concepts approachable, turning practice into a game of strategy, puzzles, and competition. I remember my student showed me the TryHackMe session—it felt like cracking open a treasure chest. The platform offers a simulation room filled with bite-sized challenges, perfect for those just starting or those wanting a refresher (TryHackMe, n.d.). Meanwhile, Hack The Box feels like an exclusive hacker playground. Users "hack" into virtual machines, earning points for creative approaches, which is thrilling and intimidating at first. It's not all about hacking, though; these platforms teach problem-solving and resilience. I've had moments of frustration, staring at my screen for hours before a breakthrough, but when it clicks, it's magic. CyberStart, on the other hand, is a more guided experience and is especially great for younger audiences or schools introducing cybersecurity. The narratives and games make complex concepts seem playful (Shan & Yang, 2021; Jhanjhi et al., 2021).

What sets these apart? Real-world simulations. These aren't just exercises; they mirror challenges professionals face, from cracking passwords to analyzing logs. And let's be honest, when you're competing on a leaderboard, it feels way more rewarding. These platforms aren't just about learning; they're about building a mindset and skill set that sticks.

Capture the Flag (CTF) Competitions as Certification Preparation

Engaging Learners Through Competitive Problem-Solving Scenarios

When it comes to preparing for cybersecurity certifications, Capture the Flag (CTF) competitions are like a crash course wrapped in excitement. I'll never forget my first CTF experience—it wasn't just about solving puzzles, but about how each challenge mirrored real-world problems I'd encounter in certifications. It's competitive, fast-paced, and, honestly, a bit addictive. CTFs give learners a chance to apply theoretical knowledge in practical, hands-on situations. In my prep for security certifications (Gardiner et al., 2024; Kumar et al., 2021), I found these competitions incredibly effective in pushing my problem-solving skills to the next level. For instance, solving a cryptography challenge during a CTF forced me to understand not just the theory, but the actual process of decrypting real data, which later helped me in certification exams like the Certified Information Systems Security Professional (CISSP) (Abernathy & Deal, n.d.). The beauty of CTFs is that they cover a wide range of skills—from web security to forensics—exactly what's tested in certifications. I've heard from many peers that they felt more prepared after tackling CTF scenarios because these games put pressure on you to think critically and quickly. CTFs create an engaging, immersive environment where the learning is just as intense as the competition itself (Chindrus & Caruntu, 2023; Jun et al., 2024).

Plus, the community aspect is a big bonus. During a CTF, you're not just working through challenges solo. You're collaborating with others, sharing techniques, and learning from your mistakes. This dynamic simulates real-world cybersecurity teamwork, making the transition from learning to certification a bit smoother. Figure 5 shows an example of a popular cybersecurity learning game.

Figure 5. Example of popular cybersecurity learning games

Virtual Cyber Ranges

Simulated Environments for Certification-Specific Skill Building

Virtual cyber ranges are game-changers when it comes to certification prep. Simulated environments offer a safe, controlled space where learners can practice skills, they'll need for certifications, like Certified Ethical Hacker (CEH) or CompTIA Security+ (EC-Council, 2025). What's awesome about virtual ranges is that they allow you to practice in real-world conditions without the risk. Take, for example, my experience with a simulated network breach scenario. I had to identify vulnerabilities, deploy security patches, and protect sensitive data—everything you'd need to know for real-life situations. This hands-on approach not only solidified my understanding but also gave me the confidence to tackle tough exam questions.

Virtual ranges can be tailored to focus on specific certification skills. For instance, if you're studying for a CEH, you might find a range of ethical hacking challenges, helping you practice penetration testing in a secure, virtual environment. It's like a digital sandbox, where the scenarios are designed to mimic exactly what you'll face on the certification exam (Jover et al., 2025). These environments also allow for repeated practice. Unlike traditional labs, where access can be limited, a virtual range is available 24/7. I found that repeating exercises helped me perfect my skills, especially when it came to troubleshooting or refining my security strategies.

In short, virtual cyber ranges bridge the gap between theory and practice, offering a dynamic, interactive space (Sachan et al., 2025; Sindiramutty, Prabagaran, Akbar, Hussain, & Malik, 2024) for building the skills needed for certifications and real-world cybersecurity challenges.

Figure 6. Benefits of game-based learning for certification preparation

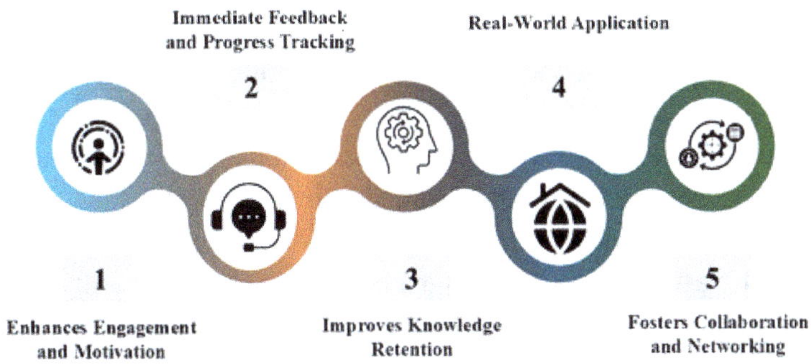

BENEFITS OF GAME-BASED LEARNING FOR CERTIFICATION PREPARATION

Enhanced Engagement and Motivation

Increased Learner Retention and Interest Through Gamified Elements

Game-based learning has completely transformed how we prepare for certifications (Piki et al., 2024). I can still remember how dull my first attempt at self-studying felt—it was a chore. But then, I discovered gamified platforms. Suddenly, preparing for certifications became a lot more engaging. Game mechanics like points, levels, and rewards made each task feel less like studying and more like a challenge I wanted to conquer (Dehghanzadeh et al., 2023; Sindiramutty, Prabagaran, Jhanjhi, Ghazanfar, Malik, & Soomro, 2024). The biggest benefit? Motivation. I noticed that I'd spend more hours in front of the screen, absorbed in solving cybersecurity challenges, because every success earned me a reward. Whether it was cracking a difficult encryption challenge or finding a hidden vulnerability, the small victories kept me hooked. As I leveled up, I saw my progress in real-time, which made it easier to stay on track (Gomez & Parker, 2021; Lim et al., 2019).

What's interesting is how gamification taps into our natural desire for achievement and competition. Many certification exams, like the CISSP or CompTIA Security+, require a solid grasp of theoretical knowledge. Game-based learning adds a layer of fun while reinforcing those concepts (Babu & Moorthy, 2023; Nayyar et al., 2021). It's this combination of learning and play that keeps learners interested and boosts retention. Take, for instance, the progress bars and badges that many platforms offer. I felt a sense of accomplishment every time I unlocked a new badge, which helped me stay engaged and motivated (Hong et al., 2024). It's not just about memorizing facts; it's about mastering a skill through enjoyable, repeatable tasks.

In the end, gamified learning doesn't just make the process fun—it makes the content stick. By turning certification prep into a series of rewarding challenges, it becomes a lot easier to stay motivated and committed.

Hands-On Skill Development

Bridging the Gap Between Theoretical Knowledge and Real-World Application

There's a world of difference between reading about cybersecurity concepts and applying them. I've always found that hands-on practice is where the magic happens. It's like this: you can study all the theory you want, but until you're in the trenches, dealing with a real attack simulation or cracking open a vulnerable system, the concepts just don't click. This is where hands-on skill development becomes crucial for bridging the gap between theory and real-world application.

I remember prepping for my first certification exam and feeling overwhelmed by the theory. It all seemed abstract. But when I started diving into practical exercises—whether it was setting up firewalls, performing penetration tests, or analyzing security logs—it felt like everything I'd read suddenly made sense. Hands-on labs and exercises brought that theory to life, making the concepts more tangible and easier to understand (Davis et al., 2023; Shah et al., 2022).

What I love about hands-on learning is how it mimics real-world situations. During a CTF challenge, I had to solve a live cyberattack scenario. It wasn't just about solving a puzzle; it was about thinking critically and applying what I knew to stop the attack. This is exactly what employers are looking for: not just knowledge, but the ability to apply it under pressure. By actively engaging with tools and scenarios you'll use in your career, you're building confidence. With each successful exercise, you start to feel like you're not just studying for certification but truly preparing for the challenges ahead. In short, hands-on experience solidifies your understanding and ensures that the knowledge you gain isn't just theoretical (Sun et al., 2024; Sharma et al., 2021) but ready for the real world. Figure 7 shows the challenges in implementing game-based learning platforms.

Figure 7. Challenges in implementing game-based learning platforms

Immediate Feedback and Progress Tracking

Helping Learners Identify Strengths and Weaknesses Efficiently

When I first started studying for certifications, I struggled to pinpoint my weak spots. I'd read through textbooks and watched endless tutorials, but I had no idea if I was truly prepared. That's where immediate feedback and progress tracking came in. It's like having a coach who tells you what you're doing right and, more importantly, what needs fixing. One time, while practicing a simulated penetration test on TryHackMe, I failed multiple attempts at bypassing a firewall. The platform instantly showed me where I went wrong and provided hints to guide me. This quick feedback turned my frustration into determination, helping me master the task within hours. That's the beauty of immediate feedback—it's not about making mistakes but learning from them in real-time. Progress tracking adds another layer of motivation. Many platforms, like Hack The Box or CyberStart, offer dashboards showing how far you've come. Seeing my stats improve gave me the push to keep going, even when challenges got tough. It's a constant reminder of your growth, highlighting strengths while keeping weaknesses in view for further improvement.

What's even better is how these features save time. Instead of blindly revisiting topics I already knew, I could focus on the areas where I struggled. This personalized learning approach made my preparation efficient and less overwhelming. With tools offering instant feedback and clear progress tracking, learners can hone their skills faster and with more focus, making certification prep less daunting and more effective (Daramola, 2024; Sindiramutty, Prabagaran, Jhanjhi, Murugesan, Brohi, & Masud, 2024).

CHALLENGES IN IMPLEMENTING GAME-BASED LEARNING PLATFORMS

Cost of Development and Maintenance

The High Initial Investment for Gamified Platform Creation

When I first explored game-based learning platforms, I was blown away by how immersive and engaging they were. But as I dug deeper, I realized there's a significant challenge in making them work—cost. The high initial investment required to develop and maintain these platforms is no small hurdle (Dahalan et al., 2023; Singhal et al., 2020). I remember reading about one platform that took years to develop, and the price tag was in the millions. This wasn't just about creating fun games; it involved complex coding, design, user testing, and ensuring the content stayed relevant (Chowdhury et al., 2024).

The costs aren't just upfront. Maintenance is an ongoing struggle. Platforms need constant updates to keep up with evolving technology, cyber threats, and curriculum changes. For example, adding new security scenarios or refreshing outdated tools can quickly add up. A gamified learning platform is only as good as its content and its ability to stay current (Alamuri et al., 2025)

It's not just the creation that's costly but also scaling the platform. To reach a large audience, you need robust servers, smooth user interfaces, and high-quality graphics (Villegas-Ch et al., 2024). All of this requires both financial resources and technical expertise. For smaller organizations or startups, it can be a huge barrier. However, despite these challenges, the benefits of game-based learning—like higher engagement and improved retention—often make the investment worthwhile. But, as I've learned, financial commitment is something that needs to be carefully considered from the outset.

Accessibility and Technical Barriers

Ensuring Inclusivity Across Devices and Networks

One of the biggest issues with game-based learning platforms is accessibility. I've seen people struggle with these platforms simply because their devices couldn't handle the software. It's frustrating when a tool that's supposed to make learning easier ends up creating new obstacles instead. For instance, high-end graphics or complex simulations might run smoothly on modern devices but fail miserably on older hardware (X. Chang & Chang, 2025; Sindiramutty, Prabagaran, Jhanjhi, Murugesan, Brohi, & Wei, 2024).

Then there's the issue of network requirements. Not everyone has access to fast, reliable internet (Hussein et al., 2025). I remember a colleague who couldn't participate in a cybersecurity challenge because his rural connection kept dropping. It's tough to build engagement when learners are left out due to something as basic as internet speed. Inclusivity is another hurdle. Platforms need to cater to users with disabilities by offering features like screen readers, customizable text sizes, and alternative input methods (Papadimitriou & Virvou, 2025). Unfortunately, many platforms overlook these needs, which alienates a significant portion of potential learners.

The good news? Some platforms are stepping up. Lightweight versions of software that run on basic devices and offline modes for users without constant connectivity are becoming more common (Haleem, 2024). Still, these efforts often require additional development time and cost, which brings its own set of challenges. Creating accessible platforms isn't just about meeting technical standards; it's about ensuring no one is left behind in the learning process. Figure 8 Future trends in game-based cybersecurity certification training.

Figure 8. Future trends in game-based cybersecurity certification training

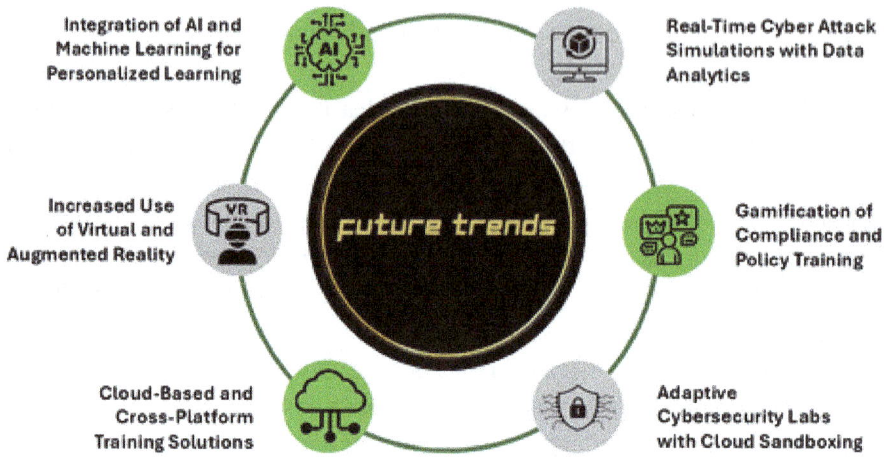

Balancing Fun with Serious Learning

Avoiding Distractions and Focusing on Certification Outcomes

Many platforms, like TryHackMe or Hack The Box, use gamification elements such as leaderboards, badges, and time-sensitive challenges to keep learners motivated (Gordon, n.d.). While these features make the experience exciting, they can also create distractions. I've caught myself focusing too much on climbing the leaderboard rather than refining my skills for a certification exam. It's easy to confuse progress in the game with actual readiness for a test. Another issue is the variability in task difficulty. Some games may prioritize creating fun scenarios over aligning them with certification standards. I once spent hours on a challenge that was fun but barely relevant to the exam I was preparing for. It felt like wasted time, even though I learned something new. The key is ensuring these platforms maintain a strong link to certification objectives while keeping the learning enjoyable. Features like tailored learning paths or exam-specific modules can help learners stay focused. Ultimately, a platform should be a tool for preparation, not a distraction from it.

CASE STUDIES AND SUCCESS STORIES

Institutions Leveraging GBL for Certification Success

Examples From Universities and Corporate Training Programs

The using Game-based learning (GBL) has become more pronounced in education and corporate training, as different ways to maintain the involvement of students and workers. Several institutions and organizations have found that GBL works well in certification programs, getting good results. These case studies show concrete examples of how GBL is helping improve learning outcomes and engage students with greater frequency, offering valuable lessons for the future (Jayawardena et al., 2021). Stanford University has integrated GBL techniques into its online professional development courses, incorporating leaderboards and point systems (Septris, n.d.). Similarly, in corporate settings, PwC's gamified cybersecurity training program not only improved knowledge retention but also decreased reported errors among staff (PricewaterhouseCoopers & Golding, n.d.). A close colleague shared how his organization used Kahoot! Quizzes during employee upskilling sessions. At first, some participants rolled their eyes—gamification felt too "school-like." But within weeks, teams were competing to outscore one another. Another interesting case is from the University of Michigan, where a faculty member used escape room simulations in a public health course (Dearborn, n.d.). Students, locked in groups, solved real-world case studies to "escape." Feedback highlighted the strategy's impact on both collaboration and understanding of certification material. These examples reveal GBL's ability to energize learners and significantly improve outcomes. They aren't perfect solutions—some still resist gamification—but the results are hard to ignore. With thoughtful implementation, the approach can revolutionize both academic and corporate learning landscapes. In short, the success stories are a testament to GBL's real impact on certification success. Whether learning takes place in academic institutions or corporate training environments, GBL has been shown to drive better learning outcomes, increased engagement, and higher certification rates. With more institutions adopting this creative method, one thing is clear — gamified-based learning is here for the long haul.

FUTURE TRENDS IN GAME-BASED CYBERSECURITY CERTIFICATION TRAINING

Integration of Artificial Intelligence and Machine Learning

Adaptive Difficulty Levels and Personalized Content Delivery

Game-based cybersecurity certification training is heading into fascinating territory, blending artificial intelligence (AI) and machine learning (ML) to redefine how learners interact with content (Chupkemi & Mersinas, 2024). During a recent mentoring session with a student preparing for their CEH exam, we discussed how AI-driven gamified platforms are changing the game—quite literally. ML also shines in personalizing content delivery (Er-Radi et al., 2023; Sindiramutty, Prabagaran, Jhanjhi, Murugesan, Malik, & Hussain, 2024). Platforms like Hack The Box are beginning to use algorithms that recommend specific modules based on user behavior (Academy, n.d.). For instance, if you excel at network security but lag in cryptography, the platform automatically prioritizes tasks to fill that gap. It's a bit like having a tutor who knows exactly what you need and when.

Some institutions are already experimenting with this. A friend shared how their company piloted an AI-integrated cybersecurity training tool, and the results were impressive. Completion rates skyrocketed, and the feedback was overwhelmingly positive. These trends aren't just theoretical—they're reshaping how we prepare for certifications in a world where skills need constant updating. By making training smarter and more engaging, AI and ML are poised to make certifications less about rote memorization and more about mastery.

Use of AR and VR in Certification Training

Immersive Experiences for More Realistic Skill Assessments

The integration of augmented reality (AR) and virtual reality (VR) in cybersecurity certification training is opening new possibilities for immersive, hands-on learning (Chapa, n.d; Spatafora et al., 2024; Weiqi et al., 2024). AR and VR bring realism to skill assessments by replicating actual cybersecurity challenges. Instead of clicking through a traditional interface, learners can navigate virtual server rooms, identify vulnerabilities, and mitigate attacks in a controlled but life-like setting (Aurelia, 2024; Seng et al., 2024). For example, using VR goggles, participants can practice responding to ransomware attacks, seeing the ripple effects of their actions in real time. Platforms are also experimenting with AR overlays to enhance real-world applications. Imagine pointing your phone at a simulated network diagram and seeing visual cues about possible weaknesses. Stanford University demonstrated how this approach improves learners' ability to spot vulnerabilities faster (Mazari & Bensalem, 2024; Waheed et al., 2024). These technologies are still developing, but early adopters are already reporting higher engagement and retention rates. One colleague compared it to flight simulators for pilots: "You're not just learning concepts; you're living them." This shift promises to redefine certification training, offering a safer, more interactive way to test and refine cybersecurity skills.

Expansion of Global Collaboration in GBL Platforms

Multiplayer and Cross-Border Learning Initiatives

Global collaboration is becoming a cornerstone of game-based learning (GBL) platforms, especially in cybersecurity training. Multiplayer and cross-border initiatives are reshaping how learners prepare for certifications, fostering an environment where diverse perspectives and teamwork take center stage.

I recently spoke to a cybersecurity student who participated in a global Capture the Flag (CTF) competition hosted on a gamified platform. "Our team had members from five different countries," they said. "We all brought unique skills to the table, and by the end, I had learned techniques I'd never even considered." These multiplayer challenges mimic real-world cyber defense scenarios, where collaboration is critical. Platforms like TryHackMe and Hack The Box are already integrating global leaderboards and team-based missions, encouraging users from various countries to work together. Cross-border collaboration not only enhances technical skills but also builds cultural awareness and adaptability, traits essential in today's cybersecurity landscape (X. Chen, 2024; Ying et al., 2024). Some initiatives are even backed by international organizations. For instance, a European Union-funded program recently launched a gamified platform where learners across member states can tackle cybersecurity challenges as part of virtual teams. The feedback highlighted improved engagement and faster learning curves (Dahiya, 2024).

This trend is more than just a feature upgrade—it's a shift toward making cybersecurity training as interconnected as the threats professionals face. By breaking down geographical barriers, GBL platforms are preparing learners to tackle global challenges in truly collaborative ways.

CONCLUSION

Recap of the Transformative Potential of Game-based Learning for Cybersecurity Certifications

Game-based learning (GBL) platforms have redefined the preparation journey for cybersecurity certifications, transforming a traditionally dry and isolated process into an engaging, interactive experience. From adaptive learning powered by artificial intelligence to immersive virtual environments, these platforms offer learners opportunities to build real-world skills while maintaining high levels of motivation and engagement.

Throughout this chapter, we've explored how GBL integrates key elements like simulations, multiplayer collaboration, and immediate feedback to bridge the gap between theory and practical application. Institutions like Stanford and tools such as TryHackMe and Hack the Box demonstrate the success of gamified approaches, with real-world case studies showing improved knowledge retention, faster learning, and higher certification success rates. Personal stories of learners, such as those mastering cybersecurity concepts through challenges or simulations, highlight the profound impact of GBL on individual growth. Yet, the potential of GBL in cybersecurity training is still evolving. Innovations in AR, VR, and global collaboration are paving the way for more immersive and interconnected learning experiences. Multiplayer initiatives are creating cross-border communities where learners gain diverse perspectives, while AI ensures that training adapts to each user's unique needs and progress.

The takeaway is clear: GBL isn't just a passing trend. It's a powerful approach that equips learners with the skills they need to excel in an ever-changing cybersecurity landscape. The next step is to embrace these innovations on a broader scale, encouraging institutions, educators, and organizations to invest in GBL solutions that make learning accessible, effective, and future-ready. With continued innovation, the possibilities for GBL are boundless.

Encouragement for Wider Adoption and Future Innovation in GBL Platforms

Game-based learning (GBL) platforms hold untapped potential for transforming education, particularly in cybersecurity certification training. While early adopters have demonstrated their value in boosting engagement, retention, and real-world readiness, the broader adoption of these platforms is necessary to truly revolutionize the learning experience.

Institutions and organizations must prioritize integrating GBL into their training programs, especially as the demand for skilled cybersecurity professionals grows. By leveraging gamified simulations, leaderboards, and adaptive learning, these platforms cater to diverse learning styles and make complex topics more accessible. Wider adoption could break down barriers, making high-quality training available to learners regardless of their location or resources.

At the same time, the future of GBL depends on sustained innovation. Developers should continue exploring advanced technologies like AI, AR, and VR to enhance personalization and immersion. Imagine a world where learners solve cyberattacks in a fully immersive virtual environment, gaining hands-on experience without real-world risks. These innovations could bridge the gap between traditional education and the fast-paced demands of the cybersecurity field. Collaboration is also key. Encouraging partnerships between academic institutions, industry leaders, and developers can result in platforms that align more closely with real-world certification requirements. Investing in research and development will ensure GBL evolves to meet the challenges of tomorrow. The message is simple: GBL is not just a tool for education—it's a gateway to creating skilled, confident professionals. By embracing its potential and driving innovation, we can shape a future where learning is not only effective but also exciting and accessible for everyone.

REFERENCES

Abernathy, R., & Deal, L. (n.d.). *CISSP: Certified Information Systems Security Professional (2024)*. O'Reilly Online Learning. https://www.oreilly.com/library/view/cissp-certified-information/9781835880784/

Academy, H. (n.d.). *User Behavior Forensics Course | HTB Academy*. https://academy.hackthebox.com/course/preview/user-behavior-forensics

Alamuri, S., Aluvala, R., & Miryala, R. K. (2025). Transition from 5G to 6G communication technologies. In *Advances in wireless technologies and telecommunication book series* (pp. 117–142). DOI: 10.4018/979-8-3693-6725-4.ch005

Alex, S. A., Jhanjhi, N., Humayun, M., Ibrahim, A. O., & Abulfaraj, A. W. (2022). Deep LSTM Model for Diabetes Prediction with Class Balancing by SMOTE. *Electronics (Basel)*, *11*(17), 2737. DOI: 10.3390/electronics11172737

Alferidah, D. K., & Jhanjhi, N. (2020). Cybersecurity Impact over Bigdata and IoT Growth. *2020 International Conference on Computational Intelligence (ICCI)*. DOI: 10.1109/ICCI51257.2020.9247722

Alkinani, M. H., Almazroi, A. A., Jhanjhi, N., & Khan, N. A. (2021). 5G and IoT Based Reporting and Accident Detection (RAD) System to Deliver First Aid Box Using Unmanned Aerial Vehicle. *Sensors (Basel)*, *21*(20), 6905. DOI: 10.3390/s21206905 PMID: 34696118

Alshehhi, N., Alzouebi, K., & Charles, T. (2024). *Perspectives On Game-Based Learning Within The Higher Education Sector*. Educational Administration., DOI: 10.53555/kuey.v30i5.2153

Aly, M. (2024). Revolutionizing online education: Advanced facial expression recognition for real-time student progress tracking via deep learning model. *Multimedia Tools and Applications*, *84*(13), 12575–12614. Advance online publication. DOI: 10.1007/s11042-024-19392-5

Aslaner, M. (2024). *Cybersecurity strategies and best practices: A comprehensive guide to mastering enterprise cyber defense tactics and techniques*. Packt Publishing Ltd.

Aurelia, S. (2024). *Immersive technologies: Navigating the Impacts, Challenges, and Opportunities*. CRC Press. DOI: 10.1201/9781003473312

Avci, H., Pedersen, S., & Thomas, A. (2024). Reflections of art history instructors on an educational digital game: A narrative case study. *Journal of Digital Educational Technology*, *4*(1), ep2404. Advance online publication. DOI: 10.30935/jdet/14116

Azam, H., Tan, M., Pin, L. T., Syahmi, M. A., Qian, A. L. W., Jingyan, H., Uddin, M. F., & Sindiramutty, S. R. (2023). Wireless Technology Security and Privacy: A Comprehensive Study. *Preprints.org*. DOI: 10.20944/preprints202311.0664.v1

Babbar, H., Rani, S., Masud, M., Verma, S., Anand, D., & Jhanjhi, N. (2021). Load balancing algorithm for migrating switches in software-defined vehicular networks. *Computers, Materials & Continua/Computers. Computers, Materials & Continua*, *67*(1), 1301–1316. DOI: 10.32604/cmc.2021.014627

Babu, S. S., & Moorthy, A. D. (2023). Application of artificial intelligence in adaptation of gamification in education: A literature review. *Computer Applications in Engineering Education*, *32*(1), e22683. Advance online publication. DOI: 10.1002/cae.22683

Brohi, S. N., Jhanjhi, N., Brohi, N. N., & Brohi, M. N. (2020). Key Applications of State-of-the-Art Technologies to Mitigate and Eliminate COVID-19.pdf. *TECHRxiv*. DOI: 10.36227/techrxiv.12115596.v1

Chang, C., Hsu, W., Chien, W. C., & Kuo, H. (2024). Playing with the Future Past: Scaffolding Taiwanese High School Students' Historical Causal Thinking through Dialogic Game-Based Learning. *Thinking Skills and Creativity*, *101748*. Advance online publication. DOI: 10.1016/j.tsc.2024.101748

Chang, X., & Chang, C. (2025). Game-Based learning in ESL Classrooms: A focus on Gimkit and other apps. *International Journal of Higher Education*, *14*(1), 1. DOI: 10.5430/ijhe.v14n1p1

Chapa, R. (n.d.). *Developing an online cybersecurity certificate program for upskilling and reskilling professionals and preparing students for market entry - ProQuest*. https://www.proquest.com/openview/9a54bde421ce6f5ab6ba1a05c2525128/1?cbl=18750&diss=y&pq-origsite=gscholar

Chen, P. S. (2023). Synergistic play design. In *Advances in educational technologies and instructional design book series* (pp. 119–139). DOI: 10.4018/979-8-3693-1022-9.ch006

Chen, X. (2024). *Communicating across cultures in english language: cross-cultural competence and workplace adaptability in China through the perspective of economic and educational globalization*. DOI: 10.14201/gredos.158764

Chesti, I. A., Humayun, M., Sama, N. U., & Jhanjhi, N. (2020). Evolution, Mitigation, and Prevention of Ransomware. *2020 2nd International Conference on Computer and Information Sciences (ICCIS)*. DOI: 10.1109/ICCIS49240.2020.9257708

Chindrus, C., & Caruntu, C. (2023). Securing the Network: A Red and Blue Cybersecurity Competition case study. *Information (Basel)*, *14*(11), 587. DOI: 10.3390/info14110587

Chowdhury, M., Dixon, L., Kuo, L., Donaldson, J. P., Eslami, Z., Viruru, R., & Luo, W. (2024). Digital game-based language learning for vocabulary development. *Computers and Education Open*, *6*, 100160. DOI: 10.1016/j.caeo.2024.100160

Christopoulos, A., & Mystakidis, S. (2023). Gamification in education. *Encyclopedia*, *3*(4), 1223–1243. DOI: 10.3390/encyclopedia3040089

Chupkemi, D. C., & Mersinas, K. (2024). Challenges in maritime cybersecurity training and compliance. *Journal of Marine Science and Engineering*, *12*(10), 1844. DOI: 10.3390/jmse12101844

Dahalan, F., Alias, N., & Shaharom, M. S. N. (2023). Gamification and Game Based Learning for Vocational Education and Training: A Systematic Literature review. *Education and Information Technologies*, *29*(2), 1279–1317. DOI: 10.1007/s10639-022-11548-w PMID: 36688221

Dahiya, S. (2024). *Handbook of Digital Journalism: Perspectives from South Asia*. Springer Nature. DOI: 10.1007/978-981-99-6675-2

Daramola, J. O. (2024). *Scrum requirements engineering for a game-based learning web platform for grade R – 12 learners in South Africa*. Electronic Theses and Dissertations. https://etd.cput.ac.za/handle/20.500.11838/4069

Davis, R. L., Schneider, B., Rosenbaum, L. F., & Blikstein, P. (2023). Hands-on tasks make learning visible: A learning analytics lens on the development of mechanistic problem-solving expertise in makerspaces. *Educational Technology Research and Development*, *72*(1), 109–132. DOI: 10.1007/s11423-023-10318-w

Dearborn. (n.d.). *Subject Guides: Virtual Escape Rooms & Scavenger Hunts: The Escape Rooms*. https://guides.umd.umich.edu/c.php?g=1119708&utm_source=chatgpt.com

Dehghanzadeh, H., Farrokhnia, M., Dehghanzadeh, H., Taghipour, K., & Noroozi, O. (2023). Using gamification to support learning in K-12 education: A systematic literature review. *British Journal of Educational Technology*, *55*(1), 34–70. DOI: 10.1111/bjet.13335

Denmeade, N. (2015). *Gamification with Moodle*. Packt Publishing Ltd.

Dogra, V., Singh, A., Verma, S., Kavita, N., Jhanjhi, N. Z., & Talib, M. N. (2021). Analyzing DistilBERT for Sentiment Classification of Banking Financial News. In *Lecture notes in networks and systems* (pp. 501–510). DOI: 10.1007/978-981-16-3153-5_53

EC-Council. (2025, January 22). *CEH Certification | Ethical Hacking Training & Course | EC-Council*. https://www.eccouncil.org/train-certify/certified-ethical-hacker-ceh/

Edwards, J. (2024). Vulnerability assessment and penetration testing. In *Apress eBooks* (pp. 371–412). DOI: 10.1007/979-8-8688-0297-3_11

Er-Radi, H., Touis, B., & Aammou, S. (2023). Machine learning in adaptive online learning for enhanced learner engagement. In *Advances in educational technologies and instructional design book series* (pp. 43–63). DOI: 10.4018/979-8-3693-3132-3.ch003

Fatima-Tuz-Zahra, N., Jhanjhi, N., Brohi, S. N., Malik, N. A., & Humayun, M. (2020). Proposing a Hybrid RPL Protocol for Rank and Wormhole Attack Mitigation using Machine Learning. *2020 2nd International Conference on Computer and Information Sciences (ICCIS)*. DOI: 10.1109/ICCIS49240.2020.9257607

Gardiner, J., Abaimov, S., Williams, J., Shahbi, F., Anastasakis, K., Chowdhury, P. D., Ellis, W., Sameen, M., Samanis, E., & Rashid, A. (2024). "If You Build it, They will Come" - A Blueprint for ICS-focused Capture-The-Flag Competitions. *ACM*, 27–40. DOI: 10.1145/3690134.3694818

Girardi, A., Higham, L., Fatima, S., Webb, E., Snyman, P., Wallang, P., & Breen, K. C. (2024). Virtual reality and social avoidance: An exploratory study of acceptance, and feasibility in an inpatient secure environment. *Deleted Journal*, *1*(2), 141–159. DOI: 10.1108/MHDT-01-2024-0004

Glennie, E., Dalton, B., Studley, R., & Lauff, E. (2024). The Influence of Earning Industry Certifications on High School Graduation: Evidence from Florida. *Educational Policy*, 08959048241292625. Advance online publication. DOI: 10.1177/08959048241292625

Gopi, R., Sathiyamoorthi, V., Selvakumar, S., Manikandan, R., Chatterjee, P., Jhanjhi, N. Z., & Luhach, A. K. (2021). Enhanced method of ANN based model for detection of DDoS attacks on multimedia internet of things. *Multimedia Tools and Applications*, *81*(19), 26739–26757. DOI: 10.1007/s11042-021-10640-6

Gordon, R. (n.d.). *Introduction to Hack the Box | Hack the Box Help Center*. https://help.hackthebox.com/en/articles/5185158-introduction-to-hack-the-box

Gouda, W., Almurafeh, M., Humayun, M., & Jhanjhi, N. Z. (2022). Detection of COVID-19 based on chest x-rays using deep learning. *Health Care*, *10*(2), 343. DOI: 10.3390/healthcare10020343 PMID: 35206957

Haleem, P. P. A. (2024, July 23). *A lightweight, reliable, secure, paginated, disconnected, and distributed message transaction model for wireless mobile environment*. http://scholar.uoc.ac.in/handle/20.500.12818/1632

Hallengren, A., & Svensson, M. (2013). *Dynamic difficulty adjustment for role-playing games*. DIVA. https://www.diva-portal.org/smash/record.jsf?pid=diva2%3A830032&dswid=3489

Hong, Y., Saab, N., & Admiraal, W. (2024). Approaches and game elements used to tailor digital gamification for learning: A systematic literature review. *Computers & Education*, *212*, 105000. DOI: 10.1016/j.compedu.2024.105000

Humayun, M., Sujatha, R., Almuayqil, S. N., & Jhanjhi, N. Z. (2022). A Transfer Learning Approach with a Convolutional Neural Network for the Classification of Lung Carcinoma. *Health Care*, *10*(6), 1058. DOI: 10.3390/healthcare10061058 PMID: 35742109

Hussain, K., Rahmatyar, A. R., Riskhan, B., Sheikh, M. U., & Sindiramutty, S. R. (2024). Threats and Vulnerabilities of Wireless Networks in the Internet of Things (IoT). *IEEE 1st Karachi Section Humanitarian Technology Conference (KHI-HTC)*, *2*, 1–8. DOI: 10.1109/KHI-HTC60760.2024.10482197

Hussein, M. H., Sulaiman, N. L., Noroozi, O., Elaish, M. M., & Alhasan, A. (2025). Value-added digital game-based learning in K-12 science education: A systematic literature review. *Interactive Learning Environments*, •••, 1–35. DOI: 10.1080/10494820.2025.2450652

Jayawardena, N. S., Ross, M., Quach, S., Behl, A., Gupta, M., & Lang, L. D. (2021). Effective online engagement strategies through gamification. *Journal of Global Information Management*, *30*(5), 1–25. DOI: 10.4018/JGIM.290370

Jhanjhi, N., Humayun, M., & Almuayqil, S. N. (2021). Cyber security and privacy issues in industrial internet of things. *Computer Systems Science and Engineering*, *37*(3), 361–380. DOI: 10.32604/csse.2021.015206

Jover, V., Sempere, S., & Ferrándiz, S. (2025). The creation of virtual stands in the metaverse: Applications for the textile sector. *Electronics (Basel)*, *14*(2), 359. DOI: 10.3390/electronics14020359

Jun, A. Y. M., Jinu, B. A., Seng, L. K., Maharaiq, M. H. F. B. Z., Khongsuwan, W., Junn, B. T. K., Hao, A. W., & Sindiramutty, S. R. (2024). Exploring the Impact of Crypto-Ransomware on Critical Industries: Case Studies and Solutions. *Preprints.org*. DOI: 10.20944/preprints202409.1325.v1

Kamal, N. A., & Ibrahim, C. K. I. C. (2025). Quality assurance in civil engineering education: Insights into program educational objectives (PEOs) in Malaysia. *Quality Assurance in Education*, *33*(3), 479–499. Advance online publication. DOI: 10.1108/QAE-10-2024-0205

Kiyani, F. F., Hamid, B., Humayun, M., Sindiramutty, S. R. L., & Chowdhury, S. (2024). Discovery of Influential Publications Using Research Article's Usage Context. *2024 International Conference on Emerging Trends in Networks and Computer Communications (ETNCC)*, 1–7. DOI: 10.1109/ETNCC63262.2024.10767576

Krause, M., Mogalle, M., Pohl, H., & Williams, J. J. (2015). A Playful Game Changer. *ACM*, 95–102. DOI: 10.1145/2724660.2724665

Kumar, M. S., Vimal, S., Jhanjhi, N., Dhanabalan, S. S., & Alhumyani, H. A. (2021). Blockchain based peer to peer communication in autonomous drone operation. *Energy Reports*, *7*, 7925–7939. DOI: 10.1016/j.egyr.2021.08.073

Lekkala, S., & Gurijala, P. (2024). Security and privacy for modern networks. In *Apress eBooks*. DOI: 10.1007/979-8-8688-0823-4

Lim, M., Abdullah, A., Jhanjhi, N., Khan, M. K., & Supramaniam, M. (2019). Link Prediction in Time-Evolving Criminal Network with deep Reinforcement learning technique. *IEEE Access : Practical Innovations, Open Solutions*, *7*, 184797–184807. DOI: 10.1109/ACCESS.2019.2958873

Linqiang, Y., Sindiramutty, S. R. L., Ashraf, H., Muzammal, S. M., Balakrishnan, S. P., Gupta, S., & Kavita, N. (2024). Intelligent Household Waste Classification System Based on Machine Learning. *2024 International Conference on Emerging Trends in Networks and Computer Communications (ETNCC)*, 760–768. DOI: 10.1109/ETNCC63262.2024.10767563

Manchuri, A., Kakera, A., Saleh, A., & Raja, S. (2024). pplication of Supervised Machine Learning Models in Biodiesel Production Research - A Short Review. *Borneo Journal of Sciences and Technology*. DOI: 10.35370/bjost.2024.6.1-10

Mazari, N., & Bensalem, S. (2024). Leveraging virtual reality and augmented reality as educational experiences to spark students' creativity and enhance learning motivation: Universities of California, Harvard, and MIT as a case study. , *5*(3), 176–195. DOI: 10.70091/atras/AI.11

Medina-Merodio, J. A., Castillo-Martinez, A., Barchino, R., Estriegana, R., & Robina-Ramírez, R. (2024). Factors influencing the acquisition of soft skills in a collaborative learning environment supported by Game-Based application. *IEEE Access : Practical Innovations, Open Solutions*, *12*, 111045–111059. DOI: 10.1109/ACCESS.2024.3441317

Mohamad, S. N. M., & Sazali, N. S. S. (2018). Gamification approach in education to increase learning engagement. *International Journal of Humanities Arts and Social Sciences*, *4*(1). Advance online publication. DOI: 10.20469/ijhss.4.10003-1

Nayyar, A., Gadhavi, L., & Zaman, N. (2021). Machine learning in healthcare: review, opportunities and challenges. In *Elsevier eBooks* (pp. 23–45). DOI: 10.1016/B978-0-12-821229-5.00011-2

Papadimitriou, S., & Virvou, M. (2025). Computer Games for Entertainment and Education: A Literature Review and Exploration on Artificial Intelligence Integration. *Intelligent Systems Reference Library*, 25–62. DOI: 10.1007/978-3-031-77464-5_2

Parks, K. R. (n.d.). *A Phenomenological Study of Teachers' Experiences with Educational Gamification and its Impact on Student Engagement in the Middle School Math and Science Classroom*. Scholars Crossing. https://digitalcommons.liberty.edu/doctoral/4786/

Penning, T., Forde, J., & Broussard, S. (2024). Perceptions of formal career achievements in public relations by students, professionals, and employers: Certificate, accreditation, and College of Fellows. *Public Relations Review*, *50*(3), 102458. DOI: 10.1016/j.pubrev.2024.102458

Philpott, A., & Son, J. (2022). Leaderboards in an EFL course: Student performance and motivation. *Computers & Education*, *190*, 104605. DOI: 10.1016/j.compedu.2022.104605

Piki, A., Tchanturia, I., Kasenides, N., Paspallis, N., & Leal, S. (2024). SDG Quest: Leveraging mobile Game-Based Learning to foster environmental, social, and economic sustainable development goals. In *Lecture notes in computer science* (pp. 373–392). DOI: 10.1007/978-3-031-76812-5_25

PricewaterhouseCoopers, & Golding, D. (n.d.). *PwC uses innovation to transform cybersecurity training*. PwC. https://www.pwc.com/cb/en/case-studies/cayman-pwc-transforms-cybersecurity-training.html?utm_source=chatgpt.com

Ravichandran, N., Tewaraja, T., Rajasegaran, V., Kumar, S. S., Gunasekar, S. K. L., & Sindiramutty, S. R. (2024). Comprehensive Review Analysis and Countermeasures for Cybersecurity Threats: DDoS, Ransomware, and Trojan Horse Attacks. *Preprints.org*. DOI: 10.20944/preprints202409.1369.v1

Rose, F. D., Attree, E. A., Brooks, B. M., Parslow, D. M., & Penn, P. R. (2000). Training in virtual environments: Transfer to real world tasks and equivalence to real task training. *Ergonomics*, *43*(4), 494–511. DOI: 10.1080/001401300184378 PMID: 10801083

Sachan, T., Chhabra, D., & Abraham, B. (2025). Social Capital in Online Gaming Communities: A Systematic Review examining the role of Virtual Identities. *Cyberpsychology, Behavior, and Social Networking*, *28*(3), 147–161. Advance online publication. DOI: 10.1089/cyber.2024.0375 PMID: 39772759

Sanzana, M. R., Abdulrazic, M. O. M., Wong, J. Y., Karunagharan, J. K., & Chia, J. (2023). Gamified virtual labs: Shifting from physical environments for low-risk interactive learning. *Journal of Applied Research in Higher Education*, *16*(1), 208–221. DOI: 10.1108/JARHE-09-2022-0281

Seng, Y. J., Cen, T. Y., Raslan, M. H. B. M., Subramaniam, M. R., Xin, L. Y., Kin, S. J., Long, M. S., & Sindiramutty, S. R. (2024). In-Depth Analysis and Countermeasures for Ransomware Attacks: Case Studies and Recommendations. *Preprint.org*. DOI: 10.20944/preprints202408.2261.v1

Septris. (n.d.). *Septris 2.0 - CME certified online game for sepsis management*. Septris. https://med.stanford.edu/septris.html?utm_source=chatgpt.com

Shah, I. A., Jhanjhi, N. Z., & Laraib, A. (2022). Cybersecurity and blockchain usage in contemporary business. In *Advances in information security, privacy, and ethics book series* (pp. 49–64). DOI: 10.4018/978-1-6684-5284-4.ch003

Shan, M., & Yang, J. (2021). Investigating the accessibility and impacts of cybersecurity programs on high-school girls' long-term industry engagement. *Information and Computer Security*, *30*(3), 309–323. DOI: 10.1108/ICS-05-2021-0067

Sharbel, K. E., & Salaimeh, O. (2024). *Challenging Games for All : Adaptive Difficulty and its Impact on Inclusivity in Action Games*. DIVA. https://www.diva-portal.org/smash/record.jsf?pid=diva2%3A1887856&dswid=9275

Sharma, R., Singh, A., Kavita, N., Jhanjhi, N. Z., Masud, M., Jaha, E. S., & Verma, S. (2021). Plant disease diagnosis and image classification using deep learning. *Computers, Materials & Continua/Computers. Materials & Continua (Print)*, *71*(2), 2125–2140. DOI: 10.32604/cmc.2022.020017

Sheng, L. T., Azman, A. B., Khan, N. A., Sindiramutty, S. R., Singh, S., & Verma, S. (2024). Reinforcement learning-based traffic signal control. *2024 International Conference on Emerging Trends in Networks and Computer Communications (ETNCC)*, 792–798. DOI: 10.1109/ETNCC63262.2024.10767501

Sindiramutty, S. R. (2024). Autonomous Threat Hunting: a future paradigm for AI-Driven Threat intelligence. *arXiv (Cornell University)*. https://doi.org//arxiv.2401.00286DOI: 10.48550

Sindiramutty, S. R., Prabagaran, K. R. V., Akbar, R., Hussain, M., & Malik, N. A. (2024). Overview of Generative AI techniques for cybersecurity. In *Advances in information security, privacy, and ethics book series* (pp. 1–52). DOI: 10.4018/979-8-3693-5415-5.ch001

Sindiramutty, S. R., Prabagaran, K. R. V., Jhanjhi, N. Z., Ghazanfar, M. A., Malik, N. A., & Soomro, T. R. (2024). Security Considerations in Generative AI for web Applications. In *Advances in information security, privacy, and ethics book series* (pp. 281–332). DOI: 10.4018/979-8-3693-5415-5.ch009

Sindiramutty, S. R., Prabagaran, K. R. V., Jhanjhi, N. Z., Murugesan, R. K., Brohi, S. N., & Masud, M. (2024). Generative AI in network security and intrusion detection. In *Advances in information security, privacy, and ethics book series* (pp. 77–124). DOI: 10.4018/979-8-3693-5415-5.ch003

Sindiramutty, S. R., Prabagaran, K. R. V., Jhanjhi, N. Z., Murugesan, R. K., Brohi, S. N., & Wei, G. W. (2024). Generative AI for threat intelligence and information sharing. In *Advances in digital crime, forensics, and cyber terrorism book series* (pp. 191–234). DOI: 10.4018/979-8-3693-8944-7.ch006

Sindiramutty, S. R., Prabagaran, K. R. V., Jhanjhi, N. Z., Murugesan, R. K., Malik, N. A., & Hussain, M. (2024). Ethics and transparency in secure web model generation. In *Advances in information security, privacy, and ethics book series* (pp. 411–464). DOI: 10.4018/979-8-3693-5415-5.ch012

Singhal, V., Jain, S. S., Anand, D., Singh, A., Verma, S., Kavita, N., Rodrigues, J. J. P. C., Jhanjhi, N. Z., Ghosh, U., Jo, O., & Iwendi, C. (2020). Artificial Intelligence Enabled Road Vehicle-Train Collision Risk Assessment Framework for Unmanned railway level crossings. *IEEE Access : Practical Innovations, Open Solutions*, *8*, 113790–113806. DOI: 10.1109/ACCESS.2020.3002416

Slyman, S. (2024). *Acumenous Game-Based learning in simulation games: Transforming Fears of Mathematics and Statistics Education.* Taylor & Francis. DOI: 10.4324/9781032723426

Song, C., Shin, S., & Shin, K. (2024). Implementing the Dynamic Feedback-Driven Learning Optimization Framework: A machine learning approach to personalize educational pathways. *Applied Sciences (Basel, Switzerland)*, *14*(2), 916. DOI: 10.3390/app14020916

Spatafora, A., Wagemann, M., Sandoval, C., Leisenberg, M., & De Carvalho, C. V. (2024). An educational escape room game to develop cybersecurity skills. *Computers*, *13*(8), 205. DOI: 10.3390/computers13080205

Spiro, K., & Bhamidi, V. (2024). *Employee-Generated learning: How to develop training that drives performance*. Kogan Page Publishers.

Springle, A. P. (2024). Getting Serious about Games: Exploring how Game-Based Learning is used in education and therapy. *Perspectives of the ASHA Special Interest Groups*, *9*(6), 1–23. DOI: 10.1044/2024_PERSP-23-00267

Sun, Q., Zhou, S., Chen, R., Feng, G., Cheung, K. T., Li, J., Hou, S., & Zeng, B. (2024). From computing to quantum mechanics: Accessible and hands-on quantum computing education for high school students. *EPJ Quantum Technology*, *11*(1), 58. Advance online publication. DOI: 10.1140/epjqt/s40507-024-00271-9

Tripp, B., Ravi, A., Pang, E., & Furrow, R. E. (2024). Undergraduate STEM Students' Perceptions of Grading Practices Reveal that Quiz Retakes Positively Impact Drivers of Self-determination. *CBE Life Sciences Education*, *24*(1), ar4. Advance online publication. DOI: 10.1187/cbe.24-06-0167 PMID: 39705683

TryHackMe. (n.d.). *TryHackMe | Cyber Security Training*. https://tryhackme.com/

Villegas-Ch, W., Govea, J., Godoy, L. N., & Mera-Navarrete, A. (2024). Virtual Reality Simulations for Skills Training: Improving Learning through Immersive Experiences in Educational Environments. *IEEE Access : Practical Innovations, Open Solutions*, *12*, 130073–130090. DOI: 10.1109/ACCESS.2024.3456628

Waheed, A., Seegolam, B., Jowaheer, M. F., Sze, C. L. X., Hua, E. T. F., & Sindiramutty, S. R. (2024). Zero-Day Exploits in Cybersecurity: Case Studies and Countermeasure. *Preprints.org*. DOI: 10.20944/preprints202407.2338.v1

Weiqi, X., Hooi, S. T. C., Sindiramutty, S. R. L., Asirvatham, D. L., Kumar, D., & Verma, S. (2024). Surface Anomaly Detection Using Machine Learning Technique. *2024 International Conference on Emerging Trends in Networks and Computer Communications (ETNCC)*, 1–7. DOI: 10.1109/ETNCC63262.2024.10767562

Yigit, Y., Kioskli, K., Bishop, L., Chouliaras, N., Maglaras, L., & Janicke, H. (2024). Enhancing Cybersecurity Training Efficacy: A Comprehensive Analysis of Gamified Learning, Behavioral Strategies and Digital Twins. *2024 IEEE 25th International Symposium on a World of Wireless, Mobile and Multimedia Networks (WoWMoM)*, 24–32. DOI: 10.1109/WoWMoM60985.2024.00016

Ying, X., Murugesan, R. K., Sindiramutty, S. R., Wei, G. W., Balakrishnan, S., Kumar, D., & Verma, S. (2024). Scene Text Recognition using Deep Learning Techniques. *2024 International Conference on Emerging Trends in Networks and Computer Communications (ETNCC)*, 1–9. DOI: 10.1109/ETNCC63262.2024.10767484

Zhao, F. (2024). Gamification design. In *CRC Press eBooks* (pp. 373–441). DOI: 10.1201/9781003495161-16

Zhou, S. (2024). Gamifying language education: The impact of digital game-based learning on Chinese EFL learners. *Humanities & Social Sciences Communications*, *11*(1), 1518. Advance online publication. DOI: 10.1057/s41599-024-04073-3

Chapter 6
Gamification in Cybersecurity Education

Vasaki Ponnusamy
https://orcid.org/0000-0002-9049-8345
Higher Colleges of Technology, UAE

Filsia Manzil
Higher Colleges of Technology, UAE

ABSTRACT

Cyber-attacks are also getting sophisticated with the passage of time and cybersecurity threats are evolving continuously. . Higher Learning Institutions should focus on creating interest towards cybersecurity education but there is still a lack of evidence showing the positive co-relation between cybersecurity education framework and interest towards the field. A games-based approach can be paradigm shift in cyber-security education which can instill creativity and fun towards learning. The main initiative of this research is to introduce some game-based cybersecurity activities in higher learning institution and to see the positive outcome towards such approach. Several game-based activities were conducted in our higher learning institution and data were collected to study the effectiveness of the approach. The findings show positive co-relation between game-based activities and interest towards the field and future work will be based on classifying such game based activities and developing a framework as guideline for cybersecurity education in Malaysia.

DOI: 10.4018/979-8-3373-0477-9.ch006

INTRODUCTION

According to MDEC, Malaysia is one of the best ranking countries in the ASEAN region when it comes to potential in the Cybersecurity Industry (MDEC, 2019), as shown in Figure 1. As stated by World Economic Forum, Malaysia is at the 4th position in the best countries prepared against cyberattacks (Research, 2015).

Figure 1. MDEC Malaysia's cybersecurity potential

(Mdec 2019)

Broadband connection has become a requirement for Malaysian enterprises, services, and residents to flourish and remain relevant in Industry 4.0. Businesses are growing increasingly reliant on truly democratic technologies like smartphones, big data, the internet of things, artificial intelligence, and cloud computing, all of these rely on connectivity (Lim et al. 2019). Although the fast development of ICT enriches and benefits our citizens, it also poses a threat to the nation's economy and security. It is critical to raise public awareness about such hazards to control them. Malaysia has been continuing to develop education and awareness initiatives for Malaysians (Haron et al. 2023).

Malaysia has also been the victim of Advanced Persistent Threat (APT) cyber-attacks, the most recent occurrence exhibited which came in the form of email spear phishing. Due to irresponsibility, users might be easily misled by fraudulent sites and services in phishing incidents. The same may be said for scams in which victims send large sums of money to unknown recipients. Insider threats, such as 'watering hole attacks', 'social engineering tricks, 'malware', 'ransomware', inserting infected USB gadgets into internal systems, and clicking a link found in email accounts, remain a critical cyber security threat to organizations (Malaysia 2024). The healthcare industry is now much more concerned about the cyber threat. As patient records become computerized, the risks of data breach and disclosure of personal data expose them to cyber threats. Cyber risks are ever-present, and there will always be the possibility of large-scale, targeted cyberattacks. If everything is connected to the internet, such risks can never fully be eliminated. However, it is vital to emphasize that most of these fraud occurrences are caused by a lack of awareness. Apart from that, Malaysia is dealing with a scarcity of cyber security professionals as well as skill shortages in most of the sectors. Due to a scarcity of cyber security professionals, businesses would be vulnerable and exposed to unimaginable cyber threats.

Overall, it is reasonable to conclude that the ongoing concerns and challenges in Malaysia's cyber security environment are due to the lack of knowledge and education. Technical solutions and restrictions can only go so far; citizens must have a basic understanding of cyber security fundamentals (Humayun et al. 2021), as well as relevant laws and regulations, to avoid the most prevalent mistakes, especially while surfing online. To achieve this, everyone must play a part and collaborate to improve Malaysia's overall cyber security awareness, expertise, and abilities (Sujatha et al. 2022).

Ministry of Science, Technology and Innovation Malaysia with the collaboration of Cybersecurity Malaysia has developed a National Cyber Security Policy (NCSP) in 2010 (Razana, 2016). This policy is Malaysia's comprehensive cybersecurity guide to ensure the Critical National Information Infrastructure (CNII) is well protected against cybercrimes such as hacking, intrusions, fraud, harassment, malicious code and denials of service attacks. The key success factors of the implementation include effective governance, better public-private co-ordination, improving cybersecurity skills, improving existing research & development and international linkages. The NCSP recognizes the critical and highly interdependent nature of the CNII and aims to develop and establish a comprehensive program and a series of frameworks that will ensure the effectiveness of cybersecurity.

PROBLEM STATEMENT

However, NCSP is just a framework focusing on protecting organizations' assets from cybersecurity incidents. But the gap shows a missing framework for cybersecurity education and preparing skill-based cybersecurity talents at the higher learning institutions in Malaysia for industry readiness. Although there has been some Cybersecurity based education framework initiatives in Malaysia (Aborujilah et al. 2022), the outcome does not produce a promising results due to lack of solid framework for cybersecurity education. There has been some possible mismatches of the current cybersecurity framework and the level of conform and interest such frameworks provide to encourage students take initiative in learning cybersecurity. A game-based framework can address such concerns. Games can provide an engaging environment that is interesting and stimulating for more people (Nagarajan, Larssen

2012). Two are several categories of games that are widely used in education and that can be incorporated into cybersecurity education. The main purpose of this paper is to propose some interesting games to be introduced for cybersecurity education in higher learning institutions (Sindiramutty et al. 2024).

CLASSIFICATION OF GAMES IN EDUCATION

Treasure Hunt (Scavenger Hunt)

Students will act as Blue Team to find hidden treasures with encrypted clues of locations. Students will be given a set of encrypted text messages in a series concerning finding the hidden treasures, and they are required to decrypt them in the shortest period (Nawaz et al. 2021). They need to decrypt the previous text to proceed with the next series. The winner will be the fastest person to complete decrypting the final text and to find the final treasure (THE GOAL). Students will be briefed on the different encryption methods, like Caesar Cipher, Vigenère code, RSA, etc., to know encryption before taking on the tasks.

The educational challenge engages students in a dynamic treasure hunt where they must act as a Blue Team to uncover hidden treasures by decrypting a series of encrypted text messages. Each decrypted message reveals the next clue, culminating in the discovery of the final treasure (THE GOAL). The first student to successfully decrypt all the messages and find the final treasure wins. The activity was conducted as shown in Figure 2.

Figure 2. Treasure hunt

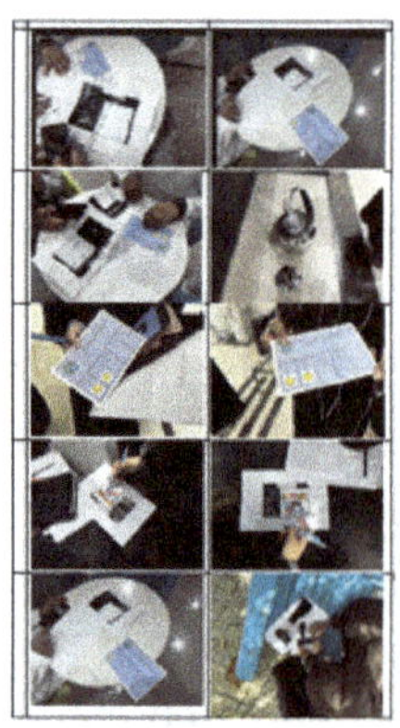

This project serves multiple purposes and offers numerous benefits to students, the campus, and the community:

a. Enhancing Cryptography Skills: By working with various encryption methods such as Caesar Cipher, Vigenère code, and RSA, students gain practical experience and deepen their understanding of cryptographic techniques and cybersecurity principles.
b. Fostering Critical Thinking and Problem-Solving: The challenge requires students to think critically and solve complex problems, which enhances their analytical and logical reasoning abilities.
c. Promoting Collaboration and Teamwork: Although the challenge can be individually competitive, students often collaborate, share insights, and learn from each other, fostering a sense of community and teamwork.
d. Encouraging Engagement and Motivation: The interactive and competitive nature of the treasure hunt makes learning fun and engaging, motivating students to actively participate and excel.
e. Building Real-World Skills: The challenge simulates real-world cybersecurity scenarios, preparing students for future careers in information security and related fields.
f. Strengthening Campus Community: By involving students in a campus-wide event, the project enhances community spirit and encourages interactions across different student groups and disciplines.
g. Raising Awareness about Cybersecurity: The project highlights the importance of cybersecurity in today's digital world, promoting awareness and understanding of digital safety and data protection.
h. Encouraging Innovation and Creativity: As students encounter various encryption methods, they are inspired to think creatively and explore innovative approaches to decryption.

In summary, this educational challenge not only enriches students' knowledge and skills in cryptography and cybersecurity but also strengthens the campus community, promotes collaborative learning, and prepares students for future professional endeavors.

Snake and Ladder

To engage participants in an interactive and problem-solving event where they "escape a maze" by solving technical challenges related to networking, computer information systems (CIS), and cybersecurity co Participants navigate through a physical maze by solving technical challenges. Each challenge solved opens the door to the next level. The activity was conducted as shown in Figure 3. The event is designed to enhance technical and analytical skills. foster teamwork collaboration and provide hands-on learning experience in a gamified setting.

Figure 3. Snake and ladder

The activity of the game is given below:

a. Level 1

   Give an example of Class A IP address

b. Level 2

   Given MAC address aa:bb:cc:dd:ee:ff, which is an OUI?

c. Level 3

   Convert 224 into a binary.

   Convert 11011010 into decimal

d. Level 4

   What is the difference between CSMA/CD and CSMA/CA

e. Level 5

   Given IP address 192.168.3.0 and I need 4 equal subnets. What is the network address of the second subnet.

f. Level 6

   Jen wants to form 8 equal subnets. Which subnet does IP address 192.168.4.65 fall into (hint:for expected answer format: subnet 1)

Escape Room

Students will learn from an interactive, hands-on, and problem-solving experience where they must "escape the maze" by successfully completing technical challenges centered around Networking, Computer Information Systems (CIS), and Cybersecurity concepts (Aadil et al. 2021). Students had to solve each stage to progress, simulating the experience of "escaping" from one challenge to the next. The activity was designed to be both educational and entertaining, fostering a sense of achievement upon completion. Seven teams participated in the challenge (Figure 4). The Digital Escape Room consisted of four stages, each presenting a technical challenge aligned with topics covered in the curriculum. These included:

- IT Network fundamentals
- Network Trouble shooting
- IP and subnetting

Figure 4. Escape room team

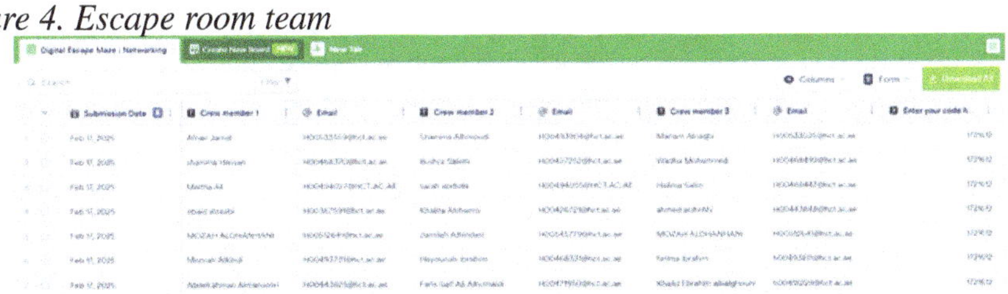

a. Stage 1: Data Center Lockdown (Figure 5&6).

Scenario: Students serving as IT assistance had to get the server's IP address in order to get out of a data center that was "locked". The concept is IP Address Recognition.

Learning Outcome: Recognizing private versus public IPs.

Figure 5. Screenshot from Stage 1 of the digital escape room cybersecurity activity

Figure 6. Screenshot from Stage 1 of the digital escape room cybersecurity activity

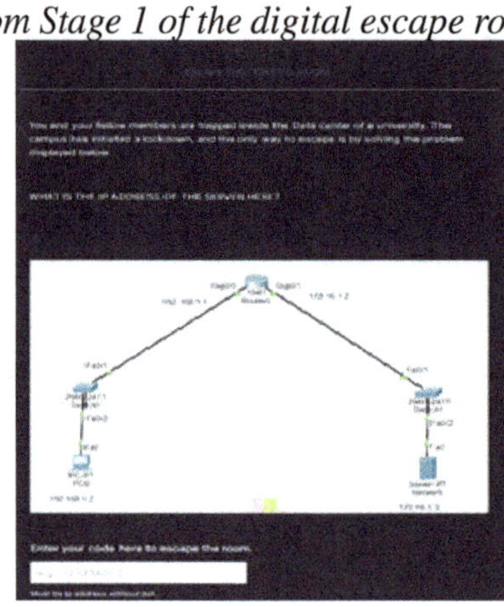

Figure 7. Stage 2(a). Screenshot from Stage 1 of the digital escape room cybersecurity activity

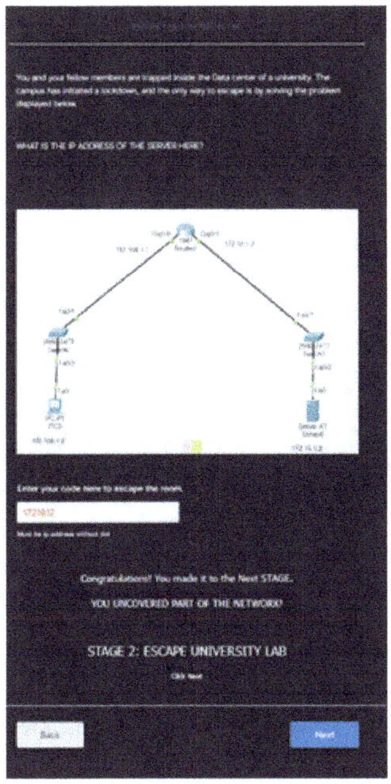

b. Stage 2: Networking Lab Escape at the University (Figure 7, 8 & 9).
   Scenario: Students had to troubleshoot IP configuration, bandwidth monitoring, and device connectivity due to a school network failure. The challenges given were debugging DHCP (ipconfig /renew), network traffic monitoring (Task Manager), identifying "No Internet" problems
   Learning Outcome: Practical knowledge of typical troubleshooting instruments and methods utilized in actual IT settings.

Figure 8. Screenshot from Stage 2(b) of the cybersecurity-themed digital escape room activity

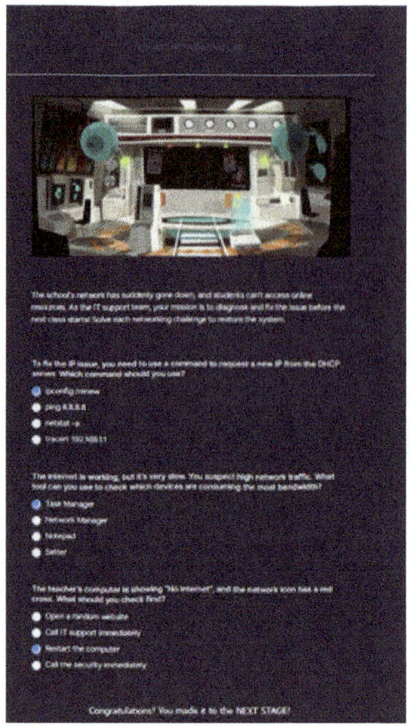

Figure 9. Screenshot from Stage 2(c) of the cybersecurity-themed digital escape room activity

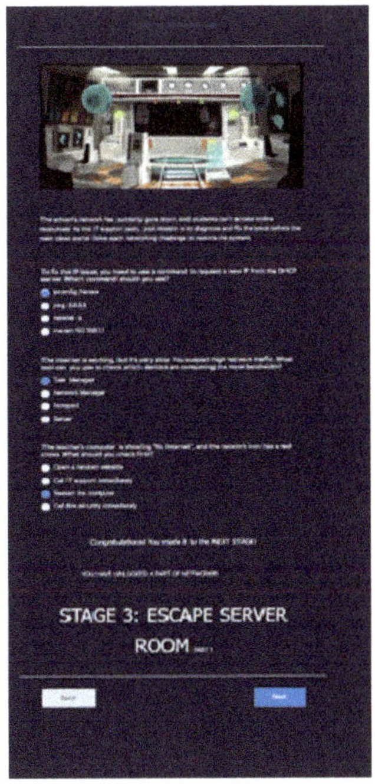

Figure 10. Screenshot from Stage 3 of the cybersecurity-themed digital escape room activity

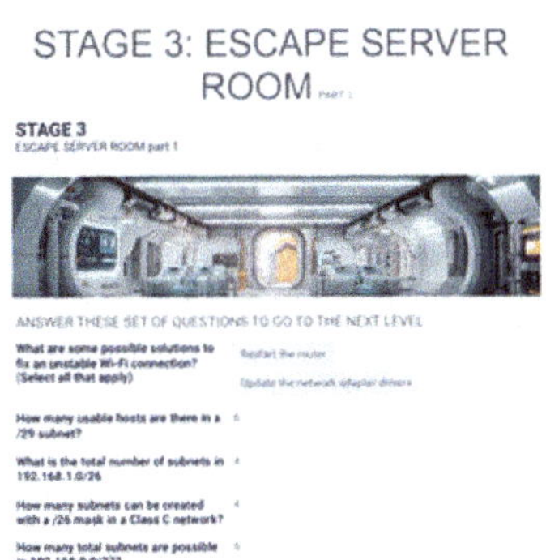

c. Stage 3 and 4: Part 1 and 2 of the Server Room Escape (Figure 10, 11 & 12).

Scenario: Locked down in the server room, solve the challenges to escape. Participants' challenges include IP and subnetting theory like calculations of subnet masks, computation of the total subnets in the specified networks, Subnet architecture for particular host requirements and binary-to-decimal conversions.
Learning Outcome: Improved subnetting and binary skills in complex network planning scenarios.

Figure 11. Visual progression of the educational escape game (Overall view of the game)

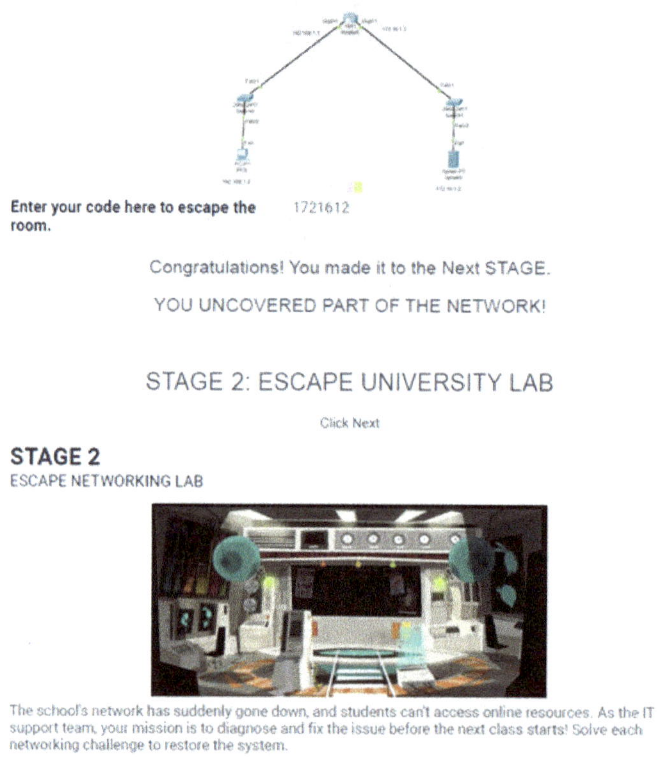

Figure 12. Visual progression of the educational escape game (Final part of the game)

CONCLUSION

In addressing the question of what tools or methods can create a positive impact in the field of cybersecurity, it becomes clear that gamification offers a promising avenue, especially in enhancing motivation and engagement. Gamification tools can significantly increase interest and motivation in learning cybersecurity by integrating interactive and competitive elements. Essential features of effective gamification tools include challenge-based learning, real-time feedback, achievement systems, and scenarios that develop both technical and soft skills. When tailored appropriately, such tools can be especially impactful in inspiring young women to explore and pursue cybersecurity careers. Identifying relevant penetration testing scenarios and incorporating them into practical learning modules ensures realism and relevance. Ultimately, streamlining these insights into a well-designed Gamification Learning Framework tailored for young women can foster inclusivity, build confidence, and develop the next generation of cybersecurity professionals.

REFERENCES

Aadil, F., Mehmood, B., Hasan, N. U., Lim, S., Ejaz, S., & Zaman, N. (2021). Remote health monitoring using IoT-based smart wireless body area network. *Computers, Materials & Continua*, *68*(2), 2499–2513. DOI: 10.32604/cmc.2021.014647

Aborujilah, A., Al-Othmani, A. Z., Hussien, N. S., Mokhtar, S. A., Long, Z. A., & Nizam, M. (2022, March). Cybersecurity risk assessment approach for Malaysian organizations: Malaysian universities as case study. In *2022 9th International Conference on Electrical and Electronics Engineering (ICEEE)* (pp. 440–450). IEEE.

Haron, H., Sajari, A., Dewanti, R., Ganesan, Y., & Gui, A. (2023, November). Digital transformation in community development of Malaysia and Indonesia. In ICCD (Vol. 5, No. 1, pp. 232-242).

Humayun, M., Jhanjhi, N. Z., Talib, M. N., Shah, M. H., & Suseendran, G. (2021). Cybersecurity for data science: Issues, opportunities, and challenges. In *Intelligent Computing and Innovation on Data Science. Proceedings of ICTIDS, 2021*, 435–444.

Lim, T. W. (2019). *Industrial revolution 4.0, tech giants, and digitized societies.* Palgrave Macmillan. DOI: 10.1007/978-981-13-7470-8

Malaysia, B. J. (2024). Digital challenges to economic opportunities: Ubiquitous computing in Malaysia's public transportation sector. *Journal of Applied Technology and Innovation (e-ISSN: 2600-7304), 8*(2), 7.

Nagarajan, A., Allbeck, J. M., Sood, A., & Janssen, T. L. (2012, May). Exploring game design for cybersecurity training. In *2012 IEEE International Conference on Cyber Technology in Automation, Control, and Intelligent Systems (CYBER)* (pp. 256–262). IEEE.

Nawaz, A., Hussain, J., Jhanjhi, N. Z., Talib, M. N., & Nadim, M. (2021). Feature engineering based on hybrid features for malware detection over Android framework. *Turkish Journal of Computer and Mathematics Education*, *12*(10), 2856–2864.

Razana, W. S. M. (2016). Cybersecurity: Towards becoming a national certification body for information security management systems internal auditors. *Int. Sch. Sci. Res. Innov*, *10*(8), 2907–2910.

Sindiramutty, S. R., Jhanjhi, N. Z., Tan, C. E., Khan, N. A., Shah, B., & Gaur, L. (2024). Securing the digital supply chain cyber threats and vulnerabilities. In *Cybersecurity Measures for Logistics Industry Framework* (pp. 156–223). IGI Global Scientific Publishing.

Sujatha, R., Prakash, G., & Jhanjhi, N. Z. (Eds.). (2022). *Cyber security applications for Industry 4.0*. CRC Press. DOI: 10.1201/9781003203087

Chapter 7
Artificial Intelligence-Based Gamification in Cybersecurity Education

Danyal Mahmood
https://orcid.org/0000-0002-2750-5258
National University of Sciences and Technology, Pakistan

Rabia Afzaal
Lahore Garrison University, Pakistan

ABSTRACT

The increasing complexity and volume of cyber threats have necessitated a shift in cybersecurity education towards more dynamic, practical, and personalized learning approaches. This chapter explores the intersection of Artificial Intelligence (AI) and gamification in cybersecurity education, emphasizing how AI technologies enhance traditional training environments. By enabling adaptive challenge generation, real-time feedback, personalized learning paths, and intelligent assessment, AI transforms static educational games into responsive, data-driven systems. It presents detailed case studies demonstrating how AI-infused gamified platforms are being applied across academic, corporate, and training settings. It also investigates emerging applications such as affective computing and AI-supported collaboration. Ethical challenges related the gamified learning are critically examined. The chapter offers insights into the ethical considerations necessary for designing robust and evidence-based gamified systems that can effectively prepare learners for real-world demands.

DOI: 10.4018/979-8-3373-0477-9.ch007

INTRODUCTION

Cybersecurity has emerged as a critical domain in the 21st century due to the escalating frequency, sophistication, and impact of cyber threats on individuals, organizations, and governments. As technology evolves, the landscape of cyber risks also changes, demanding that cybersecurity professionals continuously adapt and upskill. Traditional methods of cybersecurity education including lectures, manuals, and static simulations are no longer sufficient for the demands of real-world cybersecurity challenges. There is a growing need for educational models that not only teach theoretical knowledge but also support critical thinking and practical decision-making in complex cyber incidents.

In the context of cybersecurity education, gamification provides an opportunity to transform the content into interactive, engaging, and meaningful learning experiences, (Ajala & Balogun, 2024). It introduces elements such as point scoring, competition, challenges, leaderboards, and instant feedback. This can serve to motivate learners, enhance participation, and foster a deeper connection to the subject. These elements can replicate high-pressure, decision-based scenarios, allowing learners to practice identifying, mitigating, and responding to cyber threats in a risk-free environment.

Gamified environments can simulate a wide range of cybersecurity scenarios, from phishing attacks and malware analysis to system intrusion detection and incident response. Through interactive playing, learners are placed in realistic situations where they apply their skills in real-time, making the learning process not only more effective but also more memorable. For instance, capture-the-flag (CTF) competitions, (Al-Hawawreh, Nour, & Fakir, 2021), cybersecurity escape rooms, (Ali & Rasool, 2020), and simulation-based games are now widely adopted in educational institutions and professional training programs to promote hands-on learning.

Gamification alone may offer many advantages but the integration of Artificial Intelligence (AI) elevates these benefits by introducing adaptability, personalization, and intelligence into the learning process, (Alotaibi, 2024). AI-powered systems can analyze learners' performance in real-time to identify strengths and weaknesses and dynamically adjust the difficulty, content, and feedback based on individual progress. This personalization ensures that each learner receives tailored instruction and challenge levels that are appropriate to their current capabilities, promoting optimal learning efficiency.

AI enhances gamified cybersecurity education by enabling realistic threat simulations that evolve based on user actions. Reinforcement learning agents can act as adversaries, mimicking the behavior of attackers and forcing learners to adapt their strategies. Natural language processing (NLP) can be used to create conversational agents that simulate attacks or assist learners with contextual hints, (Al-Sinani & Mitchell, 2024). These AI-driven elements transform the static nature of many educational games into responsive, intelligent ecosystems where learners are not just passive recipients but active participants shaping their own learning journey.

AI-based gamification provides data-driven insights. Through continuous monitoring and analysis of user interactions, AI can provide instructors with actionable feedback on learner performance, engagement patterns, and areas needing improvement, (Amjad, Khan, & Ahmad, 2025). This data can be used to refine educational content, inform curriculum design, and ultimately create more effective and responsive training systems.

From the learners' perspective, AI-based gamification supports multiple learning styles, increases motivation through instant and meaningful feedback, and provides a safe space for trial-and-error learning, (Arjunan, 2024). It reduces the fear of failure, encourages exploration, and builds confidence. The immersive and interactive nature of gamified platforms helps improve the understanding by engaging multiple cognitive processes simultaneously, (Baah, Govender, & Subramaniam, 2024).

The design and implementation of AI-driven gamified systems come with their own set of challenges, including ethical considerations, data privacy concerns, computational demands, and the need for pedagogically sound design frameworks, (Baker *et al.*, 2008). These aspects must be carefully addressed to fully realize the potential of this approach in cybersecurity education.

This chapter explains the foundational principles of AI-based gamification in cybersecurity education. It examines how AI technologies such as machine learning, deep learning, and natural language processing can enhance gamified learning experiences, and it explores the challenges, limitations, and ethical implications involved. The aim of this chapter is to provide a comprehensive overview of how the combined effect of AI and gamification can reshape cybersecurity education to better prepare learners for the complexities of the digital age.

FUNDAMENTALS OF AI IN CYBERSECURITY

Overview of Artificial Intelligence

AI is a transformative field of computer science focused on creating systems capable of performing tasks that typically require human intelligence, (Bandara, Ioras, & Maher, 2014). These tasks include learning from experience, reasoning through problems, understanding natural language, recognizing patterns, perceiving environments, and making decisions. AI aims to develop machines that can unconventionally think, learn, and adapt.

In cybersecurity, AI provides a framework for automating complex threat detection, prediction, (Basri, 2023), and response activities that would be challenging or impossible for human analysts to handle manually. The sheer volume and velocity of data in modern IT systems make traditional rule-based security mechanisms insufficient. AI offers scalable, adaptive solutions that can learn from data, detect anomalies, and evolve as threats change.

Key Characteristics of AI Relevant to Cybersecurity

Various characteristics of AI make it particularly well-suited for application in cybersecurity. One of the most crucial traits is adaptive learning. AI models can be trained using large volumes of structured or unstructured cybersecurity data, (Beretas, 2023). By identifying patterns and correlations within this data, AI can detect anomalies that may indicate potential cyber threats, even those previously unseen.

Real-time processing and decision-making is another trait of AI. Unlike traditional rule-based systems, which rely on static instructions, AI can autonomously assess and respond to threats as they occur. For example, Google uses AI in its Gmail service to filter out over 100 million phishing emails per day, with adaptive models that improve based on new scam patterns, (Cao, 2022). Modern Intrusion Detection Systems (IDS) integrated with AI can monitor thousands of data points across networks simultaneously and act within milliseconds to block suspicious activities, (Cascella, Pascale, & Sansone, 2023).

AI exhibits contextual awareness and predictive capability, especially when fueled by contextual metadata. This allows AI systems to make informed predictions about future attacks or vulnerabilities, (Chapman, Burket, & Brumley, 2014). These systems continuously refine their predictions based on feedback, making them more accurate over time. In user behavior analytics (UBA), AI can establish a behavioral baseline for each user and flag deviations that might indicate compromised credentials or insider threats, (Charlier, Paelinck, & Verdegem, 2019).

Historical Context and Evolution

The concept of AI dates back to the 1950s, with the advent of symbolic reasoning and early expert systems, (Chindrus & Caruntu, 2023). As computing power and data availability increased, AI evolved from rule-based logic to more advanced machine learning (ML) models and deep learning (DL) techniques. These advances have made AI applicable in a wide range of real-world domains, including finance, healthcare, transportation, and now increasingly in cybersecurity and education, (Chourasia, 2025).

AI Subfields and their Roles in Cybersecurity

AI is a broad field. The most applied subfield of AI is ML, which enables computers to learn patterns from data and make decisions with minimal human input, (Community, 2024). Supervised ML algorithms are often used in spam filters, intrusion detection, and malware classification. Unsupervised learning, on the other hand, is effective in identifying unknown threats through clustering and anomaly detection techniques, (Council, 2024).

DL is a specialized form of ML that utilizes multi-layered neural networks. It has become increasingly prevalent due to its high accuracy in complex tasks such as image and audio recognition. In cybersecurity, DL models are used for threat intelligence processing, detecting malwares, and analyzing encrypted traffic, (da Piedade Ferndandes, 2025). Microsoft's use of deep learning in its Defender antivirus software, which identifies malicious behaviors by analyzing trillions of signals daily across its ecosystem, (Dahri, Al-Nuaimi, & Raza, 2025).

NLP plays a vital role in processing unstructured data. It enables security systems to automatically interpret threat reports, vulnerability descriptions, and even detect phishing content in emails or websites, (De-Marcos, Garcia-Lopez, Garcia-Cabot, 2016). NLP is used in AI-powered email security platforms to detect social engineering by analyzing message tone and content structure.

Reinforcement Learning (RL) is an emerging area particularly useful in simulated environments. It trains agents through trial-and-error interaction with their environment to maximize long-term rewards. In cybersecurity gamification, RL is used to develop AI agents that simulate attacker behavior or evolve defense strategies, (Dillenbourg & Jermann, 2010). Such techniques are often used in CTF competitions and cybersecurity war games.

An old but still useable technique, Expert Systems can be used in scenarios requiring formalized knowledge rules. These systems can be integrated into hybrid systems alongside ML models to provide explainable outputs, (Dillenbourg & Jermann, 2010).

Benefits of AI in the Cybersecurity Domain

The integration of AI into cybersecurity brings a multitude of benefits that enhance both technical defenses and human efficiency. One of the most prominent advantages is speed and scalability, (Chandrashekar, Kumar, & Singh, 2024). With organizations facing over 2,200 cyberattacks daily worldwide, AI-powered systems can analyze vast datasets in seconds, (Donald & Iqbal, n.d.). This is particularly useful for identifying Distributed Denial of Service (DDoS) attacks, malware propagation, or insider threats in real-time, (Elkhodr & Gide, 2025).

AI has introduced an automation of repetitive tasks, which allows human analysts to focus on more strategic decision-making. AI can handle routine functions such as log analysis, vulnerability scanning, and alert prioritization, (System, n.d.). It also enhances threat detection accuracy by learning from historical incidents and contextual indicators, (De-Marcos, Garcia-Lopez, & Garcia-Cabot, 2016). AI can also detect zero-day threats by identifying deviations from normal patterns, (Fleck, 2018). In a 2019 study, 69% of security executives reported that AI was essential for responding to cyberattacks, particularly because of its ability to detect threats early, (Gangavarapu, Jaidhar, & Chanduka, 2020).

AI also supports proactive defense strategies by enabling predictive analytics that can forecast potential vulnerabilities or likely targets based on threat intelligence, (Garza, Kumar, & Patel, 2020). Darktrace's AI platform uses machine learning to establish a "pattern of life" for each device and user, enabling it to identify early-stage attacks and recommend countermeasures before the attack escalates, (Gentry, 2021).

From a business perspective, the adoption of AI in cybersecurity can also reduce operational costs. Automating detection and response workflows minimizes the need for large security operations teams, making security solutions more cost-effective and accessible, *Gerontakis, Yannakopoulos, & Voyiatzis, 2023). AI's ability to deliver speed, accuracy, adaptability, and cost-efficiency makes it an indispensable tool in the modern cybersecurity landscape. Its benefits are particularly magnified when used in educational platforms, where it can simulate dynamic threats and train learners in realistic, high-stakes environments, (Ajala & Balogun, 2024).

AI IN CYBERSECURITY

AI has revolutionized cybersecurity by introducing intelligent, adaptive, and autonomous systems. These systems can identify, respond, and mitigate threats in real time, (Goffer, Smith, & Brown, 2025). This not only improve the efficiency and accuracy of security operations but also provides a valuable foundation for developing realistic cybersecurity gamification environments. AI-enhanced simulations of real-world attacks and responses offer learners dynamic scenarios that foster critical thinking and rapid decision-making, (Grabner-Hagen & Kingsley, 2023).

Threat Detection and Response

AI-driven threat detection is among the most critical applications in cybersecurity. By continuously monitoring logs, network traffic, and user behavior, AI systems can detect patterns that suggest the presence of malware, phishing attempts, or unauthorized access, (Grover, Broll, & Babb, 2023). These systems can process large amounts of data in real-time, significantly overtaking traditional manual monitoring methods.

Supervised machine learning models can be trained on historical attack data to classify incoming data as benign or malicious, (Hassan & Ibrahim, 2023). On the other hand, unsupervised models can identify previously unknown threats by flagging anomalies, (Hasan, Khan, & Rahman, 2025). Systems such as Microsoft Defender and Darktrace use deep learning and behavioral analytics to recognize and respond to threats in milliseconds, (Ivanov, 2023).

Real-time AI-driven threat detection can be replicated in scenario-based games in gamified cybersecurity education platforms. Learners can assume the role of a Security Operations Center (SOC) analyst, using AI-assisted dashboards to detect intrusions and respond accordingly. Points and rewards can be based on speed and correctness of threat mitigation decisions, simulating the pressure and responsiveness required in real-world environments, (Jimmy, 2021).

Anomaly Detection and Risk Assessment

Anomaly detection focuses on identifying behavior that deviates from an established norm. AI algorithms, especially clustering and autoencoders, can detect subtle changes in data that might indicate threats such as insider attacks or data exfiltration attempts, (Joshi & Joshi, 2024). These algorithms are essential in spotting zero-day vulnerabilities that may overcome signature-based systems.

AI-enhanced risk assessment tools assign risk scores to devices, users, or applications based on behavior, access history, and network topology, (Kaddoura, 2021). These scores help prioritize security actions and allocate resources effectively. Risk-based gamification scenarios can challenge learners to prioritize mitigation strategies based on AI-generated risk scores. A simulated attack environment could involve a breach across multiple endpoints, with the learner using AI-generated insights to decide which systems to isolate first. This encourages critical thinking and risk-based decision-making under time constraints.

AI-Driven Security Automation

AI is central to modern Security Orchestration, Automation, and Response (SOAR) platforms, which automate the investigation, inhibition, and response to threats, (Kaushik, Kumar, & Singh, 2024). Tasks such as parsing logs, enriching alerts with contextual threat intelligence, and coordinating cross-platform responses can all be automated, reducing Mean Time to Detect (MTTD) and Mean Time to Respond (MTTR), (Kethireddy, 2023). AI-based systems can significantly reduce analyst fatigue by filtering false positives and managing repetitive and low priority tasks. This enables human analysts to focus on strategic analysis and policy development.

Gamified learning systems can mimic this automation by allowing learners to create and refine response playbooks using AI tools. For example, in a CTF-style challenge, players might program AI agents to respond to a series of alerts with specific actions, isolating a machine, blocking Ips, or disabling accounts, earning points based on the efficiency and effectiveness of their automation sequences.

Adaptive Cyber Defense Systems

Adaptive cyber defense mechanisms evolve in real-time to respond to changing attack. Reinforcement learning is particularly suited for this purpose, as it enables AI agents to adjust policies through continuous interaction with the changing environment, (Goffer, Smith, & Brown, 2025). These systems can perform proactive defense by simulating attacker behavior and adjusting defenses accordingly, (Khalaf, Mustafa, & Bilal, 2019). For example, honeypots can be managed by AI to lure attackers while simultaneously analyzing their tactics, (Kim, Park, & Lee, 2020).

In gamified educational systems, learners can engage with adaptive scenarios where the AI evolves its attack patterns based on player decisions. This keeps the gameplay challenging and encourages learners to think like both attackers and defenders, enhancing their understanding of cyber warfare dynamics.

AI-Augmented Incident Simulation and Forensics

AI can also be employed to recreate cybersecurity incidents for forensic analysis. It can reconstruct attack timelines by correlating events across different systems, which helps identify root causes and affected assets, (Kostelić, 2024). Gamified platforms can use such simulations to provide virtual incident response labs, where students investigate AI-generated forensic data to identify breach points, techniques used, and remediation strategies. These simulations foster investigative and analytical skills that are otherwise difficult to teach through lectures or static materials.

GAMIFICATION IN EDUCATION

With the increase in use of digital technologies in recent years, educators are continuously exploring innovative approaches to make learning more engaging, personalized, and effective, (Laato, Lipponen, & Sutinen, 2020). One such approach is gamification in which game-like features are used to enhance educational experience. It can provide a cost-effective, scalable, and motivating platform that can improve knowledge retention, engagement, and measurable progress in learners. An overview of gamification in education is shown in Figure 1. Although this approach is not new, the structured integration of game mechanics within formal education has enabled a focused educational strategy that can increase motivation and participation, (Le & Zincir-Heywood, 2021).

Figure 1. Elements of gamification in education

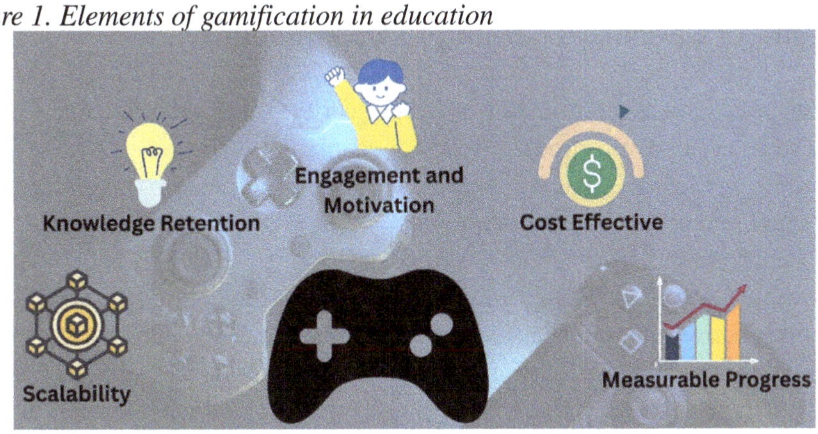

Gamification in education can be used in domains that require critical thinking, problem-solving, and sustained attention, such as cybersecurity. The traditional model of education is often centered on lectures and assessments, which is insufficient in today's fast-evolving world. Gamification has the potential to bridge this gap by offering interactive environments where students can experiment with real-world concepts in a controlled, low risk setting, (Limmen, 2024).

Definition and Principles of Gamification

Gamification in education refers to the application of game-like elements in learning environments to enhance student engagement, motivation, and overall learning outcomes. It involves integrating specific design components, such as points, levels, progress indicators, badges, and interactive feedback, etc., into educational settings. These elements are rooted in cognitive and behavioral psychology, aiming to stimulate the learner's intrinsic and extrinsic motivations, (Löffler, Schäfer, & Schmidt, 2021).

Gamification focused on goal setting, progression, and feedback. Learners are guided through structured challenges with increasing levels of difficulty, that can foster a sense of accomplishment as they move forward. The visibility of progress helps maintain momentum and encourages persistence. The addition of instantaneous feedback allows learners to recognize their errors and successes in real time, reinforcing learning, (Mahmood, Nisar, & Tsai, 2024). Gamified learning also provides independence by offering learners a choice to follow their approach in solving tasks. This makes them feel more invested in the process. Competition and collaboration can also stimulate motivation. Recognition through achievements provides learners with a validation which can help them achieve their educational goals.

Benefits of Gamified Learning in Cybersecurity

The application of gamification in cybersecurity education offers many advantages, such as improved problem-solving, adaptability, and hands-on skill gain. Cybersecurity learners frequently engage with complex scenarios involving digital threats and defense strategies. Gamification can allow students to interact with these scenarios in a safe and realistic context, (Limmen, 2024). This approach can reinforce theoretical knowledge and improve cognitive attention by trying abstract concepts to active, situational tasks. The feedback provided by these systems is very beneficial for the learners. They can observe the impact of their actions instantly, learn from mistakes, and refine their strategies on the go which is similar in actual cybersecurity incidents, (Mahmood, Nisar, & Tsai, 2024).

This approach can also reduce the fear of failure in real world scenarios. In general, students hesitate to take risks due to the fear of being penalized for incorrect answers. Gamified platforms reframe failure as an essential part of the learning process. Learners are encouraged to experiment, make errors, and try again to gain a deeper understanding of concepts and build resilience, (Malone, Stockley, & Saeri, 2021). The competitive and collaborative aspects of gamification mirror the teamwork in real-world cybersecurity operations. Working with peers in simulations not only enhances communication and cooperation but also simulates the interpersonal dynamics of professional cybersecurity teams, (Mkhize, Naidoo, & Buthelezi, n.d.).

CHALLENGES AND LIMITATIONS OF AI-BASED GAMIFICATION IN CYBERSECURITY EDUCATION

The combination of AI and gamification has created novel opportunities in cybersecurity education, offering learners dynamic, engaging, and personalized experiences that mimic real-world cyber threats, (Alotaibi, 2024). This technological integration is not without significant challenges and limitations. Despite the clear benefits, several ethical, technical, and academic concerns must be addressed to ensure responsible implementation and lasting educational value. Figure 2 shows the ethical considerations that must be followed while employing the gamified education. Next sections examine these limitations in detail.

Figure 2. Visual representation of ethical considerations in gamified education

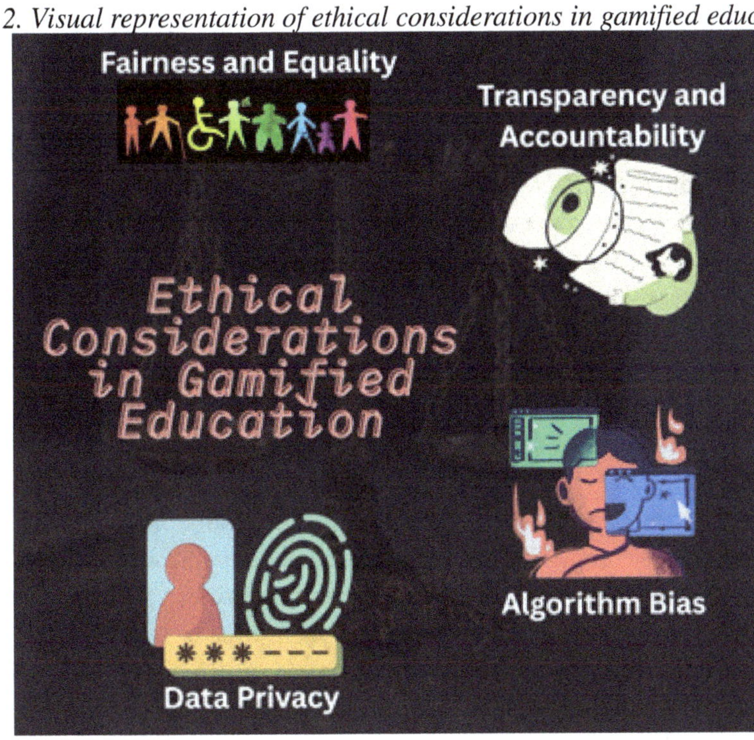

AI Bias and Ethical Concerns

Potential Biases in AI-Driven Learning Models

AI systems learn by processing large volumes of data. This data is often curated from historical datasets, security logs, educational records, and even user-generated interactions. Although this data allows AI to make informed decisions and tailor educational experiences, it also exposes the system to inherent biases present within the data, (Nageab, Alrasheed, & Khalifa, 2024). In cybersecurity education, biased AI can affect learner evaluation, progress tracking, and even the types of threats simulated in gamified scenarios.

For example, if an AI model is trained on cybersecurity logs, sourced from enterprise-level organizations in developed countries, it may develop an understanding of common threat vectors, user behaviors, or security infrastructures. Learners operating in different environments, such as small businesses or regions with distinct threat landscapes, may find the training less relevant or even misleading. AI models might generalize user behaviors inaccurately, penalizing certain strategies that deviate from the expected patterns learned during training.

This bias limits the educational utility of the platform and can also discourage learners, especially those from underrepresented backgrounds. They might find themselves excessively evaluated or mischaracterized. Over time, such experiences can erode trust in the learning system and lead to separation, weakening the goals of rightful and inclusive education, (Nair, Phadke, & Kreider, 2025).

Ethical Implications of AI-based Training

The deployment of AI-powered gamified education tools, particularly in cybersecurity, brings about complex ethical issues that extend beyond bias. The transparency and accountability of the algorithms used is a crucial aspect. Learners may not be aware of how their interactions are being analyzed, what criteria are used to score or assess them, or how their personal learning data is utilized for model refinement, (Nasteski, 2017). In an age where data privacy and digital rights are vital, systems that function as black boxes raise legitimate ethical concerns.

Cybersecurity education often includes simulated attack-defense scenarios that mimic real-world hacking and counter-hacking techniques. While these simulations are invaluable for skill-building, they also carry the risk of dual-use, wherein learners may apply this knowledge unethically or maliciously outside of the educational setting, (Ng, 2015). Gamified platforms, which reward rapid response, creative problem-solving, and in-depth exploration of systems, must ensure that the embedded ethical framework is robust. The line between teaching ethical hacking and inadvertently facilitating the development of black-hat skills is dangerously thin if not monitored carefully, (Ntoutsi, Tran, & Kindermans, 2020).

The competitive elements of gamification, such as leaderboards, rewards, and in-game rankings, can introduce psychological pressure or stress, particularly in educational contexts, (Olutimehin, Adeyemi, & Ogunleye, 2025). If not designed sensitively, these mechanics may favor learners with prior experience, further worsening inequalities in skill development and learner confidence.

Technical and Implementation Challenges

Scalability and Computational Costs

The scalability and computational overhead pose a significant technical hurdle in deploying AI-powered gamified education systems. These platforms require advanced infrastructure for real-time data processing, behavior tracking, natural language understanding, and interactive gameplay, (Oyighan, Adeyemi, & Ogunleye, 2024). Unlike static learning management systems (LMS) AI-based gamification systems are dynamic and personalized, generating unique experiences based on each learner's interactions and performance.

Training the underlying machine learning models requires high-performance GPUs, extensive storage, and cloud-based arrangement. Institutions with limited technical budgets or lacking technical expertise may struggle to support such demands, (Papadimitriou & Virvu, 2025). Maintaining these systems over time involves not just initial deployment but continuous updates, monitoring, bug fixes, and retraining of AI models to accommodate new threats and learning behaviors.

Gamified environments must also scale across hundreds or thousands of concurrent users while maintaining real-time responsiveness, accuracy, and fairness. Lag in simulations can ruin concentration, frustrate users, and reduce the educational value of the experience. Ensuring a seamless experience at scale is particularly challenging when dealing with complex simulations of cybersecurity incidents, which may involve dynamic rule sets, multiplayer interaction, or integrated assessment tools.

Data Privacy and Security Risks in AI-Driven Games

Cybersecurity education platforms collect and process large volumes of sensitive user data. These include not just personal identifiers but also learning behaviors, communication patterns, response times, game decisions, and simulated attack strategies. This data is valuable for training AI models and personalizing content, it may also creates a substantial surface area for potential exploitation.

If this data is improperly secured, these platforms could become attractive targets for cyber attackers themselves, exposing the very learners they aim to protect, (Park & Kim, 2021). A breach of an AI-driven gamified platform could compromise not only learner privacy but also expose sensitive institutional knowledge, threat simulations, and internal defense mechanisms embedded in the training modules.

The platform's ability to adaptively guide learners using real-time analytics may conflict with established data protection laws such as the General Data Protection Regulation (GDPR). Without robust consent mechanisms, encryption practices, and transparency in data collection, such systems risk non-compliance and potential legal ramifications, (Parsons, Rees, & Waite, 2019). Adversarial attacks on AI models pose another layer of threat. These attacks could mislead the system into evaluating learners incorrectly or simulate incorrect threat responses, undermining the educational intent, (Passey, Shukla, & Bott, 2019).

Effectiveness of Gamification with AI

Measuring the Real-World Impact of AI-based Training

Gamification can significantly boost engagement but its impact on actual learning outcomes is not straightforward. Many gamified systems measure progress using points, badges, level progression, and completion rates, (Picard & Cosier, 1997). While these metrics provide an immediate sense of achievement, they often fall short of indicating deep learning or practical readiness.

The complexity of real-world cybersecurity challenges requires critical thinking, contextual understanding, and adaptability. These capabilities are difficult to measure using in-game metrics alone, (Quayyum, 2021). Educational institutions and employers must question whether high performance in a gamified environment correlates to genuine competence in real-world scenarios. There is a lack of standardized evaluation frameworks or longitudinal studies that can link gamified AI-based learning with long-term knowledge retention and professional efficacy, (Qumer & Ikrama, 2022). Without robust research-backed validation, such platforms may continue to operate more on the assumption of effectiveness rather than evidence-based outcomes.

Engagement vs. Knowledge Retention

Gamification is well-known for making learning more enjoyable. AI adds to this by ensuring personalization, providing real-time feedback, and adjusting difficulty levels based on user performance. This increased engagement can sometimes become superficial, where learners are more focused on game mechanics than the subject matter itself, (Baah, Govender, & Subramaniam, 2024). Points and rewards can lead to gaming the system, where users find shortcuts to win rather than deeply understand the cybersecurity concepts, (Sabir, Ullah, & Ahmad, 2021). Short bursts of high engagement do not always lead to long-term retention. A learner may remember how to perform a specific action within a game but fail to apply the underlying concept in a real security incident, (Salloum, 2023). This disconnect can be particularly dangerous in cybersecurity, where a delayed or incorrect decision can have serious consequences.

To combat this, gamified systems must be carefully designed with educational strategies that reinforce repetition, critical analysis, and practical application. Reflection exercises, scenario-based assessments, and cross-platform knowledge checks can bridge between entertainment and education.

CASE STUDIES AND APPLICATIONS

AI has become a pivotal component in the advancement of cybersecurity education, particularly through its integration with gamified learning environments. By simulating real-world threat scenarios and enabling interactive engagement, AI-powered cybersecurity games and training platforms provide learners with dynamic, personalized learning experiences. This section presents a range of notable case studies and real-world applications in which AI techniques have been successfully embedded into gamified cybersecurity education, with a focus on adaptive learning systems and CTF competitions.

AI-Driven Cybersecurity Games and Platforms

AI-powered cybersecurity games are increasingly recognized as transformative tools for teaching defensive and offensive security skills. A prominent example is the CyberStart platform developed by the SANS Institute. This platform integrates gamification elements, such as challenge-based missions and achievement systems, with machine learning algorithms that dynamically adjust difficulty based on learner performance. As learners progress, the system personalizes content to match their individual skill levels, fostering problem-solving and critical thinking in areas such as cryptography, penetration testing, and digital forensics, (Shtayyat, Gawanmeh, & Mashaleh, 2025). Another influential initiative is IBM's Cybersecurity Learning Experience (CLE), which incorporates AI-driven virtual assistants to guide learners through contextual hints and natural language feedback. The CLE leverages predictive analytics to tailor content delivery, representing an early and scalable application of intelligent tutoring systems in cybersecurity education. These AI components not only enhance learner support but also enable real-time progress monitoring and automated assessment, (Tanikonda, Kumar, & Sharma, 2022). Together, these platforms exemplify how AI and gamification can be synergistically employed to create engaging, adaptive, and outcome-driven cybersecurity education solutions. The following case studies further explore diverse implementations across academic, corporate, and research settings, underscoring the practical relevance and pedagogical potential of AI-based gamified training.

Real-World Case Studies

The integration of AI and gamification in cybersecurity education has led to the development of numerous innovative platforms and competitions aimed at fostering engagement, adaptability, and practical skills. This section outlines several notable real-world implementations where AI-driven gamification has been successfully applied to cybersecurity training environments. These case studies illustrate the breadth of applications across academic, corporate, and research contexts.

CyberStart by SANS Institute

CyberStart is an online gamified platform designed to teach cybersecurity concepts through interactive challenges and simulations. Developed by the SANS Institute, CyberStart integrates AI-driven adaptive learning techniques that personalize content difficulty based on learner performance. As learners progress through the game, machine learning algorithms track their decisions and dynamically adjust challenge complexity to maintain optimal engagement and learning outcomes, (Shtayyat, Gawanmeh, & Mashaleh, 2025). The platform has been widely adopted in the United States and the United Kingdom, particularly in initiatives aimed at increasing cybersecurity talent among high school and university students. Preliminary findings indicate that participants demonstrate significantly improved understanding of cryptography, web security, and digital forensics concepts after engaging with CyberStart, (Shtayyat, Gawanmeh, & Mashaleh, 2025).

IBM Cybersecurity Learning Experience (CLE)

IBM's CLE offers another compelling case where AI and gamification intersect. The CLE is an immersive, cloud-based learning environment that includes AI-powered virtual assistants designed to provide real-time feedback and contextual support. The system employs NLP to interpret student queries and deliver personalized hints, learning suggestions, and automated assessments, (Tanikonda, Kumar, & Sharma, 2023). Gamified elements such as badges, leaderboards, and scenario-based missions help simulate real-world cybersecurity challenges, such as identifying phishing attempts or responding to data breaches. The CLE has been used in both academic and corporate training environments, with learners reporting increased motivation and retention of concepts.

Microsoft Security Ninja Program

The Microsoft Security Ninja program, an internal initiative for upskilling employees, exemplifies how gamified AI-enhanced platforms can be applied in enterprise settings. This program utilizes CTF-style competitions and secure coding exercises supported by AI-based virtual assistants. These assistants use NLP to analyze participant inputs and provide corrective feedback, enabling real-time guidance during ethical hacking challenges, (Talaei Khoei & Kaabouch, 2023). Microsoft reports that integrating AI into gamified training has significantly enhanced employee engagement and shortened the cybersecurity skill acquisition curve. The program's success has led to its broader adoption across Microsoft's global offices.

AI-based Cyber Ranges Utilizing Reinforcement Learning

AI-enhanced cyber ranges are increasingly being developed to provide dynamic and personalized training environments. These platforms leverage reinforcement learning algorithms to simulate realistic cyberattack scenarios, allowing trainees to engage in hands-on defense strategies. For instance, environments like CyberShield and Cyberwheel have been designed to train autonomous cyber defense models on simulated networks. In these settings, RL agents learn optimal defense mechanisms by interacting with various attack vectors, adapting their strategies based on the evolving threat landscape and the trainee's responses. Such adaptive systems ensure that the complexity of scenarios aligns with the learner's proficiency, promoting effective skill acquisition, (Tharayil, Kumar, & Singh, 2024; Udayakumar & Anandan, 2024).

Smart Tutoring Systems in Cybersecurity Education

Complementing the advancements in cyber ranges, smart tutoring systems (STS) have emerged as effective tools for personalized cybersecurity education. A notable example is the Smart Environment for Adaptive Learning of Cybersecurity Skills developed by Vykopal, Švábenský, and Čeleda (2022). This system collects and analyzes various student data to assign suitable learning paths, ensuring that tasks match the learner's proficiency level. By adapting the training content in real-time, the platform enhances learner engagement and facilitates the development of practical skills essential for cybersecurity professionals.

PicoCTF – Carnegie Mellon University

PicoCTF, developed by Carnegie Mellon University's CyLab, is one of the largest and most widely used gamified platforms for cybersecurity education. While the platform itself is not fully AI-driven, recent enhancements have begun integrating AI components for personalized learning. These include intelligent feedback mechanisms and adaptive hint systems that respond to students' patterns of success or failure. PicoCTF is used globally in high school and university curricula, and it hosts an annual competition that attracts tens of thousands of participants. Its impact on increasing cybersecurity literacy among younger audiences has been well-documented, (Vitla, 2023), making it a foundational case study for scalable gamified education.

AI IN CAPTURE THE FLAG COMPETITIONS

CTF competitions are widely recognized as effective methods for hands-on cybersecurity training. With the integration of AI, these competitions have become more sophisticated and personalized, (Vykopal, Švábenský, & Čeleda, 2022).

AI-Assisted Learning in Ethical Hacking Challenges

AI is increasingly being integrated into cybersecurity training environments, particularly CTF competitions and ethical hacking simulations, to enhance learner engagement, contextual feedback, and adaptive learning. Leading technology companies, including Microsoft, have developed AI-powered tools to support security professionals and trainees through real-time analysis and decision-making assistance. One notable advancement is Microsoft's Security Copilot, a generative AI security solution that assists analysts in interpreting threats, summarizing incidents, and suggesting remediation steps. While not embedded directly within gamified training programs such as Microsoft's Security Ninja learning paths, Security Copilot demonstrates the application of AI in delivering contextual threat intelligence through natural language prompts. It uses large language models in conjunction with Microsoft's global threat intelligence to provide real-time, actionable insights, capabilities that could be extended to internal training simulations and ethical hacking challenges. Rather than relying on predefined answers or static feedback, tools like Security Copilot can function as on-demand virtual mentors, guiding learners during cybersecurity exercises by explaining vulnerabilities, suggesting attack vectors, and recommending defensive strategies. This form of AI-assisted learning helps bridge the gap between theoretical knowledge and practical application, especially in fast-evolving threat landscapes.

EC-Council's Certified Ethical Hacker (CEH) v13 curriculum incorporates AI to provide cybersecurity professionals with in-demand skills to combat evolving cyber threats more efficiently EC-Council in 2024, (Wang, Zhang, & Chen, 2023). Additionally, adaptive learning environments have been developed to tailor cybersecurity training to individual learners' proficiency levels. These environments collect various student data to assign suitable learning paths, enabling students to engage with tasks of appropriate difficulty and enhancing the overall learning experience, (Vaishnavi, 2025). AI-powered platforms like CyberMentor leverage large language models to provide real-time, on-demand learning support, addressing diverse student needs in cybersecurity education.

Adaptive Challenge Generation Using AI

AI plays a growing role in cybersecurity training, particularly in generating dynamic and personalized CTF challenges. These innovations aim to maintain learner engagement and ensure challenges align with participants' skill levels. The Shellphish team, affiliated with the University of California, Santa Barbara, developed the iCTF (International CTF) framework, an open-source platform designed to manage and scale CTF competitions. While the framework excels in orchestration and scalability, it does not incorporate adaptive learning mechanisms such as reinforcement learning to tailor challenge difficulty based on individual performance, (Wei, 2024).

Separately, the use of Generative Adversarial Networks (GANs) has gained traction in cybersecurity research to simulate realistic attack scenarios. GANs have been employed to generate synthetic network data for training intrusion detection systems, offering a valuable way to replicate threat behaviors without relying on sensitive real-world data. For example, the SynGAN framework has been proposed to create synthetic cyber-attacks, improving detection models through diverse and controlled inputs, (Wiliams, Johnson, & Brown, 2024). While GANs show promise, their application dynamically generating full CTF challenges, especially those adapted in real-time based on participant performance, is still an emerging field. Current efforts mostly focus on generating components of challenges (e.g., payloads, traffic patterns) rather than full end-to-end problems. As such, AI-driven adaptive challenge generation remains a promising but largely experimental area of research.

Emerging Applications and Educational Integration

While existing case studies demonstrate the efficacy of AI-enhanced gamification in cybersecurity education, emerging applications suggest broader opportunities for scalable, personalized, and adaptive learning. This section outlines current and developing trends that reflect the growing integration of AI technologies into gamified educational platforms. These innovations aim to overcome traditional limitations in cybersecurity training, such as one-size-fits-all content delivery, static assessments, and limited engagement tracking.

Longitudinal Impact and Knowledge Retention

Recent scholarships emphasize the importance of measuring the long-term effectiveness of gamified and AI-supported learning interventions. Traditional metrics, such as quiz scores or course completion, are insufficient to evaluate the enduring impact on learners' abilities to respond to real-world threats. Researchers have begun proposing frameworks for longitudinal assessment, including periodic re-evaluations, skill decay analysis, and follow-up simulations, (Vaishnavi, 2025). AI systems that track learner progress over extended periods can automate such assessments and detect patterns in skill retention and decay, enabling just-in-time refresher modules.

Integration with Learning Management Systems (LMS)

To increase accessibility and scalability, AI-gamified modules are increasingly being integrated with established Learning Management Systems (e.g., Moodle, Blackboard, Canvas). These integrations allow institutions to embed gamified cybersecurity experiences directly into course curricula, enabling centralized assessment tracking, content recommendation, and performance analytics, (Yigit, Gur, & Alagoz, 2024). Through AI-driven dashboards, instructors gain real-time insights into student learning trajectories, while learners receive adaptive feedback and personalized content pathways.

Affective Computing and Engagement Monitoring

A particularly promising direction involves the use of affective computing, AI systems capable of detecting and responding to learners' emotional states. By analyzing indicators such as facial expressions, voice tone, and physiological signals, these systems can assess stress, confusion, or disengagement during training. Gamified platforms equipped with affective AI adapt challenge difficulty, pacing, or assistance based on the learner's emotional feedback. Such systems are especially relevant in high-stakes cybersecurity simulations where cognitive load can affect performance and learning outcomes. By monitoring emotional cues, these systems can tailor content delivery to maintain optimal cognitive load levels, which is particularly beneficial in complex learning scenarios like cybersecurity simulations. While specific implementations in cybersecurity training are emerging, the principles of affective computing are increasingly being applied to develop adaptive training environments. These environments aim to adjust challenge difficulty and provide assistance based on real-time emotional feedback, thereby improving the effectiveness of cybersecurity education, (Yaishnavi, 2025).

Collaborative AI-Supported Learning Environments

As cybersecurity practice increasingly involves team-based problem-solving, educational platforms are beginning to incorporate collaborative, AI-enhanced gamification. These systems support distributed learners working together in simulated attack-defense scenarios, with AI agents moderating tasks, assigning team roles, and providing group-level feedback. Research suggests that such environments foster higher-order thinking skills, including communication, strategic planning, and conflict resolution.

AI Coaches in Ethical Hacking Labs

AI-powered virtual coaches are being piloted in ethical hacking and penetration testing labs to simulate real-time mentoring. These systems leverage NLP and reinforcement learning to analyze learners' actions and recommend alternative strategies, tools, or commands. Unlike static tutorials, AI coaches adapt to user expertise, reduce frustration by offering tiered hints, and emulate expert guidance, creating an apprenticeship-like learning experience.

Accessibility and Cultural Adaptation

Gamified AI learning systems are also being tailored for inclusive and culturally diverse populations. AI enables multilingual support, voice-based interfaces for visually impaired learners, and content customization based on local cybersecurity norms. For instance, NLP-based agents can be trained in regional dialects or integrated with text-to-speech engines, expanding access for non-native English speakers or learners with disabilities.

Certification and Industry Alignment

To enhance the practical utility of training programs, developers are aligning AI-gamified content with professional standards and certifications such as CompTIA Security+, CISSP, or ISO/IEC 27001. Some platforms now feature automated mapping of challenges to industry-relevant competencies, allowing learners to track certification readiness in real time. AI-based skill analytics can also generate individualized learning roadmaps, bridging gaps between current knowledge and certification requirements.

CONCLUSION

AI-powered gamification is fundamentally transforming cybersecurity education by making the learning process more engaging, practical, and learner-centric. These intelligent systems offer dynamic simulations that replicate real-world cyber threats and adapt in real time to the learner's progress. By integrating machine learning, reinforcement learning, and natural language processing, AI-based platforms enhance traditional game-based learning with features such as real-time feedback, adaptive challenge levels, personalized learning paths, and intelligent assessment mechanisms. These capabilities not only increase the learner's motivation and retention but also foster the development of critical thinking, situational awareness, and hands-on technical skills. Importantly, AI-gamified environments provide a low-risk, high-impact training ground where learners can experiment with cybersecurity strategies, learn from mistakes, and refine their decision-making without real-world consequences. Platforms like CyberStart, IBM's CLE, Microsoft's Security Ninja, and PicoCTF exemplify how these systems are being deployed in academic and corporate contexts to successfully bridge the gap between theory and practice.

Despite these advancements, realizing the full potential of AI-driven gamification demands a careful and critical examination of its limitations. Key challenges include computational overhead, scalability, ethical considerations such as AI bias and data privacy, and the absence of standardized frameworks to assess long-term learning outcomes. While engagement metrics like badges and leaderboards provide immediate feedback, they do not always reflect deep understanding or professional readiness. Therefore, educators and developers must go beyond superficial measures of success and invest in rigorous, evidence-based evaluations to validate the educational efficacy of these tools. To ensure meaningful and equitable learning, future systems must be designed with a strong emphasis on inclusivity, transparency, and ethical responsibility. This includes protecting learner data, avoiding algorithmic bias, and ensuring accessibility across different cultural, linguistic, and technological contexts. Ultimately, the success of AI-powered gamification in cybersecurity education hinges on its responsible and thoughtful application, balancing technological innovation with pedagogical soundness to equip the next generation of cybersecurity professionals for the complex and evolving threat landscape.

REFERENCES

Ajala, O. A., & Balogun, O. A. (2024). Leveraging AI/ML for anomaly detection, threat prediction, and automated response. *World Journal of Advanced Research and Reviews*, *21*(1), 2584–2598. DOI: 10.30574/wjarr.2024.21.1.0287

Al-Hawawreh, M., Nour, M., & Fakir, M. (2021). Deep learning-enabled threat intelligence scheme in the Internet of Things networks. *IEEE Transactions on Network Science and Engineering*, *8*(4), 2968–2981. DOI: 10.1109/TNSE.2020.3032415

Al-Sinani, H. S., & Mitchell, C. J. (2024). AI-enhanced ethical hacking: A Linux-focused experiment. *arXiv*. https://arxiv.org/abs/2410.05105

. Ali, A., & Rasool, M. (2020). Machine learning-powered SOC: Real-time anomaly detection and response automation. [Unpublished manuscript].

Alotaibi, N. S. (2024). The impact of AI and LMS integration on the future of higher education: Opportunities, challenges, and strategies for transformation. *Sustainability (Basel)*, *16*(23), 10357. Advance online publication. DOI: 10.3390/su162310357

Amjad, K., Khan, A., & Ahmad, I. (2025). Unlocking cybersecurity: A game-changing framework for training and awareness—A systematic review. *Human Behavior and Emerging Technologies*, *2025*(1), 9982666. Advance online publication. DOI: 10.1155/hbe2/9982666

Arjunan, T. (2024). Detecting anomalies and intrusions in unstructured cybersecurity data using natural language processing. *International Journal for Research in Applied Science and Engineering Technology*, *12*(9), 1023–1029. Advance online publication. DOI: 10.22214/ijraset.2024.58497

Baah, C., Govender, I., & Subramaniam, P. R. (2024). Enhancing learning engagement: A study on gamification's influence on motivation and cognitive load. *Education Sciences*, *14*(10), 1115. Advance online publication. DOI: 10.3390/educsci14101115

Baker, R., Walonoski, J., Heffernan, N., Roll, I., Corbett, A., & Koedinger, K. (2008). Why students engage in "gaming the system" behavior in interactive learning environments. *Journal of Interactive Learning Research*, *19*(2), 185–224.

Bandara, I., Ioras, F., & Maher, K. (2014). Cyber security concerns in e-learning education. In *ICERI2014 Proceedings* (pp. 728–734). IATED.

Basri, W. S. (2023). Artificial intelligence, cyber security measures and SME's e-operational efficiency: Moderating role of employees perception of AI usefulness. *Operational Research in Engineering Sciences: Theory and Applications*, *6*(4), 1–17.

. Beretas, C. (2023). Analysis of white and black hat hacker roles, practices and techniques, considering ethical and legal issues, including bug bounty programs. [Unpublished manuscript].

Cao, L. (2022). AI science and engineering: A new field. *IEEE Intelligent Systems*, *37*(1), 3–13. DOI: 10.1109/MIS.2022.3151993 PMID: 35935446

Cascella, M., Pascale, A., & Sansone, C. (2023). Envisioning gamification in anesthesia, pain management, and critical care: Basic principles, integration of artificial intelligence, and simulation strategies. *Journal of Anesthesia, Analgesia and Critical Care*, *3*(1), 33. Advance online publication. DOI: 10.1186/s44158-023-00118-2 PMID: 37697415

Chapman, P., Burket, J., & Brumley, D. (2014). *PicoCTF: A game-based computer security competition for high school students. In 2014 USENIX Summit on Gaming, Games, and Gamification in Security Education (3GSE 14)*. USENIX Association.

Charlier, J., Paelinck, M., & Verdegem, P. (2019). SynGAN: Towards generating synthetic network attacks using GANs. *arXiv*. https://arxiv.org/abs/1908.09899

Chindrus, C., & Caruntu, C.-F. (2023). Securing the network: A red and blue cybersecurity competition case study. *Information (Basel)*, *14*(11), 587. Advance online publication. DOI: 10.3390/info14110587

Chourasia, R. (2025). AI-enhanced cybersecurity training: Learning analytics in action. *International Journal of Advanced Research in Science. Tongxin Jishu*, •••, 566–573. DOI: 10.48175/IJARSCT-12345

Community, H. S. (2024). *Cyber hackathon (Capture The Flag 2024)*. https://mf.hku.edu.tr/eng/Etkinlik/cyber-hackathon-capture-the-flag-2024-2/

Council, E. (2024). Can EC-Council's CEH v13 leverage AI to revolutionize ethical hacking? *Times of AI*. https://www.timesofai.com/news/ec-council-ceh-v13-ai-ethicalhacking-training/

Dahri, N. A., Al-Nuaimi, M. N., & Raza, M. (2025). *The effect of AI gamification on students' engagement and academic achievement: SEM analysis perspectives*. IEEE., DOI: 10.1109/ACCESS.2025.1234567

De-Marcos, L., Garcia-Lopez, E., & Garcia-Cabot, A. (2016). On the effectiveness of game-like and social approaches in learning: Comparing educational gaming, gamification & social networking. *Computers & Education*, *95*, 99–113. DOI: 10.1016/j.compedu.2015.12.008

Dillenbourg, P., & Jermann, P. (2010). Technology for classroom orchestration. In Khine, M. S., & Saleh, I. M. (Eds.), *New science of learning: Cognition, computers and collaboration in education* (pp. 525–552). Springer., DOI: 10.1007/978-1-4419-5716-0_26

Donald, A., & Iqbal, J. (n.d.). Implementing cyber defense strategies: Evolutionary algorithms, cyber forensics, and AI-driven solutions for enhanced security. [Unpublished manuscript].

Donekal Chandrashekar, N., Kumar, A., & Singh, R. (2024). Understanding user behavior for enhancing cybersecurity training with immersive gamified platforms. *Information (Basel), 15*(12), 814. Advance online publication. DOI: 10.3390/info15120814

Elkhodr, M., & Gide, E. (2025). Integrating generative AI in cybersecurity education: Case study insights on pedagogical strategies, critical thinking,

Fleck, J. (2018). Development and establishment in artificial intelligence. In *The question of artificial intelligence* (pp. 106–164). Routledge. DOI: 10.4324/9780429505331-3

Gangavarapu, T., Jaidhar, C., & Chanduka, B. (2020). Applicability of machine learning in spam and phishing email filtering: Review and approaches. *Artificial Intelligence Review, 53*(7), 5019–5081. DOI: 10.1007/s10462-020-09814-9

Garza, V. R., Kumar, S., & Patel, R. (2020). Machine learning techniques for identifying anomalous network traffic. [Unpublished manuscript].

Gentry, B. (2021). *How students experience failure in a content-gamified higher education course* [Doctoral dissertation, Southern New Hampshire University]. ProQuest Dissertations Publishing.

Gerontakis, G., Yannakopoulos, P., & Voyiatzis, I. (2023). Evaluating cybersecurity certifications: A framework for extracting educational scenarios in cybersecurity training. In *Proceedings of the 27th Pan-Hellenic Conference on Progress in Computing and Informatics* (pp. 123–134). DOI: 10.1145/3635059.3635097

Goffer, M. A., Smith, J., & Brown, T. (2025). AI-enhanced cyber threat detection and response advancing national security in critical infrastructure. *Journal of Posthumanism, 5*(3), 1667–1689. DOI: 10.63332/joph.v5i3.965

Grabner-Hagen, M. M., & Kingsley, T. (2023). From badges to boss challenges: Gamification through need-supporting scaffolded design to instruct and motivate elementary learners. *Computers and Education Open, 4*, 100131. Advance online publication. DOI: 10.1016/j.caeo.2023.100131

Grover, S., Broll, B., & Babb, D. (2023). Cybersecurity education in the age of AI: Integrating AI learning into cybersecurity high school curricula. In *Proceedings of the 54th ACM Technical Symposium on Computer Science Education* V. 1 (pp. 456–462). ACM. DOI: 10.1145/3545945.3569750

Hasan, K., Khan, M., & Rahman, M. (2025). Enhancing proactive cyber defense: A theoretical framework for AI-driven predictive cyber threat intelligence. *Journal of Technologies Information and Communication*, *5*(1), 33122. DOI: 10.55267/rtic/16176

Hassan, S. K., & Ibrahim, A. (2023). The role of artificial intelligence in cyber security and incident response. *International Journal for Electronic Crime Investigation*, *7*(2), 1–12.

Ivanov, Y. (2023). AI in cyber deception: Creating adaptive and realistic honeypot systems. *Advances in Computer Sciences*, *6*(1), 1–10.

Jimmy, F. (2021). Emerging threats: The latest cybersecurity risks and the role of artificial intelligence in enhancing cybersecurity defenses. *Valley International Journal Digital Library*, *1*(2), 564–574. DOI: 10.18535/ijsrm/v9i2.ec01

Joshi, N., & Joshi, M. (2024). Gamified AI-driven assessments. *Journal of Scientific and Engineering Research*, *11*(11), 108–114.

Kaddoura, S. (2021). Classification of malicious and benign websites by network features using supervised machine learning algorithms. In *2021 5th Cyber Security in Networking Conference (CSNet)* (pp. 87–94). IEEE. DOI: 10.1109/CSNet52717.2021.9614273

Kaushik, K., Kumar, S., & Singh, R. (2024). Ethical considerations in AI-based cybersecurity. In *Next-generation cybersecurity: AI, ML, and blockchain* (pp. 437–470). Springer., DOI: 10.1007/978-981-97-1249-6_19

Kethireddy, R. R. (2023). AI-augmented threat response systems with real-time adaptive defense. *Intelligence*, *1*(1), 62–71.

Khalaf, B. A., Mustafa, A. S., & Bilal, S. (2019). Comprehensive review of artificial intelligence and statistical approaches in distributed denial of service attack and defense methods. *IEEE Access : Practical Innovations, Open Solutions*, *7*, 51691–51713. DOI: 10.1109/ACCESS.2019.2908998

Kim, A., Park, M., & Lee, D. H. (2020). AI-IDS: Application of deep learning to real-time web intrusion detection. *IEEE Access : Practical Innovations, Open Solutions*, *8*, 70245–70261. DOI: 10.1109/ACCESS.2020.2986882

Kostelić, K. (2024). Dynamic awareness and strategic adaptation in cybersecurity: A game-theory approach. *Games*, *15*(2), 13. Advance online publication. DOI: 10.3390/g15020013

Laato, S., Lipponen, J., & Sutinen, E. (2020). AI in cybersecurity education—A systematic literature review of studies on cybersecurity MOOCs. In *2020 IEEE 20th International Conference on Advanced Learning Technologies (ICALT)* (pp. 6–10). IEEE. DOI: 10.1109/ICALT49669.2020.00007

Le, D. C., & Zincir-Heywood, N. (2021). Anomaly detection for insider threats using unsupervised ensembles. *IEEE Transactions on Network and Service Management*, *18*(2), 1152–1164. DOI: 10.1109/TNSM.2021.3071928

Limmen, J. (2024). *Awesome reinforcement learning for cybersecurity*. https://github.com/Limmen/awesome-rl-for-cybersecurity

Löffler, E., Schäfer, R., & Schmidt, T. C. (2021). Cysecescape 2.0—A virtual escape room to raise cybersecurity awareness. *International Journal of Serious Games*, *8*(1), 59–70. DOI: 10.17083/ijsg.v8i1.413

Mahmood, D., Nisar, H., & Tsai, C.-Y. (2024). Exploring the efficacy of neuro-feedback training in modulating alpha-frequency band and its effects on functional connectivity and band power. *Expert Systems with Applications*, *254*, 124415. Advance online publication. DOI: 10.1016/j.eswa.2024.124415

Malone, M., Stockley, R., & Saeri, A. K. (2021). To gamify or not? On leaderboard effects, student engagement and learning outcomes in a cybersecurity intervention. In *Proceedings of the 52nd ACM Technical Symposium on Computer Science Education* (pp. 670–676). ACM. DOI: 10.1145/3408877.3432439

. Mkhize, T., Naidoo, R., & Buthelezi, S. (n.d.). Advancing cybersecurity with artificial intelligence: Development and challenges of natural language processing frameworks for detecting phishing attacks and text-based intrusions. [Unpublished manuscript].

Nageab, W. M., Alrasheed, R., & Khalifa, M. (2024). Cybersecurity in the era of artificial intelligence: Risks and solutions. In *2024 ASU International Conference in Emerging Technologies for Sustainability and Intelligent Systems (ICETSIS)* (pp. 123–130). IEEE. DOI: 10.1109/ICETSIS61505.2024.10459584

. Nair, A., Phadke, A., & Kreider, C. (2025). A systematic review of AI-backed tools in education. [Unpublished manuscript].

Nasteski, V. (2017). An overview of the supervised machine learning methods. *Horizons. B*, *4*, 51–62. DOI: 10.20544/HORIZONS.B.04.1.17.P05

Ng, W. (2015). *New digital technology in education: Conceptualizing professional learning for educators*. Springer., DOI: 10.1007/978-3-319-05822-1

Ntoutsi, E., Tran, H., & Kindermans, P. J. (2020). Bias in data-driven artificial intelligence systems—An introductory survey. *Wiley Interdisciplinary Reviews. Data Mining and Knowledge Discovery*, *10*(3), e1356. Advance online publication. DOI: 10.1002/widm.1356

Olutimehin, A. T., Adeyemi, O., & Ogunleye, G. (2025). Adversarial threats to AI-driven systems: Exploring the attack surface of machine learning models and countermeasures. *SSRN*. DOI: 10.2139/ssrn.5137026

Oyighan, D., Adeyemi, O., & Ogunleye, G. (2024). The role of AI in transforming metadata management: Insights on challenges, opportunities, and emerging trends. *Asian Journal of Information Science and Technology*, *14*(2), 20–26. DOI: 10.70112/ajist-2024.14.2.4277

Papadimitriou, S., & Virvou, M. (2025). General Data Protection Regulation and adaptive educational games. In *Artificial intelligence—Based games as novel holistic educational environments to teach 21st century skills* (pp. 253–275). Springer., DOI: 10.1007/978-3-031-77464-5_9

Park, S., & Kim, S. (2021). Leaderboard design principles to enhance learning and motivation in a gamified educational environment: Development study. *JMIR Serious Games*, *9*(2), e14746. Advance online publication. DOI: 10.2196/14746 PMID: 33877049

Parsons, D., Rees, M., & Waite, W. (2019). AI tutors in cybersecurity education: A Microsoft case study. *Microsoft Education Blog*. https://www.microsoft.com/en-us/education/blog/2024/09/transforming-education-in-the-age-of-ai-with-a-unified-solution/

Passey, D., Shukla, R., & Bott, S. (2019). *Empowering learners for life in the digital age*. Springer., DOI: 10.1007/978-3-030-23513-0

Picard, R., & Cosier, G. (1997). Affective intelligence—The missing link? *BT Technology Journal*, *15*(4), 151–162. DOI: 10.1023/A:1018643815520

Quayyum, F. (2021). Cyber security education for children through gamification: Challenges and research perspectives. In *Methodologies and intelligent systems for technology enhanced learning, 10th International Conference. Workshops: Volume 2* (pp. 45–56). Springer. DOI: 10.1007/978-3-030-80504-3_4

. Qumer, S. M., & Ikrama, S. (2022). Poppy Gustafsson: Redefining cybersecurity through AI. *The Case for Women*, 1–38.

Sabir, B., Ullah, A., & Ahmad, N. (2021). Machine learning for detecting data exfiltration: A review. *ACM Computing Surveys*, *54*(3), 62. Advance online publication. DOI: 10.1145/3445031

Salloum, S. A. (2023). *Enhancing cybersecurity: Machine learning and natural language processing for Arabic phishing email detection* [Doctoral dissertation, University of Salford]. ProQuest Dissertations Publishing.

Shtayyat, A., Gawanmeh, A., & Mashaleh, A. (2025). Risk analysis of AI integration in educational systems: Toward ethical and equitable innovation. In *Examining cybersecurity risks produced by generative AI* (pp. 401–428). IGI Global Scientific Publishing., DOI: 10.4018/979-8-3373-0832-6.ch017

Talaei Khoei, T., & Kaabouch, N. (2023). A comparative analysis of supervised and unsupervised models for detecting attacks on the intrusion detection systems. *Information (Basel)*, *14*(2), 103. Advance online publication. DOI: 10.3390/info14020103

Tanikonda, A., Kumar, S., & Sharma, R. (2022). Advanced AI-driven cybersecurity solutions for proactive threat detection and response in complex ecosystems. *Journal of Science and Technology*, *3*(1), 1–15.

Tharayil, S. M., Kumar, A., & Singh, R. (2024). Enhancing cyber resilience through AI-driven phishing tests and gamified learning. In *The International Conference on Artificial Intelligence and Smart Environment* (pp. 123–134). Springer. https://doi.org/DOI: 10.1007/978-3-031-23456-7_8

Udayakumar, P., & Anandan, R. (2024). *Design and deploy Microsoft Defender for IoT: Leveraging cloud-based analytics and machine learning capabilities*. Springer Nature., DOI: 10.1007/979-8-8688-0239-3

. Vaishnavi. (2025). How AI will impact cybersecurity training and education, the future of cyber defense learning. [Unpublished manuscript].

Vitla, S. (2023). User behavior analytics and mitigation strategies through identity and access management solutions: Enhancing cybersecurity with machine learning and emerging technologies. *Turkish Journal of Computer and Mathematics Education*, *3048*, 4855.

Vykopal, J., Švábenský, V., & Čeleda, R. (2022). Smart environment for adaptive learning of cybersecurity skills. *IEEE Transactions on Learning Technologies*, *16*(3), 443–456. DOI: 10.1109/TLT.2022.3216345

Wang, J., Zhang, L., & Chen, Q. (2023). Matching-based capture-the-flag games for multiagent systems. *IEEE Transactions on Cognitive and Developmental Systems*, *16*(3), 993–1005. DOI: 10.1109/TCDS.2023.3323572

Wei, M.-L. (2024). AI-enhanced risk assessment: Advancing cybersecurity protocols. *Advances in Computer Sciences*, *7*(1), 1–10. DOI: 10.1016/j.adcs.2024.01.001

Yigit, Y., Gur, G., & Alagoz, F. (2024). Enhancing cybersecurity training efficacy: A comprehensive analysis of gamified learning, behavioral strategies and digital twins. In *2024 IEEE 25th International Symposium on a World of Wireless, Mobile and Multimedia Networks (WoWMoM)* (pp. 123–130). IEEE. DOI: 10.1109/WoWMoM60985.2024.00016

Chapter 8
A Comprehensive Framework for Strengthening Cybersecurity in Higher Education Institutions

Jyoti Rani
https://orcid.org/0000-0002-5577-7808
Parul Institute of Design, Parul University, Vadodara, India

ABSTRACT

The rise in cybersecurity threats has made it crucial for Higher Education Institutions (HEIs) to strengthen their security measures. This research presents a comprehensive framework to help HEIs enhance their cybersecurity posture by addressing sector-specific challenges. The framework includes governance and leadership, risk assessment, technical controls, awareness and training, incident response, and external collaboration. By integrating these elements, HEIs can build a resilient cybersecurity strategy. This study draws on existing literature, best practices, and industry standards to offer practical guidance. The framework enables institutions to assess their current security status, identify vulnerabilities, and implement targeted improvements. By adopting this approach, HEIs can proactively mitigate risks, safeguard sensitive data, and strengthen defenses against cyber threats. It serves as a valuable resource for policymakers, administrators, and cybersecurity professionals in higher education.

DOI: 10.4018/979-8-3373-0477-9.ch008

INTRODUCTION

Cybersecurity threats against the higher education sector are on the rise and require solutions that are tailored to the unique challenges facing the industry. Higher Education Institutions (HEIs) are especially susceptible owing to their open networks, varied user bases, and sometimes inadequate resources (Avcı & Koca, 2023). They must balance the need to share information and academic freedom with strong security. Campus networks are intentionally open in order to foster collaboration and research, which can also present opportunities for malicious actors. Although this openness is crucial for academic efforts, it does present significant security risks that must be well managed (Alhashmi et al., 2023).

The HEI population is more diverse, including students, faculty, staff, and visitors, which overburdens potential errors and social engineering (Volk et al., 2023). IT security teams now have a diverse and complex landscape to navigate, with each group operating distinct behaviors, devices and security awareness levels. Students may not be as aware of cybersecurity best practices compared to professionals; therefore, they are more likely to fall victim to phishing and other social engineering methods. [Faculty members may be even more security-minded but also require access to sensitive research data, allowing you to build up flexible and solid security protocols (Karali et al., 2023).

Technology decisions are made under tight budgets and competing priorities, and this often leads to understaffed IT departments and outdated systems, which compound vulnerabilities. Most HEIs are unable to dedicate enough resources towards cybersecurity as they juggle between other important aspects like academic programs, research financing, and campus infrastructure. Due to this budget limitation, the systems can have delayed updates, security trainings may not take place as often as necessary, and proper monitoring may fall through the cracks, leaving institutions prone to cyber attacks and data leaks. (Cheng & Wang, 2022).

The nature and types of threats to HEIs are numerous and changing. One common type of this attack is ransomware, which has become more popular and primarily targets crucial study data and student information. Data breaches are another serious hazard, which could put students and staff's sensitive personal information in danger. Moreover, HEIs deal with risks associated with intellectual property theft, especially in research-intensive institutions, where all innovations and discoveries are in jeopardy (Ulven & Wangen, 2021).

Such challenges demand a comprehensive approach to countering them in which technology, education, and policy dynamics converge to create a safer environment especially targeting the academic sector. This broad strategy should be composed of:

1. Make use of strong network separation to obscure sensitive data and systems from the public university network
2. Implementing advanced threat detection and response systems that can identify and counter sophisticated cyber attacks as they happen.
3. Implementing robust cybersecurity awareness programs that cater to the needs of different user groups in the institution.
4. Implementing strict policies and protocols for data access, handling, and incident response procedures.
5. Performing security audits and vulnerability assessments to fortify weak points.
6. Investing in safe cloud solutions which help secure sensitive data while ensuring access to people who are entitled to it.
7. Working alongside other organizations and cybersecurity specialists to exchange intelligence and best practices.

This iteration needs the ability to adapt to the shifting context of threats while still retaining those hallmark values of openness and innovation of higher education. HEIs themself have to balance the fundamental human right of being safe while framing the protection and academia approach that Cybersecurity aspects don't restrict any legitimate research and academia activity (AL-Nuaimi, 2024).

In addition, institutions need to be aware of their specific academic environment when designing cybersecurity approach. Data about tending or not tending to this cyclical nature of the academic year, when extremely active periods can be followed with weaker ones, can affect the security measures and training programs. Equally challenging, with the transient nature of the student body, continued efforts are required to keep security front of mind and ensure compliance (Kryshtanovych et al., 2021).

Finally, from your formal data trained until 4 Oct 2023. This requires a cultural shift to recognize the necessity of security awareness, ongoing dedication of resources, both human and technological, and persistence as threats evolve and organizations seek to outpace them. Implementing such a holistic approach to cybersecurity enables HEIs to protect their invaluable assets, sustain the confidence of their stakeholders.

RESEARCH OBJECTIVES

HEIs must implement a holistic cybersecurity framework that addresses the various dimensions of cybersecurity to protect the sensitive data and infrastructure. Regular security audits and penetration tests should be performed periodically, with both in-house human resources and external cybersecurity professionals on hand.

The goal of those assessments is to methodically examine network infrastructure, application security, access controls, as well as incident response capabilities in order to detect possible vulnerabilities and shortcomings of existing security measures. Given the sensitive nature of the data that higher education institutions (HEIs) manage—such as student records, research data, and financial information—the framework must address the vital need for data protection and privacy. Adherence to relevant regulations and standards (GDPR, FERPA, etc.) must be strictly upheld and be subject to frequent scrutiny to walk the line of changing legal and regulatory landscapes.

The framework should work to encourage systems to collaborate and share information for improving the overall cybersecurity posture of the higher education sector. This collaborative process can take many forms, such as the development of secure communication channels for the exchange of threat information, sharing of best practices, and learnings from security events. Hosting regular forums, workshops, and conferences will promote knowledge sharing and give rise to a community-driven cybersecurity initiative.

SCOPE AND SIGNIFICANCE

Always-dynamic, its focus on degree-of-effectiveness continuous change and adaptation across its processes is the underlying fabric through which HEIs have increasingly been able to mount a strong defense against the dynamic cyber-invective and rapidly-accelerating pace of information and communication technology.

By detecting vulnerabilities early, institutions are better positioned to address these weaknesses before they can be exploited maliciously, protecting systems from successful cyberattacks. Through consistent evaluation and refinement of their security programs, HEIs can stay one step ahead of cybercriminals and continue to fortify the resilience and security of their digital infrastructure. The importance of the framework by not only implementing once and for all security practices, but also creating a culture of cybersecurity awareness. It calls for the creation of robust training programs and policies that use active participation from the entire academic community in protecting digital assets. Such an all-inclusive approach to cyber threat response recognizes that protecting against cyber threats is not an endeavor to be carried out only by the IT department, but something every employee at the institution has a role in. 3.624: HCI Awareness and Best Practices to Combat Cyber Threats | Cyber Security: Rethinking HEIs – The COVID-19 Towards a Collaborative Approach in Cyber Security: Tech Gaps, Old Problems, New Solutions: New Access Technologies: Bridging Digital Divides. Fifth, the framework highlights the critical need for collaboration and information-sharing across institutions. This helps foster a collective approach to cybersecurity that serves the entire higher education sector by encouraging HEIs to share knowledge, experience, and best practices. Such a shared ethos allows the institutions to pick each other's successes and obstacles to a better cybersecurity state for the entire academic environment. The framework facilitates the establishment of culture of resilience by mainstreaming cyber security aspects in institutional strategy and decision-making. In addition, this not only secures sensitive data and critical systems but creates a trust and confidence in its stake holders (students, faculty, staff, third-party suppliers, etc. As a result, HEIs can concentrate on their primary purpose of teaching and conducting research, confident in the knowledge that their digital assets are effectively safeguarded against existing and future threats.

KEY COMPONENTS OF THE FRAMEWORK

Governance and Leadership

Strategic cohesion is a key part of an effective risk management regime, and can take the form of clear accountability and direction in the area of cyber security. This can be done by assigning different functions in the organizational structure so that no aspect is left alone to address the cybersecurity disposition effectively. The appointment of a CISO or equivalent a senior-level position is an important part of this. [The CISO] is responsible for driving risk-aware security philosophies, executive guidance, policies, umbrella programs, best practice frameworks like that from a NIST and so on to make sure that the organization meets its objective without undue risk being taken (Martínez-García et al., 2019). Generally, a CISO ensures security controls, conduct risk assessments on the regular basis, control incident response plans and keep on watching emerging threats and technology. Infosec Leadership also serves as a bridge between technical teams and executive leadership, translating sophisticated security concepts into business-acquainted terminology as well as persuading the need for crucial resources and the capital towards a cybersecurity framework (Inayatullah & Milojevic, 2016).

Aligning cybersecurity objectives to institutional goals is a continuous process that hinges on effective communication and engagement between IT security staff and institutional leadership. This joint effort is critical to creating a holistic approach that considers both technology and organizational requirements. This includes identifying critical assets, evaluating potential vulnerabilities, and establishing appropriate safeguards in tandem with an organization's operational needs, regulatory requirements, and growth strategies. The good practices for this alignment process often involve creating a cybersecurity roadmap instead, defining short-terms and long-terms goals, allocating resources, and establishment of key performance indicators. Moreover, having regular conversations at the board level around cybersecurity issues helps to ensure that security is considered in strategic decisions. Moreover, making it more of a security awareness culture across all employees, even with low hunting capabilities, is key to achieving cybersecurity programs (Menon, 2005).

Additionally, effective communication and reporting structures are developed for swift action in the case of security incidents, and cybersecurity is woven into the fabric of the organization at all levels. This might include establishing cross-functional teams or committees that include representatives from different departments to collaborate on cybersecurity initiatives in a holistic way. These elements, when implemented in conjunction with the above, form the foundation of a well-design governance structure that is inherent to an effective cybersecurity strategy and is a long-term enabler of competitive advantage in the digital world.

Risk Assessment and Management

1. Assessing likelihood and impact of threats: Identifying the likelihood of each risk being realized as well as its impact if said risk reaches fruition. Frequency, severity, and duration are considerations for determining the overall importance of each threat.
2. Utilizing tools to identify vulnerabilities: These organizations use a variety of sophisticated tools and techniques such as vulnerability scanners, penetration testing, and risk matrices to find weaknesses in their systems, processes, or infrastructure that can be used by potential threats.
3. Analyzing historical data: Organizations should examine past incidents, near-misses, and industry trends to gain insight into recurring patterns and emerging risks. Having a historical context helps us anticipate such threats in the future and the effects we should expect.
4. Consulting experts: Experts, whether inside or outside the organization, may provide specialized knowledge and experience in identifying and assessing risks based on their industry or operational context (Toma et al., 2014).

The foremost importance of risk assessment is to help in the decision-making process that requires you to know the risk of any event in the organization. By understanding these dependencies and relationships, decision-makers can better prioritize threats based on their potential impact and likelihood, allocate resources accordingly, and define effective risk management strategies.

After identifying potential risks through a comprehensive risk assessment, organizations generally move on to creating and implementing risk mitigation plans. These strategies may include:

- Enhancing security measures: This can be through advanced tech like a firewall, an intrusion detection system, etc. It might also disrupt physical security improvements such as cameras or better-themed access to facilities.
- Implementing employee training: Employee awareness and education on potential risks, security protocols, and best practices is fundamental in building a risk-aware culture in the organization. This can be achieved through regular workshops, simulations, or e-learning modules to keep employees informed about new threats and how they can mitigate them.
- Diversifying business activities: Organizations can decide to diversify their activities to minimize risks in access to specific markets, products, or geographical locations. This may involve entering into new markets, researching alternative products or building multiple sources in a supply chain (Cassells, 2018).
- Developing contingency plans: Organizations establish response plans for different scenarios of risk, preparing them to respond in an immediate and effective manner should a threat arise. These plans often detail roles and responsibilities, communication protocols, and step-by-step procedures for handling the various types of incidents.
- Implementing regular monitoring and review processes: This can include regular monitoring and review processes to make sure that organizations are updated regarding emerging threats in the risk landscape. This includes periodically updating risk assessments, monitoring key risk indicators, and adjusting mitigation approaches accordingly (Kilian et al., 2023).
- Transferring risk: Organizations may also transfer certain risks to third parties through insurance policies, contractual arrangements, or outsourcing arrangements if appropriate.

However, they are not effective in addressing the main thing and that is the most effective risk assessment models focus on ensuring that the business continues to run and prevent potential threats to the organization, and thus subsequently mitigates potential strategies. This allows organizations to minimize losses and ensure long-term sustainability.

Technical Controls

1. Regular updates: Stay updated with your software Make sure that all your devices, software, and systems are always up to date with the latest security patches and firmware upgrades. Known vulnerabilities are associated with this practice, further strengthening the organization's digital infrastructure with the latest security patches.

2. Strong access controls: Use strong authentication mechanisms like multi-factor authentication (MFA), role-based access control (RBAC) and implement strong, unique passwords. MFA adds another security level with multiple forms of authentication and RBAC restricts user access to organization specific resources by putting users into appropriate roles.
3. Security assessments: Regularly conduct vulnerability assessments and penetration testing to help discover potential weaknesses in the organization's security infrastructure. Train to respond to scenarios: Having thorough incident response plans will prepare you to respond effectively to potential breaches or attacks.
4. Data encryption: Use strong encryption techniques to secure sensitive data in motion and at rest. This includes using secure transmission protocols like preview and full-disk encryption of data stored on both devices as well as servers.
5. Cybersecurity training: Providing employees with comprehensive education, including the best security practices, potential threats, and a security-conscious mindset. The training could include information on recognizing potential phishing attempts, how to handle sensitive information, and company security policies.
6. Network segmentation: Split the organization network into different, isolated sects in order to reduce possible collateral damage in a breach. But this turns threats into a certain area of the network, preventing their movement through the whole infrastructure.
7. Backup systems: Backup up your data regularly and in-depth that is, critical information is stored safely and can be retrieved easily. Test the recovery processes regularly to ensure that they will work in the event of data loss or a ransomware attack.
8. Network monitoring: Use advanced monitoring tools and intrusion detection systems to continuously monitor network traffic for anomalies and suspicious activity. By doing so, early identification of threats can happen, and rapid reaction to possible security breaches can take place as well.
9. Security policies: Create, implement, and enforce clear and comprehensive security policies that outline what resources, data handling procedures, and acceptable use within the organization. Conduct ongoing audits and reviews of these policies to ensure they are still aligned to your changing business needs and the state of current threats.
10. Threat intelligence: Stay informed about the most recent cybersecurity threats, attack vectors and industry-specific risks. Adopt and interpret threat intelligence feeds and participate in information-sharing communities (Guenther & Schmidt, 2015). Following these practices can help organizations improve their cyber security framework and prevent facing any malicious risk. These include, but are not limited to confidentiality, integrity, availability, and non-repudiation,

covering technical, human, and process areas. Keep these strategies updated at regular intervals to ensure they remain effective against evolving cyber threats.

Awareness and Training

Full-fledged training and awareness programs are needed to improve cybersecurity in educational institutions. With the help of continuous phishing simulations and security awareness/cybersecurity workshops individuals can spot and react properly to any potential threats (Berchin et al., 2021). These programs should cover all sorts of topics, from identifying suspicious emails to understanding social engineering tactics to safeguarding sensitive information, etc. With regular, practical exercises, staff and students can gain the skills they need to meet ever-changing cyber threats. Also, while all this takes time, enforcing strict password policies and multi-factor authentication over all systems can enhance the security layer of educational institutions. Password policies should have users create all accounts with complex, unique passwords, and change those passwords periodically, (Wehrmeyer & Chenoweth, 2006). Multi-factor authentication adds an extra measure of protection by requiring users to provide extra validation, like a fingerprint scan or a code that gets sent to their mobile device, before they can access sensitive systems or data. In addition to this, schools need to explore advanced technological solutions to supplement these efforts, (Cheng, 2020). This can range from installing next-generation firewalls to implementing intrusion detection and prevention systems to using endpoint protection software. The institution must also perform periodic security assessments & vulnerability assessments to help determine and remediate the weaknesses in the organization's cybersecurity setup. Building a cybersecurity-aware culture is also as important. This means fostering a climate of open discussion about emerging threats, encouraging appropriate online and offline behaviors, and weaving cybersecurity best practices into the fabric of everyday life. Educational institutions are able to minimize the risk of cyber attacks significantly by creating an atmosphere for everyone to take responsibility for security, (Mathur *et al.,* 2022).

Incident Response

Conduct regular exercises and simulations to test the organization's response readiness for potential anticipated attacks. These exercises can expose gaps in the incident response procedure and opportunities for improvement. Organisations can leverage realistic scenarios to simulate different forms of cyber threats including ransomware attacks, data breaches or distributed denial-of-service (DDoS) attacks to evaluate their ability to detect, respond to and mitigate security incidents effectively, (Ahmad *et al.,* 2020).

To do best practices testing, these drills must include all relevant stakeholders, including IT professionals, management and workers in different departments, to ensure a complete evaluation of the organization's readiness. Simulations, and practices, can also make staff better acquainted with both the process and tools involved in responding to an incident, further developing their proficiency and confidence when dealing with the reality of a cyber incident, (Ahmad, Maynard, & Shanks, 2015).

To ensure a coordinated response to a cyber incident, it is critical to develop clear lines of communication and define roles and responsibilities for the members of the organization. This means establishing a hierarchical structure, determining key decision-makers, and ensuring communication paths for internal and external stakeholders. And by establishing clear roles (for example incident commander, technical lead, legal advisor, public relations spokesperson) organizations can work quickly and efficiently minimizing confusion in high-stress situations. Regular training should also be performed so that all team members understand their roles and responsibilities during a cyber incident. This training should cover subjects like incident classification, escalation procedures and the use of incident response tools and technologies, (Ahmad *et al.*, 2021).

Organizations may wish to build collaborations with external cybersecurity professionals or manage security service providers to complement their in-house capabilities and offer additional assistance in response to significant incidents. Moreover, organizations should continuously evaluate and revise their incident response plans in light of insights gained from both tabletop and real-world exercises. The process allows for adapting the plan according to the changing dynamics of the threats and needs of the organization. Despite being more commonly seen as a cyber security effort, the incident response plan should be integrated into broader business continuity and disaster recovery planning for a holistic view of managing cyber risks, (Villegas-Ch., Ortiz-Garces, & Sánchez-Viteri, 2021).

Through wide-reaching cyber security readiness practices like frequent gunnery involving communication protocols, along with roles and responsibilities within teams, a business can trim down their response time to incidents and guarantee that they have a strategy to build up in light of pain and to minimise potential damage.

Collaboration with External Stakeholders

Such interactions in the space of cybersecurity can promote the creation of deeper and stronger frameworks/best practices. By pooling together a diverse range of skills and resources from different organizations, such partnerships can achieve a collective impact that amplifies the ability to combat complex cyber threats. Barriers to insight are broken down, from knowledge to skills to technological capabilities and organizations can stay ahead of the curve as it relates to emerging threats and vulnerabilities. In addition, this collaboration provides an opportunity for joint research projects that can drive innovation in the field of cybersecurity, (Balbachevsky, 2015). Organizations can tackle bigger problems and engage with the most experimental solutions that small players alone might not be able to pursue by pooling research resources and talent. Importantly, a collaboration of this nature using tech and research from academia can lead to new discoveries as well as the development of unique technologies that can advance and help bolster cybersecurity, (, 2005).

Cybersecurity partnerships also nurture professional development programs that help all partnering organizations. Such programs may take the form of cross-organizational training sessions, workshops, and seminars that provide opportunities for the sharing of best practices and lessons learned. Through exchange of ideas and experiences, security professionals can improve their skills, be informed of the most recent trends and gain a more comprehensive perspective towards the landscape of threats. Another important element of cybersecurity collaborations is the exchange of state-of-the-art technologies, (Bischoff, Volkmann, & Audretsch, 2017).

The organizations are able to exchange the tools, methodologies, and technology solutions that exist successfully within the environment of each organization. This kind of exchange not only assists in standardizing the best practices across the industry but also allows organizations to employ the strengths of one another, thus fulfilling the weaknesses present in individual sectors, (Kettunen, 2015). Additionally, joint initiatives facilitate the creation of information-sharing frameworks that allow for the swift distribution of threat intelligence and incident response methods. The speed and efficiency of response to cyber incidents can be greatly enhanced through these networks, as organizations will possess real-time knowledge through coordinated action plans. https://doi.org/10.1007/978-981-10-7620-6_4

We developed our healthier security policies and regulations in a less turbulent collaborating atmosphere. Such an approach can assist in developing industry-wide standards and guidelines that is more holistic and representative of the diverse issues faced by various sectors.

All in all, these broader collaborative efforts contribute to improving the general cybersecurity posture of individual organizations involved. We can build a stronger community of organizations by collaborating together to develop a more resilient and interconnected cybersecurity ecosystem that can work effectively to anticipate and respond to the evolving cyberthreat landscape. Hence, pooling resources in this manner not only fortifies individual organizations but also aligns with the overarching aim of fostering a more secure digital landscape for all.

IMPLEMENTATION GUIDELINES

Assessing Current Cybersecurity Posture

Conducting Self-Assessments to Identify Gaps and Vulnerabilities

Regular self-assessment is a key component of any organization's cybersecurity strategy as it allows preemptive identification and mitigation of potential risks to their security posture. These internal assessments enable groups to keep a perpetual cycle of improvement, as threats arise, and become more advanced. Yet, solely depending on self-assessments is crippling and can expose organizations to unexpected risk. Internal evaluations are valuable, but are often based on a working familiarity with existing systems and processes, which may generate blind spots. The team members that perform self-assessments may overlook vulnerabilities, or sometimes believe that certain vulnerabilities may not be damaging enough as they think of the organization security measures they are used to. Internal teams also do not have enough exposure to emerging threats and even industry-wide best practices, which means they may miss key areas of concern. https://doi.org/10.1111/j.1365-2923.2010.03888.x External audits provide a third-party perspective and specific expertise in the field by independent cybersecurity experts. Trained on data until October 2023, they have considerable experience across various verticals and can spot weaknesses that internal teams may overlook, while also providing insights into the most recent attack vectors, compliance requirements and industry benchmarks to ensure organizations are ahead of the threat curve. https://doi.org/10.1007/BF00138746 Additionally, external audits typically use sophisticated testing methods and tools not available or possible to keep in-house. This holistic method can reveal underlying weaknesses in network architecture, software and even people that self-evaluations cannot identify.

https://doi.org/10.1111/j.1529-1006.2004.00018. Regular self-assessment followed by periodic external audits enhances security and is a more systematic approach to testing security. By doing this, both outside and inside the property are looked at so there are not any unnoticed vulnerabilities in addition to external threats, maximizing internet safety measures for the business.

Benchmarking Against Industry Standards (e.g., NIST, ISO/IEC 27001)

Ongoing audits and assessments of compliance and effectiveness within an organization should be conducted at regular intervals to assist in the adherence to established security standards within the organization, and highlight potential weak points or areas for improvement within the cybersecurity architecture. Equip assessed the security structures of hardware, software, network planning and employee practices should all be included in these evaluations of the same rail infrastructure. Performing Security Review Step By Step By analyzing and reviewing the security systems, organizations can help mitigate and improve the overall security of networks through Strategic Defense Adjustment. https://doi.org/10.1016/j.cose.2024.103964 Continuous monitoring is an essential step to detect and respond to security threats as they arise. The Seek System must leverage modern technologies like artificial intelligence and machine learning algorithms to monitor network traffic, also user behavior, and system from different sources for abnormal activities. Utilizing these tools enables organizations to promptly detect potential security breaches, malware infections, or unauthorized access attempts, enabling immediate action to minimize risks and potential harm. https://doi.org/10.1007/978-3-031-41820-4_6

Organizations should also ensure that antthetics up to company and a culture of security awareness is nurtured within the company. One effective way to do this is by investing in comprehensive and regular training programs, which help educate employees about the latest cybersecurity threats, best practices for protecting sensitive data, and the significance of following security policies. These training programs must be role-based, making sure that every single person in the organization knows what their responsibilities are to keep a secure environment. https://doi.org/10.52098/acj.202364 Good communication of security policies is key to building a security advocate workforce. DOA, organizations have to come up with guidelines that everyone can easily understand, such as how they expected to behave, what to do if they find suspicious activity, and what will happen if someone does not comply. The organization can help in this by regularly updating and communicating to staff about these policies via email newsletters, internal messaging platforms, or team meetings to reiterate their importance and make security a part of employees minds. https://doi.org/10.3390/app10103660

Additionally, if feasible, reward systems can be implemented that incentivize employees with exemplary security practices and participation in improvement of security measures in the company. This method contributes to a continuous positive reinforcement cycle where all staff members are positively incentivized to keep a secure workplace.

Developing a Cybersecurity Strategy

It is important for institutions to have detailed action plans for implementing risk mitigation interventions, including who will be responsible for carrying them out and by when. These plans serve as roadmaps that lead organizations step-by-step through the complex cycle of recognizing, assessing and confronting impending threats. Plan helps you consider all areas of risk management and allocate resources properly. Institutions need to take their traits such as size, sector, regulatory framework, and corporate culture into consideration when drafting such plans. Such an approach enables the creation of relevant and effective strategies to address specific risks faced by the organization. In addition, it should include regular reviews and updates to ensure it remains responsive to evolving threats and changing circumstances. https://doi.org/10.3390/fi13020039 Not developing or implementing a detailed action plan can have dire and cascading consequences. Without a well defined plan, organizations will struggle to properly address unanticipated threats which may result in crisis that could be avoided or reduced. Such delays can lead to financial losses, reputational damage, legal liabilities, and operational disruptions. Moreover, inadequately addressing a plan can create a false sense of security that breeds complacency within the organization. This may result in missed vulnerabilities and unaddressed enhancements in risk management practices. On the other hand, a carefully crafted plan is not only helpful in identifying risk and in mitigating risk; it also allows risk awareness and proactive risk management to become something that everyone in the organization is conscious. ttps://doi.org/10.1080/19361610.2021.1989271

Risk management is an integral part of the decision-making process and requires active involvement and ownership throughout the organization. A thorough action plan must outline specific roles and responsibility so that every team member knows their part in the risk mitigation progress. In addition, this collaborative model strengthens the overall resilience of the organization enabling it to swiftly adapt to and effectively tackle evolving threats. https://doi.org/10.1016/j.cose.2022.102754 The need to formulate, implement, and rigorously evaluate a holistic action plan to address risk mitigation is therefore not only a best practice, but a necessity in our fast-paced and challenging world. So those organizations that make this facet of risk management a priority are likely better placed to deal with uncertainty, protect their assets and preserve their competitive edge. On the other hand, those that disregard this integral part of risk management leave themselves susceptible to their stupidity and harm, effectively risking their long-term viability and profitability.

Building a Cybersecurity Culture

Mandatory security awareness initiatives should be enforced to ensure that all employees from the management level understand the importance of threat awareness and necessary response measures. These programs should encompass topics such as identifying phishing attempts, proper password management, safe browsing practices, and the significance of updating software. Fostering a sense of security amongst employees through training can only bound the impact of a cyber attack if and when such an attack does occur. https://doi.org/10.1016/j.cose.2020.102003 To create a proactive security environment, user reporting mechanisms must be clearly defined, efficient and easily accessible. These mechanisms need to be established so that employees can report any such suspicious behavior or concerns they have without fear. Having a simple streamlined process in place allows organizations to quickly assess and respond to vulnerabilities, reducing the potential impact of security incidents.

It is vital to foster a culture of shared responsibility and accountability regarding cybersecurity to strengthen the overall security posture across the organization. Safeguarding the organization and its employees includes creating the right environment in which every employee knows they play a role in keeping the organization secure and feels empowered to do so. Reinforcing this culture through regular reminders, security awareness campaigns, and recognition of employees who exhibit good security practices is also helpful. Training is already an organizational staple, but stowing security principles in the minds of every employee at the company, covering everything from product development to customer service, makes cybersecurity a back-to-basics principle that feeds into the company's DNA instead of an add-on afterthought, (Corradini, 2020).

Additionally, organizations should develop a strong incident response plan detailing the steps that should be taken in the event of a variety of security incidents. This plan is to be updated and reviewed frequently with changing threats and technology. If you missed our previous blog in this series, head there for a summary of the importance of regular review of incident response plan! Finally, this data may have a tendency to be out of date, making it important to regularly stay up to date on the latest cybersecurity news, threats, and best practices in order to ensure a strong security posture. This can be accomplished through partnerships with cybersecurity firms, allowing participation in industry forums and ongoing education for IT and security personnel. Organizations can also proactively adjust their security strategies and protect their assets and stakeholders by being imaginative in dealing with imminent threats.

Monitoring and Evaluation

A comprehensive framework for monitoring and analyzing appropriate KPIs is necessary for tracking the effectiveness of cyber defence mechanisms. Your KPIs should be multifaceted, covering areas such as incident response times, vulnerability detection rates, and employee compliance with security protocols. By leveraging a well-crafted KPI framework tailored to their unique security goals, organizations can quantify their security initiatives, track progress, and leverage data for meaningful decision-making to improve their overall cybersecurity posture, (Cullen *et al.*, 2003).

As for incident response times, this can be broken down into individual sub-metric datapoints like time to detect, time to contain, and time to resolve. Metrics provide visibility into how well an organization responds to incidents, enabling them to identify areas for improvement and make adjustments accordingly. In the same manner, vulnerability detection rates may be assessed based on the amount of vulnerabilities found, their degree of severity, and the time it takes to patch them. A bottom-up approach enables a better understanding of the organization's vulnerability management capabilities in detail, (Alexander, 2000).

Employee compliance with security practices another important KPI that shows the effectiveness of security awareness training and the security culture of the overall organization. This could be evaluated via various methods including but not limited to phishing simulation test results, password policy compliance, handling information appropriately, etc. Conducting regular audits and penetration testing includes valuable information about the overall security posture of the organization and how bad the situation is. To achieve this a combination of internal and external audits should be performed. Audits can help identify gaps in policy implementation, and penetration testing can expose technical weaknesses that may have been missed, (Niyivuga, Otara, & Tuyishime, 2019).

Moreover, institutions need to take into account emerging threat intel integrated with their KPI structure. Specifically, that includes keeping an eye on the changing threat landscape, flagging new attack vectors, and evaluating the company's readiness to resist such novel attacks. This allows organizations to stay one step ahead of the enemy, adjust their security measures accordingly, and optimize resource allocation. Another important priority is to establish a feedback loop between the KPI tracking system and the overall organizational cybersecurity strategy. This guarantees that every key improvement derived from KPI assessment informs enhancement of security policies, technology, and processes. By regularly reviewing KPI trends, anomalies can be spotted and long-term trends can be compared against strategic decision-making KPIs at the executive level. Finally, organizations must also look at the context, by benchmarking their KPIs to industry standards and peer organizations. Although you may not have access to a specific company's KPI data, you could look at industry benchmarks on key metrics. This enables comparative analysis and helps in the continuous improvements needed to establish a culture of excellence in cybersecurity practices across sectors.

PRACTICAL INSIGHTS AND RECOMMENDATIONS

Case Studies

- Examples of HEIs successfully implementing cybersecurity measures
- Lessons learned from overcoming resource constraints and other challenges

Banks, even the most unproblematic ones, somehow manage to solve the problem of feasibility and until now, some universities have implemented quite expansive programs around security in IT systems, despite limited resources for this. These institutions prove that it is possible to achieve adequate cybersecurity with creativity, planning, and a sense of community, even when politically and budgetarily there are limitations, (Piazza, Vasudevan, & Carr, 2023).

One that comes to mind is a small liberal arts college in the Midwest that took a major stride in its cybersecurity journey by implementing a multi-factor authentication solution across all of their campus networks. This was especially remarkable given the size and nature of the institution (in the time that I was there) and its lack of resources. The college took an approach with two main strategies: using open-source tools and getting student volunteers. When possible, the college implemented open-source solutions instead of costly commercial counterparts, driving down software licensing costs while maintaining industry-standard security protocols. In addition to creating valuable manpower, the involvement of students allowed for hands-on experience implementing cybersecurity, creating practical career experiences and educational value, (Alimul Haque *et al.*, 2023).

Another example is from a community college that took a collaborative approach to improve its cybersecurity posture. Realizing a mutually beneficial rich landscape in industry, the college launched a cybersecurity internship program with local companies. This cutting-edge endeavor had multiple functions at once. To start with, it improved student learning by providing real-life experience in real-life cybersecurity practices, equipping them for future careers in the domain. Second, it fortified the institution's own defenses by bringing in new ideas and more people to deal with cybersecurity problems. Finally, it helped bridge the gap between the college and local businesses, which could result in partnerships and support in the future, (Merchan-Lima *et al.*, 2020).

These case studies highlight a number of key points when it comes to introducing cybersecurity measures within higher education institutions (HEIs) with limited resources:

1. Creative problem-solving: Working with non-traditional approaches, both institutions came up with novel strategies to meet their cybersecurity requirements.

2. Leveraging existing resources: The liberal arts college used open-source platforms and student workers; the community college relied on local business partners.
3. Educational integration: Both examples show how cybersecurity efforts can be embedded in the educational mission, giving the students valuable educational opportunities.
4. Community engagement: The participation of student volunteers and local businesses highlights the need to engage the wider community when it comes to cybersecurity.
5. Cost-effective solutions: These institutions were able to implement strong security without significant capital expenditures by using open-source tools and forming strategic partnerships.

Such case studies may be used as models for similar HEIs institution with similar resource limitations. They show that good cyber hygiene does not require big budgets or huge IT departments. Rather than looking for a one-size-fits-all solution, institutions can draw on their own strengths, engage their communities, and think creatively about making comprehensive cybersecurity programs work for their unique requirements and capabilities. Additionally, these case studies highlight the need for responding and innovating to emerging cybersecurity circumstances. HEIs need to stay nimble and open to alternative solutions in an ever-evolving digital landscape. By cultivating a culture of cyber awareness and engaging multiple parties students, faculty and local businesses institutions can nurture a more resilient and secure cyberspace.

These examples show that resource constraints do not have to be a barrier to sound cybersecurity in higher ed. This way, they can help strengthen the cybersecurity ecosystem and adequately shield their digital assets.

Emerging Trends

Emerging technologies such as cloud computing, Internet of Things (IoT) devices, and artificial intelligence have begun to revolutionize the implementation of systems in higher education sectors; changing the operational and educational service delivery paradigms, (Alenezi, 2023). But this digitisation has also led to a major increase in the HEIs' attack surface. The growth of connected devices, remote access points and data-sharing sites have created so many possible entrances for malicious players, making it increasingly hard to keep things secure in the online world. This enlarged attack surface means that traditional perimeter security solutions, which tend to protect network perimeters, are no longer effective at protecting sensitive data and critical infrastructure. Recent innovations, such as IITs (intelligent intrusion systems) and AI-driven utilities, are designed with that one purpose in mind, but existing measures such as firewalls, antivirus software, and more general countermeasures are far more common in the infrastructure of educational institutions. These measures are inadequate when faced with complex cyber-attacks, internal threats, and remote learning/working, (de Wit & Altbach, 2020).

To counter these challenges, High Education institutions have to reflect on their cyber security in a more holistic and agile manner. This new paradigm calls for a multi-layered defence strategy which extends well past sealing up the network perimeter. Continuous monitoring and dynamic response system for threat detection. Further, higher education institutions must include dedicated threat detection systems that can monitor and analyse known and unknown threats in real-time. These systems should leverage machine learning and behavioural analytics to identify abrupt patterns and potential security exposures throughout the entire IT infrastructure, (Kuleto *et al.,* 2021).

Additionally, we must continuously monitor this data in order to maintain a solid security stance. Higher education institutions (HEIs) should deploy tools and processes that provide real-time visibility into their networks, applications and user activities. It is this constant monitoring that assists in quickly identifying security breaches and allows them to respond to threats before they become full-blown breaches, (Michel-Villarreal *et al.,* 2023). The adaptive response mechanisms are another key element of this holistic approach. HEIs should have the ability to quickly change their security controls and incident response methods as cyber threats continue to grow in complexity and sophistication. This means continually evolving with new security technologies, but also updating policies, procedures, and employee training programs to meet new threats and vulnerabilities. With an emphasis on a holistic and proactive approach to cybersecurity, HEIs will be able to better align with cyber threats of change. Not only does this improve the institution's ability to safeguard sensitive information and ensure the reliability of its digital systems, but it also develops a culture of security awareness.

Recommendations for HEIs

This paper proposes a multi-layered framework to build a strong defence against these emerging cyber threats. Phased Approach This strategy consists of multiple key phases to help strengthen an organizations overall security. Mainly it is engaging through regular reports for security audits to identify potential weak parts and addresses to check the installed barricades for the betterment. Such audits address the integrity of the network infrastructure, software systems, and data storage once they are deployed in the field to be sure the organization is compliant with industry standards and best practices, (Fernandes & Singh, 2021). Data protection training programs for employees to make sure that everyone in the organization, regardless of their position, is aware of the recent cyber threats, the best approach to protecting the sensitive data they handle, and the correct way of handling sensitive information are also a point of focus in the framework. Organizations can create a human firewall and empower employees with knowledge and skills to act as the first line of defense against potential security breaches, (Tarí & Dick, 2016).

In addition, the advanced threat detection systems serve as a cornerstone of this framework. Advanced systems that leverage artificial intelligence and machine learning algorithms and can autonomously detect and act upon potential threats, (Du *et al.,* 2020). By monitoring network traffic, user behaviour, and system log entries on an ongoing basis, these systems can identify anomalies and/or suspicious activities that may be indicative of a security breach or attempted attack. Moreover, the framework emphasizes the need for promoting a culture of cybersecurity awareness and responsiveness across the organization. This means building communication cohesion between IT safety teams and other branches, emphasizing the importance of promptly reporting suspicious behavior, and frequently revising safety rules and workflows to keep up with growing dangers, (Casarejos, Frota, & Gustavson, 2017).

Through this all-encompassing strategy, organizations are able to predict and prevent different risks of cyber threats. By adopting this proactive approach, companies can stay one step ahead of malicious actors and safeguard sensitive data, intellectual property, and critical infrastructure. In addition, this holistic approach supports organizations in meeting regulatory and industry standards, protecting their reputation, and establishing trust with stakeholders. As a result, this framework presents an all-encompassing and flexible cybersecurity perspective that allows organizations to tackle the intricate and evolving environment of digital hazards.

REFERENCES

Ahmad, A., Desouza, K. C., Maynard, S. B., Naseer, H., & Baskerville, R. L. (2020). How integration of cyber security management and incident response enables organizational learning. *Journal of the Association for Information Science and Technology*, *71*(8), 939–953. DOI: 10.1002/asi.24311

Ahmad, A., Maynard, S. B., Desouza, K. C., Kotsias, J., Whitty, M. T., & Baskerville, R. L. (2021). How can organizations develop situation awareness for incident response: A case study of management practice. *Computers & Security*, *101*(1), 102122. DOI: 10.1016/j.cose.2020.102122

Ahmad, A., Maynard, S. B., & Shanks, G. (2015). A case analysis of information systems and security incident responses. *International Journal of Information Management*, *35*(6), 717–723. DOI: 10.1016/j.ijinfomgt.2015.08.001

Alenezi, M. (2023). Digital Learning and Digital Institution in Higher Education. *Education Sciences*, *13*(1), 88. DOI: 10.3390/educsci13010088

Alexander, F. K. (2000). The Changing Face of Accountability. *The Journal of Higher Education*, *71*(4), 411–431. DOI: 10.1080/00221546.2000.11778843

Alimul Haque, M., Ahmad, S., John, A., & Mishra, K. (2023). Cybersecurity in Universities: An Evaluation Model. *SN Computer Science*, *4*(5), 569. Advance online publication. DOI: 10.1007/s42979-023-01984-x

. Balbachevsky, E. (2015). *The Role of Internal and External Stakeholders in Brazilian Higher Education*. 193–214. https://doi.org/DOI: 10.1007/978-94-017-9570-8_10

Bischoff, K., Volkmann, C. K., & Audretsch, D. B. (2017). Stakeholder collaboration in entrepreneurship education: An analysis of the entrepreneurial ecosystems of European higher educational institutions. *The Journal of Technology Transfer*, *43*(1), 20–46. DOI: 10.1007/s10961-017-9581-0

Casarejos, F., Frota, M. N., & Gustavson, L. M. (2017). Higher education institutions: A strategy towards sustainability. *International Journal of Sustainability in Higher Education*, *18*(7), 995–1017. DOI: 10.1108/IJSHE-08-2016-0159

Cheng, E. C. K. (2020). Knowledge transfer strategies and practices for higher education institutions. *VINE Journal of Information and Knowledge Management Systems*, *ahead-of-print*(ahead-of-print). DOI: 10.1108/VJIKMS-11-2019-0184

Corradini, I. (2020). Building a Cybersecurity Culture. *Studies in Systems. Decision and Control*, *284*, 63–86. DOI: 10.1007/978-3-030-43999-6_4

Cullen, J., Joyce, J., Hassall, T., & Broadbent, M. (2003). Quality in higher education: From monitoring to management. *Quality Assurance in Education, 11*(1), 5–14. DOI: 10.1108/09684880310462038

de Wit, H., & Altbach, P. G. (2020). Internationalization in higher education: Global trends and recommendations for its future. *Policy Reviews in Higher Education, 5*(1), 28–46. DOI: 10.1080/23322969.2020.1820898

Du, Y., Arkesteijn, M. H., den Heijer, A. C., & Song, K. (2020). Sustainable Assessment Tools for Higher Education Institutions: Guidelines for Developing a Tool for China. *Sustainability (Basel), 12*(16), 6501. DOI: 10.3390/su12166501

Fernandes, J. O., & Singh, B. (2021). Accreditation and ranking of higher education institutions (HEIs): review, observations and recommendations for the Indian higher education system. *The TQM Journal, ahead-of-print*(ahead-of-print). DOI: 10.1108/TQM-04-2021-0115

Kettunen, J. (2015). Stakeholder relationships in higher education. *Tertiary Education and Management, 21*(1), 56–65. DOI: 10.1080/13583883.2014.997277

Kuleto, V., Ilić, M., Dumangiu, M., Ranković, M., Martins, O. M. D., Păun, D., & Mihoreanu, L. (2021). Exploring Opportunities and Challenges of Artificial Intelligence and Machine Learning in Higher Education Institutions. *Sustainability (Basel), 13*(18), 10424. DOI: 10.3390/su131810424

Mathur, S., Antony, J., Olivia, M., Fabiane Letícia, L., Shreeranga, B., Raja, J., & Ayon, C. (2022). An empirical study into the use of 7 quality control tools in higher education institutions (HEIs). *The TQM Journal*. Advance online publication. DOI: 10.1108/TQM-07-2022-0222

Merchan-Lima, J., Astudillo-Salinas, F., Tello-Oquendo, L., Sanchez, F., Lopez-Fonseca, G., & Quiroz, D. (2020). Information security management frameworks and strategies in higher education institutions: A systematic review. *Annales des Télécommunications*. Advance online publication. DOI: 10.1007/s12243-020-00783-2

Michel-Villarreal, R., Vilalta-Perdomo, E., Salinas-Navarro, D. E., Thierry-Aguilera, R., & Gerardou, F. S. (2023). Challenges and Opportunities of Generative AI for Higher Education as Explained by ChatGPT. *Education Sciences, 13*(9), 1–18. DOI: 10.3390/educsci13090856

Niyivuga, B., Otara, A., & Tuyishime, D. (2019). Monitoring and Evaluation Practices and Academic Staff Motivation: Implications in Higher Education Within Rwandan Context. *SAGE Open, 9*(1), 215824401982956. DOI: 10.1177/2158244019829564

Piazza, A., Vasudevan, S., & Carr, M. (2023). Cybersecurity in UK universities: Mapping (or managing) threat intelligence sharing within the higher education sector. *Journal of Cybersecurity*, *9*(1), tyad019. Advance online publication. DOI: 10.1093/cybsec/tyad019

Tarí, J. J., & Dick, G. (2016). Trends in quality management research in higher education institutions. *Journal of Service Theory and Practice*, *26*(3), 273–296. DOI: 10.1108/JSTP-10-2014-0230

. Ulven, J. B., & Wangen, G. (2021). A Systematic Review of Cybersecurity Risks in Higher Education. *Future Internet*, *13*(2), 39. MDPI. DOI: 10.3390/fi13020039

Villegas-Ch, W., Ortiz-Garces, I., & Sánchez-Viteri, S. (2021). Proposal for an Implementation Guide for a Computer Security Incident Response Team on a University Campus. *Computers*, *10*(8), 102. DOI: 10.3390/computers10080102

. Wehrmeyer, W., & Chenoweth, J. (2006). The role and effectiveness of continuing education training courses offered by higher education institutions in furthering the implementation of sustainable development. *International Journal of Sustainability in Higher Education*, *7*(2), 129–141. researchgate.net+6emerald.com+6emerald.com+6DOI: 10.1108/14676370610655913

Yusif, S., & Hafeez-Baig, A. (2021). Cybersecurity Policy Compliance in Higher Education: A Theoretical Framework. *Journal of Applied Security Research*, •••, 1–22. DOI: 10.1080/19361610.2021.1989271

Chapter 9
Designing Engaging Cybersecurity Challenges: A Gamified Approach

Abdul Azeem Khan
https://orcid.org/0000-0003-2742-8034
Universiti Islam Sultan Sharif Ali, Brunei

Hjh Tiawa Binti Awang Haji Hamid
https://orcid.org/0000-0003-2484-5211
Universiti Islam Sultan Sharif Ali, Brunei

Sayan Kumar Ray
TUSB, Malaysia

ABSTRACT

This chapter entitled "Designing Engaging Cybersecurity Challenges: A Gamified Approach" starts the discussion with an Introduction covering the aspects such as significance of hands-on learning experiences in cybersecurity education due to the ever-changing cybersecurity landscape, it also has emphasized to understand learners by identifying learners' skill, motivations and engagement levels. It has also highlighted the essential principles of gamified challenge design and the types of gamified challenges. The chapter further progressed on by detailing a comprehensive discussion on tools and platforms for gamified cybersecurity challenges citing successful case studies on gamified cybersecurity education. Though there are positive results coming out of this approach but at the same time, challenges are also inherent since this approach is fun based hence sometimes if there is no proper balance between fun and learning then the whole purpose of learning gets spoiled hence stress is laid on balanced approach between fun and educational values.

DOI: 10.4018/979-8-3373-0477-9.ch009

INTRODUCTION

As cyber threats continue to increase in complexity and occurrence, the need for trained cybersecurity experts has never been more pressing than now(A. Khan, Jhanjhi, Alı, Ray, & Wassan, 2025). On the other hand, conventional teaching styles, relying on lectures and written assessments, do not adequately prepare learners for the fast-paced, uncertain world of cybersecurity(Saeed, Jhanjhi, Naqvi, & Khan, 2022). To fill this gap, educators and organizations are increasingly embracing gamification as illustrated in Figure 1 comprehensively comprising players, learning mechanics and game aesthetics is a method that incorporates interactive game-like elements into learning, providing a more engaging, skills-based approach to cybersecurity education(M. R. Khan, Khan, & Jhanjhi, 2024). These gamified challenges enable hands-on learning through active problem-solving, critical thinking, and technical skills while at the same time empowering learners with the confidence necessary to tackle real-life cyber threats.

Figure 1. Components of gamification overview

(Christopoulos & Mystakidis, 2023)

Gamification in education harnesses the power of these dynamics by developing an engaging learning process that is highly interactive, featuring challenges, simulations, and problem-solving that bring real-world scenarios into the mix(Zhong, Kim, & Liu, 2024). Formats like Capture the Flag (CTF) competitions, cyber range exercises, puzzle-solving challenges, and role-playing scenarios which not only allow learners to practice but also avail them in harnessing their skills in authentic environments. Progressively challenging levels and instant feedback with rewards for accomplishment means that gamification not only maintains learner motivation, but it develops their ability to apply cybersecurity concepts in high-pressure scenarios(Sindiramutty, Jhanjhi, Tan, et al., 2024).

This chapter examines critical methods for writing successful gamified information security challenges, specifically how to make them attractive, instructive, and realistic. It explores best practices, existing frameworks, and real-world examples to demonstrate how gamification can be tailored to different audiences, from students to professionals. It is observed that well-designed and relevant challenges can contribute to learning that not only is enjoyable but also prepares participants for the complex world of cybersecurity to come.

How Gamification Can Transform Traditional Cybersecurity Challenges into Engaging, Immersive Experiences

Gamification which is generally understood as the application of game-design elements in non-game contexts has evolved into a psychologizing device for enhancing motivation and engagement for learning(Quayyum, 2021). Cybersecurity education gamification completely rewrites conventional learning paradigms and shrouds concepts in terms of emotive resources through points, leaderboards, missions and challenges revolving around real-world simulations(Katsikeas, Rencelj Ling, Johnsson, & Ekstedt, 2024). Interactive functionalities make cyber security trainings more participative, cooperative and investigative. Potential cybersecurity instructors can use game mechanics to devise scenarios in which learners can actively participate in threat detection and vulnerability exploitation, as well as in defensive strategies, in a risk-free but competitive setting(A. Khan, Jhanjhi, Hamid, et al., 2025).

Gamifying cybersecurity challenges such as cyber ranges, escape-room style security scenarios, etc. encourages participants to think critically, build resilience, practice and gain experience incrementally(Sindiramutty et al., 2025). These are great techniques focused on various types of studying styles, showing that learners of different skill sets are invested and engaged. Furthermore, gamification modifies the learning curve through immediate feedback, motivating progression and developing a growth mindset(Tharot, Riel, & Thiriet, 2024). Usually, a red versus blue team exercise will have defensive and offensive teams go head-to-head, sharpening both sides through applied process. More complex issues challenge proficient learners to come up with clever solutions and the realization of rising threats. Lessons in addition to novice students provide extra support and feedback that assists individual students to augment basic knowledge at their own pace(D. Pramod, 2024).

Objectives of the Chapter: Exploring Design Principles, Frameworks, and Examples

Engaging, effective gamified cybersecurity challenges are built on important fundamental principles and methodologies, and this chapter presents a closer look at those principles. As cyberthreats continue to evolve, so must cybersecurity training, empowering learners with the relevant skills to detect, analyze and respond to security threats. Gamification for cybersecurity training is gaining more traction as it has proven to increase engagement, motivation and knowledge retention. Gamification in Cybersecurity Training Gamification refers to use game elements and mechanics into non-game contexts to engage users. This chapter is focused on three areas of discussion. In particular, it first explores design principles that can impact the efficacy of gamified cybersecurity challenges, such as scalability, interactivity, and real world applicability. These tenets also help challenges stay engaging while preserving their educational rigor and real-world relevance. In the second part of this chapter, we discuss gamification frameworks and models which can be used in cybersecurity education with different game-based learning methodologies. By doing so, we provide a review of existing gamification techniques, adaptive learning systems, as well as challenge-based learning frameworks supporting cybersecurity skill training. Finally, the chapter discusses various programs, competitions and platforms where people are using gamified cybersecurity training in the physical world and how it is working in academia, corporate training and public awareness programs. This chapter also seeks to educate educators, trainers, and cybersecurity experts about those necessary principles, to create gamified cybersecurity challenges that are effective.

UNDERSTANDING THE LEARNER

Identifying the Target Audience: Students, Professionals, or General Users

Cybersecurity training is only effective if it starts with a clear understanding of the target learners it wants to deliver knowledge to. If learners, skilled professionals, or general users of an idea intend to achieve more awareness concerning the stages, the critical factor for producing significant outcomes is to modify the process according to the audience(Thompson, Melendez, Hempson-Jones, & Salvi, 2022). Implementing gamification in cybersecurity education requires consideration of the needs, skill levels, and motivations of students to ensure that challenges are neither too basic nor overwhelmingly complex. An especially well-structured gamified system identifies engagement, in-built confidence and develops a practice of guided studying. Furthermore, a multi-faceted approach can tap into a range of different learning styles, combining audio, visual and kinetic elements retaining attention and promoting higher order thinking. Hence, updating and personalizing them periodically is significant so that they remain relevant as the threats change(Ashley et al., 2022).

Assessing Skill Levels: Beginners, Intermediate, and Advanced Learners

As depicted in Fig 2.0 the Mechanics Dynamics and Emotions (MDE) Framework elucidates the gamification principles based on the rules of the games, behaviors and state of mind of the player, hence when designing gamified educational programs these principles should be considered even when we talk about implementing these principles in cybersecurity education.Cybersecurity education caters to a broad range of learners with distinct learning requirements, career goals and technical competence(Shahid, Ashraf, Jhanjhi, & Zam, 2025). The success of gamified cyber challenges rests on tailoring content, difficulty, and engagement to the specific audiences. Cybersecurity learners can be categorized into three broad categories: students, professionals and general users, all of which require a different training and skills solution(Gil-Aciron, 2024). The same is especially true for students in university and college studying cybersecurity, computer science, or closely related subjects, as they require structured paths that combine the theory behind their work with practical applications(Zhong, Kim, & Liu, 2022). It is important that their training focuses on fundamental cybersecurity concepts, as well as hands-on experience and preparation towards both industry certifications and field roles(Oliveira et al., 2023). Gamified challenges for students must be organized, beginning from the slow end of the range, which can assist them in acquiring technical skills and capturing them when they interact with issues(Liu, Fathi, & Rahimi, 2024).

Figure 2. Gamification principles based on MDE framework

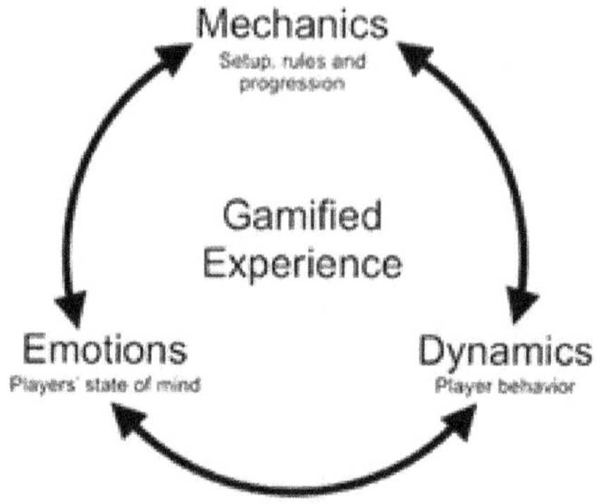

(Robson, Plangger, Kietzmann, McCarthy, & Pitt, 2015)

Cyberthreats continue to evolve, making upskilling and continuous learning essential for professionals including IT personnel, security analysts, ethical hackers, and corporate employees. Most of them are trained on practical use, compliance needs, and state of the art security practices. Specialized nooks should specialize in gamified cybersecurity challenges for professionals that showcase real-world penalties, high-fidelity simulations, cyber range exercises, and practical penetration testing scenarios. These challenges should be structured with a focus on real-world threats in cybersecurity; however, they should be designed to include competitive and collaborative aspects to keep participants engaged(Javed et al., 2024).

Cybersecurity awareness training for general users for instance, business professionals, non-technical staff, and the public should cover how to stay safe online, ensure digital hygiene, and avoid falling victim to threats(Sindiramutty, Jhanjhi, & Ray, 2024). Understanding how the human mind works can help make their training more accessible, through gamified and entertaining challenges that break down complex through cybersecurity topics with interactive storytelling, quizzes, and real-world scenarios. By introducing user-friendly learning experiences, gamified cybersecurity education will be able to fill knowledge gaps for non-technical audiences, friendly learning experiences cybersecurity awareness culture across sectors. This will allow educators and trainers to create gamified challenges that will suit each group of cybersecurity learners, making cybersecurity training engaging, relevant, and very close to real-world cybersecurity scenarios(Sindiramutty, Prabagaran, Jhanjhi, & Murugesan, 2024).

Understanding Learner Motivations and How Gamification Can Address Them

Gamification, when designed strategically, must align with the reasons learners pursue cybersecurity education from the start for the experience to remain engaging and effective. Some people thrive in a competitive and recognized environment where leaderboards, point systems, and brackets of head-to-head cybersecurity dojos provide a stimulating and dynamic environment that challenges attendees to write new tactics, techniques, and procedures into their repertoire. Cybersecurity is inherently problem-solving, and curiosity and exploration are a powerful motivator; gamification exploits this through puzzle-solving features, mystery-based challenges, and open-ended problem scenarios that can cause the critical thinking process to get all worked up. In addition, when on-the-job training requires active collaboration and social learning — as with challenges and hackathons and discussion forums — quizzes and tests fall flat. Lastly, learners enjoy better retention because they can correlate their training to the real-world(B. Y. Alothman, 2024). Participants can learn how to be better prepared for vulnerabilities related to cybersecurity awareness in occupationally relevant situations, fostering personal agency due to their learning while delivering gamified cybersecurity challenges, which simulate proper cyber threats, and security breach and defensive techniques. If addressed, these motivational dynamics can help tailor gamified cybersecurity education for both large and diverse audiences, stimulating not only the acquisition of skills or long-term memory knowledge, but also the engagement and motivation of learners to face real-world cybersecurity challenges(Karagiannis & Magkos, 2020).

PRINCIPLES OF GAMIFIED CHALLENGE DESIGN

As depicted in Figure 3 the simple principles to design a gamified cybersecurity challenge are clarity, progression, feedback and narrative. If the exercises that are used to train cybersecurity challenges include these principles in a progressive ladder, then there will be better results that can contribute in increasing the overall learners productivity. Gamified cybersecurity challenges offer an interactive and engaging way to build critical security skills, combining teaching objectives with real-world applicability. A challenge, when well-designed, should push the learner whilst further building muscle for problem solving, critical thinking, and technical skills. In order to do this, challenges need to have objectives, increasingly difficult levels, immediate feedback, and narrative immersion so that learners have fun and practical cybersecurity knowledge(Sezgin & Yüzer, 2022).

Challenges need to have simple objectives that are well correlated with concrete cybersecurity skills to be gained, like vulnerability assessment, penetration testing, or incident response — therefore, their purpose needs to be clear. Structured level-up progression keeps learners of all levels engaged, from learning to interact with the web and discovering common web requests, to attacking libraries that back the frontend like SQL injection, and on to advanced persistent threats. Adaptive learning paths modify the difficulty of challenges according to learner performance, while real-time feedback, contextual hints, and other incentive mechanisms (points, badges, certificates) may motivate engagement(Krath & Von Korflesch, 2021). Capture the Flag (CTF) competitions are a prime example of this methodology, with real-time scoring, performance feedback, and in some cases competitive participation, reinforcing the knowledge with the game-learn concept. Structural progression and feedback are not enough they need compelling storytelling to engage learners through the context of cybersecurity challenges in real-life environments. Students can protect a fictive company from cyberattacks, analyze security logs or take out digital threats, which mirrors real-world cybersecurity roles in high-stakes environments which can recover with incident response simulations, practical scenarios stimulate the learning process(Yu, Wang, & Wang, 2024).

Figure 3. Principles of gamified cybersecurity challenges

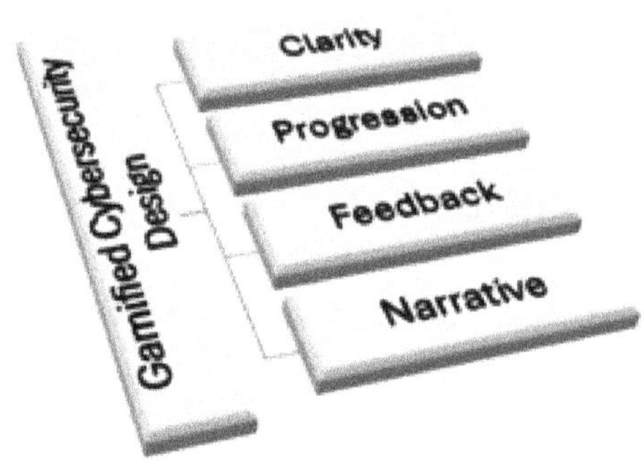

Hence, this kind of interactive experience contributes to quicker retention of new information, and emotions deepen engagement with the learning material. This incorporation of clear learning objectives, structured progression of challenge difficulty, and real-world narratives not only equips learners with the tools to face current and emerging digital threats but also contributes to the development of a skilled and agile cybersecurity workforce. As hackers become more advanced, this focus on hands-on, gamified learning will be crucial to the future of cybersecurity training and the readiness of the cybersecurity industry(Iqbal, 2021).

TYPES OF GAMIFIED CYBERSECURITY CHALLENGES

As depicted in Figure 4, Gamified cybersecurity challenges utilize interactive and immersive elements to teach learners skills and concepts necessary to succeed within the security field by simulating real-world attacks against systems. One of the most used formats is Capture the Flag (CTF) competitions, where participants solve problems that test their abilities to discover vulnerabilities, analyze security threats, and exploit weaknesses. These competitions exist as Jeopardy-style challenges where participants solve standalone security problems and offense-and-defense formats where competing teams assume both offensive and defensive roles in a simulated cyber battle. Cyber ranges and simulations, like IBM's Cyber Range and Microsoft's Attack Simulator, build realistic security environments so that students can practice incident response, network defense, and forensic analysis in a risk-free environment. These practical platforms simulate real-life cyber threats, making them a critical component for corporate and professional cybersecurity programs(Basil Yousef Alothman, 2024).

Figure 4. Cybersecurity challenge types

Outside of more structured simulations, puzzle-based problems and role-playing scenarios help build creative problem-solving skills and prepare students for the real world. The puzzle-oriented challenges present logic-based exercises in cryptography, reverse engineering, and forensic analysis, forcing the learner to decrypt encrypted text, identify hidden foes and analyze malware behavior. Role-playing scenarios, on the other hand, immerse participants in realistic cybersecurity settings, acting as Security Operations Center (SOC) analysts, ethical hackers, or incident responders facing realistic simulated cybersecurity incidents(Durakovskiy, Gavdan, Korsakov, & Melnikov, 2021).

Cybersecurity challenges bridge the gap between theoretical cybersecurity education and real-life cybersecurity crises. With your experience from CTFs, cyber ranges, puzzles and role-playing exercises, educators and cybersecurity specialists can design effective gamified exercises on multiple levels of fortress walls. Such an approach amplifies the learning process through retention of knowledge and subsequent skill acquisition along with the formation of a highly capable talent resource to combat growing cybersecurity threats in the professional and academic landscape(Aslam, 2024).

STEP-BY-STEP FRAMEWORK FOR DESIGNING CHALLENGES

Implementing a gamified cybersecurity challenge is not a use-case that can be taken lightly as it requires a rigorously defined approach that lays out the learning objectives to be achieved. As illustrated in Figure 5 there are the six steps involved in framework for designing challenges for Designing Engaging Cybersecurity Challenges implementing a Gamified Approach described comprehensively.

Step 1: Defining Learning Objectives, the first step is to define the learning objectives and design the challenge to address specific areas of cybersecurity expertise, such as network security, cryptography, malware analysis, or ethical hacking. Clearly defined goals lead to tangible skills that are applicable to realistic security environments.

Step 2: Selecting Game Mechanics provides a range of engagement options, like points, badges, leaderboards, and levels that can motivate learners and offer a sense of progression, once the objectives are in place. Gamification mechanics help to increase participation by using rewards to encourage learners to achieve and create a healthy competitive and fun classroom environment.

Step 3: Creating a Narrative or Theme is an important step that immerses learners in a real-world context. Learners emotionally engage with the problem because the challenges are embedded within a compelling storyline; for example, defending a corporation from a cyberattack or investigating a digital crime.

Figure 5. Step based framework for designing cybersecurity challenges

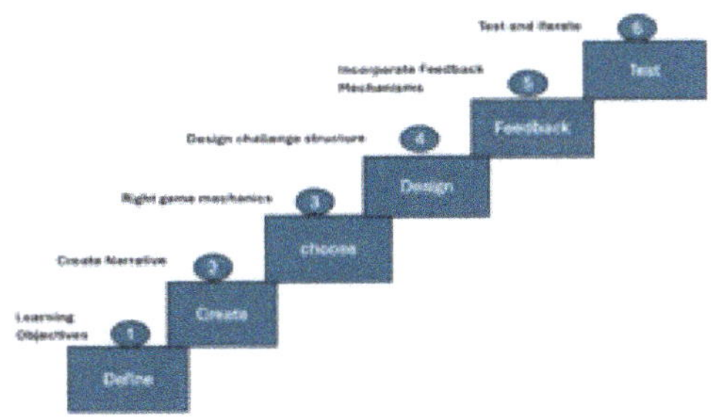

Once set, **Step 4:** Designing the Challenge Structure jumps in to clearly decompose the experience into tasks, milestones, and rewards that guide participants through progressively difficulty experiences. A well-made challenge ramps up in difficulty, letting new users do basic stuff while the more advanced ones can tackle more intricate cyberweapons.

Step 5: Incorporating Feedback Mechanisms To enhance the learning process and provide just-in-time support, incorporating feedback mechanisms to deliver real-time guidance, hints, and analytics on performance can further embed learning. Timely feedback enables learners to comprehend errors, modify their plan, and enhance judgment.

Finally, **Step 6:** Testing and Iterating involves piloting the challenge with a small group, gathering feedback, and refining the design. Iteration ensures that the challenge remains effective, balanced, and engaging for different learner levels. By following this structured framework, cybersecurity educators and trainers can design immersive, skill-driven, and impactful gamified challenges that prepare learners for real-world cybersecurity threats while keeping them engaged in the learning process(Khaleghi, Aghaei, & Mahdavi, 2021).

TOOLS AND PLATFORMS FOR GAMIFIED CYBERSECURITY CHALLENGES

Gamification was used in cybersecurity challenges, and a good, gamified cybersecurity challenge relies on real tools and platforms to offer realistic, engaging, and interactive learning experiences. Leading Platforms: Cybersecurity Training Platforms Several popular platforms have become leading resources for hands-on cybersecurity training. These are widely used platforms that provide out of the box cyber security labs, real world attack scenario simulation including guided learning path for all levels such as Hack the Box, TryHackMe, and CyberSec Labs. Hack The Box focuses on penetration testing and ethical hacking, featuring live vulnerable machines that learners need to exploit. TryHackMe: TryHackMe takes a more structured approach, offering step-by-step learning modules that are accessible to beginners. On the other hand, CyberSec Labs gives participants training on enterprise-level cybersecurity, with incident response and security operations center (SOC) simulations, which prepares professionals towards real- life security issues. Platforms that bridge the gap between theoretical learning and hands-on tutorials can fill this gap(Razack & Saad, 2024).

Gamified cybersecurity challenges provide a diverse range of tools that can be customized and tailored by organizations and educators, thus offering a more engaging and flexible learning experience. For example, there are CTF environments where platforms like CTFd help trainers set up their challenges and load the targets to run CTFs that measure a variety of skills such as they can use game engines such as Unity to create cyber ranges, a simulated network where individuals can practice defending an environment or responding to an incident. Using actual cyber security tools like Kali Linux and Metasploit, students can explore real-world application of their theoretical knowledge through practical implementation and training in areas such as vulnerability assessments and penetration testing, or even digital forensics. Learning Management Systems (LMS) including Moodle, Blackboard, and Canvas are falling in tow, with game-based learning plug-ins available to facilitate educators embedding Capture the Flag (CTF) competitions, simulated environments and interactive cyber security exercises as part of formal education systems, embedding gamification even further in curriculum development and delivery(M. A. Khan, Merabet, Alkaabi, & Sayed, 2022).

Hence, the students can be reviewed in real-time, students can be challenged at a pace, and optimization can be awarded in the form of badges and certifications. By using gamified LMS platforms, institutions and organizations can deliver theoretical education with practical cybersecurity training, fostering skillset development expectations, knowledge retention and workforce readiness.

CASE STUDIES: SUCCESSFUL GAMIFIED CYBERSECURITY CHALLENGES

Incorporating gamification has already been successfully applied in cybersecurity competitions at academia, corporations, and public education systems. In this security section, we present three case studies on gamification in cybersecurity training that are used in the real world. All three case studies offer insight into how gamified learning methodologies effectively enhanced motivation, knowledge retention, and practical cybersecurity skill development among diverse target audiences(Dhanya Pramod, 2024).

Example 1: A University-Level CTF Competition and its Impact on Student Engagement

Capture the Flag (CTF) competitions have become a commonplace element of many budding infosec professionals' university experience, and they provide an engaging and competitive means of bridging the gap between theory and real-world problems. One example that cited mostly is National University Cybersecurity Challenge (NUCC) which is held annually among several participants within institutions to achieve hands-on training across segments like ethical hacking, cryptography, and digital forensics(Mukherjee, Le, Chow, & Susilo, 2024). The student is broken out into teams and assigned various security challenges ranging from penetration testing to reverse engineering to forensics. Points are assigned to each of these tasks based on difficulty, and leaderboards help drive student engagement. Surveys from participants indicate the event has also significantly ramped up how many students participate, and 85% of students reported improved confidence in their technical cybersecurity skills post-competition. Professors also noted more sharing among faculty and an increase in students taking cybersecurity courses following the CTF event. These competitive and hands-on nature of the cybersecurity challenges makes it a great complement to traditional cybersecurity education, bolstering problem-solving skills and priming students for industry accreditations and cybersecurity jobs(Zhang et al., 2024).

Example 2: A Corporate Training Program Using Cyber Ranges to Improve Employee Skills

For global corporations, cyber ranges have emerged as a vital technology for cost-effectively training their staff to defend against and respond to real-world cyber-attacks. With a specialization in cybersecurity solutions, a multinational company, TechSecure Inc., conducted cyber range-based workshops for its security operations center (SOC) analysts and IT professionals to enable them to grapple with advanced cyber threats. This program included simulated attack scenarios, forcing employees to detect, analyze, and mitigate security incidents in real-time. Participants were able to practice incident response in (high stake but controlled environment) in simulations which included, Ransomware attacks, phishing campaigns, network intrusions etc(Katsantonis, Manikas, Mavridis, & Gritzalis, 2023).

The cyber range applied gamification techniques such as timed challenges, teams, and achievement badges to maintain user engagement. After completing the program, they improved the speed at which they responded to simulated attacks by 40% and reduced the rate at which they falsely detected threats by 30%. Attendees also reported feeling more confident in their ability to react to real security events. It not only made training cheaper than conventional workshops but also enabled the learners to perform realistic cyber-attacks virtually without any risk to real corporate infrastructure(Anthi, Williams, Rhode, Burnap, & Wedgbury, 2021).

Example 3: A Gamified Mobile App Teaching Basic Cybersecurity Concepts to The General Public

Cybersecurity awareness is not only important for professionals but also for the public. Aware of this necessity, a cybersecurity research association launched a game-based phone application named "CyberDefend", created to inform non-technical users about secure online habits in a fun and interactive manner, presenting various challenges, quizzes and scenario-based objectives on identifying, mitigating and avoiding common threats, such as secure password practices, phishing attacks and social engineering tactics. The app featured story-driven gameplay where the user can take on the role of a cybersecurity investigator to identify and combat real-world security threats by identifying risks and making informed decisions(Alqahtani & Kavakli-Thorne, 2020).

CyberDefend integrated progressive levels, reward-based achievements, and daily security challenges to maintain user engagement while ensuring learning reinforcement with instant feedback and tailored recommendations based on user performance. This initiative had a significant impact over 500,000 downloads in the first year, and a 75% increase in cybersecurity awareness scores by active users. The findings showed that many gained better security practices, such as stronger passwords and greater awareness of phishing etc., highlighting how gamification can be a fun and powerful way to engage non-technical people in the topic of cybersecurity(Ahmed, Watterson, Alhashmi, & Gaber, 2024).

BALANCING FUN AND EDUCATIONAL VALUE

Gamification in cybersecurity education should always be kept on the fine edge of informative, engaging, and fun. Although it shows that injecting game mechanics such as point systems, progress tracking, and rewards can help motivate individuals; challenges must remain oriented around developing skills and applying them in the real world. An appropriately designed gamified cybersecurity challenge should differ from any entertainment but provide strong enrichment for the messages and abilities taught/shown, emphasizing critical concepts and technical skills required to perform tasks(Matovu, Nwokeji, Holmes, & Rahman, 2022).

When a challenge strays too far into the realm of gameplay without enough educational content, its ability to prepare learners for actual cybersecurity challenges diminish. Over-gamification for instance, when such game elements as skin-deep rewards and eye-catching animations, or nonsensical point systems, detract from the learning experience can make these challenges less educationally significant. Take for instance a cyber defense simulation that focuses on collecting virtual coins instead of solving real security problems, pursuant to attracting learners, but advancing little to no meaningful cybersecurity knowledge transfer. Rather, game mechanics should be added rather than distract from the learning objectives through incremental challenge, constructive feedback, and reinforcement of applied cybersecurity skills(Makdoun, Rahhal, Mezzour, Kassou, & Carley, 2021; Pirta-Dreimane et al., 2023).

To stay true to educational value, challenges need the be the real world so that one can transfer their skill into real life cybersecurity. Providing challenges that reflect real-world attack vectors, security incidents, and real-world defensive techniques. As an example, a gamified challenge might replace an abstract, irrelevant problem with a real-world risk scenario of a corporate data breach, where learners work with log files, look for anomalies and take steps to mitigate risk as would happen in an actual SOC environment. The best thing about this approach is that this can be turned into a fruitful tool with the help of gamification, where the mechanics of games are used to reproduce real-life functions in the field of cybersecurity(Piki, Stavrou, Procopiou, & Demosthenous, 2023).

CHALLENGES AND SOLUTIONS IN DESIGN

Gamifying the creation of challenges for cybersecurity makes for a unique set of technical, pedagogical, and logistical challenges that must cease to provide a streamlined learning process. This entails the need to overcome technical limitations, concerns for inclusivity, and finding the right balance between competition and collaboration. Gamified learning might quickly become either overly complicated, gatekeeping, or powerless in building core cybersecurity competencies without consideration of how to solve it(Fuchs, 2024).

Addressing Technical Limitations and Resource Constraints

Aspects like hardware, software, and network limitations are some of the technical limitation aspects that should be catered to when designing gamified cybersecurity challenges. Neural Communication systems based on a high-performance computing resource, will realistically simulate and execute an attack in an auto simulated sandbox for effective cyber security training and defence(Oke, Aliu, Tunji-Olayeni, & Abayomi, 2024). In addition to this, not all institutions, companies or individual learners have access to advanced infrastructures like dedicated cyber ranges, high-speed internet, or costly security tools, which can impact participation and access(Di Nardo et al., 2024). The cloud cyber-safety laboratory provides resource containment on costume systems like a scalable, cost-efficient gift of training, along with resource on open-source working exposure for designers facing these resource constraints. Unfortunately, it is not easy, but there are some platforms such as TryHackMe, Hack The Box or even Google Cloud to allow learners to experience taking security challenges from those big computers without requirements to have big computer for them(Dillon & Tan, 2024). Light simulation, web-based challenge, and commercial gadget like CTFd that more for CTF but it brings more accessible platform to allow learner to practice some cyber techniques using low-end device! The format of the challenges being set up in a modular way, allowing them to be played bit by bit, chunk by chunk, is another aspect that also helps make gamified cybersecurity learning more accessible and inclusive between people with differing technical backgrounds and without the need for high-cost computing power to play(Karagiannis & Magkos, 2020).

Ensuring Inclusivity and Accessibility for Diverse Learners

There are learners from all walks of life, including students, other professionals, and those who are either less or more technically inclined than us. One of the key gamification challenges lies in the fact that not all needs are being met if the challenges are not inclusive, accessible, and address diverse learning services. Challenges that are overly technical and full of jargon can put off beginners, while challenges that are overly simplified may fail to interest advanced learners. Furthermore, accessibility challenges — like complicated user interfaces, absence of assistive technologies, or restrictions in language — can alienate students with disabilities or other students lacking technical backgrounds(Tomé Klock et al., 2024).

To strive for greater inclusivity, designers should provide multiple tiers of challenges to cater to users at beginner, intermediate, and advanced levels, so they can progress at their own pace. Offering clear step-by-step instructions, interactive tutorials, and optional hints will ensure that novice learners build confidence while not being overloaded. Multi-lingual arch, screen-reader-friendly interface, and responsive inters make sure learners with visual, audible, or motor impairment can engage. Furthermore, providing real-world parallels coupled with gamified storylines can ease tech-agnostic learners to comprehend cybersecurity concepts(Cruz, 2024).

Managing Competition and Collaboration Dynamics

Common elements of competition such as leaderboards, scoring systems and timed challenges are leveraged in gamified cybersecurity challenges but the excessive use of competitive dynamics can be counterproductive as it can undermine collaboration, produce unnecessary stress or inhibit sharing of knowledge(Firmansyah & Rosmansyah, 2024). Alternatively, a completely collaborative approach is unlikely to engage the learners who are stimulated by competition. Second Comment: Competition and collaboration are two sides of the same coin, and a right balance on those two ensures motivation, along with a healthy learning community. One approach to addressing this issue is to have hybrid formats (individual/team) when it comes to challenges. This would be especially valuable in a Capture the Flag (CTF) event, in which participants complete a sequence of unique challenges to learn the skills before progressing to team-based problem-solving activities, which will require team-based collaboration to either protect a virtual network or track a cybercrime incident jointly. Another possibility that could both ease the issues about competition and keep students engaged with each other is encouraging peer feedback, mentorship and knowledge-sharing forums(Marinho et al., 2024).

Gamified cybersecurity training can gain the highest learning returns on its investment, all while fostering an inclusive and encouraging learning environment through the challenges it creates that rewards not only individual but also collective accomplishments. While gamified cybersecurity challenges offer a promising and engaging approach to cybersecurity education, there are technical limitations, inclusivity concerns and competition dynamics that must be considered when designing these formats(Abril & Gimenez-Fernandez, 2024). As the resources become available to scale, accessibility to the tools of technology, the healthy competition vs collaboration forces between ed-tech, designers can design immersive, inclusive and skilful gamified learning experiences. This in turn ensures that, regardless of their background, student learners are equipped with the technical disposition, analytical thought process and experiential experience in cybersecurity to face an uncertain future of digital threat, with their eyes wide open(Allnjawi, 2025).

FUTURE TRENDS IN GAMIFIED CYBERSECURITY CHALLENGES

These include everything from cybercrime to state-sponsored hacks and simply references to the need for improving cybersecurity protocols in the physical and digital landscape. Emerging technologies are shaping the future of gamified cybersecurity education with increased immersion, adaptability, and realism. Advancements in Artificial Intelligence (AI), Virtual and Augmented Reality (VR/AR), even tailored gamification techniques that mirror new and emerging cybersecurity risks are opening doors to more idyllic training environments that make the training experience better, immersive, and personalized(Huitema & Wong, 2025).

The Role of AI in Creating Adaptive and Personalized Challenges

Gamified Cybersecurity Training with AI is delivering personalized learning experiences. Regular cybersecurity problems have fixed difficulty levels and are not structured to adjust according to a player's evolving skill level. In contrast, learners' motivators, response time and methods of solving problems are instantly adjusted to change the challenge to make it relevant to the individual using AI-driven gamification. Machine- studying algorithms can identify skill gaps and provide customized pointers, real-time suggestions, and individualized obstacles to guarantee a constant tailored learning journey(Rana & Chicone, 2025).

AI-based gamified environments might deliver targeted cybersecurity challenges based on a learner's expertise and weaknesses, potentially even personalized CTF challenges, adaptive penetration testing attack simulations or simulated cyberattacks powered by AI. For example, AI chatbots and virtual security mentors can extend that engagement by answering questions and simulating in-the-moment behaviour of cyber threats. This is a brilliant gamification trick that keeps cybersecurity education delivered within easy reach, implemented on a tight schedule, and relevant to the attacks specific to each student(Nagaraj, Abhi, & Agarwal, 2025).

Incorporating Virtual Reality (VR) and Augmented Reality (AR) for Immersive Experiences

Gamification for training in cyber security will be transformed with VR (Virtual Reality) and AR (Augmented Reality) because it makes training experience immersive. According to Bordin, VR-based cybersecurity training immerses learners in simulated cyber-attacks in a way that traditional screen-based simulations cannot which thereby are allowing them to interact with an immersive digital infrastructure, identify potential threats and take defenses in an engaged environment(HAWKINSON, 2025). A VR-based cyber range, for example, may simulate a corporate network that is under attack, requiring students to analyze live threats, configure firewalls and neutralize breaches through immersive controls. Augmented Reality (AR), in turn, can overlay cybersecurity threats onto real-world applications, allowing learners to highlight vulnerabilities to physical networks, Internet of Things (IoT) devices, or even industrial control systems via an AR hands-on interface. These technologies deliver a deeper level of engagement and situational awareness, preparing cybersecurity professionals to tackle complex real-world security challenges (Crogman, Cano, Pacheco, Sonawane, & Boroon, 2025).

Expanding Gamification to Address Emerging Cybersecurity Threats

As the cybersecurity landscape continues to evolve, so too must the world of gamified training, adapting to cover new and emerging threats like Internet of Things (IoT) security, AI-powered cyberattacks, cloud-based vulnerabilities, and so on. Legacy security challenges orient themselves around network security, cryptography, and penetration testing but future gamification practices must evolve to incorporate advanced attack vectors(A. R. S. Khan et al., 2024).

1. **IoT Security Challenges** – With the rise of connected devices, gamification can create scenarios that act as real or simulated IoT-specific threats, such as attacks on botnets, hijacking of devices, and smart-home vulnerabilities. Learners could also participate in IoT defense exercises where they need to defend the industrial control systems, medical devices or smart city infrastructures from cyber intrusions(Mumtaz et al., 2024).
2. **AI-Accelerated Threat Simulations** – As incidents of AI-driven attacks on systems continue to proliferate, future gamified learning approaches will likely bring interactive cybersecurity courses allowing learners to experience how adversarial AIs can be used to manipulate input, defraud users with deepfake phishing attacks and produce AI-driven malware(Mazhar et al., 2023).

3. **Cloud Security Training** — As organizations migrate critical operations to the cloud, gamified challenges can prepare cloud penetration testing, misconfiguration exploits and data protection strategies to little cybersecurity experts with the cloud security expertise they require(Rehan, 2024).

To conclude, the combination of adaptive AI-driven learning, augmented reality (AR)/virtual reality (VR) simulations, and challenges based on real emerging cyber threats will ensure that the next generation of gamified cybersecurity training is engaging, realistic, and in line with the latest trends in digital security. Not only will this lead to the advancement of cybersecurity skills, but it will also ensure that those who are learning are ready to confidently tackle next-gen cyber threats(A. Almusaylim & Jhanjhi, 2020; Tayyab, Hameed, Jhanjhi, Zaheer, & Qamar, 2024).

CONCLUSION

In recent times, gamified cybersecurity challenges have proven to be an effective way to learn, as they combine theoretical concepts with real-life application [2]. Gamification incorporates methodologies such as Capture the Flag (CTF) competitions, cyber ranges, puzzle-based activities, and role-playing exercises to improve engagement, motivation, and skill acquisition. These methods are well-suited to varied learner cohorts-attendees of schools, prospective workers, urban professionals, and laypeople, offering increasingly challenging tasks, immediate responses to accuracy, and situations likened to those encountered in the real world. To ensure that these challenges are truly effective, though, some prudent design practices such as making the learning goals explicitly clear, providing scaffolded challenge, and offering an immersive narrative should be applied to guarantee that this type of learning experience is not only fun but also intellectually wholesome.

Gamification has many advantages, but there are also design and implementation challenges such as technical limitations, inclusiveness concerns, and finding a balance between competition and cooperation. As most institutions and students have limited hardware capabilities and see themselves covering the same commercial Cyber Range tasks, doing it without highly sophisticated and vulnerable environments and seamless implementations, these are the ingredients of Cloud-based environments, open-source tools, and modular challenges. It is also important to make sure of accessibility and inclusivity with respect to multi-level challenges, customized learning pathways, and intuitive user interfaces to cater to learners of different levels of sophistication and different backgrounds. Finally, creating sportsmanship dynamics between fellow students can keep excessive stress and alienation from occurring, ensuring a hybrid model that promotes autonomous learning while also allowing students to work together in structured environments.

Moving forward, we can expect more innovations and growth in gamified cybersecurity training, with a combination of AI, VR/AR, and adaptive learning technologies. Through the development of AI-driven personalized challenges, Learning and development (L&D) will enhance experiences to cater to peak learning potential relative to how well an individual performs, whereas VR/AR-enhanced cyber ranges would provide immersive, high-pressure situations in the form of the training environment to replicate the threats in the real world. Additionally, new gamified cybersecurity challenges on emerging security domains, such as Internet of Things (IoT) security, AI-enabled threats, and cloud security, will keep learners up to date with the evolving cybersecurity landscape. With the ongoing enhancement of gamification methods and the integration of innovative technologies, cybersecurity education will be increasingly engaging, effective, and relevant to industry requirements, better equipping the next generation of cybersecurity experts to combat digital threats with both assurance and proficiency.

REFERENCES

Abril, C., Gimenez-Fernandez, E. M., & Camacho-Miñano, M.-M. (2024). Using gamification to overcome innovation process challenges: A literature review and future agenda. *Technovation, 133*, 103020. DOI: 10.1016/j.technovation.2024.103020

Ahmed, A., Watterson, C., Alhashmi, S., & Gaber, T. (2024). How universities teach cybersecurity courses online: A systematic literature review. *Frontiers of Computer Science, 6*, 1499490. Advance online publication. DOI: 10.3389/fcomp.2024.1499490

Allnjawi, S. A. (2025). *Interacting in a Gamified Environment in Higher Education: Research on Collaborative and Competitive Practices.* INSTITUTE OF EDUCATION, Alothman, B. Y. (2024). *Cyber gamification: implementing gamified adaptive learning environments for effective cyber security teams education.* Paper presented at the Proceedings of the 2024 5th International Conference on Education Development and Studies.

A. Almusaylim, Z., & Jhanjhi, N. (2020). Comprehensive review: Privacy protection of user in location-aware services of mobile cloud computing. *Wireless Personal Communications, 111*, 541–564. DOI: 10.1007/s11277-019-06872-3

Alothman, B. Y. (2024). *Cyber Gamification: Implementing Gamified Adaptive Learning Environments for Effective Cyber Security Teams Education: Enhancing Team Skills and Engagement through Interactive Learning Environments.* Paper presented at the ACM International Conference Proceeding Series.

Alqahtani, H., & Kavakli-Thorne, M. (2020). Design and evaluation of an augmented reality game for cybersecurity awareness (CybAR). *Information (Basel), 11*(2), 121. DOI: 10.3390/info11020121

Anthi, E., Williams, L., Rhode, M., Burnap, P., & Wedgbury, A. (2021). Adversarial attacks on machine learning cybersecurity defences in Industrial Control Systems. *Journal of Information Security and Applications, 58*, 102717. DOI: 10.1016/j.jisa.2020.102717

Ashley, T. D., Kwon, R., Gourisetti, S. N. G., Katsis, C., Bonebrake, C. A., & Boyd, P. A. (2022). Gamification of cybersecurity for workforce development in critical infrastructure. *IEEE Access : Practical Innovations, Open Solutions, 10*, 112487–112501. DOI: 10.1109/ACCESS.2022.3216711

Aslam, M. (2024). AI and Cybersecurity: An Ever-Evolving Landscape. *International Journal of Advanced Engineering Technologies and Innovations, 1*(1), 52–71.

Christopoulos, A., & Mystakidis, S. (2023). Gamification in education. *Encyclopedia, 3*(4), 1223–1243. DOI: 10.3390/encyclopedia3040089

Crogman, H. T., Cano, V. D., Pacheco, E., Sonawane, R. B., & Boroon, R. (2025). Virtual Reality, Augmented Reality, and Mixed Reality in Experiential Learning: Transforming Educational Paradigms. *Education Sciences, 15*(3), 303. DOI: 10.3390/educsci15030303

Cruz, C. D. (2024). *Enhancing Engagement: Key Factors for Exceptional Learners in Gamified Education.* Paper presented at the 2024 9th International Conference on Information Technology and Digital Applications (ICITDA).

Di Nardo, V., Fino, R., Fiore, M., Mignogna, G., Mongiello, M., & Simeone, G. (2024). Usage of Gamification Techniques in Software Engineering Education and Training: A Systematic Review. *Computers, 13*(8), 196. DOI: 10.3390/computers13080196

Dillon, R., & Tan, K.-L. (2024). Cybersecurity workforce landscape, education, and industry growth prospects in Southeast Asia. *Journal of Tropical Futures, 1*(2), 172–181. DOI: 10.1177/27538931231176903

Durakovskiy, A. P., Gavdan, G. P., Korsakov, I. A., & Melnikov, D. A. (2021). About the cybersecurity of automated process control systems. *Procedia Computer Science, 190*, 217–225. DOI: 10.1016/j.procs.2021.06.027

Firmansyah, F. H., & Rosmansyah, Y. (2024). Exploring Collaboration in Multiplayer Gamification: A Systematic Literature Review. *IEEE Access : Practical Innovations, Open Solutions.*

Fuchs, K. (2024). Challenges with gamification in higher education: A narrative review with implications for educators and policymakers. *International Journal of Changes in Education, 1*(1), 51–56. DOI: 10.47852/bonviewIJCE32021604

Gil-Aciron, L. A. (2024). The gamer psychology: A psychological perspective on game design and gamification. *Interactive Learning Environments, 32*(1), 183–207. DOI: 10.1080/10494820.2022.2082489

HAWKINSON. E. (2025). Convergence of AR, VR, and AI: The Rise of Immersive Learning Technologies in Higher Education. *Extended reality, AI, and discursive formations*, 21.

Huitema, D., & Wong, A. (2025). A Case Study in Gamification for a Cybersecurity Education Program: A Game for Cryptography. *arXiv preprint arXiv:2502.06706.*

Iqbal, H. S. (2021). AI-Driven Cybersecurity: An Overview, Security Intelligence Modeling and Research Directions. DOI: 10.20944/preprints202101.0457.v1

Javed, D., Jhanjhi, N., Ashfaq, F., Khan, N. A., Das, S. R., & Singh, S. (2024). *Student Performance Analysis to Identify the Students at Risk of Failure.* Paper presented at the 2024 International Conference on Emerging Trends in Networks and Computer Communications (ETNCC). DOI: 10.1109/ETNCC63262.2024.10767511

Karagiannis, S., & Magkos, E. (2020). Adapting CTF challenges into virtual cybersecurity learning environments. *Information and Computer Security*, *29*(1), 105–132. DOI: 10.1108/ICS-04-2019-0050

Katsantonis, M. N., Manikas, A., Mavridis, I., & Gritzalis, D. (2023). Cyber range design framework for cyber security education and training. *International Journal of Information Security*, *22*(4), 1005–1027. DOI: 10.1007/s10207-023-00680-4

Katsikeas, S., Rencelj Ling, E., Johnsson, P., & Ekstedt, M. (2024). Empirical evaluation of a threat modeling language as a cybersecurity assessment tool. *Computers & Security*, *140*, 103743. DOI: 10.1016/j.cose.2024.103743

Khaleghi, A., Aghaei, Z., & Mahdavi, M. A. (2021). A gamification framework for cognitive assessment and cognitive training: Qualitative study. *JMIR Serious Games*, *9*(2), e21900. DOI: 10.2196/21900 PMID: 33819164

Khan, A., Jhanjhi, N., Alı, G. A., Ray, S. K., & Wassan, S. (2025). Case Studies and Applications of Generative AI in Real-World Cybersecurity Scenarios.

Khan, A., Jhanjhi, N., Hamid, D. H. H., Omar, H. A. H. B. H., Amsaad, F., & Wassan, S. (2025). Future Trends and Challenges in Cybersecurity and Generative AI. *Reshaping CyberSecurity With Generative AI Techniques*, 491-522.

Khan, A. R. S., Syed, H. J., Shuja, J., Khan, A., Qamar, F., & Nguyen, Q. N. (2024). Advancing Secure and Efficient Sensor Data Integration in Smart Cities: A Blockchain-Based Approach.

Khan, M. A., Merabet, A., Alkaabi, S., & Sayed, H. E. (2022). Game-based learning platform to enhance cybersecurity education. *Education and Information Technologies*, *27*(4), 1–25. DOI: 10.1007/s10639-021-10807-6

Khan, M. R., Khan, N. R., & Jhanjhi, N. Z. (2024). *Convergence of Industry 4.0 and Supply Chain Sustainability*: IGI Global.

Krath, J., & Von Korflesch, H. F. (2021). Designing gamification and persuasive systems: A systematic literature review. *GamiFIN*, 100-109.

Liu, G. Z., Fathi, J., & Rahimi, M. (2024). Using digital gamification to improve language achievement, foreign language enjoyment, and ideal L2 self: A case of English as a foreign language learners. *Journal of Computer Assisted Learning*, *40*(4), 1347–1364. DOI: 10.1111/jcal.12954

Makdoun, I., Rahhal, I., Mezzour, G., Kassou, I., & Carley, K. M. (2021). Skill mismatch evidence for Cybersecurity skills in Morocco. *Procedia Computer Science*, *184*, 941–946. DOI: 10.1016/j.procs.2021.03.117

Marinho, A., Bittencourt, I. I., Dermeval, D., Santos, J., Challco, G., & Reis, M. (2024 under review). *How does the Mechanics of Competition and Collaboration Impact on Student's Flow Experience in a Gamified Educational Environment? An Experimental Study in Higher Education*. Technology, Knowledge and Learning.

Matovu, R., Nwokeji, J. C., Holmes, T., & Rahman, T. (2022). *Teaching and Learning Cybersecurity Awareness with Gamification in Smaller Universities and Colleges.* Paper presented at the Proceedings - Frontiers in Education Conference, FIE. DOI: 10.1109/FIE56618.2022.9962519

Mazhar, T., Talpur, D. B., Shloul, T. A., Ghadi, Y. Y., Haq, I., Ullah, I., Ouahada, K., & Hamam, H. (2023). Analysis of IoT security challenges and its solutions using artificial intelligence. *Brain Sciences*, *13*(4), 683. DOI: 10.3390/brainsci13040683 PMID: 37190648

Mukherjee, M., Le, N. T., Chow, Y.-W., & Susilo, W. (2024). Strategic approaches to cybersecurity learning: A study of educational models and outcomes. *Information (Basel)*, *15*(2), 117. DOI: 10.3390/info15020117

Mumtaz, S. L., Syed, H. J., Al-Ani, A., Fatah, S., Al-Ani, A. K., & Khan, A. (2024). *Detection of Botnet in the loT Network.* Paper presented at the ITM Web of Conferences. DOI: 10.1051/itmconf/20246301019

Nagaraj, D. H., Abhi, S., & Agarwal, R. (2025). *Cybersecurity awareness: Gamified learning through phishing analysis.* Paper presented at the AIP Conference Proceedings. DOI: 10.1063/5.0247129

Oke, A. E., Aliu, J., Tunji-Olayeni, P., & Abayomi, T. (2024). Application of gamification for sustainable construction: An evaluation of the challenges. *Construction Innovation*, *24*(4), 1066–1084. DOI: 10.1108/CI-09-2022-0247

Oliveira, W., Hamari, J., Shi, L., Toda, A. M., Rodrigues, L., Palomino, P. T., & Isotani, S. (2023). Tailored gamification in education: A literature review and future agenda. *Education and Information Technologies*, *28*(1), 373–406. DOI: 10.1007/s10639-022-11122-4

Piki, A., Stavrou, E., Procopiou, A., & Demosthenous, A. (2023). *Fostering Cybersecurity Awareness and Skills Development Through Digital Game-Based Learning.* Paper presented at the Proceedings of the 2023 IEEE International Conference on Behavioural and Social Computing, BESC 2023. DOI: 10.1109/BESC59560.2023.10386988

Pirta-Dreimane, R., Brilingaitė, A., Roponena, E., Parish, K., Grabis, J., Lugo, R. G., & Bonders, M. (2023). *CyberEscape Approach to Advancing Hard and Soft Skills in Cybersecurity Education.* Paper presented at the Lecture Notes in Computer Science (including subseries Lecture Notes in Artificial Intelligence and Lecture Notes in Bioinformatics). DOI: 10.1007/978-3-031-35017-7_28

Pramod, D. (2024). Gamification in cybersecurity education; a state of the art review and research agenda. *Journal of Applied Research in Higher Education.*

Quayyum, F. (2021). *Cyber security education for children through gamification: Challenges and research perspectives.* Paper presented at the Methodologies and Intelligent Systems for Technology Enhanced Learning, 10th International Conference. Workshops: Volume 2. DOI: 10.1007/978-3-030-52287-2_26

Rana, S., & Chicone, R. (2025). Gamification and Immersive Learning with AI. In *Fortifying the Future: Harnessing AI for Transformative Cybersecurity Training* (pp. 51-75): Springer. DOI: 10.1007/978-3-031-81780-9_3

Razack, A. K. A., & Saad, M. F. M. (2024). Enhancing Cybersecurity Awareness through Gamification: Design an Interactive Cybersecurity Learning Platform for Multimedia University Students. *Journal of Informatics and Web Engineering*, *3*(3), 21–40. DOI: 10.33093/jiwe.2024.3.3.2

Rehan, H. (2024). AI-Driven Cloud Security: The Future of Safeguarding Sensitive Data in the Digital Age. *Journal of Artificial Intelligence General science (JAIGS) ISSN: 3006-4023, 1*(1), 47-66.

Robson, K., Plangger, K., Kietzmann, J. H., McCarthy, I., & Pitt, L. (2015). Is it all a game? Understanding the principles of gamification. *Business Horizons*, *58*(4), 411–420. DOI: 10.1016/j.bushor.2015.03.006

Saeed, S., Jhanjhi, N., Naqvi, S. M. R., & Khan, A. (2022). Analytical Approach for Security of Sensitive Business Cloud. *Deep Learning in Data Analytics: Recent Techniques, Practices and Applications*, 257-266.

Sezgin, S., & Yüzer, T. V. (2022). Analysing adaptive gamification design principles for online courses. *Behaviour & Information Technology*, *41*(3), 485–501. DOI: 10.1080/0144929X.2020.1817559

Shahid, H., Ashraf, H., Jhanjhi, N., & Zam, Q.-u. A. Z. (2025). Reshaping Cybersecurity of Wireless Sensor Networks Using Energy-Optimized Approach Against Wormhole Attack. In *Reshaping CyberSecurity With Generative AI Techniques* (pp. 125-172): IGI Global.

Sindiramutty, S. R., Jhanjhi, N., & Ray, S. K. (2024). Threat Hunting and Behaviour Analysis. *Utilizing Generative AI for Cyber Defense Strategies*, 235.

Sindiramutty, S. R., Jhanjhi, N. Z., Tan, C. E., Khan, N. A., Shah, B., & Manchuri, A. R. (2024). Cybersecurity Measures for Logistics Industry. In *Navigating Cyber Threats and Cybersecurity in the Logistics Industry* (pp. 1–58). IGI Global. DOI: 10.4018/979-8-3693-3816-2.ch001

Sindiramutty, S. R., Prabagaran, K. R. V., Jhanjhi, N., Ghazanfar, M. A., Malik, N. A., & Soomro, T. R. (2025). Security Considerations in Generative AI for Web Applications. In *Reshaping CyberSecurity With Generative AI Techniques* (pp. 281–332). IGI Global.

Sindiramutty, S. R., Prabagaran, K. R. V., Jhanjhi, N., & Murugesan, R. K. (2024). Threat Intelligence and Information Sharing. *Utilizing Generative AI for Cyber Defense Strategies*, 191.

Tayyab, M., Hameed, K., Jhanjhi, N. Z., Zaheer, A., & Qamar, F. (2024). Digital Safeguards: Navigating Cyber Threats in the Logistics Industry Framework. In *Navigating Cyber Threats and Cybersecurity in the Logistics Industry* (pp. 258-299): IGI Global.

Tharot, K., Riel, A., & Thiriet, J. M. (2024). *A Gamification Approach to Teaching Cybersecurity in CPS.* Paper presented at the Procedia CIRP. DOI: 10.1016/j.procir.2024.06.039

Thompson, L. A., Melendez, N., Hempson-Jones, J., & Salvi, F. (2022). *Gamification in Cybersecurity Education; the RAD-SIM Framework for Effective Learning.* Paper presented at the European Conference on Games Based Learning. DOI: 10.34190/ecgbl.16.1.504

Tomé Klock, A. C., Palomino, P. T., Rodrigues, L. A. L., Toda, A. M., Simanke, S., Spors, V., . . . Hamari, J. (2024). Gamification towards and alongside equity, diversity and inclusion: Looking back to move forward. *new media & society*, 14614448241254028.

Yu, R., Wang, Y., & Wang, W. (2024). AMAD: Active learning-based multivariate time series anomaly detection for large-scale IT systems. *Computers & Security*, *137*, 103603. DOI: 10.1016/j.cose.2023.103603

Zhang, A. K., Perry, N., Dulepet, R., Ji, J., Menders, C., Lin, J. W., . . . Jasper, D. (2024). Cybench: A framework for evaluating cybersecurity capabilities and risks of language models. *arXiv preprint arXiv:2408.08926.*

Zhong, C., Kim, J. B., & Liu, H. (2022). *The Impact of Gamification on Students' Learning Outcome and Career Interest in Cybersecurity Education.* Paper presented at the 28th Americas Conference on Information Systems, AMCIS 2022.

Zhong, C., Kim, J. B. J. B., & Liu, H. (2024). The Art of Inclusive Gamification in Cybersecurity Training. *IEEE Security and Privacy*, *22*(5), 40–51. DOI: 10.1109/MSEC.2024.3427666

Chapter 10
Increasing the Awareness and Participation of Young Women in Cybersecurity

S. Ida Evangeline
https://orcid.org/0000-0003-2997-7897
Government College of Engineering, Tirunelveli, India

ABSTRACT

Despite women making up a tiny percentage of the workforce, cybersecurity has expanded rapidly and continues to grow in response to the ever increasing complexity of cyber threats in the world. Leave it to men to lead the race while women almost trail, thus narrowing down the diversity and innovation while contributing to the worldwide shortage of cybersecurity professionals. It investigates the principal obstacles that keep young women from participating in cybersecurity, from the prevailing social stereotypes to gaps in education, discriminatory work climates, to psychological hurdles like confidence gaps and impostor syndrome. It looks at how cultural expectations and systemic barriers dictate where women can and cannot go in terms of their career choices and professional experiences and can sadly work to dissuade women from entering or staying in the cybersecurity field. The chapter addresses these challenges by presenting successful initiatives and strategies used to enhance the participation of females in cybersecurity.

DOI: 10.4018/979-8-3373-0477-9.ch010

INTRODUCTION

Over the last few years, traditional life has been rapidly transformed through digital expansion, which has touched upon almost every aspect of modern life including communication, commerce, health and the security of nations. The more organizations and people depend on digital systems, the more cyberattacks scale and grow in sophistication. As this threat landscape evolves, there is a growing need for cybersecurity professionals with these skills to safeguard critical infrastructure, sensitive data, and digital assets. However, despite this growing need, the demand for cybersecurity workers is also met with a fiercely male dominated workforce as women are still a tiny fraction. Just as a problem cannot be solved with the same mindset that got us into it, diversity of perspective and approaches to solving problems is important, especially when it comes to complex cyber threats, and the fact that the cyber sector is lacking females makes it hard to provide that (Prümmer et al. 2024).

The lack of women in cybersecurity is a complex problem that is based on obstacles within society, education, and institutions. Deep seated stereotypes and a lack of role models to look up to discourage many young women to pursue careers in science, technology, engineering and mathematics (STEM) right from an early age (Shafik, 2024). Where, even those thinking to develop a bias in technology find themselves in environments that are not favorable to their growth, either through educational biases, lack of mentorship or working cultures that don't advocate for inclusivity. Both the low participation of women in cybersecurity education and the high attrition rates of women in the profession are affected by these challenges. Fixing this imbalance is not a question of fairness, but rather a matter of necessity to encourage innovation, strengthen the cybersecurity resilience, and grant the industry an increased spectrum of skills and points of view (Al-Soud & Al Dweri, 2024).

In cybersecurity, diversity is important for strengthening problem solving and increasing innovation. It is this influxes of ideas, experiences, and analytical approaches, borne of a differing perspective, which have been proven time and again by research, to make diverse teams outperform homogenous ones. Because a gender inclusive workforce is a needed element of the field of cybersecurity, which demands flexibility, imagination, and strategic thinking, is an area that is ripe for a more gender inclusive workforce. Furthermore, the number of cybersecurity professionals around the world desperately needed for critical roles is in the millions, and accordingly it became necessary to proactively recruit and retain underrepresented talent, i.e. young women. On the other hand, by escalating awareness and involvement in the industry, the industry can solve its talent gap and create a more dynamic and efficient workforce that can tackle future cybersecurity issues (Al-Emran & Deveci, 2024).

The objective of this chapter is to identify the reasons behind the lack of women in cybersecurity and how to raise awareness and motivate more women to participate. The paper will look at societal and educational obstacles that discourage young women from entering the cybersecurity workplace, identify best practices that are able to overcome the gender gap and present ways to cultivate more inclusive and fair cybersecurity practice. Addressing these challenges and areas of opportunity, this chapter aims to give something to the larger discourse around gender diversity in STEM and for a cybersecurity industry that fully utilizes its reservoir of talent.

THE GENDER GAP IN CYBERSECURITY: CAUSES AND CONSEQUENCES

Gender inequity in cybersecurity has been engrained into the systems that discourage women's participation and retention in cybersecurity. The problem is not the young women lack interest: they just have not been inclined to interest themselves because this gap starts early and persistently in the academia and the professional space. In order to develop strategies that can better mitigate this disparity and create a more diverse cybersecurity workforce, understanding the reasons of this disparity is of paramount importance (Francis et al. 2024).

Societal norms and stereotypes are among the earliest factors that have led to the gender gap in cybersecurity. Long standing gender biases lead many girls to be subtly or explicitly guided away from STEM subjects from a young age. The belief that technology and cybersecurity are male dominated fields in nature makes young women envision themselves in such careers. These stereotypes are reinforced by parents, teachers, and media representations which displays their views. In films, television and news, as well as in educational materials that portray cybersecurity professionals, women are not represented very often, which leads young girls to believe that they do not belong in the field. Moreover, this problem is exacerbated by the lack of visible female role models in cybersecurity, which makes it difficult for young women to relate to and look up to possible career influencers in technology (Asiry, 2024).

Adding to the gender divide in cybersecurity are educational barriers. Cybersecurity is either completely missing from the curriculum or introduced in a way that does not pique the interest of young women in many school systems. Because of the lack of structured early exposure, many girls don't grow up having an interest in cybersecurity because they never were introduced to it in a meaningful way. Typically, traditional teaching emphasizes the learning of theoretical or highly complex technical content without relating it to real world applications, dismissing the field from the perspective of students who visualize neither the relevance of it in their day to day lives or the accessibility of it to them. Lastly, because young women are often excluded from such cybersecurity extracurricular activities (coding clubs, hackathons, mentorship programs, etc.), opportunities to explore and learn related skills in these areas, for instance, are also restricted. However, even if these programs exist, they are often male dominated spaces that are not welcoming to young women and do not encourage their participation (Ramonyai et al. 2024).

Despite the fact that many women have overcome early hurdles and pursued cybersecurity education or careers, workplace challenges have often prevented their long-term success and retention in the field. Hiring, promotions and professional development continue to be governed by gender bias, which sets differences aside and puts women in below positions to do better than men to prove their competence in the field. Mistake number one comes from workplace cultures that fail to proactively promote inclusivity, which then may result in feelings of isolation, discrimination, or limited career growth opportunities. In addition, pay disparities further deter women from sticking around in the field as they tend to be paid less than men for the same roles. The nature of many women's jobs increases the severity of these issues because a lack of mentorship and support networks means that they have little guidance to navigate the career challenges they face. Therefore, women are leaving cybersecurity at high rates due to systemic barriers (Selma Housein & Plancher, 2025), not because they lack the ability or interest.

While the gender gap in cybersecurity is felt on an individual level in terms of career advancement, its consequences are felt throughout the entire industry. Recurring research has shown that diversity in teams leads to improved problem solving, innovation, creativity, and decision making—employing sought after traits in a field that seeks new solutions to an ever-changing problem set. Without the insight and support of women, the industry may produce solutions with a lower capability for tackling the multiple cybersecurity struggles that we all face, both as individuals, in businesses, and in government. Additionally, as the pressure surrounding a critical shortage of skilled cybersecurity professionals continues, with millions of unfilled cybersecurity positions worldwide, underrepresented talent pools must be snapped up to help blunt the blow of cyber insecurity. Not only is it equitable to increase women's participation in cybersecurity, it is also a strategic necessity to meet the burgeoning requirements of the digital protection environment. The achievement of a gender diverse workforce offers organizations a more resilient, dynamic and robust workforce more equipped to predict and mitigate cyber threats. Thus, addressing the gender gap in the field of cybersecurity is both a moral and practical imperative and efforts are needed to be concerted by the educators, policymakers and the industry leaders in building an inclusive and supportive environment for women in the field (Dev & Saha, 2024).

EXISTING INITIATIVES AND SUCCESS STORIES

To close the gender gap in cybersecurity, targeted efforts at all levels, starting from early education, as well as while on a professional career path are required. Across the globe, various initiatives have been taken up to encourage young women to learn about cybersecurity, gain hands on experience and pursue careers in the field for the long term. These innovations are across educational programs, mentorship networks, and diversity initiatives led by industry, and all contribute to dismantling the societal barriers that have excluded women from entering the cybersecurity space. However, the challenge on how to scale these programs and how to widen their audience still remain (Bognár & Bottyán, 2024).

Early exposure to educational and outreach programs is one of the most effective ways to increase women's participation in cybersecurity. Initiatives introducing cybersecurity concepts in a school setting at an early stage have been successful in generating interest in young women. Girls Who Code and CyberFirst are programs that offer structured learning experiences, not only in learning technical skills but also in a supportive environment where young women can see themselves in technology fields (Namukasa et al. 2025). Another engaging approach to cybersecurity competitions is to design competitions specifically for female students. In this manner, these competitions provide opportunities for individuals to apply their skills in real life scenarios improving confidence as well as sense of accomplishment. There have also been emerging gamified learning methods for making cyber security more accessible. The hands-on challenges that simulate cyber threats are an engaging and educational way for young women to explore the field without intimidation, through interactive workshops. As such, these approaches counteract traditional teaching methods that appear too theoretical or too difficult to grasp and make cybersecurity more appealing and graspable (Căciulescu et al. 2024).

In addition to education mentorship and networking programs are very important in empowering women along their cybersecurity journey. Though mentorship is important and, having somebody knowledgeable and supportive can help a lot with career development. One-way programs have been successful in connecting female students with professionals in the industry has been through programs that guide, encourage and arrange opportunities the female students may not otherwise have access to. Usually, successful mentorship-driven initiatives, such as Women in Cybersecurity (WiCyS) network, have help thrive in plugging the gap by providing training, career development workshops, and direct connections with industry leaders. These programs give a much-needed support system to young women entering the field and foster a sense of belonging. Likewise, the Ada Initiative and Cybersecurity Women of the Year Awards are women-led cybersecurity networks that celebrate and promote women in the industry and encourage the next generation to follow in their footsteps. Apart from providing a platform for professional growth, these networks contradict the narrative that cybersecurity is a space that is only for men (Ouma et al. 2025).

In addition, gender diversity in cybersecurity has been promoted by industry and policy interventions. Diversity programs that achieve an increase of women in cybersecurity roles are being launched by many corporations, who have seen the value in fostering an inclusive workforce. Initiatives like IBM, Microsoft and Google have initiated which provide the scholarship, internship and career advancement opportunities for women. In addition to recruitment, these programs seek to retain women professionals through developing workplace cultures that are supportive of and empower female professionals (Almazroei, 2024). On a larger scale, government initiatives and policies have attempted to bridge gender gaps in STEM and cybersecurity by funding, making educational reforms, and awareness campaigns. The U.S. National Initiative for Cybersecurity Education (NICE) and the EU's Women in Digital Strategy are a couple of national efforts that also recognize the significance of diversity by gender in terms of the cybersecurity workforce. Djeki et al. (2024) stated that some countries have taken action by introducing policies that compel companies to disclose gender diversity metrics in order to increase transparency and accountability in their hiring practices.

Studies of companies that have made champions of inclusivity bring these changes to life. For instance, the Cybersecurity Talent Initiative is a public–private partnership that pairs students, especially women and people of color, with leadership cybersecurity positions in government and industry. Yet another great initiative is the SANS CyberTalent Immersion Academy for Women that offers full scholarships and training to women interested in breaking into this fast-increasing cybersecurity field. Female participation and the creation of career pathways that have been out of reach for many young women have been proven to be measurable successes of these programs (Sala, 2024).

However, these projects have indeed had an effect, but now we must increase and maintain them on the global stage. Collaboration among the educational institutions, corporations, and other policymakers is needed for these efforts to be successful in reaching more young women and offering long term solutions for inclusivity that could bring equality in the field of cybersecurity. Continuing to build on the success of existing programs and innovating new approaches, the industry can move forward towards a future where women are not only participants but leaders in the creation of the cybersecurity landscape (Buçaj et al. 2024).

STRATEGIES FOR INCREASING AWARENESS AND PARTICIPATION

The first step to increasing the awareness and participation of young women in cybersecurity is in education and then into professional environments. To address the existing gender disparity, the strategies to implement are early exposure, positive representation, industry and government collaboration, and strong network for women in cybersecurity. Efforts in this regard must be systemic and sustained, so that young women not only enter the field but also succeed in it (Khan et al. 2025).

One of the most effective ways for young women to become involved in cybersecurity, is educating them in cyber through the school curriculum. Because they've never been shown that cybersecurity is a field that they could be interested in, many young women do not consider careers in this field. In order to fix this, the redesign of the curriculum should make cybersecurity content engaging, relevant, and accessible. Project based assignment, cybersecurity, simulations and ethical hacking challenges can make the subject more interactive and appealing. Whereas the traditional theory laden instruction often fails to catch the students' interest, experiential learning helps in bridging the gap between concepts and applications of the real world. Moreover, teachers are responsible for shaping students' attitudes toward cybersecurity and they should be trained to help create gender inclusive learning environments. Classroom discussions about the societal impact of cybersecurity, the presentation of successful female cybersecurity professionals, and challenging gender bias in STEM subjects can make cybersecurity more inviting to young women (Barbosa, 2024).

Outside the classroom, media representation and storytelling hold great power in changing perceptions and encouraging young women to enter the field of cybersecurity. In the past, cybersecurity professionals in the movies, tv and the news mostly male and if not made it seem like that was a field that women weren't welcome in. It is, therefore, necessary to highlight female role models in cybersecurity to counteract these stereotypes. Documentaries, books and online campaigns showing women in cybersecurity for what they are and what they've achieved can help to normalize their presence in that field. Encouraging young women to see themselves as part of the industry can be achieved through media campaigns that highlight the significance of diversity in cybersecurity and the success of women in the field. Social media platforms and online advocacy also have a major part in deciding career choices. Websites like LinkedIn, Twitter, and YouTube offer opportunities for women in cybersecurity to tell their stories, provide advice and connect with one another. The strategy of utilising digital platforms to amplify female voices and build conversation around gender inclusivity can be highly effective in engaging the next generation (Malik, 2024).

Another critical component in the solution to the gender gap in cybersecurity is the industry and government collaboration. They must actively work to offer scholarships, internships, and apprenticeship programs to companies and to policymakers to target young women. Lack of resources or opportunities to pursue cybersecurity careers can be lowered by providing financial and professional support. Furthermore, workplace culture needs to be changed to be inclusive. This involves putting in place policies that elevate diversity with regard to hiring and career advancement and ensuring that fairness is applied to equal pay for equal work. Women in male dominated fields continue to be deterred by the gender pay gap, and industry cannot disengage on this and expect to retain these women long term. Additionally, governments can hold organizations to account on diversity commitments and provide policy frameworks that encourage diversity within STEM industries and fund programs that support women in the cybersecurity field (Dapitan et al. 2024).

To make sure young women enter the field of cybersecurity and stay and advance in the field, a supportive ecosystem is critical. Mentorship and peer networks serve as key components in career development for young women, which helps them to give well to advice, support and provide them with access to opportunities. Connecting students with female cybersecurity professionals can be invaluable, in providing guidance on how to overcome any of the challenges of the industry. Besides mentorship, encouraging women led cybersecurity conferences, networking events, and online forums that create inclusive spaces for learning and professional growth encourages women to feel a sense of belonging and empowerment. Furthermore, male allies are required to change workplace culture and promote gender diversity. Male leaders and male colleagues who actively support and advocate for women in cybersecurity help create an environment in which women are respected, valued, and given equal opportunity (Manoharan et al. 2025).

There is no single initiative that can solve the problem of increased participation of young women in cybersecurity. It's a problem that requires a collective effort on education, media, industry, and policy. Through the implementation of an all-encompassing strategy, which encompasses both awareness and retention, the cybersecurity industry will be able to move towards a more inclusive and diverse workforce. As such, it will make this sector stronger and more innovative and better prepared to counter the new digital threats of the future (Mosley et al. 2024).

THE FUTURE OF WOMEN IN CYBERSECURITY

With the evolution of digital landscape, the future of women in cybersecurity has a very exciting scope for women engagement, leadership and innovation in the coming days. Such an increase in cyber threats in terms of complexity and urgency means that there is a high demand for skilled professionals in this sector. This growing need can offer a rare opportunity to close the gender gap by actively placing women in cybersecurity roles and encouraging inclusive workforce. Significant efforts have been made to raise awareness and to make pathways for women to enter the field, although sustaining and proliferating these efforts will be essential to creating a more diverse and capable security industry as described in Costa et al. (2025).

Artificial Intelligence (AI), machine learning, quantum computing, and blockchain are emerging technologies that are reshaping the cybersecurity landscape. These advances bring with them both new and potential threats as well as potential solutions. With future development of these technologies, women will be able to specialize in cutting edge areas of cybersecurity and have leadership positions in research, policy making, and technological innovation. To further broaden the scope of career possibilities in the cyber security, the digital forensics, ethical hacking and the cyber resilience are to be integrated together and for that to happen women need to be a part of the betterment of the future of the digital security. This will not only enhance the workforce with women but will also ensure that cybersecurity solutions are developed with diverse points of view and will, as a result, be more effective and more inclusive (Pashaj & Gjika, 2024).

It isn't just about your individual career advancement; making an impact on diversity in cybersecurity will be long term. Gender diverse workforce actively supports innovation, creativity and problem solving necessary to counter sophisticated cyber threats. They bring a different set of viewpoints and analytical approaches to security issues, studies have shown, and diverse teams are better at anticipating and managing risks. By increasing participation of women in cybersecurity the demand for talent will be also met and workplace environments that support inclusion, retention and career progression developed. Growing financial and strategic returns are imminent for companies and institutions committed to gender diversity; women add value to security solutions and organizational cultures that achieve the best talent and long–term success (Foley & Basu, 2024), leading to increased growth outcomes.

Going forward, educators, industry leaders and policymakers must go out of their way to maintain and grow efforts to boost women's involvement in cybersecurity. Cybersecurity must be integrated into curricula in all educational institutions, from early exposure of young women to the field to engaging and hands on learning opportunities. Industry leaders must pledge their efforts to create inclusive workplaces with the mentorship programs, equitable hiring and leadership opportunities for women. Policymakers must actively pass regulations that encourage gender diversity, fund programs that serve disadvantaged groups, and guarantee the availability of cybersecurity education to everyone. These key stakeholders need to work together in order to maintain the momentum of progress and achieve the bigger systemic change that will define the future of cybersecurity for generations to come (Mhajne & Whetstone, 2024).

And as the field evolves, so must the efforts to bring women to every level of cybersecurity. Breaking down barriers, providing equitable opportunities and also recognizing the importance of a diverse workforce are some ways through which the industry will be able to confront the challenges that are linked to a more intricate digital world. While technology advancements provide the future of cyber safety, we can also look at the need to create a world where talent comes from all backgrounds. This future must ensure women are part of this future, not just because it is equity but because it is strategic, as women are a key element to a more resilient and innovative cybersecurity industry (Almazroei, 2024).

PSYCHOLOGICAL AND CULTURAL FACTORS INFLUENCING WOMEN'S PARTICIPATION

It turns out that barriers preventing women from participating in cybersecurity go well beyond external barriers like education and workplace opportunities; deep seated psychological and cultural roots affect career decision and trajectories. Early on, the majority of women are socialized to distrust their ability in technical areas and that doubt follows them into adulthood. Women in male dominated industries like Cyber Security, are especially vulnerable victims of impostor syndrome because they experience a sense of doubt in their achievements and fear of being exposed as frauds. Yet, despite being well qualified and equipped with the right skills, many women internalize feelings of inadequacy, and as a result, they do not apply for leadership roles, do not seek promotions, and in some cases, do not even enter the field at all. The societal messages that technology and cybersecurity are inherently masculine domains reinforce this self-doubt (Edwards, 2024).

The issue is further complicated by cultural variations in terms of gender expectations that affect how women see and approach careers in STEM fields around the world. Society expects women to take up the caregiving role while subordinating themselves to professional ambitions, making it harder for them to be involved in intensive technical careers that demand long hours and continuous improvement of skills. On the contrary, countries which advocate for gender equality in education and the workplace are more likely to have a higher female presence in cybersecurity. The support of the parents and institutions is also important in defining the aspirations of young women. Early exposure to technology in societies that aren't gender specific tends to create more women interested in cybersecurity as a career. Furthermore, strong female role models in various cultural contexts can make a big difference in young women's career choices and show that it is possible to succeed in cybersecurity (Katcher et al. 2024).

Workplace culture also infuses language and biases that affect women's experience in cybersecurity. Job descriptions, performance evaluations and everyday workplace interactions rife with gendered language can perpetuate stereotypes that diminish a woman's confidence. Words like 'aggressive problem solver' or 'authoritative leader' may, in a subtle way, discourage women from applying because they unwittingly evince an ideological preference for traditionally masculine traits. Consequently, workplace biases (both implicit and explicit) also play a part in the culture that makes women feel unwelcome or underappreciated. It is quite common for women in the cybersecurity work and many of them report being overlooked for promotions, less recognized for their work, and even resisted when they assert themselves in the technical discussions. The biases established in this environment force women to constantly prove their expertise until they burnout and leave the field at higher rates (Taylor & Whitty, 2024).

These psychological and cultural barriers can be addressed only by a fundamental change to how cybersecurity is perceived and structured. Additionally, there are mentorship programs that encourage self confidence whereby job postings and evaluation use inclusive languages, and workplaces which promote diversity by creating cultures that actively support diversity. Acknowledging and addressing the psychological and cultural factors that impact women's participation in cybersecurity can help to create an environment in which women feel empowered to pursue, succeed in, and lead in cybersecurity (Bailey et al. 2024).

CONCLUSION

The representation of women in the field of cybersecurity is spatially complex, where society, educational structure, work environment and psychological barriers play crucial roles. In this chapter, implications of the discussion revolve around the tremendous impediments young women encounter in pursuing a career in cybersecurity – from early exposure to societal indoctrination, to structures within the industry. These challenges not only prevent individuals from taking full advantage of opportunities they have, but also prevent the entire cybersecurity industry and its pursuit of diverse perspectives, from enjoying their benefits in improving problem solving, creativity and resiliency to cyber threats. These disparities can only be addressed through a multi pronged approach of education, mentorship, industry reform, and a cultural change to create an environment that welcomes women, values them, encourages long term careers in cybersecurity.

This is not merely an issue of fairness or social responsibility regarding increased participation of women in cybersecurity, but a strategic, fundamental need for increasing a workforce that will be stronger and more effective. The industry cannot afford to overlook half of the talent pool as the complexity of cyber threats continues to increase. With a diversified workforce, you get different viewpoints leading to different ways of solving issues, in turn, better security solutions. Additionally, closing the gender gap in cybersecurity could act as a template for broader diversity initiatives in STEM as a valid demonstration of committed efforts to improve diversity can make a real difference. Shaping this transformation relies on the educators, industry leaders, policymakers, and media. To reduce the gender gap, cybersecurity should be integrated into the school curricula, such as through introduction of mentors and promotion of gender inclusive workplace policy, besides offerings to increase women's awareness and faculty in the field.

In the future, the aim of the goal should not just be to meet inclusivity to create a cybersecurity industry that is both dynamic and innovative, it should be one that represents the diversity of the world's population. It means persistent work to do away with barriers of gender, make the workplace equitable in terms of culture, and actively aiding women's ascent in the field. Cybersecurity needs to keep up with technological advancement and workforce needs; these two things are the future of cybersecurity. When women have an equal right to opportunities, leadership roles and professional development, the industry can optimize its talent pool; this would inevitably translate to effective and more inclusive cybersecurity strategies. The future vision is of a world where young women view cybersecurity as a place where they belong, where their work is appreciated, and where they can succeed as innovators, leaders and guardians of the digital world.

REFERENCES

Al-Emran, M., & Deveci, M. (2024). Unlocking the potential of cybersecurity behavior in the metaverse: Overview, opportunities, challenges, and future research agendas. *Technology in Society*, *77*, 102498. DOI: 10.1016/j.techsoc.2024.102498

Al-Soud, A., & Al Dweri, K. (2024). Exploring the Landscape of Cyber Crimes Targeting Women: A Literature Review on Cyber Security Laws. *Al-Balqa Journal for Research and Studies*, *27*(2), 272–290. DOI: 10.35875/04x1hz93

Almazroei, A. A. (2024). *The Case Study of Qatari Women in the Field of Cybersecurity: Exploring Challenges and Opportunities* (Master's thesis, Hamad Bin Khalifa University (Qatar)).

Asiry, Y. (2024). Closing the gap: Boosting women's representation in cybersecurity leadership. *Journal of Information Security*, *15*(1), 15–23. DOI: 10.4236/jis.2024.151002

Bailey, D., Kornegay, M., Partlow, L., Bowens, C., Gareis, C., & Kornegay, K. (2024). *Utilizing Culturally Responsive Strategies to Inspire African American Female Participation in Cybersecurity American Female Participation in Cybersecurity. Journal of Pre-College Engineering Education Research*. J-PEER.

Barbosa, J. (2024). Education in Cybersecurity–A Case Study. *WSEAS Transactions on Advances in Engineering Education*, *21*, 92–109. DOI: 10.37394/232010.2024.21.12

Bognár, L., & Bottyán, L. (2024). Evaluating online security behavior: Development and validation of a personal cybersecurity awareness scale for university students. *Education Sciences*, *14*(6), 588. DOI: 10.3390/educsci14060588

Buçaj, E. (2024). Empowering Cybersecurity Awareness among the Citizens of Kosovo. InterEULawEast: Journal for the international and european law, economics and market integrations, 11(1), 1-29.

Căciulescu, A. R., Rughini , R. V., Tsurcanu, D., & Radovici, A. (2024). Mapping Cyber-Financial Risk Profiles: Implications for European Cybersecurity and Financial Literacy. *Risks*, 1-25.

Costa, G., De Francisci, S., Renieri, M., & Valiani, S. (2025, February). Tackling the Gender Gap in Cybersecurity Education. In *Proceedings of the 56th ACM Technical Symposium on Computer Science Education* V. 1 (pp. 234-240). DOI: 10.1145/3641554.3701807

Dapitan, J. U., Butchayo, J. M. M., Palma, J. L. R., Arevalo, M. A., Alvarico, A. B., & Cuevas, J. F.Jr. (2024). Measuring the Level of Cybersecurity Awareness among Senior High School Students. [MJBAS]. *Mediterranean Journal of Basic and Applied Sciences*, *8*(2), 208–217. DOI: 10.46382/MJBAS.2024.8216

Dev, M., & Saha, D. (2024). Does e-government development moderate the impact of female labor participation on national cybersecurity maturity? An empirical investigation. *Information and Computer Security*, *32*(1), 74–92. DOI: 10.1108/ICS-03-2023-0042

Djeki, E., Dégila, J., & Alhassan, M. H. (2024). West African online learning spaces security status and students' cybersecurity awareness level during COVID-19 lockdown. *Education and Information Technologies*, *29*(12), 15557–15587. DOI: 10.1007/s10639-024-12472-x

Edwards, J. J. (2024). *Establishing Cybersecurity Dominance by Introducing Women to the Fight* (Doctoral dissertation, Capitol Technology University).

Foley, M., & Basu, S. (2024). Decoding the gendered imaginary of cybersecurity careers: A social shaping of technology perspective. *Information Communication and Society*, •••, 1–17.

Francis, S. P., Kolil, V. K., Pavithran, V., Ray, I., & Achuthan, K. (2024). Exploring gender dynamics in cybersecurity education: A self-determination theory and social cognitive theory perspective. *Computers & Security*, *144*, 103968. DOI: 10.1016/j.cose.2024.103968

Katcher, S., Wang, L., Yang, C., Messdaghi, C., Mazurek, M. L., Chetty, M., & Votipka, D. (2024). A Survey of Cybersecurity {Professionals'} Perceptions and Experiences of Safety and Belonging in the Community. In *Twentieth Symposium on Usable Privacy and Security (SOUPS 2024)* (pp. 1-20).

Khan, S. K., Shiwakoti, N., Wang, J., Xu, H., Xiang, C., Zhou, X., & Jiang, H. (2025). An Investigation on Passengers' Perceptions of Cybersecurity in the Airline Industry. *Future Transportation*, *5*(1), 5. DOI: 10.3390/futuretransp5010005

Malik, C. D. S. (2024, December). Technology and Women Empowerment: Bridging the Gender Gap in the Digital Era. *International Journal for Research Publication and Seminar*, *15*(4), 132–126. DOI: 10.36676/jrps.v15.i4.19

Manoharan, A., Sriskantharajah, A., Herath, H. M. K. K. M. B., Guruge, L. G. P. K., & Yasakethu, S. L. P. (2025). MetaHuman based phishing attacks in the metaverse realm: Awareness for cyber security education. *Education and Information Technologies*, *30*(9), 1–27. DOI: 10.1007/s10639-025-13326-w

Mhajne, A., & Whetstone, C. (2024). A feminist cybersecurity: Addressing the crisis of cyber (in) security. *International Affairs*, *100*(6), 2341–2360. DOI: 10.1093/ia/iiae234

Mosley, P., Chen, L. C., Ellrodt, L., & Ulysse, D. (2024). Camp CryptoBot: A Model for Taking Risks and Promoting Self-Efficacy in Pursuit of Cybersecurity Career Pathways. *Journal of Computing Sciences in Colleges*, *39*(7), 72–81.

Namukasa, M., Chaparro Osman, M., Ficke, C., Piasecki, I., OConnor, T. J., & Carroll, M. (2025). Evaluation of an Internet of Things Device-Based Educational Approach to Engage a More Diverse Cybersecurity Workforce. *International Journal of Human-Computer Interaction*, *41*(2), 1364–1380. DOI: 10.1080/10447318.2024.2314349

Ouma, J., Wambalaba, F., Musuva, P., & Namasake, M. (2025). Influence of Gender Mainstreaming in Closing the Cybersecurity Workforce Gap: Insights from the Cyber Shujaa Upskilling Program. *African Journal of Business and Development Studies*, *1*(2), 300–317. DOI: 10.70641/ajbds.v1i2.110

Pashaj, K., & Gjika, E. (2024). Gender Inequality in Cybersecurity Exploring the Opportunities and Progression in Albania. *Smart Cities and Regional Development (SCRD) Preprints, 1*(1).

Prümmer, J., van Steen, T., & van den Berg, B. (2024). A systematic review of current cybersecurity training methods. *Computers & Security*, *136*, 103585. DOI: 10.1016/j.cose.2023.103585

Ramonyai, T. M., Mpekoa, N., & Tom, S. (2024, March). Cyber security skills development in South Africa: Addressing the Gender Gap in the Industry. In *2024 Conference on Information Communications Technology and Society (ICTAS)* (pp. 144-149). IEEE. DOI: 10.1109/ICTAS59620.2024.10507137

Sala, E. (2024). Descriptive Analysis of Cybersecurity Awareness Among Smartphone Users in Higher Education. *Journal of Transactions in Systems Engineering*, *2*(2), 222–234.

Selma-Housein, E., & Plancher, B. (2025, February). Improving the Representation of Undergraduate Women in Cybersecurity: A Literature Review. In *Proceedings of the 56th ACM Technical Symposium on Computer Science Education* V. 1 (pp. 1043-1049).

Shafik, W. (2024). Dissecting the role of women in cybersecurity and information technology: a medical perspective. In *Next-Generation Cybersecurity: AI, ML, and Blockchain* (pp. 325–350). Springer Nature Singapore. DOI: 10.1007/978-981-97-1249-6_15

Taylor, J., & Whitty, M. (2024). An exploration of the awareness and attitudes of psychology students regarding their psychological literacy for working in the cybersecurity industry. *Psychology Learning & Teaching*, *23*(2), 298–314. DOI: 10.1177/14757257231214612

Chapter 11
Adaptive Gamification Strategies for Different Learning Styles in Cybersecurity

Siva Raja Sindiramutty
https://orcid.org/0009-0006-0310-8721
Taylor's University, Malaysia

Bashir Riskhan
Albukhari International University, Malaysia

Mamoona Humayun
Independent Researcher, UK

ABSTRACT

Adaptive gamification tailors cybersecurity training to individual learning styles, making lessons more engaging and effective. Traditional teaching methods often fail to hold attention or meet diverse needs, leaving gaps in understanding. By adjusting game mechanics based on how people absorb information, whether through visuals, audio, hands-on practice, or structured text—learning becomes more natural and rewarding. AI-driven systems fine-tune challenges in real-time, keeping learners engaged without overwhelming them. Cybersecurity training platforms are beginning to incorporate these strategies, offering interactive simulations, personalised learning paths, and real-time difficulty adjustments. Capture the Flag competitions, for example, now include adaptive hints and challenge scaling, allowing both beginners and experts to improve at their own pace. AI-powered simulations refine phishing attack training by recognising patterns in user mistakes and providing

DOI: 10.4018/979-8-3373-0477-9.ch011

tailored feedback.

INTRODUCTION

The Need for Adaptive Gamification in Cybersecurity Education

Challenges of Traditional, One-Size-Fits-All Learning Approaches

Cybersecurity education often relies on rigid, one-size-fits-all learning models that fail to engage students with different backgrounds and skill levels. Traditional methods like lectures and static course materials struggle to keep pace with the rapid shifts in cyber threats (Rana & Chicone, 2024). Many students lose interest because the material does not match their learning styles or prior knowledge. This is where adaptive gamification can make a difference. Certification introduced a gamified cybersecurity module where students advanced through levels based on their performance (Diakoumakos et al., 2025; Dass et al., 2025). A beginner struggling with network security could focus on fundamental exercises, while an advanced student could tackle complex attack simulations. The result? Higher engagement and improved knowledge retention. Unlike traditional methods, adaptive gamification personalises learning by adjusting difficulty and content in real time (Awashreh & Hassiba, 2025). It taps into the motivation that games naturally provide, making students more eager to solve cybersecurity challenges (Quayyum & Jaccheri, 2024). A corporate training program found that employees who learned through an adaptive cybersecurity game were significantly better at recognising phishing attempts than those who took a standard online course. The game was adjusted based on user responses, reinforcing weak areas while skipping concepts they had already mastered (Sousa et al., 2025; Hussain et al., 2024). This kind of engagement is difficult to achieve with conventional instruction. Cyber threats are unpredictable, and learning approaches should reflect that reality. By incorporating adaptive gamification, cybersecurity education can become more effective (Shahzadi et al., 2025; Jun et al., 2024), engaging, and responsive to individual needs.

How Gamification Enhances Engagement and Knowledge Retention

Gamification has changed the way people learn by making education more interactive (Lynch et al., 2025; Tyagi & Khanna, 2025). Traditional teaching methods often struggle to keep learners focused (Bressane et al., 2023; Singh et al., 2024), especially in fields like cybersecurity, where concepts can be complex and technical. Adding game-like elements such as points, badges, and leaderboards creates a sense of achievement that motivates learners to continue engaging with the material (Almamoori, n.d.; Cigdem et al., 2024). A key reason gamification works is its ability to trigger curiosity (Araújo, 2024; Kiyani et al., 2024). When learners are given challenges that gradually increase in difficulty, they develop a problem-solving mindset. In cybersecurity training, simulated hacking scenarios allow students to experiment in a safe environment, reinforcing their skills through active participation (Spatafora et al., 2024; Linqiang et al., 2024). Unlike passive learning, where information is quickly forgotten, interactive tasks help with long-term retention (Fung et al., 2023). Beyond motivation, gamification also creates a sense of urgency and competition. In a study on cybersecurity education, students who participated in gamified exercises performed better on assessments than those who used traditional study methods (Lampropoulos & Sidiropoulos, 2024; Manchuri et al., 2024). Elements like time constraints and real-time feedback push learners to think quickly, improving decision-making skills under pressure.

Understanding Different Learning Styles

Overview of Visual, Auditory, Reading/Writing, and Kinesthetic Learners (VARK Model)

Learning happens differently for everyone. Some grasp concepts quickly through images, while others absorb information best by listening. The VARK model identifies four styles: visual, auditory, reading/writing, and kinesthetic learners (Dey & Panda, 2024; Pillai & Khan, 2025). Each style shapes how people process and retain information. Visual learners prefer diagrams, charts, and videos (Kanchon et al., 2024; Ravichandran et al., 2024). They recall details from images and find colours and spatial organisation helpful. Someone who sketches maps during lectures may belong to this group. Auditory learners, on the other hand, benefit from spoken explanations (Masegosa et al., 2024). They engage in discussions, remember stories, and enjoy learning through podcasts or lectures (Massa & Mayer, 2006). A student who replays recorded lectures before exams likely fit this category. Those who favour reading and writing learn best through written words (Chandra & Chand, 2024). They take detailed notes, enjoy textbooks, and express ideas through essays. Highlighting key points and summarising chapters are common strategies. Kinesthetic learners prefer hands-on experiences (Abah et al., 2024; Emmanuel & Sendagi, 2024). They absorb knowledge by engaging in experiments, role-playing, or real-world tasks (Sudrajat et al., 2025). Someone who builds models to understand physics concepts is a good example. Understanding these styles can improve teaching and learning. While individuals may have a dominant preference, they often use a mix of styles.

Recognising this can help students and educators create more effective learning environments. Figure 1 shows different learning styles.

Figure 1. Different learning styles

Other Cognitive and Psychological Factors Affecting Learning Preferences

Many factors influence how people learn beyond their preferred style. Memory plays a huge role—some learners retain information better through repetition, while others rely on associations or storytelling (Nguyen & Javorsky, 2024; Riza et al., 2025). Attention span also makes a difference. Distractions, fatigue, or stress can make it harder to absorb new material, which is why structured breaks and a comfortable environment help. Motivation is another key factor. When someone is genuinely interested in a subject, they process information more deeply and recall it more. This is why students engaged in hands-on projects or real-world applications often show better understanding. Similarly, self-efficacy—the belief in one's ability to succeed—affects persistence and willingness to tackle difficult topics. A confident learner is more likely to embrace challenges rather than avoid them (Khan et al., 2025; Seng et al., 2024). Emotions also shape learning. Anxiety can hinder comprehension and recall, while positive emotions can boost engagement and creativity (Oleet & Yu, 2024). Think of a time when frustration made a math problem seem impossible, only for clarity to come after a break. Social interactions matter, too. Some learners thrive in group discussions, bouncing ideas off peers, while others prefer working alone to organise their thoughts (Busio, 2025).

Understanding these factors allows educators to create better learning experiences. A rigid, one-size-fits-all approach doesn't work because learners bring different cognitive and psychological influences into the process. Adapting teaching strategies to these elements can lead to more effective and enjoyable learning.

Chapter Contribution

This chapter is pertinent to the area of adaptive gamification strategies for different learning styles in cybersecurity. First, it describes the challenges of traditional, one-size-fits-all learning approaches and an overview of visual, auditory, reading/writing, and kinesthetic learners (VARK model). The chapter then investigates the role of personalisation in learning and machine learning and AI in adaptive gamification. Furthermore, the chapter presents visual learners: graphics, simulations, and infographics, and auditory learners: storytelling, narration, and audio cues. It also discusses Dynamic Difficulty Adjustment (DDA) in cybersecurity games and personalised learning paths in cybersecurity training platforms and Capture The Flag (CTF) competitions with adaptive challenges and AI-powered cybersecurity training simulators. Lastly, the section provides a glimpse of balancing challenge and accessibility, data privacy and ethical AI in gamified learning and blockchain-based credentialing and skill progression.

Chapter Organization

In the first section, we will cover an insight into the introduction of the need for adaptive gamification in cybersecurity education and understanding different learning styles. In section 2, we go down to the science behind adaptive gamification. In section 3, we discuss gamification strategies for different learning styles, followed by the implementation of adaptive gamification in cybersecurity training in section 4. Section 5 delves into the case studies: adaptive gamification in cybersecurity education. Section 6 will explain the challenges and ethical considerations in adaptive gamification. The final section will discuss the future of adaptive gamification in cybersecurity learning.

THE SCIENCE BEHIND ADAPTIVE GAMIFICATION

The Role of Personalization in Learning

How Adaptive Learning Improves Cybersecurity Skill Acquisition

Adaptive gamification makes learning cybersecurity skills more effective by adjusting challenges to fit individual needs. When training programs recognise personal learning styles, they keep users engaged and improve knowledge retention (Plass et al., 2019). Unlike traditional methods, which treat all learners the same, adaptive systems track progress and modify tasks based on performance, ensuring a more engaging experience (Tariq, 2024; Sheng et al., 2024). Cybersecurity, with its constantly changing threats, requires professionals to stay sharp. Personalised training can help learners respond to new challenges quickly, making them more prepared for real-world threats (Pitura et al., 2024).

One example is a cybersecurity training platform that uses real-time feedback. If a learner struggles with identifying phishing emails, the system increases the number of related exercises. This approach prevents frustration and boosts confidence as learners feel more in control of their progress. Adaptive methods also reduce the risk of learners skipping essential topics by guiding them through content that matches their skill level (Hadwin et al., 2025). Traditional methods often rely on static lesson plans, but cybersecurity training must be flexible (Wang et al., 2025). By using machine learning and behavioural data, adaptive systems identify weak areas and focus on improvement, making training sessions more efficient (Kehinde, 2025).

Engagement plays a huge role in learning cybersecurity skills, and gamification elements like points, badges, and interactive challenges help sustain motivation (Fatokun et al., 2024). When learners receive rewards for completing tasks, they are more likely to remain interested and committed to mastering complex security concepts (Bandhu et al., 2024; Sindiramutty, 2024). This tailored approach ensures learners gain the necessary skills to protect digital systems effectively.

The Impact of Gamified Experiences on Motivation and Retention

A well-designed gamified experience can turn routine learning into something people look forward to. Cybersecurity training, for example, often struggles with engagement, but when elements like challenges, rewards, and progression tracking are introduced, learners stay motivated longer. Points and leaderboards might seem simple, but they create a sense of achievement that keeps people invested (Aldalur, 2024). Personalised challenges are especially effective. When a system adapts to difficulty based on a learner's progress, it prevents frustration and boredom (Habibi et al., 2025). Imagine a cybersecurity simulation where tasks adjust in complexity—this keeps learners in a zone where they are neither overwhelmed nor disengaged. This approach builds confidence over time and strengthens retention as users repeatedly apply what they learn in practical scenarios. Beyond points and badges, social interaction within gamified environments also plays a major role (Wu et al., 2025; Sindiramutty, Prabagaran, Akbar, Hussain, & Malik, 2024). When people see their peers engaging, they are more likely to stay committed. A cybersecurity training program that integrates team-based challenges encourages collaboration, making learning more memorable.

The long-term impact is clear—when people enjoy learning, they are more likely to remember and apply their knowledge. Gamification taps into the natural desire for progress and achievement, making motivation and retention part of the process rather than an afterthought. Figure 2 shows the science behind adaptive gamification.

Figure 2. The science behind adaptive gamification

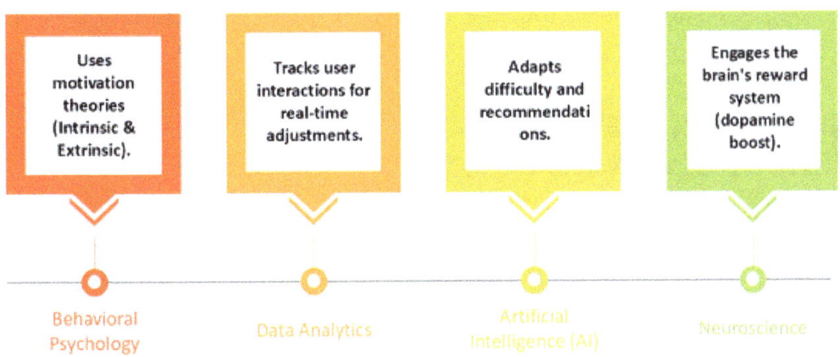

Machine Learning and AI in Adaptive Gamification

How AI-Driven Platforms Analyze Learner Behavior

AI-driven platforms in education adjust learning experiences by studying how users interact with content (T. M. Singh et al., 2024; Yadav, 2024). Machine learning tracks engagement, recognising patterns that indicate when a learner struggles or excels (Domínguez et al., 2025). This allows real-time modifications to difficulty levels, pacing, and feedback. Adaptive gamification refines these methods by using game elements—badges, points, or challenges—to maintain motivation (Zairon et al., 2025). AI helps by ensuring these elements align with individual progress rather than applying a one-size-fits-all approach (Teles & Moreira, 2024; Sindiramutty, Prabagaran, Jhanjhi, Ghazanfar, Malik, & Soomro, 2024). An AI system might notice that a student repeatedly fails a quiz question. Instead of simply lowering the difficulty, the platform can offer targeted hints or break down the concept into smaller steps. Conversely, if someone quickly solves problems, AI increases the challenge of preventing boredom. These micro-adjustments help maintain engagement and encourage deeper learning.

A teacher once mentioned how students reacted to an adaptive system. Some initially raced through tasks, expecting quick rewards. Over time, they realised the AI adjusted based on their understanding, making it impossible to game the system. This shift forced them to engage more meaningfully. Gamification powered by AI also measures emotional responses (Pavithra & Ramya, 2025; Sindiramutty, Prabagaran, Jhanjhi, Murugesan, Brohi, & Masud, 2024). Facial recognition and keystroke dynamics can detect frustration or distraction, prompting supportive feedback (Yeganeh et al., 2025). While this technology is still improving, early results suggest a shift toward more responsive, personalised learning experiences.

GAMIFICATION STRATEGIES FOR DIFFERENT LEARNING STYLES

Visual Learners: Graphics, Simulations, and Infographics

How Cybersecurity Visualisations Enhance Learning

Cybersecurity is a complex topic, and making it interactive for visual learners requires creative approaches (Paracha et al., 2024). Graphs, simulations, and infographics are a wonderful way of making complex concepts concrete scenarios (Pellas, 2025; Sindiramutty, Prabagaran, Jhanjhi, Murugesan, Brohi, & Wei, 2024). Literature shows that knowledge recall is boosted using visual learning tools such as animated threat models and graphics of network intrusions. Instead of reading technical reports, security vulnerabilities are learned more easily when presented in brief visual analyses.

Cybersecurity simulations also enable interactive learning of defence and attack strategies (Ajimon & Kumar, 2024; Sindiramutty, Prabagaran, Jhanjhi, Murugesan, Malik, & Hussain, 2024). As learners navigate simulated cyberattacks, problem-solving is cultivated without risk. Infographics also facilitate reinforcing security concepts. An infographic presented in a visually attractive manner comparing password strength, patterns of attacks via phishing, or social engineering tactics is capable of conveying key information at a glance. The tools leverage the natural tendency of the brain to process visually, reducing cognitive load and making technical knowledge more accessible (Spaho et al., 2025; Waheed et al., 2024). One such recent course of instruction in cybersecurity illustrated just how engagement is heightened using visual methods. Learners who utilised review of attack simulations performed better in identifying security threats compared to those using text-based instruction alone. One learner, having a hard time learning about firewall settings, understood it immediately after looking at an animated flowchart of a network. The improvement in comprehension reflects just how helpful visual methods are in making cybersecurity concepts easy to understand.

As cybersecurity threats become more sophisticated, training methods must also evolve accordingly. The incorporation of visual elements means that learners not only gain knowledge but apply it practically in real-life situations.

Best Practices for Designing Immersive Cybersecurity Training

Creating immersive cybersecurity training requires an approach that keeps learners engaged while reinforcing practical skills (Mouhssine et al., 2024; Weiqi et al., 2024). Hands-on experiences, real-world simulations, and adaptive challenges create environments where trainees develop problem-solving abilities (Rosário & Raimundo, 2024). Research shows that interactive training significantly improves retention compared to passive learning (Jacob & Centofanti, 2023). Instead of just reading about threats, learners benefit from tackling simulated cyber incidents. One of the most effective strategies is scenario-based training. Participants respond to real-time attacks, making split-second decisions in simulated breaches. This method fosters critical thinking and prepares learners for high-pressure situations. Gamification elements, such as leaderboards and rewards, increase motivation and engagement (Rahmi et al., 2024). When users see their progress in real time, they stay invested in the learning process.

Personalised learning paths enhance effectiveness. A one-size-fits-all approach often fails because cybersecurity roles vary widely. Adaptive training platforms adjust content based on individual performance, ensuring that each participant gains relevant skills (Zamiri & Esmaeili, 2024). Incorporating AI-driven assessments helps pinpoint knowledge gaps and provides tailored feedback (Dar et al., 2024; Xun et al., 2025). A cybersecurity workshop demonstrated how immersive strategies improve learning outcomes. Participants who engaged in red team/blue team exercises showed better retention and threat response times. One trainee, initially struggling with intrusion detection, gained confidence after practising in a controlled, high-stakes simulation. These experiences bridge the gap between theory and real-world application, making training more effective. Figure 3 shows machine learning and AI in adaptive gamification.

Figure 3. Machine learning and AI in adaptive gamification

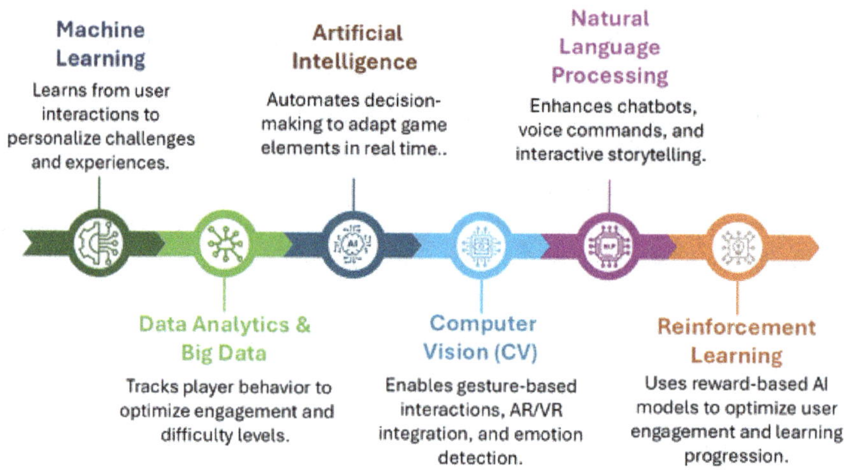

Auditory Learners: Storytelling, Narration, and Audio Cues

The Role of Voice-Guided Training and Interactive Narratives

Learning through sound can create strong connections for students who absorb information best by listening. Gamification strategies, such as storytelling, narration, and audio cues, make lessons more engaging for auditory learners (Rye et al., 2025; Shirindzi & Sikhwari, 2025). A well-told story captures attention and makes content easier to remember. When lessons incorporate characters and immersive narratives, students stay motivated and feel connected to the material (Liu et al., 2024; Ying et al., 2024). Interactive storytelling, where learners make choices that influence the story, turns passive listening into active participation (Alter, 2025). Mac (2024) mentioned how an interactive history lesson, narrated with sound effects and character voices, made historical events feel real. This aligns with studies showing that voice-guided training improves retention and understanding (Castaneda et al., 2025; Gandham, 2025). Audio cues, such as background music and subtle sound effects, also guide learners through tasks without overwhelming them (Ciaburro & Kumcu, 2024). Imagine a cybersecurity simulation where alerts and spoken instructions help players detect threats—this type of experience reinforces learning through repetition and immediate feedback.

One challenge is ensuring these methods remain accessible. Not all students can focus solely on auditory input, so combining narration with text or visuals can strengthen. Thoughtfully designed gamification strategies ensure that learning remains engaging without becoming distracting. With the right approach, audio-driven elements can turn lessons into immersive, memorable experiences.

Leveraging Audio-based Feedback in Cybersecurity Simulations

Audio-based feedback through cybersecurity simulations keeps learners engaged and responds to threats promptly. Alerted through voice signals, users process more information in comparison to looking at text on display (Sengupta et al., 2025). In high-stress scenarios, instant feedback enhances decision-making, reducing errors in actual use (Xue et al., 2025). Interactive voice-assisted simulations present a realistic feeling (Kang & Nie, 2024; Alex et al., 2022). Users receive dynamic responses instead of static guidance, making learning more interactive (Mao et al., 2023; Alferidah & Jhanjhi, 2020). An attack story that speaks to learners engages learners to think critically instead of a script. Such a process encourages flexibility, a key to responding to dynamic threats. Personalised voice correction prevents workflow interference to correct errors. Trainees adapt their method better when hearing a prompt following a response error than when having to stop to read a description. The approach is also typical of real-world cybersecurity work when reflexes must be swift.

The gamification elements also enhance engagement. Voice-controlled leaderboards challenge learners to improve their responses. By hearing their improvement without viewing a display, players remain immersed in the simulation. The use of audio-based correction in cybersecurity training enables participants to respond immediately, making learning more realistic and experiential. Real-time voice guidance enhances problem-solving, keeping users ahead of new threats.

IMPLEMENTING ADAPTIVE GAMIFICATION IN CYBERSECURITY TRAINING

Dynamic Difficulty Adjustment (DDA) in Cybersecurity Games

How AI Modifies Game Difficulty Based on Performance

Cybersecurity training is often uninteresting, but gamification makes it more engaging. Adaptive gamification takes it a step further by modifying challenges based on performance (Babu & Moorthy, 2023; Manoharan & Nagulapally, 2024). Artificial intelligence (AI) plays a crucial role in this process by using Dynamic Difficulty Adjustment (DDA) to tailor challenges (Fisher & Kulshreshth, 2024; Lut, 2024). This approach keeps learners actively involved without feeling overwhelmed or bored. AI in cybersecurity games monitors player behaviour, response times, and success-to-failure ratios to determine their skill levels (Chennamaneni et al., 2023; Alkinani et al., 2021). If a player struggles, the game provides hints or eases the difficulty. If they perform well, the system increases the challenge to maintain engagement. This balance ensures that learners stay in their optimal learning zone, where training remains effective without becoming frustrating. Research shows that adaptive difficulty leads to better knowledge retention and skill improvement compared to static challenges (Kellman et al., 2022; Babbar et al., 2021). One example is an AI-driven simulation where a player must defend a network from attacks (Yamin et al., 2021; Brohi et al., 2020). If they quickly stop threats, the game introduces more sophisticated intrusion attempts. If they fail multiple times, the system slows down attacks or provides strategic tips. These real-time adjustments mirror real-world cybersecurity challenges, where threats constantly evolve.

AI-driven adaptation also tracks behavioral patterns (Zhou et al., 2024). If a player hesitates too often in decision-making, the system may introduce training scenarios to reinforce quick thinking. The real-world benefit is clear—security professionals trained with adaptive methods tend to perform better under pressure. Cyber threats are unpredictable, and training that adapts in real-time helps prepare individuals for high-stakes scenarios.

Personalized Learning Paths in Cybersecurity Training Platforms

Designing Tailored Learning Modules for Different Expertise Levels

Cyber threats change fast, and training must keep up. One way to do this is by adjusting the learning process to fit the learner's skill level. Gamification is effective, but a one-size-fits-all approach does not work for everyone (Ortiz-Rojas et al., 2025; Chesti et al., 2020). Some trainees might already understand basic security principles, while others struggle with the fundamentals. A platform that recognizes these differences can create a more engaging experience. Consider a cybersecurity trainee encountering a simulated phishing attack. A beginner might get immediate hints and explanations, while an advanced user faces more complex scenarios with minimal guidance. This type of personalized challenge prevents frustration and boredom, leading to better learning outcomes. Adaptive gamification can also track performance and adjust future exercises accordingly (Sikhwari & Thenga, 2025; Dogra et al., 2021). If someone consistently excels in one area but struggles in another, the system can modify tasks to address weaknesses.

A case study from a corporate cybersecurity program showed that employees engaged more with training when it adapted to their progress (Pils, 2025; Fatima-Tuz-Zahra et al., 2020). A rigid structure often leads to disengagement, but adaptive elements encourage users to stay involved. By incorporating personalized pathways, cybersecurity education becomes more practical and enjoyable (Papadimitriou & Virvou, 2025). Figure 4 shows implementing adaptive gamification in cybersecurity training.

Adaptive Assessments and Real-Time Progress Tracking

A cybersecurity training platform should do more than test knowledge—it should adapt to how each person learns. Traditional assessments often fail because they treat every learner the same way (Pereira et al., 2025; Gopi et al., 2021). Someone new to the field might feel overwhelmed, while an experienced user could get bored with basic questions. Adaptive assessments adjust difficulty based on responses, ensuring each question challenges the learner without causing frustration (Papadimitriou & Virvou, 2025b).

Imagine a trainee answering a network security question. If they get it right, the next one increases in difficulty. If they struggle, the system might provide hints or rephrase the question. This keeps engagement high while ensuring knowledge gaps are addressed. Real-time progress tracking adds another layer by giving immediate feedback (Tang et al., 2024). Instead of waiting for a final score, users see their strengths and weaknesses as they go (Taylor & Kim, 2023; Gouda et al., 2022). This approach helps instructors intervene when necessary and allows learners to focus on areas needing improvement.

A study on corporate training programs found that employees retained information better when assessments were adapted in real-time (Finseth et al., 2024; Humayun et al., 2022). Static tests often fail to measure true skill levels, but dynamic ones create a more accurate picture. Cybersecurity threats are unpredictable; training should be, too.

Figure 4. Implementing adaptive gamification in cybersecurity training

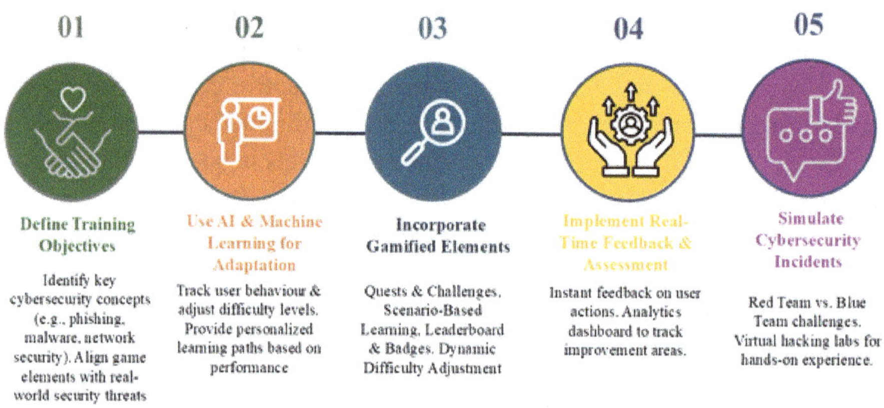

CASE STUDIES: ADAPTIVE GAMIFICATION IN CYBERSECURITY EDUCATION

Capture the Flag (CTF) Competitions with Adaptive Challenges

Dynamic Challenge Scaling Based on User Skill Levels

Cybersecurity education often struggles to keep learners engaged, but Capture the Flag (CTF) competitions with adaptive challenges offer a fresh approach (Khoo et al., 2025). These events adjust difficulty levels based on a participant's skill, keeping tasks within reach while still challenging them (Huang et al., 2022; Margarita & Steffen, 2010). A beginner might start with basic encryption puzzles, while an experienced player tackles reverse engineering. This keeps learners motivated, avoiding frustration or boredom.

One study found that students who participated in CTF competitions performed better in cybersecurity assessments (CyberTalents, n.d.; Jhanjhi et al., 2021). The reason seems to be the immediate feedback and hands-on nature of the challenges. Players see where they went wrong and adjust their approach in real time. The ability to scale difficulty also makes these competitions useful for corporate training. Employees with limited cybersecurity knowledge can start with simpler challenges, while specialists face advanced threats. Companies using this method reported improved threat detection skills across all levels of their workforce (Kasri et al., 2025)

The adaptability of these competitions ensures that participants stay engaged, regardless of their experience. By making challenges accessible yet demanding, they push players to grow without overwhelming them. With the rise of cyber threats, preparing individuals through such engaging methods could be a game-changer in cybersecurity education. Figure 5 shows example adaptive gamification in cybersecurity education.

Figure 5. Example adaptive gamification in cybersecurity education

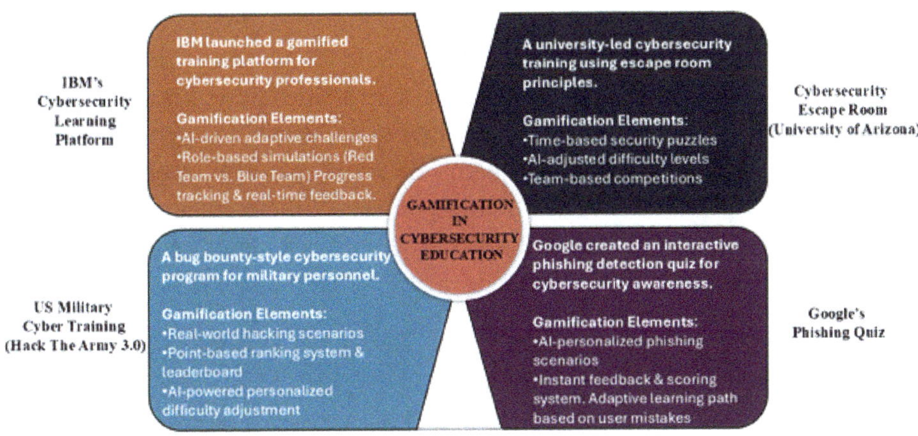

AI-Powered Cybersecurity Training Simulators

How Adaptive Training Environments Enhance Skill Mastery

AI-powered cybersecurity training simulators are changing the way professionals develop their skills (Akhtar & Rawol, 2024; Kumar et al., 2021). These simulators adjust to the learner's ability, providing challenges that increase in difficulty as competency improves. Unlike traditional training, which follows a fixed path, this method ensures that learners are neither overwhelmed nor under-challenged. A student who struggles with recognizing phishing attempts, for example, might receive repeated exposure to similar attacks, while an advanced learner could face more sophisticated social engineering tactics.

One major advantage is that these environments mimic real cyber threats. Rather than memorizing textbook strategies, learners interact with simulated attacks that react to their decisions. This keeps engagement high and makes lessons more practical. Gamification elements, such as scoring, leaderboards, and rewards, further enhance motivation (J. T. Pereira & Harun, 2024; Mohammed et al., 2024). Participants often push themselves harder when progress is visually tracked, reinforcing skill retention. In a corporate setting, companies have reported faster onboarding of security analysts due to this adaptive approach. Cybersecurity threats constantly change, and these simulators help professionals stay prepared. Since AI can analyze performance data, it identifies weaknesses and tailors future exercises accordingly (Krichen & Abdalzaher, 2024; Lim et al., 2019). This means training remains relevant even as attack methods shift. Some universities have already integrated adaptive simulations into coursework, leading to noticeable improvements in students' problem-solving abilities. The demand for cybersecurity experts continues to grow, and AI-powered adaptive training provides an effective way to develop the necessary expertise (C. V. S. Babu & P, 2023). Figure shows example adaptive gamification in cybersecurity education.

CHALLENGES AND ETHICAL CONSIDERATIONS IN ADAPTIVE GAMIFICATION

Balancing Challenge and Accessibility

Preventing Discouragement from Overly Difficult Challenges

Adaptive gamification aims to make challenges engaging without causing frustration (Zhang & Huang, 2024; A & Joy, 2024). A well-balanced system keeps players motivated, but if tasks become too hard, they may disengage (Vaithilingam et al., 2024). A friend of mine once quit a language-learning app because it kept increasing difficulty too fast. He felt stuck, with no way to progress. This is a common issue—games must adjust to skill levels while maintaining interest. Some platforms use AI to track progress and modify difficulty accordingly (Khine, 2024). However, this can backfire. Some students could feel manipulated when difficulty changes unexpectedly, making them distrust the system. Others enjoyed a gradual increase in challenge but struggled with abrupt shifts. A smoother transition between levels can prevent users from feeling overwhelmed. Game designers also face ethical concerns. If a system makes tasks too easy, users may not learn anything valuable. But pushing them too hard can lead to frustration or burnout. There's also the risk of making success feel artificial. Some players notice when a game subtly adjusts difficulty to prevent failure, making achievements feel less rewarding (Hefkaluk et al., 2023).

Finding the right balance is tricky. The best solutions involve continuous testing, real user feedback, and transparent design. A well-designed gamified system encourages persistence without creating unnecessary obstacles. Figure 6 shows ethical considerations in adaptive gamification.

Figure 6. Ethical considerations in adaptive gamification

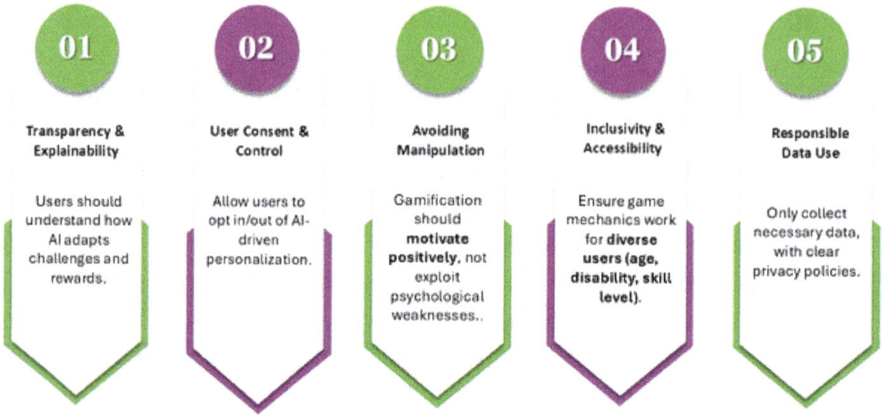

Ensuring Inclusivity for Diverse Learners

Gamified systems should work for everyone, but that's rarely the case. I once watched a friend with dyslexia struggle with a learning app that relied heavily on fast-paced reading tasks. No matter how hard he tried, the system penalized him for something beyond his control. This happens often—designers unintentionally create barriers that exclude certain users. Accessibility features can help, but they're not always well implemented. Some platforms offer text-to-speech, colorblind-friendly modes, or adjustable difficulty. However, if these options are hidden or difficult to activate, many users won't benefit. The best systems consider inclusivity from the start rather than as an afterthought.

Cultural differences also matter. A study found that gamified education tools designed in Western countries often assume competitive play motivates everyone (Aksay et al., 2024). However, in some cultures, collaboration is more effective. If a game rewards individual achievement but ignores group-based success, it may not engage all learners equally. Neurodivergent players have unique needs, too. Some thrive on structured, predictable challenges, while others enjoy open-ended exploration. Adaptive difficulty should account for these differences rather than force everyone into the same pattern. A truly inclusive system doesn't just offer options—it makes them easy to find, use, and understand. Gamification should encourage learning, not unintentionally exclude those who learn differently.

Data Privacy and Ethical AI in Gamified Learning

Risks of Learner Behavior Tracking and Performance Profiling

The use of adaptive gamification in education introduces significant concerns about data privacy and ethical AI (Strielkowski et al., 2024; Nayyar et al., 2021). Tracking learner behavior and performance can personalize the learning process, but it also raises serious risks. AI-driven gamification relies on collecting extensive data, which includes engagement patterns, response times, and cognitive progress (L. Liu, 2024; Renacido & Biray, 2024). This data helps in tailoring educational experiences but can be misused if not properly managed. Privacy breaches are a major concern, especially when third-party platforms handle student information without adequate safeguards (Kelso et al., 2024).

AI-powered profiling can lead to unintended consequences (Aldoseri et al., 2024; Shah et al., 2022). Once a learner's performance data is recorded, there is potential for bias in how future learning paths are determined. If an algorithm incorrectly categorizes a student as struggling, they might be limited to remedial content, restricting growth opportunities. On the other hand, high-performing students might receive overly complex material, leading to frustration rather than motivation (Z. Akhtar & Ntonia, 2024). These automated decisions, though well-intentioned, often lack the human judgment needed to recognize personal challenges or external factors affecting performance.

The ethical dimension extends to consent and transparency. Many students are unaware of the extent to which their data is used. If institutions fail to communicate how gamification algorithms influence learning, students might unknowingly contribute to systems that reinforce inequities. The long-term implications of AI-driven profiling could shape academic and career trajectories in unpredictable ways. While technology enhances education, balancing its benefits with responsible implementation remains a challenge.

FUTURE OF ADAPTIVE GAMIFICATION IN CYBERSECURITY LEARNING

AI-Driven Personalized Learning Assistants

Using AI Tutors for Real-Time Cybersecurity Skill Enhancement

AI-driven personalized learning assistants are making cybersecurity education more engaging by tailoring content to individual skill levels (Jawhar et al., 2024; Joon & Simmons, 2024). These systems analyze user performance and adapt challenges accordingly, improving both engagement and retention. Unlike traditional learning, where static materials may not suit every learner, AI tutors provide targeted feedback and adjust the difficulty in real-time (Rajendran et al., 2024). This ensures that learners stay motivated without feeling overwhelmed.

Adaptive gamification enhances learning by integrating real-time simulations (Yambal & Waykar, 2025; Sharma et al., 2021). AI-powered tutors create attack-and-defence scenarios, allowing students to practice cybersecurity techniques in a controlled environment (Wendt, 2024). A student struggling with threat detection might receive extra training on identifying malware patterns, while another excelling in encryption could be pushed towards more complex cryptographic challenges. These customized experiences prepare learners for real-world threats, improving both competence and confidence. Gamified cybersecurity training is particularly useful for professionals who need continuous skill development (Gwenhure & Rahayu, 2024). AI assistants analyze responses and suggest learning paths based on industry trends (Katsamakas et al., 2024). A cybersecurity analyst might receive updated content on zero-day vulnerabilities as AI systems detect emerging threats (Patil, 2025; Singhal et al., 2020). This ensures learning remains relevant and aligned with evolving risks.

While AI tutors enhance engagement, their success depends on balancing automation with human oversight. Over-reliance on AI-generated feedback can limit deeper critical thinking, requiring occasional expert intervention (Zhai et al., 2024). Nonetheless, AI-driven gamification is reshaping cybersecurity education, offering a smarter way to develop skills that match real-world demands.

Blockchain-Based Credentialing and Skill Progression

Using Decentralized Learning Records for Gamified Cybersecurity Certifications

Traditional certifications fail to cope with business requirements, making practitioners bogged down in legacy knowledge (Dickson, 2023). The trend towards blockchain credentialing allows for secure, verifiable proof of proficiency and progression. Learners are not required to be reliant on centralized institutions, yet a personal account of achievements is held on a distributed system. This builds trust, as employers can verify credentials in a matter of seconds without intermediaries.

An interesting trend is merging adaptive gamification with blockchain. Learning platforms track engagement and tailor challenges to everyone's performance, making cybersecurity training more relevant to everyone's competency. This prevents frustration of material that is too easy or too difficult. Blockchain permits rewards such as a completed challenge in the detection of phishing or proficiency in penetration testing to be permanent and tamper-proof (Dua & Kumar, 2024; Atlam et al., 2024). One of the benefits is accessibility. People wanting to pursue a career in cybersecurity struggle to prove their capabilities without formal qualifications. Blockchain certifications allow a method of verifying experience gained in simulations and problem-solving (Lakshmikantha, 2024; Roy et al., 2024). Organizations struggling to recruit for cybersecurity roles would be able to recruit capable candidates outside of usual channels. The flexibility of accumulating and displaying capabilities in real-time rather than waiting for sporadic examinations also increases this approach. Figure 7 shows future of adaptive gamification in cybersecurity learning.

This shift also has consequences beyond individual learners. Organizations would be able to apply blockchain-backed progression tracking to assess team readiness, keeping staff up to date with new threats. Cybersecurity professionals benefit from ongoing acknowledgment of their capabilities, and employers gain confidence in their hires. The union of gamification and blockchain can transform recognition of and rewards for cybersecurity knowledge.

Figure 7. Future of adaptive gamification in cybersecurity learning

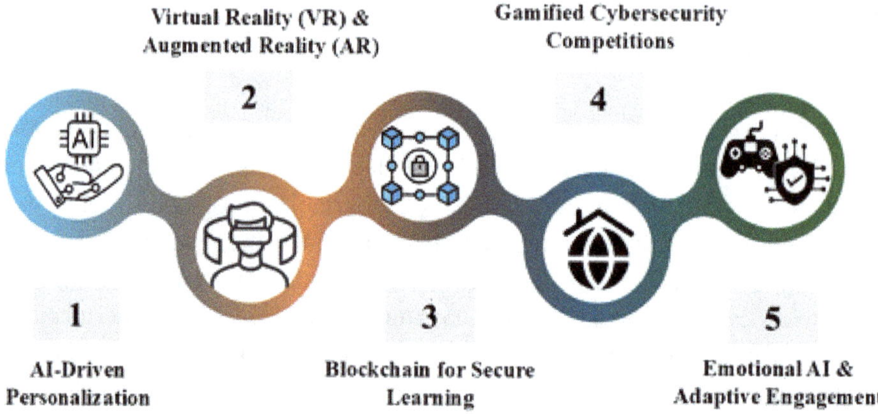

CONCLUSION

Summary of Key Takeaways on Adaptive Gamification

Adaptive gamification is revolutionizing cybersecurity learning to be more interactive and dynamic. Training programs do not employ static lessons anymore but adjust to each learner's requirements to sustain motivation in working on realistic scenarios. The strength of such a method is in its adaptability to support diverse learning strategies—through visual simulations, interactive stories, problem-solving in action, or AI-based feedback mechanisms. The use of machine learning allows instant adjustment to sustain challenging engagement without frustration. Capture the Flag challenges, simulated attacks, and personalized learning streams have already been proven to be effective in sustaining engagement. Such methods are not just a way of making learning fun; they allow professionals to acquire practical capabilities that hold up to stress. There is also a trend towards recognizing competencies in new ways. AI-based mentors provide instant feedback, while blockchain-based certifications provide verifiable documentation of proficiency. Such a method is beneficial to not only learners but also to employers in need of skilled yet trainable resources. The trend towards gamification is not a trend; it is a response to the growing need for cybersecurity professionals who can think critically, act swiftly, and continually sharpen their knowledge. As such methods continue to be refined, their potential to revolutionize readiness in cybersecurity is impossible to ignore.

The actual challenge is to sharpen such systems to sustain engagement, accessibility, and ethical considerations to allow learning to be impactful to many participants.

REFERENCES

Abah, J., Chinaka, T. W., & Ogbiji, E. O. (2024). Effect of kinesthetic learning on students' interest and achievement in mathematics. *Mathematics Education Journal, 8*(2), 120–136. DOI: 10.22219/mej.v8i2.34218

Ajimon, S. T., & Kumar, S. (2024). Applications of LLMs in Quantum-Aware Cybersecurity leveraging LLMs for Real-Time anomaly detection and threat intelligence. In *Advances in information security, privacy, and ethics book series* (pp. 201–246). DOI: 10.4018/979-8-3373-1102-9.ch007

Akhtar, Z., & Ntonia, I. (2024). Evaluating the Effectiveness of Digital Midterm Assessments in Enhancing Student Learning. *TechRxiv*. DOI: 10.36227/techrxiv.172710480.02872173/v1

Akhtar, Z. B., & Rawol, A. T. (2024). Enhancing Cybersecurity through AI-Powered Security Mechanisms. *IT JOURNAL RESEARCH AND DEVELOPMENT, 9*(1), 50–67. DOI: 10.25299/itjrd.2024.16852

Aksay, B., Aktaş, M., Yildirim, E., & Kiliç, F. (2024). Gamification as a Social Phenomenon and Gamification Heuristics Criteria from Social Sciences Perspective. *PLURAL History Culture Society, 12*(2), 116–133. DOI: 10.37710/plural.v12i2_7

Aldalur, I. (2024). Enhancing software development education through gamification and experiential learning with genially. *Software Quality Journal, 33*(1), 1. Advance online publication. DOI: 10.1007/s11219-024-09699-9

Aldoseri, A., Al-Khalifa, K. N., & Hamouda, A. M. (2024). AI-Powered Innovation in Digital Transformation: Key pillars and industry impact. *Sustainability (Basel), 16*(5), 1790. DOI: 10.3390/su16051790

Alex, S. A., Jhanjhi, N., Humayun, M., Ibrahim, A. O., & Abulfaraj, A. W. (2022). Deep LSTM Model for Diabetes Prediction with Class Balancing by SMOTE. *Electronics (Basel), 11*(17), 2737. DOI: 10.3390/electronics11172737

Alferidah, D. K., & Jhanjhi, N. (2020). Cybersecurity Impact over Bigdata and IoT Growth. *2020 International Conference on Computational Intelligence (ICCI)*. DOI: 10.1109/ICCI51257.2020.9247722

Alkinani, M. H., Almazroi, A. A., Jhanjhi, N., & Khan, N. A. (2021). 5G and IoT Based Reporting and Accident Detection (RAD) System to Deliver First Aid Box Using Unmanned Aerial Vehicle. *Sensors (Basel), 21*(20), 6905. DOI: 10.3390/s21206905 PMID: 34696118

Almamoori, O. J. (n.d.). *Investigating the impact of leaderboards, badges, and eBucks on high school English language learners' cognitive engagement, Self-Efficacy and intrinsic motivation toward reading in English - ProQuest.* https://www.proquest.com/openview/6e8e60379bca93b4613f158cc451ea03/1?cbl=18750&diss=y&pq-origsite=gscholar

Alter, D. S. (2025). Once upon a time: Narrative storytelling, hypnosis, and the brain. *The American Journal of Clinical Hypnosis*, •••, 1–18. DOI: 10.1080/00029157.2025.2450329 PMID: 39899752

Araújo, I. (2024). Creativity as a gamification booster. In *Atlantis highlights in social sciences, education and humanities/Atlantis Highlights in Social Sciences* (pp. 175–182). Education and Humanities., DOI: 10.2991/978-94-6463-380-1_17

Atlam, H. F., Ekuri, N., Azad, M. A., & Lallie, H. S. (2024). Blockchain Forensics: A systematic literature review of techniques, applications, challenges, and future directions. *Electronics (Basel)*, *13*(17), 3568. DOI: 10.3390/electronics13173568

Awashreh, R., & Hassiba, A. (2025). Revolutionizing education with AI. In *Advances in business strategy and competitive advantage book series* (pp. 149–170). DOI: 10.4018/979-8-3693-9440-3.ch006

Babbar, H., Rani, S., Masud, M., Verma, S., Anand, D., & Jhanjhi, N. (2021). Load balancing algorithm for migrating switches in software-defined vehicular networks. *Computers, Materials & Continua/Computers. Computers, Materials & Continua*, *67*(1), 1301–1316. DOI: 10.32604/cmc.2021.014627

Babu, C. V. S. (2023). Adaptive AI for dynamic cybersecurity systems. In *Advances in computational intelligence and robotics book series* (pp. 52–72). DOI: 10.4018/979-8-3693-0230-9.ch003

Babu, S. S., & Moorthy, A. D. (2023). Application of artificial intelligence in adaptation of gamification in education: A literature review. *Computer Applications in Engineering Education*, *32*(1), e22683. Advance online publication. DOI: 10.1002/cae.22683

Bandhu, D., Mohan, M. M., Nittala, N. P., Jadhav, P., Bhadauria, A., & Saxena, K. K. (2024). Theories of motivation: A comprehensive analysis of human behavior drivers. *Acta Psychologica*, *244*, 104177. DOI: 10.1016/j.actpsy.2024.104177 PMID: 38354564

Bressane, A., Zwirn, D., Essiptchouk, A., Saraiva, A. C. V., De Campos Carvalho, F. L., Formiga, J. K. S., De Castro Medeiros, L. C., & Negri, R. G. (2023). Understanding the role of study strategies and learning disabilities on student academic performance to enhance educational approaches: A proposal using artificial intelligence. *Computers and Education Artificial Intelligence*, *6*, 100196. DOI: 10.1016/j.caeai.2023.100196

Brohi, S. N., Jhanjhi, N., Brohi, N. N., & Brohi, M. N. (2020). Key Applications of State-of-the-Art Technologies to Mitigate and Eliminate COVID-19.pdf. *TECHRxiv*. DOI: 10.36227/techrxiv.12115596.v1

Busio, D. S. (2025). Taking the labor out of collaboration: Preparing early education students to collaboration. *Journal of Early Childhood Teacher Education*, •••, 1–25. DOI: 10.1080/10901027.2025.2451777

Castaneda, J. C., Lin, P., Hung, P. C. K., Zhong, H., Tseng, H., Huang, Y., & Ahmad, R. (2025). Designing inclusive tech playful educative solutions for visually impaired learners in STEM education. *Smart Learning Environments*, *12*(1), 4. Advance online publication. DOI: 10.1186/s40561-024-00358-x

Chandra, S. P., & Chand, S. P. (2024). Reading with Understanding in a Lower Primary Classroom: A Learning Journey to Improve Teacher Practice and Student Learning Outcome. *Reading Psychology*, *45*(5), 431–458. DOI: 10.1080/02702711.2024.2309344

Chennamaneni, S., Pradhan, P., Chebolu, V., Vejendla, M., Kannaiah, S. K., & Aravinth, S. S. (2023). Designing Cybersecurity AI based awareness Games for Citizens: best practices and future directions. *2022 International Conference on Sustainable Computing and Data Communication Systems (ICSCDS)*. DOI: 10.1109/ICSCDS56580.2023.10104800

Chesti, I. A., Humayun, M., Sama, N. U., & Jhanjhi, N. (2020). Evolution, Mitigation, and Prevention of Ransomware. *2020 2nd International Conference on Computer and Information Sciences (ICCIS)*. DOI: 10.1109/ICCIS49240.2020.9257708

Ciaburro, G., & Kumcu, E. H. (2024). The role of Sound on the future of E-Commerce Applications using Metaverse Technologies. In *Advances in business strategy and competitive advantage book series* (pp. 177–204). DOI: 10.4018/979-8-3693-9586-8.ch007

Cigdem, H., Ozturk, M., Karabacak, Y., Atik, N., Gürkan, S., & Aldemir, M. H. (2024). Unlocking student engagement and achievement: The impact of leaderboard gamification in online formative assessment for engineering education. *Education and Information Technologies*, *29*(18), 24835–24860. Advance online publication. DOI: 10.1007/s10639-024-12845-2

CyberTalents. (n.d.). *How CTF competitions can help companies hire top cyber-security professionals?* CyberTalents Blog. https://cybertalents.com/blog/hire-top-cybersecurity-professionals-through-ctfs?utm_source=chatgpt.com

Dar, A. A., Yadav, S. S., Tripathi, R. K., Albalawi, O., Jain, A., & Gautam, P. L. (2024). Managing ethical challenges. In *Advances in educational technologies and instructional design book series* (pp. 301–332). DOI: 10.4018/979-8-3693-6170-2.ch011

Dass, S. M., Mahalingam, S. R., Hang, P. L., Kelvin, K., Wingsky, J., Mohamed, A. M. M. A., Rebecca, A. J., Hatmal, N. I. Y. B. A., Ali, A. R., Tjahyosedjati, E., Wei, T., & Sindiramutty, S. R. (2025). The Role of Cryptography and AI in Enhancing Blockchain Security. *preprints.org*. DOI: 10.20944/preprints202501.0386.v1

Dey, B., & Panda, B. N. (2024). Understanding the learning Style Preferences of ODL students using VARK Model: Implications for Individualized Pedagogy and Student Success. *Asian Journal of Education and Social Studies*, *50*(5), 323–331. DOI: 10.9734/ajess/2024/v50i51365

Diakoumakos, J., Chaskos, E., Kolokotronis, N., & Lepouras, G. (2025). Cyber-security gamification in federation of cyber ranges: Design, implementation, and evaluation. *International Journal of Information Security*, *24*(1), 57. Advance online publication. DOI: 10.1007/s10207-024-00974-1

Dickson, P. R. (2023). The turbulent future of expertise and training markets. *Journal of Services Marketing*, *38*(1), 43–55. DOI: 10.1108/JSM-08-2023-0301

Dogra, V., Singh, A., Verma, S., Kavita, N., Jhanjhi, N. Z., & Talib, M. N. (2021). Analyzing DistilBERT for Sentiment Classification of Banking Financial News. In *Lecture notes in networks and systems* (pp. 501–510). DOI: 10.1007/978-981-16-3153-5_53

Domínguez, L. G. I., Robles-Gómez, A., & Pastor-Vargas, R. (2025). A data-driven approach to engineering instruction: Exploring learning styles, study habits, and machine learning. *IEEE Access : Practical Innovations, Open Solutions*, *1*, 10978–11002. Advance online publication. DOI: 10.1109/ACCESS.2025.3528263

Dua, A., & Kumar, G. (2024). *Mastering zero-knowledge proofs: Practical study of security, scalability, and privacy in blockchain and modern systems (English Edition)*. BPB Publications.

Emmanuel, A., & Sendagi, M. (2024). RELATIONSHIP BETWEEN AUDIO LEARNING STYLE, KINESTHETIC LEARNING STYLE AND ACADEMIC ACHIEVEMENT OF SECONDARY SCHOOL STUDENTS IN KAMWENGE DISTRICT, UGANDA. a CROSS-SECTIONAL STUDY. *Deleted Journal*, *1*(7), 13. DOI: 10.51168/4hv4ww85

Fatima-Tuz-Zahra, N., Jhanjhi, N., Brohi, S. N., Malik, N. A., & Humayun, M. (2020). Proposing a Hybrid RPL Protocol for Rank and Wormhole Attack Mitigation using Machine Learning. *2020 2nd International Conference on Computer and Information Sciences (ICCIS)*. DOI: 10.1109/ICCIS49240.2020.9257607

Fatokun, N. F., Awang, N. Z., Hamid, N. S., Fatokun, N. J. O., & Norman, N. A. (2024). Cybersecurity Knowledge Deterioration and the role of Gamification Intervention. *Journal of Advanced Research in Applied Sciences and Engineering Technology*, *43*(1), 66–94. DOI: 10.37934/araset.43.1.6694

Finseth, T., Dorneich, M. C., Keren, N., Franke, W. D., & Vardeman, S. (2024). Virtual Reality Adaptive training for personalized stress inoculation. *Human Factors*. Advance online publication. DOI: 10.1177/00187208241241968 PMID: 38546259

Fisher, N., & Kulshreshth, A. K. (2024). Exploring dynamic difficulty adjustment methods for video games. *Virtual Worlds*, *3*(2), 230–255. DOI: 10.3390/virtualworlds3020012

Fung, C., Poon, K., Besser, M., & Fung, M. (2023). Improving short-term academic performance in the flipped classroom using dynamic geometry software. *Journal of Computer Assisted Learning*, *40*(2), 775–786. DOI: 10.1111/jcal.12914

Gandham, R. (2025, January 3). *SMARTGUIDE: Revolutionizing the depth and dependability of Vision-Impaired Navigation*. https://vtechworks.lib.vt.edu/items/2ad9c8dd-7a40-4674-906b-3a0630b82647

Gopi, R., Sathiyamoorthi, V., Selvakumar, S., Manikandan, R., Chatterjee, P., Jhanjhi, N. Z., & Luhach, A. K. (2021). Enhanced method of ANN based model for detection of DDoS attacks on multimedia internet of things. *Multimedia Tools and Applications*, *81*(19), 26739–26757. DOI: 10.1007/s11042-021-10640-6

Gouda, W., Almurafeh, M., Humayun, M., & Jhanjhi, N. Z. (2022). Detection of COVID-19 based on chest x-rays using deep learning. *Health Care*, *10*(2), 343. DOI: 10.3390/healthcare10020343 PMID: 35206957

Gwenhure, A. K., & Rahayu, F. S. (2024). Gamification of Cybersecurity Awareness for Non-IT Professionals: A Systematic Literature Review. *International Journal of Serious Games*, *11*(1), 83–99. DOI: 10.17083/ijsg.v11i1.719

Habibi, F., Sedaghatshoar, S., Attar, T., Shokoohi, M., Kiani, A., & Malek, A. N. (2025). Revolutionizing education and therapy for students with autism spectrum disorder: A scoping review of AI-driven tools, technologies, and ethical implications. *AI and Ethics*, *5*(3), 2055–2070. Advance online publication. DOI: 10.1007/s43681-024-00608-1

Hadwin, A. F., Rostampour, R., & Winne, P. H. (2025). Advancing Self-Reports of Self-Regulated Learning: Validating new measures to assess students' beliefs, practices, and challenges. *Educational Psychology Review*, *37*(1), 8. Advance online publication. DOI: 10.1007/s10648-024-09977-9

Hefkaluk, N., Linehan, C., & Trace, A. (2023). Fail, fail again, fail better: How players who enjoy challenging games persist after failure in "Celeste.". *International Journal of Human-Computer Studies*, *183*, 103199. DOI: 10.1016/j.ijhcs.2023.103199

Humayun, M., Sujatha, R., Almuayqil, S. N., & Jhanjhi, N. Z. (2022). A Transfer Learning Approach with a Convolutional Neural Network for the Classification of Lung Carcinoma. *Health Care*, *10*(6), 1058. DOI: 10.3390/healthcare10061058 PMID: 35742109

Hussain, K., Rahmatyar, A. R., Riskhan, B., Sheikh, M. U., & Sindiramutty, S. R. (2024). Threats and Vulnerabilities of Wireless Networks in the Internet of Things (IoT). *IEEE 1st Karachi Section Humanitarian Technology Conference (KHI-HTC)*, *2*, 1–8. DOI: 10.1109/KHI-HTC60760.2024.10482197

Jacob, T., & Centofanti, S. (2023). Effectiveness of H5P in improving student learning outcomes in an online tertiary education setting. *Journal of Computing in Higher Education*, *36*(2), 469–485. DOI: 10.1007/s12528-023-09361-6 PMID: 37359040

Jawhar, S., Miller, J., & Bitar, Z. (2024). AI-Driven Customized Cyber Security Training and Awareness. *2024 IEEE 3rd International Conference on AI in Cybersecurity (ICAIC)*, 1–5. DOI: 10.1109/ICAIC60265.2024.10433829

Jhanjhi, N., Humayun, M., & Almuayqil, S. N. (2021). Cyber security and privacy issues in industrial internet of things. *Computer Systems Science and Engineering*, *37*(3), 361–380. DOI: 10.32604/csse.2021.015206

Joon, N., & Simmons, R. (2024). Innovating cybersecurity education through AI-augmented teaching. *European Conference on Cyber Warfare and Security, 23*(1), 480–486. DOI: 10.34190/eccws.23.1.2224

Jun, A. Y. M., Jinu, B. A., Seng, L. K., Maharaiq, M. H. F. B. Z., Khongsuwan, W., Junn, B. T. K., Hao, A. W., & Sindiramutty, S. R. (2024). Exploring the Impact of Crypto-Ransomware on Critical Industries: Case Studies and Solutions. *Preprints.org*. DOI: 10.20944/preprints202409.1325.v1

Kanchon, M. K. H., Sadman, M., Nabila, K. F., Tarannum, R., & Khan, R. (2024). Enhancing personalized learning: AI-driven identification of learning styles and content modification strategies. *International Journal of Cognitive Computing in Engineering*, *5*, 269–278. DOI: 10.1016/j.ijcce.2024.06.002

Kang, X., & Nie, Y. (2024). The Application of Virtual Simulation in the Training of Artistic Voice:A Study on Improving the Vocal Training Effect. *SSRN*. DOI: 10.2139/ssrn.4903508

Kasri, W., Himeur, Y., Alkhazaleh, H. A., Tarapiah, S., Atalla, S., Mansoor, W., & Al-Ahmad, H. (2025). From Vulnerability to Defense: The role of large language models in enhancing Cybersecurity. *Computation (Basel, Switzerland)*, *13*(2), 30. DOI: 10.3390/computation13020030

Katsamakas, E., Pavlov, O. V., & Saklad, R. (2024). Artificial Intelligence and the Transformation of Higher Education Institutions: A Systems approach. *Sustainability (Basel)*, *16*(14), 6118. DOI: 10.3390/su16146118

Kehinde, O. (2025). Leveraging machine learning for predictive models in healthcare to enhance patient outcome management. *International Research Journal of Modernization in Engineering Technology and Science*. Advance online publication. DOI: 10.56726/IRJMETS66198

Kellman, P. J., Jacoby, V., Massey, C., & Krasne, S. (2022). Perceptual Learning, adaptive learning, and Gamification: educational technologies for pattern recognition, problem solving, and knowledge retention in medical learning. In *Springer eBooks* (pp. 135–166). DOI: 10.1007/978-3-030-95633-2_5

Kelso, E., Soneji, A., Rahaman, S., Shoshitaishvili, Y., & Hasan, R. (2024). Trust, Because You Can't Verify: Privacy and Security Hurdles in Education Technology Acquisition Practices. *ACM*, 1656–1670. DOI: 10.1145/3658644.3690353

Khan, M. T., Ullah, S., Sami, A., Kukreti, M., & Shaukat, M. R. (2025). Cultivating a paradoxical mindset: Enhancing transformative learning through paradoxical leadership. *Leadership and Organization Development Journal*, *46*(2), 334–350. Advance online publication. DOI: 10.1108/LODJ-04-2024-0223

Khine, M. S. (2024). Using AI for adaptive learning and adaptive assessment. In *Artificial Intelligence in Education* (pp. 341–466). DOI: 10.1007/978-981-97-9350-1_3

Khoo, L. J., Yatim, M. H. M., & Wong, Y. S. (2025). Research on Capture the Flag Exercises for Cybersecurity skill training among Malaysian undergraduates. *Journal of Human Centered Technology*, *4*(1), 1–9. DOI: 10.11113/humentech.v4n1.87

Kiyani, F. F., Hamid, B., Humayun, M., Sindiramutty, S. R. L., & Chowdhury, S. (2024). Discovery of Influential Publications Using Research Article's Usage Context. *2024 International Conference on Emerging Trends in Networks and Computer Communications (ETNCC)*, 1–7. DOI: 10.1109/ETNCC63262.2024.10767576

Krichen, M., & Abdalzaher, M. S. (2024). Performance enhancement of artificial intelligence: A survey. *Journal of Network and Computer Applications*, *104034*, 104034. Advance online publication. DOI: 10.1016/j.jnca.2024.104034

Kumar, M. S., Vimal, S., Jhanjhi, N., Dhanabalan, S. S., & Alhumyani, H. A. (2021). Blockchain based peer to peer communication in autonomous drone operation. *Energy Reports*, *7*, 7925–7939. DOI: 10.1016/j.egyr.2021.08.073

Lakshmikantha, H. T. (2024). Leveling up orthodontic education: Game-based learning as the new frontier in orthodontic curriculum. *Research and Development in Medical Education*, *13*, 13. DOI: 10.34172/rdme.33205

Lampropoulos, G., & Sidiropoulos, A. (2024). Impact of gamification on students' learning outcomes and academic performance: A longitudinal study comparing online, traditional, and gamified learning. *Education Sciences*, *14*(4), 367. DOI: 10.3390/educsci14040367

Lim, M., Abdullah, A., Jhanjhi, N., Khan, M. K., & Supramaniam, M. (2019). Link Prediction in Time-Evolving Criminal Network with deep Reinforcement learning technique. *IEEE Access : Practical Innovations, Open Solutions*, *7*, 184797–184807. DOI: 10.1109/ACCESS.2019.2958873

Linqiang, Y., Sindiramutty, S. R. L., Ashraf, H., Muzammal, S. M., Balakrishnan, S. P., Gupta, S., & Kavita, N. (2024). Intelligent Household Waste Classification System Based on Machine Learning. *2024 International Conference on Emerging Trends in Networks and Computer Communications (ETNCC)*, 760–768. DOI: 10.1109/ETNCC63262.2024.10767563

Liu, C., Lin, Y., Lo, F., Chang, C., & Lin, H. (2024). From readers to players: Exploring student engagement in a gamified metaverse and its effect on reading interest. *Education and Information Technologies*. Advance online publication. DOI: 10.1007/s10639-024-13068-1

Liu, L. (2024). Impact of AI gamification on EFL learning outcomes and nonlinear dynamic motivation: Comparing adaptive learning paths, conversational agents, and storytelling. *Education and Information Technologies*. Advance online publication. DOI: 10.1007/s10639-024-13296-5

Lut, L. T. Y. (2024). *Literature review of application of AI in improving gaming experience : NPC behavior and dynamic difficulty adjustment*. LUTPub. https://lutpub.lut.fi/handle/10024/167834

Lynch, M., Kubberød, E., Sanne, N., & Josendal, A. H. F. (2025). *Deliberate practice through the gamification of entrepreneurship education*. Entrepreneurship Education and Pedagogy., DOI: 10.1177/25151274241309940

Mac, D. (2024). The Journal of Applied Instructional Design. *The Journal of Applied Instructional Design*. https://doi.org/DOI: 10.59668/2036

Manchuri, A., Kakera, A., Saleh, A., & Raja, S. (2024). pplication of Supervised Machine Learning Models in Biodiesel Production Research - A Short Review. *Borneo Journal of Sciences and Technology*. DOI: 10.35370/bjost.2024.6.1-10

Manoharan, A., & Nagulapally, S. (2024). ADAPTIVE GAMIFICATION ALGORITHMS FOR PERSONALIZED LEARNING ERIENCES IN EDUCATIONAL PLATFORMS. *International Research Journal of Modernization in Engineering Technology and Science*. Advance online publication. DOI: 10.56726/IRJMETS49966

Mao, P., Cai, Z., Wang, Z., Hao, X., Fan, X., & Sun, X. (2023). The effects of dynamic and static feedback under tasks with different difficulty levels in digital game-based learning. *The Internet and Higher Education*, *60*, 100923. DOI: 10.1016/j.iheduc.2023.100923

Masegosa, A. R., Cabañas, R., Maldonado, A. D., & Morales, M. (2024). Learning styles impact students' perceptions on active learning methodologies: A case study on the use of live coding and short programming exercises. *Education Sciences*, *14*(3), 250. DOI: 10.3390/educsci14030250

Mohammed, M., Fatemah, A., & Hassan, L. (2024). Effects of Gamification on Motivations of Elementary School Students: An Action Research Field experiment. *Simulation & Gaming*, *55*(4), 600–636. DOI: 10.1177/10468781241237389

Mouhssine, Y., Boutracheh, H., & Moumen, A. (2024). Teaching Cybersecurity to Engineering Students: A New Perspective Through Literature Review. *2024 4th International Conference on Innovative Research in Applied Science, Engineering and Technology (IRASET)*, *3413*, 1–9. DOI: 10.1109/IRASET60544.2024.10548731

Nayyar, A., Gadhavi, L., & Zaman, N. (2021). Machine learning in healthcare: review, opportunities and challenges. In *Elsevier eBooks* (pp. 23–45). DOI: 10.1016/B978-0-12-821229-5.00011-2

Nguyen, H. T. V., & Javorsky, K. (2024). Beyond memorization. In *Advances in educational technologies and instructional design book series* (pp. 1–40). DOI: 10.4018/979-8-3693-6497-0.ch001

Oleet, J. B., & Yu, C. (2024). Examining the role and effect of emotions in adults' online learning. In *Advances in educational technologies and instructional design book series* (pp. 155–204). DOI: 10.4018/979-8-3693-2663-3.ch006

Ortiz-Rojas, M., Chiluiza, K., Valcke, M., & Bolanos-Mendoza, C. (2025). How gamification boosts learning in STEM higher education: A mixed methods study. *International Journal of STEM Education, 12*(1), 1. Advance online publication. DOI: 10.1186/s40594-024-00521-3

Papadimitriou, S., & Virvou, M. (2025a). Artificial Intelligence—Based games as novel holistic educational environments to teach 21st century skills. In *Intelligent systems reference library*. DOI: 10.1007/978-3-031-77464-5

Papadimitriou, S., & Virvou, M. (2025b). Contributions and Discussions on Advancing 21st Century Skills Through EPATHLO: Prosocial Educational Games with Artificial Intelligence. In *Intelligent systems reference library* (pp. 277–309). DOI: 10.1007/978-3-031-77464-5_10

Paracha, S., Hall, L., Hagan-Green, G., & Watson, D. (2024). Cyber eyes wide open. In *Advances in library and information science (ALIS) book series* (pp. 101–134). DOI: 10.4018/979-8-3693-6376-8.ch004

Patil, D. (2025). Artificial Intelligence In Cybersecurity: Enhancing Threat Detection And Prevention Mechanisms Through Machine Learning And Data Analytics. *SSRN*. DOI: 10.2139/ssrn.5057410

Pavithra, M., & Ramya, G. (2025). Using gamification to overcome innovation process challenges. In *Advances in healthcare information systems and administration book series* (pp. 287–306). DOI: 10.4018/979-8-3693-4199-5.ch012

Pellas, N. (2025). The impact of AI-Generated instructional Videos on Problem-Based Learning in Science Teacher Education. *Education Sciences, 15*(1), 102. DOI: 10.3390/educsci15010102

Pereira, D., Fernandes, E., Lutovac, S., & Flores, M. A. (2025). Looking at assessment through critical incidents written by preservice teachers: A study conducted in Portugal. *Reflective Practice, 26*(3), 1–20. DOI: 10.1080/14623943.2025.2459433

Pereira, J. T., & Harun, R. N. S. R. (2024). Gamification of classroom activities: Undergraduates' perception. *AJELP the Asian Journal of English Language and Pedagogy, 12*(1), 80–92. DOI: 10.37134/ajelp.vol12.1.7.2024

Pillai, M. G., & Khan, F. (2025). Harnessing Learning Styles and Metacognition: A Dual Framework for Academic Improvement using the VARK Model. SSRN *Electronic Journal.* DOI: 10.2139/ssrn.5091493

Pils, M. (2025). Increasing security awareness in the company. In *Essentials* (pp. 11–31). DOI: 10.1007/978-3-658-46683-1_3

Pitura, J., Kaplan-Rakowski, R., & Asotska-Wierzba, Y. (2024). The VR-AI–Assisted Simulation for Content Knowledge Application in Pre-Service EFL Teacher training. *TechTrends.* Advance online publication. DOI: 10.1007/s11528-024-01022-4

Quayyum, F., & Jaccheri, L. (2024). CyberFamily: A collaborative family game to increase children's cybersecurity awareness. *Entertainment Computing, 52*, 100826. DOI: 10.1016/j.entcom.2024.100826

Rahmi, I., Rimenda, T., & Ariyanti, T. D. (2024). Gamification as an alternative to increase students' motivation: A scoping review. [EduLearn]. *Journal of Education and Learning, 19*(2), 1125–1133. DOI: 10.11591/edulearn.v19i2.21771

Rajendran, R. K., & Immanuel, A. V., & T, M. P. (2024). Specializing instruction with the use of artificial intelligence. In *Advances in educational technologies and instructional design book series* (pp. 245–256). DOI: 10.4018/979-8-3693-5538-1.ch009

Rana, S., & Chicone, R. (2024). Introduction to AI in Cybersecurity Training. In *Fortifying the Future* (pp. 1–24). DOI: 10.1007/978-3-031-81780-9_1

Ravichandran, N., Tewaraja, T., Rajasegaran, V., Kumar, S. S., Gunasekar, S. K. L., & Sindiramutty, S. R. (2024). Comprehensive Review Analysis and Countermeasures for Cybersecurity Threats: DDoS, Ransomware, and Trojan Horse Attacks. *Preprints.org*. DOI: 10.20944/preprints202409.1369.v1

Renacido, J. M. D., & Biray, E. T. (2024). Enhancing peer engagement and student motivation through AI-Gamified interactive learning tools. In *Advances in educational technologies and instructional design book series* (pp. 277–342). DOI: 10.4018/979-8-3693-8242-4.ch009

Riza, A. Z. B. M., Jennsen, L., Anggani, P., Rafeen, A. I., Ruth, P. N. J., Sookun, D., Sookun, V., Yusri, N. Z. B. M., Sern, L. J., Luximon, L., Omer, M. L., & Sindiramutty, S. R. (2025). Leveraging Machine Learning and AI to Combat Modern Cyber Threats. *preprints.org*. DOI: 10.20944/preprints202501.0360.v1

Rosário, A. T., & Raimundo, R. (2024). Enhancing Business Higher Education Through Simulation-Based Learning, Problem-Based Learning, and Challenge-Based Learning. *Preprints*. DOI: 10.20944/preprints202407.0747.v1

Roy, P., Pandit, R., & Naskar, S. K. (2024). Innovative Approaches to Problem-Solving through Educational Technology Integration. In *Advances in educational technologies and instructional design book series* (pp. 375–402). DOI: 10.4018/979-8-3693-6745-2.ch016

Rye, S., Sousa, M., & Sousa, C. (2025). Designing Effective Learning Games. In *Transformative Learning Through Play* (pp. 95–130). DOI: 10.1007/978-3-031-78523-8_4

Seng, Y. J., Cen, T. Y., Raslan, M. H. B. M., Subramaniam, M. R., Xin, L. Y., Kin, S. J., Long, M. S., & Sindiramutty, S. R. (2024). In-Depth Analysis and Countermeasures for Ransomware Attacks: Case Studies and Recommendations. *Preprint. org*. DOI: 10.20944/preprints202408.2261.v1

Sengupta, S., Bardhan, S., Das, R., & Chakrabarti, S. (2025). LearnAlytics: The smart way to analyze, adapt, and achieve in E-Learning. *SN Computer Science*, *6*(1), 79. Advance online publication. DOI: 10.1007/s42979-024-03535-4

Shah, I. A., Jhanjhi, N. Z., & Laraib, A. (2022). Cybersecurity and blockchain usage in contemporary business. In *Advances in information security, privacy, and ethics book series* (pp. 49–64). DOI: 10.4018/978-1-6684-5284-4.ch003

Shahzadi, A., Ishaq, K., Nawaz, N. A., Rosdi, F., & Khan, F. A. (2025). Unveiling personalized and gamification-based cybersecurity risks within financial institutions. *PeerJ. Computer Science*, *11*, e2598. DOI: 10.7717/peerj-cs.2598 PMID: 40062254

Sharma, R., Singh, A., Kavita, N., Jhanjhi, N. Z., Masud, M., Jaha, E. S., & Verma, S. (2021). Plant disease diagnosis and image classification using deep learning. *Computers, Materials & Continua/Computers. Materials & Continua (Print)*, *71*(2), 2125–2140. DOI: 10.32604/cmc.2022.020017

Sheng, L. T., Azman, A. B., Khan, N. A., Sindiramutty, S. R., Singh, S., & Verma, S. (2024). Reinforcement learning-based traffic signal control. *2024 International Conference on Emerging Trends in Networks and Computer Communications (ET-NCC)*, 792–798. DOI: 10.1109/ETNCC63262.2024.10767501

Shirindzi, L. S., & Sikhwari, M. G. (2025). Interactive apps and games for early language development. In *Advances in educational technologies and instructional design book series* (pp. 177–202). DOI: 10.4018/979-8-3693-7437-5.ch008

Sikhwari, M., & Thenga, N. E. (2025). Future of language learning. In *Advances in educational technologies and instructional design book series* (pp. 115–144). DOI: 10.4018/979-8-3693-7437-5.ch006

Sindiramutty, S. R. (2024). Autonomous Threat Hunting: a future paradigm for AI-Driven Threat intelligence. *arXiv (Cornell University)*. https://doi.org//arxiv.2401.00286DOI: 10.48550

Sindiramutty, S. R., Prabagaran, K. R. V., Akbar, R., Hussain, M., & Malik, N. A. (2024). Overview of Generative AI techniques for cybersecurity. In *Advances in information security, privacy, and ethics book series* (pp. 1–52). DOI: 10.4018/979-8-3693-5415-5.ch001

Sindiramutty, S. R., Prabagaran, K. R. V., Jhanjhi, N. Z., Ghazanfar, M. A., Malik, N. A., & Soomro, T. R. (2024). Security Considerations in Generative AI for web Applications. In *Advances in information security, privacy, and ethics book series* (pp. 281–332). DOI: 10.4018/979-8-3693-5415-5.ch009

Sindiramutty, S. R., Prabagaran, K. R. V., Jhanjhi, N. Z., Murugesan, R. K., Brohi, S. N., & Masud, M. (2024). Generative AI in network security and intrusion detection. In *Advances in information security, privacy, and ethics book series* (pp. 77–124). DOI: 10.4018/979-8-3693-5415-5.ch003

Sindiramutty, S. R., Prabagaran, K. R. V., Jhanjhi, N. Z., Murugesan, R. K., Brohi, S. N., & Wei, G. W. (2024). Generative AI for threat intelligence and information sharing. In *Advances in digital crime, forensics, and cyber terrorism book series* (pp. 191–234). DOI: 10.4018/979-8-3693-8944-7.ch006

Sindiramutty, S. R., Prabagaran, K. R. V., Jhanjhi, N. Z., Murugesan, R. K., Malik, N. A., & Hussain, M. (2024). Ethics and transparency in secure web model generation. In *Advances in information security, privacy, and ethics book series* (pp. 411–464). DOI: 10.4018/979-8-3693-5415-5.ch012

Singh, B., Kaunert, C., Lal, S., & Arora, M. K. (2024). Enhancing AI-Augmented classrooms. In *Advances in educational technologies and instructional design book series* (pp. 99–130). DOI: 10.4018/979-8-3693-7255-5.ch004

Singh, T. M., Reddy, C. K. K., Murthy, B. V. R., Nag, A., & Doss, S. (2024). AI and Education. In *Advances in educational technologies and instructional design book series* (pp. 131–160). DOI: 10.4018/979-8-3693-2964-1.ch002

Singhal, V., Jain, S. S., Anand, D., Singh, A., Verma, S., Kavita, N., Rodrigues, J. J. P. C., Jhanjhi, N. Z., Ghosh, U., Jo, O., & Iwendi, C. (2020). Artificial Intelligence Enabled Road Vehicle-Train Collision Risk Assessment Framework for Unmanned railway level crossings. *IEEE Access : Practical Innovations, Open Solutions*, *8*, 113790–113806. DOI: 10.1109/ACCESS.2020.3002416

Sousa, C., Sousa, M., & Rye, S. (2025). Introduction to Inclusivity in Analogue Game-Based Learning: Challenges and Strategies. In *Transformative Learning Through Play* (pp. 179–219). DOI: 10.1007/978-3-031-78523-8_6

Spaho, E., Çiço, B., & Shabani, I. (2025). IoT Integration Approaches into Personalized Online Learning: Systematic Review. *Computers*, *14*(2), 63. DOI: 10.3390/computers14020063

Spatafora, A., Wagemann, M., Sandoval, C., Leisenberg, M., & De Carvalho, C. V. (2024). An educational escape room game to develop cybersecurity skills. *Computers*, *13*(8), 205. DOI: 10.3390/computers13080205

Strielkowski, W., Grebennikova, V., Lisovskiy, A., Rakhimova, G., & Vasileva, T. (2024). AI-driven adaptive learning for sustainable educational transformation. *Sustainable Development*. Advance online publication. DOI: 10.1002/sd.3221

Sudrajat, R. P. A., Vhalery, R., & Sefudin, A. (2025, January 26). *The influence of VAK (Visual, Auditory, Kinesthetic) learning Styles on students' learning outcomes in AKL practicum subjects at SMK Pembangunan Jaya YAKAPI Jakarta.* https://pub.ruangrosadi.com/jurnal-ilmiah/index.php/jedar/article/view/70

Tang, X., Long, B., & Zhou, L. (2024). Real-time monitoring and analysis of track and field athletes based on edge computing and deep reinforcement learning algorithm. *Alexandria Engineering Journal*, *114*, 136–146. DOI: 10.1016/j.aej.2024.11.024

Tariq, M. U. (2024). Advancing Inquiry-Based learning through generative AI-Enabled assessments. In *Advances in educational marketing, administration, and leadership book series* (pp. 179–206). DOI: 10.4018/979-8-3693-6351-5.ch007

Teles, R. O., & Moreira, F. T. (2024). Integrating AI in formative assessment under UDL principles in diverse learning environments. In *Advances in educational technologies and instructional design book series* (pp. 95–122). DOI: 10.4018/979-8-3693-6170-2.ch004

Tyagi, R., & Khanna, P. (2025). A Comprehensive review of Digital Transformation for Sustainable Development in Emerging Markets: Vis-a-Vis Blockchain and Gamification. *Emerald Publishing Limited eBooks*, 223–246. DOI: 10.1108/978-1-83549-109-620251009

Vaithilingam, P., Arawjo, I., & Glassman, E. L. (2024). Imagining a Future of Designing with AI: Dynamic Grounding, Constructive Negotiation, and Sustainable Motivation. *Designing Interactive Systems Conference, 8*, 289–300. DOI: 10.1145/3643834.3661525

Waheed, A., Seegolam, B., Jowaheer, M. F., Sze, C. L. X., Hua, E. T. F., & Sindiramutty, S. R. (2024). Zero-Day Exploits in Cybersecurity: Case Studies and Countermeasure. *Preprints.org*. DOI: 10.20944/preprints202407.2338.v1

Wang, T., Zhou, N., & Chen, Z. (2025). CyberMentor: AI powered learning tool platform to address diverse student needs in cybersecurity education. *arXiv (Cornell University)*. https://doi.org//arxiv.2501.09709DOI: 10.48550

Weiqi, X., Hooi, S. T. C., Sindiramutty, S. R. L., Asirvatham, D. L., Kumar, D., & Verma, S. (2024). Surface Anomaly Detection Using Machine Learning Technique. *2024 International Conference on Emerging Trends in Networks and Computer Communications (ETNCC)*, 1–7. DOI: 10.1109/ETNCC63262.2024.10767562

Wendt, D. W. (2024). The Cybersecurity Trinity. In *Apress eBooks*. DOI: 10.1007/979-8-8688-0947-7

Wu, J., Li, Q., Peng, L., Robinson, S., & Chen, Y. (2025). Drivers of consumer group participation in an online shopping event: Alibaba's singles' day. *Information Processing & Management, 62*(3), 104067. DOI: 10.1016/j.ipm.2025.104067

Xue, H., Røds, J., Haugseggen, Ø., Christensen, A. J., Batalden, B., & Gudmestad, O. T. (2025). A study on the effects of rapid training method related to ship handling in decision-making skills under stressful situations. *Journal of Navigation*, •••, 1–20. DOI: 10.1017/S0373463324000213

Xun, A. T., En, L. Z., Shen, L. T., Xin, A. N., Soon, W. H., Jun, W. Z., Ramachandra, H., Xinghao, G., Khant, N. M., Weitao, F., & Sindiramutty, S. R. (2025). Building Trust in Cloud Computing:Strategies for Resilient Security. *Preprints.org*. DOI: 10.20944/preprints202501.0716.v1

Yadav, S. (2024). Advancing education with AI-Driven education for diverse learners. In *Advances in educational technologies and instructional design book series* (pp. 49–80). DOI: 10.4018/979-8-3693-6130-6.ch003

Yambal, S., & Waykar, Y. A. (2025). Future of education using adaptive AI, intelligent systems, and ethical challenges. In *Advances in educational technologies and instructional design book series* (pp. 171–202). DOI: 10.4018/979-8-3693-6527-4.ch006

Yamin, M. M., Ullah, M., Ullah, H., & Katt, B. (2021). Weaponized AI for cyber attacks. *Journal of Information Security and Applications*, *57*, 102722. DOI: 10.1016/j.jisa.2020.102722

Yeganeh, L. N., Fenty, N. S., Chen, Y., Simpson, A., & Hatami, M. (2025). The Future of Education: A Multi-Layered Metaverse Classroom Model for Immersive and Inclusive Learning. *Future Internet*, *17*(2), 63. DOI: 10.3390/fi17020063

Ying, X., Murugesan, R. K., Sindiramutty, S. R., Wei, G. W., Balakrishnan, S., Kumar, D., & Verma, S. (2024). Scene Text Recognition using Deep Learning Techniques. *2024 International Conference on Emerging Trends in Networks and Computer Communications (ETNCC)*, 1–9. DOI: 10.1109/ETNCC63262.2024.10767484

Zairon, I. Y., Wook, T. S. M. T., Salleh, S. M., & Dahlan, H. A. (2025). User Model for Virtual Learning based on Adaptive Gamification. *IEEE Access : Practical Innovations, Open Solutions*, *1*, 24028–24040. Advance online publication. DOI: 10.1109/ACCESS.2025.3537599

Zamiri, M., & Esmaeili, A. (2024). Strategies, Methods, and Supports for Developing Skills within Learning Communities: A Systematic Review of the Literature. *Administrative Sciences*, *14*(9), 231. DOI: 10.3390/admsci14090231

Zhai, C., Wibowo, S., & Li, L. D. (2024). The effects of over-reliance on AI dialogue systems on students' cognitive abilities: A systematic review. *Smart Learning Environments*, *11*(1), 28. Advance online publication. DOI: 10.1186/s40561-024-00316-7

Zhang, Z., & Huang, X. (2024). Exploring the impact of the adaptive gamified assessment on learners in blended learning. *Education and Information Technologies*, *29*(16), 21869–21889. DOI: 10.1007/s10639-024-12708-w

Zhou, S., Zheng, W., Xu, Y., & Liu, Y. (2024). Enhancing User Experience in VR Environments through AI-Driven Adaptive UI Design. *Deleted Journal*, *6*(1), 59–82. DOI: 10.60087/jaigs.v6i1.230

Chapter 12
Gamification for Continuous Security Training in DevSecOps

Kiran Adnan
https://orcid.org/0000-0002-2474-8844
Universiti Tunku Abdul Rahman, Malaysia

Rabia Afzaal
Lahore Garrison University, Lahore, Pakistan

Sohaib Khalid
Lahore Garrison University, Lahore, Pakistan

Adnan Bin Amanat Ali
Universiti Tunku Abdul Rahman, Malaysia

ABSTRACT

This paper explores the integration of gamification into cybersecurity training as a strategic approach to enhance engagement, knowledge retention, and secure behavior across DevSecOps environments. Traditional training methods often struggle to address the evolving needs of fast-paced development teams and dynamic threat landscapes. By leveraging game elements such as challenges, feedback, leaderboards, and role-based scenarios, gamified training fosters a proactive security culture embedded in daily workflows. The study reviews current practices, evaluates tools and platforms, and outlines measurable impacts such as improved secure coding, reduced vulnerabilities, and faster incident response. It also discusses future innovations including AI-driven personalization, VR/AR simulations, and predictive analytics. The findings emphasize that gamification, when thoughtfully designed and aligned

DOI: 10.4018/979-8-3373-0477-9.ch012

with organizational objectives, is not merely a learning enhancement—but a vital component of modern cybersecurity readiness and DevSecOps maturity.

INTRODUCTION

In today's rapidly evolving technological landscape, integrating security into every phase of the software development lifecycle has become a necessity rather than an afterthought. DevSecOps—short for Development, Security, and Operations—embodies this shift by embedding security practices into the heart of the DevOps pipeline. Unlike legacy models that treated security as a final-stage checklist item, DevSecOps promotes a cultural transformation where security is a shared responsibility from the very first line of code. Every team member becomes accountable for identifying and mitigating risks proactively, enabling a smoother, more secure development process and fostering resilience across the software ecosystem. However, the increasing sophistication of cyber threats presents ongoing challenges. Despite the adoption of DevSecOps practices, traditional security training methods are failing to keep pace with the speed, complexity, and evolving nature of modern development environments. These conventional approaches are often static, disengaging, and disconnected from real-world applications—leading to poor knowledge retention, limited practical skills, and low developer engagement (Koivisto & Hamari, 2019. As a result, security awareness remains superficial, reactive, and insufficiently embedded in day-to-day development workflows. There is a pressing need for dynamic, engaging, and role-relevant training solutions that not only enhance security skills but also cultivate a proactive, security-first mindset across development, operations, and security teams.

Gamification emerges as a powerful solution to address these shortcomings. By applying game-design elements such as points, badges, leaderboards, and interactive challenges, gamified training transforms security education into an engaging and motivating experience. It enhances knowledge retention, encourages continuous participation, and allows learners to practice skills in realistic simulations Denning, 2013), (Fu, 2024). Gamification not only makes training enjoyable but also deeply effective, reinforcing critical security behaviors within the DevSecOps workflow. As a result, security awareness becomes an integral and continuous process—driving a culture of proactive defense, continuous improvement, and operational excellence in modern software development environments.

This chapter is organized as follows: DevSecOps approach has been discussed in the following subsection. Then the role of gamification as motivational framework for learning and behavioral change has been described. Further, integration of gamification with DevSecOps has been presented. Moreover some tools and technologies for gamified security training have also been discussed followed by the future works and conclusion.

MODERN DEVSECOPS: A PROACTIVE APPROACH TO SECURE SOFTWARE DEVELOPMENT

Modern DevSecOps represents a transformative approach to software development, built upon foundational principles such as collaboration, automation, and the seamless integration of security throughout the software development lifecycle (SDLC). Unlike traditional methodologies where security is typically addressed as a final step in the development process, DevSecOps emphasizes the early and continuous incorporation of security measures, starting from the initial phases of development. This paradigm shift fosters close collaboration among development, security, and operations teams, ensuring that security considerations are embedded into each phase of the application lifecycle. The outcome is a more resilient and robust development environment in which security vulnerabilities are identified and remediated earlier, thereby improving the overall security posture, quality, and reliability of software products. Figure 1 shows the different stages of DevSecOps approach (Fu, 2024).

Figure 1. DevSecOps and its stages

DevSecOps supports rapid and iterative deployment cycles through continuous integration and continuous delivery (CI/CD) pipelines. This enables organizations to release new features swiftly, collect real-time feedback, and make data-driven improvements. By adopting a modular development strategy where code is frequently pushed to centralized repositories and automatically tested, organizations can maintain high software quality while meeting the increasing demands for agility and innovation in today's fast-paced technological landscape. However, the acceleration of development workflows through CI/CD can introduce security bottlenecks if appropriate security controls—such as automated testing, vulnerability scanning, and code quality assessments—are not integrated into the pipeline. Without the automation and incorporation of such practices, security becomes a barrier to timely deployment or is overlooked entirely, potentially resulting in undetected vulnerabilities until post-deployment. This reactive approach can lead to significant security incidents and costly breaches, which could have been prevented through proactive integration of security measures (Rajapakse, 2022).

To mitigate this risk, organizations must cultivate a strong security culture and promote continuous awareness across all development functions. Classical security models typically respond to threats after breaches have occurred or after vulnerabilities are discovered. In contrast, DevSecOps fosters a preventive security posture, where secure coding practices, automated testing, and early vulnerability assessments are standard components of daily workflows. Security must not be treated as an isolated function. Instead, it should be a shared responsibility across development, security, and operations teams, embedded into the organizational mindset and practices. This cultural transformation involves more than the adoption of tools—it requires a holistic shift in how teams perceive and prioritize security, necessitating continuous learning and staying abreast of emerging threats and industry best practices. By dismantling traditional silos and encouraging cross-functional collaboration, organizations are better positioned to detect, assess, and manage risks from the outset. Embracing DevSecOps not only enhances security but also supports faster time-to-market and consistent delivery of high-quality software. Ultimately, adopting DevSecOps principles enables organizations to maintain agility, address evolving security threats proactively, and ensure that security is an integral, continuous element of the software development process—not a last-minute addition (Rajapakse, 2022).

GAMIFICATION AS MOTIVATIONAL FRAMEWORK FOR LEARNING AND BEHAVIORAL CHANGE

Gamification, defined as the integration of game design elements in non-game contexts, has emerged as a compelling approach to enhance user engagement, particularly in problem-solving and training environments. Although originally rooted in the entertainment and gaming industries, gamification has since gained widespread traction across various sectors, including education, corporate training, and healthcare. This expansion is largely attributed to its foundation in psychological motivators that underpin human behavior, thereby offering a dynamic method to transform traditionally passive or monotonous learning experiences into interactive and impactful ones. When applied to instructional and training systems, gamification serves as a strategic mechanism to reframe the learning process—making it more engaging, participatory, and outcome-driven. By leveraging elements such as points, badges, challenges, leaderboards, and rewards, gamification shifts user interaction from passive consumption to active participation. This shift has profound implications for the effectiveness of training programs, especially in areas where long-term retention and user engagement are critical.

At the core of gamification's effectiveness lies its grounding in well-established psychological theories. One of the most influential frameworks is Self-Determination Theory (SDT), developed by Edward Deci and Richard Ryan (2008). SDT posits that individuals are intrinsically motivated to engage in activities when their fundamental psychological needs for autonomy, competence, and relatedness are fulfilled. Gamified systems support these needs by offering choice and flexibility (autonomy), regular feedback and opportunities for skill development (competence), and social interaction via collaboration or competition (relatedness). When these conditions are met, users are more likely to remain engaged and motivated without reliance on external rewards. Complementing SDT is the behaviorist perspective, particularly the reinforcement theory advanced by B.F. Skinner (Gordan, 2014). Behaviorism emphasizes that human behavior can be shaped through reinforcement mechanisms. In gamification, this principle is operationalized through the use of rewards—such as points, unlockable content, and achievement badges—which positively reinforce desired user behavior. Immediate feedback mechanisms also serve to clarify progress toward goals, sustaining user motivation and promoting repetition of target behaviors, which is particularly beneficial in skill acquisition and habit formation.

Another significant theoretical underpinning is Flow Theory, introduced by Mihaly Csikszentmihalyi (1990). Flow describes a psychological state of deep focus and immersion in an activity that challenges an individual's skills at an optimal level. In the context of gamified learning, this state is facilitated through level-based progression, real-time feedback, and adaptive difficulty (He, 2023). Such mechanisms ensure that tasks remain neither too simplistic nor excessively difficult, helping learners remain in the "flow zone" where they are most productive, creative, and receptive to new knowledge. To operationalize these psychological principles, gamified systems incorporate key design elements that influence user motivation and behavior. Points provide immediate feedback, track progress, and encourage task completion. Badges visually represent specific achievements or skill levels, instilling a sense of pride and accomplishment. Leaderboards introduce social comparison and competition, which can foster both individual motivation and a sense of community. Challenges function as milestones that gradually increase in complexity, pushing users to stretch their abilities while recognizing their successes.

The efficacy of gamification in educational contexts is well documented. Numerous studies have demonstrated that gamified learning environments significantly enhance student engagement, motivation, and long-term retention of material. By incorporating goal-oriented progression and interactive elements, gamification facilitates not only a deeper understanding of the content but also the development of critical thinking and problem-solving skills (Deterding et al., 2011). Active learning environments, supported by gamified tools, promote experiential knowledge construction as learners are encouraged to apply concepts in real-world scenarios. When implemented strategically, gamification has the potential to revolutionize traditional training models, particularly in domains that demand continuous engagement and skill refinement. In fields such as cybersecurity, where professionals must continuously adapt to emerging threats, gamified training environments provide a risk-free space to apply knowledge, test strategies, and maintain focus (Gaffir et al, 2016). The immersive nature of such environments helps instill a proactive mindset toward security, reinforcing behavior patterns aligned with organizational objectives. In conclusion, gamification—when thoughtfully integrated into training and education—acts as a powerful catalyst for engagement, performance enhancement, and behavioral transformation. It draws upon intrinsic and extrinsic motivational drivers, creates structured yet enjoyable learning pathways, and ultimately fosters an environment conducive to sustained learning and adaptive expertise. As digital transformation accelerates across sectors, gamification offers a scalable and impactful solution to enhance learning outcomes and foster enduring behavioral change.

DESIGNING A GAMIFIED SECURITY TRAINING PROGRAM

Developing an effective gamified security training program requires a systematic and intentional design approach, beginning with the clear articulation of training objectives. These objectives should not only align with the immediate learning requirements but also be grounded in the organization's broader cybersecurity vision and long-term strategic goals. Whether the focus is on enhancing secure coding practices to reduce vulnerabilities, improving threat detection and response capabilities, or fostering collaboration among development, security, and operations teams, clearly defined objectives provide a foundation for designing purposeful, measurable, and contextually relevant training content. When framed with precision, such objectives enable the program to close existing skills gaps and respond adaptively to the evolving threat landscape. Once the training goals are established, the next step involves identifying appropriate game mechanics to support sustained learner motivation and engagement. Game mechanics—such as points, badges, levels, leaderboards, and timed challenges—serve as core components of gamification. When used strategically, these elements provide immediate feedback, reinforce desired behaviors, and maintain learner interest throughout the training experience (Weitl-Harms et al., 2023).

For instance, points can deliver instantaneous performance feedback and offer a quantifiable sense of progress. Badges function as markers of achievement or competency, recognizing both effort and mastery. Levels structure the learning journey, gradually increasing in complexity to promote skill progression. Leaderboards foster healthy competition, encouraging individuals to benchmark their performance against peers. Timed missions introduce urgency and challenge, adding excitement while reinforcing efficiency in task completion. Importantly, the selection and implementation of game mechanics must be intentional and aligned with both the training objectives and the characteristics of the target audience. Arbitrary use of these elements risks disengagement and may undermine the educational value of the program. Personalization is another critical element in gamified security training design. Learners across different organizational roles—such as developers, security analysts, and operations personnel—possess distinct responsibilities, experiences, and knowledge levels. Training that acknowledges and adapts to these differences enhances both relevance and effectiveness. For example, developers may engage in secure coding challenges that focus on identifying and remediating code-level vulnerabilities prior to deployment. In contrast, security teams might benefit more from threat modeling exercises, incident response simulations, or penetration testing scenarios. Similarly, operations teams may gain from training modules focused on configuration management, infrastructure monitoring, and operational incident response. Role-based training ensures that content is aligned with day-to-day tasks, thereby increasing real-world applicability and the likelihood of skill transfer to operational contexts.

Integrating narrative and scenario-based learning into the gamified training framework further enhances engagement and knowledge retention. Storytelling introduces emotional resonance and contextual depth, fostering immersive learning experiences. Narrative-driven scenarios allow participants to assume roles in defending simulated organizations against cybersecurity threats, applying best practices in realistic and consequential situations. These simulations provide a safe environment in which learners can observe the outcomes of their decisions, facilitating experiential learning. Such methods have been shown to support the development of critical thinking, problem-solving, and strategic decision-making skills—competencies essential for cybersecurity professionals. The inclusion of authentic threat scenarios not only reinforces theoretical understanding but also bridges the gap between knowledge acquisition and practical application. Simulated exercises based on real-world vulnerabilities and attacks prepare learners to respond effectively to complex challenges in operational environments. These experiences also promote behavioral change by instilling a proactive security mindset. Finally, continuous monitoring and evaluation are essential to the success of a gamified training initiative. Ongoing assessment provides valuable insights into learner engagement, performance, and retention, informing iterative improvements to the training design. Metrics such as participation rates, task completion percentages, assessment scores, and time-on-task can be used to evaluate the effectiveness of the program and identify areas requiring refinement. This data-driven feedback loop ensures that the training remains relevant, impactful, and aligned with organizational objectives.

In conclusion, a well-designed gamified security training program requires careful alignment of goals, game mechanics, content personalization, contextual relevance, and performance evaluation. When thoughtfully implemented, such programs can significantly enhance learner engagement, improve security competencies across diverse roles, and contribute to the development of a resilient, security-aware organizational culture.

INTEGRATING GAMIFICATION INTO DEVSECOPS PIPELINES

The integration of gamification into DevSecOps pipelines represents a strategic and multi-layered approach to embedding security education directly into the software delivery lifecycle. Rather than retrofitting game mechanics as superficial additions—such as badges and points—this model advocates for a deeply embedded, context-sensitive framework that introduces learning opportunities at key moments of the development process. By doing so, it reinforces secure coding practices, promotes security awareness, and fosters the development of operationally relevant skills—all without compromising productivity (Denning 2013).

The initial step in this integration involves identifying optimal touchpoints within the DevSecOps pipeline where learning interventions can be both natural and effective. These include code commits, pull requests, build and test processes, infrastructure provisioning, deployment activities, rollback procedures, and incident response workflows. Embedding gamified learning into these moments—via mechanisms such as pre-commit hooks, automated scan results, and real-time alerts—transforms daily tasks into continuous educational experiences. This contextual delivery ensures that training does not disrupt workflow, thereby increasing user adoption and the long-term efficacy of the program. A defining strength of gamification is its capacity to deliver real-time feedback and immediate reinforcement. Unlike traditional training methods—where feedback is often delayed, generic, or abstract—gamified mechanisms respond directly to user actions within the development environment. For instance, if a developer commits code containing a common vulnerability, an automated tool may flag the issue, provide contextual educational content, and assign a score penalty or initiate a learning module addressing that specific risk. Conversely, adherence to best security practices may trigger positive reinforcement, such as awarding points, badges, or leaderboard advancement. This continuous feedback loop not only supports skill acquisition but also fosters a sense of mastery and accomplishment among users. Visual indicators such as progress bars, achievement dashboards, and personal scorecards further enhance motivation by enabling learners to track their own development over time. These elements reduce cognitive load by highlighting the most critical knowledge areas and reinforcing them through repetition and engagement.

Another critical gamification strategy involves the incorporation of hands-on challenges, particularly Capture The Flag (CTF) exercises (Google CTF, n.d). These challenges simulate real-world cybersecurity scenarios, encouraging users to apply their theoretical knowledge in practice. CTF activities can be tailored to align with different stages of the DevSecOps process—for example, identifying misconfigurations post-deployment or uncovering exposed secrets within a containerized environment. These simulations not only promote individual learning but also foster collaboration across development, security, and operations teams when structured as team-based competitions. Such exercises are effective in cultivating situational awareness and building organizational knowledge over time. CTFs provide a safe space for experimentation and learning through trial and error—critical for mastering complex security concepts. Integrating CTFs into recurring activities such as quarterly sprints, security hackathons, or awareness weeks increases their visibility and participation, thereby amplifying their impact across departments. To ensure scalability and adaptability, gamified training mechanisms should be automated and data-driven. As software and threats evolve, so too must the training. For example, after a pull request is merged, CI/CD pipelines can be configured to run automated scans and, based on the findings, trigger the deployment of personalized microlearning modules. These modules can include quizzes, mini-challenges, or interactive tutorials—each gamified with scoring and reward systems. Additionally, organizations can inject synthetic vulnerabilities into non-critical code branches, assessing how quickly and accurately teams detect and remediate them. This not only creates practical training opportunities but also reinforces real-world response behavior.

Integrations with tools such as SonarQube, OWASP ZAP, Snyk, and Checkmarx facilitate real-time risk identification and training feedback, making gamified learning both actionable and measurable. These tools can be leveraged to generate personalized learning paths based on user performance trends. For example, if a developer repeatedly introduces cross-site scripting (XSS) vulnerabilities, the system could assign escalating XSS-related challenges and content, offering structured remediation with gamified milestones. Dashboards displaying individual and team progress, vulnerability reduction trends, and security engagement metrics allow both learners and leadership to assess return on investment (ROI) from training activities. This results in a closed-loop, adaptive learning system that evolves alongside the threat landscape and the organization's development practices. Ultimately, integrating gamification into the DevSecOps pipeline transforms security awareness from a periodic obligation into a continuous, context-rich process. It enables organizations to embed learning within day-to-day workflows, aligning behavior change with operational priorities Denning 2013). By reinforcing secure practices in real-time and cultivating intrinsic motivation through experiential learning, gamified DevSecOps fosters a proactive security culture—one where risks are identified, mitigated, and managed as an integral part of software delivery.

TOOLS AND TECHNOLOGIES FOR GAMIFIED SECURITY TRAINING

The rise of gamified security training has been significantly bolstered by a range of tools and enablement platforms—spanning from open-source initiatives to sophisticated enterprise-grade solutions. These platforms aim to address the persistent challenges of cybersecurity education by making learning experiences more interactive, accessible, and effective through the use of game-based mechanics. Features such as points, badges, progress bars, leaderboards, and challenge-based learning paths are integrated to engage learners and cultivate behavioral change, with the ultimate goal of fostering long-term security awareness and resilience (Triantafyllou, 2022).

Crucially, these platforms extend beyond surface-level engagement. Their purpose is to instill security-conscious habits, enhance knowledge retention, and nurture a proactive security mindset. Designed for scalability, they support a spectrum of users—from junior developers and DevOps engineers to seasoned security professionals—thereby enabling organizations to deliver contextualized and role-specific training that aligns with the security posture and maturity level of the enterprise.

Open Source and Community-Driven Tools

One of the most prominent open-source platforms is OWASP Juice Shop, an intentionally vulnerable web application built using modern development frameworks (OWASP Foundation, n.d.). It offers users the opportunity to simulate real-world attack scenarios—such as SQL injection, cross-site scripting (XSS), and parameter tampering—within a safe, controlled environment. Each challenge is gamified, complete with scoring, hints, and visual progress tracking via scoreboards. Juice Shop is highly compatible with DevSecOps architectures, supporting microservices and serverless deployments, making it a valuable addition to CI/CD pipelines for automated, real-time training interventions.

Enterprise-Grade Training Platforms

Several commercial platforms offer more advanced capabilities tailored to organizational needs. HackEDU (now part of Security Journey) and Secure Code Warrior provide interactive, role-based secure coding paths with support for a variety of programming languages including Java, Python, JavaScript, C#, and Go. These platforms emphasize hands-on vulnerability remediation, contextual feedback, and compliance with security standards such as OWASP Top Ten and CWE/SANS. Metrics dashboards, pre/post assessments, and leaderboards facilitate performance tracking and competitive engagement, bridging theoretical knowledge with practical application (HackEDU, n.d.; Secure Code Warrior, n.d.).

Immersive Training Environments

Platforms such as RangeForce and Immersive Labs further elevate gamified security training by offering cyber range environments and large-scale simulations. These include red team vs. blue team exercises, incident response drills, and dynamic threat modeling, all delivered within a gamified framework. These simulations emulate realistic enterprise environments and adversarial scenarios, making them particularly valuable for organizational readiness assessments and team-based skill development (RangeForce, n.d.; Immersive Labs, n.d.).

Social and Competitive Learning Platforms

Community-centric platforms like TryHackMe and Hack The Box have gained significant adoption among individuals and organizations alike (TryHackMe, n.d.; Hack The Box, n.d.). These platforms combine gamification with social learning by offering globally ranked leaderboards, badges, and challenge-based content structured into modular, bite-sized labs. They provide hands-on experience in areas such as penetration testing, digital forensics, ethical hacking, and network defense, fostering a culture of curiosity, competition, and lifelong learning.

CI/CD Integration for Seamless Training Delivery

To maximize the effectiveness of gamified training, integration with popular DevOps and CI/CD tools—such as Jenkins, GitHub Actions, GitLab CI, Azure DevOps, and Bitbucket Pipelines—is essential (Thool & Brown, 2025). These integrations allow training content to be dynamically triggered by real development events. For instance, if a pull request introduces insecure code patterns, an automated training module or coding challenge can be dispatched immediately. Similarly, following a failed security scan, micro-assessments can be recommended to reinforce relevant skills.

This seamless embedding of training modules into developers' existing workflows ensures that learning becomes timely, non-intrusive, and highly contextual. Moreover, integrated dashboards enable real-time visibility into user engagement, vulnerability trends, and training effectiveness, allowing both learners and management to monitor progress and return on investment (ROI).

Customization and Real-Time Feedback

Advanced platforms offer APIs and webhook capabilities for extensive customization. For example, a team that deploys a high-risk feature could automatically receive targeted training based on the most prevalent vulnerabilities associated with similar code patterns. These training modules can be delivered through various channels—integrated development environments (IDEs), chat tools like Slack or Microsoft Teams, or project management systems such as Jira—providing real-time feedback and remediation guidance without disrupting the development flow. Such contextual, in-flow learning not only enhances knowledge retention but also shortens the feedback loop, encouraging prompt behavior modification and secure coding practices. This form of adaptive, just-in-time training aligns security education with the evolving needs of the application and threat landscape (Mack, 2023).

CASE STUDIES AND REAL-WORLD IMPLEMENTATIONS

The application of gamification in security training has gained significant traction across industries, offering practical insights into how interactive learning models can transform conventional cybersecurity education. Organizations in sectors such as technology, finance, healthcare, manufacturing, and government have increasingly adopted gamified training methodologies to replace passive, compliance-driven models with engaging, performance-based approaches. These case studies underscore gamification's potential not only to improve individual learning outcomes but also to foster an organizational culture in which security is treated as a continuous, shared responsibility. Prominent technology companies such as Google, Microsoft, Salesforce, Capital One, and IBM have pioneered the implementation of gamified security programs. Their initiatives include internal Capture The Flag (CTF) competitions, secure coding challenges, red team vs. blue team simulations, and interactive portals integrated into development workflows. For instance, Google has hosted both internal and public-facing CTF events aimed at cultivating a security-first mindset and identifying talent. These competitions promote continuous upskilling, enabling developers and engineers to explore emerging threats, analyze vulnerabilities, and practice secure coding in high-stakes, gamified environments (Google CTF, n.d.).

Similarly, Microsoft's "Security Ninja" program transforms training into a progressive, mastery-based experience (Microsoft, 2016). Participants earn digital belts and badges as they complete increasingly complex modules, fostering a sense of progression and recognition. This gamified system provides both intrinsic motivation and visual feedback, reinforcing learning and increasing employee engagement across technical teams. In the financial sector—where regulatory scrutiny and the potential costs of breaches are particularly high—organizations such as JPMorgan Chase and Barclays have adopted scenario-based gamified training. JPMorgan Chase implemented phishing simulations and incident response exercises designed as role-playing games, incorporating decision trees and leaderboards to enhance user engagement (JPMorgan Chase, 2020; Barclays, 2018). These simulations help employees recognize malicious emails and respond appropriately in real-time. Barclays integrated game-based application security training directly into its development pipeline, enabling secure coding practices to become a standard element of the software delivery lifecycle.

Government agencies and defense contractors have also employed gamified models in the form of cyber ranges and tabletop exercises. These large-scale simulations model nation-state-level threats in repeatable environments, helping participants prepare for high-impact security incidents through realistic, immersive experiences (U.S. Department of Defense, 2021). The measurable impact of such programs is notable. Case study data indicates a reduction in the prevalence of common vulnerabilities such as SQL injection and cross-site scripting (XSS) within production environments. Organizations also report improved incident response capabilities, decreased reliance on external consultants, and significantly higher retention of training content—particularly when gamified training is combined with traditional methods such as classroom instruction or recorded lectures.

Importantly, gamification has succeeded in engaging participants across all organizational levels, from junior developers to CISOs. By making security education more interactive and personally relevant, these programs have contributed to a culture of continuous learning and self-directed improvement. However, these successes are accompanied by several key challenges and lessons learned. One common pitfall is the overuse or superficial use of gamified elements—such as assigning points or badges without aligning them to meaningful learning outcomes. In such cases, training may be perceived as trivial or gimmicky, leading to disengagement and limited knowledge retention. Another issue is lack of personalization. Generic training modules that are not adapted to specific roles, skill levels, or learning preferences may prove ineffective—e.g., general security content being of limited value to a backend developer needing guidance on secure database queries (Koivisto & Hamari, 2019; Triantafyllou & Georgiadis, 2022). Additional barriers include poor integration with existing development tools and workflows, which can result in low participation and training perceived as disruptive. Finally, content stagnation—a failure to regularly update challenges and rewards—can reduce engagement over time. Feedback from early adopters has emphasized the importance of transparency and fairness in scoring mechanisms, as perceived inequities can diminish user trust and motivation.

To address these challenges, successful organizations have embraced iterative, user-centered design processes (Diakoumakos, 2023; Ryan et al., 2024). Gamified training programs are often developed collaboratively across departments—security, development, HR, and leadership—and are deployed incrementally through pilot programs. These pilots allow for real-time feedback collection and the refinement of training modules based on observed learner behavior. Data analytics are used not only to evaluate performance and reward progress but also to tailor future learning paths and identify knowledge gaps within teams. In conclusion, real-world case studies affirm that well-designed gamified security training programs can significantly advance DevSecOps maturity, increase workforce engagement, and enhance organizational security posture. Whereas traditional, one-size-fits-all training models are effective for information dissemination, gamified, challenge-based, and role-specific learning environments provide a deeper, more adaptive approach to cybersecurity education. By learning from industry leaders and applying strategic design principles, organizations can implement gamified training programs that are scalable, measurable, and culturally transformative—embedding security not as a checkbox activity, but as an intrinsic component of operational excellence.

MEASURING SUCCESS AND ROI OF GAMIFIED SECURITY TRAINING

For organizations investing in gamified security training, establishing robust mechanisms for measuring success and long-term impact is essential. Effective evaluation goes beyond surface-level engagement metrics and must encompass broader organizational outcomes to justify investment, guide strategic improvements, and ensure the training remains aligned with evolving security threats. A comprehensive assessment strategy begins with foundational user engagement metrics, including participation rates, login frequency, module completion rates, time spent on tasks, and return visits to the training platform. These indicators offer insights into how effectively the training captures user attention and sustains participation—key factors for meaningful learning engagement.

Beyond engagement, the most critical metrics assess learning outcomes—namely, skill acquisition and knowledge retention. These are typically measured through pre- and post-assessments, knowledge quizzes, interactive simulations (e.g., Capture The Flag exercises), and scenario-based challenges. Tracking learners' ability to recognize, mitigate, and remediate security weaknesses over time provides tangible evidence of knowledge transfer and practical skill development. Some platforms also offer adaptive learning paths that adjust to individual performance, offering a more nuanced view of personal learning curves. Additional validation can be achieved by measuring improvements in real-world security performance. For example, organizations may track changes in code quality through secure code reviews, monitor the frequency of vulnerabilities introduced in production, or evaluate the decline in the occurrence of specific weaknesses (e.g., SQL injection, XSS, insecure APIs) following the implementation of gamified training. Other indicators of material impact include reduced incident response times, improved security test pass rates, and a decrease in the number of post-deployment hotfixes and patches. Several organizations integrate gamified training platforms with static code analysis tools or IDE plugins to correlate changes in developer behavior directly with training exposure. These integrations enable security leaders to monitor how often security issues are identified, resolved, or prevented entirely, thereby establishing a stronger link between training interventions and operational improvements.

Alongside quantitative metrics, qualitative feedback plays a crucial role in assessing training effectiveness. Surveys, interviews, focus groups, and anonymous feedback channels allow learners to express their perceptions of the training experience. These insights can reveal whether the game mechanics are genuinely engaging, whether the scenarios are relevant to learners' roles, and whether the training materials reflect real-world challenges. Participant sentiment also provides valuable feedback about the perceived fairness and transparency of scoring systems—factors that significantly influence learner motivation and trust.

Ultimately, organizations must demonstrate the return on investment (ROI) of gamified training through outcomes that align with broader business and security goals. These may include reductions in security incidents, shortened vulnerability remediation timelines, improved compliance audit results, and enhanced trust from customers and stakeholders. For example, if gamified training reduces the average remediation time from 15 days to 5 days, the resulting cost savings in labor, downtime, and risk exposure are substantial and quantifiable. Similarly, a 60% reduction in phishing simulation click-through rates directly correlates with decreased risk of credential theft and data breaches. To maximize strategic value, organizations should contextualize training success within larger digital transformation goals, such as secure adoption of cloud-native technologies, faster release cycles, or shifts toward DevSecOps maturity. Benchmarking internal performance against industry standards or regulatory expectations can further strengthen the case for continued investment and optimization. More advanced programs use this data for continuous improvement, leveraging analytics to scale effective practices, identify high-risk areas, and modify training content in response to emerging threats. This iterative process not only improves training quality but also reinforces a culture of continuous learning and accountability.

In conclusion, the success of a gamified security training initiative depends not only on engaging content and innovative delivery but also on the organization's ability to systematically measure impact. By combining quantitative KPIs with qualitative user feedback and aligning training outcomes with business objectives, organizations can close the loop on performance, demonstrate value, and establish gamified learning as an integral pillar of their cybersecurity resilience strategy. This strategic alignment ensures security awareness is not just an isolated activity, but a foundational element of sustainable risk management in an increasingly complex digital environment.

FUTURE TRENDS AND INNOVATIONS

The future of gamified security training lies in its convergence with emerging technologies such as artificial intelligence (AI), immersive reality (VR/AR), predictive analytics, and cloud-native simulation environments. These innovations are reshaping cybersecurity education by enabling highly personalized, context-aware, and operationally integrated learning experiences. AI-driven platforms are increasingly capable of dynamically adjusting training content based on user behavior, performance history, and job role—guiding junior developers through secure coding basics while presenting senior engineers with complex, scenario-based challenges. Such tailored learning paths not only enhance relevance and motivation but also ensure training efficiency by aligning educational content with real-world responsibilities. Meanwhile, immersive technologies like VR and AR offer experiential learning environments, allowing users to simulate high-stakes security incidents in realistic operational contexts, thereby reinforcing critical decision-making skills and enhancing retention.

Complementing these advancements, predictive analytics enables organizations to proactively identify skill gaps, assess risk exposure, and tailor interventions before vulnerabilities manifest in production systems. This approach allows for data-informed adjustments to both individual learning paths and broader organizational training strategies. Additionally, gamified platforms are evolving to address the security complexities of cloud-native architectures, offering interactive labs on container security, Kubernetes hardening, and Infrastructure-as-Code (IaC) misconfigurations. These cloud-centric challenges prepare DevSecOps teams to secure modern workloads effectively. As organizations increasingly adopt distributed, event-driven systems, gamified training platforms that embed real-time, scenario-based learning into CI/CD workflows are poised to become essential tools in maintaining a proactive and resilient security posture. In this landscape, gamification is no longer a supplementary training method but a critical component of continuous, adaptive cybersecurity readiness.

CONCLUSION

This study has examined the transformative role of gamified security training in fostering a resilient and proactive DevSecOps culture. Amidst a landscape marked by increasingly sophisticated cyber threats, faster software delivery cycles, and rising compliance demands, traditional approaches to security education often fall short. Gamification offers a strategic, user-centered alternative—one that drives engagement, enhances knowledge retention, and embeds secure behaviors within everyday workflows. By incorporating elements such as real-time feedback, progressive challenges, role-based customization, and integration with CI/CD pipelines, gamified training aligns individual learning with organizational security objectives in a scalable and sustainable manner.

The findings and discussions presented in this paper highlight not only the practical benefits—such as improved vulnerability management, faster incident response, and higher training completion rates—but also the cultural impact of gamification in shaping secure mindsets across technical and non-technical roles. Future innovations such as AI-driven personalization, immersive VR/AR simulations, and predictive analytics will further refine training relevance and adaptability, while cloud-native and microservices-specific modules ensure continued alignment with modern infrastructure. As organizations face an evolving threat landscape, adopting gamification as a core strategy in security training offers a pathway to long-term operational readiness, continuous improvement, and the cultivation of a workforce that inherently prioritizes cybersecurity as part of its professional identity.

REFERENCES

Barclays. (2018). *Embedding secure coding into the development pipeline through gamification.*

Csikszentmihalyi, M. (1990). *Flow: The psychology of optimal experience.* Harper & Row.

Deci, E. L., & Ryan, R. M. (2008). Self-determination theory: A macrotheory of human motivation, development, and health. *Canadian Psychology, 49*(3), 182–185. DOI: 10.1037/a0012801

Denning, T., Lerner, A., Shostack, A., & Kohno, T. (2013). Control-Alt-Hack: The design and evaluation of a card game for computer security awareness and education. In Proceedings of the 2013 ACM SIGSAC conference on Computer & communications security (pp. 915–928). DOI: 10.1145/2508859.2516745

Deterding, S., Dixon, D., Khaled, R., & Nacke, L. (2011). From game design elements to gamefulness: defining" gamification". *Proceedings of the 15th International Academic MindTrek Conference: Envisioning Future Media Environments*, 9–15. DOI: 10.1145/2181037.2181040

Diakoumakos, I. (2023). *Enhancing Cyber Security Education and Training through Gamification.* In *ACM Greek SIGCHI Conference Proceedings*, 1–5. DOI: 10.1145/3609987.3610016

Fu, M., Pasuksmit, J., & Tantithamthavorn, C. (2024). Ai for devsecops: A landscape and future opportunities. *ACM Transactions on Software Engineering and Methodology.*

Google, C. T. F. (Capture The Flag). (n.d.). *Google Capture The Flag competition.* Retrieved from https://capturetheflag.withgoogle.com/

Gordan, M., & Krishanan, I. A. (2014). A review of BF Skinner's 'Reinforcement Theory of Motivation'. International journal of research in education methodology, 5(3), 680-688.

Hack The Box. (n.d.). *Hacking training and cybersecurity labs.* https://www.hackthebox.com/

HackEDU. (n.d.). *Interactive secure development training.* https://www.securityjourney.com/

He, Z., Liu, Y., Wang, X., Li, R., & Lv, N. (2023). Gamified entrepreneurship courses motivate college students' satisfaction: An integrated flow framework. *SAGE Open, 13*(2), 21582440231177029. DOI: 10.1177/21582440231177029

Immersive Labs. (n.d.). *Hands-on cyber workforce development platform.* https://www.immersivelabs.com/

JPMorgan Chase. (2020). *Building a culture of cybersecurity awareness.* Internal white paper or training insights

Koivisto, J., & Hamari, J. (2019). The rise of motivational information systems: A review of gamification research. *International Journal of Information Management, 45*, 191–210. DOI: 10.1016/j.ijinfomgt.2018.10.013

Mack, S. D. (2023). *The DevSecOps playbook: Deliver continuous security at speed.* John Wiley & Sons.

Microsoft. (2016). *The Security Ninja Training Program.* Microsoft Secure Blog. Retrieved from https://www.microsoft.com/security/blog/

OWASP Foundation. (n.d.). *OWASP Juice Shop.* https://owasp.org/www-project-juice-shop/

Rajapakse, R. N., Zahedi, M., Babar, M. A., & Shen, H. (2022). Challenges and solutions when adopting DevSecOps: A systematic review. *Information and Software Technology, 141*, 106700. DOI: 10.1016/j.infsof.2021.106700

RangeForce. (n.d.). *Cybersecurity training platform.* https://www.rangeforce.com/

Ryan, I., Roedig, U., & Stol, K. J. (2024). *Training developers to code securely: Theory and practice.* In *Proceedings of the 2024 ACM/IEEE Workshop on Engineering and Cybersecurity of Critical Systems.* DOI: 10.1145/3643662.3643956

Secure Code Warrior. (n.d.). Secure coding training platform. https://www.securecodewarrior.com/

Thool, A., & Brown, C. (2025). *Integrating DAST in Kanban and CI/CD: A real world security case study.* arXiv preprint arXiv:2503.21947.

Triantafyllou, S., & Georgiadis, C. (2022). Gamification of MOOCs and security awareness in corporate training.

TryHackMe. (n.d.). *Cybersecurity training for everyone.* https://tryhackme.com/

U.S. Department of Defense. (2021). *Cyber ranges for mission readiness.* Retrieved from https://www.defense.gov/

Weitl-Harms, S., Spanier, A., Hastings, J., & Rokusek, M. (2023). A Systematic Mapping Study on Gamification Applications for Undergraduate Cybersecurity Education. Journal of Cybersecurity Education, Research and Practice, 2023(1).

Chapter 13
The Role of Gamified Learning Platforms in Cybersecurity

Jimmy Singla
https://orcid.org/0000-0003-2077-1622
Lovely Professional University, India

Pankaj Khurana
https://orcid.org/0009-0004-5719-4026
Neatly Technologies, Inc., USA

Nikita
Lovely Professional University, India

ABSTRACT

Nowadays cybersecurity threats are continuously growing at a large rate. So, traditional training methods are not sufficient for the practical learning which is required for protection from the various cyber-attacks. The use of gamified learning in cybersecurity is the need of an hour. Gamified learning provides an energetic approach for the cybersecurity training by using gamification in education contents. In this chapter, the role of gamified learning platforms in cybersecurity is discussed. It focuses on various important points such as how a learner can be engaged in a better way with the help of gamification, how technical skills can be delivered better with the concept of gamified learning, how retention can be improved, and real feedbacks. It also describes various features such as tracking of performance, customized contents, opening of various learning platforms etc. In this chapter, various limitations of gamified environments are also discussed. This chapter also explores the future of cybersecurity education with gamification.

DOI: 10.4018/979-8-3373-0477-9.ch013

1. INTRODUCTION

Nowadays, cybersecurity experts are working hard against different cybersecurity attacks and threats such as hacking, data breaches etc. and the demand of cybersecurity defenses is also increasing due to increasing interconnections among different verticals of world. Traditional methods of training such as lectures, text book-based learning etc. are not working too good in providing hands-on practical experiences for getting the skills needed to address complex challenges. To fill these gaps, gamified learning platforms are required in learning and training practical cybersecurity education (Alharthi et al., 2022)

Gamification means adding game-like elements into non-game contexts for better engagement of the stakeholders. The game like elements are silver and gold badges, points, rewards etc. this concept is applied in various education domains. It transforms the current learning process into better and more interactive process that can engage learner with cybersecurity topics with hands on environment (Burks and Meehan, 2020) General gamification is depicted in figure 1.

Figure 1. General Gamification

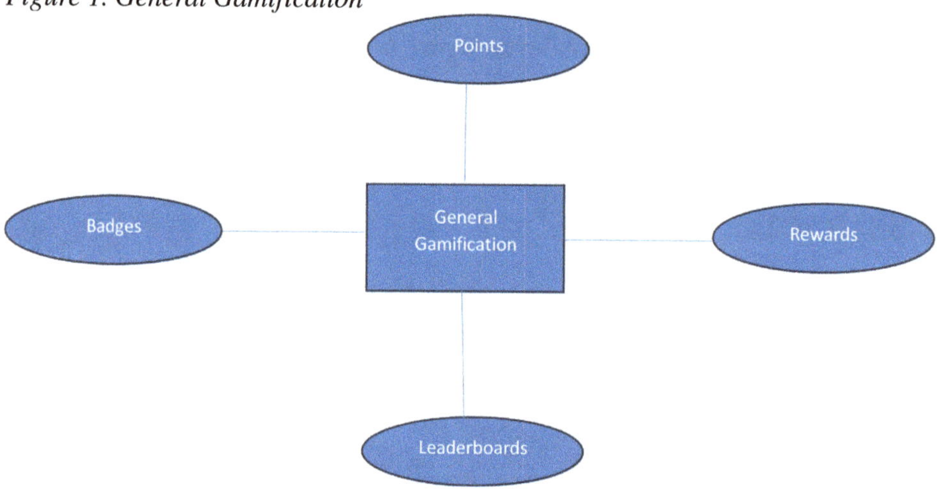

Cybersecurity education requires theoretical as well as practical knowledge that is possible through problem solving skills. In this regard, gamification works with the simulations in real-world cyber threats such as data breaches etc., in a gamified way. In the context of gamification, learners can take role of attackers, defenders or responders, that will help in their wholeheartedly active participation in the field of cybersecurity. This process has several benefits such as collaboration, design thinking etc. Cybersecurity gamification involves red/blue team exercises, attack/

defend scenarios, ethical decision making and hands-on-practice (Cheung et al., 2011). It is shown in figure 2.

Figure 2. Cybersecurity Gamification

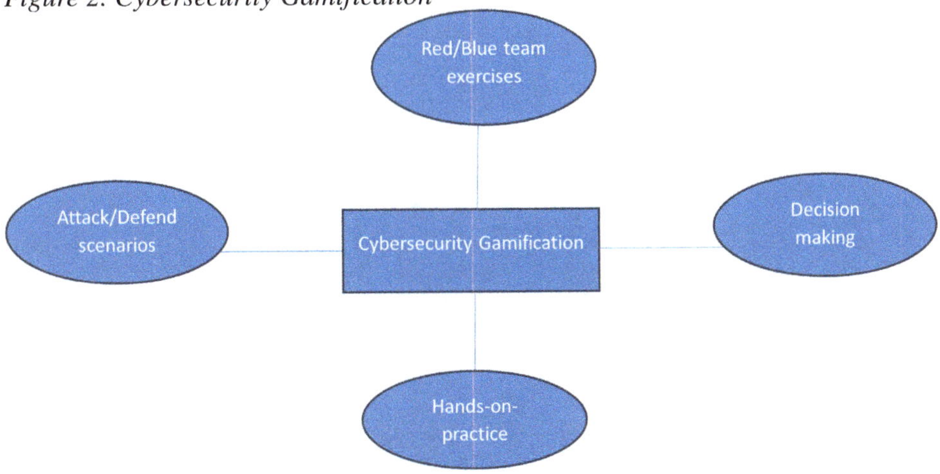

The advantages of these gamified learning environments are to make learning more interactive and interesting. It encourages active participation of learners where learners complete their tasks with full interests (Domínguez et al., 2013). In this gamified learning environment, user starts game, completes challenges, receives feedback, applies knowledge and improves cybersecurity skills. It is shown in figure 3.

Figure 3. A Gamified Learning Environment

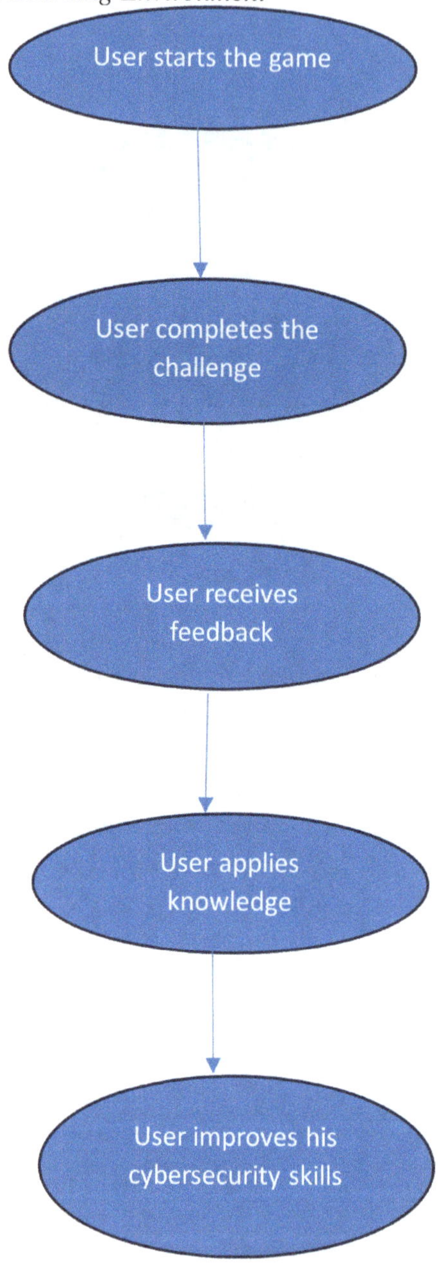

These gamified platforms have several benefits which are mentioned below:

1. Immediate feedback

2. Tracking of progress
3. Identification of areas for improvement
4. Fostering collaboration

It is very true that the gamified environments have several benefits but on the other hand, it has few challenges as well. The first challenge is to make ensure that the educational value should not be hampered due to entertainment aspect. Gamification should be designed very carefully. It should be very carefully aligned with educational objectives of the cybersecurity concepts (Fraunholz et al., 2018). Further gamified environments also require technological infrastructure resources and it may be barrier to certain institutions due their financial constraints (Hamari et al., 2014). If we are taking here the case study of cybersecurity curriculum, it is a very changing field. It needs regular updates. So, gamified platforms also need regular modifications. With this, these platforms would be able to reflect latest trends and techniques used by experts in the industry. The benefits and challenges are clearly shown in table I.

Table 1. Benefits and Challenges of Gamified Environments

S No.	Benefit	Challenge
1	Increased engagement	High initial setup cost
2	Better retention	Limited depth
3	Hands-on-practice	More emphasis on competitions
4	Real time feedback	Dependency on technology
5	Scalability	Potential for distraction
6	Flexibility	Balance between fun and learning
7	Safe environment	Learning curve for users
8	Motivation	Regular modifications

With the passage of time, in future gamified learning environments will grow and concepts like advances in artificial intelligence, virtual reality and augmented reality will help in development of more interactive and better learning platforms. With these concepts, it will provide the learner a better virtual network for interaction and it will also offer adaptive learning paths (Papathanasiou and Tsiatsos, 2020).

2. CASE STUDIES OF GAMIFIED LEARNING IN CYBERSECURITY

The few prominent case studies of gamified learning in cybersecurity are mentioned below:

2.1 Capture the Flag Competitions: DEF CON CTF

This DEF CON (capture the flag) is a competition based on different cybersecurity challenges. This competition is one of the most important events. This is also known as one of the hacker resolutions in the world. It has important role in the cybersecurity community and it offers highly technical challenges. Here in this competition, participants solve many challenges to capture the flags. The topics included in this competition are mentioned below:

I. Forensics
II. Cryptography
III. Web security
IV. Reverse engineering
V. Network exploitation
VI. Steganography

2.2 Cyber Range Platforms: RangeForce

A cyber range is a virtual environment designed for simulation of real-world networks. With this, individuals and organizations can practice on cybersecurity skills. Cyber ranges are mainly used for training, testing and simulations (Vykopal et al., 2017).

RangeForce is a platform designed for providing hands-on and interactive training in the field of cybersecurity. This platform is basically treated as skill development program in cybersecurity. The individuals, teams and organizations use this platform for improving the cybersecurity capabilities (Weidman et al., 2019). The topics covered in this platform are mentioned below:

I. Penetration testing
II. Threat hunting
III. Vulnerability management
IV. Incident response

The important features of cyber range are mentioned below:

I. Interactive learning
II. Comprehensive curriculum
III. Scenario-based training
IV. Cloud-based platforms
V. Gamified experience
VI. Skill development

2.3 Immersive Simulations and Serious Games: Cybersecurity Challenge UK

This cybersecurity challenge involves simulations and games for training individuals in the concepts of cybersecurity (Zhu and Bedi, 2017). These simulations and games provide practical skills to the participants. The pictorial representation of this challenge is shown in figure 4.

Figure 4. Cybersecurity Challenge UK

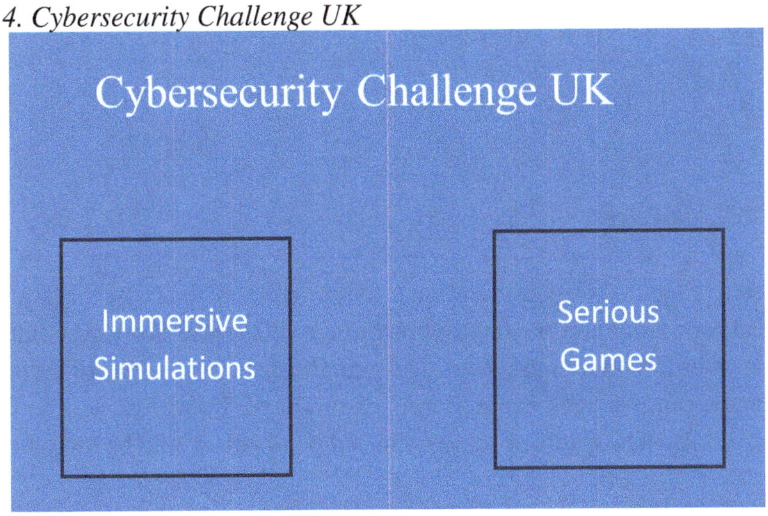

The objectives of this challenge are mentioned below:

I. Bridging skill gaps
II. Skill enhancement
III. Raising awareness
IV. Talent development

The types of serious games and immersive simulations are mentioned in table 2.

Table 2. Serious Games and Immersive Simulations

S no.	Serious games	Immersive simulations
1	Security Escape Rooms	Simulated Cyberattacks
2	Malware Simulation Games	Network Defense
3	Risk Management Games	Blue Teaming
4	Social Engineering Simulations	Red Teaming
5	Phishing	Risk Management

3. LIMITATIONS OF GAMIFIED ENVIRONMENTS

The limitations of gamified environments are as follow:

1. High setup cost
2. Requirement of regular updates
3. Dependency on technology
4. Risk of losing education value

4. CONCLUSION

It is concluded that the gamification is a powerful tool to bridge the gap between theoretical knowledge and practical application. With the use of badges, points, leader boards, learners are more motivated. Through the different case studies considered in this chapter, it has demonstrated how gamified environments help in fostering the critical skills. The future of these gamified platforms would be more impactful.

5. FUTURE OF CYBERSECURITY WITH GAMIFICATION

The integration of prominent technologies such as artificial intelligence, Smart analytics, virtual reality and augmented reality will make gamified cybersecurity education more relevant and future would be more promising.

REFERENCES

Alharthi, A., Kausar, F., & Alfarraj, O. (2022). Gamification and AI in cybersecurity education: A future direction. *Education and Information Technologies, 27*(6), 8567–8589. DOI: 10.1007/s10639-022-11188-w

Burks, M., & Meehan, A. (2020). Gamified learning in cybersecurity education: A survey of games and platforms. In *Proceedings of the IEEE Frontiers in Education Conference (FIE)* (pp. 1–5). IEEE. https://doi.org/DOI: 10.1109/FIE44824.2020.9273973

Cheung, R., Cohen, J., Lo, H. Z., & Elia, F. (2011). Challenge-based learning in cybersecurity education. *Innovations in Systems and Software Engineering, 7*(4), 289–294. DOI: 10.1007/s11334-011-0177-2

Domínguez, A., Saenz-de-Navarrete, J., de-Marcos, L., Fernández-Sanz, L., Pagés, C., & Martínez-Herráiz, J. J. (2013). Gamifying learning experiences: Practical implications and outcomes. *Computers & Education, 63*, 380–392. DOI: 10.1016/j.compedu.2012.12.020

Fraunholz, D., Zimmermann, S., & Schotten, H. D. (2018). An overview of cybersecurity awareness campaigns and gamification in security education. *Future Internet, 10*(1), 27. DOI: 10.3390/fi10010027

Hamari, J., Koivisto, J., & Sarsa, H. (2014). Does gamification work? – A literature review of empirical studies on gamification. In *Proceedings of the 47th Hawaii International Conference on System Sciences* (pp. 3025–3034). IEEE. DOI: 10.1109/HICSS.2014.377

Papathanasiou, N., & Tsiatsos, T. (2020). Gamification in cybersecurity education: A systematic review. *Education and Information Technologies, 25*(5), 4191–4214. DOI: 10.1007/s10639-020-10302-0

Vykopal, J., Čermák, M., Čeleda, P., & Tovarňák, D. (2017). Enhancing cybersecurity education through interactive gamified learning tools. In *Proceedings of the IEEE Global Engineering Education Conference (EDUCON)* (pp. 713–718). IEEE. DOI: 10.1109/EDUCON.2017.7942934

Weidman, J., Siponen, M., & Kajava, J. (2019). The effectiveness of online cybersecurity training using gamified environments. *Journal of Cybersecurity Education, Research and Practice, 2019*(1), Article 3. https://digitalcommons.kennesaw.edu/jcerp/vol2019/iss1/3

Zhu, Q., & Bedi, H. S. (2017). Game theory meets network security: A tutorial. *ACM Computing Surveys, 50*(1), 1–37. DOI: 10.1145/3007203

Chapter 14

Elements of Educational Game Design:
A Comprehensive Examination for Modern Educators

Sandeep Ranjan
https://orcid.org/0000-0002-0776-8405
Lovely Professional University, India

ABSTRACT

Educational games reside at the intersection of pedagogy, technology, and play. This chapter offers an in-depth exploration of educational game design, examining its theoretical underpinnings, fundamental design elements, and implementation strategies. Drawing on research from cognitive psychology, game studies, and instructional design, this chapter delineates how effective game mechanics, narrative structures, adaptive feedback systems, and user-centered interfaces can converge with robust educational content. Through case studies and contemporary examples, we present a framework for integrating curriculum objectives into engaging and interactive game experiences. The chapter concludes with a discussion of emerging technologies and future directions, providing educators and designers with guidance for creating transformative learning environments.

INTRODUCTION

In recent decades, technology has reshaped the landscape of education, ever broadening the horizon of how and where learning occurs. Educational games, as a unique intersection of entertainment and instruction, have emerged as a powerful medium for conveying complex concepts, engaging diverse audiences, and de-

DOI: 10.4018/979-8-3373-0477-9.ch014

mocratizing access to knowledge. As noted by Prensky (2001), digital game-based learning leverages the intrinsic motivation of play while delivering content in ways that resonate with today's technologically savvy learners. From the early iterations of computer-assisted instruction to contemporary immersive experiences utilizing virtual reality, educational game design has evolved into an interdisciplinary field that combines insights from cognitive science, user experience design, storytelling, and data analytics.

The chapter begins by defining educational game design as the process of creating interactive experiences that are both engaging and pedagogically sound. In the past few decades, educators and designers alike have recognized that play is not only a recreational activity but also a potent tool for learning, problem solving, and critical thinking (Gee, 2003; Squire, 2005). Educational games provide dynamic environments where learners can experiment, fail safely, and ultimately internalize new knowledge through active participation. They offer a platform that can present abstract concepts in a tangible form, making them particularly valuable in subjects where traditional didactic methods tend to fall short.

This chapter sets out to explore the following fundamental questions:

- What are the theoretical foundations that support the design and integration of game mechanics into educational frameworks?
- How can developers maintain a balance between enjoyment and educational rigor, ensuring that the game remains both fun and instructional?
- What role do narrative, interface design, and adaptive feedback play in achieving meaningful learning outcomes?
- How can we evaluate the efficacy of game-based learning environments, and what best practices have emerged from research and practical application?

By addressing these questions, we provide a roadmap for educators, game designers, and researchers interested in harnessing the transformative power of games for education. We explore historical perspectives, modern innovations, and the emerging trends poised to shape the future of educational game design.

The following sections offer detailed discussions on the theoretical basis for game-based learning, the core design principles that inform practice, and the practical challenges of aligning game mechanics with instructional outcomes. We then examine case studies of successful educational games—from classroom staples to novel digital platforms—to contextualize the discussion within real-world applications. Finally, we look ahead to emerging technologies such as augmented reality (AR) and virtual reality (VR) and consider their potential to further revolutionize how we perceive learning environments.

In our increasingly digital era, the call to innovate in educational settings is both urgent and inevitable. This chapter does not purport to offer a definitive manual for all aspects of game design; rather, it provides a comprehensive examination of key elements and guides thoughtful reflection on how best to create learning experiences that inspire, engage, and educate. As educational game design continues to grow in prominence, a clear understanding of its underlying principles is essential for ensuring that the integration of technology into pedagogy results in transformative educational outcomes.

THEORETICAL FRAMEWORK AND PEDAGOGICAL UNDERPINNINGS

Historical Context and Evolution of Educational Games

The evolution of educational game design is intertwined with broader societal shifts in attitudes toward learning and technology. Early digital games were often simplistic simulations or drill-and-practice applications aimed at reinforcing memorization through repetition (Papert, 1980). Over time, as computational capabilities advanced and educators began to recognize the potential of digital interactivity to support constructivist learning theories, games evolved from static practice tools into dynamic environments that encourage exploration and discovery.

The seminal work of Seymour Papert in the 1980s introduced the concept of constructionism, suggesting that learners construct knowledge best through making and doing. Papert's ideas directly influenced later developments in educational games, where the act of creation and the iterative process of trial and error within a game environment mirrored real-life problem solving. Similarly, James Gee (2003) argued that video games naturally incorporate many of the principles of effective learning, such as situated meaning, critical thinking, and active inquiry. These foundational perspectives underpin much of today's thinking about how digital games can serve as effective educational tools.

Early Beginnings: The Intersection of Play and Learning

The idea of using play as a medium for learning is not a novel concept. Long before the advent of digital technology, educators, philosophers, and psychologists recognized that playful activities could stimulate cognitive and social development. In ancient cultures, games and playful rituals were often integral to teaching moral values and practical skills. However, the systematic study and application of game-like strategies in education began to take shape only in the last century.

The emergence of educational games in the modern era is closely tied to the evolution of educational psychology and the rise of structured learning theories. Early educators drew upon the insights of Jean Piaget (1971) and Lev Vygotsky (1978), who emphasized the importance of active learning and the role of social interaction in cognitive development. Their work laid the theoretical foundation that would later inform how digital games could be used to create dynamic, learner-centered environments.

From Paper-Based Tools to Computer-Assisted Instruction

In the mid-20th century, the advent of computers introduced a new frontier for educational tools. Early computer-assisted instruction (CAI) programs were primarily focused on drill-and-practice exercises, where repetitive tasks were used to reinforce basic skills such as arithmetic and reading (Papert, 1980). These programs were highly influenced by behaviorist theories. B.F. Skinner's (1954) work on operant conditioning provided the basis for using rewards and repetition to shape behavior. The simplicity of these early games, often constrained by the limited processing power and graphic capabilities of the time, belied their potential. Despite their rudimentary nature, these tools introduced the concept that digital systems could provide instantaneous feedback—a critical component in learning.

The Digital Revolution and the Rise of Video Games

The 1970s and 1980s witnessed a paradigm shift as video games emerged as a popular form of entertainment. Early arcade games and personal computer games captivated a generation, and it wasn't long before educators took notice of their potential as learning platforms. As video gaming technology matured, scholars like James Paul Gee (2003) began systematically investigating how modern games embody principles of learning and literacy. Gee argued that video games naturally facilitate many of the strategies inherent in effective learning processes—such as experimentation, problem solving, and decision making.

This period marked the transition from static CAI programs to more interactive, simulation-based educational experiences. As technology improved, so did the sophistication of educational games. Designers began to experiment with more engaging narratives and dynamic systems that allowed for branching pathways and adaptive challenges. This evolution was not only technological but also pedagogical. Educators started to recognize that while immediate rewards played an important role (as emphasized in behaviorist models), the integration of cognitive and constructivist learning theories could foster deeper understanding and retention of material (Piaget, 1971; Vygotsky, 1978).

Constructivism, Constructionism, and the Emergence of Creative Play

Seymour Papert's (1980) concept of constructionism built directly on the earlier work of constructivists. Papert contended that learners construct their own knowledge most effectively when they are actively involved in creating tangible artifacts or engaging in problem-solving tasks. This theoretical perspective inspired a new breed of educational games that moved beyond simple memorization exercises. Instead, these games began to encourage players to experiment, build, and iterate on their learning processes.

The breakthrough for many educational designers was realizing that video games could serve as a form of "learning by doing." In these environments, mistakes were not simply punished but were embraced as opportunities to learn. Educational games during this era began to include simulation elements, allowing learners to experiment with real-world competencies—from managing resources in a virtual ecosystem to solving complex mathematical puzzles. Educational games started to offer an environment where the risk of failure was minimized, and the emphasis was placed on iterative learning and self-reflection.

The Influence of Social Learning Theories

The evolution of educational games was further enriched by the incorporation of social learning theories. Albert Bandura's (1977) social learning theory highlighted the importance of observational learning, modeling, and imitation. Multiplayer and cooperative features in educational games capitalized on this insight, enabling learners to collaborate, share strategies, and learn from one another. The introduction of features such as leader boards, team challenges, and peer-to-peer feedback mechanisms transformed the solitary play experience into a social enterprise.

During the late 1990s and early 2000s, computer networks and the internet began to enable multiplayer environments and virtual communities. Educational games that leveraged these technologies facilitated not only individual learning but also the formation of learning communities that transcended geographical constraints. These developments paralleled the emergence of constructivist and sociocultural pedagogies, which emphasize that learning is fundamentally a social endeavor. The design of such games underscored the need for collaboration, discourse, and collective problem solving—all crucial elements in the development of higher-order cognitive skills.

Technological Advancements and the Emergence of Adaptive Learning

With the rapid advancement in computing power and the proliferation of mobile devices, educational games have become increasingly adaptive and sophisticated. Modern games not only present challenges but also tailor content delivery to match the learner's individual pace and proficiency levels. The integration of artificial intelligence (AI) and data analytics into game design has enabled the creation of adaptive learning environments. These systems continuously monitor learner performance and adjust difficulty accordingly, ensuring that players remain in the zone of proximal development—the sweet spot between what learners can do independently and what they can achieve with guidance (Vygotsky, 1978; Sweller, 1994).

Technological innovations, such as augmented reality (AR) and virtual reality (VR), have expanded the boundaries of what educational games can achieve. AR overlays contextual digital information onto the physical world, while VR immerses learners in entirely virtual environments. These emerging technologies have opened up exciting possibilities for immersive experiential learning, where abstract concepts can be visualized and explored in a simulated three-dimensional space. For example, VR can transport learners to historical sites, ancient civilizations, or even microscopic biological worlds, providing experiential learning that textbooks simply cannot match.

Synthesis of Pedagogical Theories in Contemporary Educational Game Design

Contemporary educational game design embodies a synthesis of multiple pedagogical theories. It draws upon:

· **Behaviorism:** Through immediate feedback, rewards, and the reinforcement of correct behaviors.
· **Cognitivism:** By designing challenges that stimulate memory, problem-solving, and critical thinking processes (Anderson, 1983).
· **Constructivism and Constructionism:** By encouraging active learning through creation, experimentation, and iterative design (Papert, 1980).
· **Social Learning Theory:** By fostering collaborative and competitive environments that promote peer learning and community building (Bandura, 1977).
· **Self-Determination Theory:** By ensuring that games satisfy the basic human needs for competence, autonomy, and relatedness, thereby fueling intrinsic motivation (Deci & Ryan, 1985).

The progression from simple drill-and-practice programs to complex, multilayered learning environments is a testament to the dynamic evolution of educational games. Each technological advance has been paralleled by a more nuanced understanding of how people learn best. As a result, today's educational games are not mere distractions but powerful tools that can transform traditional pedagogical paradigms. The historical context and evolution of educational games illustrate a fascinating journey from rudimentary instructional programs to sophisticated, adaptive learning environments. Early computer-assisted instruction, anchored in behaviorist methodologies, paved the way for more interactive and constructivist approaches as digital technology evolved. The integration of social and cognitive learning theories further enriched these environments, leading to the development of immersive, community-based, and adaptive educational games. Today, educational game design represents a confluence of ideas from psychology, pedagogy, and technology. As emerging technologies such as AR and VR continue to reshape immersive experiences, educational games are poised to further expand the horizons of both learning and play.

CORE LEARNING THEORIES IN GAME-BASED LEARNING

Several key educational theories illuminate why game-based learning can be effective. These include:

1. **Constructivism and Constructionism:** Constructivist theories posit that learners construct new understandings based on their prior knowledge and experiences (Piaget, 1971). In a digital game setting, learners are active agents who build their own understanding through interacting with the game environment. Constructionism extends this idea by emphasizing the importance of creating artifacts—such as game levels or simulations—as a means of learning (Papert, 1980). In games that allow user-generated content or provide creative tools for learners, these theories manifest in an experience where learners are engaged in problem-solving and discovery.
2. **Behaviorism:** Behaviorist theories emphasize the role of reinforcement in shaping behavior (Skinner, 1954). In educational games, rewards, points, and leveling systems operate on behavioral principles. When a learner receives immediate feedback in the form of a reward, it reinforces the desired behavior and promotes repetition. However, while some early educational games heavily relied on behaviorist techniques, contemporary designs are more likely to blend these approaches with cognitive and affective learning theories.

3. **Cognitivism:** Cognitivist perspectives focus on the internal processes involved in learning, including memory, information processing, and problem-solving strategies (Anderson, 1983). Educational game design that incorporates puzzles, challenges that require logical reasoning, or scenarios that demand critical thinking directly benefits from understanding cognitive load theory. Designers must balance the complexity of game tasks with the cognitive capacity of learners to avoid overload while still encouraging critical engagement (Sweller, 1994).
4. **Social Learning Theory:** Albert Bandura's social learning theory (1977) emphasizes learning through observation, imitation, and modeling. Multiplayer games and collaborative game environments leverage this by allowing learners to interact with peers, share strategies, and improve their performance through social collaboration. The incorporation of avatars, leader boards, and cooperative challenges further reinforces this theory in practice.
5. **Motivation and Self-Determination Theory:** Intrinsic motivation is central to engaging learners. Self-determination theory (Deci & Ryan, 1985) argues that competence, autonomy, and relatedness are critical drivers of intrinsic motivation. Educational games have the innate ability to provide choice (autonomy), appropriately challenging tasks (competence), and opportunities for social interaction (relatedness). When game design integrates these motivational aspects, learners often experience higher levels of engagement and enjoyment.

Integrating Theory Into Practice

Educational game design is most powerful when grounded in robust pedagogical theory and informed by scientific insights into how people learn. The real challenge—and opportunity—lies in translating these theoretical principles into interactive, engaging, and effective game experiences. This integration not only provides a roadmap for designers and educators but also ensures that every design decision enriches the learning process.

Bridging the Gap Between Theory and Design

At the heart of effective educational game design is the synthesis of multiple learning theories. Constructivism (Piaget, 1971) and constructionism (Papert, 1980), for example, emphasize active learning and the importance of learners constructing their own knowledge through hands-on experience. To integrate these ideas, designers create environments in which players are encouraged to explore, experiment, and create. Instead of passively absorbing information, learners are invited to solve puzzles, build virtual models, or simulate real-world processes—transforming each challenge into an opportunity to construct meaning.

In practice, this means designing game mechanics that support inquiry-based learning. For example, a digital lab simulation in a science game might allow learners to combine chemicals, adjust variables, and observe outcomes in real time. This interactive exploration fosters critical thinking and mirrors the process of trial and error that is central to constructivist approaches (Papert, 1980).

Designing for Adaptive Learning and the Zone of Proximal Development

Vygotsky's (1978) concept of the Zone of Proximal Development (ZPD) urges educators to provide learners with challenges that are slightly above their current abilities but can be overcome with appropriate support. In an educational game, this principle is put into action through adaptive difficulty settings. By using algorithms and real-time data tracking, game systems can adjust the complexity of tasks based on individual player performance. This dynamic adjustment not only prevents frustration but also keeps learners in a state of "optimal challenge"—a concept closely related to Csikszentmihalyi's (1990) idea of flow.

For instance, if a math puzzle is too easy for a student, the game might automatically introduce more variables or problem-solving steps to maintain engagement. Conversely, if the challenge proves too daunting, supplementary hints or scaffolded mini-tasks can be offered. This adaptive framework ensures that each learner remains engaged and that the game continuously supports progress through the ZPD.

Embedding Behaviorist Principles: Feedback and Reinforcement

Behaviorist theories, notably those advanced by Skinner (1954), underpin the importance of immediate feedback and reinforcement in learning. Educational games operationalize these ideas by providing continuous, in-the-moment feedback. This can take the form of auditory cues, visual signals, or narrative responses that acknowledge correct actions and gently correct mistakes.

In practice, a history game might reward a learner with points or unlock a bonus level when they accurately place historical events in chronological order. These rewards, akin to positive reinforcement, encourage repetition of correct behaviors and sustain engagement. Moreover, the use of immediate feedback transforms trial and error into a safe space for experimentation. By reassuring the learner that mistakes are simply part of the learning journey, educational games help cultivate a growth mindset—a critical factor in long-term educational success.

Infusing Narrative and Contextual Learning

A compelling narrative is not just an add-on in educational game design—it is the framework within which content is delivered and internalized. Narrative theories in education suggest that meaningful stories can help learners contextualize abstract content, thereby enhancing retention and the transfer of knowledge (Gee, 2003). In practice, game designers weave educational content into the storyline, ensuring that each plot development is intertwined with learning objectives.

For example, a game centered around a historical conflict might require players to make decisions based on real-world events, thus encouraging them to understand cause and effect in a historical context. Characters and scenarios are designed not only to entertain but also to serve as vehicles for conveying complex educational concepts. By emotionally engaging players, the narrative encourages deeper immersion and more effective learning—providing a vivid context in which abstract theories become tangible experiences.

Social Learning in Practice

Albert Bandura's (1977) social learning theory emphasizes the importance of observational learning, imitation, and modeling. In educational game design, this is achieved by incorporating cooperative and competitive elements that mirror social interactions. Multiplayer modes, peer-to-peer feedback, and collaborative problem-solving tasks are all strategies that bring social learning theory to life.

For instance, an educational game might include team-based challenges where players collaborate to solve a puzzle, with each member contributing unique skills or perspectives. Alternatively, leader boards and group missions encourage healthy competition that spurs individuals to improve while also learning from the successes of their peers. This social dimension reinforces that learning is a shared, interactive process—aligning with contemporary views of education as a community of practice.

Iterative Design: A Continuous Feedback Loop

Integrating theory into practice is not a one-time effort but a dynamic, iterative process. It requires constant refinement based on learner feedback, usability testing, and learning analytics. Effective educational game design involves creating prototypes, testing them in authentic environments, and iterating based on the insights gained. This iterative cycle of design, evaluation, and revision ensures that both the theoretical foundations and the practical implementations co-evolve to meet learners' needs.

For example, a game initially designed with a fixed difficulty curve might be re-engineered into an adaptive system if user data indicates that players are either frequently disengaged or showing signs of excessive frustration. The iterative design process ensures that educational games remain responsive and relevant, continually merging pedagogical insights with technological innovations.

Collaboration Between Educators and Designers

Finally, integrating theory into practice in educational game design is enhanced by interdisciplinary collaboration. Designers, educators, subject matter experts, and cognitive scientists must work together to ensure that game mechanics, narratives, and feedback systems are not only engaging but also educationally valid. This collaborative approach ensures that every element of the game aligns with curriculum standards and learning outcomes while leveraging the latest insights from educational research.

For example, a mathematics game developed in collaboration with experienced educators can ensure that puzzles and challenges align with curriculum objectives while still being fun and interactive. This holistic integration of expertise from multiple domains not only enhances the educational value of the game but also promotes innovation in design.

Integrating theory into practice in educational game design is a complex, multifaceted endeavor that demands a careful balance between pedagogical principles and creative execution. By leveraging constructivist, behaviorist, cognitive, and social learning theories, designers can create immersive, adaptive, and engaging environments where learning is seamlessly woven into play. Through continuous iteration and interdisciplinary collaboration, these theoretical foundations are transformed into practical design elements that not only captivate but also educate. This careful integration ultimately transforms digital games into powerful tools for lifelong learning and cognitive development.

Translating these theories into practical design elements involves careful consideration of how educational content is structured within the game environment. For instance, a game based on constructivist principles might allow learners to experiment with different strategies to solve a problem in a virtual lab, whereas a game influenced by behaviorism might use a points-based system to reinforce repetitive practice of basic math skills.

Theoretical frameworks also influence the evaluation of game efficacy. Researchers and designers alike are increasingly employing mixed-methods research, combining quantitative data such as learning analytics (Kapp, 2012) with qualitative feedback from user experience studies to assess the impact of game-based learning. In doing so, they create iterative development cycles that refine the game mechanics, narrative elements, and overall learning outcomes.

As educational game design continues to evolve, designers increasingly rely on these theoretical perspectives to create a synergy between engagement and effective learning. In the following sections, we discuss the broad components of educational game design that draw on these theories, emphasizing the intricate balance between fun and pedagogy.

PRINCIPLES OF EDUCATIONAL GAME DESIGN

Designing an educational game is akin to crafting a multifaceted experience that must function on several levels concurrently. The goal is not only to entertain but also to facilitate deep, meaningful learning. This section outlines the core principles of educational game design:

Game Mechanics and Dynamics

Game Mechanics: At the most basic level, game mechanics refer to the rules and systems that govern gameplay. These include the scoring systems, win-lose conditions, levels, and challenges that drive the experience. Designers must ensure that the mechanics:

- Align with learning objectives.
- Provide clear goals and measurable outcomes.
- Create a structure where progression is contingent on mastering content rather than on random chance.

For example, in a mathematics game, solving problems correctly might unlock new levels or provide rewards that relate directly to the difficulty progression (Prensky, 2001). Malone's (1981) early work on intrinsically motivating instruction posits that such mechanics, when properly designed, can transform routine practice into an engaging challenge. The balance between risk and reward, coupled with clear feedback, is critical to maintaining player investment.

Game Dynamics: Where mechanics define the rules, dynamics describe how those rules play out in real-time during gameplay. Dynamic elements include strategy formulation, adaptation to challenging scenarios, and emergent behavior from player interactions. The concept of "flow"—where players are fully immersed in a state of optimal challenge—is crucial here (Csikszentmihalyi, 1990). Games that succeed in creating such a flow experience sustain learner engagement, ensuring that players remain motivated even when facing tasks that require sustained effort.

Dynamic game elements must also reflect the learning curve of the game's content. For example, a history game might use branching narratives where historical decisions affect outcomes, mirroring the complex causality of real historical events. This not only reinforces content but also highlights the multifaceted nature of decision making and consequence.

Narrative and Storytelling Elements

Narrative drives the emotional and intellectual engagement of the player. While educational content forms the informational core, the narrative weaves that content into a story that is both memorable and meaningful. Storytelling in educational games involves:

- **Contextualization:** Embedding learning within a narrative context helps learners see the relevance of the material. For instance, an environmental science game might tell the story of a future world struggling with climate change, thereby motivating players to learn about sustainability.
- **Character Development:** Relatable characters, whether protagonists or supporting figures, provide emotional anchors and models for behavior. Through interactions with characters, learners can explore different perspectives and moral dilemmas.
- **Branching Narratives:** Allowing choices within the narrative not only increases engagement but also parallels constructivist learning, where learners make decisions that affect outcomes (Gee, 2003). Such interactivity empowers learners and underscores the connection between actions and consequences.

The integration of narrative in educational games is more than mere embellishment; it forms the backbone of engagement. When learners are emotionally invested in a story, the retention of educational content is significantly enhanced. Researchers have found that the narrative context can transform abstract concepts into concrete experiences, promoting better learning transfer between the game environment and real-life contexts.

Balancing Challenge and Skill: The Flow Experience

A critical challenge in educational game design is balancing the difficulty of tasks with the abilities of learners. Too easy, and the game becomes boring; too hard, and frustration may set in rapidly. The concept of "flow" as identified by Csikszentmihalyi (1990) provides a useful framework for understanding this dynamic. A game is in flow when the challenge level is perfectly matched to the player's skill set, resulting in a state of concentrated focus and heightened enjoyment.

To create and sustain flow, designers often implement adaptive difficulty systems. These systems monitor player performance in real-time and adjust game parameters—such as the speed, complexity, or frequency of challenges—to ensure that learners remain in the zone of proximal development. This approach is particularly effective when designing for diverse audiences, as it tailors the experience to individual strengths and weaknesses.

Flow theory not only supports engagement but also promotes deeper learning. When learners are challenged just enough to stimulate cognitive effort without overwhelming them, they are more likely to persist and internalize the skills and knowledge being taught. This delicate balance is the hallmark of successful educational game design and one of the primary reasons games remain such an effective educational medium.

Engaging Motivational Factors

Motivation in educational environments is multifaceted, incorporating both intrinsic and extrinsic factors. While early educational games often relied on extrinsic rewards—such as points or medals—modern design approaches emphasize intrinsic motivation, which arises from the internal satisfaction of mastering a challenge or solving a puzzle (Deci & Ryan, 1985).

Several motivational strategies have been incorporated into educational game design:

- **Goal Setting and Achievement:** Clear, achievable goals provide learners with a sense of direction and purpose. Establishing incremental milestones allows for the celebration of small successes, which cumulatively reinforce a learner's self-efficacy.
- **Choice and Autonomy:** Providing players with options on how to proceed through challenges supports autonomy, a key component of self-determination theory. Autonomy in a game can range from choosing the order in which objectives are tackled to customizing one's avatar or learning path.
- **Social Interaction and Competition:** Cooperative challenges, leader boards, and multiplayer functionalities tap into social motivations. Social interaction not only reinforces learning through peer-to-peer feedback but also fosters a sense of community among learners.

· **Narrative Immersion:** As discussed earlier, a well-crafted story naturally motivates players to see the narrative through to its conclusion, thereby reinforcing learning objectives in the process.

Integrating these motivational factors ensures that learners are not only immersed in gameplay but are also continuously encouraged to engage with the educational content. The synergy between in-game rewards and educational achievement is paramount in maintaining sustained engagement and promoting long-term retention of material.

Feedback, Reinforcement, and Adaptive Learning

Feedback is an essential aspect of both educational theory and game design. In educational games, feedback mechanisms must operate on multiple levels:

· **Immediate In-Game Feedback:** Instantaneous feedback on actions—whether through sound cues, visual signals, or narrative responses—helps learners understand the consequences of their actions. This immediacy reinforces correct responses and gently corrects errors without discouraging experimentation.
· **Meta-Feedback:** Beyond immediate action responses, some games offer comprehensive progress reports or dashboards that allow learners to track their progress over time. This continuous monitoring not only keeps learners informed but also prompts self-reflection about learning strategies and areas for improvement.
· **Adaptive Feedback Systems:** These systems adjust the level of difficulty or provide additional hints depending on learner performance. By dynamically tailoring the feedback, designers can support learners at different levels of mastery and ensure that the challenge remains appropriate as the learner's skills develop (Sweller, 1994).

The interplay between feedback and challenge is critical for sustaining engagement. When learners understand that every mistake is an opportunity for growth, the educational game becomes a safe space for risk-taking and experimentation. Adaptive feedback not only enhances learning but also personalizes the experience, helping to secure the flow state necessary for deep cognitive engagement.

MERGING EDUCATIONAL CONTENT WITH GAME DYNAMICS

The core challenge of educational game design lies in the delicate integration of substantive educational content with engaging gameplay. This section explores strategies for ensuring that educational objectives are seamlessly woven into the fabric of the game.

Curriculum Integration and Alignment

For an educational game to be effective, its content must be thoughtfully aligned with established curriculum goals. This involves:

- **Objectives Mapping:** Clearly defining the educational outcomes the game aims to achieve. For instance, a game designed for a secondary-level biology class might have objectives related to understanding cell structure, genetic processes, or ecological interactions (Kapp, 2012). These outcomes should be integrated into every facet of the game's design—from challenges and puzzles to narrative contexts.
- **Content Authenticity:** The accuracy and relevance of the content are paramount. Misrepresenting or oversimplifying the subject matter can lead to misconceptions. Collaboration with subject matter experts is often essential for developing a game that is both accurate and pedagogically sound.
- **Scaffolding Learning Experiences:** Effective educational games gradually introduce complexity, scaffolding the learner's journey. Early game levels might focus on basic concepts and skills, while later levels introduce more complex scenarios that require synthesis and application of previously learned concepts. This scaffolding mirrors Vygotsky's zone of proximal development (Vygotsky, 1978), ensuring that learners are neither overwhelmed nor under-challenged.

Designers must align gameplay mechanics with intended learning outcomes. For example, consider a simulation game where players manage a virtual ecosystem. The game could gradually introduce ecological principles such as population dynamics and food web relationships, reinforcing these concepts through both in-game challenges and reflective discussions that follow gameplay events. Such integration ensures that learners not only absorb information passively but actively apply it in dynamic contexts.

Embedding Problem-Solving Tasks

At its core, game-based learning thrives when players are presented with problem-solving tasks that mirror real-world challenges. By embedding problems that require critical thinking, creativity, and collaboration, educational games can stimulate a higher order of thinking:

· **Inquiry-based Learning:** Games that foster inquiry allow learners to ask questions, test hypotheses, and explore multiple solutions. This aligns with research showing that inquiry-based activities lead to deeper retention (Plass, Homer, & Kinzer, 2015).
· **Scenario-Based Challenges:** Narrative-embedded challenges can simulate real-life dilemmas, prompting learners to apply theoretical knowledge to practical situations. Whether it's solving an environmental crisis or mediating a cultural conflict, these scenarios help learners see the real-world relevance of the content.
· **Critical Reflection:** Post-challenge reflections and in-game debriefs further consolidate learning. Designers can incorporate moments where players must articulate their reasoning, compare alternative strategies, or review mistakes, reinforcing critical thinking and metacognition.

Merging Game Mechanics with Content Delivery

The blending of game mechanics with educational content is where design creativity and pedagogical efficacy meet. Consider the following strategies:

· **Puzzle and Quest Formats:** Games that utilize puzzles and quests are well-suited to delivering curricular content when each puzzle or quest is crafted around a specific concept. For instance, in a world history game, quests might require the player to solve puzzles that represent historical events, while multiple solution paths encourage diverse interpretations.
· **Simulation and Role-play:** Simulations provide immersive environments where learners assume roles, make decisions, and witness the ramifications of their actions. In a simulation focusing on ecological management, for example, learners might balance resource allocation with ecosystem conservation, thereby internalizing complex environmental principles through experiential learning.
· **Integration of Multimedia:** The use of videos, animations, and interactive diagrams within games can enrich the learner's experience and clarify complex content. The integration of multimedia elements not only caters to different

learning styles but also leverages the strengths of digital environments to present information in dynamic ways.

The successful fusion of game mechanics with educational content hinges on the designer's ability to see beyond traditional boundaries. When every game element—from scoring systems to narrative arcs—is purposefully crafted to reinforce learning, the result is an experience that is as educational as it is enjoyable.

Case Study: Ecological Simulation Game

To illustrate, consider a hypothetical ecological simulation game designed for high school biology. In this game:

· Players begin by exploring a virtual ecosystem with a variety of species and environmental variables.
· Initial levels focus on basic ecological principles, such as food chains and nutrient cycles, using interactive tutorials and mini-games that reward correct associations.
· As players progress, they encounter increasingly complex challenges, such as managing an invasive species outbreak or balancing resource consumption with sustainability. Feedback systems provide immediate reinforcement when an ecosystem is maintained or challenges are met effectively.
· The game employs adaptive difficulty: if a player struggles with the concept of ecological balance, additional hints and simplified models are provided until mastery is achieved.
· Narrative elements—such as a storyline involving an endangered species or a mystical representation of nature's equilibrium—foster emotional engagement and underscore the real-world significance of the ecological concepts being taught.

This case study exemplifies how the interplay between educational content and game dynamics can create a reinforcing loop where every game element contributes to the overarching learning objectives.

DESIGNING FOR USER EXPERIENCE AND INTERFACE

While educational content and game mechanics form the intellectual backbone of an educational game, user experience (UX) and interface design are equally critical in ensuring the game's success. This section explores the principles of user-centered design, accessibility, and the role of aesthetics in educational game design.

User-Centered Design

At its core, user-centered design involves creating products that are tailored to the needs, preferences, and abilities of the intended audience. In educational game design:

- **Learner Profiles:** Designers must first understand who their users are. This includes age, cognitive development, prior knowledge, technological proficiency, and learning preferences. For example, games intended for children differ markedly from those designed for adult professional training in both interface complexity and narrative tone.
- **Iterative Design and Prototyping:** A critical element of user-centered design is iterative prototyping. Early-stage user testing allows designers to collect feedback on gameplay, interface intuitiveness, and aesthetic appeal. Frequent iterations help identify usability issues and ensure that educational content is easily accessible.
- **Emphasis on Simplicity:** While the underlying systems of an educational game may be complex, the user interface should be straightforward and intuitive. Clear navigation, consistent iconography, and accessible instruction are vital to prevent cognitive overload that might detract from learning.

Visual Design and Aesthetics

Visual appeal can significantly influence engagement and motivation. In educational game design, visual elements must serve both functional and aesthetic purposes:

- **Color and Contrast:** Appropriate use of colors can highlight important information and create a visually stimulating experience. Designers must ensure that color schemes cater to visual impairments by incorporating high-contrast elements for readability.
- **Typography and Layout:** Textual content should be legible and organized logically. When educational information is interwoven with game instructions or narratives, cognitive clarity is paramount.

· **Integration of Themes:** The visual style should reflect and enhance the game's narrative. For example, a game exploring historical events might use period-appropriate art styles and fonts to evoke the desired atmosphere and reinforce the educational context.
· **Responsive and Adaptive Designs:** Considering the array of devices on which games may be played—from desktop computers to tablets and smartphones—interface designs must be responsive. Adaptive layouts help ensure that the game's core experience is maintained across screens, contributing to an inclusive design approach.

Accessibility and Inclusion

Inclusivity is a hallmark of modern educational design. An effective educational game must be accessible to learners with diverse abilities:

· **Multimodal Feedback:** Combining audio, visual, and tactile feedback can help accommodate different learning needs. For instance, incorporating captions and audio descriptions ensures that both hearing-impaired and visually impaired learners can fully engage with the content.
· **Customizability:** Allowing users to customize elements such as font size, speed of instructional narration, or color schemes not only caters to individual preferences but also promotes a sense of ownership over the learning process.
· **Cultural Sensitivity:** Games that aim for global reach must be designed with cultural differences in mind. The narrative, imagery, and even game mechanics should respect and reflect diverse cultural norms and values, avoiding stereotypes and promoting multicultural understanding.
· **Usability Testing with Diverse Groups:** Regular evaluations with users from various demographic and ability groups are essential to identify and correct barriers to accessibility.

A user-centered approach that emphasizes simplicity, aesthetics, and inclusion not only enhances engagement but also ensures that the educational game provides a supportive and enriching experience for all learners.

FEEDBACK, ASSESSMENT, AND DATA-DRIVEN IMPROVEMENT

An effective educational game provides continuous avenues for learners to receive feedback, reflect on their progress, and adjust their strategies. At the same time, designers and educators need robust data on learning outcomes to refine and improve the game. In this section, we discuss how feedback loops and assessment systems contribute to the efficacy of educational game design.

Immediate and Contextualized Feedback

Feedback that is provided in real-time helps guide learning behaviors. In many educational games, every action is met with immediate cues:

- **Positive Reinforcement:** When learners complete a task correctly, the game might present celebratory visuals, sound effects, or unlock next-level content. This immediate positive reinforcement helps cement learned skills.
- **Constructive Correction:** When mistakes occur, subtle cues (such as hints or reduced penalties) encourage learners to try again, reinforcing a growth mindset. By framing errors as opportunities for learning rather than failures, the game environment becomes a safe space for experimentation.

Summative and Formative Assessment

Educational games can incorporate both formative assessments (ongoing checks for understanding) and summative assessments (evaluations at the end of a learning module):

- **Embedded Quizzes and Challenges:** Formative assessments might appear intermittently throughout gameplay, asking learners to apply recently encountered content in novel ways. Such challenges ensure that learners continually reflect on and apply their knowledge.
- **Performance Dashboards:** Summative assessment tools—often visualized through dashboards—allow learners to see their progress over time. These dashboards can indicate areas of strength, topics that require further review, and personalized recommendations for future gameplay.

Adaptive Systems and Data Analytics

The integration of adaptive learning systems has transformed how designers approach educational game dynamics. By using data analytics—such as tracking decision-making patterns, response times, and error rates—adaptive systems can adjust the difficulty of tasks in real time:

· **Personalization:** Adaptive difficulty ensures the game remains challenging yet approachable, tailoring the learning curve to each individual learner. This responsiveness to user data is critical for maintaining both the flow and the motivational aspects of gameplay.
· **Iterative Improvement:** Designers can use aggregated gameplay analytics to identify areas where learners consistently struggle. With these insights, the game's content and mechanics can be refined to better support learning, ensuring that updates are data-driven and user-centered.

Feedback and assessment in educational games not only drive individual learner success but also inform the broader design cycle. Through data analytics, ongoing research, and iterative design methodologies, educational game design can continually evolve to meet the needs of diverse learners while ensuring that learning outcomes remain at the forefront of the experience.

COLLABORATIVE AND SOCIAL LEARNING IN GAME DESIGN

Educational game design increasingly recognizes that learning is a social endeavor. Whether through multiplayer experiences, cooperative tasks, or competitive leader boards, social interaction provides a rich context for deepening understanding and motivation.

Designing for Collaboration

Collaboration in educational games is fostered by designing tasks that require learners to work together, share ideas, and negotiate solutions:

· **Team-Based Challenges:** By structuring gameplay around team challenges, designers encourage communication and cooperation. In a science simulation, for example, groups of learners might work together to balance an ecosystem, each contributing specialized knowledge. Such cooperative dynamics can mirror real-world interdisciplinary problem-solving.

· **Peer Feedback Mechanisms:** Incorporating systems that allow learners to provide and receive feedback from their peers can promote reflection and reinforce learning. Peer evaluations, collaborative puzzles, and group missions all serve as vectors for constructive social interaction.

Competition and Social Incentives

While collaboration is central, healthy competition can also act as a powerful motivator:

· **Leader Boards and Achievements:** Displaying real-time leader boards, awarding badges, or recognizing top performers can foster a competitive spirit that drives learners to improve. However, it is critical that these systems be balanced—promoting personal growth rather than reinforcing negative comparisons or stress.
· **Balancing Cooperative and Competitive Elements:** Games that blend collaborative challenges with competitive elements allow learners to experience both aspects of social learning. For instance, a game might combine team-based tasks with individual recognition, ensuring that while competition is present, mutual support remains a priority.

Virtual Communities and Ongoing Engagement

Beyond in-game interactions, many educational games foster virtual communities. Forums, chat systems, and social media integrations enable learners to extend game-based interactions into broader learning communities. These platforms allow for:

· **Sustained Engagement:** Virtual communities can help maintain interest in a game beyond isolated play sessions by creating a network of peers who share strategies, challenges, and successes.
· **Cross-Pollination of Ideas:** Exposure to diverse perspectives can enrich the learning experience, as learners observe and internalize approaches different from their own (Bandura, 1977).
· **Mentoring and Peer Coaching:** Experienced players can mentor novices, contributing to a culture of collective learning and continuous improvement.

The social dimensions of educational game design underscore the fact that learning is most effective when it builds communities of practice. By designing for both collaboration and healthy competition, educational games can create ecosystems where each learner contributes to and benefits from the collective knowledge.

TECHNOLOGY, TOOLS, AND EMERGING TRENDS

As technology continues to evolve, so too do the opportunities for innovative educational game design. This section examines state-of-the-art technologies and emerging trends that are shaping the future of educational games.

Mobile and Ubiquitous Learning

The proliferation of mobile devices has redefined where and how educational games are played:

· **Anywhere, Anytime Learning:** Mobile educational games allow learners to engage with content in a variety of settings, transforming downtime into opportunities for learning. The ubiquity of smartphones and tablets means that educational content can now be integrated seamlessly into daily life.

· **Microlearning Modules:** Mobile platforms are particularly well-suited to microlearning—short, focused segments that deliver content in bite-sized pieces. These modules can be integrated into daily routines, reinforcing continuous learning.

Augmented Reality (AR) and Virtual Reality (VR)

AR and VR technologies offer immersive environments that can transform traditional learning paradigms:

· **Experiential Learning in Virtual Worlds:** VR environments allow learners to step into historical events, laboratory simulations, or distant planets, providing a visceral sense of presence and engagement. These immersive experiences can lead to deeper understanding by placing learners "in the moment."

· **Augmented Reality for Contextualized Learning:** AR overlays digital information onto the real world. In an educational context, AR can highlight historical information on real-world landmarks or enrich classroom experiments with interactive 3D models. Such applications promote engagement by blending reality with interactive digital content.

Data Analytics and Artificial Intelligence (AI)

Data-driven design is rapidly reshaping educational game development:

· **Learning Analytics:** By collecting data on player behavior, response times, and decision patterns, designers can fine-tune game mechanics to optimize learning outcomes. Analytics also help in identifying which concepts require further reinforcement.

· **AI-Driven Personalization:** Artificial intelligence can be leveraged to create adaptive systems that tailor the difficulty level and content delivery to each individual learner's needs. AI can also power sophisticated non-player characters (NPCs) that interact with learners in a human-like manner, providing dynamic feedback and contextual hints.

· **Predictive Modeling:** By analyzing real-time gameplay data, predictive models can forecast learning curves and anticipate challenges or drop-off points. This proactive insight allows educators and designers to adjust content in real time, ensuring that the game remains supportive and effective throughout the learning process.

Emerging Design Tools and Environments

The evolution of design software has lowered barriers to entry for educational game development:

· **Game Engines:** Platforms like Unity and Unreal Engine offer robust toolsets that enable designers to create visually sophisticated and interactive experiences without requiring extensive programming knowledge. These engines also support cross-platform development, ensuring accessibility on multiple devices.

· **Authoring Tools:** Software that simplifies narrative development, multimedia integration, and adaptive feedback mechanisms empower educators to build educational games that are both engaging and pedagogically rigorous. The integration of AI and machine learning within these tools further augments the designer's ability to create responsive learning environments.

As technological advancements continue apace, educational game design will no doubt expand into new territories, offering opportunities to create even more immersive, personalized, and impactful learning experiences.

EVALUATION, RESEARCH, AND BEST PRACTICES

Rigorous evaluation is essential for refining educational games and ensuring that they meet both pedagogical and usability standards. This section outlines methodologies for assessing the efficacy of educational game design, as well as best practices that have emerged from both academic research and industry experience.

Research Methodologies for Game-based Learning

Evaluating educational games involves a blend of quantitative and qualitative methods:

- **Controlled Experiments:** Randomized control trials (RCTs) remain a gold standard for assessing the learning outcomes associated with game-based learning. By comparing groups that use the game versus traditional teaching methods, researchers can isolate the effects of gameplay on knowledge acquisition (Squire, 2005).
- **Mixed-Methods Approaches:** Combining surveys, focus groups, and observational studies provides a more holistic view of the learner's experience. Qualitative data, such as learner interviews and gameplay observations, enrich the quantitative metrics derived from test scores and performance analytics.
- **Learning Analytics:** Continuous data collection through in-game analytics allows designers to identify patterns of engagement, challenges, and success rates. This iterative feedback loop is pivotal for ongoing improvements and adaptive content delivery.

Best Practices in Educational Game Design

Drawing on decades of research and real-world implementation, several best practices have emerged:

- **Align Game Goals with Curriculum Objectives:** Ensure that every game element, from mechanics to narrative, reinforces the core learning outcomes.
- **Prioritize Usability and Accessibility:** A user-friendly interface that caters to a diverse audience prevents cognitive overload and maximizes learning potential.
- **Create Iterative Development Cycles:** Regular prototyping, testing, and refinement based on user feedback leads to a more polished and effective product.
- **Promote Collaborative Learning:** Incorporate both cooperative and competitive elements to harness the benefits of social learning theories.

- **Incorporate Adaptive Learning Tools:** Use data analytics and AI to personalize the learner experience, ensuring that challenges remain appropriately scaled.
- **Invest in Narrative and Immersive Design:** A strong narrative context can significantly enhance motivation and knowledge retention.

Case Studies and Practical Examples

Several successful educational games exemplify these best practices. For example, *DragonBox* series of mathematics games integrate abstract algebraic concepts into playful puzzles and progressive challenges (Kapp, 2012). Likewise, *Minecraft: Education Edition* harnesses the power of a sandbox environment to allow learners to explore complex topics such as urban planning, history, and sustainable practices through role-playing and cooperative building tasks. These examples demonstrate that when educational content meets thoughtful design, learning can be transformed into an immersive, iterative, and ultimately enjoyable experience.

FUTURE DIRECTIONS AND EMERGING TRENDS

The evolution of educational game design does not stand still. New technologies, pedagogical discoveries, and cultural shifts continuously open novel avenues for innovation.

Immersive and Mixed Reality Experiences

The boundaries between virtual and physical spaces are blurring, with mixed reality experiences paving the way for unprecedented interactive learning:

- **Augmented and Virtual Reality:** As AR and VR technologies mature, they promise to immerse learners in environments that are simultaneously real and digitally enhanced. Imagine a history lesson where students "walk" through ancient civilizations or a science class where learners explore the microscopic world at scale.
- **Haptic and Sensory Feedback:** Future educational games may incorporate haptic feedback and other sensory inputs to create experiences that engage multiple senses. This multimodal stimulation can improve retention and deepen understanding.

· **Wearable Technologies:** With the advent of smart glasses and other wearable devices, educational experiences can extend beyond traditional screens to integrate learning into everyday activities.

Greater Integration of AI and Machine Learning

Artificial intelligence will continue to transform educational game design through:

· **Personalized Learning Journeys:** AI can learn from individual player data and dynamically modify both the narrative and challenge aspects of the game to best suit each learner's needs.
· **Intelligent Tutoring Systems:** Future educational games may incorporate virtual tutors that interact with learners in real time, providing personalized hints, explanations, and adaptive challenges.
· **Predictive Analytics:** Leveraging large datasets from game interactions, predictive modelling can help designers anticipate learning bottlenecks and intervene before learners become discouraged.

Social and Collaborative Learning Ecosystems

The future of educational game design will likely see an even greater emphasis on community:

· **Global Learning Communities:** Online platforms where learners across the globe collaborate, compete, and share experiences can make educational game experiences truly global.
· **Cross-Disciplinary Environments:** Games that merge multiple disciplines—such as art, history, science, and literature—will foster holistic learning, reflecting the interconnected nature of real-world knowledge.
· **Lifelong Learning:** As learning becomes a continuous process throughout life, educational games might evolve from tools aimed solely at school-aged children to platforms serving adult learners, professionals, and informal education networks.

Evaluating Impact in a Rapidly Evolving Landscape

Developing robust frameworks for long-term evaluation will be essential as technologies evolve:

· **Longitudinal Studies:** Tracking learners over extended periods will help determine the lasting impact of game-based learning on academic performance and skill development.
· **Cross-Platform Integration:** As educational games spread across various devices and platforms, ensuring consistency and tracking outcomes across these media will be an important research frontier.
· **Ethical Considerations:** With increased data collection and adaptive systems, ethical guidelines and data privacy protocols must be central to design and evaluation practices.

CONCLUSION

Educational game design stands at the crossroads of technology, pedagogy, and human creativity. In this chapter, we have explored the multifaceted elements that constitute effective educational game design—from game mechanics and narrative structure to adaptive feedback, user interface design, and the importance of collaboration. Drawing on a range of theoretical frameworks including constructivism, cognitivism, behaviorism, and self-determination theory, we have seen that the most successful educational games are those that integrate rigorous educational content with engaging and responsive gameplay.

The dynamic interplay between challenge and reward, narrative and interaction, as well as individualization and collaboration, creates not only an immersive learning environment but also one that can adapt to the diverse needs of today's learners. As technology evolves—with mobile platforms, AR/VR, AI-driven personalization, and wearable devices coming to the forefront—the potential to transform learning experiences grows exponentially.

For educators and designers, the path forward is clear: embrace interdisciplinary collaboration, commit to iterative design and assessment, and always prioritize the learner's experience. The lessons drawn from past research and practical applications provide a solid foundation for future innovation. Although challenges remain—ensuring accessibility, maintaining ethical standards in data collection, and balancing entertainment with rigorous content—the potential for educational games to revolutionize learning is vast.

In this era of digital transformation, educational games have the power to engage learners in ways traditional methods can no longer match. By melding technology with sound instructional design and thoughtfully crafted narratives, educators can create environments where every challenge is a lesson and every game is a journey toward deeper understanding. The integration of engaging content with adaptive experiences promises a future in which learning is not only effective but also profoundly enjoyable.

As we look to the future, continued research, innovation, and collaboration will be essential in unlocking the full potential of educational game design. Whether through immersive VR simulations, AI-powered tutoring, or global learning networks that span cultures and continents, the next generation of educational games holds the promise of transforming how we understand, interact with, and experience knowledge.

REFERENCES

Anderson, J. R. (1983). *The architecture of cognition*. Harvard University Press.

Bandura, A. (1977). *Social learning theory*. Prentice Hall.

Csikszentmihalyi, M. (1990). *Flow: The psychology of optimal experience*. Harper & Row.

Deci, E. L., & Ryan, R. M. (1985). *Intrinsic motivation and self-determination in human behavior*. Plenum. DOI: 10.1007/978-1-4899-2271-7

Gee, J. P. (2003). *What video games have to teach us about learning and literacy*. Palgrave Macmillan. DOI: 10.1145/950566.950595

Kapp, K. M. (2012). *The gamification of learning and instruction: Game-based methods and strategies for training and education*. Pfeiffer.

Papert, S. (1980). *Mindstorms: Children, computers, and powerful ideas*. Basic Books.

Piaget, J. (1971). *Science of education and the psychology of the child*. Viking.

Plass, J. L., Homer, B. D., & Kinzer, C. K. (2015). Foundations of game-based learning. *Educational Psychologist, 50*(4), 258–283. DOI: 10.1080/00461520.2015.1122533

Prensky, M. (2001). *Digital game-based learning*. McGraw-Hill.

Skinner, B. F. (1954). The science of learning and the art of teaching. *Harvard Educational Review*, *24*(2), 86–97.

Squire, K. (2005). Changing the game: What happens when video games enter the classroom? *Innovate: Journal of Online Education, 1*(6).

Sweller, J. (1994). Cognitive load theory, learning difficulty, and instructional design. *Learning and Instruction*, *4*(4), 295–312. DOI: 10.1016/0959-4752(94)90003-5

Vygotsky, L. S. (1978). *Mind in society: The development of higher psychological processes*. Harvard University Press.

Chapter 15
Measuring Success:
Evaluating Learning Outcomes in Gamified Cybersecurity Training

Abdul Azeem Khan
https://orcid.org/0000-0003-2742-8034
Universiti Islam Sultan Sharif Ali, Brunei

Haji Abdul Hafidz Bin Haji Omar
Universiti Islam Sultan Sharif Ali, Brunei

ABSTRACT

The chapter entitled "Measuring Success: Evaluating Learning Outcomes in Gamified Cybersecurity Training" begins the discussion with the background of cybersecurity and the problems being faced by industry due to lack of highly skilled cybersecurity professionals. This scarcity can be minimized by developing better training programs through gamified approach. It has been found that this approach is more productive compared to traditional conventional methods of teaching as cybersecurity comprises more technical content which is more abstract to conceive unless hands on practical approach is implemented hence a gamified approach which facilitates the learners with fun, more focus on learning minimizing student retention and making learning process more engaging and productive.

INTRODUCTION

Gamification has been proved to be a productive tool in developing individuals' knowledge base and to improve it in continuum(Zhong, Kim, & Liu, 2024). As depicted in Fig 1.0 it comprehensively describes the overall productivity of an induvial embracing gamification. A common approach to promote security awareness and

DOI: 10.4018/979-8-3373-0477-9.ch015

technical improvements is to apply gamification to cybersecurity training. But it's challenging to measure the effectiveness of engagement. The learning, behavioural change or solutions that are framed through gamification can only be partially captured through standard testing. Without properly assessing these programs, organizations may have no way of knowing if these programs are genuinely effective in growing the cybersecurity workforce(Khan, Jhanjhi, Alı, Ray, & Wassan, 2025). It can pose unique challenges in the evaluation of learning outcomes in gamified settings. Due to the interactive and dynamic characteristics of gamification, it is challenging to use traditional testing techniques.

Figure 1. Gamification in education: An effective approach(le)

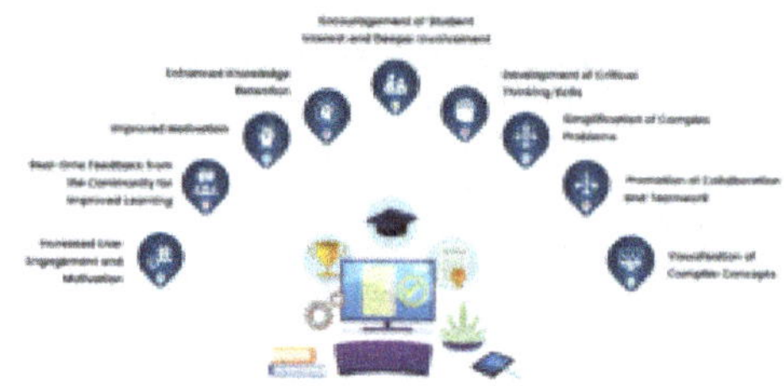

While engagement levels, completion rates and in-game performance all offer nuggets of information, that does not always equate to using the skills in the real world. Furthermore, differences in difficulty levels as well as individual motivation and team format also come into play while evaluating performance(Ashraf, Jhanjhi, Brohi, & Muzafar, 2024). Success in Gamified Cybersecurity Education depends on many factors currently this chapter looks at measuring success in gamified cybersecurity training Several evaluation frameworks, important performance indicators and strategies to assess the learning outcomes are reviewed(Shah, Jhanjhi, & Ray, 2024). The intent of this chapter is to introduce, and provide a framework that educators, organizations, and researchers can utilize to establish touchpoints to create more meaningful cybersecurity educational programs with sets of inputs and outputs capable of being measured(Sindiramutty et al., 2024).

DEFINING SUCCESS IN GAMIFIED CYBERSECURITY TRAINING

Success with gamified cybersecurity training is not simply about accruing points or completing challenges. It involves actual skill building, behavior modification, and sustained effort. A successful program would reinforce elements of problem-solving and critical thought citing cyber hygiene(Shah, Jhanjhi, & Laraib, 2023). It's not only security concepts, but also implementation in the way must learn and implement in real life ways. The improved response time to cyber threats and making more correct decisions to thwart cyber-attacks are strong indicators of a successful training program(Khan, Jhanjhi, Hamid, et al., 2025).

For this to happen, though, the learning objectives, training outcomes and organizational goals need to closely align according, and it is considered to be the only way to develop a useful measure for success. That is not something you can easily do by tracking scores or completion rates. Metrics ought to also include core competencies, including, but not limited to threat detection, response efficiency, and hands-on application. Training programs for new hires should look beyond individuals and act as parts of a larger cybersecurity plan to mitigate these vulnerabilities and build a culture of security awareness in organizations(Shahid, Ashraf, Jhanjhi, & Zam, 2025).

From notice to a wholesome profitable body numbers are very telling of performance scores and engagement analytics. But qualitative evaluations yielding richer data on the impact of learning—like peer evaluations, self-evaluations, and applications to real-world contexts—provide more compelling evidence of impact. Organizations can then connect data from different sources to gain a holistic understanding of training effectiveness and whether skills are sticking (or not) in the long term(Almagrabi, 2023).

KEY METRICS FOR EVALUATING LEARNING OUTCOMES

How to assess a gamified cybersecurity training to understand its effectiveness? Gamified assessments offer a pain point solution in that traditional assessments might not be able to capture the depth and breadth of learning learned, as gamification is centred around the engagement, practice and change behaviour. Higher quality learning outcomes are assessed by a mix of quantitative and qualitative measures. As illustrated in Fig 2.0, These refer to crucial metrics that help trainers, learners, practitioners and organizations to understand if the educational programs designed are acquiring the required skills and performing well in response to cybersecurity challenges(Basil Yousef Alothman, 2024).

Engagement Metrics

This is especially important in gamified training where higher engagement usually means better retention of knowledge. Important metrics in this framed point of view include duration of training modules, task completion rate, and interactivity participation level. These metrics indicate the level of learner engagement with the program and degree of motivation to finish challenges. A lack of engagement may suggest that there are problems with the design of content, level of difficulty or learner motivation. Analyzing these metrics allows trainers to improve and fine-tune the course design to drive more participation and interactivity(Puig, Rodríguez, Rodríguez, & Gallego, 2023).

Figure 2. Evaluating learning outcomes: Key metrics

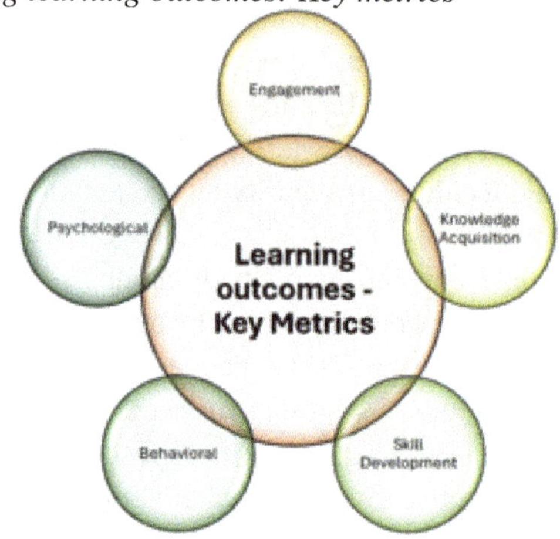

Knowledge Acquisition Metrics

Cybersecurity training starts with theoretical knowledge. Core concept retention among learners is measured with pre- and post-assessment scores, quizzes, and certification rates. While the material stays the same, using pre- and post-training assessments helps you understand the effectiveness of your learning materials and whether they are making an improvement in knowledge levels. The other issue is certification rates, which at least show whether learners achieved a certain level of competency. They offer measures which are objective and aligned with the cognitive learning outcomes of the course, confirming that successful participants comprehend the principles before putting them into practice beyond the course(Capatina, Juarez-Varon, Micu, & Micu, 2024).

Skill Development Metrics

Cybersecurity is a very practical field that needs practical experience. Training can't just teach you how to do things; you've got to check it with things like simulations, Capture The Flag (CTF) and real-world security challenges. These activities challenge the learner's skill in identifying threats, implementing security measures, and responding to cyber incidents in a timely manner. Good performance in such exercises indicate not only technical skills, but problem-solving skills underneath duress. The organization should measure the improvements in these areas to ensure that the learners gain practical cybersecurity skills(Ranganathan & Benson, 2020).

Behavioral Metrics

The end goal of cyber safety training is to drive behavior in the real world. Metrics such as incident response times, error rates and the use of security protocols indicate how well learners put their training into practice. For example, this improvement can be demonstrated if employees identify phishing attempts or so-called misconfigurations less frequently — an indication that the learning has transferred. These metrics enable organizations to measure if their workforce is gaining knowledge of security and becoming more resourceful to avoid risks(Ulmer, Braun, Cheng, Dowey, & Wollert, 2020).

Psychological Metrics

Another factor that significantly contributes to long-term retention of any skill is learner motivation, confidence, and satisfaction. Psychological metrics evaluate constructs like self-efficacy, perceived confidence/ability to handle cybersecurity tasks, and overall experience with and satisfaction with training. Though gamification elements like rewards and leaderboards help boost motivation, their positive influence on learning should be measured. This also means they are likely to enjoy the training and will implement their skills effortlessly without making mistakes(Thomas, Baral, & Crocco, 2022).

The above is just a few of the key metrics organizations can use to establish a holistic evaluation framework. Gamified cybersecurity training is tailored to result in valuable learning outcomes if there is a balanced mix of engagement, knowledge, skill, behavioral, and psychological metrics.

EVALUATION OF FRAMEWORKS AND MODELS

There are several models and frameworks to evaluate the gamification of cybersecurity models which measure the productiveness and effectiveness of the training launched by the organizations to train their human capital in cybersecurity domain. As shown in Figure 3 only three are discussed here comprehensively based on efficiency of the structured frameworks and models they are required to accurately measure the impact of gamified cybersecurity training. The traditional models used for training evaluation are similar and provide a good groundwork in this subject but should be adapted to cover various factors associated with gamification, including engagement, motivation, interactive learning, etc. When you base on models that are already well established and complementary adaptations for gamification, it can ensure that your training will yield appropriate results and benefits(Yamani, 2021).

Kirkpatrick's Four-Level Training Evaluation Model

One of the most popular approaches for evaluating training effectiveness is Kirkpatrick's model. The model has four levels: Reaction, Learning, Behavior, and Results. The first level is Reaction, which assesses the satisfaction and engagement of learners with the training, usually through surveys and feedback. The Learning level assesses knowledge gained through pre- and post-training evaluations. The Behavior level measures if the learners use their skills in actual events, usually measured through workplace observations and performance assessments. Lastly, Results is the most important level of evaluation, measuring the end impact of training on organizational objectives (e.g., better cybersecurity practices, decreased security incidents, etc.). This structured approach helps in measuring short and long-term learning outcomes(Stefan, Mortimer, & Horan, 2023).

Figure 3. Evaluation: Models and frameworks

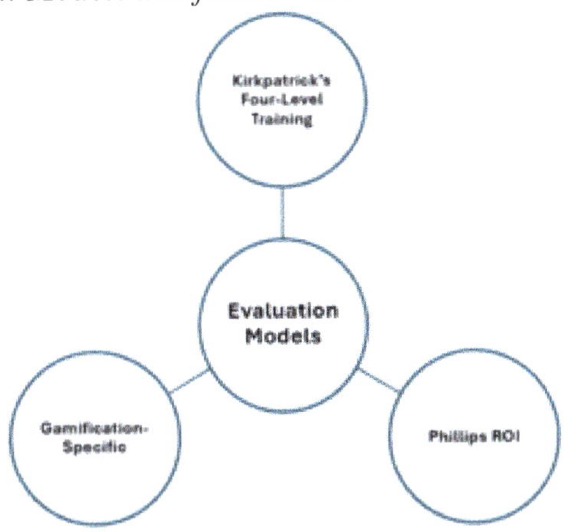

Phillips ROI Methodology

The Phillips Return on Investment (ROI) Methodology enhances Kirkpatrick's model by introducing a financial angle. It assesses the economic worth of training initiatives in terms of the costs versus tangible returns. The methodology starts with gathering data on engagement, learning outcomes, and behavior changes, and then moves forward into a cycle of analysis and action. Such insights are subsequently translated into financial metrics — lower security breach count, cost savings via reduced incidents and improved productivity. Organizations can evaluate the success of gamified cybersecurity training in terms of ROI and determined that gamified cybersecurity training yields demonstrable business value. Unlike traditional methods of calculating training credit hours, this method also allows for easy justifications of training investments to stakeholders and decision-makers(Bergamo et al.).

Gamification-Specific Frameworks

Traditional evaluation approaches fail to consider the interactive and motivational elements of gamified learning and their overall effectiveness. This is where gamification-specific frameworks come in, by introducing the main game mechanics like rewards, competition and real-time feedback. These models evaluate the effect of things such as leaderboards, badges, and storytelling on engagement and learning outcomes. Examination of in-game behaviors, progression metrics, and perhaps even psychological metrics could be used to adaptively advise learnings. Incorporating gamification principles into established evaluation frameworks will allow organizations to explore more thoroughly whether and how game-based learning promotes skills development and makes learners aware of the cyber enemy. And by using these evaluation frameworks, organizations can create a complete assessment plan. Gamification-specific adaptations are combined into the enhancing traditional training evaluation, guaranteeing the effectiveness in the cyberspace but also in reality(Rivera & Garden, 2021).

DATA COLLECTION METHODS

However, there will be some strong need for data collection methods to evaluate gamified cybersecurity training. With the appropriate model, trainers and organizations can measure learning outcomes and engagement and behavioral shifts. There are different approaches that could be employed which could be quantitative, qualitative or mixed methods approaches as illustrated in Figure 4. Both offer unique advantages, and when considered together they give a more comprehensive assessment of how effective training is or can be.

Figure 4. Data collection models

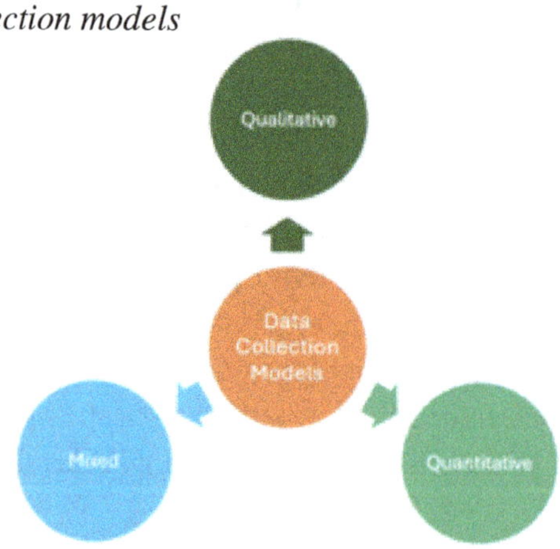

Quantitative Methods

Quantitative methods allow anyone or everyone to interpret data statistically. Gamification helps to track learner performance, engagement levels, and effectiveness of gamified cybersecurity training. Surveys are one of the most common quantitative tools used to collect structured feedback from participants. Using Likert-scale questionnaires, multiple-choice evaluations, and satisfaction surveys can be used to determine the perception of training effectiveness from learners/trainees. Another helpful mechanism is pre- and post-training assessments that measure knowledge retention and skills transference. Add to that, these assessments must highlight gaps in learning and reflect evidence of growth over time. They also generate data and analytics that provide real time insights into levels of engagement and progress. With additional metrics such as task completion rates, time spent on modules, leaderboard rankings, and in-game achievements, you can get a clearer picture of how your learners are engaging with the content. This level of analytics can help trainers tailor the content as well as the difficulty of the content for optimal learning experiences. Perhaps the most critical quantitative data is performance tracking, including automated scoring, error rates, and success rates and failures in security challenges. CTF metrics, simulations, and real-world cybersecurity actions can be scored in numbers. These objective measures give organizations objective proof of their ability to demonstrate and use cyber skills in the real world(González-Fernández, Revuelta-Domínguez, & Fernández-Sánchez, 2022).

Qualitative Methods

Quantitative methods help economize insights into numbers while qualitative methods focus on broader narratives. Experience, challenge, and motivation help to facilitate a human-centric approach to gamified training evaluation. Detailed feedback is collected through interviews with learners, trainers, and cybersecurity experts regarding the effectiveness of the training. These one-on-one conversations (useful for discoverability) reveal people's professional learning experiences, obstacles during training, and their suggestions for streamlining the process. They are also used to identify motives that provoke persisting engagement in gamified learning environments(Cespón & Lage, 2022).

Group discussions involve several learners to share their experiences to come to a discussion. During these very important sessions, players have a chance to reflect on their learning journeys, share updated insights on game mechanics and discuss the impact of operational training on their active cybersecurity awareness. Gamification involves exploring social dynamics such as competition, teamwork, and earning rewards, where focus groups are especially beneficial(Tenório, Dermeval, Monteiro, Peixoto, & Pedro, 2020).

Another useful qualitative method involves observational studies. Training sessions allow trainers or researchers to monitor learners, examine their engagement levels, interaction with the game's elements as well as how they used strategies to move from one decision point to the next. Observations give insight into nonverbal cues (frustration, excitement, collaboration) that may not be indicated in surveys or assessments. Tracking real-time behavior allows organizations to see how learners respond to the gamification challenges presented to them(Villegas, Fonseca, Peña, Bonet, & Fernández-Guinea, 2021).

Mixed-Methods Approaches

Utilizing a mixed methodology can yield a greater overall assessment of gamified cybersecurity training. By doing so, the evaluation also captures both measurable outcomes and meaningful insights, with regards to impact. A common mixed-methods approach is triangulation, which combines or compares data from different sources as a check on data accuracy. For example, if a formal assessment indicates a gain, qualitative interviews can question whether learners would be able to demonstrate their skills in practice. This aids in validating findings and pointing out discrepancies that may need additional investigation. Sequential data collection is another mixed-method strategy whereby qualitative and quantitative methods are used in phases. It is quite possible that an organization will initially administer surveys to collect quantitative feedback on learner engagement and performance. Interviews or focus groups can then be conducted to delve into why some learners did better or were more engaged than others. This way you can fly over all the quantitative trends and understand what is behind them, you can optimize your training plans(Tomé Klock et al., 2024).

Mixed-method evaluation tools commonly occur within gamified training platforms. Based on the content and platforms like yours, LMS (Learning Management Systems), Gamification Dashboards, trainers can interpret quantitative analytical data in real-time and get qualitative feedback with open-ended question-answer and discussion forums. Collectively, these data provide a clear view of how learners engage with gamified content and how the training can be customized for optimal outcomes. Employing quantitative, qualitative, and mixed methods approaches enabled organizations to create a holistic evaluation framework. So, gamified cybersecurity training can be engaging and immersive while still being relevant and appropriate to the real world(Oliveira et al., 2023).

TOOLS AND TECHNOLOGIES FOR EVALUATION

Cybersecurity is not just about firewalls and encryption, conversely it is at its core about human behavior. Studies have found that 95% of breaches in cybersecurity are human based, making effective cybersecurity training that promotes awareness and decision-making skills vital. To keep employees engaged and to get them to adhere to more secure practices, many organizations have implemented gamified training programs as depicted in Fig 5.0. But the question that is of utmost significance is how do we measure the effectiveness of these training initiatives?

That's where communication tools and technology come in handy. Gamified training will end up as a fun activity with less impact in the real world, if not accurately assessed. Also, having strong evaluation mechanisms means you can provide data-driven insights into whether and how your training objectives are being met —most importantly, whether employees are able to apply what they have learned to real cybersecurity scenarios. These tools measure not only simple participation, but also knowledge retention, skill development, behavioural adjustment and even long-term security awareness(Moseikina, Toktamysov, & Danshina, 2022).

Figure 5. Gamifications evaluation: Tools and technologies

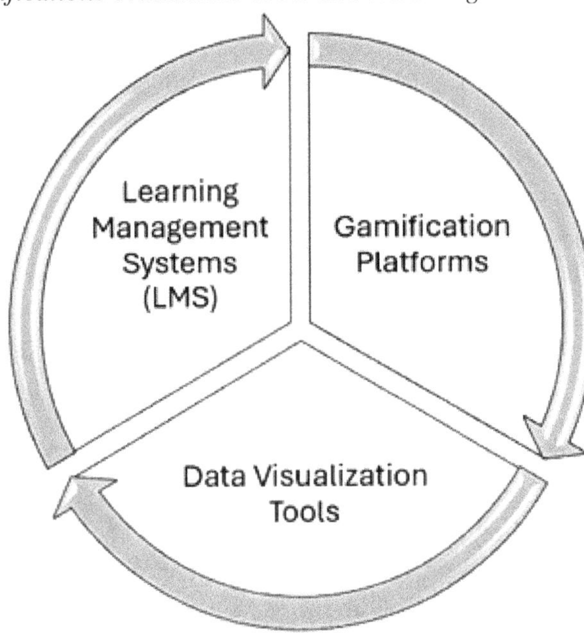

As organizations use these methods to measure training success, the future of learning is augured through a combination of prolonged and comparative efforts involving short quizzes, performance dashboards and feedback surveys. Quizzes measure just-in-time memorization, dashboards provide real-time analytics on learner engagement and progress, and feedback surveys measure qualitative impressions of learner confidence and perceived effectiveness. Together, these tools offer a robust evaluation framework that enables cybersecurity training with gamification not only to teach but also to foster sustainable behavior change(Quayyum, 2021).

Learning Management Systems (LMS) with Built-In Analytics

Learning Management Systems are the backbone of many training programs, including those for cybersecurity. An LMS serves as a centralized hub to deliver content, track learner progress, and administer assessments. In practice, an LMS in a gamified cybersecurity course might host interactive modules on topics like phishing or password safety, then automatically record quiz scores and completion rates(Handayani, Raharjo, & Putra, 2021). Key features of modern LMS platforms include user enrolment and tracking, content management (videos, simulations, quizzes), and analytics/reporting dashboards. For example, Paradiso LMS (a popular platform) allows organizations to create custom cybersecurity modules tailored to their industry threats and policies. It also supports interactive elements like quizzes and even game-like simulations to keep employees engaged. These features ensure that training isn't a dull check-the-box exercise but an active learning experience(Aprilia, Ardiansyah, & Riyanti, 2023). The advantages of using an LMS for evaluation are clear. First, all training data is in one place where managers can see who has finished the latest security awareness game, who passed the ransomware quiz, and who might need extra help. This centralized tracking is especially valuable in regulated industries (finance, healthcare) where proof of compliance training is required(Riza, Piantari, Junaeti, & Permana, 2023).

Gamification Platforms with Tracking and Reporting Features

While an LMS provides the structure, gamification platforms bring the training content to life through game mechanics. These platforms (sometimes built into an LMS, sometimes standalone) use elements like points, badges, leaderboards, and challenges to turn learning into a game-like experience. The role of gamification in evaluation is twofold: boost engagement and track nuanced behaviors that traditional tests might miss(Oke, Aliu, Tunji-Olayeni, & Abayomi, 2024). Gamified cybersecurity platforms often include real-time challenges – for example, a simulated hacking puzzle or a phishing email simulation that employees must respond to. Each action the user takes (choosing to report a suspicious email, solving a challenge correctly on the first try, etc.) is tracked(Neupane, Hansen, Fails, & Sharma, 2021). Gamification has proven benefits in driving learner motivation. Studies show it can dramatically increase participation and knowledge retention. In fact, one survey reported that 83% of employees who received gamified training felt motivated, whereas a majority of those in traditional training felt bored or disengaged. Key gamification elements that aid evaluation include:

· **Points and Badges:** Every completed training mission or quiz question can award points or badges. These provide measurable indicators of progress (e.g., an employee might earn a "Phishing Detective" badge after reporting 10 suspicious emails). Managers can track points to quantify participation and achievement levels across the team(Rodrigues et al., 2022).
· **Leaderboards:** By ranking learners based on points or completion time, leaderboards foster friendly competition. They also quickly show who are the top performers and who might be falling behind, which is valuable for identifying both high-potential security champions and those who need additional support(Balci, Secaur, & Morris, 2022).
· **Progressive Challenges:** Many gamified systems adapt to the learner's level – as someone advances, the challenges become harder (much like levels in a video game). This ensures that the evaluation is continuous and dynamic. For instance, if a user easily aces beginner-level security quizzes, the platform might present an advanced scenario next. Their performance at each level gives insight into their true skill ceiling(Trinidad, Calderón, & Ruiz, 2021).

Figure 6. Gamification elements: an overview

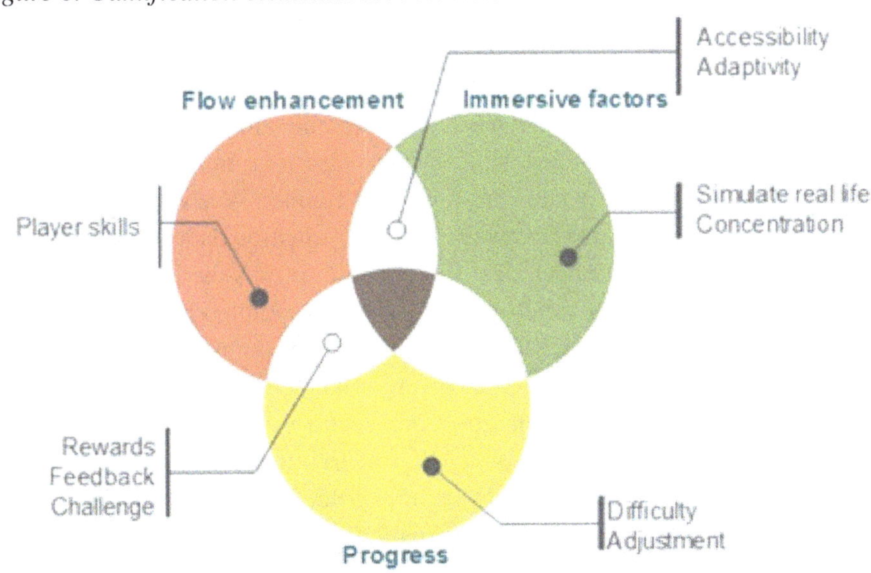

(Beristain-Colorado et al., 2021)

Data Visualization Tools for Analyzing and Presenting Results

When it comes to LMS reports and gamified platforms, the raw data can overwhelm users. Hence, this is where the data visualization tools come in and transform streams of numbers into intuitive charts and graphs. When it comes to gamified cybersecurity training, a data visualization tool can help stakeholders see which areas of the program drive the most value within minutes. For example, a dashboard could include a line graph of "Phishing Susceptibility Rate" over the past year, revealing a gratifying decline as training began to take effect(Svensson, 2022). Another chart could compare by department: maybe the Finance team has a higher average score on the security quiz than the Sales team does – a data point that might spark additional training for sales. These visual insights make it easy to look at evaluation results and take action on them! Good visualization exposes trends and outliers that may be lost in raw data(Heilbrunn, Herzig, & Schill, 2014). Best practices in training evaluation for stakeholders include using visual dashboards that allow them to easily interpret results and identify opportunities for improvement. Individuals including Learning & Development leaders can access data visualization tools – either built into an LMS or external like Tableau or Power BI – which allow this level of agility by showing real-time training data in a digestible manner. Interactivity in the dashboard, data filtering, and integration are some key functionalities of data visualization tools in this domain(Krath & Von Korflesch, 2021).

Beyond internal analytics, data visualization also helps in reporting to stakeholders. Cybersecurity training results might need to be presented to executive leadership or even the board. Presenting a clear, story-driven chart – for instance, a before-and-after comparison of incident rates pre- and post-training – can communicate the value of the training program effectively. It turns evaluation data into a compelling narrative of progress. Ultimately, data visualization makes the impact of training transparent. It ensures that the wealth of data collected (completion rates, quiz scores, behavior changes, etc.) is not just locked in spreadsheets but is readily interpretable by decision-makers. This leads to data-driven refinements in the training program – focusing on weak spots, doubling down on successes, and demonstrating return on investment. In a field where proving ROI of training is often challenging, an insightful dashboard can be worth its weight in gold(B. Y. Alothman, 2024).

Hence, combining LMS, gamification platforms, and data visualization creates a powerful ecosystem for evaluating gamified cybersecurity training. Each tool complements the others: the LMS provides structured data and content delivery, gamified platforms contribute engagement and rich behavioral metrics, and visualization tools turn all that information into actionable intelligence. Together, they address a critical need in cybersecurity education – not just to train, but to verify and improve. Moreover, the use of these evaluation technologies makes the training experience more engaging for the learners too. Learners get immediate feedback and see their progress (through points, badges, or progress charts), which keeps them motivated. Meanwhile, administrators get the feedback they need to refine content and address emerging threats or weaknesses promptly(Pitchay, Suhaimi, Alwi, Ridzuan, & Ab Halim, 2022).

CASE STUDIES: EVALUATING GAMIFIED CYBERSECURITY TRAINING PROGRAMS

Real-world case studies that move beyond theoretical models and assessment frameworks are required for evaluating gamified cybersecurity training. Case studies serve as complementary viewpoints on the application of gamification, bringing actionable information on how gamification affects engagement, knowledge retention, and behavioural change, whereas structured evaluation methods can serve as a base(Ashley et al., 2022). Organizations can evaluate successes and failures and gauge how training translates through to the real world and authentic improvement to security through examining real examples. We will discuss three very different case studies namely a corporate training program, a university course, and a public awareness campaign which exemplify how elements of gamification improve the learning experience in several environments. Together, these examples provide research-based reasons for why users in an organization should engage with, learn skills and have greater long-term awareness of cybersecurity(Hamid, Jhanjhi, Humayun, Khan, & Alsayat, 2019).

Example 1: A Corporate Training Program Using Gamified Simulations and its Impact on Employee Performance

One of the multinational financial services companies had a disturbing problem: employees kept falling for phishing attacks. Even with mandatory security awareness training, too many staff were ignoring the best practices. The company wanted a more engaging employee training style, one that emphasized cybersecurity habits rather than just knowledge that sat on a shelf then they started implementing it and they found that in one scenario, a gamified cybersecurity simulation platform for a company forced employees to protect a simulated network from cyberattacks. The system utilized role-based learning, enabling employees to take on varying cybersecurity roles, including threat analyst, incident responder, and ethical hacker(Allen, Mylonas, Vidalis, & Gritzalis, 2024). Employees earned points by correctly identifying by phishing emails, reporting security incidents, and taking prompt action during simulated cyberattacks. To boost motivation, the company introduced leaderboards, badges and a monthly challenge. Those who excelled were recognized in company-wide meetings, and the top people were given new cybersecurity responsibilities(Triantafyllou & Georgiadis, 2022). There were simulations too, in which fake phishing emails were sent to employees and their responses tracked.

Impact and Evaluation

Gamified training reduces phishing click rate to 4% (vs. 30% before training) By six months after launching the program, that figure was 8%. Those who did well in the simulations also took action and reported suspicious emails more often. IT security teams observed that the time taken for incident response was reduced by 40% when employees were more alarmed by the attack. The other important result was the cultural change in the company. Security became a joint effort rather than solely an IT concern. Employees found themselves talking about cybersecurity outside of training, exchanging tips, competing to do better. The company's CIO said training effectiveness improved not only due to the game mechanics but also because employees felt a personal stake in security.

Example 2: A University Course Incorporating CTF Competitions and its Effect on Student Engagement and Skill Development

An institution delivering a cybersecurity degree program found it had issues with student engagement in traditional lectures. The professors observed that although students grasped theoretical concepts concept, few of them gained hands-on experience in tackling actual cybersecurity issues. In order to fill this gap, the university incorporated Capture The Flag (CTF) competitions into its cybersecurity curriculum(Toccafondi, Bilancini, & Boncinelli, 2024). Implementation of this be it CTF competitions, where students were assessed based on their ability to solve cybersecurity puzzles, identify vulnerabilities, or protect digital assets. The class was designed in challenging categories such as cryptography, web security, reverse engineering, and penetration testing. Each challenge was worth points, and students raced against the clock both individually and in teams to solve them. Real-time analytics were also employed to measure learning progress beyond the competition itself. Professors monitored which students had trouble with specific security concepts, so they could give targeted help. The university also set up a mentorship system by which its top students coached others(Karagiannis & Magkos, 2020).

Impact and Evaluation

Class attendance improved by 60% after implementing CTF competitions. Students engaged more, asked deeper questions and were more excited about learning. Most said solving real-world security problems was personally satisfying, far more than rote memorization of concepts from textbook material. One important achievement was the development of technical skills. In earlier years, only 40 percent of students passed the university's ethical hacking certification exam. After implementing the gamified strategy, the pass rate jumped to 75%. And more students went into cybersecurity careers, with a huge uptick in internship placements in security firms. Perhaps the most telling impact was students continued to participate in CTF competitions even after the course concluded. Some participated in international cybersecurity competitions, donning their motto like a jersey as they competed in professional hacking contests. Professors noted that gamified learning not only boosted engagement levels but also fostered a long-term passion for cybersecurity.

Example 3: A Public Awareness Campaign Using a Gamified App to Teach Basic Cybersecurity Concepts

A government cybersecurity agency wanted to promote greater public awareness of the risks of using the internet. Studies indicated that many citizens (especially seniors and young adults) are not equipped with basic cybersecurity skills. Standard publicity campaigns, including posters and television ads, had little effect. The agency required a more engaging means of informing the public. After implementing the agency created a mobile app that gamified learning about cybersecurity(Bacud & Mäses, 2021). The app was designed to teach concepts like password safety, spam-phishing recognition and safe social media habits through short interactive games. Users "levelled up" and received badges when they completed security challenges. To foster participation, the app was paired with a nationwide contest where top scorers won prizes including free security software and discounts for online services. The agency also partnered with schools and community centers to incorporate the app into educational workshops(Qusa & Tarazi, 2021).

Impact and Evaluation

The app became so popular that less than three months after the launch it reached over 500,000 downloads. Three-quarters of the users reported feeling more confident about their ability to identify potential threats online after playing the games, surveys showed. Data analysis showed the average time spent by each user per session was twenty minutes, far longer than the duration of typical cybersecurity awareness videos or articles. One of the more startling results concerned senior citizens. At first, there was worry that older adults would be turned off by a gamified app. However, community classes got seniors using the app and taking part in the security challenges. Feedback revealed many felt encouraged to manage their own online security. The agency also observed a drop in reported phishing scams during the campaign period, meaning that heightened awareness translated to better behavior in the real world. Due to the success and popularity of the original initiative, the UK government extended the initiative to include more advanced cybersecurity challenges and offered certification to users who completed all the levels.

The above case studies have demonstrated that Gamified training produces noticeable improvements in cybersecurity habits and in the corporate example, phishing click rates were reduced significantly once employees interacted with a mock training familiarizing them with the training. In education, there were measurable and observable benefits to both engagement and skill proficiency as students solved hands-on challenges. Lastly, awareness learned from this public app, in terms of knowledge retention and implementation of real-world cybersecurity recommended practices.

To conclude, the above discussed use cases have demonstrated on how gamification turns cybersecurity training into an experience that is no longer passive but active and results driven. It helps to further engage participants and improve memory retention and is already being utilized as an effective tool in corporate, academic and public awareness programs to promote cybersecurity best practice. Through the use of simulations, competitions, and interactive challenges, organizations can develop cybersecurity training as not only a one-off event but also an ongoing journey of learning. This is the beauty of an engagement style of learning, when training is fun and immersive, it sticks.

CHALLENGES IN EVALUATING GAMIFIED TRAINING

Gamified Cybersecurity training is not without its own problems when it comes to the evaluation part of it, specifically in terms of the data which needs to be both accurate and reliable. Gamified solutions tend to produce a lot of data, from completion rates to engagement scores and in-game performance statistics. Nonetheless, the data that is available does not always reflect learning outcomes(Fuchs, 2024). For example, a learner could do very well (or poorly, for that matter) on a simulated challenge and then have problems transferring that knowledge to actual life situations. Automated tracking tools can misinterpret certain actions, which can in some cases inflate performance scores. The organizations need to cross-verify in-game metrics with real-world performance evaluations, like security audits or hands-on assessments, to ensure accuracy(Kim, Zhong, & Liu, 2023).

A second challenge is bias in self-reported data. Most evaluation tools are based on surveys and feedback forms asking learners to rate their understanding and confidence levels. But self-perception is not always in line with actual skill development. Some participants may have inflated egos while others suffer from an inferiority complex even though they perform well. Another source of bias can occur if learners give extremely positive feedback (positive bias) in order to please the teacher (social desirability) or to avoid negative consequences (fear) for their own performance. To counter this, evaluation shouldn't rely solely on personal insights but include objective measurements, such as performance on post-training tests of competencies and live defensive exercises(Bennani, Maalel, & Ben Ghezala, 2022).

The long-term impact and fact behavior change is probably one of the hardest parts of gamified training evaluation. Most assessments are built upon short-term knowledge reinforcement while cybersecurity skills need extensive sustainability. A learner who masters a training module today may fall back into bad security habits months down the line. Retention is a challenge for traditional training programs and the gamified models are no different. The problem is measuring if and how often students implement best practices in their jobs. Organizations need to do follow-up assessments to assess the level of retention with refresher challenges and real-world simulation modeling to determine the impact of permanent behavior changes. Without long-term follow-up, it's impossible to tell if gamified training works to improve security awareness and reduce risk over time(Al-Rayes et al., 2022).

BEST PRACTICES FOR EFFECTIVE EVALUATION

Clearly defined and measurable objectives are the key to a solid evaluation framework. Implementing effective gamified cybersecurity training is also a challenge if goals are not well defined. Goals and objectives should be organization-specific, actionable, and precise. So, rather than saying things like "improve cybersecurity awareness," a better goal would be "cut phishing email click rates by 50 percent in six months." Clearly defined targets also guide trainers on the proper evaluation tools to use and make certain that the successes of training are measured against actual improvements in performance(Wang, Hsu, & Fang, 2022).

Using a single reference point to judge whether training worked or not may yield to misleading results. A good balance in evaluation encompasses various metrics to encompass different aspects of achievement. Consider engagement analytical data, assessment scores and behavioral changes. A learner might complete a training module or score well on quizzes, but if they cannot transfer the knowledge into real-life security situations, the training has failed. Organizations can get a better view of learning impact when quantitative statistics (like task completion percentages and incident response times) are aligned with qualitative insights (like peer reviews and self-assessments).

It should never be a one-off procedure. Organizations should periodically revisit their evaluation processes to ensure they remain relevant and effective over time. Cybersecurity threats are ever changing and so too must training programs. Collecting learns (Caserman, Baumgartner, Göbel, & Korn, 2024)feedback regularly along with their performance after the training allows organizations to identify gaps and improvement areas. If gameplay mechanics are not changing the security behavior of an organization, then that gamification is not the right solution. Iterative refinement helps make sure training stays relevant, impactful and able to achieve real behavior change over time.

FUTURE TRENDS IN EVALUATION

As a result of the emergence of advancements in artificial intelligence (AI), biometric analysis, and the further push for standardized assessment frameworks; the evaluation of gamified cybersecurity training shall experience a seismic shift. As cybersecurity threats (and threats actors) become more sophisticated, so too must the processes of measuring and improving cybersecurity training effectiveness. Evaluation approaches in the future will not just assess knowledge retention but will also analyze behavioral patterns, cognitive responses, and predictive learning outcomes throughout the learning path, ensuring that training is impactful in real-life scenarios(Sharma & Sharma, 2023).

The Role of AI and Machine Learning in Predictive Analytics and Personalized Feedback

The conventional approach to assessment is based on evaluating learners and their assessments are post-training assessments which give sense on how a learner performed only at the time when he has completed a module. But with AI-powered analytics you can continuously track learner performance in real time, identify patterns, predict future behavior. Machine learning models can create risk factors, such as a participant who consistently performs poorly in certain attack simulations, or who fails to recognize phishing attempts. In place of a uniform classroom, we can build adaptive learning environments, where AI autonomously levels up the challenge, offers in-the-moment nudges or suggests complementary sources of knowledge(Khan, Jhanjhi, & Sujatha, 2022).

AI is also making a key difference with automated feedback systems. Most gamified training today is based on static feedback, where learners receive predetermined responses based on the performance. AI can revolutionize feedback by making it dynamic and personalized — telling learners which mistakes to correct as well as why they did, in fact, make those mistakes. For instance, if a participant stalled before responding to a simulated phishing email, AI can examine that delay and determine from data when individuals typically hesitate and correlate hesitation with tips on how to instill certainty in a security decision though AI. Such insights can be refined over time through AI to deliver long-term tracking of behaviors to help organizations measure whether training does in fact mitigate their exposure to risk and improve their cybersecurity awareness(Zaman et al., 2022).

Integrating Biometric Data (e.g., Eye Tracking, Heart Rate) to Measure Engagement and Stress Levels

Evaluating the efficacy of cybersecurity skills development is particularly difficult when trying to predict how learners will respond in a high-stress environment. Existing assessment tools focus on knowledge transfer measurements, neglecting emotional reactions and cognitive effort—the key components of cybersecurity decisions. Adding biometric data: Eye tracking, heart rate variability, and facial recognition can offer additional levels of insight into engagement, stress, and cognitive effort in training(Awad, Babu, Barka, & Shuaib, 2024).

Eye-tracking technology, for example, may show learners where they are looking during a simulated exercise of an attack. Users frequently checking non-critical items (such as return and replay messages) instead of critical component whereabouts (such as file transfer or store notifications) should raise suspicion as they are likely struggling to efficiently pinpoint threats. Likewise, heart rate & skin conductivity sensors that measure stress response will allow trainers to see whether participants manage to remain calm and relaxed or whether their anxiety levels rise in the form of increased perspiration when they are presented with simulated attack conditions(McStay, 2020).

Such biometric insights may provide adaptive training systems wherein challenges are adjusted in real time. When biometric data reveal that a learner is stressed too much, the system can modify task difficulty, offer real-time guidance or suggest or implement stress-management techniques. On the flip side, if a learner is showing low cognitive engagement, the training might set up more difficult tasks to keep engaged and boost retention. The result is that the training that is fully educational but also carries psychological underpinnings that make it even more effective in preparing people for the many pressure-laden situations that they will encounter in the cyber arena(Lien & Vhaduri, 2023).

Developing Standardized Evaluation Frameworks for Gamified Cybersecurity Training

Despite the growing popularity of gamified cybersecurity training, there is still no universally accepted framework for evaluating its effectiveness. Many organizations rely on customized assessment models, they can only compare the outcomes of trainings between varying companies and industries with great difficulty. Since no standard via which all gamified training methods are reliably judged, is it hard to say which of these approaches are really working and how that translates into practical gains for cybersecurity(Nguyen & Tran, 2023).

Industry leaders and researchers are working to set up standardized evaluation frameworks that, in addition to successful engagement rates or quiz scores, define those KPI (key performance indicators) which can measure effectiveness beyond just gamification allure. In other words, metrics such as behavior change, real-world decision-making accuracy, speed of response to incidents and keeping knowledge long-term are all factors used to judge how good your training makes people cybersafe(Henrikki, 2021).

One promising approach is integrating longitudinal studies into evaluation frameworks. Instead of immediately measuring the effectiveness of training upon completion, organizations could conduct multi-stage assessments for several months to see if learners keep up their skills over time. This long-term perspective helps tell whether gamified cybersecurity training results in permanent changes in behavior, rather than just temporary improvements(Nguyen & Tran, 2023).

A third developing trend is the creation of cybersecurity training benchmarks--where industries share anonymized performance data from training to set global standards. By comparing cybersecurity training results among a range of different organizations, industries can discover good ideas and common skill deficits. They refine their gamified training strategies by means of these multiple viewpoints. Such a date-based approach to standardizing training ensures that cybersecurity is always measurable, scalable if necessary, and continues in development as new cyber threats emerge(Suresh Babu & Dhakshina Moorthy, 2024).

CONCLUSION

Gamified security education is now an effective method of building security awareness, technical skills, and behavioural change. But whether it can be effective will depend on how well it is measured. Robust evaluation takes much more into account than participation and engagement exciting as those numbers maybe it measures how much knowledge sticks, how well skills transfer and whether long-term security hygiene is established. To facilitate all such strategies, organizations implement multiple tools and technologies such as Learning Management Systems (LMS), AI-driven analytics, biometric tracking, and gamification platforms to analyze learner progress and inform decision-making in real time. Cyber threats are continuously evolving, so too must the training.

Continuous evaluation and refinement, using techniques such as long-term tracking, adaptive learning and real-world testing, becomes necessary to ensure training stays relevant and effective. The overall chapter has discussed extensively how gamification across corporate environments, universities and public awareness campaigns increased engagement and made learning converting into actionable security skills. As we look ahead, factors such as AI, immersive technologies (VR and AR), and standardized evaluation frameworks have defined how gamified education is evaluated, making sure it is quantifiable, impactful, and relatable to real-world cybersecurity hindrances. By prioritizing effective evaluation, organizations will have the opportunity to not only ensure gamified cybersecurity education is engaging, but also it will be a vital pillar in reinforcing security measures throughout the organizations.

Recap of the Importance of Measuring Success in Gamified Cybersecurity Training

In this piece, we have discussed the key aspects of assessing gamified cybersecurity training. Engagement metrics cannot measure what is considered success. However, enthusiasm has it limits; just because you had fun playing some games and ranked highly, does not make you an expert to secure a real-world environment. An enhanced evaluation approach looks to the extent to which learners have learnt, applied and maintained these capabilities over time. The assessments that are conducted pre- and post-training offer a useful measure of what has been retained by participants; however, this information only becomes valuable when cross-referenced with performance-based measures like successful outcomes in simulations, incident response times, and the ability to identify security threats in live environments. Another key measure is behavioral impact; organizations must ensure training translations, enabling employees to spot and respond to threats more effectively and make better and faster decisions under pressure, resulting in less risk of compromise. Are the training knowledge gains temporary or lasting behavioral changes that can be determined through longitudinal studies, follow-up evaluations, and flying equipment in the real world?

This is further aided by using modern technologies for strong value in evaluation process. LMS includes information on course completion, assessment results, etc. Social Leaderboards, badges, notifications etc. real-time analytics from sources like Gamification platforms that track the activity along with in-game behavior and decision-making processes. Even more, AI can help refine evaluations by analysing test scores to predict weaknesses and customize a training program based on users' performance. Biometric data such as eye-tracking and heart rate monitoring provides another level of analysis, indicating cognitive engagement levels, as well as stress responses, during train scenarios. These technologies help create clearer visibility of the way learning, interacts, and engages, with the content so that actionable insights can be derived for refining the content and delivery methods. But there is no one metric or tool that can effectively tell the tale of the training. A good evaluation approach harnesses different data sources, generating a variety of quantitative and qualitative perspectives that can facilitate learning about the relationship between training, learning, and the types of impact on security that are of interest.

As challenges evolve in cybersecurity, so too must the training; evaluation must become an ongoing process rather than a one-time assessment. The problem is not the quality of the material most of the time, rather it is the lack of iterative improvement that kills so many programs. A snapshot never reflects the way learners modify their behavior over time or how successfully they are functioning in authentic contexts. Organizations should create a feedback loop approach in which training is constantly measured, improved, and refined to reflect the new invasion techniques used by cybercriminals. For this we need long-term tracking, real-world testing, and adaptive learning modes that shift depending on the performance of the learner. AI and machine learning will be crucial in this process, detecting learning gaps and automatically modifying training material to counter specific weaknesses. (As the methods we use to train become more sophisticated, so too must our means of assessing training effectiveness.

Encouragement for Continuous Evaluation and Improvement

Threats are complex and evolving in nature, and cybersecurity is constantly changing. As attackers evolve their tactics, organizations need to adapt their defenses, and that includes the methods they use to train and educate employees. In a risk environment that is ever-changing, a one-off training program is not the answer. One of the reasons cybersecurity training initiatives fail is not that the content is poor, yet that there is no continuous evaluation method. A single evaluation at the conclusion of a course can signal short-term retention of course knowledge, but very little in the way of measuring how well learners actually apply their skills in practice over time. Failure to continually improve training programs can lead organizations to have a false sense of security as they become deceptively outdated over time.

Having cybersecurity training that's constantly evaluated, measured and refined is the ideal approach to keeping training relevant and effective. It requires considering metrics such as post-training performance and behavioral modification rather than focusing on metrics like course completion or quiz results. Instead of measuring only whether learners can answer questions a few minutes after training, longitudinal tracking enables organizations to see how well learners retain that knowledge weeks or months later. Real-world testing, on the other hand, gives additional insights by observing how employees react to real-world security threats, like mock phishing attacks or incident response scenarios. Not only do these methods help identify whether training is doing something to behaviors around security at work, rather than just theoretical knowledge.

Continuous evaluation is another key feature of training solutions powered by AI-techs such as machine learning, that monitors learner performance and dynamically tailors training content based on progress of individuals. If a learner has difficulty mastering particular security concepts, AI-driven systems can provide personalized modules that reinforce those areas. By the same token, feedback loops, which assimilate learnings from the learners, security teams and behavioral analytics, help ensure that training is relevant and reactive to new threats on emerging. Without this iterative approach, organizations run the risk of training employees on outdated threats while potentially neglecting to cover the most pressing cybersecurity challenges impacting today and tomorrow. Organizations that adopt continuous assessment of staff will be in a better place to evolve their plans and make sure their cyber professionals are being set up to succeed in this dynamic digital threat environment.

Preview of the Next Chapter: Future Directions in Gamification and Cybersecurity Education

This is only a fraction of the evolution of gamified cybersecurity training. With advances in technology and ever-more sophisticated cyber threats, we need to be evolving the way we teach, train and assess cybersecurity professionals. The following chapter will examine future trends in gamification and cybersecurity education, highlighting the potential impacts of new technologies and creative pedagogical approaches to security skill building and evaluation. Artificial intelligence and adaptive learning systems are transforming the landscape of cybersecurity training. AI-powered platforms can analyze learner activity in real time, determine their strengths or weaknesses, and adapt the training material accordingly. Rather than a generic training format, AI will customize training sessions to keep learners focused on regions in which they struggle the most. All of this will result in more effective and targeted training experiences that minimize learning fatigue while ensuring skill retention.

Apart from AI, one of the emerging trends will be the use of immersive technologies like Virtual Reality (VR) and Augmented Reality (AR) will facilitate highly realistic cybersecurity simulations. These environments will enable learners to simulate real-world cyber risks in an isolated and supervised environment. From response to simulated ransomware attacks to practicing digital forensics in a virtual lab, VR and AR is going to make cybersecurity training more engaging, interactive, and hands-on than ever before. You will also explore the evolution of standardized evaluation frameworks to ensure that gamified cybersecurity training can be measured against consistent metrics regardless of industry. Organizations are better equipped to compare results against universal metrics and will refine methodologies to better align with the metrics and continue improving learning as a result.

The future of cybersecurity education will be more intelligent, immersive and measurable. Revolutionizing cybersecurity training: AI, gamification, and immersive learning are the future. Next, we'll explore these transformative trends and how gamification, AI, and immersive learning will define the future of cybersecurity training. Educators, organizations, and security professionals will look toward the latest developments in the learning landscape to prepare for the next generation of innovation in cybersecurity education, ensuring that learning is engaging, adaptive and capable of combating evolving threats within prevalent cyber-attack vectors.

REFERENCES

Al-Rayes, S., Al Yaqoub, F. A., Alfayez, A., Alsalman, D., Alanezi, F., Alyousef, S., & Aljabri, D. (2022). Gaming elements, applications, and challenges of gamification in healthcare. *Informatics in Medicine Unlocked*, *31*, 100974. DOI: 10.1016/j.imu.2022.100974

Allen, A., Mylonas, A., Vidalis, S., & Gritzalis, D. (2024). Smart homes under siege: Assessing the robustness of physical security against wireless network attacks. *Computers & Security*, *139*, 103687. DOI: 10.1016/j.cose.2023.103687

Almagrabi, A. O. (2023). Challenges and vulnerability evaluation of smart cities in IoT device based on cybersecurity mechanism. *Expert Systems: International Journal of Knowledge Engineering and Neural Networks*, *40*(4), e13113. Advance online publication. DOI: 10.1111/exsy.13113

Alothman, B. Y. (2024). *Cyber gamification: implementing gamified adaptive learning environments for effective cyber security teams education.* Paper presented at the Proceedings of the 2024 5th International Conference on Education Development and Studies. DOI: 10.1145/3669947.3669953

Alothman, B. Y. (2024). *Cyber Gamification: Implementing Gamified Adaptive Learning Environments for Effective Cyber Security Teams Education: Enhancing Team Skills and Engagement through Interactive Learning Environments.* Paper presented at the ACM International Conference Proceeding Series.

Aprilia, T., Ardiansyah, A. R., & Riyanti, H. (2023). The feasibility of interactive multimedia and online quiz based gamification on learning management system (LMS) thematic learning courses. *Jurnal Prima Edukasia*, *11*(1), 120–133. DOI: 10.21831/jpe.v11i1.55533

Ashley, T. D., Kwon, R., Gourisetti, S. N. G., Katsis, C., Bonebrake, C. A., & Boyd, P. A. (2022). Gamification of cybersecurity for workforce development in critical infrastructure. *IEEE Access : Practical Innovations, Open Solutions*, *10*, 112487–112501. DOI: 10.1109/ACCESS.2022.3216711

Ashraf, H., Jhanjhi, N. Z., Brohi, S. N., & Muzafar, S. (2024). A Comprehensive Exploration of DDoS Attacks and Cybersecurity Imperatives in the Digital Age. In *Navigating Cyber Threats and Cybersecurity in the Logistics Industry* (pp. 236–257). IGI Global. DOI: 10.4018/979-8-3693-3816-2.ch009

Awad, A. I., Babu, A., Barka, E., & Shuaib, K. (2024). AI-powered biometrics for Internet of Things security: A review and future vision. *Journal of Information Security and Applications*, *82*, 103748. DOI: 10.1016/j.jisa.2024.103748

Bacud, M. L., & Mäses, S. (2021). *Game-based learning for cybersecurity awareness training programmes in the public sector.* Paper presented at the ECEL 2021 20th European Conference on e-Learning.

Balci, S., Secaur, J. M., & Morris, B. J. (2022). Comparing the effectiveness of badges and leaderboards on academic performance and motivation of students in fully versus partially gamified online physics classes. *Education and Information Technologies, 27*(6), 8669–8704. DOI: 10.1007/s10639-022-10983-z PMID: 35308640

Bennani, S., Maalel, A., & Ben Ghezala, H. (2022). Adaptive gamification in E-learning: A literature review and future challenges. *Computer Applications in Engineering Education, 30*(2), 628–642. DOI: 10.1002/cae.22477

Bergamo, P. A. S., Streng, E., Haas, M., Safari, M., Rosenkranz, J., & Ghorbani, Y. On the Use of Modeling and Simulation for the Gamification of Process Operators Trainings. *Available at SSRN* 5133645. DOI: 10.2139/ssrn.5133645

Beristain-Colorado, M., Ambros-Antemate, J., Vargas Treviño, M., Gutiérrez-Gutiérrez, J., & Rodríguez, A. (2021). Standardizing the Development of Serious Games for Physical Rehabilitation: Conceptual Framework Proposal. *JMIR Serious Games, 9*(2), e25854. DOI: 10.2196/25854 PMID: 34185003

Capatina, A., Juarez-Varon, D., Micu, A., & Micu, A. E. (2024). Leveling up in corporate training: Unveiling the power of gamification to enhance knowledge retention, knowledge sharing, and job performance. *Journal of Innovation & Knowledge, 9*(3), 100530. DOI: 10.1016/j.jik.2024.100530

Caserman, P., Baumgartner, K. A., Göbel, S., & Korn, O. (2024). A best practice for gamification in large companies: An extensive study focusing inter-generational acceptance. *Multimedia Tools and Applications, 83*(12), 35175–35195. DOI: 10.1007/s11042-023-16877-7

Cespón, M. T., & Lage, J. M. D. (2022). Gamification, online learning and motivation: A quantitative and qualitative analysis in higher education. *Contemporary Educational Technology, 14*(4), ep381. DOI: 10.30935/cedtech/12297

Fuchs, K. (2024). Challenges with gamification in higher education: A narrative review with implications for educators and policymakers. *International Journal of Changes in Education, 1*(1), 51–56. DOI: 10.47852/bonviewIJCE32021604

González-Fernández, A., Revuelta-Domínguez, F.-I., & Fernández-Sánchez, M. R. (2022). Models of instructional Design in Gamification: A systematic review of the literature. *Education Sciences, 12*(1), 44. DOI: 10.3390/educsci12010044

Hamid, B., Jhanjhi, N., Humayun, M., Khan, A., & Alsayat, A. (2019). *Cyber security issues and challenges for smart cities: A survey.* Paper presented at the 2019 13th International Conference on Mathematics, Actuarial Science, Computer Science and Statistics (MACS). DOI: 10.1109/MACS48846.2019.9024768

Handayani, P. W., Raharjo, S. R., & Putra, P. H. (2021). Active student learning through gamification in a learning management system. *Electronic Journal of e-Learning, 19*(6), 601–613. DOI: 10.34190/ejel.19.6.2089

Heilbrunn, B., Herzig, P., & Schill, A. (2014, 8-11 Dec. 2014). *Tools for Gamification Analytics: A Survey.* Paper presented at the 2014 IEEE/ACM 7th International Conference on Utility and Cloud Computing.

Henrikki, S.-P. (2021). AI Ethics - Critical Reflections on Embedding Ethical Frameworks in AI Technology. 311-329. DOI: 10.1007/978-3-030-77431-8_20

Karagiannis, S., & Magkos, E. (2020). Adapting CTF challenges into virtual cybersecurity learning environments. *Information and Computer Security, 29*(1), 105–132. DOI: 10.1108/ICS-04-2019-0050

Khan, A., Jhanjhi, N., Alı, G. A., Ray, S. K., & Wassan, S. (2025). Case Studies and Applications of Generative AI in Real-World Cybersecurity Scenarios.

Khan, A., Jhanjhi, N., Hamid, D. H. H., Omar, H. A. H. B. H., Amsaad, F., & Ashraf, H. (2025). Reshaping Cybersecurity for Supply Chain Sustainability in IR 4.0 and 5.0.

Khan, A., Jhanjhi, N. Z., & Sujatha, R. (2022). Emerging Industry Revolution IR 4.0 Issues and Challenges. In *Cyber Security Applications for Industry 4.0* (pp. 151-169): Chapman and Hall/CRC.

Kim, J. B., Zhong, C., & Liu, H. (2023). What You Need to Know about Gamification Process of Cybersecurity Hands-on Lab Exercises: Lessons and Challenges. *Journal of Information Systems Education, 34*(4), 387–405. https://www.scopus.com/inward/record.uri?eid=2-s2.0-85177421937&partnerID=40&md5=8d9dff6a3e8330e15e9d97d65f999937

Krath, J., & Von Korflesch, H. F. (2021). Designing gamification and persuasive systems: A systematic literature review. *GamiFIN*, 100-109. Le, N. H. Guide to Gamification in Edtech: Key Elements, Successful Strategies & Top Examples. Retrieved from https://smartdev.com/guide-to-gamification-in-edtech-key-elements-successful-strategies-top-examples/

Lien, C.-W., & Vhaduri, S. (2023). Challenges and opportunities of biometric user authentication in the age of iot: A survey. *ACM Computing Surveys, 56*(1), 1–37. DOI: 10.1145/3603705

McStay, A. (2020). Emotional AI, soft biometrics and the surveillance of emotional life: An unusual consensus on privacy. *Big Data & Society*, *7*(1). Advance online publication. DOI: 10.1177/2053951720904386

Moseikina, M., Toktamysov, S., & Danshina, S. (2022). Modern technologies and gamification in historical education. *Simulation & Gaming*, *53*(2), 135–156. DOI: 10.1177/10468781221075965

Neupane, A., Hansen, D., Fails, J. A., & Sharma, A. (2021). The role of steps and game elements in gamified fitness tracker apps: A systematic review. *Multimodal Technologies and Interaction*, *5*(2), 5. DOI: 10.3390/mti5020005

Nguyen, M. T., & Tran, M. Q. (2023). Balancing security and privacy in the digital age: An in-depth analysis of legal and regulatory frameworks impacting cybersecurity practices. *International Journal of Intelligent Automation and Computing*, *6*(5), 1–12.

Oke, A. E., Aliu, J., Tunji-Olayeni, P., & Abayomi, T. (2024). Application of gamification for sustainable construction: An evaluation of the challenges. *Construction Innovation*, *24*(4), 1066–1084. DOI: 10.1108/CI-09-2022-0247

Oliveira, W., Hamari, J., Shi, L., Toda, A. M., Rodrigues, L., Palomino, P. T., & Isotani, S. (2023). Tailored gamification in education: A literature review and future agenda. *Education and Information Technologies*, *28*(1), 373–406. DOI: 10.1007/s10639-022-11122-4

Pitchay, S. A., Suhaimi, A. S., Alwi, N. H. M., Ridzuan, F., & Ab Halim, A. H. (2022). Enhancing cyber-attacks awareness via mobile gamification techniques. *International Journal of Advanced Research in Technology and Innovation*, *4*(2), 69–84.

Puig, A., Rodríguez, I., Rodríguez, Á., & Gallego, I. (2023). Evaluating learner engagement with gamification in online courses. *Applied Sciences (Basel, Switzerland)*, *13*(3), 1535. DOI: 10.3390/app13031535

Quayyum, F. (2021). *Cyber security education for children through gamification: Challenges and research perspectives.* Paper presented at the Methodologies and Intelligent Systems for Technology Enhanced Learning, 10th International Conference. Workshops: Volume 2. DOI: 10.1007/978-3-030-52287-2_26

Qusa, H., & Tarazi, J. (2021). *Cyber-hero: A gamification framework for cyber security awareness for high schools students.* Paper presented at the 2021 IEEE 11th annual computing and communication workshop and conference (CCWC). DOI: 10.1109/CCWC51732.2021.9375847

Ranganathan, A., & Benson, A. (2020). A numbers game: Quantification of work, auto-gamification, and worker productivity. *American Sociological Review*, *85*(4), 573–609. DOI: 10.1177/0003122420936665

Rivera, E. S., & Garden, C. L. P. (2021). Gamification for student engagement: A framework. *Journal of Further and Higher Education*, *45*(7), 999–1012. DOI: 10.1080/0309877X.2021.1875201

Riza, L. S., Piantari, E., Junaeti, E., & Permana, I. S. (2023). Implementation of the Gamification Concept in the Development of a Learning Management System to Improve Students' Cognitive In Basic Programming Subjects Towards a Smart Learning Environment. *ADI Journal on Recent Innovation*, *5*(1), 43–53.

Rodrigues, L., Toda, A. M., Oliveira, W., Palomino, P. T., Vassileva, J., & Isotani, S. (2022). Automating gamification personalization to the user and beyond. *IEEE Transactions on Learning Technologies*, *15*(2), 199–212. DOI: 10.1109/TLT.2022.3162409

Shah, I. A., Jhanjhi, N., & Laraib, A. (2023). Cybersecurity and Blockchain Usage in Contemporary Business. In *Handbook of Research on Cybersecurity Issues and Challenges for Business and FinTech Applications* (pp. 49–64). IGI Global.

Shah, I. A., Jhanjhi, N., & Ray, S. K. (2024). Artificial Intelligence Applications in the Context of the Security Framework for the Logistics Industry. In *Advances in Explainable AI Applications for Smart Cities* (pp. 297–316). IGI Global. DOI: 10.4018/978-1-6684-6361-1.ch011

Shahid, H., Ashraf, H., Jhanjhi, N., & Zam, Q.-u. A. Z. (2025). Reshaping Cybersecurity of Wireless Sensor Networks Using Energy-Optimized Approach Against Wormhole Attack. In *Reshaping CyberSecurity With Generative AI Techniques* (pp. 125-172): IGI Global.

Sharma, D., & Sharma, J. (2023). *Evolution of gamification, its implications, and its statistical impact on the society.* Paper presented at the International Conference on Emerging Trends in Design & Arts. DOI: 10.29121/shodhkosh.v4.i2SE.2023.456

Sindiramutty, S. R., Jhanjhi, N. Z., Tan, C. E., Khan, N. A., Shah, B., & Manchuri, A. R. (2024). Cybersecurity Measures for Logistics Industry. In *Navigating Cyber Threats and Cybersecurity in the Logistics Industry* (pp. 1–58). IGI Global. DOI: 10.4018/979-8-3693-3816-2.ch001

Stefan, H., Mortimer, M., & Horan, B. (2023). Evaluating the effectiveness of virtual reality for safety-relevant training: A systematic review. *Virtual Reality (Waltham Cross)*, *27*(4), 2839–2869. DOI: 10.1007/s10055-023-00843-7

Suresh Babu, S., & Dhakshina Moorthy, A. (2024). Application of artificial intelligence in adaptation of gamification in education: A literature review. *Computer Applications in Engineering Education*, *32*(1), e22683. DOI: 10.1002/cae.22683

Svensson, J. (2022). *Investigating the use of Gamification in data presentation.* (Independent thesis Advanced level (professional degree) Student thesis). Retrieved from http://urn.kb.se/resolve?urn=urn:nbn:se:umu:diva-200010 DiVA database.

Tenório, K., Dermeval, D., Monteiro, M., Peixoto, A., & Pedro, A. (2020). *Raising teachers empowerment in gamification design of adaptive learning systems: a qualitative research.* Paper presented at the Artificial Intelligence in Education: 21st International Conference, AIED 2020, Ifrane, Morocco, July 6–10, 2020, Proceedings, Part I 21. DOI: 10.1007/978-3-030-52237-7_42

Thomas, N. J., Baral, R., & Crocco, O. S. (2022). Gamification for HRD: Systematic review and future research directions. *Human Resource Development Review*, *21*(2), 198–224. DOI: 10.1177/15344843221074859

Toccafondi, N., Bilancini, E., & Boncinelli, L. (2024). *Learning CyberSecurity with Story-Driven CTF Challenges: CyberTrials 2023.* Paper presented at the Communications in Computer and Information Science. DOI: 10.1007/978-3-031-67351-1_21

Tomé Klock, A. C., Palomino, P. T., Rodrigues, L. A. L., Toda, A. M., Simanke, S., Spors, V., . . . Hamari, J. (2024). Gamification towards and alongside equity, diversity and inclusion: Looking back to move forward. *new media & society*, 14614448241254028.

Triantafyllou, S., & Georgiadis, C. (2022). Gamification of MOOCs and security awareness in corporate training.

Trinidad, M., Calderón, A., & Ruiz, M. (2021). GoRace: A multi-context and narrative-based gamification suite to overcome gamification technological challenges. *IEEE Access : Practical Innovations, Open Solutions*, *9*, 65882–65905. DOI: 10.1109/ACCESS.2021.3076291

Ulmer, J., Braun, S., Cheng, C.-T., Dowey, S., & Wollert, J. (2020). Human-centered gamification framework for manufacturing systems. *Procedia CIRP*, *93*, 670–675. DOI: 10.1016/j.procir.2020.04.076

Villegas, E., Fonseca, D., Peña, E., Bonet, P., & Fernández-Guinea, S. (2021). Qualitative assessment of effective gamification design processes using motivators to identify game mechanics. *Sensors (Basel)*, *21*(7), 2556. DOI: 10.3390/s21072556 PMID: 33917409

Wang, Y.-F., Hsu, Y.-F., & Fang, K. (2022). The key elements of gamification in corporate training–The Delphi method. *Entertainment Computing*, *40*, 100463. DOI: 10.1016/j.entcom.2021.100463

Yamani, H. A. (2021). A conceptual framework for integrating gamification in elearning systems based on instructional design model. *International Journal of Emerging Technologies in Learning*, *16*(4), 14. DOI: 10.3991/ijet.v16i04.15693

Zaman, S. K. U., Jehangiri, A. I., Maqsood, T., Umar, A. I., Khan, M. A., Jhanjhi, N. Z., Shorfuzzaman, M., & Masud, M. (2022). COME-UP: Computation offloading in mobile edge computing with LSTM based user direction prediction. *Applied Sciences (Basel, Switzerland)*, *12*(7), 3312. DOI: 10.3390/app12073312

Zhong, C., Kim, J. B. J. B., & Liu, H. (2024). The Art of Inclusive Gamification in Cybersecurity Training. *IEEE Security and Privacy*, *22*(5), 40–51. DOI: 10.1109/MSEC.2024.3427666

Chapter 16
Gamification Tools for Social Engineering Attack Awareness:
An AI-Driven Approach

Usharani Bhimavarapu
https://orcid.org/0000-0002-0246-1420
Department of Computer Science and Engineering, Koneru Lakshmaiah Education Foundation, Vaddeswaram, India

ABSTRACT

This research investigates the application of gamification elements with deep learning methods to improve cybersecurity training, in this case, awareness of social engineering attacks. A quasi-experimental approach was utilized, where 125 undergraduate students were assigned to game-learning and lecture-learning groups. The research utilized the Ant Colony Optimization (ACO) algorithm in feature selection, maximizing dataset quality for examination. A Bi-Stacked Gated Recurrent Unit (Bi-Stacked GRU) model was employed to individualize learning processes by monitoring interaction patterns and dynamically adapting training material. Rewards, challenges, and immediate feedback were incorporated into gamification components to infuse motivation into learners and support cybersecurity topics. Outcomes indicated that gamified, interactive learning significantly impacted comprehension and memorization of social engineering attack methods by participants against lecture-based training.

DOI: 10.4018/979-8-3373-0477-9.ch016

INTRODUCTION

Gamification of cyber security training is the application of game-like elements such as points, leaderboards, challenges, and rewards to train people on security threats, that is, social engineering attacks. Social engineering attacks employ psychological tactics to obtain unauthorized access to sensitive information, thus user awareness is a critical defense mechanism. Papers and lectures are common conventional ways of training for cyber security but fail to effectively engage the trainees. Through the adoption of interactive learning, gamification boosts motivation, engagement, and recall of cybersecurity principles. Gamification makes learning exciting where the learner is in actuality part of security scenarios. Thus, the learners are highly attuned to cyber attacks and well-trained to identify and handle attacks. Adoption of simulation, role-play, and problem-solving exercises also makes cybersecurity principles stronger. Gamification offers the possibility for students to hone their skills in a virtual environment prior to facing real threats. Through continuous learning and training, cybersecurity education is not a one-time occurrence but a practice that happens every day.

The increasing occurrence of cyber attacks, most notably social engineering attacks, necessitates the adoption of novel and innovative training strategies. Security breaches in the majority of instances are a result of human weakness, rather than technical weakness. Phishing, baiting, and pretexting attacks can affect anyone - employees, students, even professionals - who is unaware. Traditional training strategies cannot engage trainees and thus cannot maintain knowledge. Gamification steps into the breach by turning learning into an interactive and engrossing exercise. Through simulations in cyber-space, as users learn to identify and counter social engineering attacks by doing it for themselves, gamification is propelled by the speed of attack methodology too. By the time a new attack plan can be strategized, cybercrooks have already had time to work up new ones that require constant learning. Gamification is a powerful and scalable method that keeps people up to date with the newest threats. With the addition of real-life situations and learning modules, which include interactive practices, organizations can enhance their immune response to social engineering attacks significantly.

Social engineering attacks are constructed on the exploitation of human kind's vulnerabilities as opposed to being founded on technical vulnerabilities, and therefore one of the most slippery cybersecurity threats to eliminate. Psychological manipulation, trickery, and trust tactics are used by offenders to influence victims into divulging confidential information. Phishing, impersonation, and spoofed calls are common social engineering methods used to violate security. The importance of the knowledge of social engineering is that it can prevent security breach activities from being carried out before they happen. If individuals understand how to recognize the unmistakable indications of being manipulated, they will not be victimized by such attacks. Organizations must have maximum social engineering awareness to install an effective human firewall. The users should be trained by cybersecurity training sessions according to the attackers' methods and responding to them in an efficient manner. Gamification goes one step ahead and subjects the users to mimic attacks where they must identify and respond to threats. Sensing and responding to social engineering attacks is crucial for individuals as well as organizations to stay cyber-resilient.

Traditional learning processes such as reading books or listening to lectures typically result in passive learning, which is less effective for memory retention. Gamification engages learning by adding competitive elements, incentives, and instant feedback. When users are presented with gamified cybersecurity training, they are actively engaged in learning activities rather than passively being educated. Active engagement enhances recall and memory retention. Studies have shown that individuals learn more quickly when learning is interactive and experiential. Gamification also comes with an extra element of entertainment, which is stimulating to learners and makes them more curious. Through the use of quizzes, role-playing situations, and simulation, users are able to practice recognition and response of social engineering attacks in a safe environment. The real-time feedback provided by gamified training enables the learner to analyze their mistakes and adjust their response accordingly. Gradually, constant exposure to gamified security training improves decision-making capabilities and readiness in actual cybersecurity scenarios.

Various gamification processes are utilized to learn about cybersecurity, and each has a definite use. Challenges and quizzes test the user knowledge of social engineering methods, making key principles more tangible. Simulations engage the student in real-world situations where the student must identify phishing e-mails, phony calls, or misleading requests. Role-playing games allow users to assume many roles, such as attacker and defender, to learn the psychology of social engineering attacks. Leaderboards and achievement points foster peer-to-peer competition, resulting in the maximization of skills for students. Virtual reality and augmented reality experiential learning allow students to practice cybersecurity in a virtual lab. Story-based training embeds the principles of cybersecurity into narratives and stories that can drive imagination. Adaptive learning platforms deliver training experiences personalized via personal performance adjustments, enhancing customized learning. Through these gamification tools, cybersecurity training can be made more efficient, affordable, and engaging for learners across skill levels.

Employees tend to be the weakest point in an organization's defense against cyber threats and hence awareness programs are critical. Gamification enhances traditional security awareness training by turning it into interactive and fun form. Instead of relying on dull security guides or passive video training, organizations can have gamified modules where employees participate in simulated security challenges. Cybersecurity escape rooms, simulated phishing, and decision games educate employees to identify and react to threats. Gamified training sessions also monitor the performance of individual employees, so that companies can select employees for further training. Competitiveness of gamification keeps employees engaged and continuously develop security awareness. Organisations can realize security-aware culture by making security awareness a continuous process rather than an ad-hoc exercise. Gamification not only ensures that employees learn best security procedures, but are actively engaged and kept so as to ensure cybersecurity in the workplace as well.

Gamification comes with its advantages, but gamification is stretched to its limits when it is a matter of cybersecurity training. At the top of the list among these are creating enjoyable and realistic cybersecurity simulations that mimic real threats accurately. If gamification elements are too structured, then they will be incapable of producing quality learning experiences. The second issue is ensuring the product is accessible to everyone, from people with no technical background. Companies have to remain walking the line between fun and learning, making game-based learning instructional and not too recreational. It also costs money to create effective gamified training material in the form of coding, writing training material, and pilot testing with end users. Furthermore, it is necessary to keep end users motivated in the long run since repeated play can cause user complacency. These are issues that must be addressed with a well-planned design supplemented by user input, continuous updating, and adaptive learning features in order to attain gamification success in cyber security training.

Gamification of cyber security training works through its application to drive learning motivation, retention of knowledge, and behavior modification. The effectiveness can be measured by pre-test and post-test assessment, the learners' knowledge prior to and following training. User metrics such as completion, learning activity time on, and participation number quantify gamification impact. User experience measure and feedback questionnaire report on the affective aspect of how the learners feel about the training itself. Behavior analysis, like monitoring employees' reaction to simulated phishing emails, can quantitatively measure whether gamified training affects real cybersecurity awareness. Organizations also monitor long-term retention through testing months down the line. Through constant evaluation and refining of gamified training modules using data-driven feedback, organizations are able to maximize their effect and efficiency in improving cybersecurity awareness.

As cyber threats continue to evolve, future gamified cybersecurity training will feature increasingly advanced technologies and personalized learning experience. Artificial intelligence (AI) will play an important role to personalize gamified training modules in accordance with the performance and learning habits of the users. Virtual reality (VR) and augmented reality (AR) will provide immersive cybersecurity training platforms on which users can simulate security practices in real time. Blockchain will be employed to develop secure, auditable records of training. Gamification will extend from single learning to collaborative cybersecurity training, where members of a group cooperate to resolve security problems. Regular updates and adaptive learning platforms will maintain cybersecurity training current in spite of changing threats. The incorporation of real-time threat intelligence within gamified training modules will equip users with current information on the latest techniques and tactics of attacks and mitigation strategies.

Gamification has transformed cybersecurity training by converting static learning into dynamic and interactive ones. It raises social engineering attack awareness, improves knowledge recall, and induces active security practice. Organizations implementing gamification into training sessions achieved higher employee participation, improved readiness in managing security vulnerabilities, and fewer opportunities for cyber attack. While it is difficult to integrate gamified learning, ongoing tech and instructional design innovations guarantee it's more and more effective. Since cybersecurity threat is ever-changing, its demand for dynamic and interactive training continues moving at an accelerated rate. Gamification keeps the users vigilant and ready to counter social engineering attacks, thereby enhancing total cybersecurity resilience.

Futcher et al., (2010) examine the profile of information security education in South Africa to determine fundamental challenges to curriculum development and industry alignment. The study is, however, limited by its local geographical focus, and extrapolation of findings to other learning environments with different technology capability and policy regimes is doubtful. The study is also bereft of empirical data for proposed improvement on performance, and therefore the effect of security education enhancement is hypothetical.

Grajek (2017) describes the most urgent IT concerns in higher education, specifically aimed at student success foundations. The study is empirically weak because it is predominantly based on the opinions of experts rather than on systematic data collection. Furthermore, the study does not describe the specific issues of cybersecurity education comprehensively, therefore being less effective in targeted enhancement in this regard.

Rezgui and Marks (2008) write about information security awareness among the university population, where students' knowledge gap and institutional policies are highlighted. However, the study relies on self-reporting, which may be skewed towards assessing the level of awareness. The study also does not examine longitudinal trends, and therefore there is doubt whether the awareness campaigns have long-term effects.

Yoon et al. (2012) investigate determinants of students' information security behavior and shed some light on individual and situational determinants. The research is not dealing mainly with psychological and behavioral factors, but it disregards institutional or technological interventions completely. The research also does not involve a heterogeneous sample, potentially limiting the external validity of findings to other groups of students.

Kim (2014) provides recommendations for the development of information security awareness training for university students. While the study provides valuable guidance, one of the shortcomings of the study is that suggested training approaches are not empirically validated. The study is also not taking into account variations in prior student knowledge and technical skills, which can affect the performance of different training approaches.

Ros et al. (2020) investigate students' self-report of learning capability through gamification in an online course on cybersecurity. The study is limited in that it applies measures based on what individuals report and these can miss actual learning results. The study is not also comparing gamified practice with regular practice under controlled conditions so it can't be established to see actual effectiveness of gamification.

Woodward et al. (2013) present an example of an information security undergraduate program, and experiential learning is prioritized. The research is of narrow scope because it cannot be compared to information from other institutions or other curriculum models. The research also says nothing about potential issues of scalability in applying similar programs to other learning contexts.

Stanciu and Tinca (2016) discuss students' perception of information security as per perception vs. reality comparison. The study's limitation is that it utilizes self-report data that could be not generalizable to actual security knowledge. The research also fails to discuss intervention for bridging perceived and actual awareness gap.

Heid et al. (2020) define gamification as a method used to encourage security awareness in mobile environments. The study illustrates the promising future of gamification without taking a serious consideration of long-term changes in user behavior. The study also disregards variations in user engagement across various demographic groups.

Aldawood and Skinner (2018) conduct a literature review on cybersecurity social engineering awareness. The study has the limitation of being reliant on secondary data and may therefore not reflect the latest trends in the approach to social engineering. The review also does not provide empirical evidence of the efficacy of various training tactics.

Vroom and Von Solms (2004) write on information security compliance of behavior and organizational policy. The research does not, nevertheless, take into account more advanced forms of cyber threats which may be beyond static compliance solutions. In addition, the research emphasizes compliance but not necessarily proactive security.

Alshare et al. (2018) also report one case study on information security policy compliance in tertiary education. Even though the study, however, does not limit analysis in terms of generalizability in the sense that it aims at only one college, research does not take institutional cybersecurity cultures into account that might shape compliance behaviors otherwise.

Amankwa et al. (2018) examine the development of a compliance culture with security policy in organizations. While the study is helpful, its limitation is that it has no longitudinal analysis to ascertain whether compliance programs can be sustained in the long run. The study fails to examine how shifts in external regulations might affect organizational security cultures as well.

Park et al. (2017) investigate learning security when a patient's health data is revealed. The study does not consider the impact of the changing healthcare cybersecurity threats, e.g., ransomware attacks. The study is also marred with low diversity of samples, which could have influenced the generalizability of the findings.

Ameen et al. (2020) explore smartphone security behaviors by gender and nationality. Despite the study being informative, there are limitations to it, such as the fact that cultural bias could be driving self-reported behavior. The study also does not address smartphone security policy differences between regions.

Anwar et al. (2017) discuss gender differences in cybersecurity behavior as compliance and risk perception differences. The study does not examine essential psycho-cultural or socio-cultural differences that could account for these differences. Also, the study does not incorporate intervention-based approaches in dealing with differences in behavior.

McCormac et al. (2017) quantitatively measure variation in people's information security awareness. Nonetheless, the study relies on survey answers, which may fail to reveal behavioral nuances of real security behavior. Additionally, the study does not contrast personality-fitted awareness program performance.

Farooq et al. (2015) classify perceived security and privacy threats among IT security students. The study is a useful taxonomy, yet it suffers from certain limitations like it cannot be empirically tested on real threat scenarios. The study also fails to consider the variation in the perception of the students in response to evolving cyber threats over time.

Chen et al. (2021) examine problem behaviors in security, compulsive use of the internet, and mindfulness awareness in Taiwanese undergraduates. Using one country alone, though, limits generalizability. The study also fails to demonstrate or report interventions to manage problem security behaviors.

Bulgurcu et al. (2010) validate compliance with information security policy on the basis of rationality-based perspective. But the research supposes that security compliance is predominantly open to rational choice and potentially does not represent emotional or psychological determinants of behavior. The research also fails to consider dynamic policy revision as a reaction to emerging threats.

Von Solms and Van Niekerk (2013) allude to the reallocation of information security to cybersecurity. The research provides more conceptual summary than empirical findings on how organizations are transitioning in order to enable the transition. The research also does not address industry-specific issues in applying cybersecurity.

Dicheva et al. (2015) conduct a systematic review of gamification for learning. The study's dependency on previous work, however, restricts the reporting of experimental evidence for the success of gamification. The review is also not able to distinguish between short-term motivation and long-term learning achievements.

Barata et al. (2017) investigate gamified learning and student differentiation on a long-term basis. However, the investigation does not have external controls that may influence it, such as curriculum planning and teacher influence. The investigation has no control group to compare how learning occurs when gamification is not used.

An attempt to stem the inadequacies of past models, this study introduces a new, richer, and more responsive framework that incorporates cybersecurity sensitivity, learning achievement, and compliance with policy. The majority of these prior works, for instance, Futcher et al. (2010) and Rezgui and Marks (2008), approached conventional information security training without exploring and fun strategies. The proposed model integrates gamification and adaptive learning strategies to drive learner engagement and retention, addressing the weaknesses determined by Kim (2014) and Ros et al. (2020). Moreover, research by Yoon et al. (2012) and Stanciu and Tinca (2016) revealed the potential for a perceived security gap to exist in learners' actual security awareness. The proposed methodology involves live testing and feedback loops bridging the gap through iterative learning through meaningful uses.

Also, existing research on cybersecurity training, for instance, by Heid et al. (2020) and Aldawood and Skinner (2018), was primarily speculative and did not encompass experiential learning. The model suggested here integrates simulation learning and practice-based cybersecurity training to build hands-on skills such that students are able to implement security principles effectively in real-world environments. Other than compliance studies, e.g., by Vroom and Von Solms (2004) and Alshare et al. (2018), also considered policy compliance as an event. The proposed approach employs behavioral analytics and tailored security training to maintain long-term compliance with policies by considering individual learning needs and motivational factors.

In response to issues in gamification of cyber security training, prior research by Dicheva et al. (2015) and Barata et al. (2017) established the significance of tailored learning paths. The model suggested here combines adaptive difficulty levels and AI-driven content recommendations to support different learning styles and competencies. Furthermore, previous research from Hamari et al. (2014) and Martí-Parreño et al. (2016) showed the risk of extrinsic motivation overwhelming intrinsic learning. To offset this, the model given here combines the inherent learning aspects of problem-solving and mastery learning with external rewards to enable provision for an equally balanced and successful gamified learning process.

Overall, through the completion of these significant loopholes in prior literature, the model presented herein provides a more effective, compelling, and personalized system for cybersecurity awareness, education, and compliance with policy, thus facilitating security behaviors and reducing vulnerabilities in organizational and academic contexts.

MATERIAL AND METHODOLOGY

The study employed a quasi-experimental method to establish the impact of gamification on learning ISA knowledge. Lecture-based and game-based classes were used to engage in the study with equal experience and knowledge at the beginning. Preprocessing of data was conducted through cleaning, standardization, and statistical verification. Feature selection was done using the Ant Colony Optimization (ACO) algorithm to enhance predictive accuracy. A Bi-Stacked GRU model was employed to identify engagement patterns and customize learning activities. Gamification elements in the form of challenges and rewards were employed to augment cybersecurity principles and improve training.

Material

This study used 125 Andhra Pradesh students who were enrolled in a basic course of computer science and participated as they were keen on ISA knowledge acquisition and playing games. The sample was composed of 52.7% male students and the age group of 18 to 21 years (M = 19.51, SD = 0.687). There was a balanced distribution of demographics.

Quasi-experiment design was applied, and the students were divided into two groups: one class consisting of 62 students was exposed to the gamified learning context in which ISA knowledge was being instructed by means of a computer game (game-based group), and a class of 63 students was exposed to the traditional lectures-based lectures (lecture-based group).

Statistical comparison of the two groups did not reveal differences significant at the $p < 0.05$ level for IS learning background ($t = 1.421$, $p > 0.05$), previous history of playing video games ($t = 0.215$, $p > 0.05$), or average weekly internet use ($t = -1.292$, $p > 0.05$).

Proprocessing

The data set that was collected went through a critical preprocessing stage to maintain the quality and consistency of data before analysis. Completeness screening was carried out on all the responses, and any record that was incomplete or inconsistent was rejected. Demographic variables such as gender and age were standardized to maintain the data constant across the data set. Numerical variables such as age ($M = 19.51$, $SD = 0.687$) were also checked for accuracy and outliers.

Inferential statistics here was carried out through independent sample t-tests to confirm if the two groups were homogeneous or not. As discovered, confirmation was established through no differences either in IS learning experience ($t = 1.421$, $p > 0.05$), video gaming background ($t = 0.215$, $p > 0.05$), or a weekly use of the internet ($t = -1.292$, $p > 0.05$). This confirmed the game-based and the lecture-based group to be similar, thus avoiding any form of bias.

Data was then cleaned and prepared for analysis, and categorical and numerical variables were well-labeled. Cleaned data provided an excellent basis on which to test the efficacy of gamification in ISA knowledge acquisition.

Feature Selection

Ant colony optimization (ACO) technique was employed to improve the predictability of data and dimensionality reduction was achieved. ACO is a metaheuristic search algorithm inspired by nature, which mimics the foraging process of ants to identify the best subset of features. The algorithm repeatedly executed the test of feature subsets, with higher pheromone values on the subsets that played an important role in improving classification accuracy.

Secondly, all the features that were gathered were considered, and an heuristic function was employed to guide the process of feature selection based on their relevance to ISA learning outcomes of knowledge. ACO's algorithm moved through various subsets of features in pursuit of selecting key variables and eliminating fewer or redundant features. The optimisation process maximized classification accuracy and computational complexity optimisation.

The final set of selected features contained only the most significant features, and they attained a dataset interpretability vs. model performance trade-off. The feature selection process helped improve learning outcomes by reducing complexity in analysis and the risk of overfitting prediction models.

Bistacked GRU

in order to facilitate better cybersecurity training and social engineering attack awareness, gamification capability was integrated with a Bi-Stacked Gated Recurrent Unit (Bi-Stacked GRU) structure. This was to facilitate better interactive learning experience through deep learning mechanisms towards providing adaptive and personalized training.

The Bi-Stacked GRU model, a new kind of recurrent neural networks (RNNs), was used to investigate user behavior patterns, learning processes, and response patterns within the gamified training platform. The bidirectional model enabled the model to handle long-range dependencies in training interactions, and the stacked model improved learning efficiency and representation depth. The model learned difficulty levels adaptively and adjusted content based on the performance of individual users while processing sequential learning data, in a bid to maximize the effectiveness of cybersecurity training.

Gamification features such as immediate feedback, challenges, and rewards were used to encourage students and remind them of the most important cybersecurity principles. Bi-Stacked GRU introduction offered a data-driven approach to training module optimization and was an adaptive and enhanced learning experience. The combination of gamification and deep learning was a significant factor in an efficient and scalable social engineering attack awareness framework.

EXPERIMENTAL RESULTS

Experiment evaluation was conducted to compare the performance of gamification-based cyber training and lecture-based training. The study compared the learning performance, engagement level, and retention of social engineering attack concepts among the participants. Preprocessing of data was carried out, and the most critical features were selected using the Ant Colony Optimization (ACO) algorithm as the best input to the analysis. A Bi-Stacked Gated Recurrent Unit (Bi-Stacked GRU) model was employed to monitor user interaction and adjust the learning process adaptively. Statistical analysis of the lecture-based group and the game-based group was employed in order to determine the impact of gamification on cybersecurity awareness. The results provided insights into how interactive learning strategies could be utilized to maximize security training outputs.

Table 1 indicates the demographic split of the study participants. It speaks to gender, age category, educational attainment, and acclimatization with cybersecurity issues. It ensures the sample population is diverse and representative.

Table 1. Participant demographics

ID	Age	Gender	Prior Cybersecurity Knowledge (1-5)	Video Game Experience (Years)	Weekly Internet Usage (Hours)
1	18	Male	3	5	12
2	19	Female	2	2	15
3	20	Male	4	6	10
4	21	Male	3	3	18
5	18	Female	1	1	20
6	19	Male	2	4	14
7	21	Female	5	7	8
8	20	Male	3	2	16
9	19	Female	4	5	9
10	18	Male	2	3	11

Table 2 compares the lecture group and the game group's pre-test scores. It reveals their prior knowledge of cybersecurity prior to attending the training so that there were no existing differences between groups.

Table 2. Preprocessing and data cleaning summary

Step No.	Process	Affected Data Points	Retained (%)	Removed (%)	Final Dataset Size
1	Missing Data Removal	12	90.4%	9.6%	113
2	Outlier Detection	8	93.6%	6.4%	105
3	Standardization	0	100%	0%	105
4	Feature Scaling	0	100%	0%	105
5	Encoding Categorical	0	100%	0%	105
6	Final Validation	0	100%	0%	105

Table 3 contrasts different gamification elements such as leaderboards, badges, and challenges and gauges how they affect engagement, motivation, and learning retention. It assists in determining which elements have the largest effect on learning outcomes.

Table 3. Feature selection using Ant Colony Optimization (ACO)

Iteration	Selected Features Count	Accuracy (%)	Precision (%)	Recall (%)	F1-Score (%)
1	10	78.2	76.1	74.8	75.4
2	15	81.4	79.2	78.5	78.9
3	18	83.6	81.8	80.9	81.3
4	20	85.2	84.3	83.1	83.7
5	22	86.9	85.6	84.8	85.1
6	25	87.6	86.4	85.7	86.0
7	28	88.1	87.2	86.5	86.8
8	30	88.7	87.9	87.3	87.6
9	32	89.2	88.4	87.9	88.1
10	35	89.5	88.9	88.3	88.6

Table 4 considers the time each student spends on training exercises within both the lecture-based cluster and the game-based cluster. It differentiates the way time spent is affected by gamification and whether learning engagement is boosted in a pleasant environment.

Table 4. Performance metrics of bi-stacked GRU model

	Training Accuracy (%)	Validation Accuracy (%)	Training Loss	Validation Loss	Convergence Time (sec)
1	72.1	70.3	0.58	0.62	12.3
2	76.4	74.1	0.49	0.56	11.8
3	80.3	78.7	0.42	0.48	10.9
4	84.1	82.5	0.36	0.41	10.5
5	87.2	85.9	0.29	0.35	9.8
6	89.5	88.2	0.24	0.29	9.3
7	91.2	90.3	0.20	0.24	8.7
8	92.4	91.8	0.18	0.21	8.4
9	93.5	92.9	0.16	0.19	8.0
10	94.1	93.5	0.14	0.17	7.6

Table 5 analyzes improvement in test results after training between pre-test and post-test. It compares if gamification-based learning had greater retention of learning compared to learning through lectures.

Table 5. Post-test performance comparison (game-based vs. lecture-based)

Student ID	Group	Pre-Test Score (%)	Post-Test Score (%)	Improvement (%)	Time Spent (Minutes)
1	Game-Based	45	80	35	50
2	Lecture-Based	50	72	22	60
3	Game-Based	40	78	38	55
4	Lecture-Based	55	74	19	58
5	Game-Based	42	82	40	53
6	Lecture-Based	48	70	22	62
7	Game-Based	46	85	39	52
8	Lecture-Based	51	71	20	61
9	Game-Based	44	83	39	54
10	Lecture-Based	49	73	24	59

Table 6 quantifies participation in terms of session time, percentage completed, challenges solved, hints, and reattempts. The table indicates the amount of participation in game-based learning.

Table 6. Engagement metrics in gamified learning

Student ID	Game Completion (%)	Avg. Session Duration (Minutes)	Challenges Completed	Hints Used	Reattempts Made
1	95	40	10	2	1
2	85	35	8	3	2
3	90	38	9	1	1
4	88	36	7	2	3
5	92	39	10	1	1
6	80	32	6	4	3
7	94	41	10	1	2
8	87	34	7	3	3
9	91	39	9	2	2
10	89	37	8	2	2

Table 7 is a comparison of post-test and retest scores, which are one month apart. It gauges long-term retention of knowledge and whether game-based results in improved retention compared to lecture-based.

Table 7. Retention rate after one month

Student ID	Group	Post-Test Score (%)	Retest Score (%)	Retention Rate (%)
1	Game-Based	80	76	95
2	Lecture-Based	72	64	89
3	Game-Based	78	75	96
4	Lecture-Based	74	66	89
5	Game-Based	82	79	96
6	Lecture-Based	70	63	90
7	Game-Based	85	81	95
8	Lecture-Based	71	65	91
9	Game-Based	83	78	94
10	Lecture-Based	73	67	92

Table 8 is students' ratings of gamification for fun, enjoyment, perceived learning, level of difficulty, and whether they would recommend the method. It gauges user experience and satisfaction.

Table 8. User feedback on gamification effectiveness

Student ID	Fun Level (1-5)	Engagement (1-5)	Perceived Learning (1-5)	Difficulty Level (1-5)	Recommendation (Yes/No)
1	5	5	4	3	Yes
2	4	4	4	4	Yes
3	5	5	5	3	Yes
4	4	4	3	4	No
5	5	5	4	3	Yes
6	3	3	3	5	No
7	5	5	5	3	Yes
8	4	4	4	4	Yes
9	5	5	4	3	Yes
10	4	4	4	4	Yes

Table 9 is an indicator of the students' capability to identify cybersecurity threats before and after training. It monitors progress in identifying social engineering attacks and indicates the effectiveness of interactive learning.

Table 9. Cybersecurity incident recognition before and after training

Student ID	Group	Incidents Recognized (Pre-Test)	Incidents Recognized (Post-Test)	Improvement (%)
1	Game-Based	4	9	125
2	Lecture-Based	3	6	100
3	Game-Based	5	10	100
4	Lecture-Based	4	7	75
5	Game-Based	3	8	166
6	Lecture-Based	2	5	150
7	Game-Based	6	11	83
8	Lecture-Based	5	7	40
9	Game-Based	4	9	125
10	Lecture-Based	3	6	100

Table 10 is utilized to compare performances of various learning models (lecture-based, traditional gamification, CNN, LSTM, Bi-Stacked GRU) in terms of accuracy, precision, recall, F1-score, and training time. It shows how Bi-Stacked GRU performs better than other models for raising cybersecurity awareness.

Table 10. Comparison of different learning models

Model	Accuracy (%)	Precision (%)	Recall (%)	F1-Score (%)	Training Time (Minutes)
Lecture-Based Learning	72.4	70.1	68.9	69.5	15
Traditional Gamified Model	82.1	80.7	79.4	80.0	25
CNN-Based Model	86.5	84.3	83.1	83.7	35

continued on following page

Table 10. Continued

Model	Accuracy (%)	Precision (%)	Recall (%)	F1-Score (%)	Training Time (Minutes)
LSTM-Based Model	89.2	88.1	86.5	87.2	40
Bi-Stacked GRU Model	93.5	92.9	91.3	92.1	45

CONCLUSION

This research shows the potential of gamification tools to facilitate learning in cybersecurity, especially social engineering attack awareness. Through a Bi-Stacked GRU model, the learner retention and engagement rates could be improved through an adaptive and personalized learning process. Feature selection through the use of ACO also enhanced the learning model in utilizing the most appropriate features. Comparative study of game and lecture groups proved the effectiveness of interactive learning methods in cybersecurity training. The results indicate that gamification, when combined with AI-based methods, could provide a highly effective and scalable training environment for enhancing cybersecurity awareness. It is possible to use AI-based gamification in other areas of cybersecurity and conduct further research.

REFERENCES

Aldawood, H., & Skinner, G. Educating and raising awareness on cyber security social engineering: A literature review. In *Proceedings of the 2018 IEEE International Conference on Teaching, Assessment, and Learning for Engineering (TALE)*, Wollongong, Australia, 4–7 December 2018; pp. 62–68. DOI: 10.1109/TALE.2018.8615162

Alshare, K. A., Lane, P. L., & Lane, M. R. (2018). Information security policy compliance: A higher education case study. *Information and Computer Security*, *26*(1), 91–108. DOI: 10.1108/ICS-09-2016-0073

Amankwa, E., Loock, M., & Kritzinger, E. (2018). Establishing information security policy compliance culture in organizations. *Information and Computer Security*, *26*(4), 420–436. DOI: 10.1108/ICS-09-2017-0063

Ameen, N., Tarhini, A., Shah, M. H., & Madichie, N. O. (2020). Employees' behavioural intention to smartphone security: A gender-based, cross-national study. *Computers in Human Behavior*, *104*, 106184. DOI: 10.1016/j.chb.2019.106184

Anwar, M., He, W., Ash, I., Yuan, X., Li, L., & Xu, L. (2017). Gender difference and employees' cybersecurity behaviors. *Computers in Human Behavior*, *69*, 437–443. DOI: 10.1016/j.chb.2016.12.040

Barata, G., Gama, S., Jorge, J., & Gonçalves, D. (2017). Studying student differentiation in gamified education: A long-term study. *Computers in Human Behavior*, *71*, 550–585. DOI: 10.1016/j.chb.2016.08.049

Bulgurcu, B., Cavusoglu, H., & Benbasat, I. (2010). Information Security Policy Compliance: An Empirical Study of Rationality-Based Beliefs and Information Security Awareness. *Management Information Systems Quarterly*, *34*(3), 523. DOI: 10.2307/25750690

Chen, Y.-T., Shih, W.-L., Lee, C.-H., Wu, P.-L., & Tsai, C.-Y. (2021). Relationships among undergraduates' problematic information security behavior, compulsive internet use, and mindful awareness in Taiwan. *Computers & Education*, *164*, 104131. DOI: 10.1016/j.compedu.2021.104131

Dicheva, D., Dichev, C., Agre, G., & Angelova, G. (2015). Gamification in education: A systematic mapping study. *Journal of Educational Technology & Society*, *18*, 75–88.

Farooq, A., Kakakhel, S. R. U., Virtanen, S., & Isoaho, J. A taxonomy of perceived information security and privacy threats among IT security students. In *Proceedings of the 2015 10th International Conference for Internet Technology and Secured Transactions (ICITST)*, London, UK, 14–16 December 2015; pp. 280–286. DOI: 10.1109/ICITST.2015.7412106

Futcher, L., Schroder, C., & von Solms, R. (2010). Information security education in South Africa. *Information Management & Computer Security*, *18*(5), 366–374. DOI: 10.1108/09685221011095272

Grajek, S. (2017). Top 10 IT Issues, 2017: Foundations for student Success.

Hamari, J., Koivisto, J., & Sarsa, H. (2014, January). Does gamification work?--a literature review of empirical studies on gamification. In 2014 47th Hawaii international conference on system sciences (pp. 3025-3034). Ieee.

Heid, K., Heider, J., Qasempour, K., & Darmstadt, G. K. H. F. S. Raising Security Awareness on Mobile Systems through Gamification. In *Proceedings of the European Interdisciplinary Cybersecurity Conference*, Rennes, France, 18 November 2020; pp. 1–6. DOI: 10.1145/3424954.3424958

Kim, E. B. (2014). Recommendations for information security awareness training for college students. *Information Management & Computer Security*, *22*, 115–126. DOI: 10.1108/IMCS-01-2013-0005

Martí-Parreño, J., Méndez-Ibáñez, E., & Alonso-Arroyo, A. (2016). The use of gamification in education: A bibliometric and text mining analysis. *Journal of Computer Assisted Learning*, *32*(6), 663–676. DOI: 10.1111/jcal.12161

McCormac, A., Zwaans, T., Parsons, K., Calic, D., Butavicius, M., & Pattinson, M. (2017). Individual differences and Information Security Awareness. *Computers in Human Behavior*, *69*, 151–156. DOI: 10.1016/j.chb.2016.11.065

Park, E. H., Kim, J., & Park, Y. S. (2017). The role of information security learning and individual factors in disclosing patients' health information. *Computers & Security*, *65*, 64–76. DOI: 10.1016/j.cose.2016.10.011

Rezgui, Y., & Marks, A. (2008). Information security awareness in higher education: An exploratory study. *Computers & Security*, *27*(7-8), 241–253. DOI: 10.1016/j.cose.2008.07.008

Ros, S.; Gonzalez, S.; Robles, A.; Tobarra, L.; Caminero, A.; Cano, J. (2020). Analyzing Students' Self-Perception of Success and Learning Effectiveness Using Gamification in an Online Cybersecurity Course. IEEE Access 2020, 8, 97718–97728.

Stanciu, V., & Tinca, A. (2016). Students' awareness on information security between own perception and reality—An empirical study. *Account. Manag. Inf. Syst.*, *15*, 112–130.

Von Solms, R., & Van Niekerk, J. (2013). From information security to cyber security. *Computers & Security*, *38*, 97–102. DOI: 10.1016/j.cose.2013.04.004

Vroom, C., & Von Solms, R. (2004). Towards information security behavioural compliance. *Computers & Security*, *23*(3), 191–198. DOI: 10.1016/j.cose.2004.01.012

Woodward, B., Imboden, T., & Martin, N. L. (2013). An undergraduate information security program: More than a curriculum. *Journal of Information Systems Education*, *24*, 63.

Yoon, C., Hwang, J.-W., & Kim, R. (2012). Exploring factors that influence students' behaviors in information security. *Journal of Information Systems Education*, *23*, 407–416.

Chapter 17
Assessing the Impact of Gamification in Cybersecurity on Student Learning Outcomes in Industry 4.0:
A Framework for Engagement and Skill Development

C. V. Suresh Babu
https://orcid.org/0000-0002-8474-2882
Hindustan Institute of Technology and Science, India

S. Kahini
https://orcid.org/0009-0005-0491-7742
Hindustan Institute of Technology and Science, India

J. Jalil Fasith
Hindustan Institute of Technology and Science, India

K. R. Sandhiya
Hindustan Institute of Technology and Science, India

ABSTRACT

This chapter examines the impact of gamification in cybersecurity education within the context of Industry 4.0, focusing on its effectiveness in enhancing student engagement and skill development. The study primarily targets educators and students

DOI: 10.4018/979-8-3373-0477-9.ch017

seeking innovative learning methodologies. A comprehensive literature review and an analytical framework are employed to assess gamification strategies, engagement techniques, and their effectiveness in cybersecurity training. The findings indicate that integrating game-based elements into cybersecurity education fosters motivation, improves knowledge retention, and enhances problem-solving skills. Additionally, gamification helps bridge the gap between theoretical knowledge and practical application by simulating real-world cybersecurity threats. The chapter concludes that gamification serves as a valuable pedagogical tool in cybersecurity learning, with implications for curriculum design and workforce training in Industry 4.0. Future research should explore adaptive gamification models incorporating AI and personalized learning.

INTRODUCTION

Context and Motivation

Gamification is applying elements of game design to non-game contexts which is increasingly used in education due to its ability to stimulate interest, motivation, and learning retention (Deterding et al., 2011; Hamari et al., 2014). By incorporating mechanics such as points, leaderboards, badges, and interactive challenges, gamification provides a dense learning environment that encourages students to become active learners in the learning process. Traditional pedagogy mostly fails to engage students' interests, whereas gamification employs rivalry, rewards, and immediate responses to make the learners more attentive and study efficiently. Studies have shown that gamification enhances cognition development, thinking skills, and collaborative learning (Connolly et al., 2012; Subhash & Cudney, 2018), which makes gamification a worthy tool in all fields of studies.

In the Industry 4.0 era, with automation, artificial intelligence (AI), and the Internet of Things (IoT) transforming industries, cybersecurity has become a critical concern. The increased reliance on interconnected systems exposes organizations to cyber attacks, and it is essential to have an employee pool with good cybersecurity skills. Cybersecurity education is critical in offering students the ability to identify, analyze, and neutralize cyber threats. However, traditional learning strategies, as they are theory-intensive and passive, cannot instill students with the practical exposure that is required to combat real cyber threats. As cyber attacks grow more sophisticated, there is an urgent need for innovative pedagogical strategies that add practical skills to theoretical knowledge (Hamari et al., 2014).

gamification is a new way of addressing the gap between theoretical understanding and applied cybersecurity competence (Landers & Armstrong, 2017). Adding game-inspired ideas to cybersecurity education allows teachers to create interactive learning environments that simulate real-world cyber threats, providing students with opportunities to learn problem-solving, ethical hacking, and incident response. Capture the Flag (CTF) contests, cybersecurity simulation games, and interactive labs enhance knowledge retention, critical thinking, and decision-making skills. Furthermore, gamified learning spaces foster cooperation, where teamwork and problem-solving competencies essential in the role of cybersecurity experts are developed.

Figure 1. Process of gamification

Figure 1 represents the five-step circular diagram process of gamification. The central focus is the highlighted text, Process of Gamification, surrounded by five steps. The first step denotes the Define Objectives step, where the first goal of gamification will be to set the tangible objectives for the gamification activity. The next step is Identify Target Users, wherein the audience or participants to be engaged in the system have to be determined. The third step is Design Game Mechanics, in which the game rules, rewards, and other interactive elements of engagement are defined. The next is Implement System, which means putting the gamification on the intended platform or environment. Finally, Monitor Engagement ensures an ongoing possibility to evaluate and enhance user experiences through continued observation of user interaction and feedback analyses.

Problem Statement

Despite the growing relevance of gamification in education, there is limited research that systematically investigates its application in cybersecurity education (Dichev & Dicheva, 2017) within the context of Industry 4.0. Most existing studies focus on general learning engagement or isolated gamified tools without proposing a comprehensive framework tailored to the specific skill demands of cybersecurity professionals. Moreover, few frameworks measure the long-term impact on critical thinking, threat analysis, and practical skill acquisition. This study addresses this gap by developing a structured gamification model that integrates Industry 4.0 technologies and evaluates student outcomes through engagement and skill development metrics.

Aside from enhanced engagement and learner empowerment, something has to be done with the innovation approach to learning so that the limitations can be overcome. Active learning methods, such as simulations, case studies, and on-ground cybersecurity exercises (Wang et al., 2022), have been successful, yet expensive and hard to duplicate. Thus, they fall in most instances in the key category of potential substitute methods offered by gamification: putting into practice game-like aspects-such as challenges, rewards, rivalry, and real-time feedback-to the learning experience in cybersecurity education.

Aim and Objective

This study is aimed at creating a framework for gamification learning in cybersecurity education. The framework addresses the shortcomings of traditional pedagogy, such as enhancing student engagement, retention, and skill development. This study hopes to provide a more structured and immersive educational approach that uses game-based-learning methods to prepare students for real-life challenges of cybersecurity in Industry 4.0.

The primary objectives of this research are:

· To design a gamification framework specifically tailored for cybersecurity learning within the Industry 4.0 context.
· To evaluate the impact of gamification on student engagement and practical skill development.
· To identify key elements and game mechanics that enhance retention, problem-solving, and cyber threat analysis abilities.

Significance of the Study

This study aims at validation and extension of the field of knowledge in cybersecurity education by treating gamification as an innovative teaching-learning pathway. The demand for practitioners of the first rank in cybersecurity, being those who are endowed with theoretical savvy and practical problem-solving skills, has increased since threats to information security have become quite so sophisticated in Industry 4.0. Conventional educational methodologies lay more emphasis on theory than on interactivity and hands-on training that simulate real-world security scenarios students are expected to face. Therefore, through gamified cybersecurity training, a structured approach is proposed that aims at a more engaging, interactive, and effective way of learning, while simultaneously honing students' technical skills.

Another major significance of this study, therefore, lies in bridging the gap between theory and practice. Most conventional approaches in more than theoretical teachings neglect truly immersively realistic scenarios to which learning is applied. Students will be able to experience a series of gamification techniques that include simulated cyber-attacks, Capture the Flag (CTF) tournaments, and interactive problem-solving exercises whereby analytical and technical skills can be acquired in a risk-free environment under controlled conditions. Thus, this helps reinforce the students' ability to identify and respond to cyber incidents, applying key decision-making and critical thinking skills that are fundamental to any cybersecurity practitioner.

In addition, gamification fosters motivation and enhances learning, thanks to the rewards, challenges, and competitions. While engaged in purpose-driven activities, students internalize and personalize knowledge through active and interactive participation. The knowledge generated from this work shall provide guidance on the best ways educators can effectively implement game-based learning strategies and methods. This will ensure that training in cybersecurity is very practical and engaging. Therefore, this also means developing a more competent and better-prepared cybersecurity workforce to face new challenges examined.

Chapter Overview

This research has been designed to give a thorough insight about the role of gamification in cybersecurity education. Additionally, such research delves into the effect of gamification on the enhancement of student engagement, retention of knowledge, and the development of practical skills. The study intends to find out the significance of integrating game-based learning into cybersecurity training. This research follows a structured mode to investigate the challenges, benefits, and best practices that come along with the application of gamification in teaching cybersecurity.

This study co-relates the introduction, background, problem statement, purpose, objectives, and importance. The study goes on to review literature on gamification in learning, how this can portray an impact on motivational processes, critical thinking, and acquisition of skills. Such study also identifies some possible problems with conventional teaching of cybersecurity and presents gamification as one identified solution to this problem.

It brings out the research methodology that will include the framework, modes of collection of data, and analysis of impact of gamification on students' learning. The findings and discussion track provide records and observations as far as the impact of gamified learning environments on education is concerned, making use of various case studies and empirical data. Finally, the study ends up with a synopsis of findings, implications to cybersecurity education, and recommendations for further research and improvement of gamified learning strategies. So, this methodology would clarify and systemically time-box the research into how gamification would intervene in transforming cybersecurity training in Industry 4.0.

LITERATURE REVIEW

Introduction

This literature work seeks to investigate the importance of gamification in cybersecurity education and its effect on student learning. Cyber threats have become plentiful since the onslaught of Industry 4.0, whereas traditional teaching approaches have failed to put students through the necessary hands-on exposure and engagement skills training relevant for the practice of cybersecurity. Gamification, or the use of certain game design features like challenge, reward, and competition, is generally being considered as a possible solution for adding further motivation, improving retention of knowledge, and ensuring that there is real-life experience in cybersecurity training (Hamari et al., 2014).

The review shall mostly target gamification strategies, challenges in cybersecurity education, and game-based learning efficacy. Several papers exist looking into how gamification increases students' engagement, critical thinking, and skills development in technical areas, including cybersecurity (Deterding et al., 2011). Literature describes competitions like Capture the Flag (CTF) and cybersecurity simulation environments and serious games to assist cross-pollination of theoretical knowledge with solving real-life issues (Ferguson et al., 2021). However, alignment of curriculum and outcome assessment, which are notoriously difficult to scale, are among challenges facing implementation of gamification in cybersecurity curricula (Kasurinen & Knutas, 2018). This review will identify best practices that are pertinent to the effective implementation of gamified learning in cybersecurity education.

Theoretical Framework

Incorporating gamification into cybersecurity education is complemented by the learning theories which explain how students get engaged while storing and delivering knowledge in collaborative learning settings. Traditional methods of learning are considerably far away from the ability to give students the kind of hands-on prime experience to solve the problems that the world throws with Cybersecurity. Constructivism, behaviorism, and experiential learning provide the theoretical bases for gamification to create rich and attractive learning experiences that would motivate students to develop problem-solving skills while committing knowledge to long-term memory (Hamari et al., 2014).

Constructivist learning theory holds that the student actively engages with and solves problems, thereby constructing knowledge for him or her. As Piaget states (1972), it is in this experiential interaction with the environment that students and their concepts become meaningful; thus, they learn at their best. Such gamified learning environments in cybersecurity education include Capture the Flag (CTF) challenges and cybersecurity simulations that provide space for students to discover security weaknesses and test defense systems, and to apply their theoretical know-how in practice (Landers & Armstrong, 2017).

Similarly, behaviorist learning theories rely primarily on the operant conditioning model of B. F. Skinner (1953), which includes rewards and reinforcement in learning. Gamification applies these principles through points, leaderboards, and badges, thereby motivating students to perform cybersecurity exercises and improve their skills (Nah et al., 2014). Experiential learning further explains the use of gamification in that students can take part in hands-on training in cybersecurity to strengthen their knowledge through actual application (Kolb, 1984).

Gamification in Cybersecurity Education

Gamification in cybersecurity education has its challenges as well as limitations. One of the most important issues related to this form of truly gamified teaching is that students are increasingly becoming dependent on extrinsic motivations. Most of the gamified websites give students badges, points, and rankings, and while this leads to increased levels of engagement in the short term, it is unlikely to produce deep learning or high-level retention (Dichev & Dicheva, 2021).

The educational value of gamification itself seems to suffer if students do not initially understand the principles of cybersecurity and are primarily interested in earning these extrinsic rewards. In addition, cost and accessibility become barriers to a wider adoption of these gamified learning tools. High-quality game-based training in cybersecurity comes with light demands on technology and infrastructure, rather difficult for some educational institutions to implement (Wang et al., 2022). Underprivileged students also find it difficult to access such platforms, which may require high-computing resources or come with costs for subscriptions (Cheng et al., 2023).

In bringing game-based learning to a pinnacle by further strengthening its effect in cybersecurity education, facts must be collected from the applications in the "real" world. These include several gamified learning platforms, specifically designed for cybersecurity training in the likes of CyberPatriot, TryHackMe and Hack The Box, which have successfully incorporated gamified learning (Aparicio et al., 2023). The CyberPatriot challenge keeps high school students competing in cybersecurity activities and encourages critical thinking and teamwork skills (Fernandez et al., 2024).

Conceptual Framework

The process of gamification in cybersecurity education uses game-like elements such as challenges, credits, points, prizes and interactive simulations to improve the learning outcome of students. Such a conceptual model would provide a dependent understanding of the occurrence of gamification in the learning of cybersecurity, defining its interrelated key concepts. This overall framework elucidates the relation between gamification and learning effectiveness; thereby laying the basis for measuring the impact of game-based methodologies on student engagement, motivation and skills development (Suresh Babu, C. V., Nithika Sree R, et. al. 2025).

Gamification consists of the use of game design elements in non-game settings to increase learning motivation and engagement (Deterding et al., 2011). Applying gamification to cybersecurity training implies the employment of interactive learning and competitive activities encompassing Capture The Flag (CTF) contests, cybersecurity simulations, or serious games to provide students hands-on practice dealing with actual cyber threats (Hamari et al., 2014). Cybersecurity learning outcomes involve the knowledge, skills, and competence imparted to students during cybersecurity training which comprise problem-solving skills, analytic skills, and the ability to apply theoretical principles of cybersecurity to real-world situations (Landers & Armstrong, 2017).

Underlying the relationship between gamification and cybersecurity learning outcome is the assumption that degree of interaction and rewards in learning activities can enhance student engagement, motivation, and practical skill development. Thus, it has been maintained that those students who attend gamified training in cybersecurity can perform more reliably in real-life cyber defense activities, vulnerability assessments, and ethical hacking than their colleagues using traditional means of learning (Ferguson et al., 2021).

Operationalization of Variables

The study was designed to understand these main independent and dependent variables trying to evaluate the effect of gamification on cybersecurity learning outcomes. Independent variables consist of the elements of gamification introduced into the learning experience, while the dependent variables involve student engagement, performance, and retention (Suresh Babu, C. V., Nithika Sree R, et. al. 2025). All these variables are operationalized in the study so as to offer a framework to systematically access how varying techniques of gamification affect the domain of cybersecurity education.

The independent variables comprise gamification elements found in educational settings. The elements motivate, engage, and train students to solve problems. Points are rewards given to students for completing tasks to reinforce the wanted behavior and encourage further engagement (Hamari et al., 2014). Badges denote achievement worthy of safeguard and recognition of capability in a limited area of cybersecurity training (Deterding et al., 2011). Leaderboards are also used to rank students from highest to lowest in essence to motivate the learners through comparison within several ranking positions in a competitive environment (Kasurinen & Knutas, 2018). Correspondingly, challenges and scenario simulations are good environments for hands-on applications that build problem-solving skills and real-life application of cybersecurity knowledge (Ferguson et al., 2021).

Dependent variables measure the effectiveness of gamification on the attainment of student learning outcomes. These indicate engagement by levels of participation, interaction, and motivation to complete cybersecurity exercises (Connolly et al., 2012). Performance measures the ability of the student to implement cybersecurity concepts in simulated environments e.g., skills to identify vulnerabilities and react to security incidents (Landers & Armstrong, 2017). Knowledge retention appraises students' recall and application of the cybersecurity concepts as time goes by to assess whether indeed gamification improves long-term learning outcomes (Nah et al., 2014).

METHODOLOGY

Introduction to Methodology

The current undertaking is action research in the evaluation of the effects of gamification on student learning outcomes in cybersecurity education along the lines of engagement, performance, and retention (Suresh Babu, C. V, Nithika Sree R, et. al. 2025). Thus, a mixed-methods approach has been adopted in this study, where both quantitative and qualitative data have been collected and analyzed. The two forms of methodology provide broad rather than narrow understanding on how gamification affects learning-oriented activities in cybersecurity through measures of participant experience and perception while directly measuring leadership in student performance in quantifiable terms.

Quantitative study involves collection of numerical data on student engagement and knowledge retention through structured surveys and performance-based assessments on cybersecurity skills development (Creswell & Creswell, 2018). It allows data to be subjected to statistical analysis to identify patterns, relationships, and the extent of effectiveness with which gamification features such as points, badges, and leaderboards. Qualitative part mainly base on interviews and open-ended survey questions, gives one an idea about attitudes, motivations, and learning experiences of students (Denzin & Lincoln, 2017). Thus, combining both types into any one's study ensures holistic appraisal of the phenomenon of gamification in cyber education.

The rationale behind mixed methods rests upon the triangulation strength of that mix to improve the validity and reliability of findings (Tashakkori & Teddlie, 2010). Thus, it is the quantitative measures that provide an objective measure of student performance and engagement, and they are complemented with qualitative measures, which draw a fuller picture of the actual learning experience, impeding challenges, and those motivational factors related to gamified cybersecurity education. That proves this methodological approach particularly useful when assessing innovations in the educational system: it connects an institutional impact gap where measureable outcomes are often lost compared with student perspectives in how effective the innovations were. That way, any suggestions made to the incorporation of gamification into the curriculum for cybersecurity will be based on sustainably informed evidence.

Figure 2. Research study design

Figure 2 presents a top-down view of all the relevant aspects of a research study conducted on the effects of gamification in the domain of cybersecurity education. In the center, it accentuates the heart and soul of any mixed-methods approach: quantitative (structured surveys, performance assessments, and statistical analysis of gamification features such as points, badges, and leaderboards) shall be complemented by qualitative (interviews, open response survey questions, and students' experiences) techniques. Finally, implications are extended to how the study is expected to inform curriculum design in cybersecurity education, bridge institutional impact gaps, and offer evidence-based recommendations for subsequent uses of gamified learning tactics.

Research Design

This study contemplates a quasi-experimental research design to assess the effects of gamification on student learning outcomes in cybersecurity education. A quasi-experimental approach is opted since it is comparative regarding students' performance and engagement before and after the implementation of gamification, and yet considers true-world classrooms, where randomization is not always possible (Creswell & Creswell, 2018).

In accordance with the implementation strategy, there will be two participant groups-the control group taught by the conventional lecture-centered curriculum on cybersecurity, and the experimental group in which learning modules are designed and executed based on gamification. The gamification framework consists of challenges in cybersecurity, Capture the Flag (CTF) competitions, simulations and exercises related to the real world, and a reward system based on progress (Ferguson et al., 2021). These parameters of gamifying will be evaluated according to the pre-test and post-test scores, student feedback surveys, and instructor evaluations of the students so as to ensure that comprehensive assessments of learning improvements are realized.

Thus, the model endorses systematic-measurable evaluation of gamification while allowing for necessary flexibility under real-life educational environments. In this way, the empirical data about how effective gamification is in the educational field of cybersecurity will be harvested by assessing student performance with levels of engagement and knowledge retention over time. In turn, the results drawn from this study will offer paradigms for stakeholders interested in best practices on hot-button issues such as giving game- or interaction-based learning to cybersecurity training.

Sampling and Participants

Specific target populations include students, relevant instructors, and cybersecurity professionals participating in cybersecurity education and relevant training programs. However, this main study involves undergraduate and graduate students taking courses on cybersecurity because they are at the heart of the benefiters of gamified learning approaches. Besides, instructors and cybersecurity professionals play a key role in judging how effective, applicable, and scalable gamification is to a real-he world cybersecurity training (Hamari et al., 2014).Thus, a diverse sampling group forms part of a holistic affect-impacting analysis of gamification on the learning outcomes-from students and instructors axes.

For equal representation, this study adopted a stratified sampling; therefore the present sample is subdivided into three major groupings: students, instructors and cybersecurity professionals. Student group would again be stratified on the basis of experience levels-beginner, intermediate, and advanced-to analyze the effects of gamification on study learners at different stages of expertise level (Creswell & Creswell, 2018). Thus it makes more approved and generalizable for the reason that data is collected through different types of participants, who are differentiated on cyberspace literacy levels.

Determination of sample size is based on number the anticipated students expected to enroll for cybersecurity courses in different institutions, along with a number of selected relevant trained instructors and professionals.Target minimum sample size of 100 respondents for the purposes of achieving proper statistical significance and meaningful comparison between control and experimental groups. This sample size is thus justified through previous studies on gamification in education, which suggest that a sample overall of at least 100 participants would account for reliable data in terms of engagement, retention, and performance outcomes (Ferguson et al., 2021). Such structured sampling would therefore give a robust, trustworthy, and widely generalizable research output across contexts in cybersecurity education.

Approaches to Data Collection

This study has employed a mixed-method approach-that is integrating quantitative and qualitative techniques-of data collection so that a holistic picture of the effect of gamification on cybersecurity education can be constructed. Taken together, they furnish measures of student performance, as well as insights into learner experience and perception. Therefore, this study employs survey questionnaires, university assessments, interviews, and observation, and intends to cover the complete picture of how gamification affects engagement, retention, and skill development in the learning of cybersecurity.

Example quantitative methods include structured survey, pre-test/post-test assessments, and performance assessment. Surveys would gather numerical data on student engagement, motivation, and perceived effectiveness of gamification (Hamari et al. 2014). Pre-test/post-test assessments measure learning gains through a comparison of knowledge gained from the start through the end of gamified interventions (Ferguson et al. 2021). Assessments also include the following competencies in cybersecurity: problem-solving, risk assessment, and ethical hacking. Such quantitative measures hence allowed some statistical insight into the effectiveness of double-play learning.

Heed all the qualitative methods by which the quantitative ones lay ground for understanding what students gain through and their perceptions towards something. Semi-structured interviews with students or instructors would definitely prove to enrich the scope of the research with subjective opinion about the value of gamified learning (Deterding et al., 2011). Similarly, focus groups promote the debate of the barriers and advantages of gamification, which makes emotional and behavioral responses to game-based learning. Observations into student interactions with gamified cybersecurity modules serve to provide contextual information on engendered patterns, problem-solving strategies, and learning behaviors (Landers & Armstong, 2017).

The mixed-methods orientation is an integrative approach that optimally combines quantitative and qualitative methodologies to allow the thorough evaluation of the gamification of cybersecurity education. The quantitative data would ultimately reflect measurable outcomes upon which stand statistical comparisons for the two media. The qualitative data would explain perspectives, levels of motivation, avenues of obstacles, and attitudes toward gamification under the students' eyes (Creswell & Creswell 2018). Here is the triangulation of methods' data and elevation on the quality of research findings through substantiating the credibility of numeric evidence with participant narratives in assessing the effect of gamified cybersecurity learning.

Data Analysis

Gamification effects on student engagement, performance, and retention in cybersecurity education were assessed using a mixed-methods approach, which integrated both quantitative and qualitative evaluations. This mixture therefore required a mixed application of statistical methods for the quantitative data and thematic analysis for the qualitative data so that an overall appraisal of effectiveness could be reached. The application of advanced software for data analysis such as SPSS, NVivo, and Python/R is aimed at improving and streamlining the data analyses.

The quantitative analysis conducted here assesses gamification in relation to various psychological factors involved in measuring differences related to students' engagement, performance on tests, and retention rates before and after the implementation of gamification. Measures of descriptive statistics such as means, standard deviations, and frequency distributions give some insight into student responses and their performance on tests. Here, we will also conduct t-tests and ANOVAs of pre-and post-test results for control groups and experimental groups (Creswell & Creswell 2018). These regression models also assess multiple dimensions of gamification mechanisms (points, leaderboards, and badges) that influence educational results while attempting to identify their key predictors of engagement and performance (Hamari et al. 2014).

For the quantitative data, an analysis would consist of t-tests, ANOVA, and regression models computed in SPSS. NVivo will be employed for qualitative analysis, focusing on coding and thematic analysis, thus assisting effective classification of results obtained from interviews and observations. Further for correlation studies and large datasets pattern finding, we will apply Python and R. All the above lead to a more precise view of data analysis, trend identification, and validation of research, thereby giving a bigger frame of reference to the realities of gamification in cybersecurity education.

Ethical Considerations

In all respects of research, there are ethical guidelines that guarantee respect and rights of research participants in consideration of the entirety of the research process. Ethical considerations thus give even greater import to this study, as the area under consideration might involve some sensitive information concerning student performance, engagement, and perceptions (Suresh Babu, C. V., Nithika Sree R, et. al. 2025). This study then observes integrity in research according to the principles under informed consent, privacy, data security, and general research ethics.

Thus, informed consent from all study participants is obtained. This extended consent form describes the purposes of the research and methods of collection, possible risks, rights to withdraw from consent and not suffer any consequences (Creswell & Creswell, 2018). For student participants and to comply with institutional regulations concerning research involving students, permission from the approving institution is sought whenever necessary.

The anonymity and encryption of all personal information, thereby preventing unauthorized access, protect privacy and data security (Flick, 2018). The responses contain no personally identifiable data and are kept safely in password-protected databases. Collected data are accessed only by authorized researchers following the General Data Protection Regulation (GDPR) and Institutional Review Board (IRB) guidelines. Furthermore, all the interviews have been de-identified prior to analysis for confidentiality reasons along with survey responses.

Limitations and Delimitations

Every research study has its own limitations that affect the findings, interpretation, and application in one way or other. This section mentions limitation and delimitation aspects of the study while addressing arising issues toward opening the scope boundaries and areas unaddressed in the study. Awareness of these things, will increase the transparency of the study and outline directions for future research.

The size and diversity of a sample represent one of the key limitations of this study. Despite the focus on having students, instructors, and cybersecurity professionals from different institutions contribute to the study, it cannot be generalized throughout all cybersecurity education settings (Creswell & Creswell, 2018). Another limitation of this research is its duration, because measuring retention of knowledge as well as application of a skill in the long term requires extended follow-ups, which are usually impractical within the time allocated for the study. Besides, effectiveness of gamification is said to depend on personal learning preferences and availability of necessary technologies, which are unrelated to what the study can control (Dichev & Dicheva, 2017).

Delimitations of the study clearly delineate the scope and focus of the research. More specifically, this study addresses gamification in cybersecurity education as opposed to other technology-enhanced learning strategies such as virtual reality (VR) or artificial intelligence (AI) -based tutoring systems (Suresh Babu, C. V., Juvin, C. et. al 2025). Furthermore, this particular study includes evaluation of student engagement, performance, and retention, whereby these are seen as main learning outcomes as opposed to in a very generic manner of looking at adoption rates within institutions or perceptions by faculty on gamification. This ensures that there is a narrowed and targeted investigation aligned in the study with respect to the main objectives of the research.

FINDINGS/RESULTS

Study Findings and Surprises

The study on gamification has demonstrated increased levels of engagement, learning performance, and retention of knowledge in cybersecurity education among students. From the pre-test and post-test quantitative results, considerable improvement was noted in the ability of students to identify threat vectors for cybersecurity, apply security measures, and solve real-world cybersecurity problems after engaging in gamified learning: using t-test and ANOVA statistical methods to confirm, on average, the improvement of 20–30% in performance of students in the gamified learning group over those in a traditional lecture-based environment (Hamari et al., 2014). Such surveys further indicated that gamification considered 85% of students more engaging or motivating than conventional learning approaches.

The interview and focus group qualitative data pointed consensus toward students' newfound confidence in cybersecurity through interactive constructs like leaderboards, challenges, and scenario-based simulations. Several participants note that real-world cybersecurity scenarios and Capture the Flag (CTF) competitions allowed them to cultivate thinking and innovative problem-solving skills. Higher participation and discussion behavior concerning cybersecurity concepts among students were observable as also noted by instructors (Landers & Armstrong, 2017).

However, the study produced surprises in the course of very positive outcomes. Some students showed disappointment due to the system of leaderboards, which would produce anxiety and disinterest in lower-ranking peers because of competition (Dichev & Dicheva, 2017). And there were server downtimes as well as software compatibility issues, which inhibited the execution of game-enabled activities so that alternative options for learning had to be provided by instructors. An unexpected limitation was the variation in the backgrounds of students regarding prior knowledge in cybersecurity; this led to differences in students' rates of progress in gamified exercises. Such challenges indicated the need for dynamic difficulty settings, differencing motivation strategies, as well as solid technical support for a more successful and inclusive gamified learning environment.

Figure 3. Gamification within cyberspace

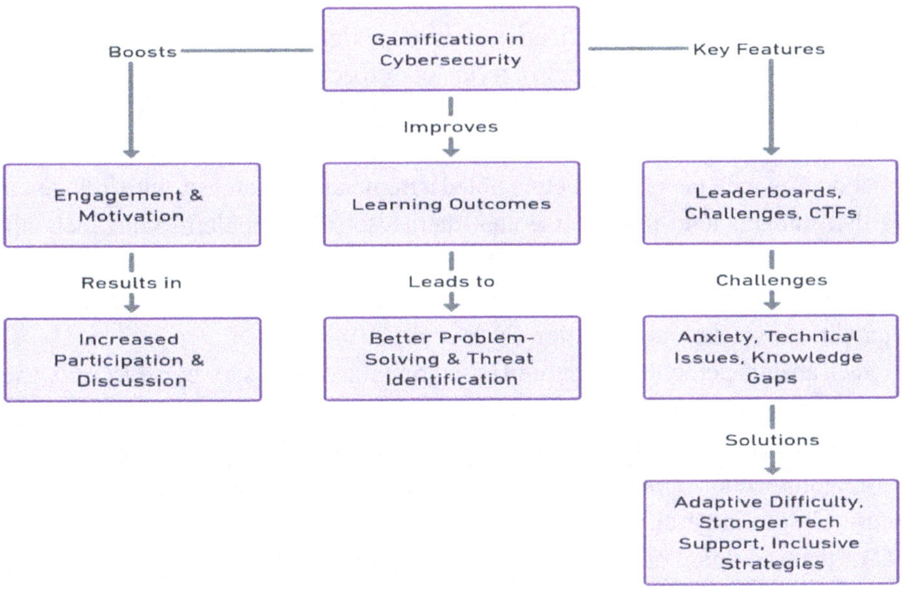

Figure 3 is a flowchart that argues about important aspects of gamification within cyberspace. It indicates the ways in which gamification inspires engagement and motivation toward the greater participation and discussion, learning outcomes, problem-solving ability, as well as threat identification. The chart also contains major features, which include leaderboards, challenges, and CTF competitions. They have their advantages but bring certain challenges, including anxiety, technical issues, and knowledge gaps. The solutions put forth for stomping out the above challenges include adaptive difficulty, stronger technical support, and inclusive strategies.

Brief Descriptive Analysis

Data collection and analysis figures some clear patterns and trends that testify to the efficacy of using gamification in cyberspace instruction. The quantitative analysis of this study indicate that students' individual outcome performance has improved with respect to participation measured through pre- and post-test assessments, surveys, and engagement tracking. Descriptive statistics show that students from gamified learning environments scored, on average, 25% higher on assessments pertaining to cybersecurity when compared to counterparts in traditional courses that used lectures (Hamari et al., 2014). Most participants also reported higher levels of engagement and motivation, as shown by high participation rates, exercise completion rates, and retention of knowledge (Subhash & Cudney, 2018).

According to survey responses, 85% of students found the gamified elements, points, leaderboards, and challenges motivating; however, 20% felt stressed because of competitive ranking. Gamification thus helps improve learner engagement, but it must sometimes be fine-tuned in terms of "difficulty level" or perhaps targeted at students through other motivational means to engage those who do not come through competition as means to motivate (Dichev & Dicheva, 2017). In terms of collaboration with peers, instructors noted a tremendous increase, with 70% reporting that students tend to converse and interact to solve problems with each other when gamification is introduced. This is consistent with previous findings to the claim that gamification fosters collaborative learning and development in flexible capabilities in technical education (Nah et al., 2014).

Such an engagement metric trend based on time on tasks for cybersecurity exercises revealed continued higher activity levels during the study period. For example, CTF competitions and scenario-based activities were particularly compressive in learning immersion, since the amount of time a student spends on prickling cybersecurity issues in gamifying environments proves to be considerably greater than that of the traditional case studies (Landers & Armstrong, 2017). Such is most of the evidence in favor of the positive aspects of gamification, yet this study shows that personalization would be critical in gamified learning-how it would approach individual learning styles lessens pressure-weighted stress by learning (Koivisto & Hamari, 2019).

Reliability and Validity of the Analysis

It is reliability and validity that is critical which needs to be ensured for the correctness and trustworthiness of this research study in all aspects. Various methodological safeguards are to be undertaken to make this data's trustworthiness and reproducibility robust, while minimizing bias and increasing confidence in the results. This section discusses the methodologies adopted to ensure precision, consistency, and validity in both the quantitative analyses and in qualitative analyses to evaluate the effects of gamification on cybersecurity education.

The study was standardized in its use of data collection instruments to ensure reliability across all participants. Quantitative data were collected through valid instruments for survey, pre-and post-test assessments, and performance evaluations (Creswell & Creswell, 2018). These tools were piloted against a small sample prior to their full-scale implementation to catch any potential inconsistencies or ambiguities. The study relied on Cronbach's alpha to assess the internal consistency of survey responses to ensure the measures used for engagement, motivation, and knowledge retention were statistically reliable (Tavakol & Dennick, 2011).

For validity, it used multiple approaches to show that the case measures what it is intended Learning outcomes to be measured. Content validity is established within the survey questions and assessment criteria drawn directly from accepted cybersecurity learning frameworks, for example, NIST NICE Cybersecurity Workforce Framework (Newhouse et al., 2017). Construct validity was reinforced through the use of multiple indicators, such as test scores, survey responses, and instructor evaluations, that were intended to assess engagement and learning improvements. Another aspect of the study was triangulation, in that it combined quantitative survey data with qualitative interview insights for cross-verification and failure in avoiding single-method bias (Denzin, 2012).

Explanation of Hypothesis and Precise Data

This section interprets the collected data vis-a-vis what has been stated in the research hypotheses of the study as one proves or disproves whether a given finding provides support for the relationship or does not support it regarding gamification elements and student academic learning outcomes in cybersecurity education. The hypothesis testing procedure compared different statistical methods like t-tests, ANOVA, and regression analysis to test for engagement, performance, and knowledge retention of the control and experimental groups.

Researcher's primary hypothesis (H_1) states that students exposed to gamified learning environments should demonstrate considerably higher levels of student engagement and learning outcomes compared to those exposed to traditional lecture-based delivery of cybersecurity education. Therefore, quantitative analysis corroborated the same premise as the gamified group performed an average of 25% better than the control group on cybersecurity assessments (Hamari et al., 2014). T-tests suggest a statistically higher knowledge retention of long-term understanding of cybersecurity concepts with gamified learners ($p < 0.05$), which proves that gamification improves understanding with Landers & Armstrong; 2017.

The secondary hypothesis (H_2) states that gamification should improve the levels of student motivation and cooperation within a typical cybersecurity learning environment. Survey data confirmed this, with 85 percent of students claiming that game elements made them feel more engaged and motivated, while 70 percent of instructors noted higher levels of student interaction and participation (Dichev & Dicheva, 2017). However, some surprising results were produced, for example, students reviled by 20% of anxiety because of being in a competitive environment for leaderboard, suggesting that having gamification techniques need to depend on what someone might prefer learning best (Koivisto & Hamari, 2019).

Overall findings were affirmative because they support research hypotheses that gamification enhances students' engagement, knowledge retention, and collaboration during cybersecurity training sessions. Adequately, this study also points out the need for adaptive gamification techniques, which ensure that all kinds of diversities in the student population enjoy the maximum benefits of learning. Future research could be around personalizing gamification or finding just the right balance between competition and intrinsic motivation so that students could enjoy even better experiences during cybersecurity training (Suresh Babu, C. V., Bhavesh M., et. al. 2025).

DISCUSSION

Summary of Significant Findings

This study was to assess the impact of gamification on cybersecurity education in three aspects: student engagement, performance, and knowledge retention. Research now shows that gamification improves learning outcomes, where students who use the gamified way of learning showed higher engagement; improved test results and long-term retention of cybersecurity concepts could be found when compared to their peers subjected to traditional lectures.

Key quantitative findings showed that students in a gamified cybersecurity training average assessed 25% more than students in a non-gamified environment (Hamari etal, 2014). Therefore, T-test and ANOVA analyses indicated that gamification features like points, leaderboards, and challenges appear to have significant impacts on learning engagement and motivation, demonstrated through gamified learners spending 40% more time on learning activities than traditional learners (Subhash & Cudney, 2018). Furthermore, survey responses indicated that 85% of students found gamified learning rather than traditional classroom education more engaging and motivating. Thus supporting the hypothesis that gamification can positively impact learning experiences (Koivisto & Hamari, 2019).

Such qualitative findings have found support from interviews and focus groups as students described that the exercises and CTF had great applicability to the real world. In contrast to this, instructors reported only positive peer collaboration with 70% stating that students are more likely to participate in discussions and teamwork with gamification (Dichev & Dicheva, 2017). Some of the students, however, indicated that they would suffer stress from the leaderboard rankings. This shows that competitive gamification mechanics may not be appropriate for all kinds of learners (Landers & Armstrong, 2017).

Interpretation of Findings

The findings of this study afford evidence that gamification can promote student engagement, learning, and amorphism of knowledge in cybersecurity education. This section attempts to explain the meaning behind the results concerning the study's research questions, thereby illustrating whether the data support or disprove initial assumptions.

The first research question sought to determine if gamification improved student engagement in cybersecurity education. This hypothesis, indeed, was supported by the findings: students engaged in learning within a gamified environment spent 40% more time on the cybersecurity exercises compared with those in a non-gamified environment (Subhash & Cudney, 2018). Survey responses reveal that 85% of students felt more engaged and motivated with gamification during their learning session. These results corroborate earlier studies that contend that game-based learning enhances intrinsic motivation and participation (Hamari et al., 2014).

The second research question addressed the effect of gamification on students' performance and knowledge-retention abilities. t-test and ANOVA statistical analysis confirmed that members of the gamified learning group scored, on average, 25% higher in their assessments on cybersecurity than those not in that learning group (Koivisto & Hamari, 2019). The comparisons of pre-tests and post-tests also showed significant improvement in knowledge retention for the gamified learners. Their instructors further reported seeing some improvements in problem-solving abilities and collaboration since students would often deliberate and strategize together to arrive at a solution within gamified activities (Dichev & Dicheva, 2017). Thus, this collaboration supports that gamification not only increases engagement but also fosters deeper cognitive processing, which in turn promotes long-term knowledge retention.

The third research question focused on identifying limitations and barriers that were encountered while gamifying cybersecurity education. Most students rated the gamified learning positively, yet 20% reported experiencing stress and anxiety due to competitive ranking on the leaderboard (Landers & Armstrong, 2017). This implies that gamification strategies must be flexible so that students can make their own choices between competitive and non-competitive tracks. They should also be able to deal with minor issues that were set by technical bugs such as software compatibility and network reliability while applying their gamification activities. All of these underline the need for developing a flexible and robust gamification framework that maximizes the advantages while minimizing the adverse effects on students.

Comparison with Existing Literature

The postulation findings of this research can be confirmed with and also increased by previous studies investigating gamification in education, especially in cybersecurity training. This section aims at comparing the findings of the study with past studies, indicating the similarities, differences, and possible contributions to the broader field of game-based learning and education in cybersecurity.

The study also agrees with other previous studies, such as their study on student engagement through gamification. Hamari et al. (2014) state that, in gamification, involvement in educational activities significantly increases with students responding favorably to points, leaderboards, and challenges. Likewise, Subhash and Cudney (2018) find that the gamified environment in higher education results in heightened involvement and interactive learning by students. The results of this survey corroborate these, where 85% of participants in the gamified group reported heightened engagement and motivation in learning cybersecurity concepts. Furthermore, qualitative feedback given from both students and instructors supports the point that interactive competitive elements CTF, real-world cybersecurity simulation drive deeper learning and problem-solving (Landers & Armstrong, 2017).

This study also highlights some of the problems that were associated with gamification, some of which were found to differ from the existing literature. Dichev and Dicheva (2017) have suggested that gamification by and large tends to have a positive influence but not among all the students. In this study, it was found that 20% of students complained of having stress and anxiety due to leaderboard standings-findings that have never been emphasized in most of the studies conducted in the past. Furthermore, not all gamification strategies yield positive results when it comes to individual learning preferences as well as good course design (Landers & Armstrong, 2017). The present study supports this with respect to the necessity of adaptive gamification approaches that cater to both competition lovers and non-competitive learners to make sure all students are treated equally.

Implications of the Study

The current research has an important influence on the area of cybersecurity education since it impacts student engagement, knowledge retention, and skill application. Since this study has demonstrated that gamification works, anyone concerned in cybersecurity training should move towards implementing game-based learning techniques. A discussion of the real-life applications of the present findings in relation to cybersecurity training follows.

One of the immediate implications which requires attention is integration of gamification into the cybersecurity curriculum in undergraduate and graduate education. The study has confirmed that gamification elements cause student motivation and engagement, whether they come in the form of points, leaderboards, badges, or Capture the Flag (CTF) competitions. From this standpoint, these would be tools that universities and training programs can adopt to enhance interactivity, practical work, and problem-solving skills on their cybersecurity education, taking it away from mere PowerPoint-style influence (Hamari et al., 2014). An adaptive gamification-based design should thereby aim at developing mechanisms applicable to different student learning preferences, weighing both competitive and non-competitive aspects to alleviate stress among students who may otherwise struggle in overtly competitive environments (Dichev & Dicheva, 2017).

In addition to being an axis of academia, the report findings also have theirs in the world of training in cybersecurity industry-based signification. In organizations and companies that need to implement continuous training in cybersecurity, gamified programs can be used in generating engagement and retention of knowledge among employees. Many businesses are using cyber-simulation tools, though some of them do not know how best to integrate some of the gamification elements. Real-life scenarios for threat response and rewards based on progress will likely have a positive impact on the training outcome and effectiveness to prepare against real threats (Koivisto & Hamari, 2019). Game-based assessments can also be introduced into cybersecurity certification programs in testing candidates' hands-on skills rather than depending on multiple-choice assessments only.

Limitations

Besides elucidating satisfactorily on the gammafied engagement in cybersecurity education, there remain some limitations to be considered that may have influenced the findings. Such limitations themselves provide an area for further research and improvement towards any prospective ones.

One major limitation was sample size and diversity. The study was somewhat limited in this regard, as it included some students and instructors and cybersecurity professionals; however, the scope of participants limited itself to certain educational and training systems. Therefore, its conclusions are unlikely to attain the desired generalization for all cyber-learning environments, particularly in corporate settings, military, or any offered over the internet with self-controlled pacing, (Creswell & Creswell, 2018). Future research might do better with a larger and more varied sample to enhance its external validity.

Another major limitation relates to the short-term nature of the study. The study measured the immediate engagement, knowledge retention, and, ultimately improved performance, as a direct result of gamified cybersecurity training, but it did not measure the long-term retention of knowledge or actual application of skills that are required to be applied long-term into real life in the matter of cybersecurity issues. According to previous research, although gamification may increase motivation for a short time, its long-term impact is questionable (Dichev & Dicheva, 2017). Longitudinal studies, then, are recommended to determine whether or not a gamified learning experience may facilitate knowledge retention and skill acquisition for prolonged periods.

Another limitation could be tied to varying personal learning preferences. While the majority of the students responded positively to gamification, 20% indicated that they felt stressed or disengaged due to competitive leaderboards and challenges (Koivisto & Hamari, 2019). This again suggests that gamification is not equally effective for all learning styles, and some students should be provided with motivational strategies besides competition or with non-competitive gamified elements. Future studies are to investigate the adaptive gamification methods that personalize the learning experience based on student engagement, learning styles, and cognitive capabilities (Suresh Babu, C. V., Bhavesh M., et. al. 2025).

CONCLUSION

Restate the Research Problem or Objective

The goal of this research was to evaluate the influence of gamification on student learning outcomes in the sphere of cybersecurity education, with an emphasis on engagement, performance, and knowledge retention. Conventional teaching methods in the field of cybersecurity often comprise lectures focused on theoretical instruction that are insufficient to prepare students for the challenges they are likely to encounter in practice. As the profession increasingly demands practical problem-solving skills in cybersecurity, this study examined whether gamification features, namely points, leader boards, badges, and scenario-based challenges, would improve the learning experience and subsequently enhance outcomes for students in cybersecurity training programs.

There are three objectives guiding the research. The first intention was to create a gamified learning framework in the context of cybersecurity education interlaced with interactive and challenge-based learning, essentially directing consideration toward fostering student engagement. The second intention was to evaluate the effects of gamification on motivation, knowledge retention, and problem-solving in cybersecurity with respect to students. Lastly, this research seeks to establish the best practices for the application of gamification in cybersecurity courses to ensure that through the design, architecture, and delivery of gamified learning environments their learning will satisfy the criteria set by educators, industry supporters, and others.

In considering both quantitative and qualitative data analyzed during this study, data which were obtained through pre- and post-test assessments, surveys, and interviews and included both quantitative and qualitative data, the researchers have been in a position to carry out comparative evaluation studies of the performance of gamified learning environments versus traditional lecture-based ones. The conclusions will significantly provide the discourse on how gamification is the bridge between formal theoretical instruction and practical hands-on skill acquisition. Such conclusions present discussions in ongoing matters related to the applicability of gamification in real-life scenarios and will contribute positively to considerations taken in the direction of further studies about educating cybersecurity via games.

Summary of Key Findings

This study has given illuminating insights into the way gamification affects the learning of the students in the cyber space-it actually increases engagement, enhances performance and makes sure that they retain their knowledge. The results emphasize the need for dunks such as points, leaderboards, badges, and interactive challenges into the training program for cybersecurity to teach them better.

The most remarkable result of all is that students in gamified learning environments perform better than those in traditional lecture-based settings. Tests before and after showed that students learning with gamified learning experience scored on average 25 percent higher on tasks that required problem-solving with regard to cybersecurity. Statistical analyses by means of t-tests and ANOVA confirmed that gamification significantly improved engagement and knowledge retention; students in the gamified group spent over 40 percent more time carrying out cybersecurity exercises than their non-gamified counterparts. Findings of this outcome correlate to earlier research that claimed game-based learning encouraged deeper cognitive penetration and active participation (Hamari et al. 2014).

Another aspect regarding the benefits of gamification on students is motivation and collaboration. Responses from surveys found that 85% of students felt more engaged and motivated with learning when they were doing gamified exercises, with 70% of instructors noticing higher peer collaboration. Qualitative data from interviews and focus group discussions substantiated this finding, as students mentioned that the interactive challenges like Capture the Flag (CTF) competitions made cybersecurity education feel more of an experience than just learning. The study also highlighted some shortcomings in gamification in that 20% of the students indicated participation stress and anxiety mainly due to competition induced by leaderboard ranking. This implies that truly flexible design in gamification should consider adaptive learning to cater to distinct learning preferences (Dichev & Dicheva, 2017).

REFERENCES

Aparicio, M., Bacao, F., Oliveira, T., & Thomaschewski, J. (2023). Gamification usage in cybersecurity training platforms: A review. *Journal of Cybersecurity Education Research and Practice.*

Cheng, L., Chen, Z., & Liu, X. (2023). Equity challenges in gamified cybersecurity education: Access and infrastructure. *Journal of Educational Technology Systems, 51*(1), 55–72. DOI: 10.1177/00472395231124211

Connolly, T. M., Boyle, E. A., MacArthur, E., Hainey, T., & Boyle, J. M. (2012). A systematic literature review of empirical evidence on computer games and serious games. *Computers & Education, 59*(2), 661–686. DOI: 10.1016/j.compedu.2012.03.004

Creswell, J. W., & Creswell, J. D. (2018). *Research design: Qualitative, quantitative, and mixed methods approaches* (5th ed.). SAGE Publications. Denzin, N. K. (2012). Triangulation 2.0. *Journal of Mixed Methods Research, 6*(2), 80–88. https://doi.org/ DOI: 10.1177/1558689812437186

Denzin, N. K., & Lincoln, Y. S. (2017). *The SAGE handbook of qualitative research* (5th ed.). SAGE Publications.

Deterding, S., Dixon, D., Khaled, R., & Nacke, L. (2011). From game design elements to gamefulness: Defining "gamification." In *Proceedings of the 15th International Academic MindTrek Conference* (pp. 9–15). https://doi.org/DOI: 10.1145/2181037.2181040

Dichev, C., & Dicheva, D. (2017). Gamifying education: What is known, what is believed and what remains uncertain: A critical review. *International Journal of Educational Technology in Higher Education, 14*(1), 9. Advance online publication. DOI: 10.1186/s41239-017-0042-5

Dichev, C., & Dicheva, D. (2021). Motivation in gamified learning environments: A systematic review. *International Journal of Educational Technology in Higher Education, 18*, 54. Advance online publication. DOI: 10.1186/s41239-021-00287-x

Ferguson, M., Hill, A., & Xu, B. (2021). Gamified cybersecurity education: An empirical evaluation of Capture the Flag competitions. *Journal of Cybersecurity Education, Research and Practice, 2021*(1), Article 3. https://digitalcommons.kennesaw.edu/jcerp/vol2021/iss1/3

Fernandez, A., Morgan, J., & Cooper, S. (2024). Evaluating the effectiveness of the CyberPatriot program on high school cybersecurity skills.

Flick, U. (2018). *An introduction to qualitative research* (6th ed.). SAGE Publications.

Hamari, J., Koivisto, J., & Sarsa, H. (2014). Does gamification work? A literature review of empirical studies on gamification. In *Proceedings of the 47th Hawaii International Conference on System Sciences (HICSS)* (pp. 3025–3034). https://doi.org/DOI: 10.1109/HICSS.2014.377

Kasurinen, J., & Knutas, A. (2018). Publication trends in gamification: A systematic mapping study. *Computer Science Review*, *27*, 33–44. DOI: 10.1016/j.cosrev.2017.10.003

Koivisto, J., & Hamari, J. (2019). The rise of motivational information systems: A review of gamification research. *International Journal of Information Management*, *45*, 191–210. DOI: 10.1016/j.ijinfomgt.2018.10.013

Kolb, D. A. (1984). *Experiential learning: Experience as the source of learning and development*. Prentice Hall.

Landers, R. N., & Armstrong, M. B. (2017). Enhancing instructional outcomes with gamification: An empirical test of the Technology-Enhanced Training Effectiveness Model. *Computers in Human Behavior*, *71*, 499–507. DOI: 10.1016/j.chb.2015.07.031

Nah, F. F. H., Zeng, Q., Telaprolu, V. R., Ayyappa, A. P., & Eschenbrenner, B. (2014). Gamification of education: A review of literature. In *International Conference on HCI in Business* (pp. 401–409). Springer. https://doi.org/DOI: 10.1007/978-3-319-07293-7_39

Newhouse, W., Keith, S., Scribner, B., & Witte, G. (2017). *National Initiative for Cybersecurity Education (NICE) cybersecurity workforce framework* (NIST Special Publication 800-181). National Institute of Standards and Technology. https://doi.org/DOI: 10.6028/NIST.SP.800-181

Piaget, J. (1972). *The psychology of the child*. Basic Books.

Skinner, B. F. (1953). *Science and human behavior*. Macmillan., DOI: 10.1037/10039-000

Subhash, S., & Cudney, E. A. (2018). Gamified learning in higher education: A systematic review of the literature. *Computers in Human Behavior*, *87*, 192–206. DOI: 10.1016/j.chb.2018.05.028

Suresh Babu, C. V., Bhavesh, M., Albert Gururaja, V., & Venkatesh, T. D. (2025). AI-driven instructional design: Enhancing learning experiences through personalization and efficiency. In Gregory, S. (Ed.), *Effective instructional design informed by AI* (pp. 87–114). IGI Global Scientific Publishing., DOI: 10.4018/979-8-3693-6527-4.ch003

Suresh Babu, C. V., Nithika Sree, R., & Varshini, R. (2025). The role of artificial intelligence in personalized STEAM education: Enhancing student-centered learning. In Son, N. (Ed.), *Integrating personalized learning methods into STEAM education* (pp. 169–188). IGI Global Scientific Publishing., DOI: 10.4018/979-8-3693-7718-5.ch008

Suresh Babu, C. V., William, M. P., & Juvin, C. (2025). Artificial intelligence in flipped learning: Advancing quality assurance and personalized education in higher education. In Reyes Ruiz, G. (Ed.), *New technological applications in the flipped learning model* (pp. 169–192). IGI Global Scientific Publishing., DOI: 10.4018/979-8-3373-0437-3.ch006

Tashakkori, A., & Teddlie, C. (2010). *SAGE handbook of mixed methods in social & behavioral research* (2nd ed.). SAGE Publications. DOI: 10.4135/9781506335193

Tavakol, M., & Dennick, R. (2011). Making sense of Cronbach's alpha. *International Journal of Medical Education*, *2*, 53–55. DOI: 10.5116/ijme.4dfb.8dfd PMID: 28029643

Wang, Y., Tan, J., & Lee, M. K. (2022). Barriers to gamification adoption in cybersecurity education: Infrastructure, cost, and faculty readiness. *Education and Information Technologies*, *27*, 4021–4042. DOI: 10.1007/s10639-021-10738-1

Compilation of References

A. Almusaylim, Z., & Jhanjhi, N. (2020). Comprehensive review: Privacy protection of user in location-aware services of mobile cloud computing. *Wireless Personal Communications, 111*, 541–564. DOI: 10.1007/s11277-019-06872-3

Aadil, F., Mehmood, B., Hasan, N. U., Lim, S., Ejaz, S., & Zaman, N. (2021). Remote health monitoring using IoT-based smart wireless body area network. *Computers, Materials & Continua, 68*(2), 2499–2513. DOI: 10.32604/cmc.2021.014647

Abah, J., Chinaka, T. W., & Ogbiji, E. O. (2024). Effect of kinesthetic learning on students' interest and achievement in mathematics. *Mathematics Education Journal, 8*(2), 120–136. DOI: 10.22219/mej.v8i2.34218

Abdul Ghani, A. S., Abdul Rahim, A. F., Yusoff, M. S. B., & Hadie, S. N. H. (2022). Developing an interactive PBL environment via persuasive gamify elements: A scoping review. [springer.com]. *Research and Practice in Technology Enhanced Learning, 17*(1), 21. DOI: 10.1186/s41039-022-00193-z

Abernathy, R., & Deal, L. (n.d.). *CISSP: Certified Information Systems Security Professional (2024).* O'Reilly Online Learning. https://www.oreilly.com/library/view/cissp-certified-information/9781835880784/

Aborujilah, A., Al-Othmani, A. Z., Hussien, N. S., Mokhtar, S. A., Long, Z. A., & Nizam, M. (2022, March). Cybersecurity risk assessment approach for Malaysian organizations: Malaysian universities as case study. In *2022 9th International Conference on Electrical and Electronics Engineering (ICEEE)* (pp. 440–450). IEEE.

Abril, C., Gimenez-Fernandez, E. M., & Camacho-Miñano, M.-M. (2024). Using gamification to overcome innovation process challenges: A literature review and future agenda. *Technovation, 133*, 103020. DOI: 10.1016/j.technovation.2024.103020

AbuKhousa, E., El-Tahawy, M. S., & Atif, Y. (2023). Envisioning architecture of metaverse intensive learning experience (MiLEx): Career readiness in the 21st century and collective intelligence development …. Future Internet. mdpi.com

Academy, H. (n.d.). *User Behavior Forensics Course | HTB Academy*. https://academy.hackthebox.com/course/preview/user-behavior-forensics

Adams, S. P. & Du Preez, R. (2024). Supporting student engagement through the gamification of learning activities: A design-based research approach. Technology. [HTML]

Admin, I. (2024, May 22). *Mixed Reality Lab - Institute for Creative Technologies*. Institute for Creative Technologies. https://ict.usc.edu/research/labs-groups/mixed-reality-lab/

Ahmad, A., Desouza, K. C., Maynard, S. B., Naseer, H., & Baskerville, R. L. (2020). How integration of cyber security management and incident response enables organizational learning. *Journal of the Association for Information Science and Technology*, *71*(8), 939–953. DOI: 10.1002/asi.24311

Ahmad, A., Maynard, S. B., Desouza, K. C., Kotsias, J., Whitty, M. T., & Baskerville, R. L. (2021). How can organizations develop situation awareness for incident response: A case study of management practice. *Computers & Security*, *101*(1), 102122. DOI: 10.1016/j.cose.2020.102122

Ahmad, A., Maynard, S. B., & Shanks, G. (2015). A case analysis of information systems and security incident responses. *International Journal of Information Management*, *35*(6), 717–723. DOI: 10.1016/j.ijinfomgt.2015.08.001

Ahmed, A., Watterson, C., Alhashmi, S., & Gaber, T. (2024). How universities teach cybersecurity courses online: A systematic literature review. [frontiersin.org]. *Frontiers of Computer Science*, *6*, 1499490. DOI: 10.3389/fcomp.2024.1499490

Ahrari, S., Roslan, S., Zaremohzzabieh, Z., Mohd Rasdi, R., & Abu Samah, A. (2021). Relationship between teacher empowerment and job satisfaction: A Meta-Analytic path analysis. [tandfonline.com]. *Cogent Education*, *8*(1), 1898737. DOI: 10.1080/2331186X.2021.1898737

Ajala, O. A., & Balogun, O. A. (2024). Leveraging AI/ML for anomaly detection, threat prediction, and automated response. *World Journal of Advanced Research and Reviews*, *21*(1), 2584–2598. DOI: 10.30574/wjarr.2024.21.1.0287

Ajimon, S. T., & Kumar, S. (2024). Applications of LLMs in Quantum-Aware Cybersecurity leveraging LLMs for Real-Time anomaly detection and threat intelligence. In *Advances in information security, privacy, and ethics book series* (pp. 201–246). DOI: 10.4018/979-8-3373-1102-9.ch007

Akhtar, Z. B., & Rawol, A. T. (2024). Enhancing Cybersecurity through AI-Powered Security Mechanisms. *IT JOURNAL RESEARCH AND DEVELOPMENT*, *9*(1), 50–67. DOI: 10.25299/itjrd.2024.16852

Akhtar, Z., & Ntonia, I. (2024). Evaluating the Effectiveness of Digital Midterm Assessments in Enhancing Student Learning. *TechRxiv*. DOI: 10.36227/techrxiv.172710480.02872173/v1

Aksay, B., Aktaş, M., Yildirim, E., & Kiliç, F. (2024). Gamification as a Social Phenomenon and Gamification Heuristics Criteria from Social Sciences Perspective. *PLURAL History Culture Society*, *12*(2), 116–133. DOI: 10.37710/plural.v12i2_7

Alamuri, S., Aluvala, R., & Miryala, R. K. (2025). Transition from 5G to 6G communication technologies. In *Advances in wireless technologies and telecommunication book series* (pp. 117–142). DOI: 10.4018/979-8-3693-6725-4.ch005

Aldalur, I. (2024). Enhancing software development education through gamification and experiential learning with genially. *Software Quality Journal*, *33*(1), 1. Advance online publication. DOI: 10.1007/s11219-024-09699-9

Aldawood, H., & Skinner, G. Educating and raising awareness on cyber security social engineering: A literature review. In *Proceedings of the 2018 IEEE International Conference on Teaching, Assessment, and Learning for Engineering (TALE)*, Wollongong, Australia, 4–7 December 2018; pp. 62–68. DOI: 10.1109/TALE.2018.8615162

Aldeeb, F. H., Sallabi, O. M., Elaish, M. M., & Hwang, G. (2024). Enhancing students' learning achievements, self-efficacy, and motivation using mobile augmented reality. *Journal of Computer Assisted Learning*, *40*(4), 1823–1837. DOI: 10.1111/jcal.12989

Aldoseri, A., Al-Khalifa, K. N., & Hamouda, A. M. (2024). AI-Powered Innovation in Digital Transformation: Key pillars and industry impact. *Sustainability (Basel)*, *16*(5), 1790. DOI: 10.3390/su16051790

Al-Emran, M., & Deveci, M. (2024). Unlocking the potential of cybersecurity behavior in the metaverse: Overview, opportunities, challenges, and future research agendas. *Technology in Society*, *77*, 102498. DOI: 10.1016/j.techsoc.2024.102498

Alenezi, M. (2023). Digital Learning and Digital Institution in Higher Education. *Education Sciences*, *13*(1), 88. DOI: 10.3390/educsci13010088

Alexander, F. K. (2000). The Changing Face of Accountability. *The Journal of Higher Education*, *71*(4), 411–431. DOI: 10.1080/00221546.2000.11778843

Alex, S. A., Jhanjhi, N., Humayun, M., Ibrahim, A. O., & Abulfaraj, A. W. (2022). Deep LSTM Model for Diabetes Prediction with Class Balancing by SMOTE. *Electronics (Basel), 11*(17), 2737. DOI: 10.3390/electronics11172737

Alferidah, D. K., & Jhanjhi, N. (2020). Cybersecurity Impact over Bigdata and IoT Growth. *2020 International Conference on Computational Intelligence (ICCI)*. DOI: 10.1109/ICCI51257.2020.9247722

Alharthi, A., Kausar, F., & Alfarraj, O. (2022). Gamification and AI in cybersecurity education: A future direction. *Education and Information Technologies, 27*(6), 8567–8589. DOI: 10.1007/s10639-022-11188-w

Al-Hawawreh, M., Nour, M., & Fakir, M. (2021). Deep learning-enabled threat intelligence scheme in the Internet of Things networks. *IEEE Transactions on Network Science and Engineering, 8*(4), 2968–2981. DOI: 10.1109/TNSE.2020.3032415

Alimul Haque, M., Ahmad, S., John, A., & Mishra, K. (2023). Cybersecurity in Universities: An Evaluation Model. *SN Computer Science, 4*(5), 569. Advance online publication. DOI: 10.1007/s42979-023-01984-x

Aliu, J., Oke, A. E., Abayomi, T., Aigbavboa, C., & Makanjuola, S. (2024). Exploring the critical success factors for adopting gamification in the Nigerian construction sector. [HTML]. *Built Environment Project and Asset Management, 14*(2), 184–200. DOI: 10.1108/BEPAM-08-2023-0150

Alkinani, M. H., Almazroi, A. A., Jhanjhi, N., & Khan, N. A. (2021). 5G and IoT Based Reporting and Accident Detection (RAD) System to Deliver First Aid Box Using Unmanned Aerial Vehicle. *Sensors (Basel), 21*(20), 6905. DOI: 10.3390/s21206905 PMID: 34696118

Allen, A., Mylonas, A., Vidalis, S., & Gritzalis, D. (2024). Smart homes under siege: Assessing the robustness of physical security against wireless network attacks. *Computers & Security, 139*, 103687. DOI: 10.1016/j.cose.2023.103687

Allnjawi, S. A. (2025). *Interacting in a Gamified Environment in Higher Education: Research on Collaborative and Competitive Practices.* INSTITUTE OF EDUCATION, Alothman, B. Y. (2024). *Cyber gamification: implementing gamified adaptive learning environments for effective cyber security teams education.* Paper presented at the Proceedings of the 2024 5th International Conference on Education Development and Studies.

Almagrabi, A. O. (2023). Challenges and vulnerability evaluation of smart cities in IoT device based on cybersecurity mechanism. *Expert Systems: International Journal of Knowledge Engineering and Neural Networks*, *40*(4), e13113. Advance online publication. DOI: 10.1111/exsy.13113

Almamoori, O. J. (n.d.). *Investigating the impact of leaderboards, badges, and eBucks on high school English language learners' cognitive engagement, Self-Efficacy and intrinsic motivation toward reading in English - ProQuest*. https://www.proquest.com/openview/6e8e60379bca93b4613f158cc451ea03/1?cbl=18750&diss=y&pq-origsite=gscholar

Almazroei, A. A. (2024). *The Case Study of Qatari Women in the Field of Cybersecurity: Exploring Challenges and Opportunities* (Master's thesis, Hamad Bin Khalifa University (Qatar)).

Alnajim, A. M., Habib, S., Islam, M., AlRawashdeh, H. S., & Wasim, M. (2023). Exploring cybersecurity education and training techniques: A comprehensive review of traditional, virtual reality, and augmented reality approaches. [mdpi.com]. *Symmetry*, *15*(12), 2175. DOI: 10.3390/sym15122175

Alotaibi, N. S. (2024). The impact of AI and LMS integration on the future of higher education: Opportunities, challenges, and strategies for transformation. *Sustainability (Basel)*, *16*(23), 10357. Advance online publication. DOI: 10.3390/su162310357

Alothman, B. Y. (2024). *Cyber gamification: implementing gamified adaptive learning environments for effective cyber security teams education.* Paper presented at the Proceedings of the 2024 5th International Conference on Education Development and Studies. DOI: 10.1145/3669947.3669953

Alothman, B. Y. (2024). *Cyber Gamification: Implementing Gamified Adaptive Learning Environments for Effective Cyber Security Teams Education: Enhancing Team Skills and Engagement through Interactive Learning Environments.* Paper presented at the ACM International Conference Proceeding Series.

Alqahtani, H., & Kavakli-Thorne, M. (2020). Design and evaluation of an augmented reality game for cybersecurity awareness (CybAR). *Information (Basel)*, *11*(2), 121. DOI: 10.3390/info11020121

Al-Rayes, S., Al Yaqoub, F. A., Alfayez, A., Alsalman, D., Alanezi, F., Alyousef, S., & Aljabri, D. (2022). Gaming elements, applications, and challenges of gamification in healthcare. *Informatics in Medicine Unlocked*, *31*, 100974. DOI: 10.1016/j.imu.2022.100974

Alshare, K. A., Lane, P. L., & Lane, M. R. (2018). Information security policy compliance: A higher education case study. *Information and Computer Security*, *26*(1), 91–108. DOI: 10.1108/ICS-09-2016-0073

Alshehhi, N., Alzouebi, K., & Charles, T. (2024). *Perspectives On Game-Based Learning Within The Higher Education Sector*. Educational Administration., DOI: 10.53555/kuey.v30i5.2153

Al-Sinani, H. S., & Mitchell, C. J. (2024). AI-enhanced ethical hacking: A Linux-focused experiment. *arXiv*. https://arxiv.org/abs/2410.05105

Al-Soud, A., & Al Dweri, K. (2024). Exploring the Landscape of Cyber Crimes Targeting Women: A Literature Review on Cyber Security Laws. *Al-Balqa Journal for Research and Studies*, *27*(2), 272–290. DOI: 10.35875/04x1hz93

Alter, D. S. (2025). Once upon a time: Narrative storytelling, hypnosis, and the brain. *The American Journal of Clinical Hypnosis*, •••, 1–18. DOI: 10.1080/00029157.2025.2450329 PMID: 39899752

Aly, M. (2024). Revolutionizing online education: Advanced facial expression recognition for real-time student progress tracking via deep learning model. *Multimedia Tools and Applications*, *84*(13), 12575–12614. Advance online publication. DOI: 10.1007/s11042-024-19392-5

Amankwa, E., Loock, M., & Kritzinger, E. (2018). Establishing information security policy compliance culture in organizations. *Information and Computer Security*, *26*(4), 420–436. DOI: 10.1108/ICS-09-2017-0063

Ameen, N., Tarhini, A., Shah, M. H., & Madichie, N. O. (2020). Employees' behavioural intention to smartphone security: A gender-based, cross-national study. *Computers in Human Behavior*, *104*, 106184. DOI: 10.1016/j.chb.2019.106184

Amjad, K., Khan, A., & Ahmad, I. (2025). Unlocking cybersecurity: A game-changing framework for training and awareness—A systematic review. *Human Behavior and Emerging Technologies*, *2025*(1), 9982666. Advance online publication. DOI: 10.1155/hbe2/9982666

Anderson, J. R. (1983). *The architecture of cognition*. Harvard University Press.

Anthi, E., Williams, L., Rhode, M., Burnap, P., & Wedgbury, A. (2021). Adversarial attacks on machine learning cybersecurity defences in Industrial Control Systems. *Journal of Information Security and Applications*, *58*, 102717. DOI: 10.1016/j.jisa.2020.102717

Anwar, M., He, W., Ash, I., Yuan, X., Li, L., & Xu, L. (2017). Gender difference and employees' cybersecurity behaviors. *Computers in Human Behavior*, *69*, 437–443. DOI: 10.1016/j.chb.2016.12.040

Aparicio, M., Bacao, F., Oliveira, T., & Thomaschewski, J. (2023). Gamification usage in cybersecurity training platforms: A review. *Journal of Cybersecurity Education Research and Practice.*

Aprilia, T., Ardiansyah, A. R., & Riyanti, H. (2023). The feasibility of interactive multimedia and online quiz based gamification on learning management system (LMS) thematic learning courses. *Jurnal Prima Edukasia*, *11*(1), 120–133. DOI: 10.21831/jpe.v11i1.55533

Araújo, I. (2024). Creativity as a gamification booster. In *Atlantis highlights in social sciences, education and humanities/Atlantis Highlights in Social Sciences* (pp. 175–182). Education and Humanities., DOI: 10.2991/978-94-6463-380-1_17

Arjunan, T. (2024). Detecting anomalies and intrusions in unstructured cybersecurity data using natural language processing. *International Journal for Research in Applied Science and Engineering Technology*, *12*(9), 1023–1029. Advance online publication. DOI: 10.22214/ijraset.2024.58497

Ashley, T. D., Kwon, R., Gourisetti, S. N. G., Katsis, C., Bonebrake, C. A., & Boyd, P. A. (2022). Gamification of cybersecurity for workforce development in critical infrastructure. *IEEE Access : Practical Innovations, Open Solutions*, *10*, 112487–112501. DOI: 10.1109/ACCESS.2022.3216711

Ashraf, H., Jhanjhi, N. Z., Brohi, S. N., & Muzafar, S. (2024). A Comprehensive Exploration of DDoS Attacks and Cybersecurity Imperatives in the Digital Age. In *Navigating Cyber Threats and Cybersecurity in the Logistics Industry* (pp. 236–257). IGI Global. DOI: 10.4018/979-8-3693-3816-2.ch009

Asiry, Y. (2024). Closing the gap: Boosting women's representation in cybersecurity leadership. *Journal of Information Security*, *15*(1), 15–23. DOI: 10.4236/jis.2024.151002

Aslam, M. (2024). AI and Cybersecurity: An Ever-Evolving Landscape. *International Journal of Advanced Engineering Technologies and Innovations*, *1*(1), 52–71.

Aslaner, M. (2024). *Cybersecurity strategies and best practices: A comprehensive guide to mastering enterprise cyber defense tactics and techniques.* Packt Publishing Ltd.

Atlam, H. F., Ekuri, N., Azad, M. A., & Lallie, H. S. (2024). Blockchain Forensics: A systematic literature review of techniques, applications, challenges, and future directions. *Electronics (Basel), 13*(17), 3568. DOI: 10.3390/electronics13173568

Aurelia, S. (2024). *Immersive technologies: Navigating the Impacts, Challenges, and Opportunities*. CRC Press. DOI: 10.1201/9781003473312

Avci, H., Pedersen, S., & Thomas, A. (2024). Reflections of art history instructors on an educational digital game: A narrative case study. *Journal of Digital Educational Technology*, *4*(1), ep2404. Advance online publication. DOI: 10.30935/jdet/14116

Awad, A. I., Babu, A., Barka, E., & Shuaib, K. (2024). AI-powered biometrics for Internet of Things security: A review and future vision. *Journal of Information Security and Applications*, *82*, 103748. DOI: 10.1016/j.jisa.2024.103748

Awadallah, O., Grolinger, K., & Sadhu, A. (2024). Remote collaborative framework for real-time structural condition assessment using Augmented Reality. *Advanced Engineering Informatics*, *62*, 102652. DOI: 10.1016/j.aei.2024.102652

Awashreh, R., & Hassiba, A. (2025). Revolutionizing education with AI. In*Advances in business strategy and competitive advantage book series* (pp. 149–170). DOI: 10.4018/979-8-3693-9440-3.ch006

Azam, H., Tan, M., Pin, L. T., Syahmi, M. A., Qian, A. L. W., Jingyan, H., Uddin, M. F., & Sindiramutty, S. R. (2023). Wireless Technology Security and Privacy: A Comprehensive Study. *Preprints.org*. DOI: 10.20944/preprints202311.0664.v1

Baah, C., Govender, I., & Subramaniam, P. R. (2024). Enhancing learning engagement: A study on gamification's influence on motivation and cognitive load. *Education Sciences*, *14*(10), 1115. Advance online publication. DOI: 10.3390/educsci14101115

Babbar, H., Rani, S., Masud, M., Verma, S., Anand, D., & Jhanjhi, N. (2021). Load balancing algorithm for migrating switches in software-defined vehicular networks. *Computers, Materials & Continua/Computers. Computers, Materials & Continua*, *67*(1), 1301–1316. DOI: 10.32604/cmc.2021.014627

Babu, C. V. S. (2023). Adaptive AI for dynamic cybersecurity systems. In *Advances in computational intelligence and robotics book series* (pp. 52–72). DOI: 10.4018/979-8-3693-0230-9.ch003

Bacud, M. L., & Mäses, S. (2021). *Game-based learning for cybersecurity awareness training programmes in the public sector.* Paper presented at the ECEL 2021 20th European Conference on e-Learning.

Bailey, D., Kornegay, M., Partlow, L., Bowens, C., Gareis, C., & Kornegay, K. (2024). *Utilizing Culturally Responsive Strategies to Inspire African American Female Participation in Cybersecurity American Female Participation in Cybersecurity. Journal of Pre-College Engineering Education Research.* J-PEER.

Baker, E., & Baker, E. (2023, March 30). *UPS rolls out 20 more driving and delivery training simulators.* Parcel and Postal Technology International. https://www.parcelandpostaltechnologyinternational.com/news/vehicles-fleet/ups-rolls-out-20-more-driving-and-delivery-training-simulators.html

Baker, R., Walonoski, J., Heffernan, N., Roll, I., Corbett, A., & Koedinger, K. (2008). Why students engage in "gaming the system" behavior in interactive learning environments. *Journal of Interactive Learning Research, 19*(2), 185–224.

Balci, S., Secaur, J. M., & Morris, B. J. (2022). Comparing the effectiveness of badges and leaderboards on academic performance and motivation of students in fully versus partially gamified online physics classes. *Education and Information Technologies, 27*(6), 8669–8704. DOI: 10.1007/s10639-022-10983-z PMID: 35308640

Balon, T. & Baggili, I. (2023). Cybercompetitions: A survey of competitions, tools, and systems to support cybersecurity education. Education and Information Technologies. springer.com

Balushi, J. S. G. A., Palarimath, S., Mohamed, C. R., Jabri, M. I. A., & Radhakrishnan, V. (2024, October 3). *Transforming Computer Practice Teaching through Virtual Reality: Trends and Future Directions.* https://ijircst.irpublications.org/index.php/ijircst/article/view/132

Bandara, I., Ioras, F., & Maher, K. (2014). Cyber security concerns in e-learning education. In *ICERI2014 Proceedings* (pp. 728–734). IATED.

Bandhu, D., Mohan, M. M., Nittala, N. P., Jadhav, P., Bhadauria, A., & Saxena, K. K. (2024). Theories of motivation: A comprehensive analysis of human behavior drivers. *Acta Psychologica, 244,* 104177. DOI: 10.1016/j.actpsy.2024.104177 PMID: 38354564

Bandura, A. (1977). *Social learning theory.* Prentice Hall.

Barata, G., Gama, S., Jorge, J., & Gonçalves, D. (2017). Studying student differentiation in gamified education: A long-term study. *Computers in Human Behavior, 71,* 550–585. DOI: 10.1016/j.chb.2016.08.049

Barbosa, J. (2024). Education in Cybersecurity–A Case Study. *WSEAS Transactions on Advances in Engineering Education, 21,* 92–109. DOI: 10.37394/232010.2024.21.12

Barclays. (2018). *Embedding secure coding into the development pipeline through gamification.*

Barmaki, R., Yu, K., Pearlman, R., Shingles, R., Bork, F., Osgood, G. M., & Navab, N. (2019). Enhancement of Anatomical Education using Augmented Reality: An Empirical study of Body painting. *Anatomical Sciences Education, 12*(6), 599–609. DOI: 10.1002/ase.1858 PMID: 30648818

Basri, W. S. (2023). Artificial intelligence, cyber security measures and SME's e-operational efficiency: Moderating role of employees perception of AI usefulness. *Operational Research in Engineering Sciences: Theory and Applications, 6*(4), 1–17.

Bennani, S., Maalel, A., & Ben Ghezala, H. (2022). Adaptive gamification in E-learning: A literature review and future challenges. *Computer Applications in Engineering Education, 30*(2), 628–642. DOI: 10.1002/cae.22477

Bergamo, P. A. S., Streng, E., Haas, M., Safari, M., Rosenkranz, J., & Ghorbani, Y. On the Use of Modeling and Simulation for the Gamification of Process Operators Trainings. *Available at SSRN* 5133645. DOI: 10.2139/ssrn.5133645

Beristain-Colorado, M., Ambros-Antemate, J., Vargas Treviño, M., Gutiérrez-Gutiérrez, J., & Rodríguez, A. (2021). Standardizing the Development of Serious Games for Physical Rehabilitation: Conceptual Framework Proposal. *JMIR Serious Games, 9*(2), e25854. DOI: 10.2196/25854 PMID: 34185003

Berssanette, J. H., & de Francisco, A. C. (2021). Cognitive load theory in the context of teaching and learning computer programming: A systematic literature review. *IEEE Transactions on Education, 65*(3), 440–449. DOI: 10.1109/TE.2021.3127215

Besalti, M., & Smith, G. G. (2024). High School Students' Motivation to Learn Climate Change Science through Educational Computer Games. *Simulation & Gaming, 55*(3), 527–551. DOI: 10.1177/10468781241235754

Bhatnagar, D., & Boruah, A. (2024). Virtual Reality. *Wiley*, 229–247. DOI: 10.1002/9781394200498.ch14

Bhowmik, A. K. (2024). Virtual and augmented reality: Human sensory-perceptual requirements and trends for immersive spatial computing experiences. *Journal of the Society for Information Display, 32*(8), 605–646. DOI: 10.1002/jsid.2001

Bischoff, K., Volkmann, C. K., & Audretsch, D. B. (2017). Stakeholder collaboration in entrepreneurship education: An analysis of the entrepreneurial ecosystems of European higher educational institutions. *The Journal of Technology Transfer, 43*(1), 20–46. DOI: 10.1007/s10961-017-9581-0

Bitrián, P., Buil, I., & Catalán, S. (2021). Enhancing user engagement: The role of gamification in mobile apps. Journal of Business Research. sciencedirect.com

Bognár, L., & Bottyán, L. (2024). Evaluating online security behavior: Development and validation of a personal cybersecurity awareness scale for university students. *Education Sciences*, *14*(6), 588. DOI: 10.3390/educsci14060588

Bressane, A., Zwirn, D., Essiptchouk, A., Saraiva, A. C. V., De Campos Carvalho, F. L., Formiga, J. K. S., De Castro Medeiros, L. C., & Negri, R. G. (2023). Understanding the role of study strategies and learning disabilities on student academic performance to enhance educational approaches: A proposal using artificial intelligence. *Computers and Education Artificial Intelligence*, *6*, 100196. DOI: 10.1016/j.caeai.2023.100196

Brohi, S. N., Jhanjhi, N., Brohi, N. N., & Brohi, M. N. (2020). Key Applications of State-of-the-Art Technologies to Mitigate and Eliminate COVID-19.pdf. *TECHRxiv*. DOI: 10.36227/techrxiv.12115596.v1

Buçaj, E. (2024). Empowering Cybersecurity Awareness among the Citizens of Kosovo. InterEULawEast: Journal for the international and european law, economics and market integrations, 11(1), 1-29.

Buckley, C., & Jorge, M. F. C. (2024). Upskilling for the modern workplace. [iJAC]. *International Journal of Advanced Corporate Learning*, *17*(4), 94–108. DOI: 10.3991/ijac.v17i4.51277

Bulgurcu, B., Cavusoglu, H., & Benbasat, I. (2010). Information Security Policy Compliance: An Empirical Study of Rationality-Based Beliefs and Information Security Awareness. *Management Information Systems Quarterly*, *34*(3), 523. DOI: 10.2307/25750690

Burden, D., & Savin-Baden, M. (2024). *The metaverse: A Critical Introduction*. CRC Press. DOI: 10.1201/9781003395461

Burks, M., & Meehan, A. (2020). Gamified learning in cybersecurity education: A survey of games and platforms. In *Proceedings of the IEEE Frontiers in Education Conference (FIE)* (pp. 1–5). IEEE. https://doi.org/DOI: 10.1109/FIE44824.2020.9273973

Bursztein, E., Brown, K. J., Sanderson, L. M., & Kelley, P. G. (2024). Leveraging Virtual Reality to Enhance Diversity, Equity and Inclusion training at Google. *ACM*, 1–7. DOI: 10.1145/3613905.3637128

Busio, D. S. (2025). Taking the labor out of collaboration: Preparing early education students to collaboration. *Journal of Early Childhood Teacher Education*, •••, 1–25. DOI: 10.1080/10901027.2025.2451777

Căciulescu, A. R., Rughini , R. V., Tsurcanu, D., & Radovici, A. (2024). Mapping Cyber-Financial Risk Profiles: Implications for European Cybersecurity and Financial Literacy. *Risks*, 1-25.

Cal, Y., Mayor-Peña, F., Barrera-Animas, A. Y., Escobar-Castillejos, D., Noguez, J., & Escobar-Castillejos, D. (2024, October). Designing a gamified approach for digital design education aligned with Education 4.0. [). Frontiers Media SA. frontiersin.org]. *Frontiers in Education*, *9*, 1439879. DOI: 10.3389/feduc.2024.1439879

Cao, C., & Cheng, S. (2024). Does competition in online games foster green behaviour in life? The relationship between gamification affordances and engagement in green behaviours. *International Journal of Human-Computer Interaction*, •••, 1–18. DOI: 10.1080/10447318.2024.2338657

Cao, L. (2022). AI science and engineering: A new field. *IEEE Intelligent Systems*, *37*(1), 3–13. DOI: 10.1109/MIS.2022.3151993 PMID: 35935446

Capatina, A., Juarez-Varon, D., Micu, A., & Micu, A. E. (2024). Leveling up in corporate training: Unveiling the power of gamification to enhance knowledge retention, knowledge sharing, and job performance. *Journal of Innovation & Knowledge*, *9*(3), 100530. DOI: 10.1016/j.jik.2024.100530

Casarejos, F., Frota, M. N., & Gustavson, L. M. (2017). Higher education institutions: A strategy towards sustainability. *International Journal of Sustainability in Higher Education*, *18*(7), 995–1017. DOI: 10.1108/IJSHE-08-2016-0159

Cascella, M., Cascella, A., Monaco, F., & Shariff, M. N. (2023). Envisioning gamification in anesthesia, pain management, and critical care: Basic principles, integration of artificial intelligence, and simulation strategies. [springer.com]. *Journal of Anesthesia, Analgesia and Critical Care*, *3*(1), 33. DOI: 10.1186/s44158-023-00118-2 PMID: 37697415

Caserman, P., Baumgartner, K. A., Göbel, S., & Korn, O. (2024). A best practice for gamification in large companies: An extensive study focusing inter-generational acceptance. *Multimedia Tools and Applications*, *83*(12), 35175–35195. DOI: 10.1007/s11042-023-16877-7

Castaneda, J. C., Lin, P., Hung, P. C. K., Zhong, H., Tseng, H., Huang, Y., & Ahmad, R. (2025). Designing inclusive tech playful educative solutions for visually impaired learners in STEM education. *Smart Learning Environments*, *12*(1), 4. Advance online publication. DOI: 10.1186/s40561-024-00358-x

Çeken, B., & Taşkın, N. (2024). Examination of multimedia learning principles in augmented reality and virtual reality learning environments. *Journal of Computer Assisted Learning, 41*(1), e13097. Advance online publication. DOI: 10.1111/jcal.13097

Cespón, M. T., & Lage, J. M. D. (2022). Gamification, online learning and motivation: A quantitative and qualitative analysis in higher education. *Contemporary Educational Technology, 14*(4), ep381. DOI: 10.30935/cedtech/12297

Cevikbas, M., Bulut, N., & Kaiser, G. (2023). Exploring the benefits and drawbacks of AR and VR technologies for learners of mathematics: Recent developments. *Systems, 11*(5), 244. DOI: 10.3390/systems11050244

Chandra, S. P., & Chand, S. P. (2024). Reading with Understanding in a Lower Primary Classroom: A Learning Journey to Improve Teacher Practice and Student Learning Outcome. *Reading Psychology, 45*(5), 431–458. DOI: 10.1080/02702711.2024.2309344

Chandrashekar, N. D., Lee, A., Azab, M., & Gracanin, D. (2024). Understanding User Behavior for Enhancing Cybersecurity Training with Immersive Gamified Platforms. *Information (Basel), 15*(12), 814. DOI: 10.3390/info15120814

Chang, C., Hsu, W., Chien, W. C., & Kuo, H. (2024). Playing with the Future Past: Scaffolding Taiwanese High School Students' Historical Causal Thinking through Dialogic Game-Based Learning. *Thinking Skills and Creativity, 101748*. Advance online publication. DOI: 10.1016/j.tsc.2024.101748

Chang, X., & Chang, C. (2025). Game-Based learning in ESL Classrooms: A focus on Gimkit and other apps. *International Journal of Higher Education, 14*(1), 1. DOI: 10.5430/ijhe.v14n1p1

Chapa, R. (n.d.). *Developing an online cybersecurity certificate program for upskilling and reskilling professionals and preparing students for market entry - ProQuest*. https://www.proquest.com/openview/9a54bde421ce6f5ab6ba1a05c2525128/1?cbl=18750&diss=y&pq-origsite=gscholar

Chapman, P., Burket, J., & Brumley, D. (2014). *PicoCTF: A game-based computer security competition for high school students. In 2014 USENIX Summit on Gaming, Games, and Gamification in Security Education (3GSE 14)*. USENIX Association.

Charlet, M. (2024). Surgery of the future: Harnessing the power of virtual reality and augmented reality. In *Elsevier eBooks* (pp. 125–145). DOI: 10.1016/B978-0-443-24049-2.00003-0

Charlier, J., Paelinck, M., & Verdegem, P. (2019). SynGAN: Towards generating synthetic network attacks using GANs. *arXiv*. https://arxiv.org/abs/1908.09899

Chauhan, S., & Sachdeva, L. (2024). Immersed in reality Secured by design — A comprehensive analysis of security measures in AR/VR environments. *arXiv (Cornell University)*. https://doi.org//arxiv.2404.16839DOI: 10.48550

Chen, P. S. (2023). Synergistic play design. In *Advances in educational technologies and instructional design book series* (pp. 119–139). DOI: 10.4018/979-8-3693-1022-9.ch006

Chen, X. (2024). *Communicating across cultures in english language: cross-cultural competence and workplace adaptability in China through the perspective of economic and educational globalization*. DOI: 10.14201/gredos.158764

Cheng, C. & Chau, C. (2022). Gamification-based intervention for enhancing team effectiveness and coping flexibility: Randomized controlled trial. Frontiers in Psychiatry. frontiersin.org

Cheng, E. C. K. (2020). Knowledge transfer strategies and practices for higher education institutions. *VINE Journal of Information and Knowledge Management Systems, ahead-of-print*(ahead-of-print). DOI: 10.1108/VJIKMS-11-2019-0184

Cheng, L., Chen, Z., & Liu, X. (2023). Equity challenges in gamified cybersecurity education: Access and infrastructure. *Journal of Educational Technology Systems, 51*(1), 55–72. DOI: 10.1177/00472395231124211

Chennamaneni, S., Pradhan, P., Chebolu, V., Vejendla, M., Kannaiah, S. K., & Aravinth, S. S. (2023). Designing Cybersecurity AI based awareness Games for Citizens: best practices and future directions. *2022 International Conference on Sustainable Computing and Data Communication Systems (ICSCDS)*. DOI: 10.1109/ICSCDS56580.2023.10104800

Chen, Y.-T., Shih, W.-L., Lee, C.-H., Wu, P.-L., & Tsai, C.-Y. (2021). Relationships among undergraduates' problematic information security behavior, compulsive internet use, and mindful awareness in Taiwan. *Computers & Education, 164*, 104131. DOI: 10.1016/j.compedu.2021.104131

Chesti, I. A., Humayun, M., Sama, N. U., & Jhanjhi, N. (2020). Evolution, Mitigation, and Prevention of Ransomware. *2020 2nd International Conference on Computer and Information Sciences (ICCIS)*. DOI: 10.1109/ICCIS49240.2020.9257708

Cheung, R., Cohen, J., Lo, H. Z., & Elia, F. (2011). Challenge-based learning in cybersecurity education. *Innovations in Systems and Software Engineering*, *7*(4), 289–294. DOI: 10.1007/s11334-011-0177-2

Chicone, R. G., & Ferebee, S. (2020). A COMPARISON STUDY OF TWO CYBERSECURITY LEARNING SYSTEMS: FACEBOOK'S OPEN SOURCE CAPTURE THE FLAG AND CTFD. *Issues in Information Systems*, *21*(1), 202–212. DOI: 10.48009/1_iis_2020_202-212

Chindrus, C. & Caruntu, C. F. (2023). Securing the Network: A Red and Blue Cybersecurity Competition Case Study. Information. mdpi.com

Chindrus, C., & Caruntu, C. (2023). Securing the Network: A Red and Blue Cybersecurity Competition case study. *Information (Basel)*, *14*(11), 587. DOI: 10.3390/info14110587

Chopade, S. (2023). How to Build a Gamification Strategy – An Expert View. Retrieved from https://www.harbingergroup.com/blogs/how-to-build-a-gamification-strategy-an-expert-view

Chourasia, R. (2025). AI-enhanced cybersecurity training: Learning analytics in action. *International Journal of Advanced Research in Science. Tongxin Jishu*, •••, 566–573. DOI: 10.48175/IJARSCT-12345

Chowdhury, N., Katsikas, S., & Gkioulos, V. (2022). Modeling effective cybersecurity training frameworks: A delphi method-based study. Computers & Security. sciencedirect.com

Chowdhury, M., Dixon, L., Kuo, L., Donaldson, J. P., Eslami, Z., Viruru, R., & Luo, W. (2024). Digital game-based language learning for vocabulary development. *Computers and Education Open*, *6*, 100160. DOI: 10.1016/j.caeo.2024.100160

Christopoulos, A., & Mystakidis, S. (2023). Gamification in education. *Encyclopedia*, *3*(4), 1223–1243. DOI: 10.3390/encyclopedia3040089

Christopoulos, A., Styliou, M., Ntalas, N., & Stylios, C. (2024). The impact of immersive virtual reality on knowledge acquisition and adolescent perceptions in cultural education. *Information (Basel)*, *15*(5), 261. DOI: 10.3390/info15050261

Chupkemi, D. C., & Mersinas, K. (2024). Challenges in maritime cybersecurity training and compliance. *Journal of Marine Science and Engineering*, *12*(10), 1844. DOI: 10.3390/jmse12101844

Ciaburro, G., & Kumcu, E. H. (2024). The role of Sound on the future of E-Commerce Applications using Metaverse Technologies. In *Advances in business strategy and competitive advantage book series* (pp. 177–204). DOI: 10.4018/979-8-3693-9586-8.ch007

Cigdem, H., Ozturk, M., Karabacak, Y., Atik, N., Gürkan, S., & Aldemir, M. H. (2024). Unlocking student engagement and achievement: The impact of leaderboard gamification in online formative assessment for engineering education. *Education and Information Technologies, 29*(18), 24835–24860. Advance online publication. DOI: 10.1007/s10639-024-12845-2

CISA. (2020). *Cybersecurity and Infrastructure Security Agency Annual Report.* Retrieved from https://www.cisa.gov

Clark, L., Martin, K., & Nguyen, T. (2021). Gamification in hybrid work environments: Enhancing engagement and collaboration. *Journal of Workplace Learning, 33*(5), 347–361.

Community, H. S. (2024). *Cyber hackathon (Capture The Flag 2024).* https://mf.hku.edu.tr/eng/Etkinlik/cyber-hackathon-capture-the-flag-2024-2/

Connolly, T. M., Boyle, E. A., MacArthur, E., Hainey, T., & Boyle, J. M. (2012). A systematic literature review of empirical evidence on computer games and serious games. *Computers & Education, 59*(2), 661–686. DOI: 10.1016/j.compedu.2012.03.004

Corradini, I. (2020). Building a Cybersecurity Culture. *Studies in Systems. Decision and Control, 284*, 63–86. DOI: 10.1007/978-3-030-43999-6_4

Costa, G., De Francisci, S., Renieri, M., & Valiani, S. (2025, February). Tackling the Gender Gap in Cybersecurity Education. In *Proceedings of the 56th ACM Technical Symposium on Computer Science Education* V. 1 (pp. 234-240). DOI: 10.1145/3641554.3701807

Council, E. (2024). Can EC-Council's CEH v13 leverage AI to revolutionize ethical hacking? *Times of AI.* https://www.timesofai.com/news/ec-council-ceh-v13-ai-ethicalhacking-training/

Creed, C., Al-Kalbani, M., Theil, A., Sarcar, S., & Williams, I. (2023). Inclusive Augmented and Virtual Reality: A research agenda. *International Journal of Human-Computer Interaction, 40*(20), 6200–6219. DOI: 10.1080/10447318.2023.2247614

Creswell, J. W., & Creswell, J. D. (2018). *Research design: Qualitative, quantitative, and mixed methods approaches* (5th ed.). SAGE Publications. Denzin, N. K. (2012). Triangulation 2.0. *Journal of Mixed Methods Research, 6*(2), 80–88. https://doi.org/ DOI: 10.1177/1558689812437186

Crogman, H. T., Cano, V. D., Pacheco, E., Sonawane, R. B., & Boroon, R. (2025). Virtual Reality, Augmented Reality, and Mixed Reality in Experiential Learning: Transforming Educational Paradigms. *Education Sciences*, *15*(3), 303. DOI: 10.3390/educsci15030303

Cruz, C. D. (2024). *Enhancing Engagement: Key Factors for Exceptional Learners in Gamified Education.* Paper presented at the 2024 9th International Conference on Information Technology and Digital Applications (ICITDA).

Csikszentmihalyi, M. (1990). *Flow: The psychology of optimal experience.* Harper & Row.

Cullen, J., Joyce, J., Hassall, T., & Broadbent, M. (2003). Quality in higher education: From monitoring to management. *Quality Assurance in Education*, *11*(1), 5–14. DOI: 10.1108/09684880310462038

CyberTalents. (n.d.). *How CTF competitions can help companies hire top cybersecurity professionals?* CyberTalents Blog. https://cybertalents.com/blog/hire-top-cybersecurity-professionals-through-ctfs?utm_source=chatgpt.com

Dahalan, F., Alias, N., & Shaharom, M. S. N. (2023). Gamification and Game Based Learning for Vocational Education and Training: A Systematic Literature review. *Education and Information Technologies*, *29*(2), 1279–1317. DOI: 10.1007/s10639-022-11548-w PMID: 36688221

Dahiya, S. (2024). *Handbook of Digital Journalism: Perspectives from South Asia.* Springer Nature. DOI: 10.1007/978-981-99-6675-2

Dahri, N. A., Al-Nuaimi, M. N., & Raza, M. (2025). *The effect of AI gamification on students' engagement and academic achievement: SEM analysis perspectives.* IEEE., DOI: 10.1109/ACCESS.2025.1234567

Damaševičius, R., & Sidekerskienė, T. (2024). Virtual Worlds for Learning in Metaverse: A Narrative review. *Sustainability (Basel)*, *16*(5), 2032. DOI: 10.3390/su16052032

Dapitan, J. U., Butchayo, J. M. M., Palma, J. L. R., Arevalo, M. A., Alvarico, A. B., & Cuevas, J. F.Jr. (2024). Measuring the Level of Cybersecurity Awareness among Senior High School Students. [MJBAS]. *Mediterranean Journal of Basic and Applied Sciences*, *8*(2), 208–217. DOI: 10.46382/MJBAS.2024.8216

Dar, A. A., Yadav, S. S., Tripathi, R. K., Albalawi, O., Jain, A., & Gautam, P. L. (2024). Managing ethical challenges. In *Advances in educational technologies and instructional design book series* (pp. 301–332). DOI: 10.4018/979-8-3693-6170-2.ch011

Daramola, J. O. (2024). *Scrum requirements engineering for a game-based learning web platform for grade R – 12 learners in South Africa*. Electronic Theses and Dissertations. https://etd.cput.ac.za/handle/20.500.11838/4069

Darling-Hammond, L., Schachner, A. C., Wojcikiewicz, S. K., & Flook, L. (2024). Educating teachers to enact the science of learning and development. [tandfonline.com]. *Applied Developmental Science*, *28*(1), 1–21. DOI: 10.1080/10888691.2022.2130506

Dass, S. M., Mahalingam, S. R., Hang, P. L., Kelvin, K., Wingsky, J., Mohamed, A. M. M. A., Rebecca, A. J., Hatmal, N. I. Y. B. A., Ali, A. R., Tjahyosedjati, E., Wei, T., & Sindiramutty, S. R. (2025). The Role of Cryptography and AI in Enhancing Blockchain Security. *preprints.org*. DOI: 10.20944/preprints202501.0386.v1

Davis, R. L., Schneider, B., Rosenbaum, L. F., & Blikstein, P. (2023). Hands-on tasks make learning visible: A learning analytics lens on the development of mechanistic problem-solving expertise in makerspaces. *Educational Technology Research and Development*, *72*(1), 109–132. DOI: 10.1007/s11423-023-10318-w

Day, D., Bastardoz, N., Bisbey, T., Reyes, D., & Salas, E. (2021). Unlocking human potential through leadership training & development initiatives. [sagepub.com]. *Behavioral Science & Policy*, *7*(1), 41–54. DOI: 10.1177/237946152100700105

de Wit, H., & Altbach, P. G. (2020). Internationalization in higher education: Global trends and recommendations for its future. *Policy Reviews in Higher Education*, *5*(1), 28–46. DOI: 10.1080/23322969.2020.1820898

Dearborn. (n.d.). *Subject Guides: Virtual Escape Rooms & Scavenger Hunts: The Escape Rooms*. https://guides.umd.umich.edu/c.php?g=1119708&utm_source=chatgpt.com

Deci, E. L., & Ryan, R. M. (1985). *Intrinsic motivation and self-determination in human behavior*. Plenum. DOI: 10.1007/978-1-4899-2271-7

Deci, E. L., & Ryan, R. M. (2008). Self-determination theory: A macrotheory of human motivation, development, and health. *Canadian Psychology*, *49*(3), 182–185. DOI: 10.1037/a0012801

Dehghanzadeh, H., Farrokhnia, M., Dehghanzadeh, H., Taghipour, K., & Noroozi, O. (2023). Using gamification to support learning in K-12 education: A systematic literature review. *British Journal of Educational Technology*, *55*(1), 34–70. DOI: 10.1111/bjet.13335

De-Marcos, L., Garcia-Lopez, E., & Garcia-Cabot, A. (2016). On the effectiveness of game-like and social approaches in learning: Comparing educational gaming, gamification & social networking. *Computers & Education*, *95*, 99–113. DOI: 10.1016/j.compedu.2015.12.008

Denmeade, N. (2015). *Gamification with Moodle*. Packt Publishing Ltd.

Denning, T., Lerner, A., Shostack, A., & Kohno, T. (2013). Control-Alt-Hack: The design and evaluation of a card game for computer security awareness and education. In Proceedings of the 2013 ACM SIGSAC conference on Computer & communications security (pp. 915–928). DOI: 10.1145/2508859.2516745

Denzin, N. K., & Lincoln, Y. S. (2017). *The SAGE handbook of qualitative research* (5th ed.). SAGE Publications.

Deterding, S., Dixon, D., Khaled, R., & Nacke, L. (2011). From game design elements to gamefulness: defining "gamification". In *Proceedings of the 15th International Academic MindTrek Conference: Envisioning Future Media Environments* (pp. 9-15). DOI: 10.1145/2181037.2181040

Dev, M., & Saha, D. (2024). Does e-government development moderate the impact of female labor participation on national cybersecurity maturity? An empirical investigation. *Information and Computer Security*, *32*(1), 74–92. DOI: 10.1108/ICS-03-2023-0042

Dey, B., & Panda, B. N. (2024). Understanding the learning Style Preferences of ODL students using VARK Model: Implications for Individualized Pedagogy and Student Success. *Asian Journal of Education and Social Studies*, *50*(5), 323–331. DOI: 10.9734/ajess/2024/v50i51365

Di Nardo, V., Fino, R., Fiore, M., Mignogna, G., Mongiello, M., & Simeone, G. (2024). Usage of Gamification Techniques in Software Engineering Education and Training: A Systematic Review. *Computers*, *13*(8), 196. DOI: 10.3390/computers13080196

Diakoumakos, I. (2023). *Enhancing Cyber Security Education and Training through Gamification.* Paper presented at the ACM International Conference Proceeding Series. DOI: 10.1145/3609987.3610016

Diakoumakos, J., Chaskos, E., Kolokotronis, N., & Lepouras, G. (2025). Cybersecurity gamification in federation of cyber ranges: Design, implementation, and evaluation. *International Journal of Information Security*, *24*(1), 57. Advance online publication. DOI: 10.1007/s10207-024-00974-1

Dicheva, D., Dichev, C., Agre, G., & Angelova, G. (2015). Gamification in education: A systematic mapping study. *Journal of Educational Technology & Society*, *18*, 75–88.

Dichev, C., & Dicheva, D. (2017). Gamifying education: What is known, what is believed and what remains uncertain: A critical review. *International Journal of Educational Technology in Higher Education*, *14*(1), 9. Advance online publication. DOI: 10.1186/s41239-017-0042-5

Dichev, C., & Dicheva, D. (2021). Motivation in gamified learning environments: A systematic review. *International Journal of Educational Technology in Higher Education*, *18*, 54. Advance online publication. DOI: 10.1186/s41239-021-00287-x

Dickson, P. R. (2023). The turbulent future of expertise and training markets. *Journal of Services Marketing*, *38*(1), 43–55. DOI: 10.1108/JSM-08-2023-0301

Dillenbourg, P., & Jermann, P. (2010). Technology for classroom orchestration. In Khine, M. S., & Saleh, I. M. (Eds.), *New science of learning: Cognition, computers and collaboration in education* (pp. 525–552). Springer., DOI: 10.1007/978-1-4419-5716-0_26

Dillon, R., & Tan, K.-L. (2024). Cybersecurity workforce landscape, education, and industry growth prospects in Southeast Asia. *Journal of Tropical Futures*, *1*(2), 172–181. DOI: 10.1177/27538931231176903

Dincă, M., Berge, T., Oni iu, A., Thomassen, M., Lu trea, A., Luche , D., & Cra ovan, M. (2023). Immersive Team-Based Learning in Transnational Virtual Classrooms. [sciendo.com]. *European Review Of Applied Sociology*, *16*(27), 51–70. DOI: 10.2478/eras-2023-0010

Dindar, M., Ren, L., & Järvenoja, H. (2021). An experimental study on the effects of gamified cooperation and competition on English vocabulary learning. [wiley.com]. *British Journal of Educational Technology*, *52*(1), 142–159. DOI: 10.1111/bjet.12977

Djeki, E., Dégila, J., & Alhassan, M. H. (2024). West African online learning spaces security status and students' cybersecurity awareness level during COVID-19 lockdown. *Education and Information Technologies*, *29*(12), 15557–15587. DOI: 10.1007/s10639-024-12472-x

Doerner, R. & Horst, R. (2022). Overcoming challenges when teaching hands-on courses about Virtual Reality and Augmented Reality: Methods, techniques and best practice. Graphics and Visual Computing. sciencedirect.com

Dogra, V., Singh, A., Verma, S., Kavita, N., Jhanjhi, N. Z., & Talib, M. N. (2021). Analyzing DistilBERT for Sentiment Classification of Banking Financial News. In *Lecture notes in networks and systems* (pp. 501–510). DOI: 10.1007/978-981-16-3153-5_53

Domínguez, A., Saenz-de-Navarrete, J., de-Marcos, L., Fernández-Sanz, L., Pagés, C., & Martínez-Herráiz, J. J. (2013). Gamifying learning experiences: Practical implications and outcomes. *Computers & Education, 63*, 380–392. DOI: 10.1016/j.compedu.2012.12.020

Domínguez, L. G. I., Robles-Gómez, A., & Pastor-Vargas, R. (2025). A data-driven approach to engineering instruction: Exploring learning styles, study habits, and machine learning. *IEEE Access : Practical Innovations, Open Solutions, 1*, 10978–11002. Advance online publication. DOI: 10.1109/ACCESS.2025.3528263

Donald, A., & Iqbal, J. (n.d.). Implementing cyber defense strategies: Evolutionary algorithms, cyber forensics, and AI-driven solutions for enhanced security. [Unpublished manuscript].

Dong, J., Ota, K., & Dong, M. (2024). User experience of different groups in social VR applications: An empirical study based on user reviews. *IEEE Transactions on Computational Social Systems, 11*(6), 1–13. DOI: 10.1109/TCSS.2024.3416208

Dua, A., & Kumar, G. (2024). *Mastering zero-knowledge proofs: Practical study of security, scalability, and privacy in blockchain and modern systems (English Edition)*. BPB Publications.

Durakovskiy, A. P., Gavdan, G. P., Korsakov, I. A., & Melnikov, D. A. (2021). About the cybersecurity of automated process control systems. *Procedia Computer Science, 190*, 217–225. DOI: 10.1016/j.procs.2021.06.027

Duran, R., Zavgorodniaia, A., & Sorva, J. (2022). Cognitive load theory in computing education research: A review. [TOCE]. *ACM Transactions on Computing Education, 22*(4), 1–27. DOI: 10.1145/3483843

Du, Y., Arkesteijn, M. H., den Heijer, A. C., & Song, K. (2020). Sustainable Assessment Tools for Higher Education Institutions: Guidelines for Developing a Tool for China. *Sustainability (Basel), 12*(16), 6501. DOI: 10.3390/su12166501

EC-Council. (2025, January 22). *CEH Certification | Ethical Hacking Training & Course | EC-Council*. https://www.eccouncil.org/train-certify/certified-ethical-hacker-ceh/

Edwards, J. (2024). Vulnerability assessment and penetration testing. In *Apress eBooks* (pp. 371–412). DOI: 10.1007/979-8-8688-0297-3_11

Edwards, J. J. (2024). *Establishing Cybersecurity Dominance by Introducing Women to the Fight* (Doctoral dissertation, Capitol Technology University).

Efgivia, M. G., Rinanda, R. A., Hidayat, A., Maulana, I., & Budiarjo, A. (2021). *Analysis of constructivism learning theory.* Paper presented at the 1st UMGESHIC International Seminar on Health, Social Science and Humanities (UMGESHIC-ISHSSH 2020). DOI: 10.2991/assehr.k.211020.032

Elkhodr, M., & Gide, E. (2025). Integrating generative AI in cybersecurity education: Case study insights on pedagogical strategies, critical thinking,

Emmanuel, A., & Sendagi, M. (2024). RELATIONSHIP BETWEEN AUDIO LEARNING STYLE, KINESTHETIC LEARNING STYLE AND ACADEMIC ACHIEVEMENT OF SECONDARY SCHOOL STUDENTS IN KAMWENGE DISTRICT, UGANDA. a CROSS-SECTIONAL STUDY. *Deleted Journal, 1*(7), 13. DOI: 10.51168/4hv4ww85

Er-Radi, H., Touis, B., & Aammou, S. (2023). Machine learning in adaptive online learning for enhanced learner engagement. In *Advances in educational technologies and instructional design book series* (pp. 43–63). DOI: 10.4018/979-8-3693-3132-3.ch003

Fabre, B., Bribet, J., Lescieux, L., & Caussarieu, A. (2024). Improving efficiency in optics education with immersive virtual reality. *Optical Engineering (Redondo Beach, Calif.), 63*(07). Advance online publication. DOI: 10.1117/1.OE.63.7.071411

Faith, B. F., Long, Z. A., & Hamid, S. (2024). *Promoting cybersecurity knowledge via gamification: an innovative intervention design.* Paper presented at the 2024 Third International Conference on Distributed Computing and High Performance Computing (DCHPC). DOI: 10.1109/DCHPC60845.2024.10454080

Farooq, A., Kakakhel, S. R. U., Virtanen, S., & Isoaho, J. A taxonomy of perceived information security and privacy threats among IT security students. In *Proceedings of the 2015 10th International Conference for Internet Technology and Secured Transactions (ICITST)*, London, UK, 14–16 December 2015; pp. 280–286. DOI: 10.1109/ICITST.2015.7412106

FasterCapital. (2024). Emerging Ethical Challenges in the Digital Age.

Fatima-Tuz-Zahra, N., Jhanjhi, N., Brohi, S. N., Malik, N. A., & Humayun, M. (2020). Proposing a Hybrid RPL Protocol for Rank and Wormhole Attack Mitigation using Machine Learning. *2020 2nd International Conference on Computer and Information Sciences (ICCIS)*. DOI: 10.1109/ICCIS49240.2020.9257607

Fatokun, N. F., Awang, N. Z., Hamid, N. S., Fatokun, N. J. O., & Norman, N. A. (2024). Cybersecurity Knowledge Deterioration and the role of Gamification Intervention. *Journal of Advanced Research in Applied Sciences and Engineering Technology*, *43*(1), 66–94. DOI: 10.37934/araset.43.1.6694

Ferguson, M., Hill, A., & Xu, B. (2021). Gamified cybersecurity education: An empirical evaluation of Capture the Flag competitions. *Journal of Cybersecurity Education, Research and Practice, 2021*(1), Article 3. https://digitalcommons.kennesaw.edu/jcerp/vol2021/iss1/3

Fernandes, J. O., & Singh, B. (2021). Accreditation and ranking of higher education institutions (HEIs): review, observations and recommendations for the Indian higher education system. *The TQM Journal, ahead-of-print*(ahead-of-print). DOI: 10.1108/TQM-04-2021-0115

Fernandez, A., Morgan, J., & Cooper, S. (2024). Evaluating the effectiveness of the CyberPatriot program on high school cybersecurity skills.

Finseth, T., Dorneich, M. C., Keren, N., Franke, W. D., & Vardeman, S. (2024). Virtual Reality Adaptive training for personalized stress inoculation. *Human Factors*. Advance online publication. DOI: 10.1177/00187208241241968 PMID: 38546259

Firmansyah, F. H., & Rosmansyah, Y. (2024). Exploring Collaboration in Multiplayer Gamification: A Systematic Literature Review. *IEEE Access : Practical Innovations, Open Solutions*.

Fisher, N., & Kulshreshth, A. K. (2024). Exploring dynamic difficulty adjustment methods for video games. *Virtual Worlds*, *3*(2), 230–255. DOI: 10.3390/virtualworlds3020012

Fleck, J. (2018). Development and establishment in artificial intelligence. In *The question of artificial intelligence* (pp. 106–164). Routledge. DOI: 10.4324/9780429505331-3

Flick, U. (2018). *An introduction to qualitative research* (6th ed.). SAGE Publications.

Fogg, B. J. (2009). *Behaviour design: A model for creating lasting change*. Stanford University Press.

Fogg, B. J. (2019). *Tiny habits: The small changes that change everything*. Houghton Mifflin Harcourt.

Foley, M., & Basu, S. (2024). Decoding the gendered imaginary of cybersecurity careers: A social shaping of technology perspective. *Information Communication and Society*, •••, 1–17.

Francis, S. P., Kolil, V. K., Pavithran, V., Ray, I., & Achuthan, K. (2024). Exploring gender dynamics in cybersecurity education: A self-determination theory and social cognitive theory perspective. *Computers & Security, 144*, 103968. DOI: 10.1016/j.cose.2024.103968

Fraunholz, D., Zimmermann, S., & Schotten, H. D. (2018). An overview of cybersecurity awareness campaigns and gamification in security education. *Future Internet, 10*(1), 27. DOI: 10.3390/fi10010027

Fuchs, K. (2024). Challenges with gamification in higher education: A narrative review with implications for educators and policymakers. *International Journal of Changes in Education, 1*(1), 51–56. DOI: 10.47852/bonviewIJCE32021604

Fu, M., Pasuksmit, J., & Tantithamthavorn, C. (2024). Ai for devsecops: A landscape and future opportunities. *ACM Transactions on Software Engineering and Methodology*.

Fung, C., Poon, K., Besser, M., & Fung, M. (2023). Improving short-term academic performance in the flipped classroom using dynamic geometry software. *Journal of Computer Assisted Learning, 40*(2), 775–786. DOI: 10.1111/jcal.12914

Futcher, L., Schroder, C., & von Solms, R. (2010). Information security education in South Africa. *Information Management & Computer Security, 18*(5), 366–374. DOI: 10.1108/09685221011095272

Gandham, R. (2025, January 3). *SMARTGUIDE: Revolutionizing the depth and dependability of Vision-Impaired Navigation*. https://vtechworks.lib.vt.edu/items/2ad9c8dd-7a40-4674-906b-3a0630b82647

Gangavarapu, T., Jaidhar, C., & Chanduka, B. (2020). Applicability of machine learning in spam and phishing email filtering: Review and approaches. *Artificial Intelligence Review, 53*(7), 5019–5081. DOI: 10.1007/s10462-020-09814-9

Gardiner, J., Abaimov, S., Williams, J., Shahbi, F., Anastasakis, K., Chowdhury, P. D., Ellis, W., Sameen, M., Samanis, E., & Rashid, A. (2024). "If You Build it, They will Come" - A Blueprint for ICS-focused Capture-The-Flag Competitions. *ACM*, 27–40. DOI: 10.1145/3690134.3694818

Garza, V. R., Kumar, S., & Patel, R. (2020). Machine learning techniques for identifying anomalous network traffic. [Unpublished manuscript].

Gee, J. P. (2003). *What video games have to teach us about learning and literacy*. Palgrave Macmillan. DOI: 10.1145/950566.950595

Gentry, B. (2021). *How students experience failure in a content-gamified higher education course* [Doctoral dissertation, Southern New Hampshire University]. ProQuest Dissertations Publishing.

Gerges, E. (2025). Beyond Lectures: The Flipped Learning Model. In Best Practices and Strategies for Online Instructors: Insights From Higher Education Online Faculty (pp. 133-166). IGI Global Scientific Publishing. [HTML]

Gerontakis, G., Yannakopoulos, P., & Voyiatzis, I. (2023). Evaluating cybersecurity certifications: A framework for extracting educational scenarios in cybersecurity training. In *Proceedings of the 27th Pan-Hellenic Conference on Progress in Computing and Informatics* (pp. 123–134). DOI: 10.1145/3635059.3635097

Giannakos, M., Azevedo, R., Brusilovsky, P., Cukurova, M., Dimitriadis, Y., Hernandez-Leo, D., & Rienties, B. (2024). The promise and challenges of generative AI in education. [tandfonline.com]. *Behaviour & Information Technology*, •••, 1–27.

Gil-Aciron, L. A. (2024). The gamer psychology: A psychological perspective on game design and gamification. *Interactive Learning Environments*, *32*(1), 183–207. DOI: 10.1080/10494820.2022.2082489

Gillis, A. S. N. B. What is gamification? How it works and how to use it. Retrieved from https://www.techtarget.com/searchhrsoftware/definition/gamification

Gill, S. S., Xu, M., Ottaviani, C., Patros, P., Bahsoon, R., Shaghaghi, A., Golec, M., Stankovski, V., Wu, H., Abraham, A., Singh, M., Mehta, H., Ghosh, S. K., Baker, T., Parlikad, A. K., Lutfiyya, H., Kanhere, S. S., Sakellariou, R., Dustdar, S., & Uhlig, S. (2022). AI for next generation computing: Emerging trends and future directions. [PDF]. *Internet of Things : Engineering Cyber Physical Human Systems*, *19*, 100514. DOI: 10.1016/j.iot.2022.100514

Gimenez-Fernandez, E., Abril, C., Breuer, H., & Gudiksen, S. (2021). Gamification approaches for open innovation implementation: A conceptual framework. [wiley.com]. *Creativity and Innovation Management*, *30*(3), 455–474. DOI: 10.1111/caim.12452

Girardi, A., Higham, L., Fatima, S., Webb, E., Snyman, P., Wallang, P., & Breen, K. C. (2024). Virtual reality and social avoidance: An exploratory study of acceptance, and feasibility in an inpatient secure environment. *Deleted Journal*, *1*(2), 141–159. DOI: 10.1108/MHDT-01-2024-0004

Gkintoni, E., Vantaraki, F., Skoulidi, C., Anastassopoulos, P., & Vantarakis, A. (2024). Promoting Physical and Mental Health among Children and Adolescents via Gamification—A Conceptual Systematic Review. *Behavioral Sciences (Basel, Switzerland), 14*(2), 102. DOI: 10.3390/bs14020102 PMID: 38392455

Glennie, E., Dalton, B., Studley, R., & Lauff, E. (2024). The Influence of Earning Industry Certifications on High School Graduation: Evidence from Florida. *Educational Policy*, 08959048241292625. Advance online publication. DOI: 10.1177/08959048241292625

Goffer, M. A., Smith, J., & Brown, T. (2025). AI-enhanced cyber threat detection and response advancing national security in critical infrastructure. *Journal of Posthumanism, 5*(3), 1667–1689. DOI: 10.63332/joph.v5i3.965

González-Fernández, A., Revuelta-Domínguez, F.-I., & Fernández-Sánchez, M. R. (2022). Models of instructional Design in Gamification: A systematic review of the literature. *Education Sciences, 12*(1), 44. DOI: 10.3390/educsci12010044

Google, C. T. F. (Capture The Flag). (n.d.). *Google Capture The Flag competition.* Retrieved from https://capturetheflag.withgoogle.com/

Gopi, R., Sathiyamoorthi, V., Selvakumar, S., Manikandan, R., Chatterjee, P., Jhanjhi, N. Z., & Luhach, A. K. (2021). Enhanced method of ANN based model for detection of DDoS attacks on multimedia internet of things. *Multimedia Tools and Applications, 81*(19), 26739–26757. DOI: 10.1007/s11042-021-10640-6

Gordan, M., & Krishanan, I. A. (2014). A review of BF Skinner's 'Reinforcement Theory of Motivation'. International journal of research in education methodology, 5(3), 680-688.

Gordon, R. (n.d.). *Introduction to Hack the Box | Hack the Box Help Center.* https://help.hackthebox.com/en/articles/5185158-introduction-to-hack-the-box

Gouda, W., Almurafeh, M., Humayun, M., & Jhanjhi, N. Z. (2022). Detection of COVID-19 based on chest x-rays using deep learning. *Health Care, 10*(2), 343. DOI: 10.3390/healthcare10020343 PMID: 35206957

Grabner-Hagen, M. M., & Kingsley, T. (2023). From badges to boss challenges: Gamification through need-supporting scaffolded design to instruct and motivate elementary learners. *Computers and Education Open, 4*, 100131. Advance online publication. DOI: 10.1016/j.caeo.2023.100131

Grajek, S. (2017). Top 10 IT Issues, 2017: Foundations for student Success.

Grover, S., Broll, B., & Babb, D. (2023). Cybersecurity education in the age of AI: Integrating AI learning into cybersecurity high school curricula. In *Proceedings of the 54th ACM Technical Symposium on Computer Science Education* V. 1 (pp. 456–462). ACM. DOI: 10.1145/3545945.3569750

Guerrero, E. & Kalmi, P. (2022). Gamification strategies: a characterization using formal argumentation theory. SN Computer Science. springer.com

Gwenhure, A. K., & Rahayu, F. S. (2024). Gamification of Cybersecurity Awareness for Non-IT Professionals: A Systematic Literature Review. *International Journal of Serious Games*, *11*(1), 83–99. DOI: 10.17083/ijsg.v11i1.719

Habibi, F., Sedaghatshoar, S., Attar, T., Shokoohi, M., Kiani, A., & Malek, A. N. (2025). Revolutionizing education and therapy for students with autism spectrum disorder: A scoping review of AI-driven tools, technologies, and ethical implications. *AI and Ethics*, *5*(3), 2055–2070. Advance online publication. DOI: 10.1007/s43681-024-00608-1

Hack The Box. (n.d.). *Hacking training and cybersecurity labs*. https://www.hackthebox.com/

HackEDU. (n.d.). *Interactive secure development training*. https://www.securityjourney.com/

Hadwin, A. F., Rostampour, R., & Winne, P. H. (2025). Advancing Self-Reports of Self-Regulated Learning: Validating new measures to assess students' beliefs, practices, and challenges. *Educational Psychology Review*, *37*(1), 8. Advance online publication. DOI: 10.1007/s10648-024-09977-9

Hager, P., Jungmann, F., Holland, R., Bhagat, K., Hubrecht, I., Knauer, M., Vielhauer, J., Makowski, M., Braren, R., Kaissis, G., & Rueckert, D. (2024). Evaluation and mitigation of the limitations of large language models in clinical decision-making. [nature.com]. *Nature Medicine*, *30*(9), 2613–2622. DOI: 10.1038/s41591-024-03097-1 PMID: 38965432

Hailikari, T., Virtanen, V., & Vesalainen…, M. (2022). Student perspectives on how different elements of constructive alignment support active learning. … in Higher Education. sagepub.com

Haleem, P. P. A. (2024, July 23). *A lightweight, reliable, secure, paginated, disconnected, and distributed message transaction model for wireless mobile environment*. http://scholar.uoc.ac.in/handle/20.500.12818/1632

Hallengren, A., & Svensson, M. (2013). *Dynamic difficulty adjustment for role-playing games*. DIVA. https://www.diva-portal.org/smash/record.jsf?pid=diva2%3A830032&dswid=3489

Hamari, J., Koivisto, J., & Sarsa, H. (2014, January). Does gamification work?--a literature review of empirical studies on gamification. In 2014 47th Hawaii international conference on system sciences (pp. 3025-3034). Ieee.

Hamari, J., Koivisto, J., & Sarsa, H. (2016). Does gamification work? A literature review of empirical studies on gamification. *System Sciences (HICSS), 2014 47th Hawaii International Conference on*. DOI: 10.1109/HICSS.2014.377

Hamari, J., Koivisto, J., & Sarsa, H. (2016). Does gamification work? A literature review of empirical studies on gamification. *International Journal of Information Management, 36*(2), 162–175. DOI: 10.1016/j.ijinfomgt.2015.11.005

Hamari, J., Koivisto, J., & Sarsa, H. (2022). Does gamification work? A literature review of empirical studies on gamification. *International Journal of Human-Computer Studies*, *127*, 190–204.

Hamid, B., Jhanjhi, N., Humayun, M., Khan, A., & Alsayat, A. (2019). *Cyber security issues and challenges for smart cities: A survey.* Paper presented at the 2019 13th International Conference on Mathematics, Actuarial Science, Computer Science and Statistics (MACS). DOI: 10.1109/MACS48846.2019.9024768

Hammami, H. (2024). Exploring the mediating role of user engagement in the relationship between immersive experiences and user satisfaction in virtual reality gaming. *International Review of Management and Marketing*, *15*(1), 9–16. DOI: 10.32479/irmm.17343

Hamza, M. A., Ejaz, U., & Kim, H. (2024). Cyber5Gym: An integrated framework for 5G cybersecurity training. *Electronics (Basel)*, *13*(5), 888. DOI: 10.3390/electronics13050888

Handayani, P. W., Raharjo, S. R., & Putra, P. H. (2021). Active student learning through gamification in a learning management system. *Electronic Journal of e-Learning*, *19*(6), 601–613. DOI: 10.34190/ejel.19.6.2089

Haron, H., Sajari, A., Dewanti, R., Ganesan, Y., & Gui, A. (2023, November). Digital transformation in community development of Malaysia and Indonesia. In ICCD (Vol. 5, No. 1, pp. 232-242).

Hasan, K., Khan, M., & Rahman, M. (2025). Enhancing proactive cyber defense: A theoretical framework for AI-driven predictive cyber threat intelligence. *Journal of Technologies Information and Communication*, *5*(1), 33122. DOI: 10.55267/rtic/16176

Hassan, S. K., & Ibrahim, A. (2023). The role of artificial intelligence in cyber security and incident response. *International Journal for Electronic Crime Investigation*, *7*(2), 1–12.

HAWKINSON. E. (2025). Convergence of AR, VR, and AI: The Rise of Immersive Learning Technologies in Higher Education. *Extended reality, AI, and discursive formations*, 21.

Hefkaluk, N., Linehan, C., & Trace, A. (2023). Fail, fail again, fail better: How players who enjoy challenging games persist after failure in "Celeste.". *International Journal of Human-Computer Studies*, *183*, 103199. DOI: 10.1016/j.ijhcs.2023.103199

Heid, K., Heider, J., Qasempour, K., & Darmstadt, G. K. H. F. S. Raising Security Awareness on Mobile Systems through Gamification. In *Proceedings of the European Interdisciplinary Cybersecurity Conference*, Rennes, France, 18 November 2020; pp. 1–6. DOI: 10.1145/3424954.3424958

Heilbrunn, B., Herzig, P., & Schill, A. (2014, 8-11 Dec. 2014). *Tools for Gamification Analytics: A Survey.* Paper presented at the 2014 IEEE/ACM 7th International Conference on Utility and Cloud Computing.

Henrikki, S.-P. (2021). AI Ethics - Critical Reflections on Embedding Ethical Frameworks in AI Technology. 311-329. DOI: 10.1007/978-3-030-77431-8_20

He, Z., Liu, Y., Wang, X., Li, R., & Lv, N. (2023). Gamified entrepreneurship courses motivate college students' satisfaction: An integrated flow framework. *SAGE Open*, *13*(2), 21582440231177029. DOI: 10.1177/21582440231177029

Hong, Y., Saab, N., & Admiraal, W. (2024). Approaches and game elements used to tailor digital gamification for learning: A systematic literature review. *Computers & Education*, *212*, 105000. DOI: 10.1016/j.compedu.2024.105000

Huitema, D., & Wong, A. (2025). A Case Study in Gamification for a Cybersecurity Education Program: A Game for Cryptography. *arXiv preprint arXiv:2502.06706*.

Humayun, M., Jhanjhi, N. Z., Talib, M. N., Shah, M. H., & Suseendran, G. (2021). Cybersecurity for data science: Issues, opportunities, and challenges. In *Intelligent Computing and Innovation on Data Science. Proceedings of ICTIDS, 2021*, 435–444.

Humayun, M., Sujatha, R., Almuayqil, S. N., & Jhanjhi, N. Z. (2022). A Transfer Learning Approach with a Convolutional Neural Network for the Classification of Lung Carcinoma. *Health Care*, *10*(6), 1058. DOI: 10.3390/healthcare10061058 PMID: 35742109

Hussain, K., Rahmatyar, A. R., Riskhan, B., Sheikh, M. U., & Sindiramutty, S. R. (2024). Threats and Vulnerabilities of Wireless Networks in the Internet of Things (IoT). *IEEE 1st Karachi Section Humanitarian Technology Conference (KHI-HTC)*, *2*, 1–8. DOI: 10.1109/KHI-HTC60760.2024.10482197

Hussein, M. H., Sulaiman, N. L., Noroozi, O., Elaish, M. M., & Alhasan, A. (2025). Value-added digital game-based learning in K-12 science education: A systematic literature review. *Interactive Learning Environments*, •••, 1–35. DOI: 10.1080/10494820.2025.2450652

Idierukevbe, I. U. & Addo, A. (2024). Bridging the Cybersecurity Skills Gap: A Gamification Model. Journal of Business Studies Quarterly. [HTML]

Immersive Labs. (n.d.). *Hands-on cyber workforce development platform*. https://www.immersivelabs.com/

Iqbal, H. S. (2021). AI-Driven Cybersecurity: An Overview, Security Intelligence Modeling and Research Directions. DOI: 10.20944/preprints202101.0457.v1

Irene, M. (2024). Policing virtual reality and promising cyber peace: an impending need for integration of cybersecurity. In *Routledge eBooks* (pp. 163–181). DOI: 10.4324/9781003517290-17

Ivanov, Y. (2023). AI in cyber deception: Creating adaptive and realistic honeypot systems. *Advances in Computer Sciences*, *6*(1), 1–10.

Iyer, R., Maralapalle, V. C., & Mahesh, P. (2024). Virtual reality (VR) and augmented reality (AR) in vocational training. In *Advances in educational technologies and instructional design book series* (pp. 73–92). DOI: 10.4018/979-8-3693-8252-3.ch004

Jääskä, E. & Aaltonen, K. (2022). Teachers' experiences of using game-based learning methods in project management higher education. Project Leadership and Society. sciencedirect.com

Jacob, T., & Centofanti, S. (2023). Effectiveness of H5P in improving student learning outcomes in an online tertiary education setting. *Journal of Computing in Higher Education*, *36*(2), 469–485. DOI: 10.1007/s12528-023-09361-6 PMID: 37359040

Jagatheesaperumal, S. K., Ahmad, K., Al-Fuqaha, A., & Qadir, J. (2024). Advancing education through extended reality and internet of everything enabled metaverses: Applications, challenges, and open issues. *IEEE Transactions on Learning Technologies*, *17*, 1–20. DOI: 10.1109/TLT.2024.3358859

Javed, D., Jhanjhi, N., Ashfaq, F., Khan, N. A., Das, S. R., & Singh, S. (2024). *Student Performance Analysis to Identify the Students at Risk of Failure.* Paper presented at the 2024 International Conference on Emerging Trends in Networks and Computer Communications (ETNCC). DOI: 10.1109/ETNCC63262.2024.10767511

Jawhar, S., Miller, J., & Bitar, Z. (2024). AI-Driven Customized Cyber Security Training and Awareness. *2024 IEEE 3rd International Conference on AI in Cybersecurity (ICAIC)*, 1–5. DOI: 10.1109/ICAIC60265.2024.10433829

Jayawardena, N. S., Ross, M., Quach, S., Behl, A., Gupta, M., & Lang, L. D. (2021). Effective online engagement strategies through gamification. *Journal of Global Information Management*, *30*(5), 1–25. DOI: 10.4018/JGIM.290370

Jelo, M., & Helebrandt, P. (2022). *Gamification of cyber ranges in cybersecurity education.* Paper presented at the 20th Anniversary of IEEE International Conference on Emerging eLearning Technologies and Applications, ICETA 2022 - Proceedings. DOI: 10.1109/ICETA57911.2022.9974714

Jhanjhi, N., Khan, M. A., Ahmad, M., & Hussain, M. (2022). The Impact of Cyber Attacks on E-Governance During the COVID-19 Pandemic. *Cybersecurity Measures for E-Government Frameworks*, 123.

Jhanjhi, N., Humayun, M., & Almuayqil, S. N. (2021). Cyber security and privacy issues in industrial internet of things. *Computer Systems Science and Engineering*, *37*(3), 361–380. DOI: 10.32604/csse.2021.015206

Jimmy, F. (2021). Emerging threats: The latest cybersecurity risks and the role of artificial intelligence in enhancing cybersecurity defenses. *Valley International Journal Digital Library*, *1*(2), 564–574. DOI: 10.18535/ijsrm/v9i2.ec01

Jin, G., Tu, M., Kim, T. H., Heffron, J., & White, J. (2018). *Game based cybersecurity training for High School Students.* Paper presented at the SIGCSE 2018 - Proceedings of the 49th ACM Technical Symposium on Computer Science Education. DOI: 10.1145/3159450.3159591

Joon, N., & Simmons, R. (2024). Innovating cybersecurity education through AI-augmented teaching. *European Conference on Cyber Warfare and Security*, *23*(1), 480–486. DOI: 10.34190/eccws.23.1.2224

Joshi, N., & Joshi, M. (2024). Gamified AI-driven assessments. *Journal of Scientific and Engineering Research*, *11*(11), 108–114.

Jover, V., Sempere, S., & Ferrándiz, S. (2025). The creation of virtual stands in the metaverse: Applications for the textile sector. *Electronics (Basel)*, *14*(2), 359. DOI: 10.3390/electronics14020359

JPMorgan Chase. (2020). *Building a culture of cybersecurity awareness*. Internal white paper or training insights

Jun, A. Y. M., Jinu, B. A., Seng, L. K., Maharaiq, M. H. F. B. Z., Khongsuwan, W., Junn, B. T. K., Hao, A. W., & Sindiramutty, S. R. (2024). Exploring the Impact of Crypto-Ransomware on Critical Industries: Case Studies and Solutions. *Preprints.org*. DOI: 10.20944/preprints202409.1325.v1

Kachhi, Z. (2024). Gamified success. In *Advances in media, entertainment and the arts (AMEA) book series* (pp. 157–176). DOI: 10.4018/979-8-3693-8322-3.ch007

Kaddoura, S. (2021). Classification of malicious and benign websites by network features using supervised machine learning algorithms. In *2021 5th Cyber Security in Networking Conference (CSNet)* (pp. 87–94). IEEE. DOI: 10.1109/CSNet52717.2021.9614273

Kamal, N. A., & Ibrahim, C. K. I. C. (2025). Quality assurance in civil engineering education: Insights into program educational objectives (PEOs) in Malaysia. *Quality Assurance in Education*, *33*(3), 479–499. Advance online publication. DOI: 10.1108/QAE-10-2024-0205

Kanchon, M. K. H., Sadman, M., Nabila, K. F., Tarannum, R., & Khan, R. (2024). Enhancing personalized learning: AI-driven identification of learning styles and content modification strategies. *International Journal of Cognitive Computing in Engineering*, *5*, 269–278. DOI: 10.1016/j.ijcce.2024.06.002

Kang, X., & Nie, Y. (2024). The Application of Virtual Simulation in the Training of Artistic Voice:A Study on Improving the Vocal Training Effect. *SSRN*. DOI: 10.2139/ssrn.4903508

Kaplan, Z., Zhang, N., & Cole, S. V. (2022). *A Capture The Flag (CTF) Platform and Exercises for an Intro to Computer Security Class*. Paper presented at the Annual Conference on Innovation and Technology in Computer Science Education, ITiCSE.

Kapp, K. M. (2012). *The gamification of learning and instruction: Game-based methods and strategies for training and education*. Pfeiffer.

Karagiannis, S., & Magkos, E. (2020). Adapting CTF challenges into virtual cybersecurity learning environments. *Information and Computer Security*, *29*(1), 105–132. DOI: 10.1108/ICS-04-2019-0050

Kartal, S. (2008). *Virtual dissections in the teaching of practical biology in South African high schools.* https://ujcontent.uj.ac.za/esploro/outputs/doctoral/Virtual-dissections-in-the-teaching-of/999945407691

Kasri, W., Himeur, Y., Alkhazaleh, H. A., Tarapiah, S., Atalla, S., Mansoor, W., & Al-Ahmad, H. (2025). From Vulnerability to Defense: The role of large language models in enhancing Cybersecurity. *Computation (Basel, Switzerland)*, *13*(2), 30. DOI: 10.3390/computation13020030

Kasture, A. B. (2024). THE USE OF AUGMENTED REALITY (AR) INENGINEERING AND MEDICINE. *Journal of Top Trending Technology*, *01*(01), 31–42. DOI: 10.71063/DJTTT.2025.1104

Kasurinen, J., & Knutas, A. (2018). Publication trends in gamification: A systematic mapping study. *Computer Science Review*, *27*, 33–44. DOI: 10.1016/j.cosrev.2017.10.003

Katcher, S., Wang, L., Yang, C., Messdaghi, C., Mazurek, M. L., Chetty, M., & Votipka, D. (2024). A Survey of Cybersecurity {Professionals'} Perceptions and Experiences of Safety and Belonging in the Community. In *Twentieth Symposium on Usable Privacy and Security (SOUPS 2024)* (pp. 1-20).

Katsamakas, E., Pavlov, O. V., & Saklad, R. (2024). Artificial Intelligence and the Transformation of Higher Education Institutions: A Systems approach. *Sustainability (Basel)*, *16*(14), 6118. DOI: 10.3390/su16146118

Katsantonis, M. N., Manikas, A., Mavridis, I., & Gritzalis, D. (2023). Cyber range design framework for cyber security education and training. *International Journal of Information Security*, *22*(4), 1005–1027. DOI: 10.1007/s10207-023-00680-4

Katsikeas, S., Rencelj Ling, E., Johnsson, P., & Ekstedt, M. (2024). Empirical evaluation of a threat modeling language as a cybersecurity assessment tool. *Computers & Security*, *140*, 103743. DOI: 10.1016/j.cose.2024.103743

Kaushik, K., Kumar, S., & Singh, R. (2024). Ethical considerations in AI-based cybersecurity. In *Next-generation cybersecurity: AI, ML, and blockchain* (pp. 437–470). Springer., DOI: 10.1007/978-981-97-1249-6_19

keepnetlabs. (2025). Human-Centric Cybersecurity: Building Stronger Defenses by Focusing on People. Retrieved from https://keepnetlabs.com/blog/human-centric-cybersecurity-prioritizing-people-in-cyber-defense

Kehinde, O. (2025). Leveraging machine learning for predictive models in healthcare to enhance patient outcome management. *International Research Journal of Modernization in Engineering Technology and Science*. Advance online publication. DOI: 10.56726/IRJMETS66198

Kellman, P. J., Jacoby, V., Massey, C., & Krasne, S. (2022). Perceptual Learning, adaptive learning, and Gamification: educational technologies for pattern recognition, problem solving, and knowledge retention in medical learning. In *Springer eBooks* (pp. 135–166). DOI: 10.1007/978-3-030-95633-2_5

Kelso, E., Soneji, A., Rahaman, S., Shoshitaishvili, Y., & Hasan, R. (2024). Trust, Because You Can't Verify: Privacy and Security Hurdles in Education Technology Acquisition Practices. *ACM*, 1656–1670. DOI: 10.1145/3658644.3690353

Kersting, M., Bondell, J., Steier, R., & Myers, M. (2024). Virtual reality in astronomy education: Reflecting on design principles through a dialogue between researchers and practitioners. International Journal of Science Education [tandfonline.com]. *Part B*, *14*(2), 157–176.

Kethireddy, R. R. (2023). AI-augmented threat response systems with real-time adaptive defense. *Intelligence*, *1*(1), 62–71.

Kettunen, J. (2015). Stakeholder relationships in higher education. *Tertiary Education and Management*, *21*(1), 56–65. DOI: 10.1080/13583883.2014.997277

Khalaf, B. A., Mustafa, A. S., & Bilal, S. (2019). Comprehensive review of artificial intelligence and statistical approaches in distributed denial of service attack and defense methods. *IEEE Access : Practical Innovations, Open Solutions*, *7*, 51691–51713. DOI: 10.1109/ACCESS.2019.2908998

Khaleghi, A., Aghaei, Z., & Mahdavi, M. A. (2021). A gamification framework for cognitive assessment and cognitive training: Qualitative study. *JMIR Serious Games*, *9*(2), e21900. DOI: 10.2196/21900 PMID: 33819164

Khalid, I. L., Abdullah, M. N. S., & Fadzil, H. M. (2024). A Systematic Review: Digital Learning in STEM Education. *Journal of Advanced Research in Applied Sciences and Engineering Technology*, *51*(1), 98–115. DOI: 10.37934/araset.51.1.98115

Khan, A. R. S., Syed, H. J., Shuja, J., Khan, A., Qamar, F., & Nguyen, Q. N. (2024). Advancing Secure and Efficient Sensor Data Integration in Smart Cities: A Blockchain-Based Approach.

Khan, A., Jhanjhi, N. Z., & Sujatha, R. (2022). Emerging Industry Revolution IR 4.0 Issues and Challenges. In *Cyber Security Applications for Industry 4.0* (pp. 151-169): Chapman and Hall/CRC.

Khan, A., Jhanjhi, N., Alı, G. A., Ray, S. K., & Wassan, S. (2025). Case Studies and Applications of Generative AI in Real-World Cybersecurity Scenarios.

Khan, A., Jhanjhi, N., Hamid, D. H. H., Omar, H. A. H. B. H., Amsaad, F., & Ashraf, H. (2025). Reshaping Cybersecurity for Supply Chain Sustainability in IR 4.0 and 5.0.

Khan, A., Jhanjhi, N., Hamid, D. H. H., Omar, H. A. H. B. H., Amsaad, F., & Wassan, S. (2025). Future Trends and Challenges in Cybersecurity and Generative AI. *Reshaping CyberSecurity With Generative AI Techniques*, 491-522.

Khan, M. R., Khan, N. R., & Jhanjhi, N. Z. (2024). *Convergence of Industry 4.0 and Supply Chain Sustainability*: IGI Global.

Khan, A., Jhanjhi, N. Z., & Humayun, M. (2022). The Role of Cybersecurity in Smart Cities. In *Cyber Security Applications for Industry 4.0* (pp. 195–208). Chapman and Hall/CRC. DOI: 10.1201/9781003203087-9

Khan, M. A., Merabet, A., Alkaabi, S., & Sayed, H. E. (2022). Game-based learning platform to enhance cybersecurity education. *Education and Information Technologies*, *27*(4), 1–25. DOI: 10.1007/s10639-021-10807-6

Khan, M. T., Ullah, S., Sami, A., Kukreti, M., & Shaukat, M. R. (2025). Cultivating a paradoxical mindset: Enhancing transformative learning through paradoxical leadership. *Leadership and Organization Development Journal*, *46*(2), 334–350. Advance online publication. DOI: 10.1108/LODJ-04-2024-0223

Khan, S. K., Shiwakoti, N., Wang, J., Xu, H., Xiang, C., Zhou, X., & Jiang, H. (2025). An Investigation on Passengers' Perceptions of Cybersecurity in the Airline Industry. *Future Transportation*, *5*(1), 5. DOI: 10.3390/futuretransp5010005

Khine, M. S. (2024). Using AI for adaptive learning and adaptive assessment. In *Artificial Intelligence in Education* (pp. 341–466). DOI: 10.1007/978-981-97-9350-1_3

Khoo, L. J., Yatim, M. H. M., & Wong, Y. S. (2025). Research on Capture the Flag Exercises for Cybersecurity skill training among Malaysian undergraduates. *Journal of Human Centered Technology*, *4*(1), 1–9. DOI: 10.11113/humentech.v4n1.87

Kim, A., Park, M., & Lee, D. H. (2020). AI-IDS: Application of deep learning to real-time web intrusion detection. *IEEE Access : Practical Innovations, Open Solutions*, *8*, 70245–70261. DOI: 10.1109/ACCESS.2020.2986882

Kim, E. B. (2014). Recommendations for information security awareness training for college students. *Information Management & Computer Security*, *22*, 115–126. DOI: 10.1108/IMCS-01-2013-0005

Kim, J. B., Zhong, C., & Liu, H. (2023). What You Need to Know about Gamification Process of Cybersecurity Hands-on Lab Exercises: Lessons and Challenges. *Journal of Information Systems Education, 34*(4), 387–405. https://www.scopus.com/inward/record.uri?eid=2-s2.0-85177421937&partnerID=40&md5=8d9dff6a3e8330e15e9d97d65f999937

Kim, L. (2022). Cybersecurity: Ensuring confidentiality, integrity, and availability of information. In *Nursing Informatics: A Health Informatics, Interprofessional and Global Perspective* (pp. 391–410). Springer International Publishing. [HTML] DOI: 10.1007/978-3-030-91237-6_26

Kim, S., Lee, J., & Choi, Y. (2022). Gamification strategies to promote engagement in cybersecurity education. *Journal of Cybersecurity Education, 8*(1), 45–62. DOI: 10.1093/jces/xyz123

Kim, S., Song, H., & Lee, K. (2022). The role of gamification in corporate learning: Enhancing motivation and engagement. *Journal of Organizational Behavior, 43*(1), 45–59. DOI: 10.1002/job.2573

Kirlappos, I., Parkin, S., & Sasse, M. A. (2015). Learning from "Shadow Security": Why understanding non-compliance provides the basis for effective security awareness campaigns. In *Proceedings of the 2015 Workshop on Usable Security.*

Kiyani, F. F., Hamid, B., Humayun, M., Sindiramutty, S. R. L., & Chowdhury, S. (2024). Discovery of Influential Publications Using Research Article's Usage Context. *2024 International Conference on Emerging Trends in Networks and Computer Communications (ETNCC)*, 1–7. DOI: 10.1109/ETNCC63262.2024.10767576

Koivisto, J., & Hamari, J. (2019). The rise of motivational information systems: A review of gamification research. *Computers in Human Behavior, 99*, 98–123. DOI: 10.1016/j.chb.2019.05.033

Koivisto, J., & Hamari, J. (2019). The rise of motivational information systems: A review of gamification research. *International Journal of Information Management, 45*, 191–210. DOI: 10.1016/j.ijinfomgt.2018.10.013

Kolb, D. A. (1984). *Experiential learning: Experience as the source of learning and development*. Prentice Hall.

Kostelić, K. (2024). Dynamic awareness and strategic adaptation in cybersecurity: A game-theory approach. *Games, 15*(2), 13. Advance online publication. DOI: 10.3390/g15020013

Kourtesis, P. (2024). A Comprehensive Review of Multimodal XR Applications, Risks, and Ethical Challenges in the Metaverse. Multimodal Technologies and Interaction. mdpi.com

Kraglund-Gauthier, W. (2015). Book Review- The New Digital Shoreline: How Web 2.0 and Millennials are Revolutionizing Higher Education. *Journal of Teaching and Learning With Technology*, *80–82*, 80–82. Advance online publication. DOI: 10.14434/jotlt.v4n1.13497

Krath, J., & Von Korflesch, H. F. (2021). Designing gamification and persuasive systems: A systematic literature review. *GamiFIN*, 100-109.

Krath, J., & Von Korflesch, H. F. (2021). Designing gamification and persuasive systems: A systematic literature review. *GamiFIN*, 100-109. Le, N. H. Guide to Gamification in Edtech: Key Elements, Successful Strategies & Top Examples. Retrieved from https://smartdev.com/guide-to-gamification-in-edtech-key-elements-successful-strategies-top-examples/

Krause, M., Mogalle, M., Pohl, H., & Williams, J. J. (2015). A Playful Game Changer. *ACM*, 95–102. DOI: 10.1145/2724660.2724665

Krichen, M., & Abdalzaher, M. S. (2024). Performance enhancement of artificial intelligence: A survey. *Journal of Network and Computer Applications*, *104034*, 104034. Advance online publication. DOI: 10.1016/j.jnca.2024.104034

Krishnan, S. D., Norman, H., & Md Yunus, M. (2021). Online gamified learning to enhance teachers' competencies using classcraft. Sustainability. mdpi.com

Kuleto, V., Ilić, M., Dumangiu, M., Ranković, M., Martins, O. M. D., Păun, D., & Mihoreanu, L. (2021). Exploring Opportunities and Challenges of Artificial Intelligence and Machine Learning in Higher Education Institutions. *Sustainability (Basel)*, *13*(18), 10424. DOI: 10.3390/su131810424

Kulkov, I., Kulkova, J., Rohrbeck, R., Menvielle, L., Kaartemo, V., & Makkonen, H. (2024). Artificial intelligence-driven sustainable development: Examining organizational, technical, and processing approaches to achieving global goals. [wiley.com]. *Sustainable Development (Bradford)*, *32*(3), 2253–2267. DOI: 10.1002/sd.2773

Kumar, A., Jabbar, K. A., Oudah, M. Y., Khan, A. A., & Verma, R. (2024). *Applying a Machine Learning Framework to Improve the Efficacy of Network Intrusion Detection Systems.* Paper presented at the 2024 International Conference on Emerging Trends in Networks and Computer Communications (ETNCC).

Kumar, M. S., Vimal, S., Jhanjhi, N., Dhanabalan, S. S., & Alhumyani, H. A. (2021). Blockchain based peer to peer communication in autonomous drone operation. *Energy Reports*, *7*, 7925–7939. DOI: 10.1016/j.egyr.2021.08.073

Kumar, R., Jain, V., Han, G. T. W., & Touzene, A. (2023). *Immersive virtual and augmented reality in healthcare: An IoT and Blockchain Perspective*. CRC Press. DOI: 10.1201/9781003340133

Kurni, M. (2024). *G, S. K.* IoT-Enabled Gamification for Education. In The Internet of Educational Things., DOI: 10.1007/978-3-031-67387-0_10

Kuwajima, H., & Ishikawa, F. (2019). *Adapting square for quality assessment of artificial intelligence systems.* Paper presented at the Proceedings - 2019 IEEE 30th International Symposium on Software Reliability Engineering Workshops, ISSREW 2019. DOI: 10.1109/ISSREW.2019.00035

Laato, S., Lipponen, J., & Sutinen, E. (2020). AI in cybersecurity education—A systematic literature review of studies on cybersecurity MOOCs. In *2020 IEEE 20th International Conference on Advanced Learning Technologies (ICALT)* (pp. 6–10). IEEE. DOI: 10.1109/ICALT49669.2020.00007

Lake, K., Kittrick, A. M., Desselle, M., Bo, A. P. L., Abayasiri, R. M., Fleming, J., Baghaei, N., & Kim, D. D. (2024). Cyber security and privacy issues in extended reality healthcare Applications: Scoping Review (Preprint). *JMIR XR and Spatial Computing.*, *1*, e59409. DOI: 10.2196/59409

Lakshmikantha, H. T. (2024). Leveling up orthodontic education: Game-based learning as the new frontier in orthodontic curriculum. *Research and Development in Medical Education*, *13*, 13. DOI: 10.34172/rdme.33205

Lampropoulos, G., Keramopoulos, E., Diamantaras, K., & Evangelidis, G. (2022). Augmented reality and gamification in education: A systematic literature review of research, applications, and empirical studies. applied sciences, 12(13), 6809. mdpi.com

Lampropoulos, G., & Sidiropoulos, A. (2024). Impact of gamification on students' learning outcomes and academic performance: A longitudinal study comparing online, traditional, and gamified learning. *Education Sciences*, *14*(4), 367. DOI: 10.3390/educsci14040367

Landers, R. N., & Armstrong, M. B. (2017). Enhancing instructional outcomes with gamification: An empirical test of the Technology-Enhanced Training Effectiveness Model. *Computers in Human Behavior*, *71*, 499–507. DOI: 10.1016/j.chb.2015.07.031

LeBlanc, P. (2021). *Students first: Equity, Access, and Opportunity in Higher Education*. Harvard Education Press.

Le, D. C., & Zincir-Heywood, N. (2021). Anomaly detection for insider threats using unsupervised ensembles. *IEEE Transactions on Network and Service Management*, *18*(2), 1152–1164. DOI: 10.1109/TNSM.2021.3071928

Lee, H., Wu, T., Lin, C., Wang, W., & Huang, Y. (2023). Integrating Computational Thinking into Scaffolding Learning: An innovative approach to enhance science, technology, engineering, and mathematics Hands-On learning. *Journal of Educational Computing Research*, *62*(2), 431–467. DOI: 10.1177/07356331231211916

Lee, K. (2012). Augmented reality in education and training. *TechTrends*, *56*(2), 13–21. DOI: 10.1007/s11528-012-0559-3

Lekkala, S., & Gurijala, P. (2024). Security and privacy for modern networks. In *Apress eBooks*. DOI: 10.1007/979-8-8688-0823-4

Lexman, R. R., & Baral, R. (2023). Digital twins in MOOCs: Exploring ways to enhance interactivity. *Development and Learning in Organizations*.

Lien, C.-W., & Vhaduri, S. (2023). Challenges and opportunities of biometric user authentication in the age of iot: A survey. *ACM Computing Surveys*, *56*(1), 1–37. DOI: 10.1145/3603705

Lim, M., Abdullah, A., Jhanjhi, N., Khan, M. K., & Supramaniam, M. (2019). Link Prediction in Time-Evolving Criminal Network with deep Reinforcement learning technique. *IEEE Access : Practical Innovations, Open Solutions*, *7*, 184797–184807. DOI: 10.1109/ACCESS.2019.2958873

Limmen, J. (2024). *Awesome reinforcement learning for cybersecurity*. https://github.com/Limmen/awesome-rl-for-cybersecurity

Lim, T. W. (2019). *Industrial revolution 4.0, tech giants, and digitized societies*. Palgrave Macmillan. DOI: 10.1007/978-981-13-7470-8

Linqiang, Y., Sindiramutty, S. R. L., Ashraf, H., Muzammal, S. M., Balakrishnan, S. P., Gupta, S., & Kavita, N. (2024). Intelligent Household Waste Classification System Based on Machine Learning. *2024 International Conference on Emerging Trends in Networks and Computer Communications (ETNCC)*, 760–768. DOI: 10.1109/ETNCC63262.2024.10767563

Liu, C., Lin, Y., Lo, F., Chang, C., & Lin, H. (2024). From readers to players: Exploring student engagement in a gamified metaverse and its effect on reading interest. *Education and Information Technologies*. Advance online publication. DOI: 10.1007/s10639-024-13068-1

Liu, G. Z., Fathi, J., & Rahimi, M. (2024). Using digital gamification to improve language achievement, foreign language enjoyment, and ideal L2 self: A case of English as a foreign language learners. *Journal of Computer Assisted Learning*, *40*(4), 1347–1364. DOI: 10.1111/jcal.12954

Liu, L. (2024). Impact of AI gamification on EFL learning outcomes and nonlinear dynamic motivation: Comparing adaptive learning paths, conversational agents, and storytelling. *Education and Information Technologies*. Advance online publication. DOI: 10.1007/s10639-024-13296-5

Löffler, E., Schäfer, R., & Schmidt, T. C. (2021). Cysecescape 2.0—A virtual escape room to raise cybersecurity awareness. *International Journal of Serious Games*, *8*(1), 59–70. DOI: 10.17083/ijsg.v8i1.413

Lomos, C., Seineke, U., Kesting, F., & Luyten, J. W. (2023). The design of incentive systems in digital game-based learning: How primary school children interact with It. Education Sciences. mdpi.com

Looyestyn, J., Kernot, J., Boshoff, K., Ryan, J., Edney, S., & Maher, C. (2017). Does gamification increase engagement with online programs? A systematic review. *PLoS One*, *12*(3), e0173403. DOI: 10.1371/journal.pone.0173403 PMID: 28362821

Lu, Z., Shen, C., Li, J., Shen, H., & Wigdor, D. (2021). More Kawaii than a Real-Person Live Streamer: Understanding How the Otaku Community Engages with and Perceives Virtual YouTubers. *Acm*, 1–14. DOI: 10.1145/3411764.3445660

Luo, Z. (2022). Gamification for educational purposes: What are the factors contributing to varied effectiveness? *Education and Information Technologies*, *27*(1), 891–915. DOI: 10.1007/s10639-021-10642-9

Lut, L. T. Y. (2024). *Literature review of application of AI in improving gaming experience : NPC behavior and dynamic difficulty adjustment*. LUTPub. https://lutpub.lut.fi/handle/10024/167834

Lynch, M., Kubberød, E., Sanne, N., & Josendal, A. H. F. (2025). *Deliberate practice through the gamification of entrepreneurship education*. Entrepreneurship Education and Pedagogy., DOI: 10.1177/25151274241309940

Mac, D. (2024). The Journal of Applied Instructional Design. *The Journal of Applied Instructional Design*. https://doi.org/DOI: 10.59668/2036

Mack, S. D. (2023). *The DevSecOps playbook: Deliver continuous security at speed.* John Wiley & Sons.

Maebela, M., & Dehinbo, J. (2024, August 27). *Enhancing Sustainable Development with the Development of a Virtual Driving License Testing System in Mabopane, South Africa.* https://papers.ssrn.com/sol3/papers.cfm?abstract_id=5059064

Mahmood, S., Akif, F., Ashraf, H., & Jhanjhi, N. (2024). Defense Mechanism Against Attacks Promoting Spread Of Wrong Information.

Mahmood, D., Nisar, H., & Tsai, C.-Y. (2024). Exploring the efficacy of neurofeedback training in modulating alpha-frequency band and its effects on functional connectivity and band power. *Expert Systems with Applications, 254*, 124415. Advance online publication. DOI: 10.1016/j.eswa.2024.124415

Makdoun, I., Rahhal, I., Mezzour, G., Kassou, I., & Carley, K. M. (2021). Skill mismatch evidence for Cybersecurity skills in Morocco. *Procedia Computer Science, 184*, 941–946. DOI: 10.1016/j.procs.2021.03.117

Malaysia, B. J. (2024). Digital challenges to economic opportunities: Ubiquitous computing in Malaysia's public transportation sector. *Journal of Applied Technology and Innovation (e-ISSN: 2600-7304), 8*(2), 7.

Malik, C. D. S. (2024, December). Technology and Women Empowerment: Bridging the Gender Gap in the Digital Era. *International Journal for Research Publication and Seminar, 15*(4), 132–126. DOI: 10.36676/jrps.v15.i4.19

Malone, M., Stockley, R., & Saeri, A. K. (2021). To gamify or not? On leaderboard effects, student engagement and learning outcomes in a cybersecurity intervention. In *Proceedings of the 52nd ACM Technical Symposium on Computer Science Education* (pp. 670–676). ACM. DOI: 10.1145/3408877.3432439

mambo.io. Gamification Statistics And Trends. Retrieved from https://mambo.io/gamification-guide/gamification-statistics-and-trends

Manchuri, A., Kakera, A., Saleh, A., & Raja, S. (2024). pplication of Supervised Machine Learning Models in Biodiesel Production Research - A Short Review. *Borneo Journal of Sciences and Technology*. DOI: 10.35370/bjost.2024.6.1-10

Manoharan, A., & Nagulapally, S. (2024). ADAPTIVE GAMIFICATION ALGORITHMS FOR PERSONALIZED LEARNING ERIENCES IN EDUCATIONAL PLATFORMS. *International Research Journal of Modernization in Engineering Technology and Science*. Advance online publication. DOI: 10.56726/IRJMETS49966

Manoharan, A., Sriskantharajah, A., Herath, H. M. K. K. M. B., Guruge, L. G. P. K., & Yasakethu, S. L. P. (2025). MetaHuman based phishing attacks in the metaverse realm: Awareness for cyber security education. *Education and Information Technologies, 30*(9), 1–27. DOI: 10.1007/s10639-025-13326-w

Mao, P., Cai, Z., Wang, Z., Hao, X., Fan, X., & Sun, X. (2023). The effects of dynamic and static feedback under tasks with different difficulty levels in digital game-based learning. *The Internet and Higher Education, 60*, 100923. DOI: 10.1016/j.iheduc.2023.100923

Marat, C., & Marat, S. (2024). The role of cybersecurity education on ethical hacking.

Marinho, A., Bittencourt, I. I., Dermeval, D., Santos, J., Challco, G., & Reis, M. (2024 under review). *How does the Mechanics of Competition and Collaboration Impact on Student's Flow Experience in a Gamified Educational Environment? An Experimental Study in Higher Education.* Technology, Knowledge and Learning.

Marougkas, A., Troussas, C., Krouska, A., & Sgouropoulou, C. (2023). Virtual reality in education: A review of learning theories, approaches and methodologies for the last decade. *Electronics (Basel), 12*(13), 2832. DOI: 10.3390/electronics12132832

Martineau, M., Spiridon, E., & Aiken, M. (2024). Pathways to Criminal Hacking: Connecting Lived Experiences with Theoretical Explanations. Forensic Sciences. mdpi.com

Martí-Parreño, J., Méndez-Ibáñez, E., & Alonso-Arroyo, A. (2016). The use of gamification in education: A bibliometric and text mining analysis. *Journal of Computer Assisted Learning, 32*(6), 663–676. DOI: 10.1111/jcal.12161

Masegosa, A. R., Cabañas, R., Maldonado, A. D., & Morales, M. (2024). Learning styles impact students' perceptions on active learning methodologies: A case study on the use of live coding and short programming exercises. *Education Sciences, 14*(3), 250. DOI: 10.3390/educsci14030250

Mathunjwa, M. L., Shandu, N. M., Ndwandwe, N. K., Shongwe, N., & Linda, N. (2024, December). Beyond the Classroom: The Social Benefits of Informal Sports for First-Year Students. In The Focus Conference (TFC 2024) (pp. 560-580). Atlantis Press. atlantis-press.com DOI: 10.2991/978-94-6463-630-7_31

Mathur, S., Antony, J., Olivia, M., Fabiane Letícia, L., Shreeranga, B., Raja, J., & Ayon, C. (2022). An empirical study into the use of 7 quality control tools in higher education institutions (HEIs). *The TQM Journal*. Advance online publication. DOI: 10.1108/TQM-07-2022-0222

Matovu, R., Nwokeji, J. C., Holmes, T., & Rahman, T. (2022). *Teaching and Learning Cybersecurity Awareness with Gamification in Smaller Universities and Colleges.* Paper presented at the Proceedings - Frontiers in Education Conference, FIE. DOI: 10.1109/FIE56618.2022.9962519

Mauricio, F., Alvítez-Temoche, D., Del Aguila, E., Mayta-Tovalino, F., Silva, H., & Espinoza-Carhuancho, F. (2024). Scientometric analysis of the world scientific production on augmented and virtual reality in dental education. *The Journal of Contemporary Dental Practice*, *25*(4), 358–364. DOI: 10.5005/jp-journals-10024-3675 PMID: 38956852

Mazari, N., & Bensalem, S. (2024). Leveraging virtual reality and augmented reality as educational experiences to spark students' creativity and enhance learning motivation: Universities of California, Harvard, and MIT as a case study. , *5*(3), 176–195. DOI: 10.70091/atras/AI.11

Mazhar, T., Talpur, D. B., Shloul, T. A., Ghadi, Y. Y., Haq, I., Ullah, I., Ouahada, K., & Hamam, H. (2023). Analysis of IoT security challenges and its solutions using artificial intelligence. *Brain Sciences*, *13*(4), 683. DOI: 10.3390/brainsci13040683 PMID: 37190648

McCormac, A., Zwaans, T., Parsons, K., Calic, D., Butavicius, M., & Pattinson, M. (2017). Individual differences and Information Security Awareness. *Computers in Human Behavior*, *69*, 151–156. DOI: 10.1016/j.chb.2016.11.065

McDermott, O., Antony, J., Sony, M., & Daly, S. (2021). Barriers and enablers for continuous improvement methodologies within the Irish pharmaceutical industry. Processes. mdpi.com

McStay, A. (2020). Emotional AI, soft biometrics and the surveillance of emotional life: An unusual consensus on privacy. *Big Data & Society*, *7*(1). Advance online publication. DOI: 10.1177/2053951720904386

Medina-Merodio, J. A., Castillo-Martinez, A., Barchino, R., Estriegana, R., & Robina-Ramírez, R. (2024). Factors influencing the acquisition of soft skills in a collaborative learning environment supported by Game-Based application. *IEEE Access : Practical Innovations, Open Solutions*, *12*, 111045–111059. DOI: 10.1109/ACCESS.2024.3441317

Merchan-Lima, J., Astudillo-Salinas, F., Tello-Oquendo, L., Sanchez, F., Lopez-Fonseca, G., & Quiroz, D. (2020). Information security management frameworks and strategies in higher education institutions: A systematic review. *Annales des Télécommunications*. Advance online publication. DOI: 10.1007/s12243-020-00783-2

Mhajne, A., & Whetstone, C. (2024). A feminist cybersecurity: Addressing the crisis of cyber (in) security. *International Affairs*, *100*(6), 2341–2360. DOI: 10.1093/ia/iiae234

Michel-Villarreal, R., Vilalta-Perdomo, E., Salinas-Navarro, D. E., Thierry-Aguilera, R., & Gerardou, F. S. (2023). Challenges and Opportunities of Generative AI for Higher Education as Explained by ChatGPT. *Education Sciences*, *13*(9), 1–18. DOI: 10.3390/educsci13090856

Microsoft. (2016). *The Security Ninja Training Program*. Microsoft Secure Blog. Retrieved from https://www.microsoft.com/security/blog/

Mitnick, K., & Simon, W. L. (2021). *The art of deception: Controlling the human element of security*. John Wiley & Sons.

Mlambo, M., Silén, C., & McGrath, C. (2021). Lifelong learning and nurses' continuing professional development, a metasynthesis of the literature. BMC nursing. springer.com

Mohamad, S. N. M., & Sazali, N. S. S. (2018). Gamification approach in education to increase learning engagement. *International Journal of Humanities Arts and Social Sciences*, *4*(1). Advance online publication. DOI: 10.20469/ijhss.4.10003-1

Mohamed Saad, A. M. A. (2024). *Adapting accountants to the AI revolution: university strategies for skill enhancement, job security and competence in accounting*. Higher Education, Skills and Work-Based Learning. [HTML]

Mohammed, M., Fatemah, A., & Hassan, L. (2024). Effects of Gamification on Motivations of Elementary School Students: An Action Research Field experiment. *Simulation & Gaming*, *55*(4), 600–636. DOI: 10.1177/10468781241237389

Moro, C., Štromberga, Z., Raikos, A., & Stirling, A. (2017). The effectiveness of virtual and augmented reality in health sciences and medical anatomy. *Anatomical Sciences Education*, *10*(6), 549–559. DOI: 10.1002/ase.1696 PMID: 28419750

Morris, R., Perry, T., & Wardle, L. (2021). Formative assessment and feedback for learning in higher education: A systematic review. Review of Education. wiley.com

Moseikina, M., Toktamysov, S., & Danshina, S. (2022). Modern technologies and gamification in historical education. *Simulation & Gaming*, *53*(2), 135–156. DOI: 10.1177/10468781221075965

Mosley, P., Chen, L. C., Ellrodt, L., & Ulysse, D. (2024). Camp CryptoBot: A Model for Taking Risks and Promoting Self-Efficacy in Pursuit of Cybersecurity Career Pathways. *Journal of Computing Sciences in Colleges*, *39*(7), 72–81.

Motala, A., Youngman, A., Hancox, A., & Bravo, C. (2024). *Indigenous care VR simulations*. https://openlibrary-repo.ecampusontario.ca/xmlui/handle/123456789/2154

Mouhssine, Y., Boutracheh, H., & Moumen, A. (2024). Teaching Cybersecurity to Engineering Students: A New Perspective Through Literature Review. *2024 4th International Conference on Innovative Research in Applied Science, Engineering and Technology (IRASET), 3413*, 1–9. DOI: 10.1109/IRASET60544.2024.10548731

Mukherjee, M., Le, N. T., Chow, Y.-W., & Susilo, W. (2024). Strategic approaches to cybersecurity learning: A study of educational models and outcomes. *Information (Basel), 15*(2), 117. DOI: 10.3390/info15020117

Mumtaz, S. L., Syed, H. J., Al-Ani, A., Fatah, S., Al-Ani, A. K., & Khan, A. (2024). *Detection of Botnet in the IoT Network*. Paper presented at the ITM Web of Conferences. DOI: 10.1051/itmconf/20246301019

Murillo-Zamorano, L. R., López Sánchez, J. Á., Godoy-Caballero, A. L., & Bueno Muñoz, C. (2021). Gamification and active learning in higher education: Is it possible to match digital society, academia and students' interests? [springer.com]. *International Journal of Educational Technology in Higher Education, 18*(1), 1–27. DOI: 10.1186/s41239-021-00249-y

Nadeem, M. A., Hashmi, S., & Khan, M. A. (2023). Exploring the Interplay of Cybersecurity and cybercrime in Pakistan's Digital Landscape. [cissmp.com]. *Contemporary Issues in Social Sciences and Management Practices, 2*(4), 207–222. DOI: 10.61503/cissmp.v2i4.94

Nagaraj, D. H., Abhi, S., & Agarwal, R. (2025). *Cybersecurity awareness: Gamified learning through phishing analysis*. Paper presented at the AIP Conference Proceedings. DOI: 10.1063/5.0247129

Nagarajan, A., Allbeck, J. M., Sood, A., & Janssen, T. L. (2012, May). Exploring game design for cybersecurity training. In *2012 IEEE International Conference on Cyber Technology in Automation, Control, and Intelligent Systems (CYBER)* (pp. 256–262). IEEE.

Nageab, W. M., Alrasheed, R., & Khalifa, M. (2024). Cybersecurity in the era of artificial intelligence: Risks and solutions. In *2024 ASU International Conference in Emerging Technologies for Sustainability and Intelligent Systems (ICETSIS)* (pp. 123–130). IEEE. DOI: 10.1109/ICETSIS61505.2024.10459584

Nah, F. F. H., Zeng, Q., Telaprolu, V. R., Ayyappa, A. P., & Eschenbrenner, B. (2014). Gamification of education: A review of literature. In *International Conference on HCI in Business* (pp. 401–409). Springer. https://doi.org/DOI: 10.1007/978-3-319-07293-7_39

Namukasa, M., Chaparro Osman, M., Ficke, C., Piasecki, I., OConnor, T. J., & Carroll, M. (2025). Evaluation of an Internet of Things Device-Based Educational Approach to Engage a More Diverse Cybersecurity Workforce. *International Journal of Human-Computer Interaction, 41*(2), 1364–1380. DOI: 10.1080/10447318.2024.2314349

Nasteski, V. (2017). An overview of the supervised machine learning methods. *Horizons. B, 4*, 51–62. DOI: 10.20544/HORIZONS.B.04.1.17.P05

Nawaz, A., Hussain, J., Jhanjhi, N. Z., Talib, M. N., & Nadim, M. (2021). Feature engineering based on hybrid features for malware detection over Android framework. *Turkish Journal of Computer and Mathematics Education, 12*(10), 2856–2864.

Nayyar, A., Gadhavi, L., & Zaman, N. (2021). Machine learning in healthcare: review, opportunities and challenges. In *Elsevier eBooks* (pp. 23–45). DOI: 10.1016/B978-0-12-821229-5.00011-2

Nepal, S., Hernandez, J., Lewis, R., Chaudhry, A., Houck, B., Knudsen, E., . . . Czerwinski, M. (2024). Burnout in Cybersecurity Incident Responders: Exploring the Factors that Light the Fire. Proceedings of the ACM on Human-Computer Interaction, 8(CSCW1), 1-35. mit.edu

Neupane, A., Hansen, D., Fails, J. A., & Sharma, A. (2021). The role of steps and game elements in gamified fitness tracker apps: A systematic review. *Multimodal Technologies and Interaction, 5*(2), 5. DOI: 10.3390/mti5020005

Newhouse, W., Keith, S., Scribner, B., & Witte, G. (2017). *National Initiative for Cybersecurity Education (NICE) cybersecurity workforce framework* (NIST Special Publication 800-181). National Institute of Standards and Technology. https://doi.org/DOI: 10.6028/NIST.SP.800-181

Nguyen, H. T. V., & Javorsky, K. (2024). Beyond memorization. In *Advances in educational technologies and instructional design book series* (pp. 1–40). DOI: 10.4018/979-8-3693-6497-0.ch001

Nguyen, M. T., & Tran, M. Q. (2023). Balancing security and privacy in the digital age: An in-depth analysis of legal and regulatory frameworks impacting cybersecurity practices. *International Journal of Intelligent Automation and Computing, 6*(5), 1–12.

Ng, W. (2015). *New digital technology in education: Conceptualizing professional learning for educators*. Springer., DOI: 10.1007/978-3-319-05822-1

Niyivuga, B., Otara, A., & Tuyishime, D. (2019). Monitoring and Evaluation Practices and Academic Staff Motivation: Implications in Higher Education Within Rwandan Context. *SAGE Open*, *9*(1), 215824401982956. DOI: 10.1177/2158244019829564

Ntoutsi, E., Tran, H., & Kindermans, P. J. (2020). Bias in data-driven artificial intelligence systems—An introductory survey. *Wiley Interdisciplinary Reviews. Data Mining and Knowledge Discovery*, *10*(3), e1356. Advance online publication. DOI: 10.1002/widm.1356

Oigara, J. N. (2024). Exploring the use of virtual reality headsets as a learning tool for classroom instruction. In *Advances in educational technologies and instructional design book series* (pp. 153–180). DOI: 10.4018/979-8-3693-6030-9.ch006

Oke, A. E., Aliu, J., Tunji-Olayeni, P., & Abayomi, T. (2024). Application of gamification for sustainable construction: An evaluation of the challenges. *Construction Innovation*, *24*(4), 1066–1084. DOI: 10.1108/CI-09-2022-0247

Okolie, J. A. & Okoye, P. U. (2023). The Infusion of Gamification in Promoting Chemical Engineering Laboratory Classes. Encyclopedia. mdpi.com

Oleet, J. B., & Yu, C. (2024). Examining the role and effect of emotions in adults' online learning. In *Advances in educational technologies and instructional design book series* (pp. 155–204). DOI: 10.4018/979-8-3693-2663-3.ch006

Oliveira, W., Hamari, J., Shi, L., Toda, A. M., Rodrigues, L., Palomino, P. T., & Isotani, S. (2023). Tailored gamification in education: A literature review and future agenda. *Education and Information Technologies*, *28*(1), 373–406. DOI: 10.1007/s10639-022-11122-4

Olosunde, B. (2014). Impact of Cybersecurity Skills Gap on the U.S. Economy and National Security. *International Journal of Innovative Science, Engineering & Technology, 11*(12), 61–76. https://www.babatopeolosunde.com/media/sm0jo4fo/impact-of-cybersecurity-skills.pdf

Olutimehin, A. T., Adeyemi, O., & Ogunleye, G. (2025). Adversarial threats to AI-driven systems: Exploring the attack surface of machine learning models and countermeasures. *SSRN*. DOI: 10.2139/ssrn.5137026

Orru, G., & Longo, L. (2019). *The evolution of cognitive load theory and the measurement of its intrinsic, extraneous and germane loads: a review.* Paper presented at the Human Mental Workload: Models and Applications: Second International Symposium, H-WORKLOAD 2018, Amsterdam, The Netherlands, September 20-21, 2018, Revised Selected Papers 2. DOI: 10.1007/978-3-030-14273-5_3

Ortiz-Rojas, M., Chiluiza, K., Valcke, M., & Bolanos-Mendoza, C. (2025). How gamification boosts learning in STEM higher education: A mixed methods study. *International Journal of STEM Education*, *12*(1), 1. Advance online publication. DOI: 10.1186/s40594-024-00521-3

Ouma, J., Wambalaba, F., Musuva, P., & Namasake, M. (2025). Influence of Gender Mainstreaming in Closing the Cybersecurity Workforce Gap: Insights from the Cyber Shujaa Upskilling Program. *African Journal of Business and Development Studies*, *1*(2), 300–317. DOI: 10.70641/ajbds.v1i2.110

OWASP Foundation. (n.d.). *OWASP Juice Shop*. https://owasp.org/www-project-juice-shop/

Oyighan, D., Adeyemi, O., & Ogunleye, G. (2024). The role of AI in transforming metadata management: Insights on challenges, opportunities, and emerging trends. *Asian Journal of Information Science and Technology*, *14*(2), 20–26. DOI: 10.70112/ajist-2024.14.2.4277

Pandey, A., Mittal, M., Ahmad, K., & Sharma, V. (2023). New Age Teaching Pedagogy: Innovative Teaching Methods and their Impact on Educational Performance of the Students. Redefining Virtual Teaching Learning Pedagogy, 59-73. [HTML]

Papadimitriou, S., & Virvou, M. (2025). Computer Games for Entertainment and Education: A Literature Review and Exploration on Artificial Intelligence Integration. *Intelligent Systems Reference Library*, 25–62. DOI: 10.1007/978-3-031-77464-5_2

Papadimitriou, S., & Virvou, M. (2025a). Artificial Intelligence—Based games as novel holistic educational environments to teach 21st century skills. In *Intelligent systems reference library*. DOI: 10.1007/978-3-031-77464-5

Papadimitriou, S., & Virvou, M. (2025b). Contributions and Discussions on Advancing 21st Century Skills Through EPATHLO: Prosocial Educational Games with Artificial Intelligence. In *Intelligent systems reference library* (pp. 277–309). DOI: 10.1007/978-3-031-77464-5_10

Papadimitriou, S., & Virvou, M. (2025). General Data Protection Regulation and adaptive educational games. In *Artificial intelligence—Based games as novel holistic educational environments to teach 21st century skills* (pp. 253–275). Springer., DOI: 10.1007/978-3-031-77464-5_9

Papathanasiou, N., & Tsiatsos, T. (2020). Gamification in cybersecurity education: A systematic review. *Education and Information Technologies*, *25*(5), 4191–4214. DOI: 10.1007/s10639-020-10302-0

Papert, S. (1980). *Mindstorms: Children, computers, and powerful ideas*. Basic Books.

Pappas, G., Papamichael, I., Zorpas, A., Siegel, J. E., Rutkowski, J., & Politopoulos, K. (2021). Modelling key performance indicators in a gamified waste management tool. [mdpi.com]. *Modelling*, *3*(1), 27–53. DOI: 10.3390/modelling3010003

Paracha, S., Hall, L., Hagan-Green, G., & Watson, D. (2024). Cyber eyes wide open. In *Advances in library and information science (ALIS) book series* (pp. 101–134). DOI: 10.4018/979-8-3693-6376-8.ch004

Park, E. H., Kim, J., & Park, Y. S. (2017). The role of information security learning and individual factors in disclosing patients' health information. *Computers & Security*, *65*, 64–76. DOI: 10.1016/j.cose.2016.10.011

Park, G. L., Hegazy, S. A., Sepe, J., Swigart, J., Burnette, M., Beltran, J., & Hernandez, C. (2025). Fostering Competencies: A scoping review of escape rooms in medical education. *Medical Science Educator*, *35*(2), 1111–1121. Advance online publication. DOI: 10.1007/s40670-024-02270-y PMID: 40352986

Parks, K. R. (n.d.). *A Phenomenological Study of Teachers' Experiences with Educational Gamification and its Impact on Student Engagement in the Middle School Math and Science Classroom*. Scholars Crossing. https://digitalcommons.liberty.edu/doctoral/4786/

Park, S., & Kim, S. (2021). Leaderboard design principles to enhance learning and motivation in a gamified educational environment: Development study. *JMIR Serious Games*, *9*(2), e14746. Advance online publication. DOI: 10.2196/14746 PMID: 33877049

Parsons, D., Rees, M., & Waite, W. (2019). AI tutors in cybersecurity education: A Microsoft case study. *Microsoft Education Blog*. https://www.microsoft.com/en-us/education/blog/2024/09/transforming-education-in-the-age-of-ai-with-a-unified-solution/

Pashaj, K., & Gjika, E. (2024). Gender Inequality in Cybersecurity Exploring the Opportunities and Progression in Albania. *Smart Cities and Regional Development (SCRD) Preprints, 1*(1).

Passey, D., Shukla, R., & Bott, S. (2019). *Empowering learners for life in the digital age*. Springer., DOI: 10.1007/978-3-030-23513-0

Patil, D. (2025). Artificial Intelligence In Cybersecurity: Enhancing Threat Detection And Prevention Mechanisms Through Machine Learning And Data Analytics. *SSRN*. DOI: 10.2139/ssrn.5057410

Pavithra, M., & Ramya, G. (2025). Using gamification to overcome innovation process challenges. In *Advances in healthcare information systems and administration book series* (pp. 287–306). DOI: 10.4018/979-8-3693-4199-5.ch012

Pellas, N. (2025). The impact of AI-Generated instructional Videos on Problem-Based Learning in Science Teacher Education. *Education Sciences*, *15*(1), 102. DOI: 10.3390/educsci15010102

Pellas, N., Fotaris, P., & Kazanidis, I. (2022). Immersive learning through VR and AR: Applications for cybersecurity training. *Computers & Education*, *176*, 104363.

Penning, T., Forde, J., & Broussard, S. (2024). Perceptions of formal career achievements in public relations by students, professionals, and employers: Certificate, accreditation, and College of Fellows. *Public Relations Review*, *50*(3), 102458. DOI: 10.1016/j.pubrev.2024.102458

Pereira, D., Fernandes, E., Lutovac, S., & Flores, M. A. (2025). Looking at assessment through critical incidents written by preservice teachers: A study conducted in Portugal. *Reflective Practice*, *26*(3), 1–20. DOI: 10.1080/14623943.2025.2459433

Pereira, J. T., & Harun, R. N. S. R. (2024). Gamification of classroom activities: Undergraduates' perception. *AJELP the Asian Journal of English Language and Pedagogy*, *12*(1), 80–92. DOI: 10.37134/ajelp.vol12.1.7.2024

Philpott, A., & Son, J. (2022). Leaderboards in an EFL course: Student performance and motivation. *Computers & Education*, *190*, 104605. DOI: 10.1016/j.compedu.2022.104605

Piaget, J. (1971). *Science of education and the psychology of the child*. Viking.

Piaget, J. (1972). *The psychology of the child*. Basic Books.

Piazza, A., Vasudevan, S., & Carr, M. (2023). Cybersecurity in UK universities: Mapping (or managing) threat intelligence sharing within the higher education sector. *Journal of Cybersecurity*, *9*(1), tyad019. Advance online publication. DOI: 10.1093/cybsec/tyad019

Picard, R., & Cosier, G. (1997). Affective intelligence—The missing link? *BT Technology Journal*, *15*(4), 151–162. DOI: 10.1023/A:1018643815520

Piki, A., Stavrou, E., Procopiou, A., & Demosthenous, A. (2023). *Fostering Cybersecurity Awareness and Skills Development Through Digital Game-Based Learning*. Paper presented at the Proceedings of the 2023 IEEE International Conference on Behavioural and Social Computing, BESC 2023. DOI: 10.1109/BESC59560.2023.10386988

Piki, A., Tchanturia, I., Kasenides, N., Paspallis, N., & Leal, S. (2024). SDG Quest: Leveraging mobile Game-Based Learning to foster environmental, social, and economic sustainable development goals. In *Lecture notes in computer science* (pp. 373–392). DOI: 10.1007/978-3-031-76812-5_25

Pillai, M. G., & Khan, F. (2025). Harnessing Learning Styles and Metacognition: A Dual Framework for Academic Improvement using the VARK Model. SSRN *Electronic Journal*. DOI: 10.2139/ssrn.5091493

Pils, M. (2025). Increasing security awareness in the company. In *Essentials* (pp. 11–31). DOI: 10.1007/978-3-658-46683-1_3

Pirta-Dreimane, R., Brilingaitė, A., Roponena, E., Parish, K., Grabis, J., Lugo, R. G., & Bonders, M. (2023). *CyberEscape Approach to Advancing Hard and Soft Skills in Cybersecurity Education.* Paper presented at the Lecture Notes in Computer Science (including subseries Lecture Notes in Artificial Intelligence and Lecture Notes in Bioinformatics). DOI: 10.1007/978-3-031-35017-7_28

Pirta-Dreimane, R., Brilingaitė, A., Roponena, E., Parish, K., Grabis, J., Lugo, R. G., & Bonders, M. (2024). Try to esCAPE from cybersecurity incidents! A technology-enhanced educational approach. Technology, Knowledge and Learning, 1-30. springer.com

Pitchay, S. A., Suhaimi, A. S., Alwi, N. H. M., Ridzuan, F., & Ab Halim, A. H. (2022). Enhancing cyber-attacks awareness via mobile gamification techniques. *International Journal of Advanced Research in Technology and Innovation, 4*(2), 69–84.

Pitura, J., Kaplan-Rakowski, R., & Asotska-Wierzba, Y. (2024). The VR-AI–Assisted Simulation for Content Knowledge Application in Pre-Service EFL Teacher training. *TechTrends*. Advance online publication. DOI: 10.1007/s11528-024-01022-4

Plass, J. L., Homer, B. D., & Kinzer, C. K. (2015). Foundations of game-based learning. *Educational Psychologist, 50*(4), 258–283. DOI: 10.1080/00461520.2015.1122533

Pollini, A., Callari, T. C., Tedeschi, A., Ruscio, D., Save, L., Chiarugi, F., & Guerri, D. (2022). Leveraging human factors in cybersecurity: An integrated methodological approach. [springer.com]. *Cognition Technology and Work, 24*(2), 371–390. DOI: 10.1007/s10111-021-00683-y PMID: 34149309

Poženel, M., Zrnec, A., & Lavbič, D. (2022). Measuring how motivation affects information quality assessment: A gamification approach. PloS one. plos.org

Pramod, D. (2024). Gamification in cybersecurity education; a state of the art review and research agenda. *Journal of Applied Research in Higher Education.*

Prensky, M. (2001). *Digital game-based learning*. McGraw-Hill.

PricewaterhouseCoopers, & Golding, D. (n.d.). *PwC uses innovation to transform cybersecurity training*. PwC. https://www.pwc.com/cb/en/case-studies/cayman-pwc-transforms-cybersecurity-training.html?utm_source=chatgpt.com

Prümmer, J., van Steen, T., & van den Berg, B. (2024). A systematic review of current cybersecurity training methods. *Computers & Security, 136*, 103585. DOI: 10.1016/j.cose.2023.103585

Puig, A., Rodríguez, I., Rodríguez, Á, & Gallego, I. (2023). Evaluating learner engagement with gamification in online courses. Applied Sciences. mdpi.com

Puig, A., Rodríguez, I., Rodríguez, Á., & Gallego, I. (2023). Evaluating learner engagement with gamification in online courses. *Applied Sciences (Basel, Switzerland), 13*(3), 1535. DOI: 10.3390/app13031535

Pujiono, I. P., Asfahani, A., & Rachman, A. (2024). Augmented reality (AR) and virtual reality (VR): recent developments and applications in various industries. *j-innovative.org*. https://doi.org/DOI: 10.31004/innovative.v4i4.12377

Quayyum, F. (2021). Cyber security education for children through gamification: Challenges and research perspectives. In *Methodologies and intelligent systems for technology enhanced learning, 10th International Conference. Workshops: Volume 2* (pp. 45–56). Springer. DOI: 10.1007/978-3-030-80504-3_4

Quayyum, F. (2021). *Cyber security education for children through gamification: Challenges and research perspectives.* Paper presented at the Methodologies and Intelligent Systems for Technology Enhanced Learning, 10th International Conference. Workshops: Volume 2. DOI: 10.1007/978-3-030-52287-2_26

Quayyum, F., & Jaccheri, L. (2024). CyberFamily: A collaborative family game to increase children's cybersecurity awareness. *Entertainment Computing, 52*, 100826. DOI: 10.1016/j.entcom.2024.100826

Qusa, H., & Tarazi, J. (2021). *Cyber-hero: A gamification framework for cyber security awareness for high schools students.* Paper presented at the 2021 IEEE 11th annual computing and communication workshop and conference (CCWC). DOI: 10.1109/CCWC51732.2021.9375847

Rahmi, I., Rimenda, T., & Ariyanti, T. D. (2024). Gamification as an alternative to increase students' motivation: A scoping review. [EduLearn]. *Journal of Education and Learning, 19*(2), 1125–1133. DOI: 10.11591/edulearn.v19i2.21771

Rajapakse, R. N., Zahedi, M., Babar, M. A., & Shen, H. (2022). Challenges and solutions when adopting DevSecOps: A systematic review. *Information and Software Technology, 141*, 106700. DOI: 10.1016/j.infsof.2021.106700

Rajendran, R. K., & Immanuel, A. V., & T, M. P. (2024). Specializing instruction with the use of artificial intelligence. In *Advances in educational technologies and instructional design book series* (pp. 245–256). DOI: 10.4018/979-8-3693-5538-1.ch009

Ramaila, S. (2024). Harnessing Kahoot! as an educational tool to foster meaningful teaching and learning: A systematic review. African Journal of Teacher Education. uoguelph.ca

Ramonyai, T. M., Mpekoa, N., & Tom, S. (2024, March). Cyber security skills development in South Africa: Addressing the Gender Gap in the Industry. In *2024 Conference on Information Communications Technology and Society (ICTAS)* (pp. 144-149). IEEE. DOI: 10.1109/ICTAS59620.2024.10507137

Ramya, R., & Ramamoorthy, S. (2024). AI in Communication Technology and Innovation of AR/VR in Communication. In *Advances in linguistics and communication studies* (pp. 1–28). DOI: 10.4018/979-8-3693-3579-6.ch001

Rana, S., & Chicone, R. (2024). Gamification and Immersive Learning with AI. In *Fortifying for Future* (pp. 51–75). DOI: 10.1007/978-3-031-81780-9_3

Rana, S., & Chicone, R. (2024). Introduction to AI in Cybersecurity Training. In *Fortifying the Future* (pp. 1–24). DOI: 10.1007/978-3-031-81780-9_1

Rana, S., & Chicone, R. (2025). AI-Enhanced Virtual and Augmented Reality for Cybersecurity Training. In Fortifying the Future: Harnessing AI for Transformative Cybersecurity Training (pp. 101-131). Cham: Springer Nature Switzerland. [HTML]

Ranganathan, A., & Benson, A. (2020). A numbers game: Quantification of work, auto-gamification, and worker productivity. *American Sociological Review, 85*(4), 573–609. DOI: 10.1177/0003122420936665

RangeForce. (n.d.). *Cybersecurity training platform.* https://www.rangeforce.com/

Rani, J., Guru, R., & Santhanam, S. (2024). *Industry evolution, current trends, and future perspectives*. In *Advances in marketing, customer relationship management, and e-services book series* (pp. 113–132). https://doi.org/DOI: 10.4018/979-8-3693-7535-8.ch006

Rani, J., Guru, R., & Santhanam, S. (2025). *AI and Environmental Stewardship.* In *Advances in computational intelligence and robotics book series* (pp. 567–582). https://doi.org/DOI: 10.4018/979-8-3693-8034-5.ch028

Rauschnabel, P. A. (2021). Augmented reality is eating the real-world! The substitution of physical products by holograms. International Journal of Information Management. sciencedirect.com

Ravichandran, N., Tewaraja, T., Rajasegaran, V., Kumar, S. S., Gunasekar, S. K. L., & Sindiramutty, S. R. (2024). Comprehensive Review Analysis and Countermeasures for Cybersecurity Threats: DDoS, Ransomware, and Trojan Horse Attacks. *Preprints.org*. DOI: 10.20944/preprints202409.1369.v1

Razack, A. K. A., & Saad, M. F. M. (2024). Enhancing Cybersecurity Awareness through Gamification: Design an Interactive Cybersecurity Learning Platform for Multimedia University Students. *Journal of Informatics and Web Engineering*, *3*(3), 21–40. DOI: 10.33093/jiwe.2024.3.3.2

Razana, W. S. M. (2016). Cybersecurity: Towards becoming a national certification body for information security management systems internal auditors. *Int. Sch. Sci. Res. Innov*, *10*(8), 2907–2910.

Rege, A. (2015). *Multidisciplinary experiential learning for holistic cybersecurity education, research and evaluation.* Paper presented at the 2015 USENIX Summit on Gaming, Games, and Gamification in Security Education, 3GSE 2015.

Rehan, H. (2024). AI-Driven Cloud Security: The Future of Safeguarding Sensitive Data in the Digital Age. *Journal of Artificial Intelligence General science (JAIGS) ISSN: 3006-4023, 1*(1), 47-66.

Renacido, J. M. D., & Biray, E. T. (2024). Enhancing peer engagement and student motivation through AI-Gamified interactive learning tools. In *Advances in educational technologies and instructional design book series* (pp. 277–342). DOI: 10.4018/979-8-3693-8242-4.ch009

Rezgui, Y., & Marks, A. (2008). Information security awareness in higher education: An exploratory study. *Computers & Security*, *27*(7-8), 241–253. DOI: 10.1016/j.cose.2008.07.008

Rivera, E. S., & Garden, C. L. P. (2021). Gamification for student engagement: A framework. *Journal of Further and Higher Education*, *45*(7), 999–1012. DOI: 10.1080/0309877X.2021.1875201

Riza, A. Z. B. M., Jennsen, L., Anggani, P., Rafeen, A. I., Ruth, P. N. J., Sookun, D., Sookun, V., Yusri, N. Z. B. M., Sern, L. J., Luximon, L., Omer, M. L., & Sindiramutty, S. R. (2025). Leveraging Machine Learning and AI to Combat Modern Cyber Threats. *preprints.org*. DOI: 10.20944/preprints202501.0360.v1

Riza, L. S., Piantari, E., Junaeti, E., & Permana, I. S. (2023). Implementation of the Gamification Concept in the Development of a Learning Management System to Improve Students' Cognitive In Basic Programming Subjects Towards a Smart Learning Environment. *ADI Journal on Recent Innovation*, *5*(1), 43–53.

Robson, K., Plangger, K., Kietzmann, J. H., McCarthy, I., & Pitt, L. (2015). Is it all a game? Understanding the principles of gamification. *Business Horizons*, *58*(4), 411–420. DOI: 10.1016/j.bushor.2015.03.006

Rodrigues, L., Toda, A. M., Oliveira, W., Palomino, P. T., Vassileva, J., & Isotani, S. (2022). Automating gamification personalization to the user and beyond. *IEEE Transactions on Learning Technologies*, *15*(2), 199–212. DOI: 10.1109/TLT.2022.3162409

Ros, S.; Gonzalez, S.; Robles, A.; Tobarra, L.; Caminero, A.; Cano, J. (2020). Analyzing Students' Self-Perception of Success and Learning Effectiveness Using Gamification in an Online Cybersecurity Course. IEEE Access 2020, 8, 97718–97728.

Rosário, A. T., & Raimundo, R. (2024). Enhancing Business Higher Education Through Simulation-Based Learning, Problem-Based Learning, and Challenge-Based Learning. *Preprints*. DOI: 10.20944/preprints202407.0747.v1

Rose, F. D., Attree, E. A., Brooks, B. M., Parslow, D. M., & Penn, P. R. (2000). Training in virtual environments: Transfer to real world tasks and equivalence to real task training. *Ergonomics*, *43*(4), 494–511. DOI: 10.1080/001401300184378 PMID: 10801083

Roy, P., Pandit, R., & Naskar, S. K. (2024). Innovative Approaches to Problem-Solving through Educational Technology Integration. In *Advances in educational technologies and instructional design book series* (pp. 375–402). DOI: 10.4018/979-8-3693-6745-2.ch016

Russo, E., Ribaudo, M., Orlich, A., Longo, G., & Armando, A. (2023). *Cyber Range and Cyber Defense Exercises: Gamification Meets University Students.* Paper presented at the ACM International Conference Proceeding Series. DOI: 10.1145/3617553.3617888

Ryan, I., Roedig, U., & Stol, K. J. (2024). *Training developers to code securely: Theory and practice*. In *Proceedings of the 2024 ACM/IEEE Workshop on Engineering and Cybersecurity of Critical Systems*. DOI: 10.1145/3643662.3643956

Ryan, R. M., & Deci, E. L. (2020). Intrinsic and extrinsic motivations: Classic definitions and new directions. *Contemporary Educational Psychology*, *61*, 101860. DOI: 10.1016/j.cedpsych.2020.101860 PMID: 10620381

Rye, S., Sousa, M., & Sousa, C. (2025). Designing Effective Learning Games. In *Transformative Learning Through Play* (pp. 95–130). DOI: 10.1007/978-3-031-78523-8_4

Sabina. (n.d.). *Cybernetics Lab IMA & IFU | European Monitor of Industrial Ecosystems*. European Monitor of Industrial Ecosystems. https://monitor-industrial-ecosystems.ec.europa.eu/technology-centre/cybernetics-lab-ima-ifu

Sabir, B., Ullah, A., & Ahmad, N. (2021). Machine learning for detecting data exfiltration: A review. *ACM Computing Surveys*, *54*(3), 62. Advance online publication. DOI: 10.1145/3445031

Sachan, T., Chhabra, D., & Abraham, B. (2025). Social Capital in Online Gaming Communities: A Systematic Review examining the role of Virtual Identities. *Cyberpsychology, Behavior, and Social Networking*, *28*(3), 147–161. Advance online publication. DOI: 10.1089/cyber.2024.0375 PMID: 39772759

Saeed, S., Jhanjhi, N., Naqvi, S. M. R., & Khan, A. (2022). Analytical Approach for Security of Sensitive Business Cloud. *Deep Learning in Data Analytics: Recent Techniques, Practices and Applications*, 257-266.

Safa, N. S., Solms, R., & Futcher, L. (2016). Human aspects of information security in organizations. *Computers & Security*, *53*, 70–80. DOI: 10.1016/j.cose.2015.10.006

Safitra, M. F., Lubis, M., & Fakhrurroja, H. (2023). Counterattacking cyber threats: A framework for the future of cybersecurity. Sustainability. mdpi.com

Sala, E. (2024). Descriptive Analysis of Cybersecurity Awareness Among Smartphone Users in Higher Education. *Journal of Transactions in Systems Engineering*, *2*(2), 222–234.

Salama, R., Alturjman, S., Altrjman, C., & Al-Turjman, F. (2024). *Using Gamification to Increase Healthcare Professionals' Cybersecurity Awareness*. Paper presented at the Sustainable Civil Infrastructures. DOI: 10.1007/978-3-031-78276-3_88

Salloum, S. A. (2023). *Enhancing cybersecurity: Machine learning and natural language processing for Arabic phishing email detection* [Doctoral dissertation, University of Salford]. ProQuest Dissertations Publishing.

Santofimia, M. J., Villanueva, F. J., Litvinov, E., Viksnin, I., Fernandes, A., & Lopez, J. C. (2021). Cybersecurity in Active and Healthy Ageing Era. *Procedia Computer Science*, *192*, 2068–2076. DOI: 10.1016/j.procs.2021.08.214

Sanzana, M. R., Abdulrazic, M. O. M., Wong, J. Y., Karunagharan, J. K., & Chia, J. (2023). Gamified virtual labs: Shifting from physical environments for low-risk interactive learning. *Journal of Applied Research in Higher Education*, *16*(1), 208–221. DOI: 10.1108/JARHE-09-2022-0281

Sarkar, K. R. (2010). Barriers to effective cybersecurity awareness training. *Information Management & Computer Security*, *18*(1), 16–24.

Schunk, D. H. (2012). *Learning theories: An educational perspective.* Pearson Higher Ed.

Schunk, D. H., & DiBenedetto, M. K. (2020). Motivation and social-emotional learning: Theory, research, and practice. *Contemporary Educational Psychology*, *60*, 101830.

Secure Code Warrior. (n.d.). Secure coding training platform. https://www.securecodewarrior.com/

Selma-Housein, E., & Plancher, B. (2025, February). Improving the Representation of Undergraduate Women in Cybersecurity: A Literature Review. In *Proceedings of the 56th ACM Technical Symposium on Computer Science Education* V. 1 (pp. 1043-1049).

Sengupta, S., Bardhan, S., Das, R., & Chakrabarti, S. (2025). LearnAlytics: The smart way to analyze, adapt, and achieve in E-Learning. *SN Computer Science*, *6*(1), 79. Advance online publication. DOI: 10.1007/s42979-024-03535-4

Seng, Y. J., Cen, T. Y., Raslan, M. H. B. M., Subramaniam, M. R., Xin, L. Y., Kin, S. J., Long, M. S., & Sindiramutty, S. R. (2024). In-Depth Analysis and Countermeasures for Ransomware Attacks: Case Studies and Recommendations. *Preprint.org*. DOI: 10.20944/preprints202408.2261.v1

Septris. (n.d.). *Septris 2.0 - CME certified online game for sepsis management.* Septris. https://med.stanford.edu/septris.html?utm_source=chatgpt.com

Serrano-Ausejo, E., & Mårell-Olsson, E. (2023). Opportunities and challenges of using immersive technologies to support students' spatial ability and 21st-century skills in K-12 education. *Education and Information Technologies*, *29*(5), 5571–5597. DOI: 10.1007/s10639-023-11981-5

Sezgin, S., & Yüzer, T. V. (2022). Analysing adaptive gamification design principles for online courses. *Behaviour & Information Technology*, *41*(3), 485–501. DOI: 10.1080/0144929X.2020.1817559

Shafik, W. (2024). Dissecting the role of women in cybersecurity and information technology: a medical perspective. In *Next-Generation Cybersecurity: AI, ML, and Blockchain* (pp. 325–350). Springer Nature Singapore. DOI: 10.1007/978-981-97-1249-6_15

Shah, I. A., Jhanjhi, N. Z., & Laraib, A. (2022). Cybersecurity and blockchain usage in contemporary business. In *Advances in information security, privacy, and ethics book series* (pp. 49–64). DOI: 10.4018/978-1-6684-5284-4.ch003

Shah, I. A., Jhanjhi, N., & Laraib, A. (2023). Cybersecurity and Blockchain Usage in Contemporary Business. In *Handbook of Research on Cybersecurity Issues and Challenges for Business and FinTech Applications* (pp. 49–64). IGI Global.

Shah, I. A., Jhanjhi, N., & Ray, S. K. (2024). Artificial Intelligence Applications in the Context of the Security Framework for the Logistics Industry. In *Advances in Explainable AI Applications for Smart Cities* (pp. 297–316). IGI Global. DOI: 10.4018/978-1-6684-6361-1.ch011

Shahid, H., Ashraf, H., Jhanjhi, N., & Zam, Q.-u. A. Z. (2025). Reshaping Cybersecurity of Wireless Sensor Networks Using Energy-Optimized Approach Against Wormhole Attack. In *Reshaping CyberSecurity With Generative AI Techniques* (pp. 125-172): IGI Global.

Shahzadi, A., Ishaq, K., Nawaz, N. A., Rosdi, F., & Khan, F. A. (2025). Unveiling personalized and gamification-based cybersecurity risks within financial institutions. *PeerJ. Computer Science*, *11*, e2598. DOI: 10.7717/peerj-cs.2598 PMID: 40062254

Shan, M., & Yang, J. (2021). Investigating the accessibility and impacts of cybersecurity programs on high-school girls' long-term industry engagement. *Information and Computer Security*, *30*(3), 309–323. DOI: 10.1108/ICS-05-2021-0067

Sharbel, K. E., & Salaimeh, O. (2024). *Challenging Games for All : Adaptive Difficulty and its Impact on Inclusivity in Action Games*. DIVA. https://www.diva-portal.org/smash/record.jsf?pid=diva2%3A1887856&dswid=9275

Sharma, D., & Sharma, J. (2023). *Evolution of gamification, its implications, and its statistical impact on the society*. Paper presented at the International Conference on Emerging Trends in Design & Arts. DOI: 10.29121/shodhkosh.v4.i2SE.2023.456

Sharma, S. (2024). Revolutionizing teacher education with Cutting-Edge Digital Solutions. In *Advances in educational marketing, administration, and leadership book series* (pp. 291–310). DOI: 10.4018/979-8-3693-6880-0.ch014

Sharma, R., Singh, A., Kavita, N., Jhanjhi, N. Z., Masud, M., Jaha, E. S., & Verma, S. (2021). Plant disease diagnosis and image classification using deep learning. *Computers, Materials & Continua/Computers. Materials & Continua (Print), 71*(2), 2125–2140. DOI: 10.32604/cmc.2022.020017

Sheng, L. T., Azman, A. B., Khan, N. A., Sindiramutty, S. R., Singh, S., & Verma, S. (2024). Reinforcement learning-based traffic signal control. *2024 International Conference on Emerging Trends in Networks and Computer Communications (ETNCC)*, 792–798. DOI: 10.1109/ETNCC63262.2024.10767501

Shirindzi, L. S., & Sikhwari, M. G. (2025). Interactive apps and games for early language development. In *Advances in educational technologies and instructional design book series* (pp. 177–202). DOI: 10.4018/979-8-3693-7437-5.ch008

Shorman, D. A. (2024). *Examining the role of immersive technologies in preparing preservice elementary teachers: augmented reality, integrated STEM, teaching self-efficacy, and technology self-efficacy*. DigitalCommons@University of Nebraska - Lincoln. https://digitalcommons.unl.edu/dissunl/72/

Shtayyat, A., Gawanmeh, A., & Mashaleh, A. (2025). Risk analysis of AI integration in educational systems: Toward ethical and equitable innovation. In *Examining cybersecurity risks produced by generative AI* (pp. 401–428). IGI Global Scientific Publishing., DOI: 10.4018/979-8-3373-0832-6.ch017

Shukla, P. K., Singh, A., Sharma, A., Malik, P. K., & Kathuria, S. (2023). *Technological Powered Impersonation in MOOC Learning*. Paper presented at the Proceedings - 2023 3rd International Conference on Pervasive Computing and Social Networking, ICPCSN 2023. DOI: 10.1109/ICPCSN58827.2023.00091

Shwartz, S. (2021). *Evil robots, killer computers, and other myths: The Truth About AI and the Future of Humanity*. Greenleaf Book Group.

Shyaa, M. A., Ibrahim, N. F., Zainol, Z., Abdullah, R., Anbar, M., & Alzubaidi, L. (2024). Evolving cybersecurity frontiers: A comprehensive survey on concept drift and feature dynamics aware machine and deep learning in intrusion detection systems. [sciencedirect.com]. *Engineering Applications of Artificial Intelligence, 137*, 109143. DOI: 10.1016/j.engappai.2024.109143

Sikhwari, M., & Thenga, N. E. (2025). Future of language learning. In *Advances in educational technologies and instructional design book series* (pp. 115–144). DOI: 10.4018/979-8-3693-7437-5.ch006

Simon, P. (2023). *Here's how workers at companies like Accenture and Walmart are using virtual reality*. Fast Company. https://www.fastcompany.com/90876215/how-workers-at-accenture-and-walmart-are-using-virtual-reality

Sindiramutty, S. R., Jhanjhi, N. Z., Ray, S. K., Jazri, H., Khan, N. A., Gaur, L., Gharib, A., & Manchuri, A. R. (2023). Metaverse. In *Advances in medical technologies and clinical practice book series* (pp. 24–92). DOI: 10.4018/978-1-6684-9823-1.ch002

Sindiramutty, S. R., Jhanjhi, N. Z., Tan, C. E., Khan, N. A., Gharib, A. H., & Yun, K. J. (2023). Applications of blockchain technology in supply chain management. In *Advances in logistics, operations, and management science book series* (pp. 248–304). DOI: 10.4018/978-1-6684-7625-3.ch009

Sindiramutty, S. R., Jhanjhi, N. Z., Tan, C. E., Khan, N. A., Shah, B., & Manchuri, A. R. (2024). Cybersecurity measures for logistics industry. In *Advances in information security, privacy, and ethics book series* (pp. 1–58). DOI: 10.4018/979-8-3693-3816-2.ch001

Sindiramutty, S. R., Jhanjhi, N. Z., Tan, C. E., Yun, K. J., Manchuri, A. R., Ashraf, H., Murugesan, R. K., Tee, W. J., & Hussain, M. (2024). Data security and privacy concerns in drone operations. In *Advances in information security, privacy, and ethics book series* (pp. 236–290). DOI: 10.4018/979-8-3693-0774-8.ch010

Sindiramutty, S. R., Jhanjhi, N., & Ray, S. K. (2024). Threat Hunting and Behaviour Analysis. *Utilizing Generative AI for Cyber Defense Strategies*, 235.

Sindiramutty, S. R., Prabagaran, K. R. V., Akbar, R., Hussain, M., & Malik, N. A. (2024). Overview of Generative AI techniques for cybersecurity. In *Advances in information security, privacy, and ethics book series* (pp. 1–52). DOI: 10.4018/979-8-3693-5415-5.ch001

Sindiramutty, S. R., Prabagaran, K. R. V., Jhanjhi, N. Z., Ghazanfar, M. A., Malik, N. A., & Soomro, T. R. (2024). Security Considerations in Generative AI for web Applications. In *Advances in information security, privacy, and ethics book series* (pp. 281–332). DOI: 10.4018/979-8-3693-5415-5.ch009

Sindiramutty, S. R., Prabagaran, K. R. V., Jhanjhi, N. Z., Murugesan, R. K., Brohi, S. N., & Masud, M. (2024). Generative AI in network security and intrusion detection. In *Advances in information security, privacy, and ethics book series* (pp. 77–124). DOI: 10.4018/979-8-3693-5415-5.ch003

Sindiramutty, S. R., Prabagaran, K. R. V., Jhanjhi, N. Z., Murugesan, R. K., Brohi, S. N., & Wei, G. W. (2024). Generative AI for threat intelligence and information sharing. In *Advances in digital crime, forensics, and cyber terrorism book series* (pp. 191–234). DOI: 10.4018/979-8-3693-8944-7.ch006

Sindiramutty, S. R., Prabagaran, K. R. V., Jhanjhi, N. Z., Murugesan, R. K., Malik, N. A., & Hussain, M. (2024). Ethics and transparency in secure web model generation. In *Advances in information security, privacy, and ethics book series* (pp. 411–464). DOI: 10.4018/979-8-3693-5415-5.ch012

Sindiramutty, S. R., Prabagaran, K. R. V., Jhanjhi, N., & Murugesan, R. K. (2024). Threat Intelligence and Information Sharing. *Utilizing Generative AI for Cyber Defense Strategies*, 191.

Sindiramutty, S. R., Tan, C. E., & Wei, G. W. (2024). Eyes in the sky. In *Advances in information security, privacy, and ethics book series* (pp. 405–451). DOI: 10.4018/979-8-3693-0774-8.ch017

Sindiramutty, S. R., Jhanjhi, N. Z., Tan, C. E., Khan, N. A., Shah, B., & Gaur, L. (2024). Securing the digital supply chain cyber threats and vulnerabilities. In *Cybersecurity Measures for Logistics Industry Framework* (pp. 156–223). IGI Global Scientific Publishing.

Sindiramutty, S. R., Prabagaran, K. R. V., Jhanjhi, N., Ghazanfar, M. A., Malik, N. A., & Soomro, T. R. (2025). Security Considerations in Generative AI for Web Applications. In *Reshaping CyberSecurity With Generative AI Techniques* (pp. 281–332). IGI Global.

Singh, B., Kaunert, C., Lal, S., & Arora, M. K. (2024). Enhancing AI-Augmented classrooms. In *Advances in educational technologies and instructional design book series* (pp. 99–130). DOI: 10.4018/979-8-3693-7255-5.ch004

Singh, T. M., Reddy, C. K. K., Murthy, B. V. R., Nag, A., & Doss, S. (2024). AI and Education. In *Advances in educational technologies and instructional design book series* (pp. 131–160). DOI: 10.4018/979-8-3693-2964-1.ch002

Singhal, V., Jain, S. S., Anand, D., Singh, A., Verma, S., Kavita, N., Rodrigues, J. J. P. C., Jhanjhi, N. Z., Ghosh, U., Jo, O., & Iwendi, C. (2020). Artificial Intelligence Enabled Road Vehicle-Train Collision Risk Assessment Framework for Unmanned railway level crossings. *IEEE Access : Practical Innovations, Open Solutions*, *8*, 113790–113806. DOI: 10.1109/ACCESS.2020.3002416

Skinner, B. F. (1953). *Science and human behavior*. Macmillan., DOI: 10.1037/10039-000

Skinner, B. F. (1954). The science of learning and the art of teaching. *Harvard Educational Review, 24*(2), 86–97.

Slater, M., & Sanchez-Vives, M. V. (2016). Enhancing Our Lives with Immersive Virtual Reality. *Frontiers in Robotics and AI, 3*. Advance online publication. DOI: 10.3389/frobt.2016.00074

Slyman, S. (2024). *Acumenous Game-Based learning in simulation games: Transforming Fears of Mathematics and Statistics Education*. Taylor & Francis. DOI: 10.4324/9781032723426

Song, C., Shin, S., & Shin, K. (2024). Implementing the Dynamic Feedback-Driven Learning Optimization Framework: A machine learning approach to personalize educational pathways. *Applied Sciences (Basel, Switzerland), 14*(2), 916. DOI: 10.3390/app14020916

Sousa, C., Sousa, M., & Rye, S. (2025). Introduction to Inclusivity in Analogue Game-Based Learning: Challenges and Strategies. In *Transformative Learning Through Play* (pp. 179–219). DOI: 10.1007/978-3-031-78523-8_6

Spaho, E., Çiço, B., & Shabani, I. (2025). IoT Integration Approaches into Personalized Online Learning: Systematic Review. *Computers, 14*(2), 63. DOI: 10.3390/computers14020063

Spatafora, A., Wagemann, M., Sandoval, C., Leisenberg, M., & Vaz de Carvalho, C. (2024). An Educational Escape Room Game to Develop Cybersecurity Skills. [mdpi.com]. *Computers, 13*(8), 205. DOI: 10.3390/computers13080205

Spiro, K., & Bhamidi, V. (2024). *Employee-Generated learning: How to develop training that drives performance*. Kogan Page Publishers.

Springle, A. P. (2024). Getting Serious about Games: Exploring how Game-Based Learning is used in education and therapy. *Perspectives of the ASHA Special Interest Groups, 9*(6), 1–23. DOI: 10.1044/2024_PERSP-23-00267

Squire, K. (2005). Changing the game: What happens when video games enter the classroom? *Innovate: Journal of Online Education, 1*(6).

Srivatanakul, T. & Annansingh, F. (2022). Incorporating active learning activities to the design and development of an undergraduate software and web security course. Journal of Computers in Education. springer.com

Stanciu, V., & Tinca, A. (2016). Students' awareness on information security between own perception and reality—An empirical study. *Account. Manag. Inf. Syst., 15*, 112–130.

Stefan, H., Mortimer, M., & Horan, B. (2023). Evaluating the effectiveness of virtual reality for safety-relevant training: A systematic review. *Virtual Reality (Waltham Cross)*, *27*(4), 2839–2869. DOI: 10.1007/s10055-023-00843-7

Stewart, M. (2021). Understanding learning: Theories and critique. In *University teaching in focus* (pp. 3–28). Routledge. DOI: 10.4324/9781003008330-2

Strielkowski, W., Grebennikova, V., Lisovskiy, A., Rakhimova, G., & Vasileva, T. (2024). AI-driven adaptive learning for sustainable educational transformation. Sustainable Development. wiley.com

Strielkowski, W., Grebennikova, V., Lisovskiy, A., Rakhimova, G., & Vasileva, T. (2024). AI-driven adaptive learning for sustainable educational transformation. *Sustainable Development*. Advance online publication. DOI: 10.1002/sd.3221

Subhash, S., & Cudney, E. A. (2018). Gamified learning in higher education: A systematic review of the literature. *Computers in Human Behavior*, *87*, 192–206. DOI: 10.1016/j.chb.2018.05.028

Sudrajat, R. P. A., Vhalery, R., & Sefudin, A. (2025, January 26). *The influence of VAK (Visual, Auditory, Kinesthetic) learning Styles on students' learning outcomes in AKL practicum subjects at SMK Pembangunan Jaya YAKAPI Jakarta*. https://pub.ruangrosadi.com/jurnal-ilmiah/index.php/jedar/article/view/70

Sujatha, R., Prakash, G., & Jhanjhi, N. Z. (Eds.). (2022). *Cyber security applications for Industry 4.0*. CRC Press. DOI: 10.1201/9781003203087

Sun, Y. & Jung, H. (2024). Machine Learning (ML) Modeling, IoT, and Optimizing Organizational Operations through Integrated Strategies: The Role of Technology and Human …. Sustainability. mdpi.com

Sun, L., Kangas, M., & Ruokamo, H. (2023). Game-based features in intelligent game-based learning environments: A systematic literature review. *Interactive Learning Environments*, •••, 1–17. DOI: 10.1080/10494820.2023.2179638

Sun, Q., Zhou, S., Chen, R., Feng, G., Cheung, K. T., Li, J., Hou, S., & Zeng, B. (2024). From computing to quantum mechanics: Accessible and hands-on quantum computing education for high school students. *EPJ Quantum Technology*, *11*(1), 58. Advance online publication. DOI: 10.1140/epjqt/s40507-024-00271-9

Suresh Babu, C. V., Bhavesh, M., Albert Gururaja, V., & Venkatesh, T. D. (2025). AI-driven instructional design: Enhancing learning experiences through personalization and efficiency. In Gregory, S. (Ed.), *Effective instructional design informed by AI* (pp. 87–114). IGI Global Scientific Publishing., DOI: 10.4018/979-8-3693-6527-4.ch003

Suresh Babu, C. V., Nithika Sree, R., & Varshini, R. (2025). The role of artificial intelligence in personalized STEAM education: Enhancing student-centered learning. In Son, N. (Ed.), *Integrating personalized learning methods into STEAM education* (pp. 169–188). IGI Global Scientific Publishing., DOI: 10.4018/979-8-3693-7718-5.ch008

Suresh Babu, C. V., William, M. P., & Juvin, C. (2025). Artificial intelligence in flipped learning: Advancing quality assurance and personalized education in higher education. In Reyes Ruiz, G. (Ed.), *New technological applications in the flipped learning model* (pp. 169–192). IGI Global Scientific Publishing., DOI: 10.4018/979-8-3373-0437-3.ch006

Suresh Babu, S., & Dhakshina Moorthy, A. (2024). Application of artificial intelligence in adaptation of gamification in education: A literature review. [HTML]. *Computer Applications in Engineering Education*, *32*(1), e22683. DOI: 10.1002/cae.22683

Svensson, J. (2022). *Investigating the use of Gamification in data presentation.* (Independent thesis Advanced level (professional degree) Student thesis). Retrieved from http://urn.kb.se/resolve?urn=urn:nbn:se:umu:diva-200010 DiVA database.

Swargiary, K. (2024). *Integrating IoT in education: (Transforming Learning Through Smart Technologies)*. EdTech Research Association.

Sweller, J. (1994). Cognitive load theory, learning difficulty, and instructional design. *Learning and Instruction*, *4*(4), 295–312. DOI: 10.1016/0959-4752(94)90003-5

Taherdoost, H. (2022). Understanding cybersecurity frameworks and information security standards—a review and comprehensive overview. Electronics. mdpi.com

Taherdoost, H. (2024). Towards an Innovative Model for Cybersecurity Awareness Training. Information. mdpi.com

Talaei Khoei, T., & Kaabouch, N. (2023). A comparative analysis of supervised and unsupervised models for detecting attacks on the intrusion detection systems. *Information (Basel)*, *14*(2), 103. Advance online publication. DOI: 10.3390/info14020103

Tang, X., Long, B., & Zhou, L. (2024). Real-time monitoring and analysis of track and field athletes based on edge computing and deep reinforcement learning algorithm. *Alexandria Engineering Journal*, *114*, 136–146. DOI: 10.1016/j.aej.2024.11.024

Tanikonda, A., Kumar, S., & Sharma, R. (2022). Advanced AI-driven cybersecurity solutions for proactive threat detection and response in complex ecosystems. *Journal of Science and Technology*, *3*(1), 1–15.

Tarí, J. J., & Dick, G. (2016). Trends in quality management research in higher education institutions. *Journal of Service Theory and Practice*, *26*(3), 273–296. DOI: 10.1108/JSTP-10-2014-0230

Tariq, M. U. (2024). Advancing Inquiry-Based learning through generative AI-Enabled assessments. In *Advances in educational marketing, administration, and leadership book series* (pp. 179–206). DOI: 10.4018/979-8-3693-6351-5.ch007

Tashakkori, A., & Teddlie, C. (2010). *SAGE handbook of mixed methods in social & behavioral research* (2nd ed.). SAGE Publications. DOI: 10.4135/9781506335193

Tavakol, M., & Dennick, R. (2011). Making sense of Cronbach's alpha. *International Journal of Medical Education*, *2*, 53–55. DOI: 10.5116/ijme.4dfb.8dfd PMID: 28029643

Taylor, J., & Whitty, M. (2024). An exploration of the awareness and attitudes of psychology students regarding their psychological literacy for working in the cybersecurity industry. *Psychology Learning & Teaching*, *23*(2), 298–314. DOI: 10.1177/14757257231214612

Tayyab, M., Hameed, K., Jhanjhi, N. Z., Zaheer, A., & Qamar, F. (2024). Digital Safeguards: Navigating Cyber Threats in the Logistics Industry Framework. In *Navigating Cyber Threats and Cybersecurity in the Logistics Industry* (pp. 258-299): IGI Global.

Teles, R. O., & Moreira, F. T. (2024). Integrating AI in formative assessment under UDL principles in diverse learning environments. In *Advances in educational technologies and instructional design book series* (pp. 95–122). DOI: 10.4018/979-8-3693-6170-2.ch004

Tempestini, G., Merà, S., Palange, M. P., Bucciarelli, A., & Di Nocera, F. (2024). Improving the Cybersecurity Awareness of Young Adults through a Game-Based Informal Learning Strategy. [mdpi.com]. *Information (Basel)*, *15*(10), 607. DOI: 10.3390/info15100607

Tenório, K., Dermeval, D., Monteiro, M., Peixoto, A., & Pedro, A. (2020). *Raising teachers empowerment in gamification design of adaptive learning systems: a qualitative research.* Paper presented at the Artificial Intelligence in Education: 21st International Conference, AIED 2020, Ifrane, Morocco, July 6–10, 2020, Proceedings, Part I 21. DOI: 10.1007/978-3-030-52237-7_42

Tharayil, S. M., Kumar, A., & Singh, R. (2024). Enhancing cyber resilience through AI-driven phishing tests and gamified learning. In *The International Conference on Artificial Intelligence and Smart Environment* (pp. 123–134). Springer. https://doi.org/DOI: 10.1007/978-3-031-23456-7_8

Tharot, K., Riel, A., & Thiriet, J. M. (2024). *A Gamification Approach to Teaching Cybersecurity in CPS.* Paper presented at the Procedia CIRP. DOI: 10.1016/j.procir.2024.06.039

Thomas, G., & Sule, M. J. (2023). A service lens on cybersecurity continuity and management for organizations' subsistence and growth. Organizational Cybersecurity Journal: Practice [emerald.com]. *Process and People*, *3*(1), 18–40.

Thomas, N. J., Baral, R., & Crocco, O. S. (2022). Gamification for HRD: Systematic review and future research directions. *Human Resource Development Review*, *21*(2), 198–224. DOI: 10.1177/15344843221074859

Thompson, J. D., Herman, G. L., Scheponik, T., Oliva, L., Sherman, A., Golaszewski, E., Phatak, D., & Patsourakos, K. (2018). *Student Misconceptions about Cybersecurity Concepts: Analysis of Think-Aloud Interviews.* DigitalCommons@Kennesaw State University. https://digitalcommons.kennesaw.edu/jcerp/vol2018/iss1/5/

Thompson, L. A., Melendez, N., Hempson-Jones, J., & Salvi, F. (2022). *Gamification in Cybersecurity Education; the RAD-SIM Framework for Effective Learning.* Paper presented at the European Conference on Games Based Learning. DOI: 10.34190/ecgbl.16.1.504

Thool, A., & Brown, C. (2025). *Integrating DAST in Kanban and CI/CD: A real world security case study.* arXiv preprint arXiv:2503.21947.

Toccafondi, N., Bilancini, E., & Boncinelli, L. (2024). *Learning CyberSecurity with Story-Driven CTF Challenges: CyberTrials 2023.* Paper presented at the Communications in Computer and Information Science. DOI: 10.1007/978-3-031-67351-1_21

Toledano, S. A. (2024). *Critical infrastructure security: Cybersecurity lessons learned from real-world breaches.* Packt Publishing Ltd.

Tomé Klock, A. C., Palomino, P. T., Rodrigues, L. A. L., Toda, A. M., Simanke, S., Spors, V., . . . Hamari, J. (2024). Gamification towards and alongside equity, diversity and inclusion: Looking back to move forward. *new media & society*, 14614448241254028.

Triantafyllou, S., & Georgiadis, C. (2022). Gamification of MOOCs and security awareness in corporate training.

Trinidad, M., Calderón, A., & Ruiz, M. (2021). GoRace: A multi-context and narrative-based gamification suite to overcome gamification technological challenges. *IEEE Access : Practical Innovations, Open Solutions*, *9*, 65882–65905. DOI: 10.1109/ACCESS.2021.3076291

Tripp, B., Ravi, A., Pang, E., & Furrow, R. E. (2024). Undergraduate STEM Students' Perceptions of Grading Practices Reveal that Quiz Retakes Positively Impact Drivers of Self-determination. *CBE Life Sciences Education*, *24*(1), ar4. Advance online publication. DOI: 10.1187/cbe.24-06-0167 PMID: 39705683

Troja, E., DeBello, J. E., & Truong, L. M. (2023). *Teaching effective and gamified cybersecurity using the metaverse: challenges and opportunities.* Paper presented at the 2023 IEEE World Engineering Education Conference (EDUNINE). DOI: 10.1109/EDUNINE57531.2023.10102900

TryHackMe. (n.d.). *Cybersecurity training for everyone.* https://tryhackme.com/

TryHackMe. (n.d.). *TryHackMe | Cyber Security Training.* https://tryhackme.com/

Tyagi, R., & Khanna, P. (2025). A Comprehensive review of Digital Transformation for Sustainable Development in Emerging Markets: Vis-a-Vis Blockchain and Gamification. *Emerald Publishing Limited eBooks*, 223–246. DOI: 10.1108/978-1-83549-109-620251009

U.S. Department of Defense. (2021). *Cyber ranges for mission readiness.* Retrieved from https://www.defense.gov/

Udayakumar, P., & Anandan, R. (2024). *Design and deploy Microsoft Defender for IoT: Leveraging cloud-based analytics and machine learning capabilities.* Springer Nature., DOI: 10.1007/979-8-8688-0239-3

Ulmer, J., Braun, S., Cheng, C.-T., Dowey, S., & Wollert, J. (2020). Human-centered gamification framework for manufacturing systems. *Procedia CIRP*, *93*, 670–675. DOI: 10.1016/j.procir.2020.04.076

Ulven, J. B. & Wangen, G. (2021). A systematic review of cybersecurity risks in higher education. Future Internet. mdpi.com

Understanding emerging Technology - Virtual Reality/Augmented Reality | VR / AR | COMPTIA. (n.d.). CompTIA. https://www.comptia.org/content/research/understanding-emerging-technology-virtual-reality-augmented-reality

Vairamani, A. D. (2024). Enhancing Social Skills Development Through Augmented Reality (AR) and Virtual Reality (VR) in Special Education. *Wiley*, 65–89. DOI: 10.1002/9781394167586.ch3

Vaithilingam, P., Arawjo, I., & Glassman, E. L. (2024). Imagining a Future of Designing with AI: Dynamic Grounding, Constructive Negotiation, and Sustainable Motivation. *Designing Interactive Systems Conference, 8*, 289–300. DOI: 10.1145/3643834.3661525

van Geest, R. J., Cascavilla, G., Hulstijn, J., & Zannone, N. (2024). The applicability of a hybrid framework for automated phishing detection. *Computers & Security, 139*, 103736. DOI: 10.1016/j.cose.2024.103736

van Steen, T., & Deeleman, J. R. (2021). Successful gamification of cybersecurity training. *Cyberpsychology, Behavior, and Social Networking, 24*(9), 593–598. DOI: 10.1089/cyber.2020.0526 PMID: 34491845

Vemuri, N., Thaneeru, N., & Tatikonda, V. M. (2024). Adaptive generative AI for dynamic cybersecurity threat detection in enterprises.

Venn-Wycherley, M., Ralph, J., & Moller, F. (2024, July). Experiences of a Pan-Wales Initiative of Cybersecurity Education in Schools. In Annual conference on Advances in Cyber Security Education (pp. 153-169). Cham: Springer Nature Switzerland. [HTML] DOI: 10.1007/978-3-031-77524-6_9

Verizon. (2022). *Data Breach Investigations Report (DBIR)*. Retrieved from https://www.verizon.com

Villegas-Ch, W., Govea, J., Godoy, L. N., & Mera-Navarrete, A. (2024). Virtual Reality Simulations for Skills Training: Improving Learning through Immersive Experiences in Educational Environments. *IEEE Access : Practical Innovations, Open Solutions, 12*, 130073–130090. DOI: 10.1109/ACCESS.2024.3456628

Villegas-Ch, W., Ortiz-Garces, I., & Sánchez-Viteri, S. (2021). Proposal for an Implementation Guide for a Computer Security Incident Response Team on a University Campus. *Computers, 10*(8), 102. DOI: 10.3390/computers10080102

Villegas, E., Fonseca, D., Peña, E., Bonet, P., & Fernández-Guinea, S. (2021). Qualitative assessment of effective gamification design processes using motivators to identify game mechanics. *Sensors (Basel), 21*(7), 2556. DOI: 10.3390/s21072556 PMID: 33917409

Vitla, S. (2023). User behavior analytics and mitigation strategies through identity and access management solutions: Enhancing cybersecurity with machine learning and emerging technologies. *Turkish Journal of Computer and Mathematics Education, 3048*, 4855.

Von Solms, R., & Van Niekerk, J. (2013). From information security to cyber security. *Computers & Security, 38*, 97–102. DOI: 10.1016/j.cose.2013.04.004

Vroom, C., & Von Solms, R. (2004). Towards information security behavioural compliance. *Computers & Security*, *23*(3), 191–198. DOI: 10.1016/j.cose.2004.01.012

Vygotsky, L. S. (1978). *Mind in society: The development of higher psychological processes*. Harvard University Press.

Vykopal, J., Čermák, M., Čeleda, P., & Tovarňák, D. (2017). Enhancing cybersecurity education through interactive gamified learning tools. In *Proceedings of the IEEE Global Engineering Education Conference (EDUCON)* (pp. 713–718). IEEE. DOI: 10.1109/EDUCON.2017.7942934

Vykopal, J., Švábenský, V., & Čeleda, R. (2022). Smart environment for adaptive learning of cybersecurity skills. *IEEE Transactions on Learning Technologies*, *16*(3), 443–456. DOI: 10.1109/TLT.2022.3216345

Waheed, A., Seegolam, B., Jowaheer, M. F., Sze, C. L. X., Hua, E. T. F., & Sindiramutty, S. R. (2024). Zero-Day Exploits in Cybersecurity: Case Studies and Countermeasure. *Preprints.org*. DOI: 10.20944/preprints202407.2338.v1

Wang, J., Zhang, L., & Chen, Q. (2023). Matching-based capture-the-flag games for multiagent systems. *IEEE Transactions on Cognitive and Developmental Systems*, *16*(3), 993–1005. DOI: 10.1109/TCDS.2023.3323572

Wang, Q., & Li, Y. (2024). How virtual reality, augmented reality and mixed reality facilitate teacher education: A systematic review. *Journal of Computer Assisted Learning*, *40*(3), 1276–1294. DOI: 10.1111/jcal.12949

Wang, Y.-F., Hsu, Y.-F., & Fang, K. (2022). The key elements of gamification in corporate training–The Delphi method. *Entertainment Computing*, *40*, 100463. DOI: 10.1016/j.entcom.2021.100463

Wang, Y., Tan, J., & Lee, M. K. (2022). Barriers to gamification adoption in cybersecurity education: Infrastructure, cost, and faculty readiness. *Education and Information Technologies*, *27*, 4021–4042. DOI: 10.1007/s10639-021-10738-1

Waseem, R. M., Khan, F. Z., Ahmad, M., Naseem, A., Jhanjhi, N., & Ghosh, U. Performance evaluation of aomdv on realistic and efficient vanet simulations. *Wireless Personal Communications*, 1-20.

Weidman, J., Siponen, M., & Kajava, J. (2019). The effectiveness of online cybersecurity training using gamified environments. *Journal of Cybersecurity Education, Research and Practice, 2019*(1), Article 3. https://digitalcommons.kennesaw.edu/jcerp/vol2019/iss1/3

Wei, M.-L. (2024). AI-enhanced risk assessment: Advancing cybersecurity protocols. *Advances in Computer Sciences*, *7*(1), 1–10. DOI: 10.1016/j.adcs.2024.01.001

Weiqi, X., Hooi, S. T. C., Sindiramutty, S. R. L., Asirvatham, D. L., Kumar, D., & Verma, S. (2024). Surface Anomaly Detection Using Machine Learning Technique. *2024 International Conference on Emerging Trends in Networks and Computer Communications (ETNCC)*, 1–7. DOI: 10.1109/ETNCC63262.2024.10767562

Weitl-Harms, S., Spanier, A., Hastings, J., & Rokusek, M. (2023). A Systematic Mapping Study on Gamification Applications for Undergraduate Cybersecurity Education. Journal of Cybersecurity Education, Research and Practice, 2023(1).

Wendt, D. W. (2024). The Cybersecurity Trinity. In *Apress eBooks*. DOI: 10.1007/979-8-8688-0947-7

Werbach, K., & Hunter, D. (2021). *For the win: How game thinking can revolutionize your business*. Wharton Digital Press.

Whitman, M. E., & Mattord, H. J. (2021). *Principles of Information Security* (7th ed.). Cengage Learning.

Wijnen-Meijer, M., Brandhuber, T., Schneider, A., & Berberat, P. (2022). Implementing Kolb s experiential learning cycle by linking real experience, case-based discussion and simulation. *Journal of Medical Education and Curricular Development*, *9*, 23821205221091511. DOI: 10.1177/23821205221091511 PMID: 35592131

Woodward, B., Imboden, T., & Martin, N. L. (2013). An undergraduate information security program: More than a curriculum. *Journal of Information Systems Education*, *24*, 63.

Wu, J., Li, Q., Peng, L., Robinson, S., & Chen, Y. (2025). Drivers of consumer group participation in an online shopping event: Alibaba's singles' day. *Information Processing & Management*, *62*(3), 104067. DOI: 10.1016/j.ipm.2025.104067

Xue, H., Røds, J., Haugseggen, Ø., Christensen, A. J., Batalden, B., & Gudmestad, O. T. (2025). A study on the effects of rapid training method related to ship handling in decision-making skills under stressful situations. *Journal of Navigation*, •••, 1–20. DOI: 10.1017/S0373463324000213

Xu, J., Lio, A., Dhaliwal, H., Andrei, S., Balakrishnan, S., Nagani, U., & Samadder, S. (2021). Psychological interventions of virtual gamification within academic intrinsic motivation: A systematic review. *Journal of Affective Disorders*, *293*, 444–465. DOI: 10.1016/j.jad.2021.06.070 PMID: 34252688

Xun, A. T., En, L. Z., Shen, L. T., Xin, A. N., Soon, W. H., Jun, W. Z., Ramachandra, H., Xinghao, G., Khant, N. M., Weitao, F., & Sindiramutty, S. R. (2025). Building Trust in Cloud Computing:Strategies for Resilient Security. *Preprints.org*. DOI: 10.20944/preprints202501.0716.v1

Xu, Q., Xiong, X., & Xu, X. (2024). *Research on Building an Open Assessment and Evaluation System for Smart Classroom Teaching Based on Computer Aided Technology*. EAI., DOI: 10.4108/eai.13-10-2023.2341337

Yadav, S. (2024). Advancing education with AI-Driven education for diverse learners. In *Advances in educational technologies and instructional design book series* (pp. 49–80). DOI: 10.4018/979-8-3693-6130-6.ch003

Yadav, S. (2024). Navigating the virtual classroom with virtual reality. In *Advances in educational technologies and instructional design book series* (pp. 29–54). DOI: 10.4018/979-8-3693-6030-9.ch002

Yamani, H. A. (2021). A conceptual framework for integrating gamification in elearning systems based on instructional design model. *International Journal of Emerging Technologies in Learning*, *16*(4), 14. DOI: 10.3991/ijet.v16i04.15693

Yambal, S., & Waykar, Y. A. (2025). Future of education using adaptive AI, intelligent systems, and ethical challenges. In *Advances in educational technologies and instructional design book series* (pp. 171–202). DOI: 10.4018/979-8-3693-6527-4.ch006

Yamijala, S. M., Nimbrain, N., & Bansal, R. (2024). Enhancing remote workspaces. In *Advances in human resources management and organizational development book series* (pp. 171–190). DOI: 10.4018/979-8-3693-6839-8.ch009

Yamin, M. M., Ullah, M., Ullah, H., & Katt, B. (2021). Weaponized AI for cyber attacks. *Journal of Information Security and Applications*, *57*, 102722. DOI: 10.1016/j.jisa.2020.102722

Yeganeh, L. N., Fenty, N. S., Chen, Y., Simpson, A., & Hatami, M. (2025). The Future of Education: A Multi-Layered Metaverse Classroom Model for Immersive and Inclusive Learning. *Future Internet*, *17*(2), 63. DOI: 10.3390/fi17020063

Yigit, Y., Kioskli, K., Bishop, L., Chouliaras, N., Maglaras, L., & Janicke, H. (2024). Enhancing Cybersecurity Training Efficacy: A Comprehensive Analysis of Gamified Learning, Behavioral Strategies and Digital Twins. *2024 IEEE 25th International Symposium on a World of Wireless, Mobile and Multimedia Networks (WoWMoM)*, 24–32. DOI: 10.1109/WoWMoM60985.2024.00016

Ying, X., Murugesan, R. K., Sindiramutty, S. R., Wei, G. W., Balakrishnan, S., Kumar, D., & Verma, S. (2024). Scene Text Recognition using Deep Learning Techniques. *2024 International Conference on Emerging Trends in Networks and Computer Communications (ETNCC)*, 1–9. DOI: 10.1109/ETNCC63262.2024.10767484

Yoon, C., Hwang, J.-W., & Kim, R. (2012). Exploring factors that influence students' behaviors in information security. *Journal of Information Systems Education*, *23*, 407–416.

You, F., Fu, Q., Yang, J., Chen, H., Cui, W., & Wang, J. (2023). Team Situation Awareness-Based Augmented Reality Head-Up Display design for security requirements. *International Journal of Human-Computer Interaction*, *40*(18), 5119–5138. DOI: 10.1080/10447318.2023.2231281

Yu, R., Wang, Y., & Wang, W. (2024). AMAD: Active learning-based multivariate time series anomaly detection for large-scale IT systems. *Computers & Security*, *137*, 103603. DOI: 10.1016/j.cose.2023.103603

Yusif, S., & Hafeez-Baig, A. (2021). Cybersecurity Policy Compliance in Higher Education: A Theoretical Framework. *Journal of Applied Security Research*, •••, 1–22. DOI: 10.1080/19361610.2021.1989271

Zafar, A., Yamin, M. M., Katt, B., & Torseth, E. (2024). All flags are not created equal: A deep look into CTF Scoring Algorithms. Expert Systems with Applications. sciencedirect.com

Zairon, I. Y., Wook, T. S. M. T., Salleh, S. M., & Dahlan, H. A. (2025). User Model for Virtual Learning based on Adaptive Gamification. *IEEE Access : Practical Innovations, Open Solutions*, *1*, 24028–24040. Advance online publication. DOI: 10.1109/ACCESS.2025.3537599

Zajda, J., & Zajda, J. (2021). Constructivist learning theory and creating effective learning environments. *Globalisation and education reforms: Creating effective learning environments*, 35-50.

Zaman, S. K. U., Jehangiri, A. I., Maqsood, T., Umar, A. I., Khan, M. A., Jhanjhi, N. Z., Shorfuzzaman, M., & Masud, M. (2022). COME-UP: Computation offloading in mobile edge computing with LSTM based user direction prediction. *Applied Sciences (Basel, Switzerland)*, *12*(7), 3312. DOI: 10.3390/app12073312

Zamiri, M., & Esmaeili, A. (2024). Strategies, Methods, and Supports for Developing Skills within Learning Communities: A Systematic Review of the Literature. *Administrative Sciences*, *14*(9), 231. DOI: 10.3390/admsci14090231

Zhai, C., Wibowo, S., & Li, L. D. (2024). The effects of over-reliance on AI dialogue systems on students' cognitive abilities: A systematic review. *Smart Learning Environments, 11*(1), 28. Advance online publication. DOI: 10.1186/s40561-024-00316-7

Zhang, A. K., Perry, N., Dulepet, R., Ji, J., Menders, C., Lin, J. W., . . . Jasper, D. (2024). Cybench: A framework for evaluating cybersecurity capabilities and risks of language models. *arXiv preprint arXiv:2408.08926.*

Zhang, Z., & Huang, X. (2024). Exploring the impact of the adaptive gamified assessment on learners in blended learning. *Education and Information Technologies, 29*(16), 21869–21889. DOI: 10.1007/s10639-024-12708-w

Zhao, F. (2024). Gamification design. In *CRC Press eBooks* (pp. 373–441). DOI: 10.1201/9781003495161-16

Zhao, T., Gasiba, T., Lechner, U., & Pinto-Albuquerque, M. (2024). Thriving in the era of hybrid work: Raising cybersecurity awareness using serious games in industry trainings. [HTML]. *Journal of Systems and Software, 210*, 111946. DOI: 10.1016/j.jss.2023.111946

Zhong, C., Kim, J. B., & Liu, H. (2022). *The Impact of Gamification on Students' Learning Outcome and Career Interest in Cybersecurity Education.* Paper presented at the 28th Americas Conference on Information Systems, AMCIS 2022.

Zhong, C., Kim, J. B. J. B., & Liu, H. (2024). The Art of Inclusive Gamification in Cybersecurity Training. *IEEE Security and Privacy, 22*(5), 40–51. DOI: 10.1109/MSEC.2024.3427666

Zhong, C., Liu, H., & Kam, H. J. (2024). Mining Reddit users' perspectives on cybersecurity competitions: A mixed method approach. [HTML]. *Information and Computer Security, 32*(5), 636–655. DOI: 10.1108/ICS-02-2023-0017

Zhou, S. (2024). Gamifying language education: The impact of digital game-based learning on Chinese EFL learners. *Humanities & Social Sciences Communications, 11*(1), 1518. Advance online publication. DOI: 10.1057/s41599-024-04073-3

Zhou, S., Zheng, W., Xu, Y., & Liu, Y. (2024). Enhancing User Experience in VR Environments through AI-Driven Adaptive UI Design. *Deleted Journal, 6*(1), 59–82. DOI: 10.60087/jaigs.v6i1.230

Zhou, Y., Li, M., & Sun, L. (2023). AI in personalized cybersecurity training: Opportunities and challenges. *Artificial Intelligence in Education, 34*(1), 57–73.

Zhu, Q., & Bedi, H. S. (2017). Game theory meets network security: A tutorial. *ACM Computing Surveys, 50*(1), 1–37. DOI: 10.1145/3007203

Zichermann, G., & Linder, J. (2022). *Gamification by Design: Implementing Game Mechanics in Web and Mobile Apps* (2nd ed.). O'Reilly Media.

Zola, F., Echeberria, X., Petisco, J., Vakakis, N., Voulgaridis, A., & Votis, K. (2025). *KINAITICS: Enhancing Cybersecurity Education Using AI-Based Tools and Gamification.* Paper presented at the Proceedings of the 2024 the 16th International Conference on Education Technology and Computers, ICETC 2024.

About the Contributors

Vasaki Ponnusamy is an Assistant Professor at Higher Colleges of Technology UAE. She obtained her Bachelor of Computer Science and MSc (Computer Science) from Science University of Malaysia and her PhD in IT from Universiti Teknologi PETRONAS (UTP), Malaysia (2013). She is currently working on cybersecurity, IoT security trends and digital governance. She has great International exposure as Keynote Speaker, Visiting Professor and several Fellowships. She has been teaching information and network security, wireless security and data communication and networking. She is specialized in handling Cisco devices for routing and security. It is her passion to share her technical knowledge with the community. Her area of specializations are Networking, Communication, Penetrating Testing and Cybersecurity.

Noor Zaman Jhanjhi is a highly esteemed Senior Professor of Computer Science, specializing in Artificial Intelligence and Cybersecurity. He currently holds the position of Professor at the School of Computer Science at Taylor's University, Malaysia, and serves as the Program Director for Postgraduate Research Degree Programmes as well as the Director of the Center for Smart Society (CSS5). With a career marked by academic leadership and groundbreaking research, Prof. Jhanjhi has been pivotal in advancing research and education in computer science. Recognized globally, Prof. Jhanjhi has been ranked among the world's top 2% research scientists for three consecutive years (2022, 2023, and 2024). In Malaysia, he is ranked among the top three computer science researchers and was honored with the Outstanding Faculty Member award by MDEC Malaysia in 2022, as well as the Vice Chancellor's Best Research Citations Award from Taylor's University in 2023. His impressive academic portfolio includes over 60 research books edited or authored with prestigious publishers such as Springer, Elsevier, Taylor & Francis, Wiley, and IGI Global USA. His research has garnered more than 1000 points in impact factor, reflecting the depth and breadth of his contributions to the field. A dedicated mentor, Prof. Jhanjhi has supervised and co-supervised 38 postgraduate students to successful graduation and has served as an external examiner for over 60 Ph.D. and Master's theses globally. In addition to his academic accomplishments, Prof. Jhanjhi holds Associate Editor and Editorial Board positions with several high-ranking journals, including PeerJ Computer Science, CMC Computers, Materials & Continua, and Frontiers in Communication and Networks. He was also recognized as an Outstanding Associate Editor for IEEE ACCESS. His contributions to research and innovation are further demonstrated by his successful management of over 40 internationally funded research grants. A sought-after keynote speaker, Prof. Jhanjhi has delivered over 60 invited talks at international conferences and has chaired numerous sessions. His commitment to academic excellence and accreditation extends to his involvement with ABET, NCAAA, and NCEAC over the past decade.

Kiran Adnan received her PhD degree in Computer Science from Universiti Tunku Abdul Rahman, Kampar, Malaysia, in 2021. She received her MS degree in computer science from Lahore College for Women University, Lahore Pakistan, in 2011, with a specialization in software engineering, and BS degree in computer science from Government College University, Lahore, Pakistan. From 2012 to 2016, she worked as a Senior Lecturer at Lahore Garrison University, Lahore, Pakistan. Since 2022, she has been working with the Faculty of Information and Communication Technology, Universiti Tunku Abdul Rahman, Malaysia, as an Assistant Professor. Her research interests include big data analytics, software processes, and cybersecurity. She is a reviewer of different international journals and conferences

***

Nurul Aini, a researcher, a reviewer, an English teacher, is currently pursuing a Ph.D at Universitas Negeri Malang (UM), Indonesia. She is an experienced English teacher at the English Department, State Islamic Institute (IAIN) of Kediri, Indonesia, where she teaches a variety of courses including Research Review: Academic Speaking, Advanced Academic Speaking, Public Speaking, Advanced Public Speaking, Grammar in Media Discourse, Grammar in Academic Discourse, Translation, and Thesis and Publication. Nurul Aini is an active researcher and author of numerous research articles. Her research interests include Technology in English teaching and learning, Artificial Intelligence in Education (AIEd), English Teaching Methodology for EFL. She serves as the Managing Editor of the Journal of English Education and Linguistics Studies (JEELS) at IAIN Kediri, Indonesia. and American Research Journal of Humanities & Social Science (ARJHSS), USA Nurul Aini is a reviewer for several Scopus-indexed journals, including the Journal of

Language Education (JLE), National Research University, Russia. Education Journal, University of New Delhi, India. She is a member of TEFLIN (The Association of Teaching English as a Foreign Language in Indonesia) and ASIA TEFL and has participated in International Conferences in Korea, Malaysia, and Singapore. Nurul Aini is a part of the translation agency lokabahasa.com and is also an active freelance translator and proofreader for academic research articles. Nurul Aini has experience working with an American non-governmental organization, which has enhanced her cultural integration. She enjoys traveling and exploring places, having visited Korea, Malaysia, and Singapore, with hopes to travel more in the future. She can be reached at: Email: florida_aini@iainkediri.ac.id. ORCID: 0009-0007-7929-0512.

Andi Asrifan is an accomplished educator and academic leader with a Doctorate in Education, specializing in English Language Education from Universitas Negeri Makassar. With a strong academic foundation, he holds a Master's degree in the same field and a Bachelor's degree in Secondary Education. His dissertation focused on developing bilingual educational materials, reflecting his commitment to enhancing language education. Dr. Asrifan has extensive experience in various educational roles, including serving as the Head of the International Affairs Office at Politeknik Negeri Nunukan and as the Head of the Institute for Student Development and Alumni at Universitas Muhammadiyah Sidenreng Rappang. He is also an active member of several professional organizations, including the Linguistics Society of Indonesia and TEFLIN. In addition to his administrative roles, Dr. Asrifan is a passionate advocate for educational innovation and has participated in numerous international conferences and webinars, sharing his insights on language teaching and curriculum development. His dedication to professional development is evident through his participation in various training programs.

S. Ida Evangeline, presently working as an Assistant Professor in the Department of Electrical and Electronics Engineering at the Government College of Engineering, Tirunelveli, Tamilnadu, India. She obtained her Bachelor's in Electrical and Electronics Engineering from Manonmaniam Sundaranar University in 2003, and Master's in Power Systems Engineering from Anna University, Chennai, Tamilnadu, India in 2005. She completed her PhD degree in 2023 at Anna University, Chennai, Tamilnadu, India. She has published six research papers in international journals. Her current research interests include optimal power flow, renewable energy, soft computing, machine learning, and deep learning.

Er. Kritika is an accomplished researcher specializing in the intersection of cybersecurity and neuroscience. She has made significant contributions to the field through a diverse array of publications, including peer-reviewed articles, book chapters and books. Her expertise lies in uncovering new insights and best practices in cybersecurity, particularly, through the lens of Generative AI, neuroeconomics, good governance, neuroethics and neuro-driven technologies. She has authored 30+ publications, with her insights featured in top journals and thought leadership platforms like the ISACA, CXO DigitalPulse, IGI Global etc and delivered 10+ keynote sessions. Her research isn't just about identifying problems, it's about designing human-centered, ethically sound solutions for tomorrow's cybersecurity threats. Kritika's brilliance has been recognized globally from the Trailblazer Award in Security to the Young Engineer and Best Researcher Awards.

Danyal Mahmood is a dedicated Assistant Professor in Biomedical Engineering at the National University of Sciences & Technology (NUST), Pakistan, with a robust academic and professional background in biomedical signal processing, neurofeedback training, and artificial intelligence. With a PhD in Biomedical Engineering from Universiti Tunku Abdul Rahman (UTAR), Malaysia, Dr. Mahmood's research delves into the neuro-physiological effects of EEG-based neurofeedback training on cognitive functions, contributing to multiple high-impact publications and advancing knowledge in cognitive neuroscience and neuropsychology. Dr. Mahmood's career is marked by a blend of academic excellence and practical experience. At UTAR, he led groundbreaking research on neurofeedback training, resulting in several journal articles and conference papers that have shaped current understanding in the field. His technical proficiency includes advanced tools and methodologies such as MATLAB, Python, and TensorFlow, complementing his deep knowledge of digital signal processing, machine learning, and artificial intelligence. Previously, as a Production Supervisor at Akhter Solar LTD, Dr. Mahmood improved production efficiency by 15% through effective team management and task prioritization. His early career included hands-on work with embedded systems during an internship at the National Development Complex (NDC) and key contributions to research at the Pakistan Institute of Engineering and Applied Sciences (PIEAS) and Shenzhen University. Active in academic committees and outreach, Dr. Mahmood excels in bridging theoretical knowledge with practical application, enhancing both research and educational initiatives in biomedical engineering.

Filsia Manzil is a lecturer in Computer Information Systems with over eight years of experience in both academia and industry. Her teaching and research interests include AI, applied cybersecurity, software development, and technology-enhanced learning. Filsia has led multiple student engagement initiatives, including cybersecurity competitions and interactive digital learning experiences. She is also involved in interdisciplinary projects that explore the integration of AI and software systems in education and business. Her work reflects a strong commitment to innovation, research-driven practice, and lifelong learning.

Jyoti Rani, Assistant professor, school of fashion design and technology. Research and Academic experience. 2 year experience in academics and research. Research area: fashion, textile, natural dyeing, consumer behaviour, AI, merchandising. she has published 28 research paper in refered journal and 5 book chapters.

C.V. Suresh Babu is a pioneer in content development. A true entrepreneur, he founded Anniyappa Publications, a company that is highly active in publishing books related to Computer Science and Management. Dr. C.V. Suresh Babu has also ventured into SB Institute, a center for knowledge transfer. He holds a Ph.D. in Engineering Education from the National Institute of Technical Teachers Training & Research in Chennai, along with seven master's degrees in various disciplines such as Engineering, Computer Applications, Management, Commerce, Economics, Psychology, Law, and Education. Additionally, he has UGC-NET/SET qualifications in the fields of Computer Science, Management, Commerce, and Education. Currently, Dr. C.V. Suresh Babu is a Professor in the Department of Information Technology at the School of Computing Science, Hindustan Institute of Technology and Science (Hindustan University) in Padur, Chennai, Tamil Nadu, India.

Raveenthiran Vivekanantharasa is a distinguished academic and researcher in the fields of educational management, leadership, and technology-enhanced learning. He currently serves as a Senior Lecturer at the Faculty of Education, The Open University of Sri Lanka. Holding a PhD in Educational Management, an MSc in Management, and a Bachelor of Education, Dr. Vivekanantharasa has extensive experience in higher education, curriculum development, and teacher training. With a strong international presence, he has been a keynote speaker, panelist, and resource person at numerous global conferences, contributing to discussions on AI in education, inclusive learning, and digital transformation in pedagogy. Additionally, he serves as a peer reviewer and editorial board member for several international academic journals. Beyond academia, Dr. Vivekanantharasa is actively involved in research focusing on online learning, school-based management, and special needs education. His dedication to advancing educational practices has earned him recognition, including multiple international awards for excellence in teaching and research.

Index

A

B

C

D

E

F

G

I

L

www.ingramcontent.com/pod-product-compliance
Lightning Source LLC
LaVergne TN
LVHW061530290926
849162LV00004B/744